WORLD REPORT 2024

EVENTS OF 2023

HUMAN RIGHTS WATCH

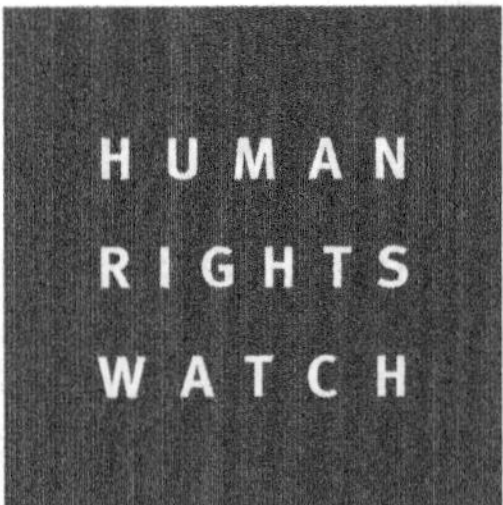

Printed in the United States of America
ISBN 978-1-64421-337-7

www.hrw.org

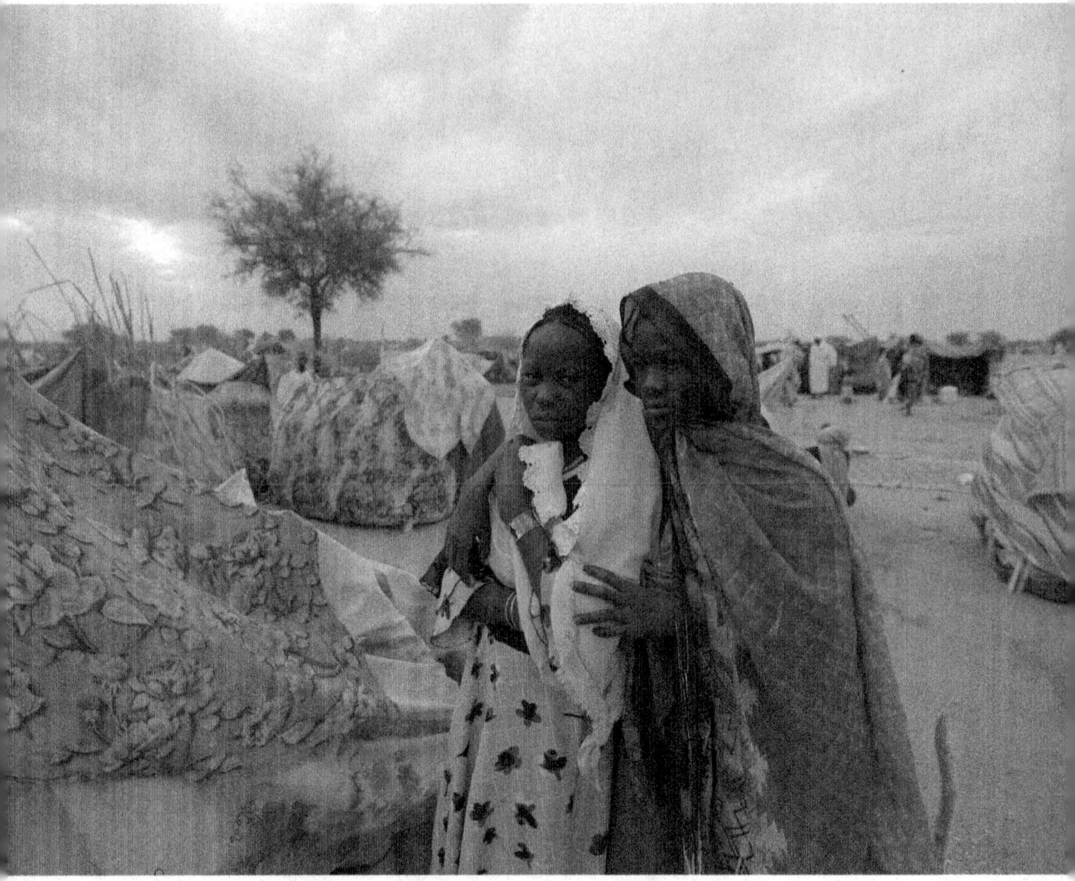

Cover photo: **Nadia, a Sudanese refugee who has fled the violence in Sudan's Darfur region, hugs her friend Khadidja, beside makeshift shelters near the border between Sudan and Chad in Koufroun, Chad on May 11, 2023.**

© 2023 Reuters/Zohra Bensemra

Cover and book design by Rafael Jiménez

Human Rights Watch defends the rights of people worldwide.

We scrupulously investigate abuses, expose facts widely, and pressure those with power to respect rights and secure justice.

Human Rights Watch is an independent, international organization that works as part of a vibrant movement to uphold human dignity and advance the cause of human rights for all.

Human Rights Watch began in 1978 with the founding of its Europe and Central Asia division (then known as Helsinki Watch). Today it also includes divisions covering Africa, the Americas, Asia, Europe and Central Asia, the Middle East and North Africa, and the United States. There are thematic divisions or programs on arms; business and human rights; children's rights; crisis and conflict; disability rights; the environment and human rights; international justice; lesbian, gay, bisexual, and transgender rights; refugee rights; and women's rights.

The organization maintains offices in Amman, Amsterdam, Beirut, Berlin, Bishkek, Brussels, Chicago, Geneva, Goma, Hong Kong, Johannesburg, Kiev, Kinshasa, London, Los Angeles, Miami, Moscow, Nairobi, New York, Paris, San Francisco, São Paulo, Seoul, Silicon Valley, Stockholm, Sydney, Tokyo, Toronto, Tunis, Washington DC, and Zurich, and field presences in more than 50 other locations globally.

Human Rights Watch is an independent, nongovernmental organization, supported by contributions from private individuals and foundations worldwide. It accepts no government funds, directly or indirectly.

Table of Contents

The Human Rights System Is Under Threat: A Call to Action

By Tirana Hassan, *Executive Director*

We only have to look at the human rights challenges of 2023 to tell us what we need to do differently in 2024. It was a formidable year not only for human rights suppression and wartime atrocities but also for selective government outrage and transactional diplomacy that carried profound costs for the rights of those not in on the deal. Yet amid the gloom, we saw signs of hope showing the possibility of a different path.

Renewed hostilities between Israel and Hamas and in Sudan caused tremendous suffering, as did ongoing conflicts in Ukraine, Myanmar, Ethiopia, and the Sahel. Governments struggled to deal with the hottest year on record and the onslaught of wildfires, drought, and storms that wreaked havoc on millions of people in Bangladesh, Libya, and Canada. Economic inequality rose around the world, as did anger about the policy decisions that have left many people struggling to survive. The rights of women and girls and lesbian, gay, bisexual and transgender (LGBT) people faced harsh backlashes in many places, exemplified by the Taliban's gender persecution in Afghanistan.

The drivers of these human rights crises and their consequences often transcend borders and cannot be solved by governments acting alone. Understanding and responding to these threats needs to be rooted in universal principles of international human rights and the rule of law. These ideas built on shared human histories agreed upon by nations across all regions 75 years ago in the Universal Declaration of Human Rights, the basis for all contemporary human rights conventions and treaties.

This foundation is needed now more than ever. But this very system we rely on to protect the human rights of people everywhere is under threat. Every time a government overlooks or rejects these universal and globally accepted principles, someone pays a price – in freedoms and liberties, in their health or livelihood, and at times their lives.

Governments that could play a role in helping to improve human rights frequently adopt double standards in applying the human rights framework, which chips away at trust in the institutions responsible for enforcing and protecting rights. Governments that are vocal in condemning Israeli government war crimes against civilians in Gaza but silent about Chinese government crimes against humanity in Xinjiang, or demand international prosecution for Russian war crimes in Ukraine while undermining accountability for past US abuses in Afghanistan, weaken the belief in the universality of human rights and the legitimacy of the laws designed to protect them.

In transactional diplomacy, governments disregard the benefits of long-term relationships built on human rights principles to achieve immediate, short-term trade or security gains. When governments pick and choose which obligations to enforce, they perpetuate injustice not only in the present but in the future for those whose rights have been sacrificed – and can embolden abusive governments to extend the reach of their repression. The moral foundation of international human rights demands consistency and steadfastness.

Governments have found it easier to disregard human rights issues in the international arena in part because the international community is not challenging their violations of human rights at home. Across regions, autocrats have worked to erode the independence of key institutions vital for protecting human rights and shrink the space for expressions of dissent with the same end game in mind: to exercise power without constraint.

But just as these threats are interconnected, so too is the power of the human rights framework to deliver on the promise of protecting people's freedom and dignity, no matter who they are or where they live. The protection of human rights has advanced on multiple fronts.

After three years of diplomatic negotiations and a decade of campaigning by civil society groups, 83 countries adopted a political declaration to better protect civilians from the use of explosive weapons in populated areas during armed conflict. The international pledge is the first to formally address the long-standing practice of warring parties to use aerial bombing, artillery, rockets, and missiles in villages, towns, and cities – the leading cause of civilian casualties in armed conflict around the world.

It goes further than simply urging better compliance with the laws of war by committing its signatories to adopt policies and practices that prevent and address harm. Six of the world's top eight arms exporters – the United States, France,

Germany, Italy, the United Kingdom, and South Korea – have adopted the declaration, as well as 25 of 31 NATO member states.

A number of countries addressed the rights of long-marginalized communities. After years of civil society pressure, the Japanese parliament passed its first law to protect LGBT people from "unfair discrimination." Nepal's Supreme Court instructed authorities to recognize same-sex marriages while it considers a case demanding full marriage equality rights. In Mexico, a civil society coalition persuaded Congress to pass a law establishing full legal capacity and the right to supported decision-making for everyone over 18, benefiting millions of people living with disabilities and older people, while the Mexican Supreme Court ruled that Congress must eliminate federal criminal penalties for abortion, meaning that all federal health facilities should provide abortion care.

The human rights and humanitarian crises have caused some to question the effectiveness of the human rights framework as a model for protection and for positive change – especially in the face of selective government outrage, transactional diplomacy seeking short-term gain, growing transnational repression, and the willingness of autocratic leaders to sacrifice rights to consolidate their power.

But this is no basis for giving up on the human rights framework, which remains the roadmap to building thriving, inclusive societies. Governments should respect, protect, and defend human rights with the urgency, vigor, and persistence needed to confront and address the global and existential challenges that threaten our common humanity.

The cost of selective outrage

The October 7 attacks by Hamas-led fighters on Israel were a terrifying assault on civilians. Hamas and other Palestinian armed groups deliberately killed hundreds of civilians, shot families in their homes, and took more than 200 people hostage, including children, people living with disabilities, and older people. Palestinian armed groups launched thousands of rockets toward Israeli communities. Many countries quickly and justifiably condemned these horrific acts.

Israel's government responded by cutting water and electricity to Gaza's 2.3 million civilians and blocking the entry of all but a trickle of fuel, food, and humanitarian aid – a form of collective punishment that is a war crime. The Israeli military ordered more than a million people in Gaza to evacuate their homes and bombarded densely populated areas with heavy weapons, killing thousands of civilians, including children, and reducing entire blocks to rubble. Attacks on populated areas using explosive weapons with wide area effects raise grave concerns of indiscriminate attacks, which are apparent war crimes. Israel used white phosphorus, a chemical that burns human flesh and can cause lifelong suffering, in both Gaza and southern Lebanon.

Many of the governments that condemned Hamas' war crimes have been reserved in responding to those by the Israeli government. These governments' unwillingness to call out Israeli government abuses follows from the refusal by the US and most European Union member countries to urge an end to the Israeli government's 16-year unlawful closure of Gaza and to recognize the ongoing crimes against humanity of apartheid and persecution against Palestinians.

Tradeoffs on human rights in the name of politics are clear when many governments fail to speak out about the Chinese government's intensifying repression, the arbitrary detention of human rights defenders, and its tightening control over civil society, media, and the internet, especially in Xinjiang and Tibet. Chinese authorities' cultural persecution and arbitrary detention of a million Uyghurs and other Turkic Muslims amount to crimes against humanity, yet many governments, including in predominantly Muslim countries, stay silent.

This selective outrage undermines the human rights not only of Palestinians in Gaza and Uyghurs in China but of anyone around the world in need of protection. It sends the message that some people's dignity is worth protecting, but not everyone's – that some lives matter more.

The ripple effects of these inconsistencies shake the legitimacy of the system of rules that we rely on to protect everyone's rights. Governments such as Russia and China then seek to weaponize this weakened legitimacy to reshape the rules-based order to strip it of human rights values and undermine the system that could hold them to account for their countless abuses.

Every government has a responsibility to apply human rights principles to address human rights crises. The people of Sudan have suffered because of the absence of international attention, commitment, and leadership to address the widespread abuses in the country's conflict.

In April 2023, an armed conflict broke out in Sudan when the two most powerful Sudanese generals began battling each other for power. The power struggle between the armed forces leader, Gen. Abdelfattah al-Burhan, and the leader of the Rapid Support Forces, Gen. Mohamed "Hemedti" Hamdan Dagalo, unleashed fighting that resulted in massive abuses against civilians, notably in the Darfur region. Their abuses have mirrored those committed over the past two decades by forces loyal to both generals, for which accountability has remained elusive.

The International Criminal Court (ICC) has brought arrest warrants for past crimes in Darfur, and the ICC prosecutor announced in July that current crimes in Darfur are in his remit. However, the Sudanese authorities have repeatedly obstructed ICC efforts, and the United Nations Security Council has done nearly nothing to tackle the government's intransigence. The resulting impunity – save for one trial of a militia leader at the ICC – has fueled repeated cycles of violence in Sudan, including the current conflict. In 2023, when African countries on the Security Council included Gabon, Ghana, and Mozambique, the UN closed its political mission in Sudan at the insistence of the Sudanese government, ending what little remained of the UN's capacity in the country to protect civilians and publicly report on the rights situation.

Calls to prioritize accountability at the UN Human Rights Council following renewed violence in Sudan were met with strong resistance from Arab states and largely rebuffed by African governments. Western governments were initially reluctant to push for an accountability mechanism in Sudan, unwilling to commit the resources or effort that they had devoted to a similar body for Ukraine immediately after Russia's full-scale invasion in 2022.

A group of countries eventually mustered enough votes to create a mechanism that can collect and preserve evidence of crimes, but not a single African government voted in favor, although some abstained. The Sudanese government has made it clear that it will not cooperate with the mechanism, which will operate outside the country.

And yet, African governments do take positive action on human rights on some issues. They have tended to overwhelmingly support Human Rights Council resolutions that address the human rights situation in Palestine, while Western states oppose them. And in November, the South African government led an effort, supported by ICC member countries Bangladesh, Bolivia, Venezuela,

Comoros, and Djibouti, to back the prosecutor's investigation in Palestine. And in December, the South African government asked the International Court of Justice to determine whether Israel violated its obligations under the 1948 Genocide Convention in its military operations in Gaza. It also asked the court to impose provisional measures directing Israel to cease acts that could violate the Genocide Convention while the court decides on the merits of the case.

All governments can demonstrate human rights leadership to protect civilians. The challenge – and the urgency – is to do so consistently, in a principled manner, no matter the perpetrator or the victim.

The myopia of transactional diplomacy

Governments should center respect for human rights and the rule of law in their domestic policies and foreign policy decisions. Unfortunately, even normally rights-respecting governments at times treat these foundational principles as optional, seeking short-term, politically expedient "solutions" at the expense of building the institutions that would be beneficial for security, trade, energy, and migration in the long term. Choosing transactional diplomacy carries a human cost that is paid not only within, but increasingly beyond, borders.

Examples of transactional diplomacy abound.

US President Joe Biden has shown little appetite to hold responsible human rights abusers who are key to his domestic agenda or are seen as bulwarks to China. US allies like Saudi Arabia, India, and Egypt violate the rights of their people on a massive scale yet have not had to overcome hurdles to deepen their ties with the US. Vietnam, the Philippines, India, and other nations the US wants as counters to China have been feted at the White House without regard for their human rights abuses at home.

Similarly, on migration, Washington has been reluctant to criticize Mexico, on whom it leans to prevent migrants and asylum seekers from entering the US. The Biden administration and that of Mexican President Andrés Manuel López Obrador have worked in tandem to expel or deport tens of thousands of migrants in the US to Mexico and block thousands more from reaching the US to seek safety, knowing they are targeted in Mexico for kidnapping, extortion, assault, and other abuse. Biden has largely remained silent while López Obrador has attempted to undermine the independence of the Mexican judiciary and other constitutional bodies, demonized journalists and human rights activists, and allowed the military to block accountability for horrific abuses.

The EU has its own brand of transactional diplomacy focused on circumventing its human rights obligations to asylum seekers and migrants, especially those from Africa and the Middle East. Member states' preferred response is to push people back to other countries or strike deals with abusive governments like Libya, Türkiye and, most recently, Tunisia to keep migrants outside of the European bloc. Perversely, some EU member states, including France, Greece, Hungary, and Italy, have even taken measures to punish those who extend humanitarian aid and assistance to migrants and asylum seekers who arrive by irregular means.

Democratic governments in the Asia-Pacific region, including Japan, South Korea, and Australia, repeatedly deprioritize human rights in the name of assuring military alliances with security partners like Thailand and the Philippines, seeking to counter Chinese government influence with governments in Sri Lanka and Nepal, and securing trade and economic deals with few, if any, human rights commitments in fast-growing economies like Vietnam and Indonesia.

Conducting transactional diplomacy with blinders is dangerous. Trying to separate human rights and the rule of law from more "pragmatic" decisions squanders valuable leverage to influence the practices and policies of rights-violating governments. It can also contribute to further human rights violations, including transnational repression.

The alarming reach of transnational repression

Governments commit acts of transnational repression, also known as extraterritorial repression, when they commit human rights abuses against their nationals living abroad or their family members at home. While this is a longstanding phenomenon, increased communications, travel, and new technologies have allowed for greater unlawful practices, including arbitrary deportations, abductions, and killings.

Under Prime Minister Narendra Modi, India's democracy has slid toward autocracy, with authorities targeting minorities, tightening repression, and dismantling independent institutions, including federal investigative agencies. During summits with Modi, his counterparts in the US, Australia, the UK, and France failed to publicly raise rights concerns, instead prioritizing trade and security. French President Emmanuel Macron even awarded Modi the Legion of Honor, France's highest order of merit, during Bastille Day celebrations.

Silence on the Indian government's worsening rights record appears to have emboldened the Modi government to extend repressive tactics across borders, including to intimidate diaspora activists and academics or restrict their entry into India.

In March, Indian authorities blocked the messages of several high-profile Canadian Twitter users who are critical of the Indian government. In September, Canada's Prime Minister Justin Trudeau described "credible allegations" that agents of the Indian government were involved in the assassination of a separatist Sikh activist in Canada, a claim that Indian officials denied. And in November, US authorities indicted a man for a failed plot with an Indian government official to assassinate a separatist Sikh activist in the US.

India's transnational repression is not an isolated example. Three decades of impunity for the Rwandan government's repression of civil and political rights at home has emboldened it to stifle dissent beyond its borders. As Rwanda has grown more prominent on the international stage, leading multilateral institutions and becoming one of the largest African contributors of peacekeeping troops, the UN and Rwanda's international partners have consistently failed to recognize the scope and severity of its human rights violations.

The Rwandan government has carried out over a dozen kidnappings or attempted kidnappings, enforced disappearances, assaults, threats, and killings, as well as harassment against Rwandan nationals who are perceived critics of the government living in Australia, Belgium, Canada, France, Kenya, Mozambique, South Africa, Tanzania, Uganda, the UK, and the US. Their relatives living in Rwanda are also under intense scrutiny and vulnerable to human rights violations.

Similarly, the failure of countries to push back against Chinese government abuses has tacitly permitted Beijing to escalate and export its repression against both Chinese and non-Chinese people and institutions critical of the ruling Chinese Communist Party. Pro-democracy students and academics at Western universities have faced harassment, surveillance, and intimidation for speaking up about Chinese government abuses in Hong Kong, Tibet, or Xinjiang. The Chinese government has pressured governments to forcibly return human rights defenders, like Lu Siwei, a lawyer, from Laos. And in a blatant effort to stymie international criticism about the Chinese government's dismantling of democracy in Hong Kong, the authorities there issued baseless arrest warrants and HK$1 million (US$128,000) bounties on eight democracy activists and former legislators in exile.

If repressive governments can get away with heavy-handed tactics to silence human rights defenders, exiled politicians, journalists, and critics beyond their borders, then nowhere is safe.

Sacrificing human rights to consolidate power

This year, nearly half the world's population will be eligible to vote in elections around the world. If free and fair, elections can be a critical expression of the public will when it comes to a country's priorities and values. But accountable governance – where governments center human rights and the rule of law in their policies and decision-making – depends on much more than a trip to the ballot box.

Independent, rights-respecting institutions, including the judiciary, ombudspersons, and human rights commissions, can effectively guard against capricious decision-making, stem legislative overreach, and uphold the rule of law. An active and independent civil society is critical to ensure that the decisions of those who exercise political power serve the public interest. But civil society and the institutions needed to protect rights and free societies have become renewed battlegrounds for autocratic leaders around the world looking to eliminate scrutiny of their decisions and actions.

In Tunisia, President Kais Saied, elected in 2019, has steadily eliminated checks and balances, including by weakening the judiciary, cracking down on political opponents and perceived critics, and targeting freedom of expression and the press.

El Salvador's President Nayib Bukele has used mass detention of mostly low-income people as an ostensible solution for high levels of crime in the country. He has used this crackdown to grab and consolidate power, an effort made easier by his purge of the Supreme Court and steady capture of the judiciary. Peru's Congress has taken measures to undermine other democratic institutions and limit lawmakers' accountability, including by seeking to remove members of the National Board of Justice, a body critical to protecting the independence of judges, prosecutors, and electoral authorities.

In Guatemala, a judiciary largely co-opted by politicians and other corrupt actors threatened to set aside the electoral victory of President-elect Bernardo Arévalo, who campaigned on an anti-corruption platform. In Nicaragua, where President Daniel Ortega and his wife, Vice-President Rosario Murillo, have virtually no checks on their power, the government has used abusive legislation to shut down over 3,500 nongovernmental organizations – roughly 50 percent of the registered groups in the country.

The slow destruction of these vital checks and balances can spell alarming consequences for human rights and the rule of law.

In Thailand, the politically compromised Constitutional Court effectively subverted the will of the Thai people in the 2023 election when it suspended the leading candidate for prime minister from parliament on bogus charges. In Bangladesh, Prime Minister Sheikh Hasina's government ordered the arrest of over 10,000 opposition leaders and supporters ahead of the January 2024 election, and a compliant judiciary has disqualified hundreds of candidates.

While elections in Poland ushered in a new government at the end of 2023, the country's previous Law and Justice government has systematically eroded the rule of law by undermining judicial independence and silencing independent civil society groups and other critics, including through the courts and the police. The Law and Justice party's capture of the justice system made possible the former government's signature attacks on women's sexual and reproductive health rights.

The cost can be measured in lives: following a 2020 ruling by the politically compromised Constitutional Tribunal, which virtually banned legal abortion in Poland, at least six women died after doctors did not terminate their pregnancies despite complications. In May 2023, an abortion rights activist was convicted of helping a woman to get abortion pills and was sentenced to eight months of community service – the first known prosecution of its kind in the EU. Poland's new government will face a challenging role to reestablish the independence of key institutions, including the judiciary, which will likely take years.

In the US, state legislatures and the courts have weakened laws to prevent racial discrimination in voting, such as the Voting Rights Act, almost to the point of ineffectiveness. In Florida and other US states, educational censorship is limiting people's ability to learn about sexuality and gender identity, as well as the history of slavery and racism in the US. Politicians know that accurate information on these issues is one factor inspiring people to participate in civic activism and hold authorities to account. Some 4.6 million people in the US, disproportionately Black, were disenfranchised under US laws as of 2022, after being convicted of a criminal offense.

Meanwhile, enhanced civic engagement to meet the urgency of the climate crisis has triggered the nefarious use of vague laws to target activists to make it harder to express dissent. Across Europe, in the US, Australia, and Vietnam, governments are imposing harsh and disproportionate measures to punish activists and deter the climate movement. The United Arab Emirates (UAE), one of the world's largest oil producers, hosted the UN Climate Conference COP28 in 2023, an apparent attempt to burnish its image while pushing the expansion of fossil fuels and undermining efforts to confront the climate crisis. People trying to speak out about the UAE's record face risks of unlawful surveillance, arbitrary arrest, detention, and ill-treatment.

Governments are increasingly using technology platforms to silence critics and censor dissent. Especially in countries lacking independent judiciaries or oversight, governments can impose laws that essentially become traps set for critics, activists, and unsuspecting internet users. An especially egregious example is Saudi Arabia's death sentence for Muhammad al-Ghamdi, a 54-year-old retired teacher, for violating the country's counterterrorism law based on his peaceful expression on X and YouTube.

Months before its May 2023 elections, Türkiye's parliament tightened control of social media and introduced a new abusive criminal speech offense, ostensibly to fight the spread of fake news online. In practice, the laws added to the existing arsenal of online censorship legislation, providing more possible restrictions on access to information and threatening severe penalties against tech companies for failing to comply with user data and content take-down demands. As a result, President Recep Tayyip Erdoğan's government equipped itself with the capacity to further limit dissenting views online before and during the elections, which the ruling party ultimately won.

How institutions delivered for human rights

For all the backsliding in 2023, we also saw shining examples where institutions and movements delivered victories for human rights. Indeed, these successes illustrate why self-serving politicians and repressive governments work so hard to curtail them – and why all governments should recognize and support these fragile successes.

In March, the ICC issued arrest warrants for Russian President Vladimir Putin and his children's rights commissioner, Maria Lvova-Belova, for war crimes relating to the deportation of children from occupied territories of Ukraine to Russia and forced transfers of children to other Russia-occupied territories of Ukraine. The warrant created a diplomatic dilemma for the South African government, which hosted a BRICS summit (Brazil, Russia, India, China, South Africa) in August. After months of conflicting messages from South African authorities about the country's obligations as an ICC member to arrest Putin if he set foot in South Africa, news broke that Putin would not attend the summit in person. Two days later, the Gauteng High Court ruled that South Africa had an obligation to arrest Putin and that the ICC arrest warrant should be carried out in the country.

In November, the International Court of Justice ordered the Syrian government to take all measures within its power to prevent acts of torture and other abuses. The case before the world court is a critical counterweight to the rush of several Arab countries to normalize ties with the Syrian government, despite continuing rights abuses, and little or no accountability for past crimes under President Bashar al-Assad. There are also efforts to hold individuals to account for torture and other atrocities in Syria before courts in Germany, Sweden, and France. These cases are critical for victims to see their abusers brought to justice and can help establish that refugees in these countries should not be sent back to a country where they face real risks to their lives.

Brazil's Supreme Court upheld all Indigenous peoples' rights to their traditional lands, thwarting efforts by Santa Catarina state to challenge land claims by the Xokleng Indigenous people if they could not prove they were physically present on the land on October 5, 1988, when Brazil's current Constitution was adopted. The ruling was a huge boost for Indigenous people in their fight to preserve their way of life. It was also relevant in the fight against climate change, as demarcating Indigenous territories has time and again shown to be one of the most effective barriers against deforestation in the Amazon. Yet, the powerful farm lobby in Congress reacted by approving a bill to limit Indigenous land claims that runs counter the Supreme Court´s decision. Congress later overturned a presidential veto of the bill. Indigenous groups and others said that they would file petitions before the Supreme Court to strike down the law.

In November, the UK's highest court unanimously found that Rwanda is not a safe third country for the government to send asylum seekers, striking down an agreement that effectively outsourced and shifted the UK's asylum responsibilities to Rwanda. Drawing attention to Rwanda's poor rights record, including threats to Rwandans living in the UK, the court found that asylum seekers sent to Rwanda could face a real risk of being returned to their home countries where they could face ill-treatment. The agreement was found to violate the UK's obligations under international and domestic law.

The UK government has since introduced a "Safety of Rwanda (Asylum and Immigration) Bill" to parliament to get around the court's ruling. But the UK cannot legislate its way around the fact that Rwanda counters criticism with violence and abuse, including against refugees.

These victories highlight the tremendous power of independent, rights-respecting, and inclusive institutions and of civil society to challenge those who wield political power to serve the public interest and chart a rights-respecting path forward. All governments, in their bilateral relations and at the multilateral level, should redouble efforts to uplift key institutions and protect civic space wherever it is under threat.

***

These human rights crises demonstrate the urgency of all governments applying longstanding and mutually agreed principles of international human rights law everywhere. Principled diplomacy, by which governments center their human rights obligations in their relations with other countries, can influence oppressive conduct and have a meaningful impact for people whose rights are being violated. Support for institutions that solidify human rights protections will help promote rights-respecting governments. Upholding human rights consistently, across the board, no matter who the victims are or where the rights violations are being committed, is the only way to build the world we want to live in.

HUMAN
RIGHTS
WATCH

"This Hell Was My Only Option"

Abuses Against Migrants and Asylum Seekers Pushed to Cross the Darién Gap

WORLD REPORT 2024

COUNTRIES

HUMAN
RIGHTS
WATCH
"Schools are Failing Boys Too"
The Taliban's Impact on Boys' Education in Afghanistan

Afghanistan

The human rights situation in Afghanistan continued to deteriorate in 2023 as the Taliban committed widespread human rights violations, particularly against women and girls. Afghanistan remained the only country where women and girls could not access secondary and higher education and were banned from most employment with international nongovernmental organizations (NGOs) and the United Nations (except in health care, nutrition, and primary education). Women also faced significant barriers to freedom of movement and speech. Human Rights Watch has concluded that the pattern of abuses against women and girls in Afghanistan amounts to the crime against humanity of gender persecution.

Taliban authorities cracked down further on local media and freedom of speech and increased arbitrary detentions of journalists, human rights defenders, and civil society activists, including women protesters. Their forces detained and executed members of the former government's security forces. On August 22, 2023, the UN reported that since August 2021 there had been at least 800 instances of extrajudicial killing, arbitrary arrests, and detentions, over 144 cases of torture and brutal treatment, 218 extrajudicial deaths, and 14 enforced disappearances of former government employees and security personnel by Taliban forces.

More than 28 million people, almost two-thirds of the population, needed humanitarian aid in Afghanistan in 2023, 14.7 million of whom needed it for basic survival, making it one of the world's worst humanitarian crises. The UN reported that by mid-2023, 4 million Afghans were acutely malnourished, including 3.2 million children under 5. The loss of most foreign assistance after August 2021, a shortfall in humanitarian assistance in 2023, and a longstanding drought exacerbated by climate change were the primary reasons for the humanitarian crisis.

A December 24, 2022 ban on women working with local and international NGOs, except in positions relating to health, nutrition, and education, continues to deprive many women of their livelihoods. The ban exacerbated the humanitarian crisis by making it more difficult to deliver aid to women and girls and assess and monitor the humanitarian needs of women and girls who generally have more difficulty accessing food and other humanitarian assistance.

Afghanistan's criminal code makes same-sex conduct a criminal offense, and the Taliban have echoed the previous government's support for the criminalization of same-sex relations, with some of their leaders vowing to punish lesbian, gay, bisexual, and transgender (LGBT) people, many of whom live in hiding as a result.

The number of attacks by the Islamic State of Khorasan Province (ISKP), the Afghan affiliate of the Islamic State, declined, but several bombings and improvised explosive devices caused civilian casualties.

Women's and Girls' Rights

The Taliban have imposed and enforced rules and policies that comprehensively bar women and girls from exercising their fundamental rights, including freedom of assembly, movement, work, and education. These rules also undermine other rights, such as the rights to life, livelihood, and access to health care, food, and water. In addition to the ban on women working in most jobs for the UN and international NGOs, Taliban authorities previously prohibited women from working in the public sector or holding senior positions within their central or provincial institutions. Most women who worked for the former government have been unable to resume their jobs.

In most of Afghanistan's provinces, the authorities have also issued regulations that forbid women from travelling or leaving their houses without being accompanied by a male relative as a chaperone, including to work. In most places, women must wear a full hijab and have their faces covered in public.

Actions by Taliban authorities through 2023 suggest the crackdown is deepening, including their refusal to allow 63 women to travel to the United Arab Emirates to accept scholarships, their closure of all beauty salons, which cost women 60,000 jobs, and their ban on women visiting the Band-e-Amir national park.

Taliban security forces have used excessive force to disperse women protesting against Taliban policies and have arbitrarily detained some female protesters, holding them for hours or days. In some cases, their family members have also been detained. Detained women protesters and their family members have sometimes been tortured. Among the women's rights protesters detained in

2023 were Neda Parwani and Zholia Parsi, both taken by the Taliban in September.

The UN special rapporteur on the situation of human rights in Afghanistan and the Working Group on discrimination against women and girls visited Afghanistan in April and May. They presented a report to the UN Human Rights Council in June describing the widespread and systematic discrimination to which women and girls in Afghanistan are subjected, concluding it "constitutes gender persecution and an institutionalized framework of gender apartheid."

Extrajudicial Killings, Enforced Disappearances, and Torture

Taliban forces carried out revenge killings and enforced disappearances of former government officials and security force personnel. In a report published in August 2023, the UN Assistance Mission in Afghanistan (UNAMA) documented 218 extrajudicial killings, 14 enforced disappearances, and over 144 cases of torture and mistreatment of detainees since August 2021. In a September report, UNAMA documented the systematic torture of detainees, particularly by the Taliban's intelligence agency, the General Directorate of Intelligence (GDI), with methods including waterboarding. UNAMA reported public floggings of at least 34 men, 8 women, and 2 boys for drug offenses, gambling, and so-called moral crimes since August 2021.

Attacks on Journalists and the Media

Taliban authorities enforced extensive censorship and used unlawful force against Afghan media and journalists in Kabul and the provinces. Hundreds of media outlets have been closed, and most female media workers across Afghanistan have lost their jobs. Foreign correspondents also face severe visa restrictions when coming to Afghanistan to report, and many Afghan journalists now live in exile due to safety concerns.

Taliban arbitrary arrests of media workers increased in 2023. On August 13, the Taliban detained Ataullah Omar, a journalist reporting for Tolo News, and accused him of working with media outlets operating from exile. On August 10, Faqir Mohammad Faqirzai, the manager of Kilid Radio, and Jan Agha Saleh, a reporter, were detained by the Taliban's GDI. On the same day, Hasib Hassas, a reporter for Salam Watandar, was arrested in Kunduz. All three journalists were released a few days later. Taliban authorities rarely provide any information about the basis for such arrests or whether those detained will be put on trial. Those in custody lack access to lawyers and in most cases family members are not allowed to visit them. On January 5, the French Afghan journalist Mortaza Behboudi was arrested; he was released on October 18 with any charges against him unknown.

Attacks on Civil Society Activists

The Taliban also continued to crack down on civil society activists. On February 2, the Taliban arrested university professor Ismail Mashal who had publicly protested the Taliban's ban on women's university education. On March 27, the GDI arrested Matiullah Wesa, an education activist and the founder of Penpath, an organization that advocates for education in Afghanistan, along with several of his family members. He was released on October 26 with no charges against him.

After Taliban authorities closed down beauty salons on July 19, security forces used water cannons and fired shots into the air to disperse a peaceful protest by salon owners and employees. Four women protesters were reportedly arrested and released later that day. The Taliban detained dozens of women's rights protesters across the country in 2023.

Economic and Humanitarian Crises

In 2023, an unprecedented number of Afghans needed humanitarian assistance. According to the UN Afghanistan Humanitarian Response Plan for 2023, acute malnutrition affected more than 4 million people, including more than 840,000 pregnant and nursing women and over 3 million children. Six million people were expected to face extreme food insecurity by the end of the year, putting them one step away from famine. The loss of millions of jobs after August 2021, the loss of most foreign aid, and a multi-year drought were the principal reasons people were unable to buy enough food to feed their families.

The ban on Afghan women working for international humanitarian NGOs and the UN exacerbated the crisis and constrained the operational capacity of humanitarian aid organizations, with long-lasting consequences for all people in need, especially women-headed households. The UN Office for the Coordination of Humanitarian Affairs (OCHA) estimated 48 percent of women-headed households have a poor Food Consumption Score (FCS) compared to 39 percent of male-headed households.

The Taliban's restrictions on women's rights are among the factors that have influenced donors' decisions to cut aid, leading to an alarming funding shortfall. The UN requested US$3.26 billion in humanitarian funding for Afghanistan for 2023, but as of November, it had received less than 25 percent of the appeal. Afghan and international NGOs cite this shortfall as the main reason for stopping aid programs. By late 2023, several organizations providing health care were either closing clinics and hospitals or withdrawing support for them due to lack of funding.

Attacks on Civilians

On January 12, the ISKP claimed responsibility for a suicide bombing at the Ministry of Foreign Affairs in Kabul that killed 33, many of them civilians, and wounded at least 45. On June 6, a car bomb killed the Taliban's provincial governor in Badakhshan; a suicide attack on June 8 during the funeral killed nine civilians and injured 37. On November 7, a minibus explosion killed seven and injured 20 members of the Hazara community. The attack occurred in the Dasht-e Barchi area of Kabul, a predominantly Shia Hazara neighborhood that has seen many ISKP attacks.

Key International Actors

In March 2023, the UN Security Council extended the mandate of UNAMA, including its role to report on human rights conditions. It also called on the secretary-general "to conduct and provide, no later than 17 November, an integrated, independent assessment, after consultations with all relevant Afghan political actors and stakeholders, including relevant authorities, Afghan women and civil society, as well as the region and the wider international community." Feridun Sinirlioğlu, the former permanent representative of Türkiye to the UN, was appointed to lead the assessment. Human Rights Watch and others stressed that the assessment should prioritize the rights of women and girls.

In October, the UN Human Rights Council in Geneva renewed and further strengthened the mandate of the UN special rapporteur on Afghanistan.

On December 21, 2022, Australia, Canada, France, Germany, Italy, Japan, the Netherlands, Norway, Spain, Switzerland, the United Kingdom, the United States, and the European Union issued a joint statement condemning the ban on women attending universities. On February 1, the US State Department announced additional travel restrictions on several Taliban officials in response to the Taliban's ban on women's university education and most jobs with international NGOs.

In Australia, the Office of the Special Investigator charged a former special forces soldier with a war crime for allegedly executing an Afghan civilian, the first of several such charges expected in the ongoing investigation of abuses by Australian military personnel against Afghan civilians and captured combatants in Afghanistan.

Following authorization by the pre-trial chamber in November 2022, the Office of the Prosecutor of the International Criminal Court resumed its investigation into alleged crimes in Afghanistan, focusing on those perpetrated by the Taliban and ISKP while continuing to de-prioritize alleged abuses by US personnel and former Afghan government forces.

On April 5, the UN issued a statement condemning the Taliban's ban on Afghan women working with the UN. The EU and many countries issued similar statements of condemnation.

Algeria

Algerian authorities have intensified their repression of freedoms of expression, the press, association, assembly, and movement, as part of their continued efforts to crush organized contestation.

They have dissolved major civil society organizations, suspended opposition political parties and independent media outlets, and continued to use restrictive legislation to prosecute—including on dubious charges of terrorism and receiving funding to harm state security—human rights defenders, activists, journalists, and lawyers, pushing some of them to flee into exile.

Between March and April, the authorities also adopted new legislation that tightens government control on the media and a new law on unions that could further limit workers' ability to organize freely.

Political Repression

In an example of wielding manifestly political charges to imprison critics, a Constantine court sentenced journalist Mustapha Bendjama and researcher Raouf Farrah on August 29 to two years of imprisonment for "receiving funding to commit actions undermining state security," under article 95 bis of the penal code, and "publishing classified information on electronic networks," under article 38 of Ordinance 09-21 on data protection. On October 26, an appeals court reduced their prison sentence to 20 months, 12 of them suspended. Both of them, along with several others, were detained in February, apparently in retribution for the irregular departure from Algeria of activist Amira Bouraoui, whom authorities have forbidden from leaving the country since August 2021. Farrah was released in October.

On November 7, a Constantine court sentenced Bendjama to six months of imprisonment in a second case for allegedly assisting Bouraoui to leave Algeria. Bendjama, who is the editor-in-chief of regional newspaper *Le Provincial*, had previously faced police and judicial harassment for his work and involvement in the Hirak protest movement. After receiving an initial sentence of one year in prison, he was sentenced on appeal on July 16 to a fine for defamation and "undermining the public interest" in connection with an article denouncing the enforcement of Covid-related restrictions.

On July 4, Algiers' Court of Appeal confirmed the sentencing of Slimane Bouhafs to three years in prison and a fine for "insulting Islam" and terrorism-related charges. In August 2021, Bouhafs—a Christian convert, an Amazigh (Berber) activist, and a refugee recognized by the United Nations refugee agency (UNHCR) living in Tunisia—was abducted from his home and forcibly returned to Algeria, where he reappeared in detention.

On March 2, an Algiers court sentenced Zaki Hannache, a human rights defender and refugee living in Tunisia since 2022, to three years in prison in absentia in relation to his peaceful activism. Hannache has been closely monitoring the arrests and trials of peaceful activists and protesters since the Hirak protest movement began in 2019.

The authorities have also increasingly imposed arbitrary travel bans on activists and perceived critics because of their associative activities or opinions, sometimes without any legal basis or time limitation. At least a dozen activists, including Bendjama and Bouraoui, have been under travel bans.

Freedoms of Assembly and Association

On March 7, Parliament adopted a new law on unions that forbids union members from participating in political activities and unions from having any ties with political parties. The law also conditions the right to strike on "not harming the principles of the continuity of public service, the protection of people's and property's security," vague concepts that authorities could interpret to arbitrarily restrict strikes.

On February 23, the State Council, Algeria's highest administrative jurisdiction, confirmed the October 2021 decision by the Algiers Administrative Court to dissolve the Rassemblement Action Jeunesse (RAJ), on the grounds that the 30-year-old association, which had supported the Hirak protest movement, had violated the law on associations. As of September, three RAJ members, including its president, Abdelouahab Fersaoui, were still facing prosecution for their activism.

On June 29, 2022, the Algiers Administrative Court dissolved the Algerian League for the Defense of Human (LADDH), Algeria's oldest independent human rights group, for holding "suspicious activities" that did not conform to its by-laws, such as collaborating with international NGOs, taking interest in migration issues, or denouncing government repression of protests. The LADDH said it was not until January 2023 that it learned of the case and dissolution order against it. As of September, six of its members were being prosecuted, including three on dubious terrorism-related charges: Kaddour Chouicha, Said Boudour, and Djamila Loukil.

In February, the State Council also indefinitely suspended the activities of the Democratic and Social Movement (MDS), a left-wing opposition party, and closed its headquarters in Algiers, allegedly for non-compliance with Law 12-04 on political parties.

The Algerian legal framework related to associations breaches the right to freedom of association. It gives authorities broad discretion to withhold legal recognition from nongovernmental associations and requires groups to obtain a registration receipt before they can legally operate. Law 12-06 also forbids associations from receiving any foreign funding or cooperating with or seeking membership in foreign organizations without the government's agreement, and it empowers the government to suspend associations that interfere with "internal affairs of the state" or violate "national sovereignty."

Authorities also use Law 12-04 on political parties to muzzle the opposition. The legislation requires prior authorization to create a party, provides for intrusive government oversight, and enables authorities to suspend parties prior to any judicial order.

Freedom of Media

On June 18, Algiers' court of appeal increased the sentence imposed on journalist Ihsane El Kadi from five to seven years in jail for "receiving funding to commit actions prejudicial to state security." El Kadi was arrested on December 24, 2022, after publishing an article on the army's reluctance to see President Abdelmadjid Tebboune serve a second term. An Algiers court that initially sentenced him on April 2 also ordered the dissolution of his media company, which encompasses the two outlets Radio M and Maghreb Emergent.

On April 13, Algeria adopted a repressive new law on information that forbids foreign funding and bans dual citizens from owning media outlets or shares in media businesses. The law also heavily relies on vaguely worded terms to regulate media activity, such as respect for "national sovereignty and unity," and other provisions that could undermine journalists' access to information and their right to inform.

Migrants' Rights

In 2023, Algerian authorities continued arbitrarily and collectively expelling to Niger migrants of multiple nationalities, including children, often without individual screenings or due process. Between January and August 2023, Algeria expelled more than 20,000 migrants to its border with Niger, according to Niger-based NGO Alarme Phone Sahara.

Migrants continued to report cases of violence, theft of their belongings, arbitrary detention, poor treatment in detention, and other mistreatment by Algerian authorities during arrests, detention, and expulsions to land borders.

While Algeria deported about 27,000 migrants to its southern border between 2015 and 2018, Algerian authorities expelled more than 36,000 migrants in 2022 alone, according to Doctors Without Borders (MSF), and 27,208 in 2021.

Women's Rights

Algeria's Family Code contains discriminatory provisions against women and restricts women's rights. The code allows men to divorce their spouses unilaterally without explanation but requires women to apply to courts for a divorce on specified grounds. It also makes fathers, not mothers, the automatic guardians of their "minor" children (under 19). Interior Ministry instructions require fathers or legal guardians to provide written permission for their "minor" children when applying for their passport.

Algeria's laws contain loopholes that allow convictions to be dropped, or sentences reduced, if victims pardon their abusers. Article 326 of the penal code, a colonial-era relic, allows a person who abducts a minor to escape prosecution if he marries his victim.

Sexual Orientation and Gender Identity

Same-sex relations remain punishable under article 338 of the penal code by up to two years in prison. Article 333 increases the penalty to up to three years in prison and a fine for public indecency if it involves "acts against nature with a member of the same sex," whether between men or women.

Angola

Angolan state security forces were implicated in serious human rights abuses, including more than a dozen extrajudicial executions and other unlawful killings, excessive use of force against peaceful protesters, and arbitrary detentions. Authorities continued to forcibly evict people and conduct demolitions without the necessary procedural guarantees or the provision of alternative adequate housing or adequate compensation for those evicted. The press was under attack on several occasions throughout the year, as authorities continued to use draconian media laws to repress and harass journalists. Freedom of association was under pressure as the government tried to pass a new nongovernmental organization (NGO) law limiting the activities of civil society groups. Women and girls, particularly street traders and migrants, continued to suffer abuses by security forces. In August, Angola assumed the one-year rotating presidency of the Southern African Development Community (SADC) regional body.

Abuses by State Security Forces

Angolan state security forces have been implicated in serious human rights abuses, including more than a dozen extrajudicial executions and other unlawful killings, excessive use of force against peaceful protesters, and arbitrary detentions, throughout 2023.

In February, men who identified themselves as Criminal Investigation Service (SIC) officials took into custody a group of young men whose bodies were found three days later at a hospital morgue in Luanda. The sister of one of the victims said that his body was found with bullet wounds and "holes in the head" and that the relatives of the other seven victims also found bullet wounds on their bodies.

In June, police officers in Huambo city fired on taxi drivers protesting an increase in fuel prices, which surged following the partial removal of government-funded fuel subsidies in the context of an ongoing International Monetary Fund (IMF) lending program. A police statement seen by Human Rights Watch confirmed the killing of five people. The media reported that as of June 7, the number of deaths had increased to eight after three people died from their injuries in the hospital.

In a statement seen by Human Rights Watch, the Huambo police said "it was not possible to avoid" the killings, as officers tried to contain "acts of violence" by protesters who destroyed properties, confronted the authorities, and used burning tires to block roads.

Also in June, police fired tear gas in the capital, Luanda, and other cities, like Benguela and Namibe, as thousands of peaceful protesters took to the streets over the fuel price increases caused by the removal of government-funded subsidies. In the same month, police detained dozens of activists and artists, including the musician Pedro Sapalo, known as "Pedrito de Bié." Sapalo told Human Rights Watch that he was accused of "inciting tribalism" for allegedly making the comparison between Bié and Bengo provinces.

Forced Evictions and Illegal Demolitions

Angolan authorities continued to forcibly evict people and conduct demolitions without the necessary procedural guarantees or the provision of alternative adequate housing or adequate compensation for those evicted.

In February, Angolan security forces raided Luanda's Zango 3 neighborhood, forcibly evicting people and demolishing over 300 homes, leaving hundreds homeless. Residents said that those who refused to abandon their houses or who gathered to peacefully demonstrate against the security forces' actions were beaten and arrested. Local authorities claimed the houses had been built illegally. In June, they acknowledged what they called "excesses" of the security forces during the evictions and pledged to relocate the homeless families to another area. At time of writing, the evicted residents had not been relocated.

Freedom of Expression and Media

The press was under attack on several occasions throughout 2023, as authorities continued to use draconian media laws to repress and harass journalists.

In September, authorities charged Angolan journalist Liberato Furtado Pereira with criminal defamation, insult, and forgery, after a complaint by prosecutor Elizete Francisco in connection with a November 2020 report alleging that Francisco used her personal account to collect payments due to the general prosecutor's office. According to the Committee to Protect Journalists (CPJ), the prosecutor filed the complaint one day after Furtado sought her comment on the allegations.

In March, the privately owned Camunda News website suspended its operations indefinitely, following months of government harassment. In October 2022, the Angolan police National Criminal Investigation Service (SIC) interrogated the owner of the publication, David Boio, about an activist and co-host of one of the outlet's shows; the activist is facing charges of rebellion and outrage against the president. According to CPJ, in February and March 2023, Boio and other Camunda News staff were again questioned for several hours about the outlet, the publication's legal status, and funding.

In October, the prison sentence of Ana da Silva Miguel, a social media influencer popularly known as Neth Nahara, was increased from six months to two years for "insulting" and "disregarding" the president, after she used her TikTok account to accuse him of anarchy and disorganization.

Freedom of Association

Freedom of association was under pressure as the government tried to pass a new law limiting the work of civil society groups.

In May, the Angolan parliament voted on the first draft of the Law on the Status of Non-Governmental Organizations, which civil society groups said contradicts Angola's international legal commitments to uphold the freedoms of expression and assembly.

Among other things, the law establishes a supervisory body with the power to dissolve NGOs without recourse to judicial proceedings and prohibits NGOs from engaging in "subversive acts or acts that could be perceived as such." The law is currently undergoing revision by a special committee of parliament before being reapproved by the parliament and subsequently sent to the president for final sign-off.

The crackdown on peaceful protesters and activists in the Cabinda enclave continued in 2023, in violation of international law. Authorities refused all the requests by Cabinda pro-independence activists to peacefully assemble. Where meetings took place, police violently interrupted them and arbitrarily detained participants.

In March, Angolan security forces in pickup trucks raided Colegio Privado, a private school in Cabinda, breaking into one of the classrooms where dozens of people were attending a human rights workshop organized by a Christian NGO.

Three organizers and forty-five participants were arrested. Most were questioned and released within 48 hours, but their lawyers said that seven were charged with criminal association and rebellion, which carries criminal punishments of up to eight years in prison.

Rights of Women and Girls, Particularly Street Traders and Migrants

Security forces continued to commit serious human rights abuses against women and girls, particularly street traders and migrants.

In February, the Women's Movement for Civil and Political Rights in Angola denounced physical attacks, mistreatment, and sexual harassment by police officers against local women street traders, also known as "Zungueiras".

Also in February, media reported that according to a doctor, officials, and the UN, Angolan security force personnel and others raped Congolese women and children and otherwise abused them during mass expulsions of migrant workers over the preceding six months. Multiple media reports in April cited a yet-to-be published United Nations report that had documented the abuses.

In May, police with dogs fired tear gas without warning at a crowd of women vendors who had gathered to march from the local Sao Paulo market to the Luanda governor's official residence to protest the city's decision to reorganize informal street markets in some areas of the capital.

According to the UN Children's Fund (UNICEF), some 30 percent of Angolan girls and 6 percent of boys are married before 18.

Key International Actors

In January, the European Union gave US$850,000 to Angola to finance four human rights projects, including on promoting sexual and reproductive rights, combating gender-based violence, and strengthening the right to information and freedom of expression.

Angola continued its efforts in conflict resolution and peacebuilding across central Africa, particularly in eastern Democratic Republic of Congo. In March, the government announced it would send troops to the region, days after the peace talks it brokered did not end the fighting. A statement from the Angolan president's office said the soldiers would be deployed to help secure areas that have been held by the M23 rebel group and to protect ceasefire monitors.

In August, Angola took up the one-year rotating presidency of the SADC regional body.

In September, United States Secretary of Defense Lloyd Austin visited Angola and pledged to deepening cooperation "on military modernization, training in maritime security, and medical readiness."

Argentina

Argentina's longstanding economic crisis, which brought soaring levels of inflation and an accelerated currency depreciation in 2023, increased poverty and hindered the realization of economic and social rights.

The government pushed for a politically motivated Congressional impeachment process against Supreme Court justices and used hostile rhetoric against judges.

For years, Congress has failed to appoint an attorney general, an ombudsperson, and a Supreme Court justice, important human rights officials whose selections would require a two-thirds majority vote in Congress. High levels of polarization, which increased during the 2023 presidential campaign, have contributed to Congressional deadlock and undermined the rule of law.

In November, Javier Milei defeated incumbent minister of economy Sergio Massa in a presidential run-off. As a candidate, Milei promised to carry out severe cuts in government spending, questioned climate change, minimized systematic human rights violations committed during the country's latest dictatorship, and criticized the decriminalization of abortion. He took office on December 10, on the 40th anniversary of Argentina's return to democracy.

Threats to Democratic Institutions

In January, then-President Alberto Fernández asked Congress to impeach all four Supreme Court justices. A Congressional committee dominated by pro-administration legislators voted in February to initiate the impeachment and as of October was deliberating and calling witnesses. A two-thirds majority in the House of Representatives and then the Senate is required for impeachment.

The proceedings focus on three rulings: the first from 2017 that opened the door to the early release of people convicted of crimes against humanity; the second from 2021 that made the Supreme Court president the president of the Council of the Judiciary, which appoints federal judges; and the third from 2022 requiring a more favorable distribution of resources to the city of Buenos Aires, which is governed by the opposition.

The impeachment request came in the context of hostile rhetoric by high-level government officials toward judges and prosecutors who ruled against the government or were investigating corruption allegations against then-Vice President Cristina Fernández de Kirchner.

In September, pro-administration senators and allies extended the mandate of a judge who handled a corruption investigation into the then-vice president. Then-President Fernández ratified the extension. The Supreme Court ruled in September that the judge's mandate had expired in August, when she turned 75, and therefore could not be extended.

The Supreme Court has had a vacancy since 2021. The constitution requires the president to nominate a candidate, whom the Senate needs to confirm with a two-thirds majority. Former President Fernández did not nominate a candidate.

The Supreme Court ruled in 2015 that delays in appointments, which leave temporary judges serving for years, undermine judicial independence. As of October, 282 federal and national judgeships remained vacant.

An interim attorney general has served since 2018, as the Senate cannot muster the two-thirds majority required for an appointment. In September, the interim attorney general complained of a "hostile environment" for his work, with dozens of attempts to remove him.

Congress has failed to appoint an ombudsperson since 2009, crippling the Ombudsperson's Office, which is supposed to be independent and investigate the federal government for human rights violations. The office stopped functioning normally when a deputy ombudsperson, whose term ended in 2013, was not replaced.

Economic and Social Rights

Year-to-year inflation was 138.3 percent as of September, the government reported, with food and non-alcoholic drink prices increasing by 150.1 percent. The Fernández administration unsuccessfully tried to slow inflation, including through price controls, tariff freezes, and export closures.

As of June 2023, 40.1 percent of the population lived in poverty, a sharp increase from 27.5 in 2019 (pre-pandemic), according to official data. People living in extreme poverty—unable to meet key elements of the right to food—amounted to 9.3 percent of the population. Almost half of children under 14 were living in poverty, and more than 1 in 10 were in extreme poverty.

As of March 2023, official data showed 36.7 percent of workers were employed in the informal labor market, lacking formal labor protections. Three out of four domestic workers, who are almost all women and girls, work informally, official data showed.

Prison Conditions and Abuses by Security Forces

In recent years, the country has seen significant increases in the prison population, which overcrowds facilities in several provinces. The government reported over 100,000 people in detention facilities in 2022, a 77 percent surge since 2010. Over 12,000 more were held in police stations.

By 2022, 41 percent of the prison population was awaiting trial, official data showed.

The National Penitentiary Office reported 316 complaints of torture or ill-treatment in federal prisons in 2022 and 66 from January through March 2023. The Attorney General's Office reported 42 deaths in federal prisons in 2022, including 10 violent deaths.

In June, Jujuy province security forces reportedly used excessive force against people protesting reforms to the provincial constitution, injuring several people. The proposed changes include provisions criminalizing roadblocks in a way that runs counter to international human rights standards on freedom of expression and association.

In July, three city of Buenos Aires police officers were sentenced to life in prison for the 2021 killing of Lucas González, 17, who was shot after leaving a football practice. Five more police were sentenced to between four and six years in prison for covering up the crime.

In August, photojournalist Facundo Morales died after police held him to the floor during a demonstration in the city of Buenos Aires. The mayor alleged that Morales died from a heart attack. Rights groups said that police were responsible. An investigation into his death was ongoing at time of writing.

Freedom of Expression

In Rosario, Santa Fe province, organized crime groups have reportedly threatened journalists and thrown explosives at their offices. The city has seen a surge in homicides and violence linked to drug trafficking.

High-level authorities, including then-President Fernández and then-Vice President Fernández de Kirchner, have used hostile rhetoric to stigmatize independent journalists and media, inaccurately accusing them of "fake news," "hate speech," and "slander campaigns."

In Salta province, legislators passed a law, supposedly to control the spread of false information, allowing jail terms of as long as 25 days for people involved in the "creation and propagation of false information with the intent to induce fear." Such overbroad provisions could easily be used to target journalists and critics.

Women's and Girls' Rights

A landmark 2020 law legalized abortion until the 14th week of pregnancy and longer in cases of rape or risk to the life or health of the pregnant person. Authorities reported over 96,000 legal abortions in 2022. Obstacles to legal abortion reportedly included lack of access to information about the law; excessive use of "conscientious objection," which allows medical staff to refuse to perform abortions; and undue delays and disparities in access to services among provinces.

In a ruling made public in January, the Inter-American Court of Human Rights found Argentina responsible for the death of Cristina Brítez Arce, who died of cardiac arrest in 1992 when induced to labor. The court found that Brítez did not receive proper medical treatment, considering several known risk factors in her pregnancy, or have adequate information on treatment alternatives. Using the term for the first time, the court called her treatment "obstetric violence."

Despite a 2009 law detailing comprehensive measures to prevent and prosecute violence against women, their unpunished killing remains a serious concern. The National Registry of Femicides reported 226 femicides—the murder of women and girls based on their gender—and only 4 convictions in 2022.

Environment and Indigenous Peoples' Rights

The Argentine Constitution protects Indigenous communal ownership of traditional lands. In 2020, the Inter-American Court of Human Rights ordered Argentina to adopt legislative measures to guarantee that right. Congress has repeatedly postponed consideration of a law to ensure these protections.

In 2021, Argentina ratified the Escazú Agreement, a regional accord to ensure access to environmental information and public participation in environmental decision-making and to protect environmental defenders. A 2022 government analysis of the agreement's implementation found the country's legal framework does not ensure effective public participation in the management of forests. Argentina lost 231,000 hectares of primary forest in 2022, Global Forest Watch reported, mostly in the biodiverse Gran Chaco region, with cattle ranching and soy cultivation being the main drivers of conversion.

Confronting Past Abuses

The Supreme Court and federal judges, in the early 2000s, annulled pardons and amnesty laws shielding officials implicated in the 1976-1983 dictatorship's crimes. As of September, the Attorney General's Office reported 3,732 people charged, 1,159 convicted, and 178 acquitted of crimes against humanity. The large number of victims, suspects, and cases makes it difficult for prosecutors and judges to bring those responsible to justice while respecting their due process rights.

As of September, 133 people illegally taken from their parents as children during the dictatorship had been identified and many had been reunited with their families, the Abuelas de Plaza de Mayo, a human rights group, reported.

Court battles continue 29 years after 85 people died and more than 300 were injured in the bombing of the AMIA Jewish Center. Nobody has been convicted. In February 2019, a court convicted a former intelligence chief and a judge of interference in the initial investigation but acquitted former President Carlos Menem. An appeal of the judge's conviction remained pending as of September 2023. In 2015, prosecutor Alberto Nisman, who had accused then-President Fernández de Kirchner of covering up Iran's role in the attack, was found dead. In 2018, a court of appeal said that he appeared to have been murdered. At time of writing, nobody has been convicted in connection with his death.

In 2021, a federal court dismissed Nisman's accusation against Fernández de Kirchner, saying her actions did not constitute a crime. In September 2023, an appeals court overturned the decision, ordering Fernández de Kirchner to trial.

Key International Actors

In 2022, the Fernández administration renegotiated a program with the International Monetary Fund (IMF) for US$44 billion. In 2018, the administration of then-President Mauricio Macri had agreed to a $57 billion program that, according to the IMF, did not deliver on its objectives. Throughout 2023, the government and the IMF rediscussed several economic targets, including fiscal deficit, social spending, and currency devaluation.

Foreign Policy

As a member of the United Nations Human Rights Council, Argentina supported scrutiny of various states' human rights records in 2023. It voted in favor of a resolution extending the mandates of a group of UN experts investigating systematic rights violations in Nicaragua, a similar group covering Syria, and the special rapporteurs on the human rights situations in Russia, in Iran, and in Belarus.

Throughout the electoral process in Guatemala, Argentina expressed its concern about attempts by political actors and several institutions to interfere with the election and urged respect for the will of the people.

In August, the BRICS—a group of emerging economies that includes Brazil, Russia, India, China, and South Africa—invited Argentina, along with five other countries, to join, starting in 2024.

President Milei said he would align with Israel and the United States. During his campaign, he said he would reject the invitation to join BRICS and sever ties with China and the administration of President Lula da Silva in Brazil.

Armenia

The Nagorno-Karabakh conflict and the eventual influx into Armenia of more than 100,000 ethnic Armenians who fled the Azerbaijani enclave dominated events in the country in 2023.

While constitutional reforms stalled, authorities continued to pursue sectoral reforms with respect to the judiciary, police, disability rights, and education.

Human rights groups raised concerns over the efficacy of judicial reforms and impartiality of the accountability process for judges suspected of alleged infractions. They also criticized the lack of comprehensive police reforms.

Areas of continuing human rights concerns include ill-treatment of detainees by law enforcement, domestic violence, discrimination against people with disabilities, and violence and discrimination based on sexual orientation and gender identity.

Aftermath of the Nagorno-Karabakh Conflict

Over 100,000 ethnic Armenians, almost the entire Armenian population of Nagorno-Karabakh, fled for Armenia in September following a military operation by Azerbaijan to regain full control over the enclave. Azerbaijan's military operation followed months of acute shortages of food, medication, hygiene products, and other essential supplies to the region due to Azerbaijan's disruption of vehicular and pedestrian traffic between Armenia and Nagorno-Karabakh since December 2022. For more information, see the Azerbaijan chapter of this report.

Police Abuses and Impunity

Lack of effective accountability for law enforcement abuses is an ongoing problem. Authorities often pursue investigations into ill-treatment allegations under "abuse of office" offenses, which carry lighter penalties.

In April 2023, during a drug prevention operation in Yerevan, police used disproportionate force against employees and visitors at a night club and briefly detained dozens of them. Several alleged that police and investigators ill treated them based on their assumed or real sexual orientation and gender identity. Authorities initiated an abuse-of-power case against police, recognizing at least six people as victims, but no charges had been brought at time of writing.

In February, two lawyers representing a detained child reported that several officers physically assaulted them following an argument at a police precinct. Authorities charged two officers with the criminal offense of manhandling; the investigation was pending at time of writing.

In June, another lawyer alleged that police used physical violence against him and his client at a Yerevan police station. Authorities charged three officers with ill-treating the defendant, but they also charged the lawyer with hooliganism and hindering lawful police actions.

In another case, Armenian law enforcement bodies dropped a criminal investigation into the April beating by a senior police officer of a 17-year-old child who was working as a waiter in a restaurant at the time. The prosecutor claimed that the perpetrator "fully regretted" his actions and apologized to the victim. Following public outcry, law enforcement bodies reopened the investigation, suspended the officer from active duty, and charged him with causing a child severe physical pain.

In June, the independent Monitoring Group of Institutions for Children, Older Persons and Persons with Disabilities reported violence against children at a child support center and alleged that a police officer mistreated one of the children. Authorities did not investigate the allegations, claiming that the report did not include enough factual information.

Freedom of Expression and Information

Although defamation is decriminalized, politicians and private businesses often bring civil cases against journalists and media outlets, dragging them into lengthy legal battles, and threatening heavy financial penalties. A local media advocacy group reported that from January through September, media outlets faced 23 new defamation suits.

In March, parliament passed amendments establishing additional grounds for denying public information requests. Under the new regulation, an agency can refuse to provide information if it contains "official information of limited distribution," vague language that opens the door to unwarranted censorship.

Disability Rights

Armenia lacks a comprehensive plan to introduce community-based services for people with psychosocial and intellectual disabilities and continues to prioritize institutions and institutional care.

The government adopted a program on social inclusion of people with disabilities, which envisages the creation of eight small group homes and an independent living center and the expansion of in-home services for people with disabilities.

In February, the authorities introduced a digital system to evaluate a person's "functionality," which uses an algorithm to determine disability status. In August, a local disability rights group filed a lawsuit against the state for failure to disclose the algorithm used for such determinations. They allege that the algorithm reflects a medical model of disability, which largely focuses on the person's medical condition, rather than the systemic barriers, derogatory attitudes, and acts of social exclusion that prevent people with disabilities from enjoying human rights on an equal basis with others.

Armenia allows courts to deprive people with psychosocial or intellectual disabilities of legal capacity and offers no supported decision-making mechanisms. As of September, courts had received about 200 requests to strip individuals of legal capacity and did so in at least 109 cases; they restored legal capacity to one individual.

Violence against Women

Authorities investigated 1,051 criminal domestic violence complaints through June, a significant increase over the 391 complaints investigated during the same period in 2022, and brought charges against 144 people. At least 12 women were killed between September 2022 and September 2023, 8 by a family member and 1 by a partner. Six of these women were over 60.

Armenia has only two shelters for domestic violence survivors, together having a capacity to shelter 24 women plus their children. According to the Women's Support Center, a local group, the shelters are continuously full, and protection of women remains ineffective and marred by court rulings invalidating police urgent intervention orders.

Sexual Orientation and Gender Identity

Lesbian, gay, bisexual, and transgender (LGBT) people continue to face discrimination, harassment, and violence.

LGBT people can apply for an exemption from military service, where they face homophobic harassment and violence. However, to do so, they must receive a "diagnosis" of "homosexualism" or "transsexualism," which is then registered in the unified healthcare electronic information system. According to LGBT groups, this "diagnosis" can later expose them to discrimination when seeking healthcare services.

Fear of discrimination and humiliation due to public disclosure of their sexual orientation or gender identity continues to prevent many LGBT people from reporting hate crimes against them. According to LGBT rights groups, investigations into such crimes are often inconclusive or ineffective and the charges brought often do not reflect the homophobic and transphobic motives of perpetrators: the Criminal Code does not explicitly recognize animus due to sexual orientation or gender identity as an aggravating circumstance in hate crimes cases.

Local LGBT rights groups and activists documented 37 cases of physical violence, including 17 cases of violence committed by family members from January through August 2023. The groups recorded 14 cases of psychological and economic violence and harassment by family members over the same period.

In a positive move, Armenian authorities in December 2022 lifted a policy prohibiting men who have sex with men from donating blood.

Key International Actors

European Council President Charles Michel hosted meetings throughout 2023 with Armenian and Azerbaijani leaders, discussing issues related to the Lachin corridor (the sole road connecting Nagorno-Karabakh to Armenia), border delimitation, transport links, and the peace agreement that would also address the rights and security of Nagorno-Karabakh's ethnic Armenian population. The United States also mediated several rounds of discussions between the Armenian and Azerbaijan foreign ministers aimed at reaching a "durable peace agreement."

In February, the European Union launched the civilian mission in Armenia (EUMA), deploying 50 observers along the Armenian side of the border with Azerbaijan and aiming to contribute to stability, build confidence in conflict-affected areas, and ensure an environment "conducive to the normalisation efforts" between the parties.

In its November 2022 Concluding Observations, the UN Committee on the Elimination of Discrimination against Women urged Armenia to ensure better representation of women in all branches of government, expedite adoption of a pending law on legal equality, and adopt a model of "substantive equality." It also called on the authorities to eliminate persistent gender stereotypes within the judiciary and law enforcement agencies, criminalize all forms of gender-based violence against women, and ensure effective investigations into all cases of domestic violence.

The Committee also recommended that authorities take measures to combat discrimination against lesbian, bisexual, transgender, and intersex women and ensure that transgender people, including women, can change the gender marker in their passport and other identity documents.

The UN Working Group on the use of mercenaries conducted its first visit to Armenia in February 2023.

During the June EU-Armenia Partnership Committee, the EU highlighted the importance of an independent and efficient judiciary and the fight against corruption. It also called on Armenian authorities to make additional efforts to eliminate all forms of discrimination.

In its March resolution on EU-Armenia relations, the European Parliament condemned the blockage of the Lachin corridor and highlighted the humanitarian crisis in Nagorno-Karabakh. It also called on Armenia to ratify the Council of Europe Convention on Preventing and Combating Violence Against Women and Domestic Violence (Istanbul Convention) and improve human rights protections, especially for women and minorities, including LGBT people.

In October, Armenia's parliament voted to ratify the Rome Statute, the founding treaty of the International Criminal Court.

Australia

Australia is a vibrant democracy that mostly protects the civil and political rights of its citizens; however, its reputation is tarnished by some significant human rights concerns. This includes the cruel treatment of refugees and asylum seekers as well as its failure to address systemic discrimination against First Nations people. Indigenous people are still overrepresented in Australian prisons. A referendum in October on The Voice, which would have allowed Indigenous people to advise Parliament in the form of an advisory committee, was defeated in every Australian state.

Australia remains the only Western country without a national human rights act or constitutional charter. However, Parliament has opened an inquiry on the country's human rights framework and is considering developing a human rights charter. In June 2023, Australia evacuated the last refugee detained on the island country of Nauru under its offshore processing policy but started sending new asylum seekers to the island just two months later. The Australian government maintains a policy of offshore detention for asylum seekers who arrive by boat and in 2023 allocated additional funds for the practice. Serious concerns surrounding the treatment of children in custody and use of "chemical restraint" in aged care have yet to be seriously addressed by the government.

In March, an Australian soldier was charged by the Office of the Special Investigator with an alleged war crime in Afghanistan, the first case of its kind in Australia. In June, a court sided with three newspapers in a defamation suit brought by a former Australian Special Forces soldier over coverage of the murders of civilians during the armed conflict in Afghanistan. These cases represent important developments for justice and authorities. The families of the victims have been waiting for over a decade for prompt and adequate compensation.

Asylum Seekers and Refugees

The year 2023 marked 11 years since the Australian government reintroduced offshore processing of asylum seekers who arrive by boat. In June, Australia evacuated what was then the last refugee detained on the island country of Nauru under its offshore processing policy. However, Australian authorities again started sending new asylum seekers to Nauru just months later, including a group of 11 in September and a group of 12 in November. In October, Papua New Guinea's chief migration officer said 64 refugees and asylum seekers exiled from Australia remained in Papua New Guinea, some of whom alleged they had been left without food and electricity and were being threatened with eviction from their accommodations following a dispute between Australia and Papua New Guinea over funding.

The Australian government has allocated 1.5 billion Australian dollars (US$1 billion) over the next four years for the continued operation of offshore operations, signaling its commitment to the practice. The "turn-back" policy of interdicting boats and summarily turning them to the high seas or returning the people onboard to countries of departure or origin has continued under the government of Prime Minister Anthony Albanese.

In February, the government permitted 19,000 refugees holding temporary protection and safe-haven enterprise visas to apply for permanent residency and citizenship, fulfilling one of Prime Minister Albanese's key election pledges. A permanent visa allows the holder to take out mortgages and higher education loans and receive social security payments. Despite this improvement, statistics from the Department of Home Affairs in August showed that 124 people had been held in immigration detention for over five years. Also in August, the government announced it would increase its annual refugee intake to 20,000 people, short of an earlier pledge to increase the intake to 27,000 people.

In July, a judge found that the government's detention of refugee Mostafa (Moz) Azimitabar in a hotel room for over 14 months was "lawful but lacking humanity." During the period of detention, Azimitabar could not access the outside world or proper medical treatment.

In September, the United Nations Working Group of Experts on People of African Descent released a report following its visit to Australia in 2022, finding "evidence of the weaponization of refugee and migrant status, placing migrants of African descent in a state of precariousness, including risk of loss of status, 'indefinite' detention, and/or deportation."

In November, the High Court of Australia ruled that indefinite immigration detention is unlawful, overturning a previous ruling that had allowed the government to hold non-citizens without valid visas even when there was no possibility of deporting them. The decision triggered the release of more than 100 people, but new laws were rushed through parliament to place additional restrictions and surveillance upon the former detainees.

Indigenous Peoples' Rights

Indigenous people are significantly overrepresented in the criminal justice system, with Aboriginal and Torres Strait Islanders comprising nearly one-third of Australia's adult prison population, but just 3 percent of the national population. In August, the Western Australia Office of the Inspector of Custodial Services found that Broome prison, where 80 percent of the inmates are Aboriginal, is "depressing, degrading and entirely inappropriate in a modern mental health service context," emphasizing that such conditions were a product of underlying systemic racism. At least 19 Indigenous people died in custody in 2023, including a 16-year-old First Nations boy who died after self-harming in pretrial detention in October following prolonged solitary confinement.

On October 14, Australians voted in a referendum to decide whether to enshrine a First Nations Voice to parliament and government in the country's constitution, which would recognize, for the first time, the Aboriginal and Torres Strait Islander people as the First Peoples of the land and allow them to give advice to the Australian Parliament and the government on issues that affect them. The referendum was defeated in every state and was considered a major setback for First Peoples' rights. Presently, Australia has no national treaty with Indigenous Australians.

Disability Rights

The Royal Commission into Violence, Abuse, Neglect and Exploitation of People with a Disability continued its hearings in 2023 and released its final report in September. It found that people with disabilities experience substantially higher rates of violence than people without disabilities. In July, the commission reported that parents with disabilities are over-represented in child protection allegations and investigations. It also found that First Nations participants in

Australia's National Disability Insurance Scheme (NDIS) are 28 percent less likely to receive care through the scheme than non-Indigenous people.

Prisons remain damaging and at times deadly for people with disabilities. A Human Rights Watch analysis of deaths in prisons from 2010-2020 found that about 60 percent of adult prisoners who died had a disability. In June, a court heard the case of Michael, an Aboriginal teenager with an intellectual disability, who spent more than 500 days in solitary confinement in the Townsville youth prison in Queensland for reasons unrelated to his behavior.

Youth Justice

In September, Queensland suspended its regional Human Rights Act for the second time to allow growing numbers of children in detention to be held indefinitely in police watch houses, which are concrete cells typically used for short-term detention of adults. Recent changes in youth justice laws, including the strengthening of punishments for breaking bail, have led to increases in the number of detained children that cannot be accommodated by the current size of youth detention centers.

Following the recommendations of a 2021 report by the Australian Human Rights Commission, the Australian Capital Territory (ACT) government passed a bill banning medically unnecessary non-consensual surgeries on children with intersex traits.

In August, the Northern Territory government raised the minimum age of criminal responsibility from 10 to 12; in April, the state of Victoria had committed to implementing the same increase. International standards, however, call for a minimum age of at least 14. In November, the ACT passed legislation adopting the age 14 minimum.

Older People's Rights

Historically, many Australian nursing homes have used dangerous drugs, often without informed consent, to control the behavior of older people with dementia, known as "chemical restraint." Even now, there are no national protocols for dementia care, including compulsory training for those who work at nursing homes.

At time of writing the Australian government was drafting a new Aged Care Act. The current act, enacted in 1997, does not guarantee protection from the use of chemical and physical restraints. It also does not specify minimum staffing levels for facilities that support older people or require mandatory dementia care training for those who work at nursing homes.

Freedom of Expression

In July, the Select Committee on Foreign Interference through Social Media found that the risk of foreign interference through social media is a material and immediate concern, and recommended that the government implement measures that would call on social media platforms to meet certain transparency requirements or face fines. The committee opened its inquiry in the wake of concerns about the influence of Chinese social media companies and the Chinese Communist Party beyond China's borders.

In May, the state of South Australia passed an anti-protest law that increased the maximum fine on "disruptive" protesters from 750 to 50,000 Australian dollars (US$500 to $33,000) and authorized potential imprisonment for offenders. This legislation was in response to a three-day climate protest.

Terrorism and Counterterrorism

In May, the families of some 40 Australian women and children unlawfully detained in life-threatening conditions in decrepit camps in northeast Syria since at least 2019 filed a lawsuit with the aid of Save the Children seeking to compel the government to bring them home. Many of these Australians were taken to Syria by family members who wanted to join the Islamic State (ISIS). Several Australian men are also unlawfully detained as ISIS suspects in the region. In November, a federal court dismissed the lawsuit.

Climate Change

As a top 20 global greenhouse gas emitter, Australia is contributing to the climate crisis and its growing toll on human rights. Despite the government's increasing support of the renewable energy sector and significant emissions reduction legislation, Australia remains the world's largest coking coal exporter and a leading exporter of liquefied natural gas or LNG. In February the Australian government blocked a new coal mine in Queensland because of risks it posed to the Great Barrier Reef, freshwater creeks, and groundwater, but in May the government approved a new coal mine and rejected requests from civil society groups to reconsider three prior approvals for other coal and gas projects.

Improvements implemented in July to the "Safeguard Mechanism" require Australia's highest greenhouse gas emitting facilities to meet emissions targets that grow increasingly stringent over time in line with Australia's goal to reach net zero emissions by 2050, or pay to offset emissions.

The government agreed with the UN Human Rights Committee's landmark 2022 finding that climate change is currently impacting the daily lives and cultural practices of Torres Strait islanders but has rejected the committee's recommendation to award compensation to the claimants.

Technology and Rights

In August, the Albanese government apologized for the Robodebt scheme, an automated debt assessment system that issued debt notices to vulnerable people and led recipients of welfare to pay more than what they owed. The government also forgave the debts of nearly 200,000 people that were being investigated under the scheme in an important acknowledgment of the human rights violations that took place due to lack of legislation.

In March, the Attorney-General's Department released the Privacy Act Review Report, which delineated over 100 recommendations for an overhaul of the 1988 act that would make it better suited to developments in modern technology, including artificial intelligence and facial recognition technology. In September, the government responded to the report and committed to enacting new privacy protections in 2024.

Foreign Policy

The Chinese government eased some trade restrictions on Australia, including barley tariffs that were imposed three years prior after Australia called for an inquiry on the origins of Covid-19. Australia still has not taken concrete actions to address human rights concerns within the Chinese government or against Australian nationals. Australia has not imposed any Magnitsky-type sanctions on Chinese officials for violations in Xinjiang or elsewhere. Australian citizen and writer Yang Hengjun remains indefinitely and arbitrarily detained in China. In October, Australian citizen-journalist Cheng Lei was finally released and returned to Australia after three years in prison. In July, Hong Kong authorities issued baseless bounties on two Australian activists, Kevin Yam and Ted Hui.

In July, Vietnamese-born Australian citizen Chau Van Kham, a democracy activist, was released from a Vietnamese jail after spending four years in prison for his political beliefs.

The Australian government's continued concern about stability in the region remains apparent. In April, Australia publicized its Defence Strategic Review, showing its investment in its defense capabilities, including maritime technology like nuclear-powered submarines.

Australia has continued to strengthen its relationship with India, its fellow Quad member, as well as with countries in Southeast Asia, including Indonesia and Vietnam. It has continued to purse "quiet diplomacy" with India, declining to publicly raise human rights concerns including recent crackdowns on civil society and the adoption of laws and policies that systematically discriminate against Muslims and Christians. Australia's parliament launched an inquiry to examine government efforts to support democracy in the region but has fallen short of pressing for accountability for human rights.

In February, Australia imposed sanctions and travel bans on those responsible for the 2021 coup and ensuing human rights violations in Myanmar, as well as two military-owned companies. In March, it imposed 14 Magnitsky-style travel bans and financial sanctions on members of the Iranian "morality police" involved in the death of 22-year-old Mahsa (Jina) Amini in September 2022, along with those involved in the supply of drones to Russia. Further sanctions targeting Iranian individuals and entities who "oppress women and girls in Iran" were announced by the government in September. In November, sanctions were imposed on eight people and one entity in response to the October 7 massacres led by Hamas in Israel.

In March, Australia became the 117th country to endorse the Safe Schools Declaration, an intergovernmental political commitment to reduce the likelihood that students, teachers, and schools are targeted for attack during armed conflict.

Azerbaijan

Long-term human rights concerns persisted in Azerbaijan in 2023. The government severely restricted freedoms of expression, assembly, and association. Despite some progress on a notorious torture case, torture and ill-treatment in police custody and places of detention persisted.

The May presidential pardon included a handful of people whose convictions were believed to be politically motivated, yet dozens remained wrongfully imprisoned. Authorities sentenced numerous critics to 30-day detention terms, following perfunctory misdemeanor trials, and arrested two civic activists, Bakhtiyar Hajiyev and Gubad Ibadoghlu, who face long prison terms.

The authorities' violent crushing of two separate grassroots protests over environmental issues highlighted their intolerance for public expression of legitimate concerns as well as public frustration with the government's failure to protect the environment.

The prosecutor's office closed criminal investigations against several NGOs targeted in 2014. Investigations against others appear to have remained open. Restrictive laws impeded civil society groups from operating independently and accessing funding.

Nagorno-Karabakh

On September 19, Azerbaijan launched a military operation to regain full control over Nagorno-Karabakh. Nagorno-Karabakh forces surrendered after one day of fighting. More than 100,000 ethnic Armenians—nearly the entire Armenian population of the area—fled to Armenia. The military operation followed months of acute shortages of food, medication, hygiene products, and other essential supplies to the area due to Azerbaijan's disruption of vehicular and pedestrian traffic between Armenia and Nagorno-Karabakh that started in December 2022.

Starting in mid-June, Azerbaijan blocked all humanitarian goods transport and periodically blocked International Committee of the Red Cross (ICRC) patient transports. Azerbaijan also cut power and gas lines, causing regular, daily blackouts. Even before the military operation in September, military skirmishes had periodically broken out in other areas along the Armenia-Azerbaijan border and in Nagorno-Karabakh, threatening the safety and livelihoods of civilians residing in those areas.

Azerbaijan refused to implement February and July interim measure decisions by the International Court of Justice (ICJ) calling on Azerbaijan to ensure "unimpeded movement of persons, vehicles and cargo along the Lachin Corridor in both directions."

Following the September military operation, Azerbaijan arrested several leaders of the de facto authorities, charging them with, inter alia, financing terrorism, establishing illegal armed formations, and illegal border crossing.

A historic December 2023 joint statement between the Armenian and Azerbaijani leaderships on steps to normalize relations announced Azerbaijan's intention to release "32 Armenian servicemen" and Armenia's intention to release "2 Azerbaijani military servicemen."

Governments and intergovernmental organizations expressed alarm about the humanitarian situation. In an October resolution, the European Parliament called on Azerbaijan to "allow the safe return of the Armenian population" and "offer solid guarantees regarding the protection of their rights" and also called for the establishment of an international monitoring mission under UN auspices.

In an October joint statement at the UN Human Rights Council, 34 countries called on Azerbaijan to "promptly create conditions for the voluntary, safe, dignified and sustainable return" of ethnic Armenians and provide for international monitoring of the situation.

Prosecutions of Government Critics

Among those freed under presidential pardon was Ali Aliyev, a politician sentenced in 2022 to 3.5 years in prison on a variety of politically motivated charges.

Authorities continued to target leading activists, opposition politicians, and rank-and-file members of opposition political parties.

In December 2022, authorities arrested Bakhtiyar Hajiyev, a prominent activist, on hooliganism and contempt charges, which Hajiyev refuted. Starting in February, Telegram and Meta accounts leaked intimate photos and messages—some of them fake, others apparently stolen from Hajiyev's private Facebook account—in what appeared to be an effort to smear his reputation. In June, Hajiyev faced four new sets of charges. Hajiyev remained in pretrial custody and faces six years in prison.

In May, a court sentenced Alizamin Salayev, senior politician with the opposition Azerbaijan Popular Front Party (APFP), to four years on criminal hooliganism charges.

In July, authorities arrested renowned economist and anti-corruption activist Gubad Ibadoghlu on charges of counterfeiting and possession of religious extremist materials. During his arrest, police assaulted Ibadoghlu and his wife; she had multiple bruises as a result. Remanded to pretrial detention, Ibadoghlu is facing 12 years in prison. Authorities denied him access to adequate medical treatment in custody, causing his pre-existing health conditions to deteriorate.

Freedom of Expression and Media

Critics whom authorities jailed for up to 30 days included: in February, APFP member Orkhan Bakhishli (detained the day after his media interview criticizing Bakhtiyar Hajiyev's arrest), Vali Shukurzade (a freelance journalist, detained shortly after he requested information from police for a journalistic investigation), and APFP activist Zaur Usubov (detained for his social media posts); and in May, social media activist Amrah Tahmazov (detained 11 days after his Facebook post called on President Ilham Aliyev to release Alizamin Salayev).

In June, a court sentenced activists Elmir Abbasov and Giyas Ibrahimov to 32 and 20 days of detention, respectively, on resisting police and other charges following their Facebook posts criticizing police brutality against protesters in Soyudlu.

In July, authorities detained Vugar Mammadov, editor-in-chief of the online news outlet Hurriyat, together with a guest of his program after they criticized corruption in the Defense Ministry. A court sentenced both to 30 days of administrative detention on charges of disseminating prohibited information online, an offense that is not strictly defined in law and that is often used against government critics.

The authorities arrested at least nine civic activists who criticized online the September 19 military operation in Karabakh. These included Amrah Tahmazov,

Nurlan Gahramanly, and Emin Ibrahimov, each sentenced to 30 days in administrative detention on charges of sharing prohibited information online; Nemat Abbasov, for allegedly disobeying police; Ruslan Vahabov, charged with drug trafficking; and Afiyeddin Mammadov, charged with hooliganism and inflicting intentional bodily harm. Vahabov and Mammadov remain in pretrial custody.

In November, authorities arrested Ulvi Hasanli and Sevinc Vagifgizi, top leaders of Abzas Media, an independent media outlet known for investigating and exposing corruption, and Mahammad Kekalov, a social entrepreneur who also worked with the outlet, on bogus smuggling charges. At time of writing, the three remained in pretrial custody.

Freedom of Assembly

The authorities remain hostile toward protests, violently dispersing several of them, in some cases unlawfully, and jailing peaceful protesters.

In February, a court sentenced activists Afiyeddin Mammadov and Samir Sultanov to 30 days' detention on disobedience charges for their involvement in an unsanctioned protest against Hajiyev's detention.

In March, police in Saatli district, central Azerbaijan, used tear gas and rubber bullets to disperse villagers who attempted to block a road to protest longstanding critical water shortages. Residents told a media outlet that two people, including a 15-year-old boy, were seriously injured by rubber bullets.

In March, a court sentenced two APFP members, Sahladar Isganderli and Jeyhun Novruzov, and journalist Nurlan Jafarli to 25, 30, and 15 days, respectively, for their involvement in an unsanctioned, peaceful protest demanding Alizamin Salayev's release.

In June, in the western Azerbaijan village of Soyudlu, riot police forcibly dispersed a peaceful demonstration against plans for an artificial lake to hold waste from a nearby gold mine. Police used tear gas and physical violence against protesters, reportedly injuring dozens. Police restricted access to and from the village for several weeks, physically removing at least three journalists and confiscating mobile phones. Authorities sentenced at least eight village residents on administrative charges and remanded three others to pretrial custody on spurious criminal drug charges. A court also sent a former parliamentarian, Nazim Baydamirli, to four months' pretrial detention on extortion charges after pro-government media accused him of coordinating the protests.

Torture and Ill-Treatment

Torture and ill-treatment remain common in police custody, with human rights groups and the media reporting on credible allegations of torture. Impunity for torture and ill-treatment remains the norm.

In February, police arrested Jeyhun Balashov, a religious activist with the Muslim Unity Movement, on what he said are bogus drug possession charges. His father, who met him later in prison, told independent media that his son had visible bruises on his arms and had difficulties standing.

In July, police beat journalist Elmaddin Shamilzadeh to compel him to remove his Facebook posts of photographs of police who he said were involved in the dispersal of the Soyudlu protest.

In an exception to the pattern of impunity for torture, proceedings continued to address the 2017 torture of hundreds of military officers in Terter region accused of spying for Armenia. In 2023, four were released by presidential pardon and one by a court ruling. In December 2022, 19 were acquitted of treason charges and released. The trial of four people accused of torture continued. At least seven other wrongly imprisoned military officers continued to serve their terms.

Sexual Orientation and Gender Identity

Lesbian, gay, bisexual, and transgender (LGBT) people continue to face ill-treatment, extortion, arbitrary detention, and discrimination by state and non-state actors.

For example, in May, police detained at least two transgender women in Baku following a confrontation with police. The next day, police detained several LGBT rights activists who had gathered in front of the police station to protest those women's arrest. At least two were sentenced to 15 days' detention on disobedience charges. Two others, who received fines on charges of hooliganism and drug possession, told the media that police used anti-LGBT slurs against them in custody, handcuffed them, and forced them to take drug tests.

Key International Actors

Numerous governments and intergovernmental organizations spoke out about the arrest of Gubad Ibadoghlu, calling for Azerbaijan to ensure his due process rights and access to needed medication. In September, the European Parliament adopted an "urgency resolution" demanding his immediate and unconditional release, stating that the finalization of a future EU-Azerbaijan partnership agreement should be conditional on the release of all political prisoners, and calling for targeted sanctions on Azerbaijani officials who have committed human rights violations. Various members of the US Congress and a Parliamentary Assembly (PACE) of the Council of Europe (CoE) official called for Ibadoghlu's immediate release. Also in September, the European Court of Human Rights adopted interim measures ordering the government to take urgent steps to ensure the protection of Ibadoghlu's health.

In its annual meeting of the Subcommittee on Justice, Freedom, Security and Human Rights and Democracy with Azerbaijan in May, the European Union expressed concerns about the continuous persecution of independent voices in the country.

Foreign governments and intergovernmental organizations condemned Bakhtiyar Hajiyev's arrest and called for his immediate release. In February, the US State Department stated that the charges against Hajiyev were "understood as politically motivated." The Baku delegation of the EU urged authorities to release Hajiyev "expeditiously."

In May, the US Embassy in Azerbaijan welcomed the presidential pardons of "Azerbaijanis incarcerated for exercising their fundamental freedoms," noted that many remained imprisoned for exercising those rights, and called for their release.

In March, a joint opinion by the CoE's Venice Commission and the Organization for Security and Co-operation in Europe (OSCE) Office for Democratic Institutions and Human Rights (ODIHR) expressed serious concern about several provisions of the Law on Political Parties, which could potentially chill pluralism in the country. The EU also called on Azerbaijan to address the report's recommendations, saying that "vibrant, accountable and inclusive multiparty systems must be guaranteed."

During their June visit, PACE co-rapporteurs raised concerns about persisting restrictions on the freedoms of assembly and association, noting that NGOs "continue to operate in a very restrictive environment." They noted continued imprisonment "on politically motivated charges" and called on the authorities to amend the Media Law.

In her July letter to the Interior Minister, the CoE Commissioner for Human Rights Dunja Mijatovic raised concerns about the use of disproportionate force in Soyudlu.

Bahrain

More than 800 inmates in Jau prison, the country's largest detention facility, participated in a hunger strike from August to September 2023 to protest abysmal conditions and Bahraini authorities' denial of adequate health care. Many of those on hunger strike were being held unjustly following manifestly unfair trials.

Ten prominent opposition leaders have remained behind bars for more than a decade for their roles in the 2011 pro-democracy protests. They include Hassan Mushaima, the head of the unlicensed opposition group Al-Haq; Abdulwahab Hussain, an opposition leader; Abdulhadi al-Khawaja, a prominent human rights defender; and Dr. Abduljalil al-Singace, the spokesman for Al-Haq. All four are serving life sentences following manifestly unfair trials. Al-Khawaja and Al-Singace continue to be denied adequate medical care.

On March 8, Bahraini authorities revoked the entry visas they had issued on January 30, 2023, to two Human Rights Watch staff members to attend the 146th Inter-Parliamentary Union (IPU). Human Rights Watch holds permanent observer status with the IPU granting access to the parliamentary organization's Assemblies, which IPU's senior leadership failed to publicly criticize.

Closure of Political Space, Freedom of Assembly, and Freedom of Association

The government of Bahrain continued imposing restrictions on expression, assembly, and association. Elections are neither free nor fair, and opposition voices are systematically excluded and repressed.

Many members of Bahrain's political opposition, as well as activists, bloggers, and human rights defenders, continue to be imprisoned for their roles in the 2011 pro-democracy protests and for more recent political activism. They have faced brutal treatment, including torture and denial of medical care. Authorities failed to hold officials accountable for torture and ill-treatment in detention.

Human Rights Watch, along with several other human rights organizations, addressed a joint letter on March 6 to delegates to the IPU highlighting human rights abuses in Bahrain and urging them to use the assembly to raise concerns about the serious repression of human rights in Bahrain and avoid using the assembly to whitewash Bahrain's dismal rights record.

Bahrain's "political isolation laws," introduced in 2018, barred former members of the country's opposition parties from running for parliament or sitting on boards of governors of civil society organizations. These laws also target former prisoners, including those detained due to their political work. Those affected by these laws routinely experience delays and denials when applying for a Good Conduct Certificate, which Bahraini citizens and residents need to apply for a job or university admission or even join a sports or social club.

Two of Bahrain's former parliament members are in prison for exercising their freedom of expression, and the government has forced many more into exile and stripped them of their citizenship.

No independent media has operated in Bahrain since the Information Affairs Ministry suspended *Al Wasat*, the country's only independent newspaper, in 2017. Foreign journalists rarely have access to Bahrain, and Human Rights Watch and other international rights groups are routinely denied access.

Death Penalty

Since 2017, Bahrain has executed six people. As of September 2023, 26 others remain on death row with their appeals exhausted. Bahraini courts have convicted and sentenced defendants to death following manifestly unfair trials, based solely or primarily on confessions allegedly coerced through torture and ill-treatment.

Human Rights Watch and the Bahrain Institute for Rights and Democracy (BIRD) examined the cases of eight men facing the death penalty, based primarily on court records and other official documents. The defendants were convicted and sentenced following manifestly unfair trials based primarily, or in some instances solely, on coerced confessions. The trial and appeal courts in these cases dismissed credible allegations of torture during interrogation, relied on secretly sourced documents, and denied or failed to protect fundamental fair trial and due process rights, including the rights to counsel during interrogation and to cross-examine prosecution witnesses. Bahraini authorities also violated their obligations to investigate allegations of torture and abuse.

Freedom of Religion

The Bahraini government has discriminated against its Shia majority population for years, including by targeting Shia clerics and arresting and prosecuting human rights defenders from Shia backgrounds, including Abdulhadi al-Khawaja in 2011. UN experts have expressed concern that members of the Shia community are "clearly being targeted on the basis of their religion."

In June, Bahraini authorities imposed restrictions and set up checkpoints in and around Al-Diraz village where Imam Al-Sadeq Mosque—the main mosque for the Shia community in Bahrain—is located, blocking worshippers from attending Friday prayers there. The access restrictions followed the Bahraini authorities' brief detention of a prominent Shia cleric, Sheikh Mohammad Sanqoor, who often gave sermons at Imam al-Sadeq Mosque.

Women's Rights

Under the unified 2017 Family Law, women are required to obey their husbands and not leave the marital home without a "legitimate excuse." She can lose her right to spousal maintenance (*nafaqa*) from her husband if she is deemed disobedient or recalcitrant by a court.

A woman cannot act as the guardian of her child even if her child's father has passed away or following divorce in which a court orders that her child reside primarily with her (custody). The 1963 citizenship act prohibits women from conferring their nationality to their children from a non-Bahraini father. Women have had problems trying to obtain passports for their children particularly when their child's father is abroad.

Women also face discrimination in practice. Some universities may require women to have parental consent to live in campus accommodation.

In February, the UN Committee on the Elimination of Discrimination against Women published their findings on women's rights in Bahrain, which included concern about the "shrinking space for women human rights defenders and reports of reprisals against them, including intimidation, harassment, threats, physical abuse, sexual violence, travel bans and arbitrary detention." The committee also noted the absence of a timeline for adopting a draft law amending the Penal Code to remove the exemption from criminal liability if a perpetrator of rape marries the victim.

Bahrain's parliament has voted to abolish a law exempting rapists from punishment if they marry their victim.

Sexual Orientation and Gender Identity

Although no law explicitly criminalizes same-sex relations, authorities have used vague penal code provisions against "indecency" and "immorality" to target sexual and gender minorities.

Migrant Workers

Bahrain continues to enforce the *kafala* (sponsorship) system that ties migrant workers' visas to their employers, which means if they leave their employer without their employer's consent, they lose their residency status and can face arrest, fines, and deportation for "absconding." In 2009, Bahrain allowed migrant workers to terminate their employment contracts after one year with their first employer if they give reasonable notice (at least 30 days) to their employer. However, in January 2022, the parliament voted to extend this to two years. The workers are also expected to bear their own fees for the two-year work permit, which has been too onerous for many, resulting in little up-take.

Bahrain's Labor Law includes domestic workers but excludes them from some protections, such as weekly rest days, a minimum wage, and limits on working hours.

Online Surveillance and Censorship

Bahraini authorities continued to block websites and forced the removal of online content, particularly social media posts criticizing the government. While social media remains a key space for activism and dissent, self-censorship is high due to the fear of online surveillance and intimidation from authorities.

In March 2023, Bahraini authorities arrested four men over social media posts. Ebrahim Al-Mannai, one of the four men arrested, was a lawyer and prominent activist who made a post on X, formerly known as Twitter, stating that the Bahraini government should reform its parliament if it is interested in highlighting the Bahraini parliament to the world.

Bahrain has purchased and used spyware, including NSO Group's Pegasus spyware, to target government critics and human rights defenders.

Key International Actors

In September 2023, Bahraini crown prince and prime minister Salman bin Hamad Al-Khalifa visited Washington, DC, and signed the Comprehensive Security Integration and Prosperity Agreement (C-SIPA), which aims to enhance cooperation between the two countries in various areas, such as defense, security, trade, investment, and emerging technology. The agreement was signed just after several human rights organizations urged the White House to use their diplomatic relations with Bahrain to push for the release of Abdulhadi Al-Khawaja.

In July, the United Kingdom prime minister also hosted the crown prince to sign a Strategic Investment and Collaboration Partnership, which "aims to facilitate additional investment of more than £1 billion into the UK." The UK Government continues to fund Bahrain-led and owned reform and capacity-building programs for agencies involved in egregious human rights violations through the Gulf Strategy Fund (GSF). The GSF has supported Bahrain's Ministry of Interior and its ombudsman, Special Investigations Unit, and security bodies implicated in the abuses of at least eight men currently on death row.

In February, Human Rights Watch and other human rights organizations released a joint statement responding to the 2021 human rights and democracy report of the Foreign, Commonwealth and Development Office (FCDO), in which the UK government gives Bahrain unreserved praise for its Restorative Justice Law for children as a "progressive step" without acknowledging the failures of this law to protect key rights enumerated by the Convention on the Rights of the Child.

Bangladesh

In 2023, Bangladesh authorities tightened repression ahead of national elections.

Security forces carried out mass arrests of opposition members and in some cases responded to protests with excessive force. The arrests appeared to reflect senior police officials' plans, stated in leaked meeting minutes, to ensure convictions of opposition members so they would be disqualified from contesting elections. The main opposition Bangladesh Nationalist Party estimated that half of its 5 million members face politically motivated prosecution.

On September 14, prominent human rights defenders Adilur Rahman Khan and ASM Nasiruddin Elan of the Dhaka-based rights group, Odhikar, were sentenced to two years in prison for a 2013 report on indiscriminate and excessive use of force against protesters.

Also in September, the government replaced the Digital Security Act 2018 (DSA) with the Cyber Security Act 2023 (CSA) after facing criticism for the use of the DSA to stifle freedom of expression and suppress dissent. However, the new law retains many of the DSA's abusive elements.

The country continues to host nearly 1 million Rohingya refugees amid rising violence by armed groups and serious donor funding shortages. Bangladesh authorities have made conditions increasingly hostile in the camps, and hundreds of refugees have embarked on perilous boat journeys to seek protection elsewhere.

Enforced Disappearances, Extrajudicial Killings, Torture, and Impunity

According to Bangladeshi human rights monitors, security forces have carried out over 600 enforced disappearances since 2009. While some people were later released, produced in court, or said to have died during an armed exchange with security forces, nearly 100 people remain missing. The government has refused to take up the offer from the United Nations to help establish a specialized mechanism to investigate allegations of enforced disappearances in line with in-

Trading Lives for Profit
How the Shipping Industry Circumvents Regulations to Scrap Toxic Ships on Bangladesh's Beaches
HUMAN RIGHTS WATCH
NGO SHIPBREAKING PLATFORM

ternational standards. Instead, Bangladesh authorities continue to harass and intimidate victims' families.

Immediately after the United States' designation of human rights sanctions against the notoriously abusive Rapid Action Battalion in 2021, some abuses dropped for a period. However, security force abuses, including enforced disappearances, appear to have resumed. Human rights monitors have also noted a disturbing rise in allegations of torture in custody.

Allegations of torture in Bangladesh are rarely investigated or prosecuted. Only one case of torture resulted in convictions under Bangladesh's Torture and Custodial Death (Prevention) Act since its passage a decade ago, according to media reports.

Bangladesh has ignored repeated requests from the UN Committee Against Torture to follow up on its recommendations, as required. The Committee's recommendations included the independent monitoring of all detention sites and investigation of all allegations of torture or ill-treatment by law enforcement officials.

Freedom of Speech

Journalists faced increasing attacks for exercising their right to freely criticize government policies and practices, undermining the conditions for open political debate ahead of elections.

Newsrooms were further driven toward self-censorship, with government authorities demanding they remove news articles from their websites and increasing judicial targeting of major outlets.

On March 30, 2023, authorities arrested Shamsuzzaman Shams, a correspondent for the leading national newspaper, *Prothom Alo*, accusing him of "tarnishing the image of the nation" in an article about the cost of living in Bangladesh. Matiur Rahman, the editor, and others were also sued under the DSA in relation to the same article. In a speech in parliament, Prime Minister Sheikh Hasina castigated *Prothom Alo* as the "enemy" of the ruling Awami League party, democracy, and the people of the country. Following her statement, the *Prothom Alo* offices were vandalized.

Prominent journalists and activists, such as Shahidul Alam and Rozina Islam, continue to face charges under the DSA.

The new CSA retains many of the abusive elements of its predecessor, the DSA, that grant wide authority to officials to criminalize and jail critics of the ruling Awami League government. For example, it maintains section 21, which criminalizes "any kind of propaganda or campaign against liberation war, spirit of liberation war, father of the nation, national anthem or national flag."

In a letter to the Bangladesh government, the UN special rapporteur on the promotion and protection of the right to freedom of opinion and expression, Irene Khan, raised concerns that the CSA "contains vague and overly broad provisions which criminalize a large variety of legitimate forms of expression. These provisions have been reproduced from the Digital Security Act, although they contravene international human rights law, have been used wrongly against journalists, human rights defenders and scholars, and have led to severe negative human rights consequences, including prolonged detention, deaths in custody and attacks on media freedom."

Labor Rights

On June 25, union leader Shahidul Islam was beaten to death after he visited a factory to secure unpaid wages for the factory's workers, following a pattern of targeted attacks against labor organizers in Bangladesh. Islam's murder underscored the inadequacy of the social audits and certifications that brands and retailers use to monitor working conditions in factories and their failure to adequately prevent and respond to threats to workers trying to organize independent unions.

The Bangladesh authorities have yet to amend the labor laws to protect workers' freedom of association and collective bargaining in line with International Labour Organization conventions and recommendations, including to curb anti-union tactics by managers and assaults on independent union organizers.

In November, the government raised the minimum wage for garment factory workers from US$75 to $113 per month following massive protests. The protesters had been calling for an increase to $208, which is still far below the livable wage estimated by Bangladesh think tanks.

Despite the high prevalence of sexual harassment at work in Bangladesh, the 2006 Labour Act does not define or effectively prevent sexual harassment at work. The authorities also have yet to ratify the ILO Violence and Harassment Convention (C190), which requires comprehensive protections to end violence and harassment, including gender-based violence, at work.

Women's and Girls' Rights

Women in Bangladesh continue to have little recourse to seek protection or services or access justice for domestic violence. Bangladesh continues to have one of the highest rates of child marriage in the world, with a shocking 51 percent of girls married before 18, and has the shameful distinction of being one of the only countries in the world to have legalized child marriage in recent years. Women and girls face widespread sexual violence with little recourse and protection; in Bangladesh, it is estimated that fewer than 1 percent of rape cases investigated by the police leads to conviction.

Sexual Orientation and Gender Identity

While Bangladesh has taken important steps toward protecting *hijras*, authorities force them to undergo abusive medical examinations to legally recognize their gender identity. (In South Asia, hijra refers to an identity category for people assigned male at birth who develop a feminine gender identity.)

On August 12, police forced eight hijras to strip naked after they were arrested in Dhaka on charges of extortion. The police then presented them to the media, saying that the detainees had disguised themselves as hijra in order to extort people.

Same-sex conduct is criminalized in Bangladesh, and LGBT people continue to face harassment and violence with little protection from the police.

Disability Rights

In June, police attacked people with disabilities who were protesting to increase their social welfare monthly allowance from 850 taka (US$7) to 5,000 taka

(US$45). The government did not increase the monthly allowance despite commitments to do so.

Human Rights Watch found that Bangladesh authorities failed to ensure that people with disabilities and older people had access to protection, services, and infrastructure during unprecedented flooding in northern Bangladesh in June 2022.

Refugees

The nearly 1 million Rohingya refugees in Bangladesh face growing restrictions by the authorities. Refugees describe new barriers to education, livelihoods, and movement. Camp authorities resumed harassing and evicting Rohingya shop owners, including by destroying their stores.

Bangladesh authorities have relocated 30,000 Rohingya to the isolated silt island Bhasan Char, where they risk food and medicine shortages, flooding, waterborne diseases, drowning, and injuries due to cyclones and rising sea levels.

Amid surging violence by armed groups and criminal gangs in the camps, Bangladesh authorities have failed to provide protection, maintain security, or prosecute those responsible. Refugees have reported facing layers of barriers to police, legal, and medical assistance.

The 2023 UN Joint Response Plan for the Rohingya humanitarian crisis has received less than one-third of the US$876 million sought in donor contributions. The funding shortfall has led the World Food Programme to cut Rohingya food rations by a third since February, down from $12 to only $8 per month per person. Rohingya and humanitarian workers reported that the ration cuts were already having medical and social consequences.

Bangladesh authorities contend that the repatriation of Rohingya is the only solution, refusing to support sustainable solutions to ensure safety, health, and livelihoods in the camps, and freedom to move outside the camps, the prerequisite for productive self-sufficiency and integration. The UN Children's Fund (UNICEF) reported that 300,000 out of more than 400,000 refugee children were enrolled in classes teaching the Myanmar curriculum, but their education was not accredited. The government has initiated steps with the Myanmar junta to return Rohingya to Rakhine State under a pilot project that has been marked by coercion and deception.

Key International Actors

On August 4, 2023, the spokesperson for the UN High Commissioner for Human Rights called on all political parties, their supporters, and the security forces to create a peaceful, inclusive, and safe environment for a free and fair election. In March, the UN High Commissioner said: "In Bangladesh, I regret the increasing incidence of political violence, coupled with arbitrary arrests of political activists, and ongoing harassment of human rights defenders and media personnel in the build up to the elections this year."

In May, the US government announced a new policy that will restrict the issuance of visas for any Bangladeshi who undermines "the democratic election process in Bangladesh." Fourteen US Congressmembers expressed their concerns over the violent crackdown on opposition parties and dissidents leading up to the elections.

On August 31, 2023, more than 170 global leaders, including former US President Barack Obama and former UN Secretary-General Ban Ki-moon, called on Prime Minister Sheikh Hasina to suspend the judicial harassment of Nobel Prize winner Muhammad Yunus and raised concerns about ongoing threats to democracy and human rights in Bangladesh.

In July, the EU special representative for human rights visited Bangladesh, holding institutional talks about human rights developments in the country and drawing attention to the situation of the Rohingya.

The UN independent expert on the rights of older people called on the government to take urgent action to mitigate the impacts of climate change on older people.

In September, the European Parliament passed an urgency resolution on the "Human rights situation in Bangladesh, notably the case of Odhikar," urging the release of Odhikar's leaders and deploring the increasing repression in Bangladesh. UN independent experts and the UN Office of the High Commissioner for Human Rights expressed concern over the intimidation and harassment of human rights defenders and civil society leaders, including the leaders of Odhikar.

Belarus

In 2023, widespread repression of government critics in Belarus continued. At time of writing, almost 1,500 people remained behind bars on politically motivated charges, including human rights defenders, journalists, lawyers, opposition politicians, culture workers, trade unionists, and activists. Authorities increasingly subjected political prisoners to incommunicado detention, torture, and other forms of ill-treatment.

Belarus continued to allow Russian forces to use the country's territory in Russia's full-scale invasion of Ukraine.

In February, the Office of the High Commissioner for Human Rights (OHCHR) reported on systematic, widespread, and gross human rights violations committed in Belarus, concluding that some may amount to crimes against humanity.

The humanitarian crisis at the European Union borders continued. Over the past year, migrants, including children, continued to be stuck on the Belarusian side of the border and faced serious abuses by Belarusian officials and risk of death.

Arrest and Detention of Perceived Opponents

Between October 2022 and September 2023, according to leading Belarusian human rights organization Viasna, more than 400 people were sentenced on politically motivated criminal charges, and another 3,300 faced politically motivated administrative charges. At time of writing, Viasna's count of political prisoners was 1,462.

Authorities used a variety of bogus charges to prosecute their critics, including "defamation" charges over insulting Aliaksandr Lukashenka or Belarusian government or state symbols, "inciting enmity" against the "social group of law enforcement officers," or "violent acts or threat of violence against law enforcement officers." Authorities also widely used charges related to "extremism" and "terrorism" against critics for actions such as leaving critical comments on social media, following "extremist" Telegram channels, or having a white-red-white tattoo.

Belarusian authorities continued detaining and prosecuting people in connection with peaceful protests in 2020, including some who returned to Belarus from abroad. Workers of state companies faced mass layoffs in connection with their alleged participation in the protests.

In 2023, authorities subjected family members of political prisoners to arbitrary searches, detentions, interrogations, and other forms of harassment. In January, a court in Brest sentenced Daria Losik to two years' imprisonment on charges of "aiding extremist activity" over an interview she gave about her incarcerated husband, a popular blogger and journalist, Ihar Losik, to independent broadcaster Belsat, which Belarusian authorities had labeled extremist. Her sentencing left the Losiks' 4-year-old daughter in the care of her grandparents.

In February 2023, a court in Zhodino handed down an additional one-and-a-half-year sentence to former presidential contender Siarhei Tsikhanouski over his supposed "malicious disobedience to the demands of the prison administration." Tsikhanouski was already serving 18 years in prison for "organizing mass protests."

In July, the Minsk regional court sentenced Eduard Babaryka, son of former presidential contender Viktar Babaryka and a member of his campaign team, to eight years in prison for "tax evasion," "enmity incitement," and "aiding activities gravely violating public order."

Between July and October, Belarusian authorities denied registration to all opposition political parties, registering only four pro-government parties.

Crackdown on Human Rights Defenders and Lawyers

In March, the Lenin District Court of Minsk handed down prison sentences to three human rights defenders from Viasna, which had been hit particularly hard by the authorities, in retaliation for their work. Ales Bialiatski, head of the group and a 2022 Nobel Peace Prize co-laureate; Valiantsin Stefanovich, his deputy; and Uladzimir Labkovich, one of the group's lawyers, were respectively sentenced to ten, nine and seven years in prison. Viasna's board member Zmitser Salauyou was sentenced to eight years in absentia.

Two other members of Viasna, Maria (Marfa) Rabkova and Andrey Chapiuk, remained behind bars, serving their respective sentences of 15 and 6 years. Leanid Sudalenka, chairman of Viasna's Homieĺ branch, was released in July, having served his three-year sentence in full.

Authorities increasingly labeled human rights organizations as "extremist." In March, the Belarusian Association of Journalists (BAJ), a leading rights group working to protect freedom of expression and the rights of journalists, and some of its individual staff members, were designated "extremist." In August, Viasna was designated as an "extremist formation."

In June, the Minsk City Court sentenced prominent human rights defender Nasta (Anastasia) Loika to seven years in prison for "inciting enmity" against law enforcement officers over her report documenting rights violations perpetrated by police. Loika had served six arbitrary administrative arrest sentences prior to facing criminal charges. During her short-term arrests and then in pretrial custody, authorities subjected her to torture and other forms of inhumane treatment, forced her to record "confession" videos, vilified her in smear campaigns, searched her mother's home, and disbarred her lawyers.

Between October 2022 and October 2023, authorities prosecuted at least 24 independent trade union members on politically motivated charges.

Authorities continued cracking down on human rights lawyers in retaliation for representing clients in politically motivated cases and expressing their views on rule of law issues. Since August 2020, more than 100 attorneys have lost their licenses following arbitrary decisions of the Justice Ministry or politically motivated disbarment procedures. At time of writing, six attorneys remained behind bars on politically motivated charges such as "call for sanctions," "creation of an extremist formation," "aiding extremist activity," and "inciting enmity."

Crackdown on Journalists and Harassment of Students

According to BAJ, between October 2022 and mid-September 2023, at least 7 media workers were detained on criminal charges and 20 more were subjected to administrative arrest. At time of writing, at least 34 media workers remained in prison on politically motivated charges varying from "discreditation of Belarus" to "creation of an extremist formation." Dozens faced police raids.

Authorities label independent media outlets and social media channels as "extremist." They characterize any form of communication with them as "aiding extremist activity" and have said that following and sharing their content constitutes "dissemination of extremist materials."

Authorities regularly prosecute those who expressed disapproval of Russia's war against Ukraine and Belarus's role in it, including by publicly speaking out or showing disagreement in other ways.

Freedom of opinion and expression in schools has also deteriorated. Children who express dissenting opinions face insults and threats of expulsion, and their parents risk job loss or the suspension of parental rights.

Torture and Ill-Treatment of Political Prisoners

Throughout 2023, political prisoners continued to face torture and ill-treatment during short-term arrests and in detention, including in pre-trial custody and penal colonies.

Law enforcement officers routinely subjected detainees in politically motivated cases to the degrading practice of "repent videos," forcing them to confess their "crimes" on camera.

Since February 2022, Belarusian authorities have held dozens of jailed opposition politicians, rights defenders, attorneys, journalists, and other political prisoners in prolonged incommunicado detention. Prolonged incommunicado detention is a form of inhuman treatment that may constitute torture or an enforced disappearance.

Political prisoners face beatings and arbitrary confinement in punishment cells for supposed violations of penitentiary regulations that are then used as a pretext for harsher prison treatment. Increasingly, political prisoners face new criminal charges, including for violating prison rules, resulting in consecutive lengthy prison sentences.

Lack of health care in penitentiary facilities has led to serious health issues for some detainees, including key opposition figure Maria Kalesnikava and opposition presidential candidate Viktar Babaryka, both of whom were admitted to a hospital for urgent surgery after being denied adequate care in custody. At least two political prisoners died behind bars in 2023 due to untreated illness.

Politically Motivated Repression of Belarusians in Exile

Since September 2022, Belarusian authorities initiated at least 31 "special procedure" criminal cases, including against opposition politicians, human rights defenders, and activists. A so-called special procedure provides for trials to take place without the presence of defendants charged with crimes under 43 different articles of the criminal code.

In July, legislative amendments to a 2002 citizenship law entered into force, allowing the president to strip Belarusians abroad of their citizenship if convicted of "participation in an extremist organization" or "grave harm to the interests of Belarus," including those convicted in absentia.

In September, Aliaksandr Lukashenka signed a decree abolishing the authority of consulates and diplomatic missions to issue, replace, or extend passports or identification cards of Belarusians abroad, making it obligatory for them to travel to Belarus. This exposes people to a risk of politically motivated prosecution upon their return and impedes their basic human rights abroad.

Death Penalty

Belarus remains the only country in Europe and Central Asia to carry out the death penalty.

In February, Human Rights Defenders Against Death Penalty in Belarus reported that Viktar Skrundzik, sentenced to death for murder and attempted murder, was executed on July 16, 2022.

In March, amendments to the Criminal Code entered into force, expanding the death penalty to cover the crime of "high treason" for state officials and military personnel.

In October, the Minsk regional court sentenced Alexander Taratuta, convicted of murder, to death.

Key International Actors

In 2023, the EU, Canada, the United States, and the United Kingdom extended and launched further sanctions against Belarus, including against individuals and legal entities, in response to continuing attacks on human rights and involvement in Russia's invasion of Ukraine.

In February, OHCHR published a report on the run-up to and aftermath of the 2020 presidential election in Belarus pursuant to its mandate to examine human rights in the country, documenting systematic, widespread, and gross human rights violations, some of which, it concluded, may amount to crimes against humanity. In April, the United Nations Human Rights Council extended this mandate for another year. In May, the UN special rapporteur on the human rights situation in Belarus published her annual report, documenting the ongoing deterioration of human rights; the Human Rights Council renewed the mandate of this special rapporteur in July. Also in May, the special rapporteur on the human rights of migrants published a report on his visit to Belarus from July 16 to 20, 2022, to assess the situation of the human rights of migrants at the border between Belarus and Poland, condemning the use of migrants as a political tool and the loss of migrants' lives due to pushbacks.

In March, 38 Organization for Security and Co-operation in Europe (OSCE) states invoked the Vienna Human Dimension Mechanism, highlighting the growing number of persons detained for politically motivated reasons. In May, the OSCE Office for Democratic Institutions and Human Rights presented an expert report documenting widespread violations in Belarus since November 5, 2020.

In June, the International Labour Organization adopted a resolution, noting Belarus' failure to comply with its 2004 Inquiry and requesting that member states review any cooperation with Belarus in response to non-respect of trade union rights in the country.

In July, the OSCE Parliamentary Assembly adopted a declaration and resolution in support of pro-democratic voices in Belarus, calling on Belarusian authorities to free political prisoners and on OSCE states to support political prisoners.

In July, the Viasna Human Rights Center was awarded the 2023 UN human rights prize.

In September, a Belarusian national stood trial in St. Gallen, Switzerland, under the legal principle of universal jurisdiction for having participated in the enforced disappearances of three major political opponents in 1999.

Bolivia

Political interference has plagued Bolivia's justice system for years. The government, both under former Interim President Jeanine Áñez and current President Luis Arce, has used an overbroad definition of "terrorism" to prosecute political opponents. Prison overcrowding, inadequate health care, and excessive use of pretrial detention continue.

In March, the Constitutional Court recognized civil unions for same-sex couples. In September, a tribunal acknowledged the serious harm that unchecked use of mercury caused to Amazon Indigenous communities and ordered the government to protect their rights.

Gender-based violence and violations of sexual and reproductive health and rights remain very serious problems. As a member of the United Nations Human Rights Council, Bolivia often sided with repressive governments and failed to uphold victims' rights.

Judicial Independence and Due Process

Bolivia's justice system has historically been exploited to accommodate the "interests of the ruling political power," the Inter-American Commission on Human Rights (IACHR) noted after a March 2023 visit. President Luis Arce has failed to fulfill his promise of judicial reform to make the system independent from politics.

In December 2022, Santa Cruz Governor Luis Fernando Camacho was detained on charges of terrorism, which has an overbroad definition in Bolivia. Camacho was accused of scheming to secure the resignation of then-President Evo Morales in 2019. Human Rights Watch reviewed the charging documents and found no supporting evidence for the terrorism charge. Camacho remains in pretrial detention as of October 2023. His family and lawyer allege he is not receiving adequate treatment for a serious chronic illness.

Former Interim President Áñez has been in prison since 2021, initially charged with terrorism. Human Rights Watch reviewed the documents and found the terrorism charge unsubstantiated and grossly disproportionate. In 2022, in a separate case, a tribunal sentenced Áñez to 10 years in prison for dereliction of duty and taking decisions contrary to the law—crimes that are also very broadly defined in Bolivian law—for her actions as she took office as interim president in November 2019. Áñez was unable to attend that trial in person, as judges said they could not guarantee her health or security in the courthouse.

César Apaza, the leader of a legal coca growers' association, has been in pretrial detention since September 2022. He suffered a stroke in February. His family complained that authorities were not providing him with adequate medical care. In July, the ombudsperson said the Attorney General's Office, at the ombudsperson's request, was investigating allegations that authorities had subjected Apaza to torture and ill-treatment.

Almost 50 percent of judges in Bolivia remain "temporary," the IACHR said in March. Almost 80 percent of prosecutors were also "temporary," as of December 2022, as showed by data obtained by Fundación Construir, a Bolivian nongovernmental organization (NGO). Justice officials who lack security of tenure may be vulnerable to reprisals, including arbitrary dismissal, if they make decisions that displease those in power.

Bolivians were scheduled to vote in 2023 for high court judges and members of the Magistrates Council, the body that appoints and dismisses judges, from lists created by Congress. In the past, the ruling party repeatedly packed the lists with people linked to the government. Elections have been delayed because for the first time, the ruling party lacks the two-thirds majority required to unilaterally select candidates. The terms of current judicial authorities end in January 2024; the constitution does not provide for temporary appointments or term extensions in case elections do not occur in a timely manner.

Detention Conditions

Detention centers in Bolivia hold more than three times more detainees than they were built to accommodate. From 2021 through 2022, the prison population grew 19 percent (to 24,824 people), as shown by official data obtained by Fundación Construir.

Bolivia's justice system uses pretrial detention excessively, including against opposition leaders. As of December 2022, 66 percent of detainees were awaiting trial, Fundación Construir said.

Justice for 2019 Abuses

As of October 2023, no one had been held responsible for 37 deaths, as well as alleged torture and other abuses by law enforcement, in the context of protests over contested October 2019 elections. A 2021 report by the IACHR-sponsored Interdisciplinary Group of Independent Experts (GIEI) documented major flaws in probes of the abuses.

Freedom of Expression and Access to Information

Página Siete, one of Bolivia's main newspapers, closed in June. Its president accused the government of denying it state-paid advertising, pressuring private companies not to advertise in *Página Siete*, and imposing arbitrary audits and fines, which depleted Página Siete's income. In March, the IACHR had expressed concern about how the government allocated paid state advertising, which is unregulated in Bolivia.

Bolivia lacks a law to implement the constitutional right of access to information.

Environment and Indigenous Peoples' Rights

A June 2023 study found that three-quarters of the members of 36 Indigenous communities in the Amazon exhibited mercury levels that were nearly double the safe limit established by the World Health Organization, based on analysis of hair samples. Such dangerous exposure to mercury may cause very serious harm to people, especially children, and result in lifelong health conditions. In high doses, mercury exposure may also be lethal. The most affected communities consumed fish that was obtained downriver from gold mining activities, which employ mercury.

In September, a court acknowledged the harm caused to these Indigenous communities and ordered the government to take protective measures and to respect their right to *free*, prior, and *informed consent* about projects that affect them.

Bolivia ratified the UN Minamata Convention on Mercury, which obligates states to protect people from the harmful effects of mercury, in 2016. However, mercury is widely used for mining in Bolivia with little or no oversight and smuggled to

Peru and other countries that have banned mercury imports, officials told Human Rights Watch. In 2021, Bolivia was the second largest importer of mercury after India, according to World Bank data.

Throughout 2023, the state-run lithium company announced agreements with Chinese and Russian firms for the industrial extraction of Bolivia's very large lithium deposits. Little information is publicly available about the terms of the agreements and their likely social and environmental impact, raising concerns in light of Bolivia's record of allowing mining without respecting the rights of Indigenous and local communities.

From 2021 to 2022, deforestation in Bolivia increased 32 percent, reaching record levels, driven mainly by the expansion of soybean cultivation, the World Resources Institute reported. Bolivia was exceeded only by Brazil and the Democratic Republic of the Congo in tropical primary forest losses.

In 2019, Bolivia ratified the Escazú agreement, which requires access to information and public participation in environmental matters and the protection of environmental defenders, but has done very little to implement it.

Economic and Social Rights

Official data showed that some 36 percent of Bolivians fell below the national poverty line and 11 percent were considered in extreme poverty as of 2021, respectively down from 42 percent and 19 percent in 2016. Inequality, as measured by the Gini index—where 0 means absolute equality and 1 absolute inequality—fell from 0.6 in 2005 to 0.4 in 2021, official data showed.

By the government's count, 724,000 children ages 5 to 17 worked in 2019, including in commercial sexual exploitation, mining, and dangerous agricultural jobs constituting the worst forms of child labor. In March 2023, in its concluding observations following its periodic review of Bolivia, the UN Committee on the Rights of the Child recommended that Bolivia increase the frequency of inspections to eliminate labor by children under 14, the country's legal minimum age to work.

Women's and Girls' Rights

Women and girls remain at high risk of violence. In 2022, prosecutors registered more than 51,000 reports of domestic violence, including 94 femicides. From

January through September 2023, there were 65 femicides. The Ombudsperson's Office denounced "discretionary" handling of judicial cases for attempted femicide, resulting in alleged perpetrators being prosecuted for less serious charges.

Under Bolivian law, abortion is a crime except in cases of rape or when necessary to protect the life or health of a pregnant person. Women and girls seeking legal abortions are likely to encounter stigma, mistreatment, and revictimization.

In March, the UN Committee on the Rights of the Child urged Bolivia to decriminalize abortion and modify the legal definition of rape, which requires violence or intimidation and does not include lack of consent to sexual intercourse.

Sexual Orientation and Gender Identity

In March, the Plurinational Constitutional Court made public a ruling recognizing civil unions for same-sex couples, a longstanding demand by activists. The court called upon the legislature to modify national legislation related to LGBTI rights in accordance with international standards. Same-sex marriage is still not legal in Bolivia.

The ruling did not address the rights of transgender people to enter into civil unions, which is prohibited by a 2017 decision by the same court. The 2017 ruling also denied their rights to adopt children and be elected to public office and curtailed their privacy rights with respect to the gender they were assigned at birth.

Disability Rights

Bolivia has not aligned its legislation with the UN Convention on the Rights of Persons with Disabilities. Its laws fail to recognize denial of reasonable accommodation as a form of disability-based discrimination. The government has failed to address discrimination against people with disabilities and ensure inclusive education, accessibility, access to justice, legal capacity, and an adequate standard of living.

Key International Actors

In January, the government decided not to renew the mandate of the local office of the UN High Commissioner for Human Rights, which, since its establishment in December 2020, had functioned as an important independent entity monitoring human rights.

As a member of the UN Human Rights Council, Bolivia consistently opposed scrutiny of various states' records and failed to protect rights. In 2023, among other actions, it abstained from voting on a resolution extending the mandate of a group of UN experts investigating systematic rights violations in Nicaragua, and it voted against renewing the mandates of a similar group for Syria and of the special rapporteurs on the human rights situations in Russia, in Burundi, in Iran, and in Belarus. Bolivia also voted against the establishment of an international fact-finding mission on Sudan.

Bosnia and Herzegovina

A European Court of Human Rights (ECtHR) judgment in August 2023 against territorial and ethnic voting restrictions underscored Bosnia and Herzegovina (BiH) authorities' lack of progress in addressing the country's discriminatory electoral system. Lesbian, gay, bisexual, and transgender (LGBT) people faced restrictions on assembly and official hostility in some parts of the country. The country lacks effective systems to protect victims of gender-based violence. New laws in Republika Srpska criminalize defamation and restrict foreign funding for civil society.

In its November 2023 enlargement report, the European Commission noted that BiH needs to make further efforts toward fulfilling the 14 integration reform priorities. It recommended opening accession negotiations with BiH once the necessary degree of compliance is achieved.

Discrimination and Intolerance

Controversial changes to the election law by the Office of the High Representative (OHR) hours after polls closed on election day in October 2022 resulted in people voting under one system but their votes being tabulated under another, leading to widespread international and domestic criticism. The electoral reform failed to address political discrimination against Roma, Jews, and others barred under the constitution from standing for the presidency.

In August, the ECtHR found that territorial and ethnic voting restrictions in Bosnian election law violated human rights by preventing citizens from voting for the candidates of their choice in 2022 legislative and presidential elections. This was the sixth ECtHR ruling on BiH's discriminatory electoral system since a landmark 2009 judgment on the residency.

The Organization for Security and Co-operation in Europe (OSCE) recorded 88 hate motivated crimes between January and August 2023, most of which were based on ethnicity and religion. At time of writing, 15 hate crime trials were ongoing, but no one had been convicted.

With several attacks on formerly war-displaced returnees in Republika Srpska in 2023 and poor investigation efforts by authorities, victims associations called on the European Union peacekeeping force in Bosnia and Herzegovina (EUFOR Operation Althea) in September to protect returnees. Also in September, the OHR called on BiH authorities to ensure safety in all parts of the country.

In July, the European Parliament urged BiH authorities to improve human rights protections, including measures to tackle inequality and ensure social protection of Roma people.

Disability Rights

The longstanding failure of BiH authorities to ensure the rights of people with disabilities and end institutionalization was highlighted in August, when a video emerged showing a staff member at a state-run institution abusing a man with a disability. It followed previous incidents of abuse at the same institution, including of children. Rather than address the root cause of the abuse by committing to ensure people with disabilities are moved out of institutions and into the community, the Minister of Labour and Social Policy of the Federation BiH (FBiH) threatened criminal charges against those who filmed the video and shared it with the media.

Accountability for War Crimes

Progress toward accountability for war crimes remains slow, with investigations, prosecutions, and court proceedings taking years. Authorities failed to meet the 2023 deadline to implement the Revised National War Crime Strategy. In March, the Council of Ministers formed a body to monitor its implementation.

Problematic laws that allow war crime sentences of up to a year to be replaced with a fine remain a concern. According to the OSCE, in the last five years, eight people convicted for war crimes have used this loophole to avoid jail time, including two men convicted of rape and attempted rape of girls. A proposal to abolish this practice did not pass the BiH Parliamentary Assembly.

According to the OSCE, 232 war crime cases against 516 defendants were pending before courts in BiH at the end of September. In the first nine months of 2023, courts in BiH rendered first instance judgments in 15 cases against 36 defendants, finding 16 guilty and acquitting 20. In the same period, 17 cases involving 20 defendants ended with final judgments; 12 were found guilty.

In August 2023, there were 55 pending cases, against 122 defendants, involving allegations of conflict-related sexual violence (CRSV). At time of writing, the courts had reached only two first instance judgments against four defendants and two final judgments against two defendants in CRSV cases.

In August, following years of advocacy by civil society and victims' groups, FBiH adopted a law recognizing children born of wartime rape as a special category of civilian victims of war with equal rights in society. Most survivors of CRSV have yet to receive reparations.

Asylum Seekers and Migrants

Between January and August 2023, the Service for Foreigners' Affairs registered 18,995 people expressing an intention to seek asylum, up from 11,881 in the same period in 2022. The UN Refugee Agency (UNHCR) reported improvements in asylum processing times.

Reports of Croatian police pushing refugees, asylum seekers, and migrants, including children, back into BiH and abusing them at the border continued.

Gender-Based Violence, Including Domestic Violence

High profile cases during the year highlighted the lack of adequate protections from gender-based violence.

In August, a man killed his ex-wife and livestreamed the murder. Before her death, the woman had reported threats and violence by her ex-husband to the authorities, but despite a police request to the municipal court to issue a restraining order against the man, the court refused the request for lack of evidence. In a separate case, Eldin Hodzic was sentenced to 35 years in prison for the murder of his wife in 2021. She reported him to the police for domestic violence 150 times before he killed her in front of their daughter.

Ten years after ratifying the Istanbul Convention, BiH authorities have yet to adopt legislative measures to prevent, investigate, and punish acts of gender-based violence. In August, Bosnian officials pledged to improve police and judicial responses and to strengthen legislation, including through the promulgation of a law on domestic violence.

In 2022, the Federation BiH House of Peoples adopted a law aiming to harmonize national legislation with the Istanbul Convention, but its implementation has been delayed by lack of consensus at the local level.

Sexual Orientation and Gender Identity

The 2023 Sarajevo Pride march went without registered incidents, but a March attack in Banja Luka on activists organizing a film screening underscored the precarious situation for LGBT rights in the country.

Prior to the attack, the film screening was banned by police following calls by Bosnian Serb President Milorad Dodik and the mayor of Banja Luka to do so two days earlier. Following the event's cancellation, the police told organizers to leave the city because the police could not guarantee their safety. According to activists present, the police stood aside while a group of men physically attacked activists. The Council of Europe Commissioner for Human Rights called on the authorities to sanction those responsible and investigate police failure to protect the activists.

Days later, Dodik announced a plan to ban LGBT content from school textbooks and LGBT activists from entering schools.

Freedom of Media

The national public radio and TV broadcaster BHRT remains in financial paralysis and under threat of closure due to an unresolved dispute with its counterpart station in Republika Srpska.

In July, Republika Srpska authorities adopted a law that criminalizes defamation and risks stifling free speech. The EU expressed concern about the law's disproportionate restrictions on independent civil society.

In September, Republika Srpska authorities adopted a draft "foreign agent" law regulating independent organizations that receive overseas funding. The EU found that the law violates EU principles and Republika Srpska's EU commitments.

The Council of Europe's Venice Commission and the OSCE jointly warned in June that the law threatens association and expression rights for civil society and media organizations.

Air Pollution and Human Rights

The burning of coal and wood in industries and homes continues to produce high levels of air pollution in BiH that negatively impacts residents' right to health and contributes to climate change. The transition from coal to renewable energy for heating and power production is slow.

In July, the Federation BiH adopted energy laws on electricity production and use of renewables and confirmed a previous ban on construction of new small hydropower plants. Republika Srpska has yet to adopt a similar ban.

HUMAN
RIGHTS
WATCH
"They Promised to Kill 30"
Police Killings in Baixada Santista, São Paulo State, Brazil

Brazil

Luiz Inácio Lula da Silva, known as Lula, took office as president on January 1, 2023. Seven days later, supporters of defeated candidate and former President Jair Bolsonaro stormed Congress, the Supreme Court, and the presidential palace, unsuccessfully calling for a military coup.

The Lula administration has reversed certain harmful Bolsonaro administration policies on the environment and sexual and reproductive rights, but it did not take decisive measures to address chronic police abuse.

Lula's government also failed to consistently defend human rights abroad.

In a landmark decision, the Supreme Court upheld the land rights of Indigenous people, but Congress reacted by approving a bill that runs counter to the ruling. Deforestation in the Amazon decreased sharply, but forest defenders continued to suffer threats and attacks.

Democratic Rule

Under orders from a Supreme Court justice, police arrested about 1,500 people in connection with the January 8 break-in and ransacking of federal buildings in Brasília. Prosecutors had charged about 1,300 people as of October and 128 remained in pretrial detention. Twenty-five had been convicted as of mid-November.

A parliamentary inquiry asked authorities to open criminal investigations against Bolsonaro and 60 other people, including former cabinet members and high-ranking military officers, in connection with the attacks.

In June, the Superior Electoral Court banned Bolsonaro from running for office for eight years, ruling that he had abused his power and misused news media. This referred to a meeting—broadcast on public television—with ambassadors less than three months before the presidential election during which he insisted, without providing evidence, that Brazil's electoral system was unreliable.

As of November, lawmakers were considering an amnesty for political parties that had violated rules requiring minimum allocations of electoral funds to female and Black candidates and that failed to account properly for the use of public electoral funds.

Corruption and Judicial Independence

Former President Bolsonaro and his associates were under investigation for falsifying health records to show he had received a Covid-19 vaccine, selling gifts he had received from foreign governments, and inciting the January 8 attacks.

In 2019 and 2021, Bolsonaro broke with a practice since 2003 of selecting an attorney general from a list of three candidates chosen by prosecutors from across the country. This practice had been intended to strengthen the attorney general's independence from politicians. The attorney general Bolsonaro appointed was widely viewed as lacking independence and making decisions that benefited Bolsonaro. In November, President Lula chose an attorney general from outside the list whose confirmation by the senate was pending as of early December.

Freedom of Expression and Access to Information

In the context of the attacks in Brasília from January 8 to 11, journalism defense organizations registered 45 cases of threats, destruction of equipment, and assaults against journalists by protesters.

In August, the government announced it would unblock more than 3,000 social media users the Bolsonaro administration had blocked from interacting with institutional accounts. It did not say whether government officials would also unblock users from personal accounts they use to discuss matters of public interest.

Detention Conditions

More than 649,000 people were in jail or prison as of June 2023, exceeding the capacity of Brazilian facilities by 34 percent. Another 190,080 people were under house arrest.

The National Mechanism for the Prevention and Combat of Torture denounced overcrowding, unhealthy conditions, collective punishment, and ill-treatment (including torture) of adults and children in detention in eight states in 2022.

The number of people aged 12 to 21 who broke the law as children and were held in youth detention—12,154 in 2022—dropped 50 percent since 2018, the non-profit Brazilian Forum of Public Security (FBSP) reported.

Public Security and Police Conduct

Homicides fell by 3 percent in the first half of 2023, compared to the same period the year before, not including killings by police.

On-duty and off-duty police killed 6,429 people nationwide in 2022, about the same number as the previous year, FBSP reported. The states of Amapá, Bahia, and Rio de Janeiro had the highest rates of police killings.

After falling 59 percent in two years, killings by on-duty police in São Paulo state went up 45 percent from January through September 2023, compared to the same period the year before. From late July through early September, police killed 28 people in the Baixada Santista region of São Paulo during an operation launched after a military police officer was shot dead. Human Rights Watch identified significant gaps in the investigations, such as deficient forensic analysis.

To comply with a Supreme Court order, Rio de Janeiro state published an updated version in December 2022 of its plan to curb killings by police. In October, the court ordered the state to take into consideration suggestions by a group of experts and other civil society members who called for explicit targets for reduction of police killings.

In August, the government conditioned the transfer of federal public security funds to states on a reduction in police killings and other factors.

In 2022, 161 police were killed nationwide, 70 percent while off duty. Another 82 police officers died by suicide.

At least two police suicides in 2023 appeared motivated by harassment at work: the June suicide of a female police clerk who had reported sexual and other harassment in Minas Gerais state, and the August suicide of a male police officer in Maranhão state who had reported harassment and discrimination based on his sexual orientation.

Military-Era Abuses

Since 2012, federal prosecutors have filed charges in more than 50 criminal cases of human rights abuses during Brazil's military rule, from 1964 to 1985. Courts have dismissed most, citing the statute of limitations or an amnesty law passed by the dictatorship and upheld by a 2010 Supreme Court ruling which the Inter-American Court of Human Rights found violated Brazil's obligations under international law.

In June, a federal court convicted a former official for helping conceal bodies during the dictatorship. The court held that the amnesty law was incompatible with the Inter-American Convention on Human Rights and did not apply to enforced disappearances, as they are continuing crimes.

Ruling on a lawsuit, a federal court in January ordered three former civil police officials should pay 1 million Brazilian reais (about US$198,404) each for the torture and killing of 25 people during the dictatorship.

The Lula administration began reassessing requests for reparations for political persecution during military rule, after finding 95 percent of requests had been denied under the Bolsonaro administration. Yet, as of mid-November, it had failed to deliver on its pledge to re-establish a commission to investigate political deaths and enforced disappearances dismantled by the Bolsonaro administration.

Women's and Girls' Rights

Gender-based violence reports increased in the first semester of 2023, FBSP reported. There were 34,000 rapes of women and girls from January through June, a 15 percent increase compared to the same period in 2022.

Killings of women went up 2.6 percent, to 1,902, in the first semester of 2023. Police registered more than a third of them as femicide, defined under Brazilian law as the killing of women "on account of being persons of the female sex."

More than one million cases of domestic violence were pending in court at the end of 2022.

As of November, judges had granted more than 350,000 protective orders, which typically require suspected abusers to stay away from targeted women. The law requires that judges decide on such requests within 48 hours, but most state courts take longer than that; courts in Sergipe took 165 days on average, the National Council of Justice (CNJ) said.

Congress approved a law requiring specialized police stations for women to stay open 24/7, and another law guaranteeing equal pay for women and men doing the same jobs. As of November, it had not yet ratified the International Labour Organization (ILO) Violence and Harassment Convention (C190).

Abortion is legal in Brazil only in cases of rape, to save a woman's life, or when the fetus has anencephaly. Women and girls who have illegal abortions risk injury, death, and up to three years in prison. People who perform illegal abortions face up to four years in prison. In September, the then Supreme Court chief justice voted to decriminalize abortion up to 12 weeks. A decision by the full court was pending as of November.

A survey published in August estimated that one in seven women had had an abortion by age 40, particularly Black and Indigenous women, those residing in poor regions, and those with low educational levels.

In January, the Lula administration revoked a 2020 regulation requiring health professionals to report to police rape survivors seeking to terminate pregnancies.

Disability Rights

About 18.6 million adults and children over 2 years old with disabilities live in Brazil. Thousands are confined in institutions—sometimes for life—where some face neglect and abuse. In 2021, the National Council of Prosecutors' Offices passed a resolution requiring prosecutors to inspect institutions for adults with disabilities yearly and take legal action in cases of abuse. The Council has not published information on the resolution's implementation.

Some 26 percent of people with disabilities had completed high school compared to almost 57 percent without disabilities, a government survey published in 2023 showed, and 29 percent of people with disabilities had a job, compared to 66 percent without disabilities.

In January, President Lula revoked a Bolsonaro administration policy that appeared aimed at establishing segregated schools for certain children with disabilities.

Education

In April, Human Rights Watch found that from 2021 to 2023, educational websites owned and operated by the education secretariats of Minas Gerais and São Paulo sent children's personal data to advertising companies.

In response, Brazilian authorities opened investigations into educational websites, the education secretariat of Minas Gerais removed all ad tracking from its website, and at least two companies took steps to shield children from their data surveillance.

In August, the government announced the resumption of an initiative to promote sexuality and reproductive health education at schools that the Bolsonaro administration had discontinued.

Rights of Indigenous People, Afro-Descendant People, and Environmental Defenders

In a landmark decision in September, the Supreme Court rejected an attempt to block Indigenous people from obtaining title to their traditional lands if they were not physically present on them when Brazil's constitution was adopted in 1988. Congress reacted by approving a bill—and later overturning a presidential veto of the bill—that runs counter to the ruling. Indigenous groups petitioned the Supreme Court to strike down the law.

President Lula appointed the first Indigenous leaders to chair Brazil's Indigenous affairs agency and the newly created Ministry of Indigenous Peoples.

The Lula administration withdrew a bill the Bolsonaro administration introduced to allow mining and other commercial activities in Indigenous territories and revoked policies facilitating encroachment. The government resumed titling of Indigenous lands.

In January, the government documented malnutrition and serious diseases associated with illegal mining activities in the Yanomami Indigenous territory and launched a large-scale operation to remove thousands of miners who operated largely unimpeded during the Bolsonaro administration. Some responded by shooting at law enforcement officials. In August, Yanomami associations reported continuing health problems and the return of some miners.

For the first time, Brazil released comprehensive demographic data on Afro-descendant rural communities, revealing more than 1.3 million inhabitants. In March, the government granted collective land titles to three communities. Yet, Afro-descendant communities continue to face violence. In August, assailants killed Bernadete Pacífico, a leader in Bahia state who was under police protection after having received death threats.

At least 11 people were killed in conflicts over land and resources in the Amazon in the first semester of 2023, the nongovernmental Pastoral Land Commission reported.

In May, President Lula sent Congress the Escazú Agreement, which requires governments in Latin America and the Caribbean to protect environmental defenders and guarantee access to information and public participation in environmental matters. As of November, ratification by Congress was pending.

In December, the Lula administration announced at the United Nations climate conference, COP 28, that Brazil plans to join the OPEC+ group of oil-producing nations as an observer.

Climate Change Policy and Impacts

Brazil contributes to the climate crisis as one of the world's top ten greenhouse gas emitters.

Increased deforestation due to weakened law enforcement in the Amazon between 2019 and 2020 drove up overall emissions, which rose 12 percent in 2021, the highest increase in almost two decades, according to the non-governmental organization, Climate Observatory.

From January through October 2023, preliminary official data show that 4,776 square kilometers of Amazon rainforest were cleared, a 49 percent decrease compared to the same period in 2022. However, over the same period, 6,802 square kilometers of a wooded savannah area known as Cerrado was deforested with a 34 percent increase.

In November, the government updated its climate action plan with more ambitious targets, pledging a 48 percent cut in emissions by 2025 and 53 percent by 2030. President Lula launched a plan to fight deforestation in the Amazon, renewing a commitment to reach zero illegal deforestation by 2030. But the government sent mixed signals about allowing offshore oil exploration at the mouth of the Amazon River. Despite pledging to boost the ecological transition and turn Brazil into "a great sustainable power," it announced investments in fossil fuels that drive climate change.

Migrants, Refugees, and Asylum Seekers

Thousands of Venezuelans have crossed the border into Brazil in recent years, fleeing hunger, lack of basic health care, or persecution.

About 499,650 Venezuelans lived in Brazil as of October 2023. Brazil had granted refugee status to 53,307 by 2022, having facilitated asylum by recognizing a "serious and widespread violation of human rights" in their country. Venezuelans can also apply for residency in Brazil.

The Lula administration adopted simplified procedures to review asylum requests based on gender identity or sexual orientation by people from countries that criminalize same-sex sexual conduct and by girls and women who have suffered genital mutilation.

Key International Actors

The UN High Commissioner for Human Rights (OHCHR), the Inter-American Commission on Human Rights (IACHR), the UN Committee on Economic, Social and Cultural Rights (CESCR), and UN special rapporteurs expressed concern over violence and land conflicts affecting Indigenous people and Afro-descendant communities.

At an Amazon Summit in August, countries sharing the rainforest committed to protecting it but did not announce deforestation reduction targets.

The UN Human Rights Committee, the Committee against Torture, OHCHR, and the IACHR denounced police violence in Brazil, expressed concern about its impact on Black Brazilians, and urged authorities to ensure thorough investigations.

In November, the UN Expert Mechanism to Advance Racial Justice and Equality in Law Enforcement visited Brazil.

The European Parliament, the EU's High Representative for Foreign Affairs, OHCHR, and the IACHR condemned the January 2023 attack on democratic institutions.

Foreign Policy

Brazil retained inconsistent positions on human rights in its foreign policy.

In June, Brazil urged the UN Human Rights Council (HRC) to adopt a treaty recognizing the right to free secondary education and to at least one year of free pre-primary education.

President Lula offered to broker peace talks to end the Russia-Ukraine war but made controversial public statements, including incorrectly suggesting that Kyiv and Moscow were equally responsible for starting it.

President Lula re-established diplomatic ties with Venezuela. In May, he called concerns about the undermining of democratic institutions there a "constructed narrative."

In March, Brazil declined to sign an HRC declaration condemning abuses in Nicaragua. Officials later said they were "extremely concerned" about human rights violations in Nicaragua and offered to receive political refugees who had been stripped of nationality. Brazil has consistently declined to support statements of concern about China's crimes against humanity against Uyghurs in Xinjiang.

In October, Brazil proposed a UN Security Council resolution aimed at facilitating humanitarian aid to civilians in Gaza amid the escalating hostilities in Israel and Palestine. The US vetoed it.

Brazil was elected to the Human Rights Council for the 2024-2026 term.

Burkina Faso

Burkina Faso's human rights situation deteriorated considerably in 2023, as deadly attacks by Islamist armed groups against civilians surged and military forces and pro-government militias committed abuses during counterinsurgency operations.

The armed conflict has killed nearly 7,900 people since 2021 and forced over 2 million people from their homes since it began in 2016.

In April, the military government, which came to power in an October 2022 coup, announced a "general mobilization" as part of a plan to recapture territory lost to the armed groups, which may control up to 50 percent of the country's territory. The plan seeks to create a "legal framework for all actions" taken against insurgents.

Burkina Faso's transitional military authorities also cracked down on the media and dissent, contributing to the shrinking of civic space.

In October 2022, the leader of the military junta, Ibrahim Traoré, promised to hold elections by July 2024, a deadline agreed on by former Burkinabè coup leader Lt. Col. Paul Henri Sandaogo Damiba with the Economic Community of West African States (ECOWAS). However, on May 30, Prime Minister Apollinaire Kyelem de Tambela said elections might be delayed given the persistent insecurity affecting the country.

In a September 27 statement, the spokesman for the military government, Rimtalba Jean Emmanuel Ouedraogo, said the Burkinabè intelligence services thwarted a coup attempt by some army officers and others. The military prosecutor said four army officers were arrested and two were on the run.

Burkinabè transitional authorities have cut relations with France—requesting in February that Paris withdraw its special forces from the country, marking the end of more than 20 years of the French military presence—and have established stronger ties with non-Western partners including Türkiye and Russia.

Abuses by Islamist Armed Groups

The Al-Qaeda-linked Jama'at Nasr al-Islam wal Muslimin (Group for the Support of Islam and Muslims, JNIM) and, to a lesser extent, the Islamic State in the Greater Sahara (ISGS) killed hundreds of civilians during attacks across the country. Some attacks targeted communities that had formed local civil defense groups. Islamist armed groups also besieged more than two dozen towns—an estimated 800,000 people—leading to severe food shortages and contributing to malnutrition.

Islamist armed groups led repeated and escalating attacks on the town of Dassa and its surroundings, Centre-Ouest region, from December 2022 to February 2023, culminating in killings that caused residents to flee the area. Dassa is in an area where the JNIM is known to operate and carry out attacks. On January 26, gunmen attacked Doh, a village about 4 kilometers from Dassa, allegedly killing 12 men and injuring 2. As a result of the attack, the population fled the area. On February 9, gunmen wearing sand-colored clothes and turbans attacked Dassa, killing two men.

Islamist armed groups carried out at least three attacks in villages in and around the town of Pissila, Centre-Nord region, in December 2022 through February 2023, killing civilians in an apparent attempt to expel its population. Pissila is in an area where JNIM operates and conducts attacks and raids. In January, about 40 gunmen on motorcycles, wearing military fatigues and turbans, entered the village of Dofinega, about 16 kilometers from Pissila, and killed 17 men. In mid-January, gunmen wearing military fatigues and turbans attacked Ouanobian, 15 kilometers north of Pissila, and burned at least one house. In February, about 100 gunmen rounded up a group of about 60 residents of Noaka village, about 12 kilometers from Pissila, and issued an ultimatum for them to leave the area.

Islamist armed groups allegedly linked to JNIM led at least three incursions into the village of Zincko, Centre-Nord region, in December 2022 and early January 2023, looting, shooting in the air, and demanding villagers tell them where they could find government security forces, residents said. They eventually issued two ultimatums for residents to leave the village. On January 4, gunmen wearing "cold-weather clothes," carrying AK-47-style assault rifles, and riding on motorcycles returned and went around the town to give residents an ultimatum to leave within 48 hours. In late January, a confrontation between Islamist fighters and local militias led to the killing of two civilian men.

On January 12, armed men abducted over 60 people, foraging for food in the department of Arbinda, Sahel region, an area mainly controlled by JNIM but where fighters from ISGS have also carried out attacks. A week later, the Burkinabè information agency announced the captives—identified as 39 children and 27 women—had been found alive. Arbinda residents have been battling extreme hunger as a direct result of a siege by the Islamist armed groups.

JNIM forces have besieged the town of Djibo, Sahel region, since February. The Islamist armed group controls the access roads to Djibo, along which they have planted explosives. They have destroyed bridges, water, and communications infrastructure, as well as prevented deliveries of market supplies, isolating the town from the rest of the country. People cannot move freely and lack access to basic goods and services, including food, water, electricity, and health care. Prices have risen so much that many people are unable to buy food staples and other necessities. Attacks by Islamist armed groups and counterinsurgency operations by the Burkinabè armed forces around Djibo have led to mass displacement, with thousands of people seeking refuge in Djibo. As of early May, of the 300,000 people living in Djibo, almost 270,000 were displaced.

Abuses by State Security Forces and Pro-Government Militias

The military authorities have relied heavily on local militias to counter the attacks. In October 2022, they opened a campaign to bolster these militias by recruiting 50,000 civilian auxiliaries, called Volunteers for the Defense of the Homeland (Volontaires pour la défense de la patrie, VDPs).

Pro-government forces, including soldiers and VDPs, unlawfully killed or forcibly disappeared hundreds of civilians during counterinsurgency operations.

On July 8, Burkinabè soldiers stopped a truck carrying 11 people, including 8 children, fleeing their village of Bekuy, western Burkina Faso, following an attack by Islamist armed groups the day before. They threatened to kill the driver and drove off with 11 people. The bodies of those 11 were found the same day a few kilometers away from Bekuy. All appeared to have been shot.

On April 3, a supply convoy heading to the town of Dori, Séno province, escorted by a large number of military vehicles, motorcycles, and armored cars, stopped in Gangaol village and dropped off soldiers around the market area. Soldiers questioned people, asking them to show their identity cards, then broke into a home and pulled out 10 men. Soldiers beat the men and later summarily executed six of them, according to witnesses.

On April 20, apparent Burkinabè military forces summarily executed at least 156 civilians, including 28 women and 45 children, burned homes, and looted property in the village of Karma and the vicinity, northern Yatenga province, in one of the worst massacres in Burkina Faso since 2015.

On March 29, soldiers killed a 47-year-old man and two children, ages 13 and 14, in Ouro Hesso, a neighborhood of Gangaol village, Séno province.

On February 15, scores of Burkinabè soldiers accompanied by militia in a counterinsurgency operation arrested 16 men in Ekeou village, Séno province, Sahel region, and then headed to Goulgountou, a nearby village, and arrested two additional men. The bodies of at least nine of those arrested, including one man with a visual disability, were found on May 26 near the VDP base in Falagountou. Soldiers also severely beat those arrested in Ekeou along with eight children between the ages of 6 and 16 in the same village. A man with a physical disability later died due to injuries he received during the military operation.

Two members of the security forces and two militia members arrested two ethnic Peul brothers on January 30 in Zoundwéogo province. One reportedly died in detention, and the other appears to have been tortured before being released.

On July 25, a group of about 30 VDPs stormed Ekeou village, killed two men, including one with a visual disability, and seriously injured two children. They also burned four homes and a barn. Witnesses said the VDPs were searching out the men of the village, whom they accused of being Islamist fighters or their accomplices.

On August 3, a Burkinabè military Bayraktar drone struck a crowded market in Bouro, Sahel region, killing at least 23 men and wounding many others. There was no evidence that the men were combatants, and the strike was far from any fighting.

On September 10, a group of VDPs stormed the grazing fields surrounding the village of Peteguersé, Sahel region, to loot livestock. During the attack, they killed 7 people, including 4 children, and looted over 100 cows and 24 goats.

On November 12, the European Union called for an investigation into a massacre in northern Burkina Faso, saying about 100 people were reportedly killed. According to the government, unidentified gunmen killed at least 70 people, mainly older people and children, in Zaongo village, Centre Nord region, on November 5, and the incident was being investigated.

On September 21, a military drone strike killed at least 20 civilian men and injured 10 others who had gathered for a funeral ceremony in Bidi, North region.

Crackdown on the Media and Dissent

On March 27, Burkinabè authorities suspended the French international television news network, France 24, for airing a 19-second clip of a March interview with Abou Obeida Youssef al-Annabi, the self-proclaimed leader of the Islamist armed group Al-Qaeda in the Islamic Maghreb (AQIM).

On March 29, the media regulatory body in Burkina Faso, the Superior Council for Communication regretted "the recurrence of threats against media outlets and media actors" and called on the authorities to "take appropriate measures to ensure the safety of the media and journalists in the course of their work."

In March, Burkinabè military authorities expelled Agnès Faivre and Sophie Douce, two journalists working for the French newspapers *Libération* and *Le Monde*. Both journalists, who possessed valid visas and accreditation, had reported on human rights abuses by government forces. National intelligence officers summoned and questioned them on March 31 in Ouagadougou about their work and gave them 24 hours to leave the country without providing any reason for their expulsion.

On August 10, Burkinabè military authorities suspended independent radio station Radio Omega for broadcasting an interview with supporters of the ousted president of Niger, Mohamed Bazoum. The journalist who conducted the interview, Abdoul Fhatave Tiemtoré, was summoned by State Security the next day and questioned for five hours. The radio started broadcasting again in September.

On September 25, military authorities ordered the suspension of *Jeune Afrique* media, accusing it of discrediting the military.

Burkina Faso's military junta has used a sweeping emergency law against perceived dissidents. Between November 4 and 5, 2023, members of the security forces notified, in writing or by telephone, at least a dozen journalists, civil society activists, and opposition party members to inform them they will be conscripted to participate in government security operations across the country. The transitional military authorities assert that the conscription orders are authorized under the April 13 "general mobilization" plan that gives the president extensive powers to combat the Islamist insurgency, including requisitioning people and goods and restraining civil liberties.

Accountability for Abuses

On June 14, Human Rights Watch sent letters to the Burkinabè justice and defense ministers, sharing the organization's research findings on the alleged abuses committed by members of the Burkina Faso armed forces between January and April 2023 in Séno and Zoundwéogo provinces and requesting responses to specific questions. The Burkinabè minister of justice and human rights responded on July 25.

The justice minister said all allegations of human rights abuses by members of the Burkinabè armed forces and security forces into systematically investigated. He provided information regarding the investigations opened into the alleged abuses in Karma and Gangaol villages and Zoundwéogo province. He said the inquiry into the massacre of 156 civilians in Karma has been finalized—with 54 people heard, including 9 military officers and sub-officers, two soldiers, and two VDPs—and transferred to the prosecutor of the high court in Ouahigouya. The justice minister also said the government is drafting a decree to compensate the victims of terrorist acts.

On February 16, the nation's transitional parliament passed a bill to strengthen the role of provost marshals, who are responsible for discipline in the armed forces. The new law, if fully implemented, will better protect detainees' rights during military operations and at military camps and contribute to accountability for human rights abuses.

Children's Right to Education

Islamist armed groups allied with Al-Qaeda and the ISGS began attacking teachers and schools in Burkina Faso in 2017, citing their opposition to "French," Western-style education and government institutions. The attacks have increased every year since. The groups have killed, beaten, abducted, and threatened education professionals; intimidated students; terrorized parents into keeping children out of school; and damaged, destroyed, and looted schools.

One-quarter of schools are closed in Burkina Faso because of the increased fighting between Islamist armed groups and government forces. As of July, 6,100 schools were closed, affecting close to 1 million students.

Most of the attacks on schools in the country have been attributed to JNIM fighters. On March 10, JNIM fighters burned a school in Sanguen village, Centre-Nord region.

Key International Actors

On September 16, Burkina Faso, Mali, and Niger signed the Liptako-Gourma charter, a security and defense agreement establishing the Alliance of Sahel States, binding the parties to assist one another in case of an attack on any one of them and to work to prevent or settle armed rebellions.

On September 15, Burkina Faso expelled the French military attaché for "subversive activities" and ordered the closure of the French military mission in Ouagadougou. France withdrew its troops from Burkina Faso after the October 2022 military coup.

On September 18, France's foreign ministry announced that new visas for students coming from Burkina Faso, Mali, and Niger will no longer be issued "for security reasons." On August 6, France also announced the suspension of development aid and budgetary assistance to Burkina Faso.

In April, the EU's external service called for an impartial and thorough investigation into the massacre of civilians in the village of Karma, warning it could constitute war crimes.

Burundi

Burundi's ruling party, the National Council for the Defense of Democracy-Forces for the Defense of Democracy (Conseil national pour la défense de la démocratie-Forces pour la défense de la démocratie, CNDD-FDD) consolidated its control over institutions and continued to weaken and quash political opposition, routinely targeting those it accuses of being "enemies" of the country. At the same time, the arrest of former Prime Minister Gen. Alain Guillaume Bunyoni on April 21 exposed divisions and shifting dynamics within the ruling party.

The government failed to implement promised reforms, tackle the country's economic crisis, and address financial mismanagement, chronic shortages of fuel, and spiraling prices. These failures, alongside the war in Ukraine and climate-related shocks, have exacerbated food insecurity in Burundi.

The government's hostility toward independent civil society and media persisted. In May, a court of appeal decided to maintain the conviction of journalist Floriane Irangabiye, who was arbitrarily arrested on August 30, 2022, and is currently serving a 10-year prison sentence for criticizing the government.

Political Space

The relentless targeting of real and suspected opposition members in recent years—through extrajudicial killings, enforced disappearances, arbitrary detention, and torture— has contributed to the ruling party's de facto monopoly of the country's political space and economy.

Internal turmoil and divisions within the leadership of the National Congress for Freedom (Congrès National pour la Liberté, CNL) came to a head when the interior minister suspended the activities of the opposition party on June 2. In a further escalation, 10 ousted members of the CNL's political bureau, also members of parliament, issued a public statement on July 4 announcing that they were suspending Agathon Rwasa from the position of president of the CNL, accusing him of "serious failures." The inability of the CNL, the main opposition party in Burundi, to operate and campaign will affect the credibility of the 2025 legislative elections.

The authorities failed to hold accountable security forces and members of the ruling party's youth league, the Imbonerakure, for abuses perpetrated against real or suspected opponents. Instead, senior party officials, including the president and the CNDD-FDD secretary general, have urged them to take action to defend the country and promoted their role as a parallel security force, emboldening them to carry out abuses.

CNDD-FDD hardliner Gen. Alain Guillaume Bunyoni was arrested in April. Although he coordinated police action as minister of public security during the demonstrations and violent repression that followed the 2015 elections, judicial authorities have shied away from investigating his role in overseeing human rights abuses during this period. He is being prosecuted for alleged offenses during his time as prime minister, including "undermining the internal security of the State" and "undermining the proper functioning of the national economy" and for "conflict of interest," "illegal possession of weapons," and "contempt of the Head of State." His close ally Désiré Uwamahoro was arrested on April 18.

Civil Society and the Media

On December 8, 2022, the Supreme Court of Burundi overturned the unjust five-year prison sentence handed down by the Ngozi Court of Appeal to lawyer Tony Germain Nkina and his client Apollinaire Hitimana. They were released on December 27, 2022.

On January 2, the Mukaza High Court in Bujumbura, the country's economic capital, convicted journalist Floriane Irangabiye of endangering the integrity of the national territory, sentenced her to 10 years in prison, and imposed a fine of 1 million Burundian francs (approximately US$482) following a deeply flawed trial during which the prosecutor failed to provide credible evidence. Irangabiye's prosecution violated her right to freedom of expression, as it was based on comments made during a radio show for Radio Igicaniro, an online platform in exile, in which she and other guests were critical of the Burundian government.

On May 2, the Court of Appeal of Mukaza upheld the conviction. Although the court found that Irangabiye's initial interrogation by the National Intelligence Service violated the criminal procedure code because it was conducted without a lawyer present and without informing her of her right to remain silent, it held that this did not nullify the procedure. Her lawyers have filed an appeal to the Supreme Court.

On February 14, five human rights defenders were arrested by national intelligence agents and accused of rebellion and of undermining internal state security and the functioning of public finances. The charges appeared to relate only to their relationship with an international organization abroad and the funding they received from this organization. Two of the defenders work for the Association of Women Lawyers in Burundi (Association des femmes juristes du Burundi, AFJB) and three for the Association for Peace and the Promotion of Human Rights in Burundi (Association pour la paix et la promotion des droits de l'Homme, APDH).

Initially, all five were also charged with rebellion, but this charge was only maintained for three of them during the trial. The charge of "undermining the functioning of public finances" was eventually dropped for all five accused. All were released on April 28: all five were acquitted of "undermining internal state security"; three were acquitted and two were convicted of rebellion, fined 50,000 Burundian francs ($25), and handed a two-year suspended sentence.

In September, Human Rights Watch and the Burundi Human Rights Initiative submitted a report to the Global Alliance of National Human Rights Institutions to request that it reviews the work of Burundi's National Independent Human Rights Commission (Commission Nationale Indépendante des Droits de l'Homme, CNIDH) ahead of its scheduled review. Burundi's commission has demonstrated a lack of independence, credibility, and effectiveness, including through its failure to publicly advocate for the release of detained human rights defenders and Irangabiye.

In October, the UN special rapporteur on the situation of human rights in Burundi expressed concern about the "shrinking civic space and a growing pressure on political parties, civil society organisations and the media" ahead of the 2025 legislative and municipal elections.

Refugee Rights

As of September 2023, there were over 250,000 Burundian refugees living in the Democratic Republic of Congo, Rwanda, Tanzania, and Uganda. According to the

UN Refugee Agency (UNHCR), as of August, about 210,000 refugees had been repatriated to Burundi since 2017 under its "voluntary repatriation" programs. The repatriations primarily took place from Congo, Rwanda, Tanzania, and Uganda, where refugees face worsening conditions and authorities encouraged refugees to repatriate, in some cases leading to coerced returns in violation of the principle of non-refoulement. The UN special rapporteur on the situation of human rights in Burundi noted the lack of essential elements of a voluntary repatriation process and urged the government to guarantee conditions for the credible return of refugees.

Girls' Rights

According to the United Nations Children's Fund (UNICEF), 19 percent of girls are married before age 18.

Sexual Orientation and Gender Identity

Burundi punishes consensual same-sex sexual relations between adults with up to two years in prison under article 567 of the penal code. Article 29 of the Constitution explicitly bans same-sex marriage.

In March, police arrested 24 delegates at a seminar on entrepreneurship and charged them with "homosexuality and incitement to debauchery and prostitution." Their case is ongoing at time of writing.

Key International Actors

Burundian authorities continued to demonstrate their disregard for the international human rights system. In July, the Burundian delegation walked out of its review by the UN Human Rights Committee, a treaty body focusing on civil and political rights, apparently protesting the presence of a duly accredited human rights defender. This followed a pattern of noncooperation with UN human rights bodies and mechanisms, including a continued refusal to cooperate with the UN special rapporteur on the human rights situation in Burundi.

The UN special rapporteur presented his report to the UN Human Rights Council in September, concluding that, despite some positive steps on the part of the

Burundian government, there remain significant challenges, including the weakness of institutions and lack of oversight of intelligence services. The government of Burundi has repeatedly rejected the special rapporteur's requests for access to the country to carry out his work. In October, the Human Rights Council extended the special rapporteur's mandate for another year.

Members of the Human Rights Council are required to "uphold the highest standards in the promotion and protection of human rights" and to fully cooperate with it and its mechanisms. Despite its rights record and refusal to cooperate with the international human rights system, Burundi was elected as a member of the council for 2024-2026 as the only candidate running on behalf of the African group.

During a visit in February, European Union Special Representative for Human Rights Eamon Gilmore stressed the need to reform the judiciary, raised individual cases of concern, and called on the authorities to facilitate country visits of the UN special rapporteur.

Cambodia

Cambodia's self-characterization as a democratic government does not reflect the reality. Cambodia is effectively a single-party state with fixed and controlled elections, a lack of independent media, ruling party interference and control of all state institutions, political control of the judiciary, and systematic harassment and targeting of critics in the political opposition and civil society.

The situation deteriorated further in the run-up to the national elections in July 2023. Then-Prime Minister Hun Sen intensified his violent rhetoric, prompting a crackdown on political opposition, independent media, land rights activists, civil society leaders, and trade union leaders.

On May 15, the government-controlled National Election Committee (NEC) barred the main opposition party, the Candlelight Party (CLP), from fielding candidates by rejecting the CLP's application documents on bogus, politically motivated grounds, ensuring that the elections were not a meaningful political process. Previously, the NEC had permitted the CLP to run in the June 2022 national elections for commune-level offices using the same registration documents it rejected in May 2023.

After the election, on August 22, Hun Sen, who had ruled Cambodia as prime minister since 1985, handed power to his son, now Prime Minister Hun Manet. Hun Sen remains head of the ruling Cambodian People's Party (CunPP) and serves as Senate president. Despite the royalist party FUNCINPEC winning 5 out of the 125 national assembly seats, Cambodia remains tightly controlled by the CPP.

Attacks against Opposition Members

Ahead of the 2023 national elections, surveillance, intimidation, judicial harassment, and violent attacks intensified against members of the political opposition, both inside and outside Cambodia.

During a speech on January 9, 2023, Hun Sen warned the opposition not to criticize the ruling CPP ahead of the upcoming elections and said defiance would be met with either punitive rulings by the courts, which are controlled by the CPP, or mob violence. In the months that followed, a number of opposition party members were assaulted in Phnom Penh in broad daylight while others were convicted or arrested on politically motivated criminal charges.

Opposition party members in Phnom Penh described to Human Rights Watch several similarities in the attacks against them: they were carried out on the street by men in dark clothes and wrap-around motorcycle helmets on motorbikes who used an extendable metal baton as a weapon. All the victims interviewed prior to the elections said they believed they were targeted because of their public participation in CLP activities.

On March 24, the Phnom Penh Municipal Court opportunistically sentenced Cambodia National Heart Party's co-founder Seam Pluk, as well as 12 other members of the political opposition, to prison for politically motivated charges connected to gathering signatures on party registration documents. On March 21, authorities arrested two former Cambodia National Rescue Party (CNRP) members for "insulting the monarchy" on Facebook. Authorities released both Yim Sinorn and Hun Kosal after they publicly apologized to both King Sihamoni and Hun Sen and agreed to resign from the opposition and join the ruling CPP.

In July, the government fined and banned 18 opposition party members from holding elected office for 10 to 20 years after being convicted in absentia for inciting voters to spoil their national election ballots. They included seven former lawmakers from the dissolved CNRP (Sam Rainsy, Mu Sochua, Long Ry, Nuth Romdul, Hou Vann, Kong Saphea, and Eng Chhai Eang) and 11 activists. Also in July, unknown assailants violently targeted five additional opposition CLP members and activists.

Attacks against Cambodian opposition activists continued after the election. Three Khmer-speaking men assaulted Phorn Phanna, a refugee recognized by the United Nations Refugee Agency (UNHCR), at about noon on August 22, 2023, in Rayong province in Thailand, injuring his face and chest. Phanna, a member of the CNRP, had fled to Thailand in July 2022 to escape government persecution.

On September 12, men with metal batons viciously attacked political critic Ny Nak and his wife Sok Synet in Phnom Penh, resulting in Nak being hospitalized with serious wounds to his head and extremities. The attack shares similarities with assaults reported earlier in 2023 against members of the opposition CLP, which were never seriously investigated. Nak said he believed the attack was triggered by a number of recent public criticisms he made about the government.

On March 3, 2023, a court found political opposition leader Kem Sokha guilty of treason and sentenced him to a 27-year prison sentence and indefinitely suspended his political rights to vote and to stand for election. UN experts said the "politically motivated" conviction provided "further evidence of an ongoing pattern of the misapplication of laws to target political opponents and any critic of the Government," urging the authorities "to restore Mr. Sokha's liberty and ensure respect for his fundamental rights." Sokha remains imprisoned at his residence in Phnom Penh.

Freedom of Media

The government effectively controls all Khmer-language national TV, radio stations, and newspapers. The few remaining independent outlets are subject to regular harassment, intimidation, and threats of shutdowns.

On February 12, Hun Sen announced the revocation of the operating license of the Voice of Democracy (VOD). The action followed the prime minister's objection to a February 9 VOD article alleging that Hun Manet had been improperly acting in place of his father by approving a financial aid package for Türkiye. The reporter, Pa Sokheng, fled the country to escape persecution and subsequently resettled as a refugee overseas. The UN High Commissioner for Human Rights and a group of UN experts expressed alarm over the move, urging authorities to reverse the decision.

In July, the government issued an order to internet service providers to block access to online websites and social media accounts of three major independent media outlets, *The Cambodia Daily*, Radio Free Asia (RFA), and Kamnotra. The action was taken under a directive authorizing the Department of Information and Audiovisual to block sites that "disseminate misleading news affecting the honor and reputation of the Royal Government."

In September, the Ministry of Agriculture, Forestry and Fisheries (MAFF) demanded in a letter posted on Facebook that *CamboJA News*, one of the last remaining independent news outlets in the country, rectify "breaches of journalistic ethics" by removing "claims and speculations" perceived as linking the ministry and its minister to an attack against and outspoken critic of the MAFF.

Union Leader Behind Bars

Since the Labor Rights Supported Union of Khmer Employees of NagaWorld (LRSU) went on strike in December 2021 to call for the reinstatement of laid-off workers, Cambodian authorities have arbitrarily arrested, detained, and prosecuted union activists.

On January 3, 2022, the authorities charged Chhim Sithar, the LRSU leader, and other trade union members with the crime of "incitement to commit a felony or disturb social security." They held Sithar for 74 days in pretrial detention before releasing her on bail in March. The authorities rearrested Sithar on November 26, 2022, for violating bail conditions on international travel. Neither she nor her lawyer had been informed by the court or prosecutors about the travel restrictions.

On May 25, 2023, a court found Sithar and 8 trade unionists guilty, sentencing her to 2 years in prison and the other union members to between 1 and 1.5 years. On October 19, 2023, the Phnom Penh Appeal Court upheld the convictions of eight of them; the ninth did not appeal the lower court's verdict.

Facebook's Actions about Hun Sen

In March, Meta's oversight board, responsible for overseeing Facebook's content policies, selected Hun Sen's January 9 speech for consideration, stating that it "raises relevant policy questions around how the company should treat speech from political leaders.... This is particularly relevant in the context of potentially violent threats against political opponents from a national leader before an election in a country with a history of electoral violence and irregularity."

The oversight board recommended in June that Hun Sen be suspended from the social media site for six months for posting a video violating rules against violent threats. The board said the company had been wrong not to remove the video.

Meta removed Hun Sen's speech but decided to reject the recommendation to suspend him from the platform.

Rights-Abusing Laws and Bills

On June 23, the effectively single-party CPP National Assembly voted unanimously to amend the election law to penalize anyone who boycotts the election from running as a candidate in future elections. Prospective candidates must have voted in at least two elections to qualify as a candidate in local and national elections. The amendments also criminalized any acts advocating for the boycott of an election or deliberately spoiling a ballot. The action was in response to CLP activists' calls on social media to spoil ballots or stay away from the election.

Cyberscam Centers

In 2023, the Office of the UN High Commissioner for Human Rights (OHCHR) released a report detailing how at least 100,000 people in Cambodia have been enslaved for the purpose of carrying out online scams. Many of the victims originate from other Southeast Asian countries or from East Africa, South Asia, and China. Senior Cambodian officials are accused of looking the other way and ignoring this criminality.

Despite government claims made in a September 2022 statement that officials have raided compounds of suspected locations, the cyberscam human trafficking gangs continue to operate with impunity.

Women's and Girls' Rights

Child marriage is prevalent in Cambodia with 19 percent of girls being married before they turn 18, and 2 percent before they turn 15. It is more common in rural areas and among ethnic minority populations. In Mondulkiri and Ratanakiri provinces, 36 percent of girls are married before they turn 18.

In recent years, the trafficking of brides from Cambodia to China has increased. Many women and girls are tricked or forced into marriages with men in China, where they are vulnerable to abuses and often held prisoner, endure forced labor and sexual slavery, and are pressured to produce babies. Brokers have increasingly been targeting girls in their teens as brides.

Women's rights and land rights defenders continue to face harassment, threats, and criminal charges from private companies and well-connected elites as well as police and other authorities. On June 29, nine land activists were arrested and charged in Koh Kong province while peacefully speaking out in defense of their local communities. That same month, the UN Committee on the Elimination of Discrimination against Women found that Cambodia's failure to protect a rural woman human rights defender from forced eviction had constituted multiple rights violations.

Key International Actors

In March, the European Parliament adopted a resolution urging the release of Kem Sokha and all others detained on politically motivated charges.

In May, the European Union condemned the Cambodian authorities' decision to disqualify the CLP. And in July, it issued a statement criticizing the government's repression of the opposition, media, and civil society ahead of the elections.

Cambodia remains the only current beneficiary of the EU's Everything But Arms—a trade scheme that grants developing countries tariff-free access to the EU market conditioned on their respect for certain human and labor rights standards—to have been stripped of part of its trade benefits. The decision was taken in 2020, following the refusal by the government to backtrack on its political crackdown and on labor and land rights abuses, despite years of enhanced engagement between EU and Cambodian authorities.

In July, the United States government issued a statement that the Cambodian national elections "were neither free nor fair," imposed visa restrictions on individuals who undermined democracy, and implemented a pause of certain foreign assistance programs.

The UN High Commissioner for Human Rights and a group of UN independent human rights experts also expressed concern about rights abuses, as well as severe restrictions on civic and political space, that the group of experts said "affected the credibility of the entire electoral process."

The UN Human Rights Council renewed the mandate of the special rapporteur on the situation of human rights in Cambodia by consensus in October.

Cameroon

Continued clashes between armed groups and government forces throughout Cameroon's Anglophone and Far North regions severely impacted civilians, with cases of unlawful killings, abductions, and raids on villages increasing in the second half of the year.

The violence across the two English-speaking North-West and South-West regions continued for a sixth year, despite President Paul Biya saying in January that many armed separatist groups had surrendered and that the threat they posed had been significantly reduced. As of mid-year, there were over 638,000 internally displaced people across the Anglophone regions and at least 1.7 million people in need of humanitarian aid.

Armed separatists, who have violently enforced a boycott on education since 2017, continued to attack schools, students, and education professionals. Assaults on school infrastructure and staff were recorded in 2023, in keeping with a pattern of attacks on education throughout the crisis.

Civilians faced killings and abductions by armed Islamist groups in the Far North region, including by Boko Haram and the Islamic State in West Africa Province (ISWAP). Between January and July, at least 169 civilians died in attacks by non-state actors. Floodings and torrential rains in early July destroyed crops and further impeded humanitarian access in a region where 1.6 million people are in need of assistance.

The political space remains closed, with the ruling party, the Cameroon People's Democratic Movement (Rassemblement démocratique du peuple camerounais, RDPC), taking the majority of contested senate seats in elections held in March, further consolidating its 40 year-long political hegemony over the country's political landscape. The RDPC and its allies also have a majority of 164 deputies out of 180 in the National Assembly.

Freedom of expression continues to be curtailed and independent journalists face risks. Three journalists, including a high profile investigate journalist, were killed in 2023.

Anglophone Crisis

At least 6,000 civilians have been killed by both government forces and separatist fighters since the violence started in late 2016. Civilians across the Anglophone regions continue to face abuses by multiple actors involved in the crisis, including sexual and gender-based violence.

Abuses by Government Forces

State forces responded to separatist attacks with counter-insurgency operations that often failed to protect civilians, or targeted them outright. In some instances, such as that outside Bamenda, North-West region, in July, victims may have been fleeing fighting when they were killed. Abusive army raids and killings of civilians may also have been perpetrated against individuals suspected of being separatists or in retaliation for attacks against army positions.

Abuses by Armed Separatists

Separatist fighters continued to target civilians, forcing people to stay at home and launching attacks around major events, including an annual race, the elections, and as schools re-opened in early September.

After Biya's announcement that senatorial elections would be held in March, several separatist groups threatened anyone who announced their intention to participate, and killed an election official on January 18, among several others. On February 5, Honourine Wainachi Nentoh, a member of parliament of the opposition Social Democratic Front (SDF), was abducted by armed separatists who allegedly demanded ransom in exchange for her liberation. She was freed days later.

On May 20, more than 30 women were abducted by separatists in a North-West village after protesting unlawful taxes imposed by armed groups. A government spokesperson said that some of the women had been tortured.

During the night from July 16 to 17, unidentified alleged separatists killed at least 10 civilians in Bamenda. The assailants who were wearing military uniforms reportedly opened fire in a bar after accusing locals of failing to support the separatists.

On August 11, separatists reportedly raided Kekukesim village, killing at least four civilians, including the village chairperson, and burning houses.

Separatist fighters disrupted the start of the 2023 academic year, planned for September 4, by enforcing a school boycott. On September 7, days after schools reopened, at least three civilians in the South-West were killed in an assault blamed on separatists, who shot at car passengers and set vehicles ablaze. According to the United Nations, at least 2,245 schools are not functioning in the Anglophone regions due to attacks and threats by armed separatists.

Attacks in the Far North

In the Far North region, Boko Haram and ISWAP have attacked civilians, carrying out killings, abductions, and lootings. In the past, government forces also committed serious abuses as they responded forcefully to the attacks.

Since January, 246 attacks have been reported, causing the deaths of 169 civilians. Most of these deaths were caused by attacks by Islamist groups.

Civic Space and Democracy

In November 2022, Cameroon's government and supporters held events across the country to celebrate President Biya's 40 years in power.

On March 12, senatorial elections were held. The electoral law provides that 70 senators out of 100 are to be elected by an electoral college of regional and municipal councilors, while the president nominates another 30. Although 10 political parties participated, the ruling party won all 70 seats. On March 31, President Biya then appointed 30 other senators, including 5 from the opposition, further consolidating the RDPC's grip on power.

Opposition parties claimed the elections were marred by irregularities, accusing Biya's ruling party of vote-buying. Three political parties filed a complaint with the Constitutional Council, asking for a revote or partial revote in the center of the country, alleging fraud and lack of transparency. The Council rejected the complaint on March 21.

In the days leading up to the election, the military said separatists launched an attack against army vehicles in an effort to disrupt voting in the Anglophone regions.

On May 7, leader of the opposition party, Cameroon Renaissance Movement (Mouvement pour la Renaissance du Cameroun, MRC), Maurice Kamto, held the party's first political meeting in Yaoundé, the capital, since the 2018 presidential election. The opposition group had not been allowed to hold a meeting in the capital since Biya was re-elected for a seventh term five years ago.

Opponents from the MRC arrested in 2020 after participating in peaceful protests and exercising their right to freedom of assembly remained in detention. These include the party's treasurer, Alain Fogue Tedom, and Kamto's spokesperson, Olivier Bibou Nissack.

On June 12, prominent Anglophone opponent and leader of the Social Democratic Front (SDF) John Fru Ndi died. Hundreds attended his funeral in a village 18 kilometers from Bamenda to pay tribute to Ndi, seen as a historical figure.

Freedom of Speech and Media

The year 2023 was a dark year for media freedoms in Cameroon, as several journalists were killed in unclear circumstances.

On January 22, Martinez Zogo's body was found in a suburb of Yaoundé, showing signs consistent with torture. Zogo, a prominent investigative journalist and director of a radio station, regularly exposed corruption. In the weeks before he was killed, he had reported on air about a case of alleged embezzlement involving a media outlet owned by the businessman Jean-Pierre Amougou Belinga.

Belinga was arrested on February 6 and charged on March 4 for complicity in kidnapping and torture on the basis of statements made by Lt. Col. Justin Danwe, a former head of operations at Cameroon's counter-espionage agency. Danwe confessed in police custody to having set up the operation to abduct Zogo and identified Belinga as the mastermind.

On February 2, Jean-Jacques Ola Bebe, an Orthodox priest and radio host, was found dead in Yaoundé. Ola Bebe, who had been a vocal advocate for justice for Zogo, regularly commented on current affairs issues, including corruption, as a guest on local radio stations.

Anye Nde Nsoh, a weekly newspaper's bureau chief in Bamenda, was killed in a separatist attack on May 7. The government announced an investigation. Capo Daniel, a separatist group leader, admitted in a video statement that one of his group's fighters had killed Nde Nsoh, but that it had been a case of mistaken identity. No one has been held accountable for Nde Nsoh's killing.

On September 12, the governor of the South-West region banned the *Post* newspaper after it ran an article on the possibility of a military coup in Cameroon. The paper resumed publication on October 18.

Sexual Orientation and Gender Identity

Cameroon's penal code punishes "sexual relations between persons of the same sex" with up to five years in prison.

Cameroonian authorities objected to a visit by the French ambassador for the rights of lesbian, gay, bisexual, transgender, and intersex (LGBTI) people, Jean-Marc Berthon, scheduled for June 27, to attend an event on gender and sexuality held by Yaoundé's French Institute. The event also sparked online hatred against sexual minorities in the country, and the planned visit was canceled.

Accountability and Justice

Hearings in the trials of three security force members accused of involvement in a massacre in Ngarbuh village, North-West region, were repeatedly postponed. Initial trial hearings are being held in a military court in Yaoundé, about 380 kilometers from the village, making it hard for victims to attend. The defendants are charged with murder, arson, destruction, and disobeying orders.

Although the beginning of the trial, following international pressure, was a positive move toward justice in Cameroon, its slow pace and irregularities in procedure have cast doubt on the government's will to ensure accountability for state forces' abuses.

Key International Actors

Journalists Zogo and Ola Bebe's death prompted strong condemnation inside and outside of Cameroon, including by the Office of the High Commissioner for Human Rights (OHCHR) and the United Nations Educations, Scientific and Cultural Organization (UNESCO), which called on the government to allow an independent effective investigation into the killings.

On January 20, Canada's minister of foreign affairs, Mélanie Joly, announced that Cameroon's government and Anglophone separatists had agreed to start negotiations toward a peaceful resolution of the crisis. Although several separatist leaders committed to participating, on January 24, Cameroon's authorities publicly disavowed Canada's initiative, claiming it had not mandated a third party to facilitate any peace process. The public denial came as a surprise, as Yaoundé initially took part in Canada-led negotiations, and dashed hopes for a peaceful resolution of the crisis.

Canada

Since assuming office in 2015, the government of Prime Minister Justin Trudeau has taken significant steps to advance human rights at home and abroad. Despite progress in a few key areas, a range of deeply entrenched challenges remain. These include wide-ranging abuses against Indigenous peoples and immigration detainees, including people with disabilities. Canada's failures to mitigate the impacts of climate change and provide adequate government support are also leading to violations in Indigenous communities across the country while compounding risks for people with disabilities, children, and older people.

The Trudeau government has failed to address serious human rights concerns beyond Canada's borders, including impunity for abuses by Canadian extractive and apparel companies overseas. Canada also continues to fail to provide consular assistance or repatriate a group of Canadian men, women, and children unlawfully detained in life-threatening conditions in northeast Syria.

Indigenous Peoples' Rights

In April 2023, police chiefs representing nine First Nations police forces in Ontario province filed a complaint against the federal government with the Canadian Human Rights Tribunal alleging discrimination due to the "chronic underfunding and under-resourcing of the safety of Indigenous communities."

Following a 16-year legal battle, in July, the Canadian Human Rights Tribunal approved a revised settlement of 23.4 billion Canadian dollars (about US$17.1 billion) to compensate victims of the First Nations child welfare system. In 2016, the tribunal found that the federal government had racially discriminated against this group "by chronically underfunding on-reserve child and family services and refusing to pay for essential health care."

In April, representatives of more than 50 Indigenous communities across North America submitted a report as part of the United Nations Human Right Council's Universal Periodic Review of Canada's human right record, condemning Canada's support of a controversial cross-border pipeline, known as Line 5, that transports crude oil through the Great Lakes region.

Ten First Nations communities in Ontario province filed a lawsuit in April against the provincial and federal government to end their "unilateral jurisdiction and decision-making control" of Treaty 9 territory in northern Ontario. The territory includes the Ring of Fire, a mineral-rich area located in the James Bay Lowlands region that is the traditional territory of more than a dozen First Nations.

In his report to the UN Human Rights Council in July, the UN special rapporteur on the rights of Indigenous peoples called on Canada to "suspend large-scale mining and other business activities in the Ring of Fire region and cease construction or operation of the Coastal GasLink, Trans Mountain and Line 5 pipelines, until the free, prior and informed consent of the Indigenous Peoples affected is secured."

In June, the federal government released its action plan for implementing the UN Declaration on the Rights of Indigenous Peoples (UNDRIP) despite calls for more consultation by the Assembly of First Nations in April. The action plan includes 181 measures the government intends to take to advance the rights of First Nations, Inuit, and Métis people in Canada.

Violence against Indigenous Women and Girls

In May, Canadian parliamentarians unanimously supported a motion declaring the deaths and disappearances of Indigenous women and girls a national emergency and called for federal funding for a new public alert system.

In response to one of the key recommendations of the National Inquiry into Missing and Murdered Indigenous Women and Girls, the federal government announced an investment of 103 million Canadian dollars (about US$75.3 million) in May to build and support 178 shelter spaces and transitional houses for Indigenous women, children, and Two-Spirit, lesbian, gay, bisexual, transgender, queer+, and intersex (2SLGBTQI+) people fleeing violence.

Immigration Detention

People in immigration detention, including people with disabilities and those seeking refugee protection in Canada, continue to be regularly handcuffed and shackled. With no time limits on immigration detention, they can be detained for months or years and are at risk of being held indefinitely. Many are held in provincial jails alongside people detained on criminal charges or convictions, and they are also sometimes subjected to solitary confinement.

The Canada Border Services Agency (CBSA) remains the only major law enforcement agency in Canada without independent civilian oversight. The federal government has introduced oversight legislation, but it has yet to pass. CBSA's unchecked exercise of its broad mandate and enforcement powers has repeatedly resulted in serious human rights violations in the context of immigration detention, including prolonged solitary confinement in maximum-security jails, child detention and family separation, indefinite detention, and the stripping of legal capacity of people with mental health conditions.

CBSA has traditionally had broad latitude to place people in immigrant holding centers, provincial jails, or other detention facilities. Following the 2021 launch of a joint Human Rights Watch and Amnesty International campaign, #WelcomeToCanada, eight of Canada's ten provinces gave notice of termination of their immigration detention contracts with the federal government. This means CBSA will no longer have the power to detain refugee claimants and migrants in those provinces' jails solely on immigration grounds.

Corporate Accountability

Canada has not taken adequate steps to ensure that authorities exercise meaningful oversight of Canadian extractive companies operating abroad. Communities and workers whose rights have been violated are often unable to access justice or remedy, and human rights defenders frequently face violence and intimidation.

In response to complaints filed in 2022 by a coalition of 28 human rights organizations, the Canadian Ombudsperson for Responsible Enterprise (CORE) announced in August the opening of investigations against three Canadian companies alleged to have used or benefited from the use of Uyghur forced labor in Xinjiang, China.

In May, a coalition of civil society organizations, including Human Rights Watch, critiqued a new forced and child labor law passed by Canadian parliamentarians for failing to require that companies both take action if they are made aware of abuses in their supply chains and offer assistance to victims.

In February, members of the House of Commons' Standing Committee on International Trade held hearings on the harmful impacts of Canadian mining companies abroad. As inputs to the proceedings, the Canadian Network on Corporate Accountability (CNCA) submitted six new reports linking Canadian companies and their subsidiaries overseas to "widespread and ongoing" abuses, including allegations of killings, torture, forced labor, arbitrary detention, and intimidation.

In September, the UN special rapporteur on contemporary forms of slavery urged the Canadian government to "bring forward legislation requiring Canadian companies to implement mandatory human rights due diligence, and expand the independence, powers, and mandate of the CORE."

Counterterrorism

In response to growing international pressure and a federal lawsuit, Canada in April and July repatriated 19 Canadian women and children who had been unlawfully detained since at least 2019 in camps holding suspected members of Islamic State (ISIS) and family members in northeast Syria. However, Canada refused to repatriate at least one Canadian mother and her six children, citing security concerns about the mother, as well as a group of Canadian children born to foreign mothers unless the mothers agreed to stay behind. Canada also refused to bring home at least eight Canadian men detained in northeast Syria for alleged ISIS ties. All are held in dire and at times life-threatening conditions.

Canada brought home the 19 citizens as part of an out-of-court settlement in January. That same month, a federal court in Ottawa ruled that Canada should also bring home four detained Canadian men, finding that the government had a positive obligation to request the return of its detained citizens, provide them with travel documents, and appoint a representative to travel to the region as soon as possible. The court found that Canada had breached the Canadian Charter of Rights and Freedoms in its failure to take all reasonable steps to bring the Canadians home.

In May, a federal court of appeal overturned the decision, upholding Canada's argument that the government is not obligated to repatriate the four Canadian men. In August, lawyers representing the families of these men said they would appeal to the Supreme Court.

In July, the UN special rapporteur on human rights and counterterrorism urged the Canadian government to reconsider its decision not to repatriate a Canadian mother from northeast Syria along with her children.

In August, a delegation, including Canadian Senator Kim Pate, visited northeast Syria and met with a group of unlawfully detained Canadians, including two men who had not been heard from in years. Following the visit, the delegation urged the government of Canada to provide consular assistance to the detainees and engage with officials in northeast Syria to repatriate all Canadians still held in the region.

Climate Change Policy and Impacts

As a top 10 global greenhouse gas emitter and one of the highest per capita emitters in the world, Canada is contributing to the climate crisis and its growing toll on human rights around the globe. Since being re-elected in 2021, the Trudeau government has repeatedly pledged to pursue ambitious actions to reduce greenhouse gas emissions.

Canada is the top public financier of fossil fuels among G20 nations and projects increased domestic oil and gas production through 2050. Extraction of oil from Canadian oil sands is among the most carbon-intensive and polluting oil production methods globally. The government continues to permit oil and gas pipeline expansions, including on First Nations' lands. Plans to increase fossil fuel production disregard the government's human rights obligation to adopt and implement robust climate mitigation policies.

Federal and provincial climate change policies have failed to put in place adequate measures to support First Nations in adapting to the current and anticipated impacts of climate change, and they have largely ignored the impacts of climate change on First Nations' right to food.

Fueled by hot, dry conditions, over 17 million hectares of forest was consumed by wildfires throughout Canada in 2023, displacing thousands and negatively impacting air quality throughout the country and into the United States.

A June 2023 report by British Columbia's Centre for Disease Control confirmed that the 2021 heat dome led to the deaths of more than 130 people with schizophrenia. This represents about 8 percent of all deaths during the heat dome, even though people with schizophrenia represent only about 1 percent of the province's population. The report also confirmed that people with schizophrenia are not usually at the forefront of public health messaging about extreme heat despite the risks.

British Columbia is currently developing a disaster and climate risk and resilience assessment and a disaster risk reduction plan and is in the process of modernizing the Emergency Management Legislation to align with the Sendai Framework for Disaster Risk Reduction, which aims to ensure full and meaningful participation of women, older people, people with disabilities, migrants, Indigenous peoples, and local communities.

Key International Actors

In July, the UN special rapporteur on the rights of Indigenous peoples presented a report on his country visit to Canada calling on the government to urgently address "the deep-set, systemic and structural racism affecting Indigenous Peoples."

Following a visit to Canada from August to September, the UN special rapporteur on contemporary forms of slavery called on the government "to promote effective human rights due diligence in the activities of Canadian companies" and reform "migration programmes that serve as a breeding ground for contemporary forms of slavery."

In August, following a visit to northeast Syria, the UN special rapporteur on human rights and counterterrorism condemned Canada's failure to take responsibility for its nationals unlawfully detained in prisons and camps holding ISIS suspects and their families.

Foreign Policy

Addressing the House of Commons in September, Prime Minister Trudeau said that Canadian authorities were investigating "credible allegations of a potential link between agents of the government of India" and the killing of Canadian Sikh leader Hardeep Singh Nijjar in British Columbia in June. The Indian government strongly denied the allegations.

In May, Canadian Foreign Minister Mélanie Joly announced Canada's intention to run for a seat on the UN Human Rights Council for the 2028-2030 term.

In September, Canada, in partnership with the Netherlands, launched a new UN declaration on misinformation aimed at "establishing global norms on disinformation, misinformation, and information integrity."

In September, Canada announced sanctions against three Haitians in "response to acts of significant corruption, which are fueling the current security, political and humanitarian crisis in the country."

In October, the International Court of Justice began hearings as part of a case brought by Canada and the Netherlands against Syria alleging it has breached the Convention against Torture and Other Cruel, Inhuman or Degrading Treatment or Punishment.

Throughout 2023, Canada imposed a series of measures against the government of Iran, including a 14th package of sanctions against Iranian officials for gross and systemic violations of human rights. In January, Canada also reaffirmed its commitment to holding Iran accountable for the 2020 downing of Ukraine International Airlines Flight 752 and ensuring reparations for the victims' families.

In August, Canada imposed additional sanctions against 4 individuals and 29 entities with "direct ties to Russia's military-industrial complex," building on sanctions announced in July targeting Russia's nuclear sector. Also in August, Canada announced new sanctions against 15 Russian individuals and 3 entities, including senior officials of the Russian government, judiciary, and investigative committee, "directly involved in human rights abuses against Russian opposition leaders."

Following the third anniversary of the Beirut blast explosion, Canada joined the United Kingdom and the US in August in imposing sanctions against three Lebanese nationals for their involvement in acts of significant corruption.

In January, on the second anniversary of the Myanmar coup, Canada imposed sanctions against six individuals and new prohibitions on the "export, sale, supply or shipment of aviation fuel to the Myanmar military regime." That same month, Canada announced targeted sanctions against four Sri Lankans, including two former presidents, responsible for gross and systematic violations of human rights during the country's armed conflict.

Central African Republic

Fighting between the national army, alongside Russian mercenaries and Rwandan forces, and elements of the Coalition of Patriots for Change (Coalition des patriotes pour le changement, CPC) decreased, but was at times intense. In some attacks, civilians were killed. Schools and hospitals remained targets, and some that had been damaged during previous fighting remained so. According to the United Nations, "more than half a million children aged 3-17 ... are out of school, or are at risk of having to leave due to a critical lack of qualified teachers and inadequate school facilities."

Security conditions have hampered humanitarian relief, and serious violations of human rights and international humanitarian law have resulted in high numbers of refugees and internally displaced people.

Russian mercenaries from Wagner, a mercenary outfit managed by Yevgeniy Prigozhin until his death in July, are deployed in the country. Prigozhin's death in Russia has not diminished Wagner's presence in the country and, to date, the group still controls mines outside Bangui, the capital, including the large Ndassima gold mine in Ouaka province. The group's control over some road checkpoints makes travel outside of Bangui difficult. The UN reported several instances in which these mercenaries participated in active fighting and were implicated in serious human rights abuses.

The country veered toward authoritarianism with crackdowns on civil society, the media, and opposition political parties ahead of a constitutional referendum designed to remove term limits for the president, Faustin-Archange Touadéra. The referendum passed in July with diverging accounts of voter turnout.

The country remained dangerous for humanitarian actors, with 123 incidents ranging from harassment to abductions of humanitarian actors registered between January and August.

Attacks

The national army, alongside Russian mercenaries and Rwandan forces, pushed non-state armed groups, including those from the CPC, further into border positions.

A new Zandé-based ethnic militia, which might, according to the UN, have received some support from South Sudan, increased attacks in the southeast border region of the country in response to other armed groups.

Gold mines were targeted, with the most serious attack occurring in March in Ouaka province, in the center of the country, where nine Chinese workers were killed. Central Africans also may have been killed in this attack, but this has not been confirmed.

Rise in Abductions

Armed groups increased hostage-taking, targeting national soldiers, UN staff, and civilians.

In January, CPC fighters captured 20 national soldiers near Sikikédé after combat. The CPC issued a set of demands for the release of the soldiers, including the departure of "Russian Wagner mercenaries" and the release of people associated with the group. The soldiers were released in early April without those demands met.

Two UN staff and a government employee were released in March after 117 days of being held hostage by members of the armed group Party for the Rally of the Central African Nation (Parti pour le rassemblement de la nation centrafricaine, PRNC).

Three Chinese workers were taken hostage on March 13 at a gold mine in Ndiba in the Nana-Mambéré province. They were released on April 2 after a ransom was paid.

Constitutional Referendum

Political tensions increased around the constitutional reform process. In 2022, Touadéra's party, the United Hearts Movement (Mouvement Cœurs unis, MCU), began the process of changing the constitution to remove the two-term limit and allow the president to run for a third term. Touadéra was first elected in 2016 and was re-elected in 2020 amid a military offensive by the CPC. In September 2022, the Constitutional Court ruled that the steps taken thus far by the MCU and the president were "unconstitutional." In October 2022, the Public Service Ministry began a process to forcibly retire the court's president, Danièle Darlan, stating she had reached the age of retirement. She was pushed out later that month by a presidential decree. In January, the Constitutional Court—under a new court president—declared that a plan to initiate a referendum was legal, clearing the way for the constitutional reform.

In response to opposition, government institutions, including the police, threatened civil society advocates, accused them of collaborating with armed groups, and refused to allow political protests. Journalists and activists became more reluctant to criticize the government to avoid being labeled as political opponents and threatened. Two pro-MCU associations that mobilize youth, the Requins (French for "sharks") and Galaxie Nationale (National Galaxy), campaigned for the referendum and harassed opponents, both online and in the streets.

The referendum was approved as the government claimed turnout was high, but reporters anecdotally spoke of a low turnout. The next presidential vote is due in 2025.

Justice for Serious Crimes

In July, the appeals chamber of the Special Criminal Court (SCC)—a war crimes court that is part of the domestic justice system but has both national and international staff and benefits from extensive UN and other international assistance—upheld the conviction of three members of the Return, Reclamation, and Rehabilitation (3R) armed group for crimes against humanity and war crimes for their roles in a massacre of 46 civilians in May 2019 in Koundjili and Lemouna in the northwest. Issa Sallet Adoum, Yaouba Ousman, and Mahamat Tahir were sentenced to prison terms ranging from 20 years to life imprisonment for the killings and other crimes.

In June, the SCC announced the death of Oumar Al Bachir in a hospital following an illness. Al Bachir was arrested in September 2022 for crimes against humanity and war crimes allegedly committed in 2014 at the Notre Dame of Fatima church in Bangui.

At the SCC, a case on crimes against humanity and war crimes committed in Ndélé in March and April 2020 was approved to go to trial following a judicial investigation. The accused are Kalite Azor, Charfadine Moussa, Antar Hamat, Wodjonodroba Oumar Oscar, Général Faché, Younouss Kalamyal, Atahir English, Abdel Kane Mahamat Salle, Fotor Sinine, and Youssouf Moustapha, alias "Badjadje."

In September, the SCC announced charges against Abdoulaye Hissène, a leader of the Front Populaire for the Renaissance of the Central African Republic (Front populaire pour la renaissance de la Centrafrique, FPRC). Hissène was an early Seleka commander and a minister while the rebels controlled Bangui in 2013. Later, he was a leader of a splinter group headed by Noureddine Adam, who is currently a fugitive suspected of war crimes and crimes against humanity, including torture, by the International Criminal Court (ICC).

Also in September, the SCC announced the arrest of Edmond Patrick Abrou, an anti-balaka leader, on charges of crimes against humanity and war crimes committed in the village of Boyo, Ouaka province. From December 6 to 13, 2021, anti-balaka fighters allegedly under Abrou's command carried out an attack on Boyo and killed at least 20 civilians, raped at least 5 women and girls, and burned and looted at least 547 houses.

Hassan Bouba, a government minister arrested under a warrant from the SCC in November 2021 but released a couple of days later despite court orders to the contrary, remained at liberty and continued his role as the minister of livestock and animal health. Bouba, a former leader of an armed group who was named a special councilor to the president in 2017 before being appointed minister, is charged with war crimes and crimes against humanity. Bouba's group started committing serious abuses in Ouaka province in 2014, which continued in 2023. Bouba was expelled from the group in January 2021. There was no attempt to re-arrest him in 2023.

In October, Maxime Mokom, a former military coordinator of a group of anti-balaka militia, was released by the ICC after the court's prosecutor withdrew charges, citing a lack of evidence and witnesses. Mokom had fled to Chad after having taken part in the CPC's unsuccessful bid to take Bangui in 2020. Mokom had been one of the highest ranked anti-balaka leaders in the country and in 2019, he was made the minister for disarmament, demobilization, reintegration, and repatriation under a failed peace deal. His arrest warrant was issued in 2018.

At the ICC, the trials of Seleka commander Mahamat Said Abdel Kani, accused of war crimes and crimes against humanity committed in Bangui in 2013, and anti-balaka leaders Patrice-Edouard Ngaïssona and Alfred Yékatom, both charged with war crimes and crimes against humanity committed between December 2013 and December 2014, continued.

In September, an appeals court in Bangui sentenced in absentia exiled former Central African Republic President François Bozizé, who became a CPC leader, to forced labor for life for conspiracy and rebellion. Bozizé was convicted with over 20 other co-accused, also found guilty in absentia, including armed group leaders Ali Darassa, Mahamat Al-Katim, Noureddine Adam, "General" Bobo, Maxime Mokom, Abakar Sabone, and Bozizé's sons Jean-Francis and Aimé-Vincent, known as "Papy." In March, François Bozizé moved from Chad to Guinea-Bissau, where he remains in exile.

Displacement and Humanitarian Needs

The year 2023 marked a decade of conflict and subsequent violence ravaging the country, and the civilian population continued to pay a heavy price. The total number of displaced people remained high because of fighting. Over 1.2 million people, according to the UN, were either refugees in neighboring countries (746,000) or internally displaced (486,000) as of September. Conditions for internally displaced people and refugees, many of whom stay in camps, remained harsh. Assistance to internally displaced people was seriously hampered by attacks on humanitarians and general insecurity in the country.

About 3.4 million people, out of a population of 6.1 million, needed humanitarian assistance. The humanitarian response plan was underfunded, with a budget gap of about US$283 million as of December.

Key International Actors

In June, the United States treasury imposed sanctions on two mining companies connected to the Wagner group and Prigozhin, Midas Ressources SARLU and Diamville SAU. Midas Ressources was given a mining exploitation permit for Ndassima in 2020, after the existing license for the area, held by Canadian company Axmin, was revoked.

The US also prohibited some military assistance to CAR under the Child Soldiers Prevention Act, based on the government's involvement in the recruitment and use of child soldiers.

In March, the United Kingdom imposed sanctions on Mahamat Salleh Adoum Kette for crimes allegedly committed by FPRC and CPC fighters under his command as part of a new package of sanctions aimed at violators, particularly those who target women and girls.

In November 2022, the UN independent expert on the situation of human rights in Central African Republic, Yao Agbetse, warned that the political situation could erode the peace and reconciliation process.

The UN peacekeeping mission, MINUSCA, deployed 13,394 military peacekeepers and 2,415 police across many parts of the country. Under Chapter VII of the UN Charter, the mission is authorized to take all necessary means to protect the civilian population from threat of physical violence and to "implement a mission-wide protection strategy." In November 2022, the UN Security Council extended the mandate of the mission for another year.

In June, a Tanzanian unit of peacekeepers deployed with MINUSCA was repatriated after sexual exploitation and abuse allegations. The UN reported that 11 members of the unit committed the abuse based on credible allegations from four victims.

Chad

April 2023 marked two years since Mahamat Idriss Déby Itno seized power and declared himself head of the Transitional Military Council (Conseil Militaire de Transition, CMT) following the sudden death of his father, Idriss Déby Itno, president of Chad since 1990. A new draft constitution proposed by the transitional government was adopted in June by 96 percent of the members of the National Transitional Council (Conseil National de Transition, CNT), which replaced the National Assembly when it was dissolved after Idriss Déby Itno's death. A public referendum on the new constitution was scheduled for December at time of writing. Presidential elections are scheduled for 2024.

Rebel movements in the far north remained active as did tensions in the north between the transitional government and the Miski self-defense group, despite a peace agreement signed in January.

Another rebel group emerged in the south in early 2023 along the border with the Central African Republic. In January, the governor of the southern Logone Oriental province confirmed the existence of this rebel group, declaring it "must be defeated." The group's emergence coincided with an uptick in violent clashes between herder and farmer communities in the south.

To date, there has been no accountability for the violent crackdown on October 20, 2022, against protests in several cities across the country, that resulted in the killing and injury of scores of people. An investigation by the Economic Community of Central African States (ECCAS), one of eight African Union regional economic communities, has yet to be published.

At least 72 party members and supporters of Les Transformateurs, an opposition party, were arrested in October and held for 3 weeks at the headquarters of the National Intelligence Service before being released. The party members were exercising in the early morning before a meeting in preparation for the return of Succès Masra, the party's president, who left the country after the crackdown on October 20, 2022. Masra returned to the country in early November after his safe return was negotiated in Kinshasa, Congo.

Fighting in Sudan, which started in April between the Sudanese Armed Forces (SAF) and the Rapid Support Forces (RSF), triggered massive displacement of people and resulted in more than 420,000 Sudanese refugees seeking safety in Chad. This added to an estimated 580,000 refugees and asylum seekers already in the country and strained an already underfunded humanitarian response.

Aftermath of the October 20, 2022 Protests

In October 2022, thousands took to the streets in the capital N'Djamena and towns in the south in protest to mark the date the military administration had initially promised to hand over power to a civilian government. The transitional government had on several previous occasions violently suppressed protests demanding civilian democratic rule.

In a February report, the National Human Rights Commission said that 128 people were killed and 518 injured. The commission found that security forces "systematically violated several fundamental human rights ... [using] disproportionate means" to quell the protests. The commission posed several questions to the government, including why authorities had failed to open judicial investigations into human rights violations and called for the prosecution of perpetrators of those violations.

In November 2022, the minister of justice said that 621 people had been arrested in relation to the protests, including 83 children. In November and December 2022, group trials of 401 of those arrested began at Koro Toro, a high security prison 600 kilometers from N'Djamena designed to house so-called violent extremists. A total of 262 people were sentenced to prison terms ranging from 24 to 36 months on several charges, including taking part in an unauthorized gathering, destroying property, arson, and disturbing public order. Eighty people were given suspended prison sentences and another fifty-nine were acquitted. In December 2022, 80 children were released on bail. The majority of protestors were subsequently pardoned and released in groups over the course of 2023.

In the days following the violence, the ECCAS announced an investigation commission. The commission has yet to publish its report.

Violence in the South

Violent clashes, attributed to conflicts between herders and sedentary farmers, increased in the south.

In April, at least 23 people around Monts de Lam, Logone Oriental province, were killed in less than 48 hours, according to media reports. On May 8, at least 17 people were killed when unidentified gunmen attacked the village of Dion. On May 17, 11 people were killed by what the government called "bandits" in the same region. Many of the victims were young children.

Retaliatory killings continued through September around Monts de Lam.

Islamist Armed Groups

The Islamist armed groups Boko Haram and the Islamic State in West Africa Province (ISWAP) continued to carry out attacks against civilians in the Lake Chad area.

Chad has provided military contributions to regional counterterrorism operations In the Sahel for years. In November, French President Emmanuel Macron declared the end of Operation Barkhane, the French-led counterinsurgency operation against Islamist armed groups in the Sahel, and headquartered in N'Djamena. Chad contributed the third-highest number of troops to the United Nations Multidimensional Integrated Stabilization Mission in Mali (MINUSMA), which the UN Security Council ended in June. MINUSMA was scheduled to leave the country by the end of 2023.

The future of the G5 Sahel, a joint counterterrorism force including Burkina Faso, Chad, Mali, Mauritania, and Niger, was put in doubt as Burkina Faso and Niger announced their intentions to leave the group after Mali exited the group in 2022.

Constitutional Reform

The 2021 creation of the Transitional Military Council (CMT) and the National Transitional Council (CNT) was in blatant contravention of a constitutional requirement that leadership should be transferred to the president of the National

Assembly until elections can be held. A national dialogue in 2022—deemed non inclusive by political opposition and civil society actors—adopted a measure to extend the transition for a maximum of 24 months. Delegates decided that Mahamat Déby would remain interim head of state. Over the course of 2023, transitional authorities pushed forward with a constitutional referendum despite calls for political inclusion and dialogue from political and civil actors.

Sexual Orientation and Gender Identity

Article 354 of the 2017 Penal Code prohibits "sexual relations with a person of one's own sex." Under the code, individuals convicted of same-sex relations face up to 2 years' imprisonment and a fine of between 50,000 to 500,000 CFA francs (approximately US$75-750).

Economic and Social Rights

According to the World Food Programme, Chad has one of the highest levels of hunger in the world: an estimated 42 percent of the population lives in poverty, and over 37 percent of children aged under 5 suffer from stunting.

Millions remain affected by underinvestment in social security while climate change and desertification negatively impact agricultural yields.

Displacement

As of early October, over 420,000 Sudanese refugees had fled into eastern Chad since the start of the crisis in Sudan. Before this, an estimated 1.9 million people in Chad's eastern provinces already needed humanitarian assistance, with malnutrition rates exceeding the WHO's critical threshold in several places.

International Justice

There was no compensation given to victims of former President Hissène Habré, who died of Covid-19 in August 2021 while serving a life sentence. Habré had been convicted of crimes against humanity, war crimes, and torture on May 30, 2016. His crimes included sexual violence, including rape and the sexual slavery of women to serve his soldiers.

In September 2022, the Chadian government announced the release of 10 billion FCFA ($16 million) to compensate victims and survivors of Habré-era abuses. In May, Mahamat Idriss Déby Itno told a victims' group delegation that he had asked the finance minister to make Chad's contribution available to victims, but the government took no subsequent action. The government also did not comply with a ruling from a Chadian court ordering additional compensation for victims as well as the creation of a monument to honor those killed under Habré and a museum in the former political police headquarters where detainees were tortured.

Although the African Union had allocated $5 million to a trust fund for the victims in 2017 in line with the Senegal appellate court's order, the fund has yet to begin work.

Key International Actors

In September, media reported that the United Arab Emirates sent arms to the Rapid Support Forces militia in Darfur, in violation of a UN arms embargo, via an airstrip in eastern Chad.

Chile

Chile has been working toward a new constitution since massive demonstrations in 2019 called for reform. In 2022, voters rejected a draft written by a constitutional convention, and in 2023, they rejected a new draft developed by a constitutional council. President Gabriel Boric said his administration would not attempt to develop another draft.

Although Chile still has one of the lowest crime rates in Latin America and the Caribbean, murders have increased in recent years, and crime is a major concern for Chileans.

Chile's laws and policies make it very difficult for migrants and asylum seekers to obtain legal status, pushing them to remain outside the law. In February, the government placed the armed forces in charge of patrolling the northern border, a hot spot for irregular migration.

President Boric has consistently promoted human rights abroad, regardless of the political ideology of the government committing the abuses.

Constituent Process

Massive protests over deficiencies in the provision of public services, an increase in the price of public transportation, and economic inequality erupted across Chile in October 2019. Police used excessive force against demonstrators and bystanders.

As an "institutional exit" from the crisis, political parties agreed to consult the citizenry on steps toward a new constitution.

In 2020, Chileans voted overwhelmingly to establish a convention to write the new constitution. However, in September 2022, almost 62 percent of voters rejected the convention's draft. In December 2022, political parties agreed to a new drafting process.

In January 2023, Congress created an expert commission to work on a new draft that was reviewed by a constitutional council with a conservative majority, which was elected by voters. The draft advanced the protection of environmental and some other rights but also included a broad right to conscientious objection that could be abused to deny access to certain human rights and provided for the expulsion of migrants with irregular status "as soon as possible."

In December more than 55 percent of voters rejected the council's draft. President Gabriel Boric said "the constitutional process is over" and called on political forces to reduce polarization and work within the framework of the current constitution to deliver on Chileans' urgent needs.

Public Security and Police Reform

A July government report counted 1,322 murders in 2022, a 56 percent increase since 2018. The report combined data from various institutions for the first time. Although Chile still has one of the lowest murder rates in Latin America and the Caribbean—6.7 per 100,000 people—polls show that insecurity is one of Chileans' main concerns.

During a 20-day period in March and April, three police officers were killed while on duty. In response, Congress approved a law establishing a legal presumption of self-defense for on-duty security force members who "repel or impede an attack" using weapons or any other means. The United Nations Office of the High Commissioner for Human Rights (OHCHR) noted that Chilean law already allowed officers to defend themselves and that the new presumption of self-defense "reduces accountability, hindering access to justice for victims of potential abuses and favoring impunity."

Chile has tried, with little success, to reform its national police, the Carabineros, since 2019, when police used excessive force against protesters and committed abuses against some detainees. Carabineros have updated various protocols, including on the use of anti-riot shotguns, but deficiencies still leave ample room for abuse. Laws granting Carabineros broad powers of detention, which they exercise with little oversight, have not been amended. Carabineros' disciplinary regime fails to guarantee independent and impartial investigations. A commission established by President Boric in 2022 to work on police reform has met only a few times and, as of October, had showed no progress.

Migrants' and Asylum Seekers' Rights

Over 1.4 million foreigners (both Chilean citizens and noncitizens) live in Chile, representing 8 percent of the country's population. They are mainly Venezuelans, followed by Peruvians, Haitians, and Colombians.

In February, for an initial period of 90 days, the Boric administration put the armed forces in charge of monitoring and detaining migrants crossing the northern border irregularly. This measure was extended three times and remained in force as of November. Security forces detained 13,256 people crossing irregularly from January through July, a significant drop compared to 23,012 during the same period in 2022, the Ministry of Interior reported.

Regularizing legal status is one of the most significant challenges for migrants and asylum seekers in Chile, affecting access to public services and formal jobs. Only 17 percent of Venezuelans had a permanent residence permit, according to a 2023 survey by a platform comprising over 200 nongovernmental organizations (NGOs) and UN agencies. As of September, no regularization program existed for those who entered the country without papers.

Applying for asylum is difficult and few claims are granted. In practice, immigration officials enjoy wide discretion in deciding to whom they give an application form. From January 2010 through August 2023, only 797 of 28,900 applicants—under 3 percent—were granted asylum.

Between June and December, Chilean authorities biometrically registered foreigners over age 18 who had entered irregularly by land before May 30 to "strengthen security" and "identify those who live in Chile," explicitly saying that this process implied "no regularization." Migration experts have raised concerns that the data could be used to facilitate expulsions.

Women's and Girls' Rights

Chile's 28-year total abortion ban ended in 2017, when the Constitutional Court upheld a law decriminalizing abortion when the life of a pregnant woman is at risk, the fetus is non-viable, or the pregnancy resulted from rape. Official statistics show that 831 people received legal abortions in 2022, and 407 did between January and September 2023.

Chile's abortion law, as interpreted by a constitutional court decision, includes an overly broad exception for healthcare providers—individuals, companies, and institutions—to refuse to perform abortions based on conscientious objection. More than 40 percent of public health obstetricians were registered as conscientious objectors in 2022 and refused to perform abortions in cases of rape. Registered as conscientious objectors, six entire private hospitals and clinics refuse to perform any abortions, and a seventh health facility only performs them in cases of rape.

On March 8, International Women's Day, Chile ratified the International Labour Organization (ILO) Violence and Harassment Convention (C190), which establishes state obligations to protect women from violence and harassment in the workforce.

Confronting Past Abuses

Chile commemorated the 50th anniversary of the 1973 coup against former President Salvador Allende, amid high polarization about those events. President Boric, along with all living former presidents, signed a commitment to promote and defend human rights "regardless of political ideology." All political parties in the Senate supported a declaration on the promotion of democracy and human rights while acknowledging the impossibility of a "common vision of history."

During the dictatorship of Augusto Pinochet (1973-1990), at least 3,200 people were killed or disappeared, by the official count. In August, the government launched a national search plan for victims of disappearance, guaranteeing participation and access to information for relatives and promising reparations and guarantees of non-repetition.

Disability Rights

People with disabilities can be deprived of their legal capacity under Chile's civil legislation. People with disabilities suffer discrimination in employment and occupation, education, housing, and health care. People with disabilities cannot access all public buildings and transportation on an equal basis with others, particularly outside Santiago.

Indigenous Peoples' Rights

In June, President Boric created an expert commission to work on land rights solutions and reparations for Mapuche communities, which is expected to issue a report by the second half of 2024.

The state of emergency that President Boric declared in May 2022 in four provinces of southern Chile with a significant Mapuche population, citing increasing violence and roadblocks, continued as of October, with repeated congressional approval. Rural violence in that region diminished 11 percent from January through August, compared to the same period in 2022, while the number of arrests increased fourfold, the government reported.

Prison Conditions and Pretrial Detention

The prison population increased more than 18 percent in a year, surpassing 51,000 people as of September 2023, about 25 percent above facilities' capacity. In May, the Justice Ministry warned that the "congestion" represented a challenge to infrastructure and penitentiary personnel capacities.

More than 100 children under 2 years old lived with their mothers in prisons, latest official data from 2019 shows. A bill that would temporarily suspend prison time for pregnant women and primary caregivers of small children until they turn 3 years old is stalled in Congress.

As of September, 37 percent of detainees awaited trial. Chile's criminal code allows broad use of pretrial detention and does not establish a maximum period for it.

Sexual Orientation and Gender Identity

In March 2022, a law recognizing same-sex couples' rights including to civil marriage, joint adoption, and assisted reproductive technology—took effect. Fundación Iguales, an NGO, reported problems with the implementation of the law, including errors in the registration of children of same-sex couples, excessive delays in the delivery of birth and marriage certificates, and the issuing of outdated forms—such as birth certificates, proof-of-delivery-care, and educational matriculation documents that refer only to a "mother" and a "father"—in civil registries, hospitals, clinics, and schools.

Foreign Policy

President Boric has consistently criticized human rights abuses in other countries—including El Salvador, Venezuela, Nicaragua, and Cuba—regardless of the political ideology of the governments. In September, he denounced a crackdown by the "dictatorial regime of [Daniel] Ortega and [Rosario] Murillo in Nicaragua, where [critics] are banned from participating in elections, persecuted, their nationalities taken, their houses searched, and their political rights taken."

Throughout the electoral process in Guatemala, Chile expressed its concern about attempts by political actors and several government institutions to interfere with the election and urged respect for the people's will.

As a member of the UN Human Rights Council, Chile supported scrutiny of various states' human rights records in 2023. It voted in favor of a resolution extending the mandates of groups of UN experts investigating systematic rights violations in Nicaragua and Syria, and of the special rapporteurs on the human rights situations in Russia, Iran, and Belarus.

In January, Chile joined Colombia in requesting an advisory opinion from the Inter-American Court of Human Rights on states' human rights obligations in responding to the climate emergency, including its varied impact on regions and particular population groups.

China

In late 2022, the Chinese government abruptly ended its draconian "zero Covid" policy. As much of the population—and the medical establishment—was unprepared, Covid-19 infections, hospitalizations, and deaths surged. Officially, the government estimated that there were 60,000 "excess deaths" in December 2022; a US academic study put the figure at 1.87 million deaths between December 2022 and January 2023. The true toll will likely remain unknown due to severe censorship.

Ten years into President Xi Jinping's rule, repression deepens across the country. The Chinese government continues its abusive policies against Uyghurs and other Turkic Muslims in Xinjiang, which amount to crimes against humanity. In both Tibet and Xinjiang, those who contact family and friends abroad, or who advocate for their culture, language, and religion, risk being treated as "separatists" and have been given harsh prison sentences. Across China, the government is further tightening social controls. There is no independent civil society; even small pockets of freedom are eliminated. In Hong Kong, the Chinese government has assumed full control over the city since imposing the National Security Law in 2020.

The Chinese government's list of political targets continues to expand. Even those who work for foreign entities in China's cosmopolitan cities find themselves in the crosshairs, with revisions to a law on "counter-espionage" in July and with the state security ministry encouraging the population to report alleged spies.

As the economy slows, small protests have flared, such as those by pensioners against cuts to their medical insurance in February. Aspirations for a fairer society continue to run deep among many, especially those who have faced injustice, including women; lesbian, gay, bisexual, and transgender (LGBT) people; Tibetans; Uyghurs; Hong Kongers; and those at the bottom of the socioeconomic hierarchy. Some who went into exile have coalesced into diaspora activist movements.

In November, crowds of people across the country mourned the unexpected death of former Premier Li Keqiang. For many, Li represented a more economically vibrant China, in contrast to Xi, who prioritized social control and is taking China backward.

Freedom of Expression

Through laws and regulations, criminal punishment, harassment, intimidation, and the use of technology, the Chinese government operates one of the world's most stringent censorship regimes.

In April, authorities released Wuhan businessman Fang Bin, who was among the first to report on the Covid-19 outbreak, after three years in detention. But Shanghai-based activist and former lawyer Zhang Zhan, who went to Wuhan to report on the outbreak in February 2020, remains in custody. In July 2023, authorities transferred her to a prison hospital due to her deteriorating health.

Authorities released on bail some protesters who took part in the White Paper protests in late 2022, including Cao Zhixin, Li Yuanjing, Zhai Dengrui, and Li Siqi. But in March, a court sentenced Uyghur college student Kamile Wayit to three years in prison for "promoting extremism" after she shared a video of the protests online. It is unknown how many protesters remain in detention.

In April, Chinese state security arrested a Taiwanese pro-independence politician Yang Chih-yuan, who was living in Zhejiang province, on suspicion of "secession."

In May, the Chinese government fined a comedy company 14.7 million renminbi (RMB) (about US$2 million) for a joke by stand-up comic Li Haoshi, who compared the People's Liberation Army to dogs. In the same month, Weibo suspended a Malaysian comedian known as Uncle Roger for joking about the Chinese government's surveillance and sovereignty claims over Taiwan.

In August, a court in Guizhou province sentenced former economics professor, Yang Shaozheng, to 4.5 years in prison for "inciting subversion" after he raised concerns about the high annual cost of government personnel in China.

In September, the Chinese government released a draft regulation that, if passed, would penalize those who wear clothes in public that "hurt the Chinese people's feelings." The regulations appear to target those who wear Japanese clothing or items that challenge gender norms.

The Chinese government continues to rely on tech companies to enforce censorship. After a roof in Heilongjiang province collapsed, killing 10 children and the coach of a middle school volleyball team, authorities swiftly censored the outpouring of grief, including the names of the children.

In April, researchers found that China's search platforms use 60,000 rules to censor online content; the most far-reaching political censorship among web search engines was by Microsoft's Bing, its rules less numerous but broader and affecting more search results than the rules applied by Chinese companies such as Baidu. Bing said it would "look into the findings." In August, Apple reportedly removed over 100 generative Artificial Intelligence (AI) apps from China's app store as Beijing cracked down on the new technology, in part to maintain social control. Apple said these apps "include content that is illegal in China." In May, LinkedIn announced that it would phase out its app for China, InCareer, becoming the latest major US social media platform to shutter in China.

In May, the *Wall Street Journal* revealed that employees at TikTok, owned by Chinese company ByteDance, reportedly monitored content accessed by users, including those who watched LGBT content. TikTok said they had terminated such practices and that "safeguarding the privacy and security" of users is one of their "top priorities." This is after a December 2022 revelation that the company tracked American journalists who were writing critically about TikTok, which the company attributed to "the misconduct of certain individuals" who were no longer its employees.

Freedom of Religion

State control over religion has grown since 2016, when President Xi called for "Sinicization" of religions. Police arrest, detain, and harass leaders and members of various "illegal" religious groups, including "house churches" (congregations that refuse to join official Catholic and Protestant churches). Authorities also disrupt their peaceful activities—whether they are preaching religion or running summer camps for children—and ban these groups outright.

Beyond dictating what constitutes legal religious activity, authorities now seek to comprehensively reshape religions to be consistent with party ideology and promote allegiance to the party and Xi.

In provinces with a high proportion of Muslims, authorities have closed down, demolished, or removed the minarets and domes of mosques to "Sinicize" them or to remove foreign influences. In Yunnan province, authorities removed Islamic features from Najiaying Mosque leading to a rare protest by hundreds of Hui Muslims in May.

The Measures on the Administration of Religious Activity Venues came into force in September. They impose further restrictions on religious activities, requiring religious venues to indoctrinate followers in Chinese Communist Party ideology, and prohibiting them from "creating conflicts ... between sects" or receiving funding other than those approved by the state.

In July, the Chinese government transferred a Catholic bishop, Joseph Shen Bin, to head the vacant Shanghai diocese, without consulting with the Vatican, in violation of the 2018 China-Vatican accord. While the Vatican publicly protested Beijing's decision, it approved the move and has remained largely silent over Beijing's religious persecution.

Attacks on Human Rights Defenders

Human rights defenders and government critics continue to face persecution.

In January, authorities released human rights lawyer Tang Jitian after forcibly disappearing him for 398 days. In March, a Guangxi court sentenced human rights lawyer Qin Yongpei to five years in prison for "inciting subversion of state power." In April, a court in Shandong province sentenced prominent legal scholar Xu Zhiyong and human rights lawyer Ding Jiaxi to 14 and 12 years in prison, respectively, for "subversion of state power."

In April, authorities arrested rights lawyer Yu Wensheng and his wife, Xu Yan, while en route to a meeting with the EU ambassador in Beijing. They placed human rights lawyers Wang Quanzhang, Wang Yu, and Bao Longjun under house arrest. Between May and June, police harassed and forced Wang and his wife, Li Wenzu, to move homes 13 times.

In May, a court in Guangzhou sentenced prominent human rights legal activist Guo Feixiong to eight years in prison for "inciting subversion of state power."

Guo was arrested in January 2021 at Shanghai airport as he tried to visit his critically ill wife in the United States; she died a year later.

Also in May, journalist-in-exile Yang Zewei was disappeared from his home in Laos and reappeared in detention in Hunan province. In July, Laotian police detained human rights lawyer Lu Siwei while en route to Thailand. Despite calls from UN experts, on September 15, Laos deported Lu to China where he awaits trial for "illegally crossing the border."

Hong Kong

Since Beijing imposed the draconian National Security Law on Hong Kong in June 2020, freedoms have sharply declined. Hong Kong authorities have arrested at least 279 people for allegedly violating that law and the colonial-era sedition law. Prosecutions under the National Security Law had a 100 percent conviction rate at time of writing.

In July, the high-profile national security trial of 47 pro-democracy politicians began. Another national security trial, of 75-year-old media tycoon Jimmy Lai, was slated to begin on December 18. In October, four former university student leaders were sentenced to two years in prison for "incitement to wound with intent." They were imprisoned for presiding over a student council meeting in 2021 that passed a resolution mourning a man who killed himself after stabbing and injuring a police officer.

In June, the Hong Kong government sought an injunction order to ban the broadcast and distribution of the protest song "Glory to Hong Kong." The court denied the request in July, but the government appealed. In August, a court sentenced a man to three months in prison for "insulting" the Chinese national anthem after he replaced the soundtrack with "Glory to Hong Kong" in an online video.

Since 2020, the Hong Kong government has removed a couple hundred titles it labeled "politically sensitive" from public libraries. In July, it set up a channel that encouraged the public to report publications that might "endanger national security." In September, police charged a man with "sedition" for allegedly receiving 18 copies of a pro-democracy children's book titled *Sheep Village* from abroad.

Self-censorship has become even more commonplace. In February, Disney's streaming platform in Hong Kong pulled an episode of *The Simpsons* that mentioned forced labor camps in China.

Since June 2020, no major public assemblies have taken place in Hong Kong. In March, police initially allowed a protest on International Women's Day, but the organizer canceled it after police stated, without giving specifics, that "violent groups" might join the protest. Organizers canceled a planned International Workers' Day protest in April after national security police briefly detained one of the organizers.

The government's targets of repression have extended beyond Hong Kong's borders. In July, police issued baseless arrest warrants and bounties on eight exiled politicians and activists who reside abroad for offenses under the National Security Law. Police froze their bank accounts, interrogated their Hong Kong-based family members, and raided the homes of activists associated with them.

In November, a Hong Kong woman was sentenced to two months in prison for "sedition" over social media posts she published while studying at a university in Japan. In 2023, immigration authorities denied entry to three Japanese journalists and artists critical of the Hong Kong government.

There was some progress on LGBT rights. In February, the Court of Final Appeal ruled that the government's requirement that transgender men undergo "full sex reassignment surgery" to change their legal gender was unconstitutional. In September, the top court ordered the government to establish a legal framework for recognizing same-sex partnerships.

Xinjiang

Beijing continues its massive abuses in Xinjiang, which Human Rights Watch has found to constitute crimes against humanity. Although some political education camps appear to have closed, an estimated half-million Uyghurs and other Turkic Muslims remain in prison, detained during China's "Strike Hard Against Violent Terrorism" crackdown that started in 2017. There have been no mass releases. In September, a court sentenced prominent Uyghur anthropologist Dr. Rahile Dawut to life imprisonment for spurious state security crimes. Many

Uyghurs abroad continue to have little to no contact with family members in Xinjiang.

Xinjiang authorities are forcibly assimilating Uyghurs, including through the Sinicization of Islam. The government has been promoting tourism to the region, where it presents a sanitized and controlled version of Uyghur culture to domestic tourists.

In August, President Xi visited Xinjiang ahead of the first anniversary of a damning United Nations report that detailed widespread abuses across Xinjiang—including targeting of cultural and religious practices, family separation, arbitrary arrests and detention, rapes, torture, and enforced disappearances—and concluded that Beijing's policies in the region "may constitute crimes against humanity." Xi pronounced that his policies in Xinjiang were a "success."

In February and April, two Uyghur men died in Thai immigration detention after being held there for nine years, highlighting the plight of Uyghurs trapped in countries susceptible to Beijing's influence even after escaping from the country.

Tibet

The authorities in Tibetan areas enforced severe restrictions on the freedoms of religion, expression, movement, and assembly. Tibetans who speak out over issues such as mass relocation, environmental degradation, or the phasing out of the Tibetan language in primary education are met with repression. Local officials are required to educate the public to "obey the law," and cash rewards are offered to citizens prepared to inform on others. Having banned content on one's phone or merely contacting Tibetans in exile can result in detention. A revered monk, Geshe Phende Gyaltsen, arrested in good health by Litang county police in March 2022, died in police custody in January 2023.

In June 2023, a group of UN special rapporteurs requested information about the cases of six Tibetans detained for possession of photos of the exiled religious leader, the Dalai Lama. The Chinese government has not responded.

Women's and Girls' Rights

On January 1, revisions to the 1992 Law on the Protection of Women's Rights and Interests came into effect, which addresses workplace discrimination and sexual harassment. However, victims still face difficulties in seeking accountability while legal experts question the amendments' effectiveness.

Largely because of the decades-long "one-child" policy, for the first time in six decades, deaths outnumbered births in China. Some local governments have shifted to promoting births, including cash rewards for brides ages 25 or younger in Zhejiang county and birth subsidy plans in several Chinese cities. Official language in some laws and policies suggests a restrictive role for women. The amendments to the Law on Protection of Women's Rights and Interests, for example, tells women to "respect social morals ... and family values."

The Women's Tennis Association returned to China in September, ending its suspension of tournaments in the country after Peng Shuai, a three-time Olympian and Grand Slam doubles champion, accused former Vice Premier Zhang Gaoli of sexual abuse in 2021.

Journalist Huang Xueqin and labor rights activist Wang Jianbing were put on trial by a Guangzhou court in September for "inciting subversion of state power" for their leading involvement in the #MeToo Movement.

Sexual Orientation and Gender Identity

LGBT people and rights activists have experienced increased harassment and censorship.

In February, two Tsinghua University students filed a lawsuit against the Ministry of Education after school authorities disciplined them in July 2022 for leaving rainbow flags in a campus supermarket.

One of the oldest LGBT organizations in China, the Beijing LGBT Center, suddenly announced its closure due to "force majeure" in May. This closure is the latest in a string of forced shutdowns of LGBT groups since 2019.

On August 22, the Chinese version of Valentine's Day, known as Qixi, several LGBT organizations, including TransBrotherhood China, Beijing Lesbian Centre, and the Beijing branch of Trueself, and other community public accounts, including Beijing Lala Salon, Wandouhuang, Transtory, Outstanding Partners, Ace, and the Flying Cat Brotherhood, found that WeChat had banned their accounts. This follows the deletion of dozens of university student-run LGBT social media accounts by WeChat in 2021.

Disability Rights

In a case that has captured national attention, in April, a court in Jiangsu province sentenced Dong Zhimin to nine years in prison for his wrongful imprisonment of a woman with schizophrenia, Xiaohuamei. In 2022, a netizen filmed Xiaohuamei shackled at the neck in a squalid shack. Local officials repeatedly tried to restrict activists' searches about her origins, but it is believed that she was trafficked, sold to Dong, held in sexual slavery— giving birth to eight children—and shackled for years. Xiaohuamei's case is a rare example where shackling of people with real or perceived psychosocial disabilities—often due to inadequate support and mental health services—have been discovered and their perpetrators punished.

Climate Change Policy and Impacts

As the world's largest emitter of greenhouse gases, with per capita emissions that rank 11th among the G20 nations, China is contributing to the climate crisis and its growing toll on human rights around the globe. China is the world's largest producer and consumer of coal, burning more coal every year than the rest of the world combined. It is the largest importer of oil and gas. A Chinese bank was the largest financier of fossil fuels between 2016 and 2022. China's plans to continue to increase production of fossil fuels are contrary to its human rights obligations, which require that all governments phase out fossil fuels.

Despite improved targets, the Climate Action Tracker rates China's domestic emission reduction target as "highly insufficient" to meet the Paris Agreement goal to limit global warming to 1.5 degrees Celsius above pre-industrial levels.

China leads the world in renewable energy production. It also processes the vast majority of the minerals and metals needed for batteries and other renewable energy technologies. Some of these materials are made by companies in Xinjiang, creating a risk of links to forced labor. Researchers have, for example, documented links between polysilicon production, a key material for solar manufacturing, and forced labor in Xinjiang.

Key International Actors

The end of China's "zero Covid" policy prompted a wave of high-level visits to China over the year, from German Chancellor Olaf Scholz to Brazilian President Lula da Silva. Few publicly raised human rights issues.

Diplomats friendly with the Chinese government from Indonesia, Iran, Mexico, North Korea, and Saudi Arabia, among others, and representatives of the League of Arab States and Islamic scholars, visited Xinjiang as part of Chinese government propaganda tours. The Chinese Foreign Ministry and state media reported that these visits affirmed "peace" and "happiness" across the region.

The German government published a long-awaited China strategy, which advanced a sober view of ties to Beijing.

In June, European Union heads of state reiterated concerns about China's record but fell short of initiating new actions. Many human rights groups questioned the relevance of the resumption in February of the EU's human rights dialogue with China. In October, EU top diplomat Josep Borrell visited Beijing, and in December, the EU and Chinese government held an EU-China summit.

In the EU, efforts proceeded in the legislative process toward the adoption of legislation on human rights and environmental due diligence for companies and on banning products made through forced labor from being imported into or exported from the EU market. Neither measure is country-specific, but import restrictions may play a key role in preventing such products from being imported from Xinjiang.

In May, UN High Commissioner for Human Rights Volker Türk urged "concrete follow up" on his office's August 2022 report on the Chinese government's severe violations in Xinjiang. However, he has yet to brief the UN Human Rights Council on the report or indicate what "concrete follow up" he intends to take to advance implementation of the report's recommendations or end the abuses.

Since the June 2022 entry into force of the Uyghur Forced Labor Prevention Act, US customs officials had, as of November 29, 2023, denied entry to goods worth US$561 million due to suspected links to forced labor in Xinjiang or elsewhere in China.

Foreign businesses in China experienced unprecedented pressure in 2023. In April, the Chinese government made vague amendments to the Counter-Espionage Law, leaving foreign firms uncertain as to whether previously acceptable business practices are now criminal. In March, Chinese authorities raided the Beijing office of the US corporate due diligence firm, Mintz Group, and detained staff. In April, authorities raided the Shanghai office of global consulting company, Bain. In June, authorities obliged staff members of financial firms Franklin Templeton and BlackRock to attend classes on "Xi Jinping Thought."

Foreign Policy

In 2023, Beijing launched its new Global Security Initiative, Global Development Initiative, and Global Civilization Initiative, each designed to challenge existing global governance, security, and human rights norms and institutions.

Xi's previous flagship global development program, the Belt and Road Initiative, which has been criticized for a lack of transparency and rights violations, has reduced in scope. But he continues to build strong coalitions with the Global South, such as prioritizing attendance at summits like BRICS in South Africa.

Xi continued to lend crucial support to Russia despite international sanctions imposed on Russia for its full-scale invasion of Ukraine. Shortly after an arrest warrant was issued against Russian President Vladimir Putin by the International Criminal Court in March, Xi traveled to Moscow to meet Putin. In September, Xi welcomed to Beijing the Syrian president, Bashar al-Assad, who is alleged to have committed war crimes.

Chinese government efforts to silence critics in other countries brought new attention from governments, including indictments by the US Department of Justice against 40 Chinese police officials.

Chinese diplomats continued their campaign to mute criticism of the government's human rights record and to weaken UN human rights bodies. They interrupted and harassed civil society representatives at the UN Human Rights Council. In September, Chinese diplomats sent one *note verbale* discouraging government attendance at a civil society event focused on Xinjiang taking place on the margins of the UN General Assembly and another with a similar message to Geneva-based missions about an event on press freedom in Hong Kong.

Colombia

Abuses by armed groups, limited access to justice, and high levels of poverty, especially among Indigenous and Afro-descendant communities, remain serious human rights concerns in Colombia.

The 2016 peace accord between the Revolutionary Armed Forces of Colombia (FARC) and the government ended a five-decade-long conflict and brought an initial decline in violence. But violence took new forms and abuses by armed groups increased in many remote areas, reaching similar levels to those that existed immediately before the peace process. A year and a half since President Gustavo Petro took office, his "total peace" strategy has achieved limited results in curbing abuses against civilians.

In a welcome move, President Petro shortlisted three women with a strong record of investigating human rights violations to become the new attorney general. The Supreme Court had not appointed a new attorney general at the time of writing.

Abuses by Armed Groups

Numerous armed groups operate in Colombia fueled by illegal economies, including drug trafficking and illegal mining. These include the National Liberation Army (ELN) guerrillas, a group formed in the 1960s; over 30 "dissident" groups that emerged from the 2017 demobilization of the FARC; and the Gaitanist Self-Defense Forces of Colombia (AGC), which emerged from the demobilization of paramilitary groups in the mid-2000s and is also known as the "Gulf Clan." Many of these groups have fluid and complex links to each other, and some are parties to non-international armed conflicts.

Armed groups continue to commit serious abuses against civilians. Reports of child recruitment and kidnappings increased in 2023. Security forces and judicial authorities have often failed to effectively protect the population, ensure victims' access to justice, and prosecute and dismantle criminal groups.

Fears of antipersonnel landmines, threats by armed groups, and the hazards of crossfire prevented 64,000 mostly Indigenous people from leaving their communities between January and October, a situation known as "confinement."

HUMAN
RIGHTS
WATCH
"We Must Ask for What Is Already Ours"
Afro-descendant Women and Access to Land in Alto Mira y Frontera, Colombia

Between January and end of June, the United Nations Office of the High Commissioner for Human Rights (OHCHR) reported 52 "massacres," defined as the intentional killing of three or more civilians in a single incident.

In the southern state of Nariño, fighting among FARC dissident groups has displaced thousands, mainly Afro-descendants and Awá Indigenous people, who also suffer threats, confinement, kidnappings, and killings.

In neighboring Cauca state, Nasa Indigenous people who oppose abuses by armed groups have been threatened and killed. Fighting by armed groups, mainly in Argelia municipality, has left more than 6,500 people displaced and confined.

Violations by Public Security Forces

Limited progress in investigating violations by security forces remains a serious concern.

On March 28, 2022, 11 people died in an army operation in Alto Remanso, Putumayo state, in southern Colombia. At least four civilians died. The Attorney General's Office announced in May 2023 it would charge 25 soldiers with the killings, but at time of writing, the Constitutional Court was analyzing a request by defense lawyers to transfer the case to the military justice system, which has historically failed to ensure justice.

Police committed serious human rights violations in response to protests across Colombia between 2019 and 2021.

In 2021, Human Rights Watch reviewed evidence linking police to 25 killings of protesters and bystanders, as well as dozens of injuries and arbitrary arrests, in the context of peaceful demonstrations. As of June, the Attorney General's Office had charged eight police officers. Nobody had been sentenced.

The Ministry of Defense ousted 10 police officers credibly linked to human rights violations during demonstrations.

The Ministry of Defense also initiated a process, with broad participation of civil society groups, to reform police protocols. But the government failed to move forward with other reforms to security forces, such as transferring the police out of the Ministry of Defense.

Violence against Human Rights Defenders and Other People at Risk

More than 1,200 human rights defenders and social leaders have been killed in Colombia since 2016, according to the Human Rights Ombudsperson's Office. Human Rights Watch documented 150 killings of human rights defenders and other social leaders committed between January and the end of November 2023.

Colombia has a broad range of policies, mechanisms, and laws to prevent abuses against human rights defenders and protect former FARC fighters. But implementation has often been poor.

In September, authorities announced a new policy to "dismantle" armed groups that attack human rights defenders, as required under the 2016 peace accord.

In a case brought by Colombian human rights groups, the Constitutional Court ordered in December broad government action to protect human rights defenders and hold those responsible for their killings to account. The court found that government action fell short of addressing these "persistent, grave and widespread" violations and described the situation as an "unconstitutional state of affairs."

Killings and other attacks against local politicians and candidates increased ahead of the October regional elections. Between January and July, 16 candidates, politicians, and other people involved in political campaigns were killed, according to the Ombudsperson's Office.

Peace Negotiations, Negotiated Disarmament, and Accountability

The 2016 peace agreement created a truth commission; the Special Jurisdiction for Peace (JEP), charged with trying violations committed during the conflict; and an agency to seek the bodies of those who disappeared during the conflict.

The JEP has made significant strides in investigating and prosecuting war crimes and crimes against humanity, charging top former FARC commanders and several army officers.

Defendants who fully cooperate with the JEP and confess to their crimes are subject to up to eight years of "special sanctions," including restrictions on liberty but no prison time. It remains unclear how the "special sanctions" will operate in practice.

In September 2023, the JEP initiated a nation-wide "macro-case" investigating gender-based violence, including sexual and reproductive violence and other crimes based on prejudice committed by the FARC and security forces.

In November 2022, the JEP indicted former FARC top commanders for their responsibility in kidnappings. The commanders had acknowledged their role in these crimes in a June hearing.

In August, the JEP indicted General Mario Montoya, who commanded the army between 2006 and 2008, for his role in 130 extrajudicial executions when he led a brigade.

In late 2022, Congress passed a Petro administration-sponsored law that allows the government to negotiate a peace accord, including new transitional justice mechanisms, with parties to the armed conflict such as the ELN, as well as with organized crime groups. In November, the Constitutional Court ruled that negotiations with organized crime groups should ensure access to justice for victims.

Throughout 2023, the government continued to negotiate a peace accord with the ELN guerrillas and a coalition of FARC dissident groups that the government calls Estado Mayor Central (EMC).

On December 31, 2022, President Petro announced a six-month bilateral ceasefire with five armed groups, including the ELN, the Gulf Clan, and the EMC. The ELN did not accept the terms of the ceasefire and the Attorney General's Office questioned the legality of ceasefire with the Gulf Clan. Preparations, including relevant protocols, were insufficient and the ceasefires produced limited results.

In July and September, the government agreed to new ceasefires with the ELN and the EMC, respectively.

A government-supported truce between two gangs in the port city of Buenaventura led to a decrease in killings between September 2022 and March 2023, followed by an increase between April and July.

Internal Displacement, Reparations, and Land Restitution

The UN Office for the Coordination of Humanitarian Affairs (OCHA) reported that over 56,000 people were displaced between January and October 2023, in "mass displacements" of 50 or more people or 10 or more families.

Municipalities and state governments often lack sufficient funding to assist displaced people, and national government assistance has often been slow and insufficient.

In 2011, Congress passed a Victims' Law to ensure redress for victims and restore millions of hectares left behind or stolen from Colombians displaced during the conflict. Less than 15 percent of more than 9 million registered victims of the armed conflict had received reparations as of August 2023. In September, the Petro administration sent a bill to Congress to renew and expand the Victims' Law.

Refugees, Asylum Seekers, and Migrants

As of November 2023, more than 2.8 million Venezuelans lived in Colombia.

In 2021, then-President Iván Duque announced temporary protection for Venezuelans, granting them 10 years of legal status. As of September 2023, authorities had granted temporary protection to over 1.8 million Venezuelans, out of more than 2.4 million who had requested it.

Hundreds of thousands of migrants crossed Colombia's Darién gap into Panama in 2023, in most cases believed to be headed to the US. The number of people crossing the gap continued to increase, in large part driven by continued migration by Venezuelans. During their days-long walk across the gap, migrants and asylum seekers of all nationalities are frequently victims of robbery and serious abuses, including rape. They receive little security, aid, or access to justice.

Gender-Based Violence

Gender-based violence, including by armed groups, is widespread. Lack of training and poor implementation of treatment protocols impede timely access to medical services and create obstacles for women and girls seeking post-violence care and justice. Perpetrators of gender-based crimes are rarely held accountable.

Sexual Orientation and Gender Identity

In August, the Constitutional Court extended labor protections during pregnancy to trans men and non-binary people who are pregnant. Despite constitutional protections based on sexual orientation and gender identity, lesbian, gay, bisexual, and transgender (LGBT) people in Colombia continue to face high levels of violence and discrimination. In 2022, Colombia Diversa reported 148 killings of LGBT people, including 28 possibly based on prejudice. Colombia Diversa also reported 97 cases of police violence that affected 107 LGBT people in 2022. Between January and November 2023, the Attorney General's Office registered homicides against 134 LGBT persons.

Access to Abortion

In February 2022, the Constitutional Court decriminalized abortion in all circumstances up to the 24th week of pregnancy and maintained access beyond that time in cases of rape, a non-viable pregnancy, or risk to a pregnant person's health or life. In early 2023, a chamber of the Constitutional Court issued two rulings that threatened to undermine access to abortion services. In October, the Constitutional Court annulled the chamber's decisions.

Economic and Social Rights

High levels of poverty, especially among Indigenous and Afro-descendant communities, remain a serious human rights concern.

The 2016 peace accord established "Territorial Development Programs" (PDET) to increase the presence of state institutions in 170 municipalities highly affected by the armed conflict, poverty, and illegal economies, such as drug trafficking. In 2021, the multidimensional national poverty rate (28.7 percent) in these areas was more than double the national rate (12.9 percent). Efforts to implement the PDET have been limited.

Between January and November 2023, at least 54 children under age 5—the majority Indigenous Wayuu—died in La Guajira state of causes associated with malnutrition and limited access to safe drinking water.

Technology and Rights

The Education Ministry failed to act following Human Rights Watch research showing that all eight online learning products recommended by the ministry during the Covid-19 pandemic surveilled or had the capacity to surveil children online outside of school hours and deep into their private lives.

Climate Policy and Impacts

In November 2022, President Petro signed a law to ratify the Escazú Agreement, a regional accord that shores up protection for ecosystems and their defenders. At time of writing, the Constitutional Court was analyzing whether the accord was consistent with Colombia's Constitution.

Colombia's national plan to reduce greenhouse gas emissions is "highly insufficient" to meet the Paris Agreement goal of limiting global warming to 1.5 degrees Celsius above pre-industrial levels, according to the Climate Action Tracker. The plan commits Colombia to reducing deforestation to 50,000 hectares per year by 2030. Colombia subsequently joined the Glasgow Declaration, which commits it to "halt and reverse forest loss and land degradation by 2030."

Government figures registered 123,000 hectares deforested in 2022, a 29 percent decrease compared to 2021, according to the most recent available information. Roughly two-thirds of deforestation occurs in the Amazon region.

Cattle ranchers and FARC dissident groups are major drivers of deforestation, pressuring residents to fell trees, extorting farmers, promoting coca crops to produce cocaine, or threatening people who defend conservation.

Key International Actors

The United States approved approximately US$487 million in assistance to Colombia in fiscal year 2023. In May, President Petro met with President Joe Biden in the White House to discuss climate change, migration policy, the human rights situation in Venezuela, and peace efforts in Colombia. In May, the US designated as ineligible for entry into the country three former Colombian military officers for gross violations of human rights.

President Petro and Venezuelan President Nicolás Maduro re-established diplomatic relations in August and reopened the border in September 2022. President Maduro agreed in September 2022 to take part in peace negotiations between the ELN and the Colombian government.

In April 2023, the Petro administration carried out a conference with foreign governments in Bogotá to seek progress in political negotiations between the Maduro government and the opposition in Venezuela. But the negotiations remained stalled as of writing.

In March, during their human rights dialogue, the EU and Colombia agreed on the "urgent need to reinforce preventive actions" to address the high rate of violence against human rights defenders. EU High Representative for Foreign Affairs Josep Borrell visited Colombia in April and said that the EU would support peace negotiations with the Estado Mayor Central. At the EU-CELAC Summit in July, Borrell issued a statement jointly with the presidents of France, Brazil, Colombia, and Argentina, urging Venezuela to hold "fair, transparent and inclusive elections" in 2024.

In July, the UN Human Rights Council passed a resolution requesting the appointment of an international human rights expert mandated with identifying and verifying obstacles to implementation of the 2016 Peace Agreement.

The Office of the Prosecutor of the International Criminal Court concluded its preliminary examination in Colombia in October 2021 but has continued to monitor developments in the country. In June, Prosecutor Karim Khan visited Colombia and agreed to provide technical assistance to the JEP.

In 2016, the UN Security Council established a political mission to monitor and verify implementation of the FARC peace accord, a mission succeeded in 2017 by the UN Verification Mission in Colombia. In August, the Council expanded the mission's mandate to include verifying a ceasefire between the government and the ELN. In October, the Council extended the mission's mandate for one year, until October 31, 2024.

In November 2022, Colombia endorsed the Safe Schools Declaration, promising to protect education during armed conflict and to avoid using schools for military purposes.

Cuba

The government continues to repress and punish virtually all forms of dissent and public criticism, as Cubans endure a dire economic crisis affecting their rights.

Hundreds of critics and protesters, including many who took to the streets in July 2021, remain arbitrarily detained. Demonstrations continued in 2023, triggered by blackouts, shortages, and the deterioration of living conditions. Cubans continued to leave the country in unprecedented numbers.

The United States continued a failed policy of isolation towards Cuba, including a decades-long embargo.

Arbitrary Detention and Prosecution

The government continued to employ arbitrary detention to harass and intimidate critics, independent activists, political opponents, and others.

Two years after the July 2021 protests, the largest since the Cuban revolution, rights groups counted over 700 people, including over 70 women, still behind bars in connection with them. Many were periodically held incommunicado. Some suffered ill-treatment and in some cases torture.

The government said over 380 people, including several children, were serving sentences. Some stood trial in military courts, contravening international law. Some stood trial in ordinary courts on "sedition" charges, accused of violence such as rock-throwing and received disproportionate prison terms of up to 25 years. Many received only summary trials on vaguely defined charges such as "public disorder" or "contempt."

Prosecutors framed as criminal behavior actions such as criticizing the government on social media or protesting peacefully, which are lawful exercises of freedoms of expression and association. Prosecutors and judges used unreliable or uncorroborated evidence.

Migration

Between January 2022 and October 2023, the US Border Patrol apprehended Cubans more than 420,000 times, which may have included multiple encounters with the same people. Many traveled north through Nicaragua, which waived visa requirements for Cubans in late 2021.

Additionally, between October 2022 and July 2023, the US Coast Guard intercepted over 6,800 Cubans at sea.

Many Cubans have also fled to countries other than the US, including in Latin America and Europe.

Travel Restrictions

Since reforms by the Cuban government in 2013, many people previously denied permission to travel to and from Cuba have been able to do so, including human rights defenders and bloggers. However, the reforms give the government broad discretionary power to restrict travel on grounds of "defense and national security" or "other reasons of public interest."

The government continued to bar critics from boarding planes to visit or return to their own country, in violation of international human rights law.

Economic and Social Rights

The economic crisis in Cuba severely impacts people's enjoyment of economic and social rights. They endure blackouts and acute shortages of food, medicine, and other basic items. In February, authorities said Cubans should expect three-hour blackouts every day for several months.

In May, the head of the Cuban pharmaceutical industry said authorities were unable to obtain medicines that Cuban people needed. She blamed the US embargo.

Also in May, Cuban authorities reported a decrease in life expectancy, from 78.07 years between 2014 and 2016 to 77.7 years between 2018 and 2020, and an increase in child mortality, from 4.9 deaths per 100,000 born alive in 2020 to 7.5 in 2022.

Political Prisoners

Cuba was holding over 1,000 people, including 34 adolescents and other children, who met the definition of political prisoners, as of November, according to Prisoners Defenders, a Madrid-based nongovernmental organization (NGO).

Cubans who criticize the government risk criminal prosecution. They are not guaranteed due process, such as the right to fair and public hearings by a competent, independent, and impartial tribunal. In practice, courts are subordinate to the executive branch.

José Daniel Ferrer, leader of the Cuban Patriotic Union, the main opposition party, remained in prison at time of writing. In April 2020, a court in Santiago de Cuba sentenced him to 4.5 years of "restrictions on freedom" for alleged "assault" in a case that the United Nations Working Group on Arbitrary Detention deemed arbitrary. On July 11, 2021, officers detained Ferrer as he was heading to a demonstration. In August 2021, a Santiago de Cuba court ruled that Ferrer had failed to comply with the "restrictions on freedom" and sent him to the Mar Verde prison. His relatives say he has been held incommunicado for long periods of time and suffers health problems.

In June 2022, a court in Havana convicted activists Luis Manuel Otero Alcántara and Maykel Castillo Pérez, who performed in the 2021 music video "Patria y Vida" (Motherland and Life), which repurposes the government's old slogan "Patria o Muerte" (Motherland or Death) to criticize repression. They were prosecuted on charges that violate freedom of expression, such as for posting a meme of President Díaz Canel. Otero Alcántara and Castillo Pérez were sentenced to five and nine years in prison, respectively.

Prison Conditions

Prisons are often overcrowded. Detainees have no effective complaint mechanism to seek redress for abuses.

The government continues to deny Cuban and international human rights groups access to prisons. In June 2022, the UN Committee against Torture expressed concern about "allegations of the systematic ill-treatment and torture of inmates."

Freedom of Expression

The government controls virtually all media in Cuba, restricts access to outside information, and periodically censors critics and independent journalists.

Increased access to the internet has enabled activists to communicate, report on abuses, and organize protests. Some journalists and bloggers publish articles, videos, and news on websites and social media, including X (formerly known as Twitter) and Facebook.

Authorities routinely block access to many news websites within Cuba and repeatedly impose targeted, and at times widespread, restrictions on critics' access to mobile phone data.

In May 2023, the National Assembly passed a Social Communication Law that severely restricts the operation of independent media and includes overly broad prohibitions, such as a ban on "promoting the communicational aggression that is occurring against the country," which could be used to censor criticism.

Labor Rights

Cuba ratified International Labour Organization standards on freedom of association and collective bargaining, but its Labor Code, updated in 2014, violates them.

In an April 2023 report, the Inter-American Commission on Human Rights found "systematic patterns of violations of labor rights," including limited occupational health and safety protection measures, and lack of freedom of expression in the workplace.

Thousands of Cuban health workers deployed abroad provide valuable services. But the government imposes rules on them that violate their basic rights, including to privacy, liberty, movement, and freedoms of expression and association.

Attacks on Human Rights Defenders

The government refuses to recognize human rights monitoring as a legitimate activity and denies legal status to Cuban rights groups. Authorities have harassed, assaulted, and imprisoned human rights defenders documenting abuses.

In June 2023, the Inter-American Commission on Human Rights concluded that the Cuban government was responsible for the 2012 deaths of democracy activists Oswaldo Payá and Harold Cepero.

Sexual Orientation and Gender Identity

The 2019 constitution explicitly prohibits discrimination based on sexual orientation or gender identity. However, many lesbian, gay, bisexual, and transgender (LGBT) people suffer violence and discrimination, particularly in Cuba's interior.

Prisoners Defenders reported in July that over 100 transgender women imprisoned in Cuba are held with men, in violation of international human rights standards.

In September 2022, a new family code that included a gender-neutral definition of marriage was approved by referendum, legalizing same-sex marriage.

Disability Rights

Cuba has not aligned its domestic legislation with the UN Convention on the Rights of Persons with Disabilities or implemented policies to address disability rights in the areas of accessibility, access to justice, legal capacity, education, independent living, and employment. Children with disabilities are sent to special segregated schools.

Women's and Girls' Rights

Cuba decriminalized abortion in 1965. It is available and free at public hospitals.

In July 2023, lawmakers reported an increase in pregnancies in women and girls under 19. Lawmakers said that almost 20 percent of pregnancies in the country were in women and girls between 12 and 19; they also said that in parts of Cuba, early pregnancies were more likely among adolescents who were Black, lived in rural areas, or had low income.

Between January and July, Yo Sí Te Creo, an NGO supporting victims of gender-based violence, reported 54 "femicides" in Cuba. The government does not publish official figures of such gender-based killings.

Key International Actors

For decades, the international community has been unable to secure sustained progress on human rights in Cuba.

The US embargo gives the Cuban government an excuse for problems, a pretext for abuses, and sympathy from governments that might otherwise condemn repressive practices.

In November 2023, the UN General Assembly voted overwhelmingly to condemn the embargo, with 187 countries in favor, the US and Israel opposed, and Ukraine abstaining.

The European Union continued its policy of "critical engagement" with Cuba. In May 2023, High Representative of the EU for Foreign Affairs and Security Policy Josep Borrell visited Cuba. He condemned the US embargo, noting that the EU and Cuba had "differences" regarding the "concept of human rights" but adding that the EU "did not have the capacity nor the will to impose changes in Cuba." In November, EU Special Representative for Human Rights Eamon Gilmore visited Cuba, where he met with the government and civil society groups and called for the release of people who have been arbitrarily detained.

In July, the European Parliament passed a resolution condemning systematic human rights violations and abuses against protesters in Cuba.

In May, the US Secretary of State again listed Cuba as a state sponsor of terrorism, a policy initially implemented by former US President Donald Trump in 2021. President Joe Biden has repeatedly condemned abuses against protesters and imposed targeted sanctions on several officials credibly linked to repression.

In January, the Biden administration announced a "humanitarian parole" program for Cubans who have a financial supporter in the US. In July, the US Department of Homeland Security said that 38,000 Cubans had been vetted and approved for travel in the first six months of the year.

Despite its abysmal human rights record, in October, Cuba was elected to the UN Human Rights Council for the sixth time.

Democratic Republic of Congo

Ongoing armed conflicts in the Democratic Republic of Congo continued to seriously affect civilians. The authorities cracked down on opposition members and the media amid heightened political tensions ahead of the December general election.

In eastern Congo, an offensive by the Rwanda-backed M23 armed group worsened the dire humanitarian situation in North Kivu, forcing more than half-a-million people to flee their homes and pushing the number of displaced people across the country to nearly 7 million—the highest number of internally displaced people in Africa—according to the United Nations. Martial law violated rights without curbing widespread violence and atrocities by armed groups against civilians in Ituri province. Government forces were also involved in serious abuses, including the killing of dozens of civilians during an operation to enforce an August 30 ban on demonstrations in Goma.

Repression against journalists, activists, government critics, and peaceful protesters continued. The authorities also targeted leaders of opposition political parties, restricting their fundamental liberties and arresting party officials.

President Felix Tshisekedi's administration made little progress on promised systemic reforms to break the cycles of violence, abuse, corruption, and impunity that have plagued the country for decades.

Freedoms of Expression, Media, and Peaceful Assembly

Police used excessive force to disrupt peaceful demonstrations, including a protest organized by a coalition of opposition political parties in Kinshasa on May 20, to denounce the high cost of living, the opacity of the electoral process, and the persistent insecurity in eastern Congo.

Authorities targeted artists, journalists, and opposition members online and on social media. On February 10 in Kinshasa, government security agents arrested Junior Nkole, a satirical comedian, because of a short comedy sketch video posted a year earlier that they considered insulting to the president. He was detained for one month before being released without charge.

On May 1, intelligence agents arrested Lens Omelonga, a member of the opposition political party Envol, whom they accused of retweeting a post criticizing the Congolese first lady's foundation. On October 30, Omelonga was sentenced to seven months in prison on a defamation charge with a release date set for December 1.

On May 30, military intelligence agents arrested Salomon Kalonda, a top advisor of one of the main opposition leaders Moïse Katumbi, on the tarmac of Kinshasa's N'djili Airport. At time of writing, Kalonda remained in detention and his trial was ongoing on treason charges. He was accused of being in contact with the M23 armed group and its Rwandan backers.

On June 20, members of the Republican Guard, a military unit that protects the president, arrested opposition member and presidential candidate Franck Diongo in Kinshasa, accusing him of illegal possession of a weapon. He was detained at the military intelligence headquarters and then transferred to Ndolo military prison on July 8 following a military hearing. He was released without charge on July 15.

The government crackdown also had an impact on media coverage of opposition parties as journalists faced threats or physical attacks while covering political events.

Chérubin Okende, a 61-year-old member of parliament and spokesman for Moïse Katumbi's political party, was found dead with gunshot wounds in his car in Kinshasa on July 13. The Congolese government made two arrests, denounced the "assassination," and set up a commission of inquiry. Forensic experts from the UN Organization Stabilization Mission in the Democratic Republic of the Congo (MONUSCO), UN police officers, and South African and Belgian experts provided assistance to the commission. However, the circumstances of Okende's murder were still unknown at time of writing.

On September 8, police arrested prominent journalist Stanis Bujakera—deputy director of the Congolese online news outlet Actualite.cd and reporter for *Jeune Afrique* and the international news agency Reuters—while he was waiting to board a flight at Kinshasa's N'djili Airport. He remained in detention, and his trial was ongoing at time of writing; he is facing several charges, including "forgery and the use of forged documents" and "spreading false information."

Authorities accused Bujakera of fabricating an intelligence note to inform a *Jeune Afrique* article, but the article did not bear his name. His arbitrary arrest and detention sparked an international outcry.

On August 30, government troops shot and killed at least 57 people, and injured scores more, in Goma in an operation to enforce a demonstration ban. A mystic religious sect called Natural Judaic and Messianic Faith Towards the Nations had planned a protest to call on the UN peacekeeping mission and the East African Community regional force to leave the country, but the authorities had banned the demonstration.

At the same gathering, the security forces also arrested several dozen people, and members of the sect stoned a police officer to death. A military court sentenced a colonel from the Republican Guard to death (converted to life imprisonment) and two lower-ranking army officers to 10 years in prison. The trial did not investigate responsibility for the shooting higher up the chain of command. Four civilians were also sentenced to death (converted to life imprisonment) and 59 others, including 8 women, were sentenced to between 10 and 20 years in prison for insurrection and murder of a police officer.

Attacks on Civilians by Armed Groups and Government Forces

More than 100 armed groups were still active in eastern Congo's Ituri, North Kivu, South Kivu, and Tanganyika provinces, including several groups with fighters from neighboring Rwanda, Uganda, and Burundi. Many of their commanders have been implicated in war crimes, including massacres, sexual violence, recruiting children, and pillaging.

In North Kivu, the Rwanda-backed M23 armed group continued its offensive against government troops and controlled large swathes of territory. A coalition of militia fought alongside Congolese soldiers against the M23. Responsible for widespread abuses in 2012 and 2013, including war crimes and crimes against humanity, and dozens of killings in 2022, the M23 committed more unlawful killings, rapes, and other apparent war crimes in areas under their control. Troops from the East African Community force did not intervene to stop the violence.

Various armed actors, some unidentified, killed at least 1,211 civilians in Ituri province between January and October, according to data collected by the Kivu Security Tracker, which documents violence in eastern Congo. This includes at least 80 civilians killed by Congolese security forces. Militia fighters continued to target camps for displaced people, killing dozens of civilians, including women and children.

Intercommunal violence continued in the western province of Mai-Ndombe between the predominantly Teke and Yaka communities over land and customary rights. Dozens of people were reportedly killed while more than 160,000 people remained displaced. The government sent hundreds of surrendered members of Mobondo militia groups to military training centers without any kind of vetting to ensure that new army recruits were not previously involved in serious human rights abuses.

Accountability and Justice

Following national consultations on a new transitional justice initiative, the government reaffirmed its commitment to accountability for serious crimes committed across the country. However, the Tshisekedi administration has not taken any concrete steps to advance justice domestically.

Militia leader Guidon Shimiray Mwissa, wanted by Congolese authorities for serious crimes, including child recruitment and rape, remained active in North Kivu, commanding a faction of the Nduma Defense of Congo-Rénové. Guidon is one of the commanders of a coalition of armed groups, some of them rivals, that fought alongside Congolese forces against the M23.

Former head of police Gen. John Numbi, involved in serious abuses and suspected to be implicated in the 2010 assassination of prominent human rights defender Floribert Chebeya and his driver Fidèle Bazana, was still at large. He fled the country in 2021 after Congolese authorities issued a warrant for his arrest.

The High Military Court made little progress in the appellate trial of dozens of defendants who were sentenced in 2022 for the 2017 murders of two UN investigators, Zaida Catalán and Michael Sharp, and the fates of their Congolese interpreter, Betu Tshintela; motorbike driver, Isaac Kabuayi; and two other unidentified motorbike drivers. So far, judicial authorities have failed to uncover the full truth about the murders.

Little progress was made in a trial to establish culpability for the December 2018 massacres in Yumbi territory in the country's northwest in which at least 535 people were killed. The trial started in 2021.

Gédéon Kyungu, a warlord responsible for atrocities in the southern region of Katanga who escaped from house arrest in Lubumbashi in March 2020, remained at large.

In June, the Congolese government requested that the International Criminal Court (ICC) investigate the upsurge of violence and abuses in North Kivu and signed a memorandum of understanding with the ICC prosecutor outlining their renewed mutual cooperation.

Key International Actors

The UN Joint Human Rights Office reported in August that "the pre-electoral environment in [Congo] is increasingly characterized by a narrowing of civic space and political and electoral violence, arbitrary arrests and detentions, abductions and threats targeting political opponents, excessive use of force against peaceful demonstrators, and hate speech and incitement to violence." The office warned that such abuses "risk damaging the credibility of the electoral process" and "increase the risk of violence."

In late September, President Tshisekedi requested an "accelerated" withdrawal of MONUSCO by the end of 2023, rather than the end of 2024. Tshisekedi said "peacekeeping missions deployed for 25 years ... have failed to cope with the rebellions and armed conflicts."

The United States and the European Union imposed targeted sanctions on several individuals—mostly militia commanders—for their roles in backing abusive armed groups in eastern Congo. The US government sanctioned a senior Rwandan commander while the EU sanctioned a Rwandan army officer, both of whom have been involved in Rwanda Defence Forces (RDF) operations supporting the M23 armed group in North Kivu. By sanctioning RDF commanders for the first time, the US and the EU sent a strong message to Rwanda that its support to the abusive M23 armed group has consequences. The EU and US both sanctioned Congolese officer Col. Tokolonga for his role in abusive militias in the fight against the M23. In July, the EU called for accountability and urged Rwanda to withdraw its troops from eastern Congo.

Troops from the East African Community regional force, which deployed in November 2022, started withdrawing from eastern Congo on December 3.

Ecuador

In a context of fragile democratic institutions, Ecuador has seen a sharp increase in violence and activity by organized crime, which took homicide rates to unprecedented levels.

Longstanding, unaddressed structural problems, including limited enjoyment of social rights, have led to chronic protests and led a growing number of migrants and asylum seekers to leave Ecuador and head north.

In an October 15 runoff election, Ecuadorians chose businessman and former legislator Daniel Noboa, of Acción Democrática Nacional, as their next president. Elections were marked by violence, including the killing of journalist and former legislator Fernando Villavicencio, who was running for president.

On August 20, Ecuadorians voted in a nationwide referendum to halt current and future oil drilling in the heart of Yasuní National Park in the Amazon rainforest.

Allegations of corruption, lack of enforcement of Indigenous peoples' rights, restrictions on access to abortion, and limited protection of children and lesbian, gay, bisexual, and transgender (LGBT) people remain serious concerns.

Violence and Crime

Ecuador's homicide rate surged from 13.7 per 100,000 people in 2021 to 25.9 in 2022. In 2023, it escalated further to about 45, placing Ecuador among the top three most violent Latin American countries, alongside Venezuela and Honduras.

Two large gangs—the Choneros and the Lobos—collaborate with Colombian, Mexican, and Albanian drug traffickers supplying Ecuador. Fighting for territorial control, the gangs have escalated their use of extreme violence, including decapitations and dismemberments, car bombings, and attacks on and killings of judges, prosecutors, journalists, and political candidates.

Extortion by criminal groups continues to grow. Between January and June 2023, the National Police received over 4,600 extortion reports, doubling the number in the same period in 2022.

On July 23, armed men killed Agustín Intriago, mayor of the western city of Manta.

On August 9, an assailant shot and killed presidential candidate Fernando Villavicencio, of the Construye party, as he was leaving a campaign event in Quito, the country's capital. Villavicencio had, for years, exposed government corruption and abuses by organized crime.

Gang violence in the streets of Ecuador is related to violence inside prisons, where overcrowding and lack of state control has enabled gang members to launch around 14 massacres that have taken the lives of more than 600 people since 2019, according to the nongovernmental organization (NGO) Comité Permanente por la Defensa de los Derechos Humanos (CDH). Overcrowding is rooted in punitive drug policies, delays in granting prison benefits, and excessive use of pretrial detention. Prison guards are poorly trained and insufficient for containing violence.

In response to the surge in violence, then-President Guillermo Lasso declared a range of localized and some nationwide states of emergency, suspending constitutional rights. The government deployed the military, conducted prison raids, and authorized civilian use of guns.

Democratic Institutions and the Rule of Law

Democratic institutions remained fragile amid allegations of corruption, interference in appointments to senior positions, and politically motivated removals of authorities. Reports of trial delays, lack of due process, and improper pressure and disciplinary sanctions on courts and judges continued.

In May, then-President Lasso, who was facing an impeachment vote on corruption allegations, invoked an article in the Ecuadorian Constitution to dissolve the legislative National Assembly and call for new elections for president, vice president, and legislators. The constitution allows presidents to govern by decree until a new president takes office, but only on "urgent economic" issues. The Constitutional Court annulled several decrees passed by then-President Lasso during this period.

In September, the president of the Council of Citizen Participation, an independent branch of the government, announced an investigation into the 2019 appointment of constitutional court magistrates. The court, whose members were selected through an independent and transparent process, issued multiple rulings upholding basic human rights. The investigation appeared to be politically motivated and, according to Ecuadorian lawyers, the council lacked the legal mandate to conduct it. On October 6, the Constitutional Court removed the council's president.

Environmental Protection and Indigenous Peoples' Rights

After decades of organizing led by a coalition of Indigenous peoples, youth, and activists, Ecuadorians voted in an August 20 referendum to halt current and future oil drilling in the Ishpingo, Tambococha, and Tiputini (ITT) area of Yasuní National Park—a United Nations World Biosphere Reserve. The ban would help protect the Amazon and the rights of the Taromenane, Tagaeri, and Dugakaeri Indigenous peoples, who live in voluntary isolation, but then-President Lasso and his Energy and Mines Ministry cast doubts on whether the government would comply with the referendum.

Voters also chose to ban all mining in the Chocó Andino reserve, near Quito.

Eduardo Mendúa, an Indigenous leader, was shot dead on February 26 outside his home in the Ecuadorian Amazon. At time of writing, one suspect was on trial while two others remained fugitives. Mendúa opposed oil drilling in an Indigenous community in Sucumbíos province.

Migrants, Asylum Seekers, and Refugees

A record 48,000 Ecuadorians crossed the Darién Gap, a dangerous jungle between Colombia and Panama, between January and September 2023, compared to about 29,000 in all of 2022. Joblessness, low income, general insecurity, and gang threats and violence are some of the factors causing people to leave.

As of late September 2023, over 201,000 foreigners, including over 193,000 Venezuelans, had registered for the regularization process launched in 2022 by then-President Lasso, for Venezuelans who had entered irregularly and for others who had overstayed their visas. Ecuadorian authorities had issued over 78,000 temporary exception residence visas (VIRTE), including over 77,000 for Venezuelan nationals. As of September, about 477,000 Venezuelan migrants and refugees lived in Ecuador.

Ecuador has recognized over 55,800 refugees between 2007 and 2023, most of them Colombian.

Children's Rights

Sexual violence remains a problem in public and private schools. In nearly 26 percent of 20,000-plus sexual violence reports received by the Ministry of Education between January 2014 and July 2023, alleged perpetrators were within the national education system.

In June 2023, Ecuador's Ombudsperson's Office opened a non-judicial investigation, in collaboration with COCASEN, a coalition of civil society organizations working on children's rights, into institutional sexual abuse against adolescents and other children.

In August, the education ministry launched the National Strategy on Comprehensive Sexuality Education, a step toward prevention of sexual violence in schools, in response to the ruling of the Inter-American Court of Human Rights in the case of Paola Guzmán Albarracín.

Ecuadorian human rights organizations and UN experts warned that, in the absence of jobs and education, an increasing number of children are being recruited by criminal groups, subjected to sexual exploitation, and coerced to engage in violence.

Women's and Girls' Rights

Abortion is criminalized in Ecuador, except when a pregnancy threatens a person's health or life or results from rape.

In a 2022 abortion law, Congress included measures that restrict access to the procedure, such as broad conscientious objection for individuals and institutions, a prerequisite to report rapes to authorities, and parental or guardian consent for girls. In 2023, the Constitutional Court maintained a temporary suspension of these measures. A final decision by the court was pending at time of writing.

Stigmatization, mistreatment, fear of criminal prosecution, and a narrow interpretation of the health exception to the abortion ban remain barriers to access.

The Attorney General's Office reported 77 femicides—murders deemed gender-related—between January and September, more than in the same period in

2022. Civil society groups reported 238 femicides between January and the end of September.

Disability Rights

Institutional and social discrimination continued to restrict access for people with disabilities to work, education, and health care.

Ecuador adopted specific procedures in 2022 for responding to emergencies related to people with disabilities.

Sexual Orientation and Gender Identity

The National Assembly has yet to comply with Constitutional Court orders to revise civil marriage provisions to include same-sex couples, allow self-determination in gender recognition procedures, regulate assisted reproduction methods, and allow same-sex couples to register children with their surnames.

The constitution discriminates against same-sex couples by excluding them from access to adoption.

Freedom of Expression

Increased violence and political instability have hampered the work of journalists and media outlets.

Attacks against media workers increased, according to the free speech organization Fundamedios. Death threats and mailed explosive devices to several journalists and media outlets forced five journalists to flee Ecuador between January and September 2023.

Key International Actors

UN High Commissioner for Human Rights Volker Türk visited Ecuador in January, identifying challenges, including socioeconomic inequality, poor prison conditions, and security issues linked to transnational crime. Later, he expressed concerns about rising violence and the killing of Fernando Villavicencio. Various UN experts echoed his concerns, highlighting attacks on justice officials and linking poverty to the increasing violence and insecurity.

The Inter-American Commission on Human Rights condemned "severe instances of violence" during the election campaigns and granted protective measures to Christian Zurita, who became Construye's presidential candidate following the assassination of Villavicencio, and his team.

On August 8, during the first day of an Amazon Summit, Ecuador, along with seven other Amazon countries, signed the Belém Declaration, establishing a collective agenda to protect the Amazon.

Ecuador became a member of the UN Security Council in January 2023 and assumed the presidency in December. Ecuador's draft resolution to strengthen the mandate of the UN Integrated Office in Haiti was adopted unanimously. Ecuador has used its Security Council seat to speak out forcefully on issues like Russian abuses in Ukraine and the importance of cross-border humanitarian aid for northwest Syria. Ecuador has been helping to lead the Security Council's work on the humanitarian situation in Ukraine.

Egypt

The Egyptian government continued to systematically detain and punish peaceful critics and activists, effectively criminalizing peaceful dissent and often equating it with "terrorism." The authorities detained and prosecuted dozens of protesters and activists participating in Palestine solidarity demonstrations in October, as well as in other protests, as the December presidential vote approached. Authorities also detained and prosecuted dozens of family members as well as perceived or actual supporters of former parliament member Ahmed Tantawy as soon as he said in March that he planned to run for president. In November, authorities referred Tantawy to trial over charges related to collecting public endorsements.

Meanwhile, thousands of detainees remained locked up in dire conditions in lengthy pretrial detention or on sentences stemming from unjust trials. Civic space remained severely curtailed as independent organizations operating under draconian laws faced continued judicial and security harassment. Key organizations and members faced criminal charges for their work as well as asset freezes and travel bans. The deteriorating economic situation hampered people's economic and social rights, such as the rights to food, health, and electricity.

August marked 10 years since the Rab'a square massacre on August 14, 2013, during which security forces killed hundreds with total impunity. In May, a national dialogue initiated by President Abdel Fattah al-Sisi the year before began, but by October, it had not resulted in any recognizable policy reforms. Egyptian authorities continued to arrest activists, including members of groups participating in the dialogue, one of whom security forces detained for roughly 10 days in September.

Between April 2022 and September 2023, the authorities released roughly 1,700 unjustly detained prisoners, including some high-profile political detainees, such as Ahmed Douma. However, authorities arrested more than 4,500 during the same period, according to a rights campaign launched by local rights defenders, including some who had just been released.

Abuses by Police and Security Forces in Prisons

Interior Ministry police and National Security agents continued to forcibly disappear critics and dissidents in official and unofficial detention places where detainees are frequently subjected to torture and forced to confess.

Prison conditions remained generally dire with widespread and systematic abuses, including in the newly built prisons that the government used in public relations campaigns to whitewash its abuses. The banning of visits by family members and lawyers and denial of adequate medical care remained pervasive. In March, Salah Soltan, the arbitrarily detained father of a prominent Egyptian-American human rights defender, said in a leaked letter from Badr 1 prison that the prison authorities had deprived him of adequate health care even though he suffers from life-threatening heart and liver diseases, among other complex medical conditions. Families of some detainees in political cases said they had not seen their detained relatives for years because prison authorities denied regular visits, including by lawyers, as well as written or phone communication.

In April, prosecutors refused a request submitted by the Association for Freedom of Thought and Expression to reopen the investigation into the forced disappearance, ill-treatment, and suspicious death in custody of Egyptian economist Aymad Hadhoud.

Military Operations in Sinai

In 2023, Human Rights Watch and the Egyptian rights group Sinai Foundation for Human Rights documented Egyptian security forces' arbitrary detention of women and girls between 2017 and 2022, all of whom were related to suspected members of Wilayat Sina' in North Sinai, the local affiliate of Islamic State (ISIS). Security forces held 12 of the 21 women and girls incommunicado for periods ranging from 2 weeks to 6 months. Relatives of three women said that National Security Agency (NSA) officers abused them at various agency sites, including with beatings and electric shocks. Two other women said that officers verbally abused the women, slapped one in the face, and blindfolded the other.

In September, the United States Department of State added Egypt to its list of countries implicated in using child soldiers based on independent reports that the Egyptian military conducted joint operations with allied militia groups in

North Sinai that recruited children. In August, the Sinai Foundation for Human Rights reported that army-aligned militias in North Sinai recruited boys, some as young as 16, for logistical and combat operations. Some of those children were injured or killed.

Freedoms of Expression and Assembly

The authorities continued their ruthless campaign to silence critics and crush freedom of expression and freedom of assembly. The United Nations Human Rights Committee said in April, in its concluding observations, that it is "concerned that restrictive criminal laws are improperly used to unduly restrict and suppress legitimate freedom of expression, including by journalists."

In October, following the escalation of hostilities in Israel and Palestine, authorities detained and prosecuted dozens of protesters and activists in pro-Palestine protests in Cairo and Alexandria. Authorities also detained dozens of protesters in several unrelated protests in Cairo, Marsa Matrouh, and North Sinai. Security forces routinely cordoned off peaceful protests to prevent more people from joining, and on several occasions, they used batons, sticks, and water cannons to violently disperse protesters.

In September, a court in Mansoura sentenced Mohamed Adel, a prominent activist and former leader of the April 6 Youth Movement, who had been held in unlawful pretrial detention since 2018, to four years in prison on charges of "spreading false news" because of Facebook posts that were critical of the government and the International Monetary Fund (IMF). An appellate court upheld the verdict against him later that month.

On August 20, Egyptian authorities detained prominent politician and veteran news publisher Hisham Kassem after prosecutors charged him with libel and slander based on Facebook posts critical of a former minister. Prosecutors also added vague, broadly worded charges of intentionally "disturbing the authorities" and slander against policemen in Cairo's el-Sayda Zainab Police Station, where Kassem was first interrogated. A Cairo court sentenced Kassem in September to six months in prison and a fine of 20,000 Egyptian pounds (EGP) (about US$647). An appeals court confirmed his sentence in October.

In February, the public prosecution referred three journalists working with *Mada Masr*, one of the few remaining independent media outlets in the country, to trial before the Mansoura Economic Court on charges of insulting members of parliament from the pro-Sisi Nation's Future Party and of misusing social media. The charges are tied to *Mada Masr*'s September 1, 2022 published report about an unannounced corruption investigation that government oversight authorities were reportedly carrying out against senior party members. The trial has not started as of writing, according to a rights lawyer.

Freedom of Association and Attacks on Human Rights Defenders

April marked the deadline set by the government for nongovernmental organizations to register under the draconian 2019 Associations Law, which allows the authorities to shut down and freeze the assets of any group that continues to operate without registration and bans work deemed to be "political" without defining what this means. Several leading human rights activists, such as Hossam Bahgat and Gamal Eid, remained under virtually indefinite travel bans and asset freezes, many stemming from Case 173 in which the major human rights organizations in the country have been prosecuted for over a decade for receiving foreign funds.

In March, a Cairo Emergency State Security court sentenced 29 rights activists belonging to the Egyptian Coordination for Rights and Freedoms, a human rights organization, to prison terms between five years and life following an unfair mass trial. Human Rights Watch and Egyptian organizations have documented that the defendants faced a number of serious due process violations, including months-long enforced disappearances, denial of visits by family members, and lack of meaningful access to legal counsel.

Extraterritorial (Transnational) Repression of Egyptians Abroad

A Human Rights Watch report released in March documented that the Egyptian authorities in recent years have systematically refused to provide or renew the identity documents of dozens of dissidents, journalists, and human rights activists living abroad, apparently in order to pressure them to return to Egypt, where they would face near-certain persecution. The inability to obtain birth certificates or renew essential documents such as passports and ID cards has undermined livelihoods and hampered access to basic rights for the individuals targeted and their dependent family members, including children.

In addition, the authorities continued the systematic targeting of the families of actual or perceived dissidents living abroad. In August, Egyptian authorities detained the fathers of Ahmed Gamal Ziada, an Egyptian journalist living in Brussels who was previously detained and tortured in Egypt, and Fagr al-Adly, a German-Egyptian doctor and activist. The Supreme State Security Prosecution kept both fathers in pretrial detention after charging them with "spreading false news." Authorities released Ziada's father on September 20, and al-Adly's father on October 19, both without trial.

Fair Trials and Due Process

The Egyptian authorities in 2023 widely deployed a videoconference system to remotely conduct pretrial detention hearings and permanently avoid bringing detainees to court in person. The system is inherently abusive as it undermines detainees' right to be brought physically before a judge to assess the legality and conditions of detention, and it curtails their ability to speak to the judge directly and to their lawyers in private. In June, the Supreme State Security Prosecution, which usually investigates political cases, started holding the detention renewal sessions remotely via videoconference as well, with detainees attending the sessions from prisons under police custody.

Economic and Social Rights

In August, the annual inflation rate hit a record of 39.7 percent, exacerbating the economic hardships facing residents of Egypt. In September, a Bloomberg analysis showed that Egypt is the second most vulnerable country to a debt crisis, after Ukraine. In January, the IMF published the details of the new loan agreement with Egypt, worth $3 billion, the fourth IMF-Egypt loan since 2016. The agreement included some improvements over previous loans, including clear conditions around transparency of military-owned businesses for the first time and by expanding coverage of the Takaful and Karama cash transfer conditional assistance programs. In September, the government said that the two programs were covering more than 5 million families (or 22 million people). However, this is only about one-third of families living in or near poverty. Currency devaluation eroded the value of the transfers, making it inadequate to protect people's economic rights from the combined impact of the IMF program's reforms, high inflation, and Egypt's low social spending baseline. Despite the agreement, the military continued to expand its enormous and opaque business ventures in civilian sectors. The first and second quarterly reviews of the agreement due around March and June were postponed to the end of 2023 as the government failed to meet transparency criteria.

Between July and November, the Egyptian government limited electricity use with daily or semi-daily power cutbacks nationwide. The cuts appeared to last longer in rural and impoverished areas and left many people without power amid soaring temperatures, hindering their ability to perform their jobs, including for some healthcare workers, and limiting access to water.

The Egyptian government and a private British company, Academic Assessment Ltd., exposed private data of over 72,000 children, including names, dates of birth, genders, home and email addresses, phone numbers, schools, grade levels, photos, and copies of their passports or national IDs online. It was left unprotected for at least eight months. The children's information was stored as part of a university-application process that some secondary school students are required to complete.

Women's Rights

A Human Rights Watch report released in July found that male guardianship policies continued to hinder women's travel and mobility. For instance, Egypt's Personal Status Law provides that a women can be deemed disobedient by a court and lose the right to spousal maintenance (*nafaqa*) from her husband if she leaves the marital home or works without her husband's consent, with some exceptions.

Authorities continued to prosecute women social media influencers on ill-defined morality charges. In April, an economic court sentenced the Egyptian model and influencer Salma al-Shimy to two years in prison and an EGP 100,000 (about US$3,237) fine on vague charges of publishing sexually provocative videos and violating family values through her social media posts.

Sexual Orientation and Gender Identity

In a report published in February, Human Rights Watch documented the far-reaching offline consequences of online targeting against lesbian, gay, bisexual, and transgender (LGBT) people in Egypt, including entrapment; online extortion, including by organized gangs; online harassment; and reliance on illegitimately obtained digital information based on arbitrary phone searches in prosecutions.

The report included 29 cases in Egypt that involved arrests and prosecutions, including against foreigners, suggesting a coordinated policy—either directed or acquiesced to by senior government officials—to persecute LGBT people.

Human Rights Watch also documented serious abuses by security officials or co-inmates in detention against LGBT people, including being placed in solitary confinement; denied food and water, contact with family, and medical services; and sexually assaulted and subjected to other physical violence.

Egypt does not explicitly criminalize same-sex relations. However, several Egyptian laws restrict the rights to freedom of expression and privacy.

Refugees and Asylum Seekers

In June, following the April outbreak of conflict in Sudan, the Egyptian government issued a decision requiring all Sudanese to obtain visas to enter Egypt. The decision—which made it more difficult for women, children, and older people, who had been previously exempted from visa requirements, to flee the conflict—violated international standards by creating unreasonable and life-threatening delays in processing asylum seekers. As of September, Egypt had received over 317,000 refugees fleeing Sudan's conflict, including 310,000 Sudanese people and over 7,000 people of other nationalities, according to the UN Refugee Agency (UNHCR).

Key International Actors

In September, the US government announced it would waive human rights conditions to provide $235 million out of $300 million in annual military assistance for Fiscal Year 2022, which Congress had previously conditioned on the Egyptian government taking actions to address human rights issues. The US government withheld only $85 million due to lack of progress in "releasing political prisoners, providing detainees with due process, and preventing the intimidation and harassment of American citizens." In the same month, Senator Bob Menendez, chairman of the Senate Foreign Relations Committee, was indicted for allegedly accepting bribes to use his influence to benefit Egypt, including by allowing US military aid despite Egypt's failure to meet human rights conditions. In early October, Senator Ben Cardin, who replaced Menendez as chairman of the committee, said he would put on hold the $235 million previously waived due to inadequate improvements in Egypt's human rights conditions.

In July, Italy's Prime Minister Giorgia Meloni invited Egypt, along with other Middle East and North Africa governments with records of abusing migrants, to a conference in Rome to address irregular migration, in an apparent move toward expanding collaboration on migration control. Between January and October, more than 8,000 Egyptians had arrived by boats in Italy, mostly through Libya. In 2022, Egyptians had constituted the highest number of migrants arriving in Italy by boats as the economic crisis in Egypt continued to deteriorate.

In October, the European Parliament adopted an urgency resolution on Egypt, the fourth in this legislature, urging the Egyptian government to end its repression ahead of the presidential elections. Apart from occasional, faint criticism at the UN Human Rights Council, the European Commission and European Union member states continued to refrain from publicly criticizing the Egyptian government's abuses and taking action to address them; instead, they continued to provide Egypt with security and military support. In October, EU Commission President Ursula von der Leyen proposed additional support to Egypt.

The United Kingdom failed to gain consular access to or secure the release of the detained Egyptian-British pro-democracy activist and blogger Alaa Abdel Fattah.

El Salvador

President Nayib Bukele and his majority in the Legislative Assembly have systematically dismantled democratic checks and balances. In October, despite a constitutional prohibition on immediate re-election, Bukele registered as a candidate for the 2024 general elections. In November, the assembly granted Bukele a six-month leave of absence from the presidency and named Claudia Rodrĭguez, the current head of the National Directorate of Municipal Works, as his substitute.

A state of emergency adopted in March 2022 that suspended basic rights remains in force. Authorities have committed widespread human rights violations, including mass arbitrary detention, enforced disappearances, ill-treatment in detention, and due process violations.

The country's longstanding high levels of gang violence, including homicides and extortion, have significantly decreased in the past two years.

Human rights challenges include high levels of poverty and social exclusion, limited transparency and accountability, and violence against women and lesbian, gay, bisexual, and transgender (LGBT) people.

Security Measures

In March 2022, after a spike in gang violence, the Legislative Assembly adopted a 30-day state of emergency that suspended certain basic rights. The state of emergency has been extended 20 times and remained in force at time of writing.

The assembly also approved a series of measures to address gang violence that allow collective trials, let judges imprison children as young as 12, and dangerously expand the use of counterterrorism legislation and pretrial detention.

During the state of emergency, police and soldiers have conducted hundreds of indiscriminate raids, particularly in low-income neighborhoods, arresting over 73,000 people, including more than 1,600 children. Authorities reported that 7,000 people had been released from prison since the start of the state of emergency.

Many arrests appear to be based on the appearance or social background of detainees or on anonymous calls, and Salvadoran and international human rights groups have documented detentions of hundreds of people with no connections to gangs. Detainees include union and community leaders as well as environmental human rights defenders.

The arrests raised El Salvador's incarcerated population to about 104,000, which is roughly 30,000 more than prisons' capacity. Historically poor conditions in detention—overcrowding, violence, and inadequate access to basic services, including food and drinking water—deteriorated.

In February, the government began holding detainees in a new mega prison, known as the "Center of Confinement of Terrorism," with a capacity of 40,000. Over 12,000 detainees were held there as of August.

At least 189 detainees have died in prison during the state of emergency, human rights groups reported in October. Attorney General Rodolfo Delgado said in June that all investigations into such deaths had been closed.

Gang Violence

Gang violence appears to have significantly decreased following the government's crackdown.

For decades, gangs exerted territorial control over areas throughout the country, committing homicides, forced recruitment of children, rapes and sexual assaults, abductions, extortion, and displacement. Official estimates place the number of gang members between 60,000 and 86,000.

The country's longstanding high homicide rate, which peaked at 105 per 100,000 people in 2015, has sharply diminished since 2019, reaching a historic low in 2022, according to official figures. Extortions have also decreased, authorities reported. However, the lack of transparency and reports of manipulation make it hard to determine the accuracy of government reports or to estimate the true extent of the decrease in violence.

Past administrations' responses to criminal violence have oscillated between obscure negotiations with gangs and iron-fisted security policies. Both have resulted in renewed cycles of violence and human rights violations.

Prior to the crackdown, the Bukele administration negotiated with the country's three largest gangs, the prestigious digital outlet *El Faro* reported, offering prison privileges and employment opportunities in exchange for lowering the homicide rate and for electoral support during 2021 elections. Collapsed government negotiations with the MS-13 gang sparked the wave of violence in March, *El Faro* reported.

The media also reported that in November 2021, a prominent MS-13 leader, Elmer Canales, known as "Crook," was released from prison, where he was serving a 40-year sentence. He was reportedly escorted to Guatemala by a high-level government official. In November, Canales was detained by Mexican authorities and sent to the United States where he was placed in custody. In 2020, Canales, along with 13 other MS-13 members, had been indicted in the US on terrorism charges relating to his alleged involvement in organized crime in the US, Mexico, and El Salvador.

According to the media, at least three other MS-13 leaders have been released, but their whereabouts are unknown.

Economic, Social, and Cultural Rights

Persistent poverty—along with limited access to services and goods, such as housing, health care, education, and food—hinders the realization of economic, social, and cultural rights, especially for women, Indigenous communities, children, older people, LGBT people, and rural people.

Between 2021 and 2022, poverty decreased by 0.5 percent, affecting 29.8 percent of Salvadorans and extreme poverty rose by 0.3 percent, affecting 8.7 percent.

In 2022, working-age Salvadorans completed an average of 8.8 years of schooling, significantly lower than the Latin American average of 10.1. Additionally, 23.5 percent of Salvadorans aged 15-24 were neither employed nor in school in 2022.

Poverty and social exclusion contribute to children and young people joining gangs, increasing risks of violence at home and leading to high levels of migration.

Judicial Independence

In May 2021, the Legislative Assembly, with Bukele's party holding a two-thirds majority, summarily removed and replaced the attorney general and all five judges of the Supreme Court's Constitutional Chamber. The assembly appointed five additional supreme court judges, for a total of 10 of the 15, although each legislative session is only allowed to appoint 5.

In September 2021, legislators passed laws allowing the Supreme Court and the attorney general to dismiss judges and prosecutors who are over 60 years old and expanding their powers to transfer judges and prosecutors to new posts. The laws contradict international human rights standards on judicial independence and have been used to dismiss or transfer independent judges or prosecutors.

A 2021 ruling by the new Constitutional Chamber allowed President Bukele to run for re-election, departing from longstanding jurisprudence interpreting the constitution as forbidding immediate re-election.

Disappearances

For years, gangs and security forces have used disappearances to hide homicides and ensure impunity for abuses.

There is no single registry of missing people, and figures vary by institution. The Attorney General's Office registered over 22,000 reports of missing people between 2014 and 2019. The National Civil Police registered over 12,000 reports during that period. The figures are higher than the estimated 8,000 to 10,000 disappeared during the 12-year civil war (between 1980 and 1992).

Transparency and Anti-Corruption

In August, the Legislative Assembly appointed Roxana Soriano as president of the Court of Accounts, which audits public finances. Soriano had run as a candidate for Congress for President's Bukele's party, Nuevas Ideas, in 2020, which prompted questions about her independence.

In January, the assembly passed a public procurement law that limits scrutiny of "strategic projects of public utility," as defined by a Council of Ministers. The law prevents oversight of public spending and increases opportunities for corruption.

At the time of his removal in May 2021, Attorney General Raúl Melara was investigating six government officials for corruption and irregular purchases related to the Covid-19 response. In January 2022, the Attorney General's Office raided prosecutors who were investigating allegations of corruption and officials' negotiations with gangs. At least four prosecutors fled the country, fearing persecution.

In June 2021, newly named Attorney General Rodolfo Delgado ended a cooperation agreement with the Organization of American States (OAS) to establish an International Commission against Impunity in El Salvador. The commission, which started operating in September 2019, said the government had hindered investigations into corruption involving government officials.

The Bukele administration has weakened the role of the Access to Public Information Agency, including by dismissing one of its members and reforming its regulations in ways that undermine its autonomy.

Freedoms of Expression and Association

The government has created a hostile environment for journalists and members of civil society and discredited their work, including by labeling them as "gang defenders."

The Association of Journalists of El Salvador (APES) reported 147 "press freedom violations" during 2022, including digital harassment, stigmatizing statements targeting journalists, and restrictions on journalists' work and access to public information. In July, APES reported that 17 journalists had fled the country fearing harassment and arbitrary arrest during the state of emergency.

In November, the assembly repealed a law that allowed criminal charges against people who reproduced messages allegedly produced by gangs.

In April, the online outlet *El Faro* announced that it was moving its staff and finances from El Salvador to Costa Rica due to intimidation and smear campaigns. In May, a judge released journalist Víctor Barahona, who was accused of the crime of "unlawful association" and had been detained for almost one year in the context of the state of emergency. He reported experiencing ill-treatment in detention.

In December 2022, El Salvador's Ministry of Economy revoked a permit that allowed Cristosal, a leading human rights organization, to be exempt from paying income tax for being a "public interest" nonprofit. Cristosal took the case to the courts, which have yet to rule.

Access to Abortion

El Salvador criminalizes abortion under all circumstances. Women and girls living in poverty are disproportionately affected. Women have been sentenced to up to 50 years in prison on related charges, including after miscarriages or obstetric emergencies.

In March 2023, the Inter-American Court of Human Rights held a hearing concerning the case of Beatriz, who was denied an abortion by El Salvador in 2013 despite her high-risk pregnancy. The ruling is still pending.

Disability Rights

El Salvador's legislative framework remains inconsistent with international disability rights law, restricting legal capacity of people with intellectual and psychosocial disabilities and lacking measures to improve physical and communications access. Criminal gangs have attacked children with disabilities with high levels of impunity. Bukele's strategy to combat gangs and criminality has disproportionately endangered the rights of people with disabilities to liberty and due process, including the provision of procedural accommodation.

Sexual Orientation and Gender Identity

LGBT people remain targets of homophobic and transphobic violence and discrimination by police, gangs, and the general public. In many cases, LGBT people flee, seeking safety abroad, often to the US.

In February 2022, the Supreme Court ordered the legislature to create a procedure for transgender people to change their names on identity documents to reflect their gender identity. Legislators failed to meet the one-year deadline given by the court and had not complied with the ruling at time of writing.

Key International Actors

For fiscal year 2023, the US provided over US$100 million in bilateral aid to El Salvador, predominantly for strengthening governance and civil society as well as for emergency humanitarian assistance.

In December 2022, the US Department of Treasury sanctioned the presidential legal secretary and the minister of labor under the Global Magnitsky Act, which targets individuals who have engaged in serious rights abuses and corruption. In July 2023, the US Department of State released its *Corrupt and Undemocratic Actors Report*, which imposed sanctions on several former Salvadoran government officials, including two of the country's former presidents.

In October, US Assistant Secretary for Western Hemisphere Affairs, Brian Nichols, traveled to El Salvador and met with President Bukele. They discussed "El Salvador's support for the international mission in Haiti ... bilateral cooperation on rule of law, and mutual efforts to address irregular migration."

More than 122,000 Salvadorans were seeking asylum in other countries in 2022, mostly in the US.

In February, a US federal indictment of MS-13 gang members said that, as part of a negotiated truce, the Bukele administration had protected gang leaders by blocking their extradition and releasing one from prison before he had finished his sentence.

Various United Nations bodies and experts have expressed concern about abuses committed during the state of emergency. In May, three UN experts said the "prolonged state of emergency ... carries the risk of mass violations of the right to a fair trial." In September, the UN High Commissioner for Human Rights expressed concern about the "excessive duration of the current state of emergency, and mass detentions which have occurred in this context." The Salvadoran government has repeatedly abstained on UN General Assembly resolutions condemning Russia's invasion of Ukraine.

In July, a memorandum of understanding between the European Union and El Salvador established a political dialogue on areas of cooperation, including "prevention of violence."

El Salvador announced it has been renegotiating a US$1.3 billion loan with the International Monetary Fund (IMF). Negotiations stalled, seemingly due to El Salvador's September 2021 adoption of bitcoin as a legal tender and concerns about the weakening of judicial independence and the reduction of transparency and accountability. The Inter-American Development Bank approved over US$1.3 billion for El Salvador for 2021-2024. The Central American Bank for Economic Integration has 14 active loans to El Salvador, with funds approved for a total of over US$1.6 billion, including some to government bodies involved in human rights violations, such as the Attorney General's Office and the National Police.

Eritrea

Eritrea continues to suppress basic rights, including to freedom of opinion, religion, and expression, with heightened restrictions in the context of forced mass conscription. Eritrean security forces continued to commit serious rights violations in Ethiopia's Tigray region.

This year marked the 30-year anniversary of President Isaias Afewerki's one-man rule over Eritrea. The country has had no elections since independence in 1993, and the unelected president has refused to implement the 1997 constitution guaranteeing civil rights and limiting executive power. Since 2010, no legislature has met. There is no free press or civil society to keep check on the executive. Impunity remains the norm and due process rights are systematically flouted.

The government continued its abusive indefinite forced military and national conscription service and has failed to either limit the duration of service or stop abuses against conscripts, including children. From mid-2022 through early 2023, it conducted a new mass conscription drive targeting alleged draft evaders. The relatives of alleged conscription evaders were collectively punished.

Eritrea is not a party to the November 2022 cessation of hostilities agreement signed between Ethiopian and Tigrayan authorities. The country's forces remained in parts of Ethiopia's Tigray region where they continued to commit serious violations, including widespread sexual violence and extrajudicial executions, and blocked humanitarian aid from reaching areas under their control.

Despite being a member of the United Nations Human Rights Council, Eritrea refused to cooperate with key UN and African Union (AU) rights mechanisms, including by denying access to the UN special rapporteur on the situation of human rights in Eritrea and ignoring African Commission on Human and Peoples' Rights (ACHPR) decisions.

Eritrea criminalizes consensual same-sex relations with up to seven years' imprisonment.

Abusive, Indefinite Military Conscription and Forced Labor

The government continued to use its uniquely abusive form of national and military service to control the population. Despite legal provisions limiting its duration to 18 months, the service—which is compulsory for all Eritreans aged 18 to 40, male and female—has often been indefinite since the start of the country's border war with Ethiopia between 1998 and 2000. The conscription has forced many Eritreans into military service for years, some decades. Releases from service, if they occur, happen arbitrarily.

Alleged draft evaders are rounded up by police through raids known as *giffas*. From mid-2022 through early 2023, the government of Eritrea conducted an intensive forced recruitment campaign, including of 50- to 60-year-old reservists called up to serve in border areas.

The government collectively punished relatives of alleged draft evaders and deserters, which is illegal under regional and international human rights law. Government security forces and officials evicted older relatives and women with young children from their homes, cut them off from critical food rations, and arbitrarily detained.

The conscription system continues to have a devastating impact on children's education. Students of Warsai Yekalo Secondary School, in the Sawa military camp, some of them still children, are pushed into military service before they finish secondary school, compelling many to drop out. Conscripts have no say about the place and duration of their assignment after Sawa. Conscientious objection is prohibited.

The UN special rapporteur on Eritrea documented a significant number of school-age children being recruited during recent mass conscription drives.

Unlawful Detentions and Enforced Disappearances

Mass roundups and prolonged arbitrary arrests and detentions without access to legal counsel, judicial review, or family visits, sometimes for decades, targeting the government's many perceived opponents are widespread. Detainees are held in horrific conditions.

Many of the alleged draft evaders rounded up near the capital, Asmara, from mid-2022 through early 2023, were initially taken to the notorious military-run Adi Abeito prison, to the north. Residents saw large crowds of people in one of the prison compounds from October 2022 through late January 2023.

Many Eritreans have been disappeared, including top government officials arrested in 2001 after they questioned Isaias' leadership, and are held incommunicado (or died in detention). Sixteen journalists were also arrested that year. Ciham Ali Abdu, daughter of a former information minister, has been held for 11 years since her arrest at age 15. Former finance minister and critic of the president, Berhane Abrehe, has remained in incommunicado detention since September 2018.

Freedom of Religion

The government continues to detain and deny religious liberty to anyone whose religious affiliation does not match the four government "recognized" denominations: Sunni Islam, Eritrean Orthodox, Roman Catholic, and Evangelical (Lutheran) churches.

In 1994, the Isaias regime revoked all Jehovah's Witnesses' Eritrean citizenship and imprisoned them for not voting on the independence referendum and for claiming their conscientious objection to military service. There are 36 Jehovah's Witnesses (10 women and 26 men) reportedly still in detention.

Even the leaders of those recognized faiths are not spared imprisonment. Three Catholic priests, including a bishop who called for peace in Tigray, were arbitrarily held for over two months in late 2022.

Throughout the year, new arrests of Christians were reported. In January, 44 people holding religious services were reportedly detained and sent to Mai Serwa prison, followed by another 103 Christians in April.

The UN special rapporteur on Eritrea said that 44 orthodox monks, supporters of the late patriarch Abune Antonios, were detained in April. A Pentecostal church leader died in detention in April, following 10 years of detention, and was, according to Christian groups, denied the burial chosen by his relatives.

Positively, the UN special rapporteur reported the release of at least 11 Christians from Mai Serwa in the first quarter of the year.

International Protection and Forced Returns of Eritrean Refugees and Asylum Seekers

Indefinite national service has continued to drive Eritreans from their country. The UN Refugee Agency (UNHCR) reported 345,000 Eritrean refugees and asylum seekers in East Africa alone, as of June, out of over 580,000 Eritrean refugees and asylum seekers globally.

Eritreans seeking protection in several countries faced threats to their safety, pushbacks, or forced returns in 2023 by the country's authorities or by Eritrean forces, including in Ethiopia, Israel, and South Sudan and reportedly in Sudan. Forcibly returned Eritreans face serious risks of persecution or other human rights violations. Egypt had previously deported Eritrean asylum seekers in 2022 who were subsequently held in incommunicado detention, according to the UN special rapporteur on Eritrea.

In Sudan, which hosted over 130,000 Eritrean refugees and asylum seekers as of February 2023, asylum space and protection for Eritreans shrank further as conflict broke out in April. Media reported on the alleged abductions and forced returns of Eritrean asylum seekers in Sudan by Eritrean security forces in the early phases of the conflict. In South Sudan, authorities turned back dozens of Eritreans fleeing the conflict in Sudan via flights to South Sudan's capital of Juba in May, despite the serious risks they faced in Sudan.

In Ethiopia, government policies and ongoing fighting since 2020 kept registrations on hold, leaving many Eritreans unregistered. UN special procedures condemned Ethiopia's summary expulsion of hundreds of Eritreans to Eritrea in late June. They called on authorities to provide information on the fates of deportees.

Eritrean asylum seekers abroad protested the celebrations to mark Eritrea's 30th anniversary of independence in various foreign embassies. In Israel, Prime Minister Benjamin Netanyahu threatened to deport Eritrean asylum seekers involved in demonstrations that turned violent outside an event sponsored by the Eritrean embassy. UNHCR urged the Israeli government to refrain from actions that could constitute unlawful refoulement.

Key International Actors

Eritrean forces remained in Ethiopia's Tigray region where they have continued to commit serious violations and to restrict civilians' access to critical aid. The Eritrean government, including President Isaias, have repeatedly denied allegations of serious abuses, calling them "a fantasy."

In June, Eritrea rejoined the regional body, the Intergovernmental Authority on Development (IGAD), almost 16 years after it withdrew in protest of the Ethiopian intervention in Somalia.

Despite its resumption of diplomatic relations with Djibouti in 2018, a decade after border skirmishes, Eritrea continues to withhold information about 13 Djiboutian prisoners of war allegedly captured in 2008.

In July, during a visit to Moscow, Isaias accused the United States' "unipolar world order" of spreading "crises and destruction" around the world.

The US renewed an executive order related to the crisis in Ethiopia and, with it, the sanctions on Gen. Filipos Woldeyohannes, Chief of Staff of Eritrean Defense Forces (EDF), for serious human rights abuses committed by the Eritrean forces in Tigray. In September, the US government added Eritrea for the first time to its list of governments implicated in the recruitment and use of child soldiers and prohibited military assistance to Eritrea under the US Child Soldiers Prevention Act. The European Union maintained individual sanctions, first issued in March 2021, on Eritrea's national security agency head, Maj. Gen. Abraha Kassa, for serious human rights abuses in Eritrea, including killings, arbitrary arrests, enforced disappearances, and torture.

Eswatini

In Eswatini, an absolute monarchy ruled by King Mswati III since 1986, the year 2023 started with the brutal killing of Thulani Maseko, a prominent human rights lawyer and opposition activist. More than two years after a series of protests, there has been no accountability for the security forces' crackdown on pro-democracy protesters. As in past elections where political parties were banned from participating, general elections were held in September with little expectation that they would bring about any meaningful change in the country. Two members of parliament, Mduduzi Bacede Mabuza and Mthandeni Dube, who were arrested in July 2021 were found guilty of all charges against them, including murder and terrorism.

Civic space continues to be under threat as the expression of dissent is routinely restricted. There has been no progress toward instituting the much-awaited multi-stakeholder national dialogue, despite recommendations from regional bodies such as the Southern African Development Community (SADC) and the African Commission on Human and Peoples' Rights (ACHPR).

Conduct of Security Forces

Eswatini authorities have failed to ensure accountability for the security forces' crackdown on pro-democracy protesters that began two years ago, which led to the death of at least 46 people as well as other serious human rights abuses. Since pro-democracy demonstrations began in May 2021, the government has intensified its clampdown on dissenting views by arresting government critics on bogus charges, interfering with peaceful assembly, and resisting calls for democratic reforms. It has failed to conduct a transparent, independent, and impartial investigation into the killings and other human rights violations resulting from the security forces' excessive use of force. Despite repeated calls by Eswatini's international partners and other actors for rights reforms, the government has made no progress in addressing the country's deteriorating human rights record.

Rule of Law

On January 21, Thulani Maseko was fatally shot through the window at his home, where he sat with his wife and two children, in Luhleko, Bhunya, 50 kilometers from the capital, Mbabane. Hours earlier, during an address to his Traditional Regiments at Engabezweni Royal Residence in Matsapha, King Mswati warned those calling for democratic reforms that mercenaries would deal with them, adding that pro-democracy activists have made the country unstable. Human rights activists, on the other hand, accused the government of having a hand in the killing of Maseko, the chairperson of the pro-democracy Multi-Stakeholder Forum (MSF), a coalition of civil society groups and political parties leading the campaign for democracy in Eswatini. The government has denied the allegations of involvement in Maseko's killing. However, nearly a year on, no independent investigation has been initiated and his killers have not been apprehended.

Political dissent and civic and labor activism are subject to harsh punishment under the Terrorism Act of 2008 and the Sedition and Subversive Activities Act of 1938. In July 2021, the authorities arrested two members of parliament, Mduduzi Bacede Mabuza and Mthandeni Dube, on spurious charges of terrorism for supporting pro-democracy protests and calling for democratic reforms. The government also charged them with two killings. Their trial concluded on January 31, and on June 1, they were found guilty of all charges against them, including murder and terrorism. Mabuza and Dube, who pleaded not guilty to all counts, face up to 20 years in prison. A sentencing date has yet to be announced at time of writing.

The murder convictions relate to the deaths of two men, Siphosethu Mntshali and Thando Shongwe, who were hit by a car on June 29, 2021, at one of a number of roadblocks around the country where residents were stopping vehicles and demanding money. Critics have described the verdict as baseless and aimed at stifling dissent in a context where the judiciary is neither impartial nor independent.

Freedoms of Assembly and Association

General elections were held in September as part of the country's Tinkhundla constituency system, under which political parties are banned from participating and nearly all individual candidates are loyal to the king and have his support.

King Mswati exercises absolute authority over all branches of national government and controls local governance structures through his influence over traditional leaders. Political parties have been banned in the country since 1973, which does not meet regional or international standards for the conduct of democratic elections.

While political activists are divided over whether to contest or boycott the elections, what has become apparent is that the MSF, once led by Maseko, has considerably weakened and is unable to speak with a united voice. In early August, the Swaziland Liberation Movement (SWALIMO) and the Swazi Democratic Party (SWADEPA) withdrew from the MSF, accusing the forum of "bullying" and siding with members calling for a boycott of the elections.

Women's and Girls' Rights

While section 28 of the constitution protects women's rights, in reality, women and girls experience cultural norms that marginalize them in a patriarchal society. In 2023, the global Gender Gap Index for Eswatini recorded an index of 0.73. This index quantifies the gap between women and men in four key areas: health, education, economy, and politics and gives them a score from 0 to 1. A score of 1 indicates full equality between women and men, and a score of 0 indicates full inequality.

Eswatini has the highest HIV rate globally, reporting a prevalence of 19.58 percent, and is confronted with many challenges contributing to this rate, including limited availability of stigma-free sexual and reproductive health education, low condom use, the normalization of polygamous marriages and multiple intimate partners, limited access to healthcare services, and HIV/AIDS-related stigma. Disproportionately affected by HIV, girls and young women in Eswatini are five times more likely to be living with HIV compared to boys and young men. This can be attributed to girls and women having limited power to negotiate safe sex practices. Violence against women and girls remains a persistent challenge in the country, with approximately 1 in 3 women and girls experiencing some form of sexual violence by age 18, and 48 percent experiencing some form of sexual violence in their lifetime. In November, a local women's rights group called on the government to declare violence against women a national emergency due to rising incidences of brutal intimate partner violence, rape, and femicide.

Sexual harassment at work remains prevalent. Eswatini has yet to ratify the International Labour Organization (ILO) Violence and Harassment Convention (C190), which requires comprehensive protections to end violence and harassment, including gender-based violence, at work.

Key International Actors

On May 23, 2023, the ACHPR adopted Resolution 554 on the political crisis in Eswatini and the ongoing extrajudicial killings by King Mswati's security forces and mercenaries. The ACHPR expressed concern about the violent killing of Maseko and allegedly many other human rights defenders in Eswatini. The resolution also raised concerns about allegations of the violations of the rights to life, dignity, and freedoms of movement, assembly, and expression, enshrined in the African Charter and international instruments.

Among its recommendations to the Eswatini authorities, the ACHPR called on them to "refrain from any form of victimization, harassment, intimidation and targeting of human rights defenders, political parties, protesters, pro-democracy leaders and campaigners through the arbitrary use of the police and security forces"; withdraw all politically motivated charges and release all political prisoners, including Mabuza and Dube; and establish an independent panel of inquiry to conduct a thorough, transparent, and expeditious investigation into the violence committed against human rights defenders, particularly Maseko's assassination. Other international actors, such as the United Nations and the United States, also condemned Maseko's killing and the targeting of other human rights activists in Eswatini.

The special envoys established in 2021 by South African President Cyril Ramaphosa in his capacity as chairperson of the SADC Organ on Defense, Politics, and Security have not shown any sustained engagement or concrete progress in mediating the crisis in Eswatini. King Mswati agreed to hold a national dialogue under the advisement of President Ramaphosa with the aim of deliberating on the democratic challenges confronted by the country. However, two years later, the dialogue still has not taken place and there appears to be a lack of political will to hold this much-awaited dialogue.

The king decided in 2021 that the national dialogue would be held through the Sibaya or "people's parliament," an annual traditional gathering of the nation. Human rights activists in the country argue that the Sibaya format has traditionally been a monologue where the king talks down to his people while they sit in silence, rather than a meaningful and constructive dialogue. They have also argued that the royal kraal, where the Sibaya takes place, is not a neutral venue for a national conversation about the country's democratic future.

At the special summit of SADC's Organ Troika in Namibia in January to discuss, among other issues, the deteriorating political and security situation in Eswatini, King Mswati was represented by his prime minister, Cleopas Dlamini, who said it would be impossible to hold a national and inclusive multi-stakeholder dialogue in the current climate of ongoing violence in the country.

Ethiopia

The human rights situation in Ethiopia remained precarious, with government security forces, militias, and non-state armed groups responsible for systematic abuses, with impunity remaining the norm.

In August, clashes between the Ethiopian military and militias in the Amhara region escalated, resulting in hundreds of civilian deaths and injuries, the destruction of civilian infrastructure, and displacement. In response, the federal government passed a sweeping state of emergency for the region, but in practice, its provisions have been applied throughout the country.

A November 2022 cessation of hostilities agreement between the federal government and Tigrayan authorities, two of the main warring parties to the conflict in northern Ethiopia, ended active fighting in the Tigray region. However, serious rights abuses against civilians in Tigray continued throughout the year, notably in Western, Northwestern, and Eastern Tigray Zones.

As of September, there were 2.9 million internally displaced people in Ethiopia due to conflict and over 141,000 Ethiopian refugees and asylum seekers in neighboring countries, according to the UN Refugee Agency (UNHCR).

Journalists, civil society organizations, and outspoken public figures faced an increasingly hostile and restrictive reporting environment.

Lesbian, gay, bisexual, and transgender (LGBT) people in Ethiopia faced online harassment and physical attacks. The Addis Ababa Peace and Security Administration Bureau said it was taking action "against institutions where homosexual acts are carried out," such as hotels and other businesses, following massive online reporting. Consensual same-sex relationships are outlawed and carry a penalty of up to 15 years in prison.

Government efforts toward accountability for past and ongoing abuses, including atrocities carried out during the conflict in northern Ethiopia, have been inadequate and lacked transparency and independent oversight.

Conflict in Northern Ethiopia

Since the November 2022 cessation of hostilities agreement, human rights abuses have continued in Tigray.

Months after the truce, Eritrean forces in Tigray committed rape and sexual violence, including sexual slavery, against Tigrayan women and girls, extrajudicial executions, abductions, and pillaged civilian property in areas they occupied. In May, Eritrean forces blocked a humanitarian mission from entering two villages where reports of rape, looting, and destruction of property continued. That same month, Eritrean forces reportedly hindered the work of the African Union Monitoring, Verification, and Compliance Mechanism (AU-MVCM), established to oversee the implementation of the truce.

In Western Tigray Zone, local authorities, Amhara regional forces, and militias known as "Fano" continued an ethnic cleansing campaign and forcibly expelled Tigrayans in November 2022 and January 2023. Reports of detentions and expulsions of Tigrayans from the zone continued through August.

In March, the United Nations World Food Programme (WFP) and the United States Agency for *International* Development (*USAID*) suspended food aid to Tigray after reports emerged that food aid was being "diverted and sold in the local markets." The agencies extended the suspension to all of Ethiopia in June after an investigation uncovered "a widespread and coordinated scheme" by federal and regional government actors to divert food assistance.

Reports of hunger-related deaths increased in June, as the pause severely restricted access to food for an estimated 20 million people requiring food assistance, with people in displacement and refugee camps particularly impacted. In October, WFP and USAID resumed food aid to refugees while maintaining the suspension of assistance to other food-insecure populations.

Abuses by Security Forces and Attacks by Armed Groups

In April, the security situation in the Amhara region deteriorated following the federal government's decision to integrate regional police forces into the federal military. On April 9, two Catholic Relief Services staff members were shot and killed.

In August and September, heavy fighting was reported in and around cities and towns throughout the Amhara region, resulting in hundreds killed and injured, including children and refugees, and damage to civilian property and infrastructure such as hospitals. On August 29, the Office of the UN High Commissioner for Human Rights (OHCHR) found that at least 183 people had been killed in fighting since July. Government security forces also arrested individuals during house-to-house searches in the Amhara region.

On August 5, Ethiopia's parliament declared a sweeping state of emergency in the Amhara region that could be extended to any part of the country as deemed necessary. The emergency declaration grants the government far-reaching powers to arrest criminal suspects without a court order, impose curfews, ban public gatherings, and carry out searches without a warrant.

In February, government security forces responded to unrest following a split within the Ethiopian Orthodox Tewohedo church, resulting in killings and arrests as protesters gathered in Shashemene, Oromia.

The government relaunched its counterinsurgency campaign against the Oromo Liberation Army (OLA) in May after the collapse of peace talks in April. Reports of attacks against the population in Oromia, including Oromo and Amhara communities, continued through August. In June, the International Committee of the Red Cross (ICRC) said the fighting damaged critical infrastructure, including healthcare centers and water systems.

In March, Oromia authorities demolished homes and businesses in Shegar city, a newly formed area near Ethiopia's capital, Addis Ababa, rendering scores of residents in the area homeless. Security forces reportedly beat and shot individuals that protested the demolitions.

In September, Somali civilians in Qoloji displaced persons camp in Ethiopia's Somali region died as a result of clashes involving security forces from the Oromia and Somali region.

Freedoms of Expression, Media, and Association

Civic space continued to erode in the country, with the federal government tightly controlling the environment for reporting on critical issues.

Authorities harassed and detained critical voices, forcing journalists, opposition members, and civil society activists into silence or exile.

On January 5, Ethiopian police arrested and forcibly disappeared for several hours four Ethiopian Human Rights Council (EHRCO) staff members—three human rights staff members, Daniel Tesfaye, Bezuayehu Wondimu, and Bereket Daniel, and their driver Nahom Husen—who were investigating cases of forced evictions outside Addis Ababa. On January 12, an Oromia court released the four staff on bail.

Since the August state of emergency declaration, mass arrests of ethnic Amharas have been reported in the Amhara region and in Addis Ababa. In early August, federal police arrested Christian Tadele, an opposition member of parliament and outspoken critic of the ruling party and the government's actions in the Amhara region; Yohannes Buayelew, a member of the Amhara regional council; and Kassa Teshager, a member of Addis Ababa city council. Christian Tadele and Kassa Teshager were initially held incommunicado.

Between April 3 and 18, Ethiopian authorities arrested eight journalists who had reported on the deteriorating situation in the Amhara region. In August, authorities arrested three more journalists following the state of emergency declaration. In early September, the Ethiopian Human Rights Commission visited detainees held at Awash Arba military camp in the Afar region. Detainees included political figures, such as Christian Tadele, Kassa Teshager, and Sentayehu Chekol, and journalists, such as Abay Zewdu.

In September, police in Tigray region beat and arrested opposition leaders and supporters calling for demonstrations against the interim administrations led by the Tigray People's Liberation Front (TPLF) after authorities refused to authorize the demonstrations.

The federal government repeatedly restricted access to the internet and social media. In Tigray, after years of a prolonged internet shutdown in the region, phone and internet access slowly resumed.

In early February, authorities restricted access to social media platforms after protests broke out in the Oromia region following tensions in the Ethiopian Orthodox church. Authorities disrupted mobile internet at least twice as fighting intensified in the Amhara region.

Due Process and Fair Trial Rights

Ethiopia's federal and regional authorities exerted control over certain judicial processes, with investigative authorities routinely appealing or ignoring court decisions in cases involving critics of the government or opposition figures.

Ethiopian authorities continued to arbitrarily detain seven Oromo Liberation Front figures held since 2020 despite multiple judicial orders directing their release.

Migrants, Refugees, and Asylum Seekers

Public reports began to emerge in June that Ethiopian security forces had rounded up and arbitrarily detained Eritrean refugees, migrants, and asylum seekers in Addis Ababa and other parts of the country. Ethiopian authorities stopped registering newly arriving Eritrean asylum seekers in March 2020.

A group of independent UN experts condemned Ethiopia's summary expulsion of hundreds of Eritreans at the end of June and urged authorities to end further arbitrary arrests and deportations of refugees, asylum seekers, and migrants.

Eritrean refugees in Alemwach camp in the Amhara region also faced attacks by unidentified armed men following the outbreak of fighting in the Amhara region.

The suspension of UN and USAID food assistance operations severely limited access to food for many of the over 900,000 refugees and asylum seekers hosted by Ethiopia as of mid-2023, including Sudanese refugees who arrived since the outbreak of conflict in Sudan in April.

Accountability and Justice

Meaningful accountability for past and present serious abuses, including those committed during the conflict in northern Ethiopia, was lacking.

Following the November 2022 cessation of hostilities agreement, the Ethiopian government committed to implement a national transitional justice policy framework to ensure accountability, truth, reconciliation, and healing. In January 2023, the Ethiopian government released a draft "Policy Options for Transitional Justice" (Green Paper) as a starting point for public consultations. The government began seeking public input in February, including in the Amhara region and parts of the Oromia region still affected by fighting. In September, the second report of the UN-mandated International Commission of Human Rights Experts on Ethiopia (ICHREE) found that the government "failed to effectively investigate violations" and "initiated a flawed transitional justice process."

Political opposition groups, civil society groups, Ethiopian human rights experts, and consultation participants criticized the draft policy document, pointing to its focus on the principle of sovereignty, and the lack of inclusiveness of the consultations. They also questioned the timeliness of the discussion while fighting was ongoing. In Tigray, participants reportedly raised concerns about the document's failure to address Eritrean forces' accountability.

The government continued its campaign against independent rights scrutiny when, in March, it threatened to introduce a resolution at the UN Human Rights Council prematurely terminating the ICHREE's mandate. The government also refused to cooperate with and resisted the work of the African Commission on Human and Peoples' Rights (ACHPR) Commission of Inquiry on Tigray, whose investigation ended in May without the release of a public report on its findings and recommendations.

Key International Actors

In January, the French and German foreign ministers traveled to Ethiopia and pressed for accountability for widespread abuses committed during the two-year armed conflict as a condition for the European Union to normalize its relations with the government. In March, the US and EU member states folded to Ethiopia's threats to prematurely end the ICHREE mandate, agreeing to refer to ICHREE's forthcoming September report as its "final" one. In October, the EU, which previously led the resolution establishing the commission in December 2021, failed to introduce any draft resolution at the UN Human Rights Council session that would either renew ICHREE's mandate or maintain international scrutiny of the human rights situation in Ethiopia.

The EU's Foreign Affairs Council adopted conclusions in April reaffirming the importance of accountability; however, it set the bar for EU's future engagement with Ethiopia low, including by failing to call for Ethiopia's cooperation with ICHREE, and overlooked the lack of progress on key requests, including on justice, that the EU made early in the conflict. In October, the EU announced a €650 million aid package for Ethiopia that had been suspended in late 2020 due to the outbreak of conflict in Tigray as a step toward normalizing relations.

In March, the US government formally recognized that atrocity crimes, including war crimes and crimes against humanity, were committed during the conflict in northern Ethiopia. Three months later, President Joe Biden's administration notified Congress in June that it believed the Ethiopian government was no longer engaging in a "pattern of gross violations of human rights," allowing the country to qualify again for US and international loans and other financial assistance.

In September, the US renewed a 2021 executive order that established a sanctions regime on individuals and entities responsible for human rights abuses in northern Ethiopia. To date, it has only sanctioned Eritrean entities and individuals.

HUMAN
RIGHTS
WATCH
"Like We Were Just Animals"
Pushbacks of People Seeking Protection from Croatia
to Bosnia and Herzegovina

European Union

European Union (EU) member states and institutions made new and renewed existing commitments to uphold and protect rights in 2023. In practice, however, the willingness of the EU to give effect to those commitments too often fell short, particularly when it came to the rights of people at its external borders and members of marginalized communities and in its response to the troubling spread of curbs on civil society.

Migrants, Refugees, and Asylum Seekers

Amid an increase in people arriving at EU borders, particularly by sea, the EU and its member states doubled down on repressive deterrence measures and alliances with abusive countries without regard for human rights.

According to the United Nations Refugee Agency (UNHCR), by November 19, more than 240,800 people arrived irregularly at the EU's southern borders and at least 2,594 died or went missing in the attempt, both figures well over the total for the previous year. UN Children's Fund (UNICEF) estimated that 11 children died or went missing every week in the first half of the year while attempting to cross the central Mediterranean. Major shipwrecks near Italy in February and Greece in June highlighted the deadly consequences of the EU's approach to boat migration.

The European Parliament called in July for a "comprehensive" EU search and rescue mission by member states and the EU border agency Frontex, measures to ensure disembarkation only in places of safety, and assessment by the European Commission of whether individual member states' activities in relation to rescue at sea comport with the Charter of Fundamental Rights and EU and international law. The EU's Fundamental Rights Agency (FRA) called in July for the establishment of independent border monitoring, while mechanisms established so far in Croatia and Greece are neither independent nor effective, according to nongovernmental groups.

EU member states, including Bulgaria, Croatia, Poland, Greece, Hungary, Lithuania, and Latvia, continued to engage in unlawful pushbacks at external borders while Italy and Malta facilitated interceptions at sea and returns to Libya. The

Council of Europe's Committee for the Prevention of Torture called on European countries in March to end unlawful pushbacks and ill-treatment in immigration detention and removal operations. In September, the Court of Justice of the EU ruled that France's systematic refusal of entry of undocumented migrants at the Italian border was unlawful.

The EU continued to support security forces in multiple African countries for migration control purposes. In February, the European Commission handed over the first of five boats to Libyan coast guard forces, deepening its complicity in abuses against migrants in Libya, which the UN called possible crimes against humanity. In July, the EU pledged €105 million to Tunisia for border management despite serious risks to refugees and asylum seekers and racist and xenophobic hate speech at the highest levels of the Tunisian government, as denounced by UN experts. In September, the EU ombudsman opened an inquiry into the agreement. Nongovernmental rescue organizations, already facing obstruction and criminalization, received instructions by Italy to disembark in Tunisia.

In September, the European Commission adopted a "10-point plan for Lampedusa" after the Italian island experienced high numbers of arrivals within a short period of time, overwhelming its perennially inadequate capacity. In addition to rehashing abusive and ineffective policies, the Commission said it was open to considering expanded naval missions in the Mediterranean after the Italian prime minister requested a naval blockade against people on the move.

As of September, 4.2 million people who fled Russia's full-scale invasion of Ukraine enjoyed temporary protection in the EU. Citing difficulties with respect to education, housing, and particularly employment for those fleeing Ukraine, the EU FRA called for long-term measures. In September, EU countries agreed to extend temporary protection until March 2025.

In June, EU states endorsed expedited border procedures despite the lack of sufficient safeguards, increased use of detention, and discretionary approach to what constitutes a "safe third country" to which people can be deported. EU states agreed in October on a proposed regulation that would allow governments to derogate from key rights and safeguards in ill-defined emergency situations. There was no meaningful progress on reforming the dysfunctional system for sharing responsibility for migrants and asylum seekers among EU states. As of August, a total of 2,503 people had been relocated out of Cyprus, Greece, Italy, Malta, and Spain to other EU countries since the 2022 Voluntary Solidarity Mechanism was agreed, about 30 percent of its modest goal.

In July, the European ombudsman launched an inquiry into whether Frontex respects rights during its joint maritime operations and aerial surveillance of the Mediterranean Sea. In a case brought by a Syrian family returned to Türkiye from Greece in 2016 in a joint operation with Frontex, the General Court of the EU ruled in September that Frontex cannot be held responsible for damages because only member states assess asylum applications and make removal decisions.

In its annual report 2023, the FRA noted increased pressure on civil society groups protecting migrants' and refugees' rights at borders in Greece, Italy, Hungary, and Latvia, among others. Civil society organizations face similar pressure in Poland.

Discrimination and Intolerance

Efforts by European institutions to develop and improve standards for tackling different forms of discrimination and intolerance in the European Union were not always matched by the actions of member states.

Many EU governments failed to make sufficient progress to implement or adequately translate into national policy the European Commission's Action Plan Against Racism 2020-2025. Giving effect to the action plan requires states to address structural racial inequities and inequalities—including their historical roots—and to strengthen protection and accountability for victims of racism.

In June, the Council of Europe's European Commission against Racism and Intolerance (ECRI) annual report identified continued discrimination against lesbian, gay, bisexual, transgender, and intersex (LGBTI) people and Roma and Travellers as key trends in Europe, including in EU member states.

Roma children face school segregation, and Roma live in poor housing conditions or face eviction, according to ECRI. In August, ECRI made recommendations to Council of Europe member states to tackle discrimination against Roma and Travellers.

The ECRI annual report identified the undermining of free speech and assembly of LGBTI persons as well as hate speech by politicians and hate-motivated violence directed against LGBTI people as key concerns, while state efforts to combat discrimination were insufficient. In July, ECRI adopted a general recommendation "on preventing and combating intolerance and discrimination against LGBTI persons."

In April, the European Parliament adopted a resolution calling for concrete progress on the adoption of an EU anti-discrimination directive. This directive is needed to address the currently fragmented EU approach to anti-discrimination policies, with some forms of discrimination, such as age, only covered when it comes to employment. The European Parliament called on the EU Council to adopt a new comprehensive anti-discrimination directive that would expand EU-level legal protection against discrimination across the board, including on grounds of gender, racial or ethnic origin, religion or belief, disability, age, and sexual orientation. Previous efforts in the council have been blocked by some member states.

In June, the EU Council approved the EU's accession to the convention on preventing and combating violence against women and domestic violence (the Istanbul Convention), requiring EU institutions to uphold comprehensive standards on prevention, protection, and prosecution in legislation and policies. All EU member states have signed the convention, but six—Bulgaria, Czechia, Hungary, Latvia, Lithuania, and Slovakia—have yet to ratify it, and Poland has threatened to withdraw.

Negotiations on an EU directive to combat violence against women and domestic violence—the first EU-wide measure to address the issue—were ongoing at time of writing.

In September, the EU Council adopted a draft decision calling on member states to ratify the International Labour Organization (ILO) Violence and Harassment Convention (C190).

In September, the European Parliament adopted a resolution against "prostitution," but rejected some harmful parts of a previous draft, indicating a growing understanding of the dangers of criminalization for sex workers and their rights.

In May, the European Parliament Working Group against Antisemitism stressed the need for further education to counter antisemitism and all forms of intolerance and discrimination in the EU. A European Commission-funded joint project by the UN Education, Scientific and Cultural Organization (UNESCO) and the Organization for Security and Co-operation in Europe (OSCE) Office for Democratic Institutions and Human Rights (ODIHR) already seeks to develop the educational dimension of national strategies to combat antisemitism in 12 EU member states.

In October, the FRA published a report on anti-Black racism in the EU based on a survey in 15 member states. It shows that despite EU anti-discrimination legislation and other policy tools to tackle racism, Black people face increased racism, discrimination, and hate crimes in EU member states.

The same month, the head of the FRA described antisemitism as "deeply ingrained racism in European society," with reports of it significantly increasing in France and Germany following the October 7 attacks by Hamas and Israel's response. There are also concerning reports of an increase in Islamophobic incidents in EU states during the same period.

In February, the European Commission appointed Marion Lalisse as the new EU anti-Muslim hatred coordinator; the post had been vacant for over 18 months.

Poverty and Inequality

EU data from June 2023 showed that 95.3 million people (21.6 percent of the population) were "at risk of poverty or social exclusion" during 2022, conditions that threatened their rights. The primary factor contributing to the risk of poverty was unemployment. Poverty rates in Romania, Bulgaria, Greece, Spain, and Latvia exceeded 25 percent, according to EU data. The risk of poverty or social exclusion was slightly higher for women (22.7 percent) than it was for men (20.6 percent).

Mid-year data showed that inflation fell across the bloc in 2023 in relation to food, energy, and the general consumer price index, softening the negative impact on rights of sharp price rises in 2022. However, some countries continued to experience high rates of inflation. June 2023 consumer price inflation in Hungary (19.9 percent) was more than three times the EU average (6.4 percent).

Many EU countries continued to earmark financial support to households and businesses to meet electricity and gas costs.

A European Commission report published in June, based on 2020-2022 living standards data, raised serious concerns about the obstacles people at risk of poverty or social exclusion in some member states face in accessing public services essential to realizing their rights, including water and sanitation, energy, digital communications, bank accounts, and transport. The report highlighted obstacles to accessing these services for marginalized groups, including homeless people, Roma, people with disabilities, single-parent (mostly women-headed) households, and families with three or more children.

In January, the European Commission adopted a report examining member states' progress toward implementing a 2019 recommendation on social protection for workers and self-employed people. The report found that across the 12 EU states reporting data, an estimated 5.6 million "non-standard workers" and 15.3 million self-employed people had no access to unemployment benefits. Data released in November showed that expenditure on social protection increased in 2022 compared to the prior year in all EU states except Malta and Ireland; however, it decreased by 1.5 percent overall as a proportion of total state expenditure (in GDP terms).

In February, an expert group appointed by the Commission published recommendations for improving social protection and addressing poverty, including the establishment of a minimum package of social rights guaranteed at the national level in every EU state.

In February, the European Anti-Poverty Network presented findings showing that while all EU member states had minimum income schemes in place, none meet the actual needs of beneficiaries. The network called on the EU to progress from the 2022 Council recommendation on minimum income toward a binding directive and establish a "right to adequate minimum income" in EU law.

In September, FEANTSA and the Abbé Pierre Foundation, two anti-homelessness organizations, estimated that around 895,000 people are homeless in Europe. The survey included most EU states and the UK.

At time of writing, two EU states, Austria and Latvia, had yet to meet a March 2022 deadline to submit a national action plan on implementing the European Child Guarantee. The EU-wide measure aimed at tackling child poverty requires states to ensure free access to early childhood education and care, free education with one free healthy meal each school day, health care, and housing for all children facing social exclusion or other disadvantages.

In July, the European Parliament, Commission, and Council began negotiating legislation to prevent the employment misclassification of some gig economy workers, who are often subject to precarious work arrangements and low pay.

Rule of Law

Two EU member states, Hungary and Poland, continue to face scrutiny under article 7 of the Treaty on European Union (TEU) over their governments' persistent disregard for the democratic and human rights values on which the EU is founded. Concerns about declining democratic freedoms and shrinking civil society space deepened in many member states while legislative initiatives at the EU level compounded threats to civil society.

Despite persistent concerns over rule of law, on December 13 the European Commission concluded that Hungary had met benchmarks linked to judicial independence and announced it was unfreezing €10 billion in EU cohesion funds. The Commission maintained a freeze on €21 billion in other funds linked to ongoing breaches of rule of law principles in Hungary.

Neither Hungary nor Poland have received EU COVID-19 recovery funds because of their failure to meet core benchmarks. In Poland, these relate to the justice system, and in Hungary to corruption, judicial independence, and transparent decision-making.

An EU Council hearing on Hungary, and a "state of play" update on Hungary and Poland under the article 7 procedure took place in May and November, respectively. While EU member states continued to engage in political dialogue around the procedure, they avoided putting to a vote whether either state's actions constituted a "clear risk of a serious breach" of EU values or to adopt recommendations to addresses these breaches. This is despite another European Parliament resolution in June calling on the Council to do so.

While both governments continued to flout rulings of the EU Court of Justice with little consequence, the European Commission continued efforts to use infringement proceedings to address their breaches of EU law.

In June, the commission launched legal infringement proceedings against Poland over its new law against "Russian influence" that could lead to opposition party members being banned from public office. As of mid-November, 16 EU member states and the European Parliament had joined the European Commission's 2021 infringement against Hungary for its anti-LGBT child protection law. These proceedings are noteworthy in that they target Hungary and Poland for their breach of EU fundamental values and principles as enshrined in article 2 of TEU rather than breaches of individual EU laws.

The European Commission's 2023 *Rule of Law* report and the country-specific recommendations under the 2023 European Semester criticized Hungary's continued use of emergency powers and raised concerns about the independence of the judiciary in Poland.

The *Rule of Law* report highlighted that the concentration of news media ownership remains a "high risk" across the EU, and levels of political independence of media stayed unchanged at "medium risk" overall. The report put media pluralism at "high risk" in five member states in particular—Croatia, Cyprus, Greece, Slovenia, and Malta—and at "very high risk" in Bulgaria, Poland, Romania, and Hungary. It also noted that civil society and human rights defenders faced increasing challenges linked to the narrowing of civic space and highlighted Greece, Spain, Italy, France, Hungary, and Poland.

The European Parliament's Democracy, Rule of Law and Fundamental Rights

Monitoring Group continued its scrutiny of member states, including on the follow-up of court cases concerning the murders of journalists in Malta and Slovakia; ongoing corruption investigations and the dismissal of the prosecutor general in Bulgaria; freedoms of expression and demonstration and policing in France; and the undermining of independent public bodies, freedom of the press, and civil society in Greece. The monitoring group criticized the European

Commission for failing to launch or pursue infringement procedures despite serious democracy and rule of law challenges in member states.

The use of spyware against journalists, lawyers, politicians, and others in Greece, Hungary, Spain, and Poland remains a concern. In a June resolution, the European Parliament called on the council, commission, and individual member states to implement reforms to curb spyware exports and to investigate cases of abuse.

Negotiations on an EU draft Artificial Intelligence (AI) Act are underway in an attempt to regulate AI and related technology across member states. The draft includes provisions that threaten human rights, including through exemptions for protections around AI use in law enforcement and migration and asylum contexts.

The EU is currently developing a regulation on political advertising, expected to be agreed on in 2024, which aims to increase transparency around political advertising online, including during election processes, by setting limitations on how personal data is used in political contexts.

The European Commission's proposed "Defence of Democracy Package" aimed at addressing malign foreign influence, generated intense push-back from civil society over potential stigmatization of foreign-funded groups and the chilling effect such legislation could have on civil society in Europe and abroad.

Foreign Policy

The EU and its member states remained the world's biggest humanitarian donors and leading actors on human rights in multilateral fora. However, Europe's stance in the wake of the hostilities in Israel and Palestine since October 7 and its open support to some repressive governments in pursuit of short-term stability, migration control, and other trade or geopolitical interests highlighted major double standards undermining its standing as a principled global actor.

Russia's invasion of Ukraine remained the EU's top priority. The EU has provided unprecedented financial and humanitarian assistance to Ukraine and supported initiatives for the country's reconstruction. The EU backed unparalleled efforts for accountability, including in international fora, and renewed and expanded the use of sanctions for crimes committed in Ukraine. At time of writing, EU leaders were scheduled to discuss in December the European Commission's recommendation to open EU accession negotiations with Ukraine.

European Council President Charles Michel facilitated talks between Armenia and Azerbaijan over the situation in Nagorno-Karabakh until the September 19 military takeover by Azerbaijan, which resulted in an almost complete depopulation of ethnic Armenians from the region.

The EU or its member states commendably led on several resolutions at the UN Human Rights Council and General Assembly, including on North Korea, Russia, Belarus, Myanmar, Eritrea, Burundi, and Afghanistan, and supported other country-specific and thematic initiatives. However, EU member states' record at the UN was stained by their mixed voting on key resolutions on the hostilities in Israel and Palestine as well as by their reluctance to initiate or support initiatives to address serious human rights abuses in Libya, Egypt, China, Saudi Arabia, Yemen, and Bahrain, among others. In October, the EU did not present a follow-up resolution on the situation in Ethiopia, despite the alarming conclusions of a UN inquiry, which the EU had initiated at the peak of the conflict.

At the end of 2022, Czechia, on behalf of the EU, proposed an amendment to the UN General Assembly's draft budget resolution for 2023 aimed at countering efforts by Russia, China, and like-minded UN member states to defund UN human rights mechanisms. The EU amendment was adopted.

Most EU governments and commissioners failed to acknowledge, let alone address, Israeli authorities' crimes of apartheid and persecution against Palestinians. The EU's response to the hostilities in Israel and Palestine that started in October exposed biases and divisions within the bloc. Commission President Ursula von der Leyen and other officials condemned Hamas' heinous deadly attacks on civilians in Israel but not Israel's cutting off of basic services and aid to civilians in Gaza, and they showed little regard for the loss of Palestinian lives amid Israel's relentless bombardment of Gaza. Efforts by the EU's foreign policy chief, Council President Michel, and some EU governments were key to rejecting efforts to cut vital EU aid to Palestinians and to securing EU calls on Israel to respect international humanitarian law.

The EU's top foreign policy priority in relations with neighbors to the south remained containing migrants' departures toward Europe at any cost, persevering in a failed approach that has exposed the erosion of the bloc's human rights commitments.

Emblematically, in July, the European Commission concluded a deal with Tunisia pledging increased financial support in exchange for cooperation on curbing irregular departures toward Europe. Regrettably hailed as a "blueprint" for the region by EU President von der Leyen, the deal showed no regard for serious abuses against Black African migrants in the country nor to Tunisia President Kais Saied's increasing authoritarianism.

The EU's focus on curbing irregular migration extended to other foreign policy areas, such as development aid and trade. At time of writing, the European Parliament and Council were still negotiating a reform of the EU's Generalised Scheme of Preferences (GSP), which grants trade benefits to developing countries linked to their respect of human rights and labor standards. The reform has stalled due to the council's attempts, rightly opposed by the European Parliament, to condition GSP benefits on migration cooperation. In October, a precautionary four-year rollover of the current GSP regulation was approved, while negotiations for reform continue. Pressure through the GSP was key to securing some positive developments in Sri Lanka and in Bangladesh, but the EU was overly indulgent toward other GSP beneficiaries, such as the Philippines and Pakistan, highlighting the need for a reform to make the scheme more transparent, predictable, and impactful.

In May, the EU adopted the Deforestation-Free Products Regulation, putting the onus on companies registered in EU member states to ensure seven agricultural commodities they import or export have not been produced on land deforested after December 31, 2020, and that the production complied with key human and labor rights standards. Other key pieces of business and human rights-related legislation—notably a directive on mandatory corporate human rights and environmental due diligence and a regulation banning goods made through forced labor from the EU market—remained in the making. Both will likely have a particular impact on the EU's trade and business relations with China, where forced labor is pervasive as part of Beijing's crimes against humanity against Uyghurs and other Turkic Muslims.

While divisions among states persist, the EU seems determined to pursue a "de-risking" approach to China, reducing critical supply chain dependency and strengthening trade ties with other partners in the region. EU statements on China at the UN Human Rights Council remained strong, but the EU did not take further steps, such as leading efforts at this council toward accountability for crimes against humanity in Xinjiang and serious violations elsewhere or expanding the use of the EU's human rights sanctions regime.

Self-censorship continued to underpin the EU's approach to human rights abuses in the Persian Gulf. The EU prioritizes trade, economic, and political ties with governments in the region and remains reluctant to publicly criticize abuses, leaving the matter to yearly, ineffective human rights dialogues.

The same applies to India, with the EU and its governments reluctant to speak openly and exert public pressure over deteriorating human rights conditions under Prime Minister Narendra Modi.

In July, the EU held a summit to reengage with Latin American and Caribbean leaders. The EU continued to play an important role for human rights in Guatemala and Venezuela, but its actions remain insufficient to address other human rights crises in the region, including in Haiti, Nicaragua, Cuba, and El Salvador.

In February, the EU Foreign Affairs Council renewed its Great Lakes Strategy, committing to strengthen support for human rights and international humanitarian law in the region and to speak out actively against violations. The EU's slow and limited response to the renewed crisis in Sudan questioned its capacity to prevent and address atrocities. Continued disengagement from the Sahel region, following a series of military coups, was accompanied by greater attention to Gulf of Guinea states.

In November, in Samoa, the EU signed a new agreement with 79 African, Caribbean and Pacific (ACP) countries to replace the 2000 Cotonou agreement, making human rights one of its engagement priorities. Previously, the signature of the agreement had been blocked since 2021 by Hungary over references to gender and migration.

The EU expanded listings under its Global Human Rights Sanctions regime and ad hoc country regimes to target individuals and entities involved in human rights violations.

Following corruption allegations involving some of its members, the European Parliament adopted new rules aimed at preserving its integrity and transparency. Some political groups took the chance to call into question the integrity of all NGOs and tried to halt the parliament's human rights work. However, the parliament continued to play an important role in advancing human rights, challenging, among others, the European Commission's deal with Tunisia, adopting resolutions on human rights situations of concern around the world, voicing human rights issues during country visits, and adopting principled negotiating positions on important legislation. The Parliament's position in October on the hostilities in Israel and Palestine exposed biases similar to those that characterized the European Council's response. Parliament awarded the 2023 Sakharov Prize for Freedom of Thought to Jina Mahsa Amini and the Woman, Life, Freedom Movement in Iran.

France

Excessive use of force by law enforcement against protesters and detainees persisted in 2023, a year marked by demonstrations and strikes. Actions taken to curb civil society activities raised concerns about the erosion of the rule of law.

Spillover from the hostilities in Israel and Palestine negatively impacted human rights in France with an increase in antisemitic incidents, restrictions on pro-Palestinian protests, and threats to limit rights of asylum seekers and migrants.

Government measures to mitigate the effects of inflation were inadequate to protect the right of many, particularly in economically vulnerable communities, to an adequate standard of living. Migrants and asylum seekers, including children, continued to face inhumane living conditions, detention, and police abuse. Discriminatory identity checks remained widespread.

France continued to reaffirm its commitment to the multilateral human rights protection system but did not consistently prioritize human rights in its foreign policy.

Rule of Law

The European Commission's July 2023 *Rule of Law* report noted that civic space in the country had narrowed. The report noted that authorities suspended public funding for some associations and denied them authorization to conduct certain activities.

In June, the government dissolved Les Soulèvements de la Terre, an umbrella group of environmental activists protesting the construction of a giant water reservoir in Sainte-Soline in western France, adding to growing concerns about curbs on civil society. The Council of State, France's highest administrative court, overturned the dissolution in November, ruling that the decision to shut down the group was an infringement of freedom of association.

In April, France's interior minister threatened to withdraw government funding from the prominent rights group Ligue des droits de l'Homme after it denounced police violence during the Sainte-Soline protests. The European Commission noted in its *Rule of Law* report that several announcements by the interior minister about dissolution proceedings and review of subsidies to certain groups "could be perceived as a means to exert pressure."

Thirty-eight civil society organizations, including Human Rights Watch, and the National Consultative Commission on Human Rights (CNCDH) voiced concerns that a law adopted in March authorizing the use of controversial surveillance technology at the 2024 Olympic and Paralympic Games poses risks to fundamental rights.

The Council of State ruled in October against the interior minister's blanket ban on pro-Palestinian protests in the wake of hostilities in Israel and Palestine, emphasizing that risks of disturbance to public order should be assessed on a case-by-case basis.

In July, the European Commission criticized the frequent use of accelerated procedures for the adoption of laws and noted the often-negative impact on freedoms and rights.

Freedom of Media

In May, Reporters Without Borders (RSF) moved France up from 26th to 24th place in its press freedom index, citing a positive legal and regulatory framework for press freedom and editorial independence, while noting an insufficient legislative framework "to prevent vertical media concentrations in the hands of just a few owners." In its *Rule of Law* report, the European Commission highlighted the persistent problem of media concentration.

In September, after police detained journalist Ariane Lavrilleux and raided her home, media organizations denounced the threat to confidentiality of sources and press freedom. Lavrilleux had co-authored a 2021 investigative article using leaked classified documents on France's alleged complicity in unlawful airstrikes by the Egyptian military.

Prison Conditions

In May, the Controller General of Places of Deprivation of Liberty (CGLPL) again denounced prison overcrowding, a major cause of prisoners' rights violations. The European Court of Human Rights condemned France in July for inhuman and degrading detention conditions and for the lack of an effective remedy for abuses at Fresnes prison.

Discrimination and Intolerance

Interior ministry data published in July showed a 23 percent decrease in racist and antisemitic incidents in 2022 compared to 2021. CNCDH's annual report, released in July, noted "the rise of xenophobic identity-based rhetoric" in public debate and the persistence of racist, antisemitic, anti-Roma, and anti-migrant prejudices.

The interior minister said in early November that the escalation of hostilities in Israel and Palestine had triggered an "explosion" in antisemitic acts on French territory and that the police had carried out almost 500 arrests for such acts since October 7.

In January, the government presented its overdue national plan to combat racism, antisemitism, and discrimination. While a positive step, the plan has significant shortcomings, including a lack of measures to address ethnic profiling and systemic racism.

In July, the UN Committee on the Elimination of Racial Discrimination called on France to address the structural and systemic causes of racial discrimination, including by the police, following the killing of Nahel M., a 17-year-old French citizen of Algerian descent, during a traffic stop. The UN Office of the High Commissioner for Human Rights (OHCHR) called on France to address "deep issues" of racism in policing.

In June, the Council of State upheld a ban on players wearing the hijab in football competitions, rejecting an appeal by the Muslim women's collective "Les Hijabeuses" against the French Football Federation (FFF).

At the end of August, the government banned from schools the abaya, a long robe worn by some Muslim women and girls. The Council of State upheld the ban, rejecting complaints that the ban was discriminatory and could incite hatred against Muslims.

In May, the rights group SOS Homophobia said the number of cases of transphobia sharply increased from 2021 to 2022.

Law Enforcement Abuse

Numerous rights groups and independent bodies, including the CNCDH and the Defender of Rights, criticized law enforcement abuse, particularly during demonstrations and strikes. According to RSF, several clearly identified journalists were "assaulted by security forces while covering protests." The UN special rapporteur on freedom of association; the Council of Europe Commissioner for Human Rights; and a group of seven UN experts, including the special rapporteur on freedom of association, reminded France of the duty to protect the rights to freedom of expression and assembly.

In October, the Council of State issued a decision in a class action suit against police ethnic profiling, brought in 2021 by six rights groups, including Human Rights Watch. While recognizing that ethnic profiling is a serious problem that is taking place and cannot be explained away as isolated cases, the court failed to order French authorities to take necessary measures to end it.

Poverty and Inequality

The government implemented measures to mitigate the effects of the cost-of-living crisis, but the impact on the most vulnerable remained a major concern.

France's National Institute of Statistics (INSEE) said that at the beginning of 2022, 9 million people in metropolitan France—14 percent of the population—were living in material and social deprivation, with 10 percent of people living in households lacking the financial means to heat their homes properly.

In its annual report on housing in France, the Abbé Pierre Foundation found that low-income and precarious workers are disproportionately affected by the rising costs of energy and food.

Migrants and Asylum Seekers

In November, the Senate toughened a highly controversial government bill on immigration that threatens to limit the rights of asylum seekers and migrants. At time of writing, the bill was still pending before parliament.

A police operation launched in Mayotte in April to dismantle informal settlements of undocumented migrants was met with widespread criticism that it violated the rights of migrants and vulnerable people, including children. The CNCDH urged the government to cease the operation, as did United Nations Children's Fund (UNICEF) France, citing the risk of harm to children, particularly unaccompanied children.

People continue to make the dangerous journey across the English Channel in the absence of safe migration and asylum routes to the United Kingdom. France and the UK signed agreements focused on increased surveillance, securitization of the border, and new detention centers.

In May, migrants' rights groups denounced the forcible evictions of migrants and asylum seekers in northern France.

Children's Rights

In August, 18 nongovernmental groups denounced "the pushbacks, confinement, and the lack of care" for unaccompanied children in Menton and Nice and the deterioration of their situation in Alpes-Maritimes department.

The UN Committee on the Rights of the Child in May and the Committee on Economic, Social and Cultural Rights in October pressed France to urgently improve the situation of child asylum seekers and migrants.

In its annual report for 2022 published in April, the Defender of Rights voiced concerns about the number of children held in administrative detention. France continued to detain children, despite repeated calls against it by the CGLPL and two European Court of Human Rights judgments in May, which ruled that detaining migrant children, including infants, violated their rights to liberty and security and constituted inhuman and degrading treatment.

In April, the Defender of Rights highlighted to the Committee on the Rights of the Child violations of children's rights in Mayotte, including the separation of migrant children from their families, their treatment afterward, and reports that police had altered birth dates on official paperwork to facilitate the administrative detention or deportation of unaccompanied minor children.

In August, UNICEF and the Fédération des acteurs de la solidarité highlighted the increasing number of migrant children left to sleep in the streets and voiced concerns about closures of emergency housing units.

Repatriations of French Citizens from Syria

In January and July, France repatriated a total of 57 children and 25 women, who were held in northeast Syria as suspected members of Islamic State (ISIS) or family members of ISIS fighters. In January, the UN Committee against Torture found that France's failure to take steps to protect French women and children in northeast Syria violated its obligations under the Convention against Torture and Other Cruel, Inhuman or Degrading Treatment or Punishment. At time of writing, about 80 French women and 100 French children were reportedly still being held in Syrian camps. 80 French women and 100 French children were reportedly still being held in Syrian camps.

Women's and Girls' Rights

Oxfam said in January that women in France earn on average 28.5 percent less than men, earn 15.8 percent less than men for the same work, and are disproportionately affected by rising prices.

In March, French President Emmanuel Macron announced plans to enshrine in the Constitution "the freedom of women to resort to voluntary termination of pregnancy" as part of a broader constitutional reform. In November, he announced that the proposed constitutional change would be presented to the Council of Ministers by the end of the year.

The High Council for Equality said in its annual report that sexual violence against women in France had increased by nearly one-third in recent years.

France ratified the International Labour Organization (ILO) Violence and Harassment Convention (C190) in April.

Government figures released in September show that intimate partner femicides occur every 2.5 days in France.

Disability Rights

The UN Committee on the Rights of the Child voiced concerns in June that children with disabilities, notably children with intellectual and psychosocial disabilities, continue to face discrimination, particularly in overseas territories and rural areas. It also criticized France for institutionalizing children with disabilities, urging it to take measures to decrease institutionalization and ensure regular monitoring.

International Justice

In October, the French parliament voted to remove a provision from a 2010 law, thus allowing French judicial officials to prosecute individuals for serious international crimes even if those crimes were not criminalized in the domestic legislation of the country where the crimes were committed. The parliament did not, however, address other restrictions that hamper France's justice system from pursuing the prosecution of serious crimes, such as the requirement that an accused be habitually resident in France.

Two May decisions by France's Court of Cassation, related to atrocity crimes in Syria, recognized France's ability to prosecute perpetrators of serious crimes committed outside of France under the principle of universal jurisdiction.

Climate Change Policy and Impacts

France remains one of the EU's biggest greenhouse gas emitters and contributors to the global climate crisis that is taking a growing toll on human rights around the globe. According to government data published in June, greenhouse gas emissions in France fell by 2.7 percent in 2022 compared to 2021. This pace is insufficient to achieve France's 2030 reduction targets, according to the High Council for the Climate. In May, the Conseil d'Etat asked the prime minister to "take all necessary additional measures" to reduce greenhouse gas emissions in line with its commitments.

The National Observatory on the Effects of Global Warming said in August that 2022 was the hottest year on record since 1900, with an average temperature of

14.5 degrees Celsius over mainland France (2.7 degrees higher than the historical average).

Foreign Policy

France reaffirmed its commitment to the multilateral human rights protection system, the protection of civilians in conflict, international criminal justice, women's rights and the fight against sexual violence, the protection of journalists, and the rights of lesbian, gay, bisexual, and transgender (LGBT) people.

However, concrete implementation of these commitments continued to be uneven, with government actions too often failing to match the gravity of global human rights challenges.

At the UN Security Council, France supported the renewal of cross-border delivery of vital humanitarian aid for 4 million Syrians, particularly in the context of the February 2023 earthquake in southern Türkiye and northern Syria, and deplored Russia's veto of this renewal in July.

In October, France voted in favor of a UN Security Council resolution condemning all violence against civilians in Israel and Palestine and calling on all parties to comply with international humanitarian law (IHL). The resolution was vetoed by the United States. France also voted for a resolution adopted at the UN General Assembly calling for a "humanitarian truce," the parties to respect international law, unimpeded aid to the Gaza Strip, and the "immediate and unconditional release" of all civilians held hostage. According to French authorities, 40 French nationals were killed during the October 7 Hamas-led attack in Israel; 8 others were missing or taken hostage, 4 of whom had been released at time of writing. France condemned Israeli settler violence against Palestinians in the West Bank, calling it a "policy of terror." In November, France voted in favor of a second UN Security Council resolution focused on the plight of children in the Gaza Strip and Israel that also called for humanitarian pauses and full compliance with IHL. This second council resolution passed, with the US, UK, and Russia abstaining.

At the UN Human Rights Council, France supported accountability for serious crimes in Ukraine and the renewal of the mandate of the special rapporteurs on Russia and Belarus. France also voted in favor of a resolution establishing a fact-finding mission for Sudan, but it did not support the continuation of the international commission of human rights experts on Ethiopia, despite ongoing serious abuses there and France's international commitment to fight impunity for the most serious crimes.

France has pursued or strengthened its commercial and strategic ties with grossly abusive governments at the expense of the defense of rights.

In April, during his visit to China with European Commission President Ursula Von der Leyen, President Macron remained silent on Chinese crimes against humanity against Uyghurs and other Turkic communities in Xinjiang and other serious abuses by Chinese President Xi Jinping's government.

In June, for the second time in less than a year, Macron received the crown prince and de facto ruler of Saudi Arabia, Mohammed bin Salman, known as MBS, at the Elysée Palace, with the aim of boosting France's partnership with Saudi Arabia. Their meeting took place despite ongoing brutal repression under MBS and his approval of the murder of journalist Jamal Khashoggi, according to US intelligence.

The French president made Indian Prime Minister Narendra Modi his guest of honor for the July 14 military parade and awarded him the highest rank of France's Legion of Honor, despite the Modi government's increasing repression of Muslims and other minorities, and crackdown on civil society and media freedom. During the visit, India announced a multibillion-dollar arms deal with France.

France also pursued its close partnership with the United Arab Emirates (UAE) despite widespread human rights abuses under President Mohammed bin Zayed al-Nahyan. France's annual report on arms exports lists the UAE as its biggest arms buyer in 2022.

France pulled out its troops from Burkina Faso in February and announced its withdrawal from Niger in late September in the wake of military coups in these countries and against a backdrop of growing hostility to the French military presence in the region. The French journalist Olivier Dubois, kidnapped in Mali in April 2021, was released in March.

In September, President Macron presented a new plan to meet the government's commitment to reduce greenhouse gas emissions by 55 percent compared to

1990 levels by 2030. Despite some positive measures, such as investments in public transport, the plan does not phase out oil and gas and was criticized for its lack of ambition.

In October, France was re-elected, on a closed slate for the Western Group, to the UN Human Rights Council for the period 2024-2026.

Georgia

Georgia's human rights record remained uneven in 2023. Tensions over the government's implementation of the 12 priorities set by the European Union for Georgia's EU candidacy—which include important human rights benchmarks—dominated political developments.

Authorities attempted to adopt "foreign agent" legislation that would have undermined freedom of expression. Lack of accountability for law enforcement abuses, especially related to freedom of assembly, persisted. Other human rights concerns included restrictions and attacks on media freedom as well as unfair labor conditions. The National Human Rights Strategy failed to include the rights of lesbian, gay, bisexual, and transgender (LGBT) people.

In November, the European Commission recommended Georgia be granted EU candidate country status "on the understanding" that it would undertake further reforms.

Freedoms of Association and Expression

In February, a faction from the ruling Georgian Dream (GD) parliamentary majority initiated two versions of a controversial bill: one requiring nongovernmental groups and media that receive 20 percent or more of their annual revenue from abroad to register as "agents of foreign influence"; the other imposing similar requirements on individuals. Failure to comply would have resulted in harsh penalties, including criminal prosecution. The bills drew widespread criticism from the Public Defender's Office (PDO), Georgian civil society, the United Nations, the Council of Europe, the EU, and others. While the authorities claimed that they intended the bills to boost funding transparency, their public statements suggested that they intended to stigmatize and penalize independent groups, media, and critical voices.

On March 7, despite overwhelming public opposition, GD hastily passed one of the bills on the first reading. After two days of massive protests, GD withdrew the bill, citing their failure to explain it to the public.

The government's hostile rhetoric toward civil society organizations persisted throughout the year, particularly targeting watchdog groups. The UN special rapporteur on human rights defenders, after an official country visit, expressed concern about "systematic efforts to undermine human rights defenders," including government smear campaigns against civil society members on social media.

In September, the State Security Service launched an investigation into an alleged "plot" funded by the US development agency (USAID) to recruit activists to foment civil unrest and overthrow the Georgian government. The US embassy flatly denied the allegations. At time of writing, the Georgian security services had questioned a dozen activists, making them sign non-disclosure statements to prevent them from discussing the case publicly.

Law Enforcement Abuses and Lack of Accountability

The PDO and civil society organizations reported several instances of excessive use of police force and unlawful state interference with freedom of assembly in 2023.

Riot police used water cannons and massive amounts of tear gas to disperse thousands of peaceful demonstrators who spontaneously gathered to protest the "foreign agents" bill. The PDO said these measures were disproportionate and unnecessary. The Special Investigation Service (SIS), which investigates instances of abuse of office, launched an investigation into police conduct during the protests after receiving 124 complaints about abuse. The investigation was pending at time of writing.

Georgian rights groups criticized the persistent problem of police use of administrative charges to detain peaceful protest participants. Court rulings on administrative offenses are often based solely on the testimonies of police officers and disregard fair trial norms.

In June, police detained several activists, including members of prominent human rights groups, on charges of petty hooliganism and disobeying police order for holding banners that intentionally distorted the first name of the prime minister, blank posters, and a copy of the constitution. After 48 hours, police released them. In September, courts fined them for petty hooliganism and disobeying police.

In July, police detained about 20 participants of an anti-war protest against a Russian cruise ship in Batumi. In August, the SIS began investigating alleged physical and verbal abuse by the police during these detentions. The investigations were pending at time of writing.

In October, the GD rushed through amendments to the law on rallies and demonstrations, granting police broad discretion to disband or detain protesters who try to erect non-permanent "structures," such as tents and stages. Failure to comply would result in a 500 Georgian lari (GEL) (about US$190) fine or up to 15 days' detention.

From January to October, the SIS received 1,775 complaints of alleged abuses by law enforcement and launched criminal investigations into 178 cases. Over the same period, the PDO received 72 complaints of alleged ill-treatment by law enforcement.

Attacks on Journalists and the Media

Numerous threats and attacks targeted media professionals. By October, the SIS had received 37 complaints and launched 12 investigations into unlawful interference with journalistic activities.

In June, an assailant beat Misha Mshvildadze, a Formula TV co-founder and host. The assailant later claimed in his social media post that the attack was in response to Mshvildadze's criticism of the Georgian Patriarchate. Police arrested the perpetrator, and in September, the SIS closed any further investigation, referring the case to court. In October, a court sentenced the perpetrator to 6 months in prison. Mshvildadze raised concerns about the SIS investigation, saying it failed to properly examine CCTV video footage that allegedly placed a Security Service employee at the attack site, indicating potential state involvement.

In February, the parliament passed new, restrictive regulations on media accreditation, which, among other things, allow the authorities to ban journalists from parliament for asking members of parliament (MPs) questions after they refuse to be interviewed. Officials cited alleged harassment of MPs by the media to justify the amendments. The PDO criticized the rules for restricting media freedom and lacking an effective appeals mechanism. After the rule's adoption, parliament suspended the accreditation of nine journalists and cameramen from leading critical media outlets. The journalists claimed this was due to their critical questions.

In June, the president of Georgia pardoned Nika Gvaramia, director of Mtavari Arkhi TV, a leading critical television channel. The pardon followed a June Supreme Court decision upholding Gvaramia's highly contested criminal conviction for abuse of office charges over managerial decisions he made while leading another private TV company.

In October, parliament rapidly adopted controversial amendments expanding the power of the Georgian National Communications Commission to penalize broadcast content allegedly containing obscenity, incitement to hatred, or terrorism. The amendments empowered the commission to impose sanctions, including hefty fines and suspension of an outlet's broadcasting authorization. Previously, the commission could take such action only in response to complaints. Georgian rights groups condemned the amendments as posing serious risks of censorship and arbitrary interference with the work of broadcasters who criticize the authorities, due in part to the commission's low level of independence.

Labor Rights

Despite some legislative improvements, labor rights remain a concern. Overtime regulations are weak, wage theft is common, social protections are minimal, and unions lack legal guarantees that would allow them to effectively bargain for systemic changes.

There were numerous protests and strikes in 2023 by metro workers, app-based workers, video journalists, doctors, culture workers, factory workers, construction workers, and miners. They called for better pay, improved working conditions, and the enforcement of existing labor laws and collective bargaining agreements.

Georgia's Labor Inspectorate regained its full mandate to enforce both labor and safety rights in 2021, but its effectiveness has been hampered by a lack of resources, limited public trust, and a failure to conduct systemic preventative inspections. In April 2023, the inspectorate began redacting employers' names from its public inspection reports, effectively shielding rights-abusing employers from public scrutiny. In August, it reverted to disclosing names after engaging with civil society.

The government has largely abandoned wage regulation. The monthly minimum wage has been 20 GEL (about US$7) since 1999 and is 12 times lower than the subsistence minimum and 88.5 times lower than the estimated living wage of 1,770 GEL (about US$660). In a positive development, the government instituted an increased minimum wage for healthcare workers in clinics that participate in the state's universal healthcare program.

Workplace safety remains problematic. Construction remains the most dangerous sector for workers.

Sexual Orientation, Gender Identity, and Gender Equality

The Tbilisi Pride Festival, planned for July 8, was abruptly canceled after far right-wing hate groups violently stormed the venue. They looted and vandalized festival property in the presence of police and journalists. Although hate groups had called for anti-LGBT protests at the festival ahead of time, authorities failed to stop violent groups from entering the venue.

The authorities launched an investigation but did not arrest anyone in connection with the attack. Tbilisi Pride organizers' request for victim's status in the investigation was pending at time of writing.

The 2023-2030 National Human Rights Strategy adopted in March does not mention the rights of LGBT people, in contrast to the previous strategy. Following criticism from Georgian groups and international partners, the government's Human Rights Secretariat promised to cover missing topics in the strategy's action plan.

In December 2022, the European Court of Human Rights ruled against Georgia for failing to allow transgender individuals to change the gender marker on their official documents without undergoing medical sex reassignment procedures.

The State Concept on Gender Equality, adopted in December 2022, fails to embrace the concept of gender in all its diversity, thereby not recognizing the rights of all women. During parliamentary review, members dropped language addressing the needs and priorities of LGBT individuals.

Georgia has not ratified the International Labour Organization (ILO) Violence and Harassment Convention (C190), which establishes international legal standards for preventing and responding to violence and harassment, including gender-based violence, at work.

Key International Actors

In November, the European Commission published its "Enlargement Report" on Georgia, marking as fulfilled 3 of 12 reform priorities: progress on gender equality and gender-based violence, Georgian courts' proactive consideration of European Court of Human Rights judgments, and the nomination of an independent public defender. The Commission recommended Georgia be granted EU candidate country status "on the understanding" that Georgia would address the remaining priorities, including to guarantee a free and pluralistic media environment, strengthen rights protections for "vulnerable groups," and involve civil society in decision-making processes at all levels. The European Commission also highlighted that Georgia is expected to considerably increase its alignment with EU foreign policy. At time of writing, the final decision by EU member states on whether to grant Georgia candidate status was pending and expected in December 2023.

In a February 2023 resolution, the European Parliament expressed "grave concern" about the deteriorating health of imprisoned former President Mikheil Saakashvili, calling for his release and access to "proper medical treatment" abroad.

A number of embassies and international partners condemned the attack on Tbilisi Pride in July.

In its March concluding observations, the UN Committee on the Elimination of Discrimination against Women urged the government to ensure that all forms of gender-based violence against women and girls, including domestic and sexual violence, are effectively investigated and that perpetrators are prosecuted. It also criticized the government for slow progress on amending legislation to adopt a definition of rape based on lack of consent in line with the Istanbul Convention, rather than on the use of violence or threat of violence.

In its April concluding observations, the UN Committee on the Rights of Persons with Disabilities welcomed legislative and policy progress made by Georgia but criticized the "prevalence of the medical approach to disability" in the country's disability assessment system. It called on Georgia to adopt a comprehensive strategy and national action plan to implement the Convention on the Rights of Persons with Disabilities.

In October, the UN Subcommittee on the Prevention of Torture visited Georgia. While noting "significant progress," the subcommittee called, inter alia, for additional measures to reduce the prison population and strengthen rehabilitation programs.

In April, the US State Department sanctioned four Georgian judges for "their involvement in significant corruption," banning them and their immediate families from entering the United States.

Germany

Germany's rights record in 2023 was marred by a large increase in far-right motivated demonstrations as well as a rise in attacks against migrants, Jews, Muslims, Sinti, Roma, and lesbian, gay, bisexual, and transgender (LGBT) people, often constituting hate crimes.

Following the extension of the European Union's Temporary Protection Directive for displaced people fleeing Russia's full-scale invasion of Ukraine, the government extended special protection for refugees from Ukraine, with over 1 million counted in Germany, while a new humanitarian program for Afghans in response to the Taliban takeover was plagued with problems and delays in implementation.

Germany failed to uphold its international obligations in its pursuit of a bilateral reparations process to address colonial crimes it committed in Namibia between 1904 and 1908.

Discrimination and Intolerance

In January 2023, the Commissioner for Integration and Anti-Racism called for more data collection and protective and preventive measures to fight racism, drawing attention to how racist attacks and structural racial inequalities continue to impact people's everyday lives, including in the education, housing, employment, and health sectors.

Official data showed a record high 58,916 politically motivated crimes in 2022, including 4,043 acts of violence. Antisemitic crimes slightly decreased in 2022 by 12.75 percent (2,641 reported acts) compared to the previous year (3,027 acts), but the Interior Ministry warned that 84 percent of these acts had been committed with right-wing motifs. In its 2023 annual report, Germany's main antisemitism network counted 2,480 reported cases of antisemitism in 2022.

There were three times as many right-wing demonstrations in the first half of 2023 as in the first half of 2022, many featuring anti-migrant themes.

The final report of the Independent Expert Council on anti-Muslim hatred, based on three years of monitoring, concluded that anti-Muslim hatred is widespread, with openly identifiable Muslims like women or girls wearing headscarves particularly affected. Anti-Muslim racism is present in everyday life, particularly at school, at work, and online.

In June, state-level interior ministers committed to strengthening their prevention of anti-LGBT hate crimes and violence, including through law enforcement training and the introduction of designated contact persons at police stations throughout Germany. The federal interior minister said the police registered over 1,400 hate crimes against members of the LGBT communities in Germany. Several attacks occurred at Christopher Street Day Pride parades, one of which ended in the death of a man who defended two lesbian women. In May, the federal human rights commissioner expressed worries about setbacks for LGBT rights.

The Independent Federal Anti-Discrimination Agency said it received 8,827 requests for advice in 2022, an increase of 14 percent over 2021 and 50 percent over 2019. Of all complaints, 43 percent related to racial discrimination, 27 percent to disability-based discrimination, 21 percent to gender-based discrimination, and 10 percent to age discrimination. Most people seeking advice experienced discrimination in the labor market (27 percent). The agency called for reforms to Germany's anti-discrimination law to make it applicable to public institutions, including the police and judiciary. In its coalition agreement 2021-2025, the three-party coalition government promised reforms to strengthen and widen the scope of the law but had not taken action at time of writing.

In December, the government amended the national police law, which, among other reforms, introduced mandatory receipts of police stops to tackle racial profiling.

International Justice

German judicial officials continued to collect witness testimony about serious crimes committed in Ukraine as part of a structural investigation opened in 2022.

The trial on charges of crimes against humanity of Alaa M., who allegedly worked as a physician in two military hospitals in Syria, continued in Frankfurt.

In January, the NGO Fortify Rights and 16 individuals filed a criminal complaint with German judicial officials against senior Myanmar military generals and others for genocide, war crimes, and crimes against humanity.

In February, the Higher Regional Court of Berlin convicted and sentenced to life imprisonment a member of the Syrian Free Palestine Movement, Moafak D., for his involvement in war crimes and murder committed in Syria in 2014.

The Federal Court of Justice upheld the Higher Regional Court of Koblenz's conviction of Eyad al-Gharib, a former Syrian intelligence official, for aiding and abetting crimes against humanity. The appeal of Anwar R., a former member of Syria's General Intelligence Directorate, of his conviction for crimes against humanity was pending at time of writing.

Refugees, Asylum Seekers, and Migrants

According to government data, 188,967 people applied for asylum in Germany in the first six months of 2023, an increase of 78.1 percent over the previous year. Most applicants came from Syria, Afghanistan, Türkiye, Iran, and Iraq.

There were 1.1 million Ukrainians in Germany in April, the largest group of foreign nationals in the country. The Interior Ministry said that by July, 243,000 people fleeing war in Ukraine had left Germany, either returning to Ukraine or moving elsewhere.

Following the extension of the EU Temporary Protection Directive, the government extended its exceptional policy allowing people fleeing the war in Ukraine to reside in Germany, allowing them to work and access social protection, until March 3, 2024.

Asylum seekers and refugees spent weeks or months in large reception centers due to a lack of affordable housing in various regions. Despite a significant increase in reception capacity throughout the country in the aftermath of the war in Ukraine, many centers are almost full.

After the Taliban takeover in Afghanistan in 2021, according to the Interior Ministry, Germany accepted over 28,000 former local staff and their family members and thousands of human rights defenders and journalists via other admission programs or on humanitarian grounds. In March, the government temporarily suspended a special program to bring to Germany up to 1,000 at-risk Afghans per month, citing concerns with screening procedures. Though the government reinstated the program, not a single Afghan had benefited at time of writing.

In January, German authorities deported Tajik opposition activist Abdullohi Shamsiddin despite serious concerns of persecution and torture upon his return to Tajikistan. In March, following an unfair trial, a Tajik court convicted him of inciting violent government overthrow and sentenced him to seven years' imprisonment.

Sexual Orientation and Gender Identity

In August, the government agreed on a draft self-determination law (Selbstbestimmungsgesetz), which will allow transgender, intersex, and non-binary people to change their name and gender on official documents to reflect their gender identity via a simple administrative procedure and without the need for discriminatory "expert reports."

Rule of Law

In its annual *Rule of Law Report*https://commission.europa.eu/document/download/6a02c9dc-e9c3-4aef-a12e-633f80b670d7_en?filename=16_1_52572_coun_chap_germany_en.pdf, the European Commission noted a lack of adequate resources for the justice system and recommended improved monitoring of lobby activities around legislative texts and the creation of a legal basis for journalists' right to information from federal authorities.

Germany dropped to rank 21, down from rank 16 last year, in Reporters Without Borders' press freedom rankings for 2023 due to rising violence and verbal attacks against journalists, decreasing media pluralism, fragmented access to information, and draft bills that "threaten the protection of journalistic sources."

In October, Berlin authorities imposed blanket bans on pro-Palestine protests following an escalation of hostilities in Israel and Palestine and a sharp rise in civilian casualties. They failed to conduct individual assessments of whether the restrictions on free assembly were necessary and proportionate.

In May, Berlin police had already banned several Palestinian Nakba Day protests citing cases of violence and antisemitic statements. Police intervened in a protest held in defiance of the ban, organized by Israeli and German Jews and Palestinians, reportedly over antisemitic statements and unlawful activities. In other cities, like Frankfurt, demonstrations were allowed.

Also in May, prosecutors ordered the seizure of assets linked to the organization Last Generation, known for blocking roads and targeting artwork to press for action against climate change, as part of an investigation into its finances.

Business and Human Rights

The Supply Chain Act came into force in January. While an important step, the law—which obliges companies to identify, prevent, address, and publicly report on human rights risks in their supply chains—only allows regulators to initiate administrative action or impose penalties in limited situations set out in the act. The law does not include any provisions to hold companies liable in courts and has only limited application to entities in the value chain.

Women's and Girls' Rights

According to government statistics published in July, police registered 240,547 cases of domestic violence in 2022, an increase of 8.5 percent over 2021. Women comprised over 70 percent of victims. A study showed that the number of reported cases perpetrated by an intimate partner rose by 9.4 percent compared to 2021, with women comprising 80 percent of victims. Intrafamily violence, particularly affecting children, increased by 7.7 percent. Experts suggest precarious socioeconomic situations following the Covid-19 pandemic or greater reporting of cases to the police may be responsible for the increase.

Authorities pledged more support for those affected, including investment in shelters for domestic violence victims; according to a statement made by the Association of Women's Shelters in July, 14,000 more places needed. In a survey commissioned by Plan International Germany, 33 percent of men aged 18 to 35 said violence against women could be "acceptable" and 34 percent said they had previously used violence against a woman partner.

In June, Germany ratified the International Labour Organization (ILO) Violence and Harassment Convention (C190), which sets out global standards for preventing and responding to violence and harassment at work.

Abortion remains illegal under the criminal code except in the first 12 weeks of pregnancy where there is a risk to the health of the mother, a pregnancy resulting from rape, or a doctor's certification following mandatory counseling. Women's rights groups continued to call for the decriminalization of abortion and elimination of barriers such as mandatory counseling. In a case brought by the group 40 Days for Life, a high court ruled in June that banning peaceful protests, including prayer vigils, outside of abortion clinics is unconstitutional. Service providers said that such protests intimidate patients and deter them from seeking care.

Poverty and Inequality

In January, the "Citizen's Income" scheme replaced a previous form of social security support with marginally higher allowances. Anti-poverty groups said the amount remained insufficient and criticized the punitive sanctions against recipients deemed non-compliant. At time of writing, proposed measures to tackle rising child poverty and impose caps on rent increases had not been adopted.

An increase in the cost of living, including food prices, left many unable to afford an adequate standard of living. Single-parent households, 88 percent of which are women-led, were particularly affected.

Climate Change and Policy Impacts

As the EU's biggest greenhouse gas emitter, Germany is a significant contributor to the climate crisis and its growing toll on human rights around the globe.

In July, the German Environment Agency said total greenhouse emissions in 2022 decreased by 1.9 percent compared to the previous year, but raised concerns about an increase in the use of coal. Germany is still among the world's top 10 coal producers and supports new fossil fuel infrastructure inside and outside of Germany. According to the Climate Action Tracker, the government has to do more to meet its commitments under the Paris Agreement goal to stay below 1.5°C of warming, which is necessary to limit the most catastrophic climate outcomes. The government is planning to draw up a new heat action plan to prevent heat wave deaths.

Foreign Policy

Human rights are included as a guiding principle of foreign policy in the 2021 coalition agreement of the three parties that form the current German government. German Foreign Minister Annalena Baerbock promoted human rights and a value-based foreign policy as central pillars of Germany's foreign policy. And in March 2023, the Foreign Office presented guidelines for a feminist foreign policy.

In reality, human rights are too often a secondary concern, outweighed by other interests. Germany's foreign policy in 2023 also sought, among other things, to contain Russia's security threats against Europe, diversify access to energy supplies and economic markets, confront the climate crisis, and realign relations with the so-called Global South.

In response to the hostilities between Israel and Hamas starting in October, the German government publicly condemned Hamas' deadly attacks on civilians in Israel. It did not condemn publicly Israeli violations of international humanitarian law in Gaza. The German government did not highlight the need for accountability for international crimes, including at the International Criminal Court. Germany as one of Israel's key allies provided military assistance to Israel, which risks making German authorities complicit in war crimes.

Germany continued to play a central role in coordinating the international condemnation of Russia's full-scale invasion of Ukraine. The German government provided extensive assistance to Ukraine and also supported the investigation of war crimes by the International Criminal Court and Ukrainian judicial authorities.

In July, Germany published its first China strategy. The strategy describes China's rights abuses and prioritizes human rights conceptually, but it does not characterize Chinese government policies in the Uyghur region as crimes against humanity and remains vague about implementation. On her visit to China in April, Baerbock publicly raised human rights concerns; but when Chinese Prime Minister Li Keqiang met with Chancellor Olaf Scholz in Berlin, journalists were not allowed to ask questions at the press conference.

Germany did too little to raise human rights concerns in its relations with other governments with poor rights records. Germany strengthened its relations with India despite the Modi government's escalating crackdown on civil society and the media and its growing discrimination against religious minorities. In February and for the G20 summit in September, Scholz traveled to India without prominently raising human rights violations.

Germany also strengthened its ties with Arab Gulf countries. The government eased arms exports to Saudia Arabia and the United Arab Emirates but continued to block fighter jet deliveries. On her trip to Saudi Arabia in May, Baerbock promoted closer economic ties but also raised human rights concerns. The German Interior Ministry stopped its training program for Saudi border forces after reports of Saudi killings of hundreds of Ethiopian migrants at the border with Yemen.

At the United Nations Human Rights Council, Germany continued to provide important leadership on a number of key issues, including on a resolution to ensure continued scrutiny of Russia's domestic rights record and another to launch a probe into serious abuses committed in the conflict in Sudan. However, Germany failed to make serious efforts to ensure the renewal of a crucial probe on Ethiopia, and it joined a minority of countries voting against a resolution on racism, racial discrimination, xenophobia, and related intolerance.

Germany expressed human rights concerns about an EU-Tunisia migration deal announced in July but did not take any concrete action to condition its implementation on human rights improvements.

In February, seven UN special rapporteurs expressed grave concern about Germany's failure to uphold its obligations under international human rights law, requiring a rights-respecting reparations process—including meaningful participation and representation of affected communities—to address the ongoing impact of crimes committed during Germany's colonial rule of Namibia.

Germany is one of the main shareholders of the International Monetary Fund (IMF). But it has not taken steps within its power to reform IMF policies that threaten rights, such as conditioning its support to austerity programs that do not include prior assessments of their human rights impacts, that encourage low social spending floors, or that promote means-tested rather than universal social security.

Greece

During 2023, abuses against asylum seekers and migrants continued, including violent pushbacks, abuses in detention, and vigilante violence. The government also smeared and judicially harassed civil society groups working with asylum seekers and migrants. Media freedom curbs continued to raise concerns about the rule of law, as did a surveillance scandal. Victims of hate crimes were reluctant to report attacks to the police. The New Democracy Party was returned to government following June elections.

Attacks on Civil Society

The European Commission's 2023 *Rule of Law Report* noted shrinking space for civil society. CIVICUS, a nongovernmental group assessing civic freedoms globally, downgraded civic space in Greece from "narrowed" to "obstructed" due to "the repeated targeting of civil society and activists working with refugees and asylum seekers, disproportionate responses to protests and continuous legal harassment and surveillance of journalists."

United Nations special rapporteur on human rights defenders, Mary Lawlor, noted in a March report to the UN Human Rights Council that migrant rights defenders "have been subjected to smear campaigns, a changing regulatory environment, threats and attacks and the misuse of criminal law against them, to a shocking degree."

Judicial review applications challenging a problematic 2020 regulatory legal framework for nongovernmental groups working with migrants were pending before the Council of State—Greece's highest administrative court—as of late October.

At the end of 2022, Greek authorities brought unfounded charges against two migrants' rights defenders, Panayote Dimitras and Tommy Olsen, for their work shedding light on human rights violations taking place at Greece's borders and seeking justice for those affected. In May 2023, Dimitras learned via leaks in the media that Greece's Anti-Money Laundering Authority had ordered a freezing of his assets pending an investigation of alleged misuse of European Union and other funding related to his organization's work. He was notified of the decision to freeze one bank account in July.

In January 2023, the Court of Appeal of Mytilene found procedural flaws in what a European Parliament report called the "largest case of criminalization of solidarity in Europe" against Sarah Mardini, Séan Binder, and 22 other defendants, and it rejected part of the case. The case relates to efforts in 2018 to help rescue migrants and asylum seekers in the Aegean Sea.

In February, the prosecution appealed the decision, and an appeal hearing took place in May. In June, the Supreme Court recognized that there had been major procedural flaws and rejected the prosecution's appeal. A linked investigation against a group of humanitarians, including Mardini and Binder, for alleged smuggling and money laundering was ongoing at time of writing.

In January, Council of Europe human rights commissioner, Dunja Mijatovic, warned against the prosecutions of Dimitras, Mardini, and Binder and urged Greek authorities "to ensure that human rights defenders and journalists can work safely and freely, by providing an enabling environment for their work and publicly recognizing their important role in a democratic society."

Freedom of Media

For the second year in a row, Greece was last among EU countries in Reporters Without Borders' (RSF) 2023 World Press Freedom Index. Problems include a major ongoing surveillance scandal, government interference, and abusive lawsuits. A government spokesperson dismissed RSF as "unreliable."

In its *Rule of Law Report* published in July, the European Commission noted that threats and attacks against journalists persist.

In a resolution adopted in June related to an ongoing major spyware scandal and revelations that the government surveilled independent journalists, an opposition leader, and others, the European Parliament found Greek authorities had contravened EU law and urged them to conduct urgent reforms to tackle the illicit use of Predator spyware. According to a media report, the European Public Prosecutor's Office (EPPO) opened an investigation in April into Greece's illegal use of Predator spyware in the wiretapping scandal.

In July, the Greek Data Protection Authority announced the initial results of its investigation into the use of Predator spyware, confirming that attempts were made to install spyware on multiple peoples' devices. So far, the DPA has not identified those responsible.

In a European Parliament plenary debate in February, numerous Members of the European Parliament (MEPs) warned against a backsliding of the rule of law in Greece, particularly due to the spyware scandal and state of media freedom.

In a development welcomed by media freedom organizations, authorities announced in April the arrests of two suspects in connection with the 2021 murder of crime reporter Giorgos Karaivaz. RSF added that full accountability for the murder of Karaivaz requires that "all those responsible for the crime including the mastermind must be apprehended."

A September report by press freedom groups criticized Greek authorities for inaction and inadequate investigations into the unsolved 2010 murder of journalist Sokratis Giolias. The groups called on the authorities to independently review the Giolias and Karaivaz cases and improve investigative practices in all cases involving crimes against journalists.

Migrants and Asylum Seekers

Over 38,400 asylum seekers and migrants arrived by sea and land from January to early November, compared with 18,780 in all of 2022.

A fishing vessel carrying an estimated 750 people sank on June 14 off the coast of Pylos. In the aftermath, several of the 104 survivors alleged that the vessel sank after being towed by a Greek coast guard boat. Greek authorities have denied these claims. Forty survivors filed a criminal complaint in September against Greek authorities, alleging that they failed to take adequate rescue measures and towed the vessel, causing it to capsize and sink. The survivors have demanded an immediate, thorough, and reliable investigation into the shipwreck.

In a July letter to the prime minister, Council of Europe Commissioner for Human Rights Dunja Mijatovic noted Greece's legal obligation to conduct effective investigations into the Pylos shipwreck to establish the facts and, where appropriate, to ensure the punishment of those responsible.

In response to the Hellenic Coast Guard's decision to forgo an internal disciplinary investigation into the actions of its personnel during the Pylos shipwreck, the Greek Ombudsman's office initiated an independent inquiry in November to examine the acts and potential omissions of coast guard members. Human rights commissioner Mijatovic commended this action and urged Greek authorities to provide full cooperation with the Ombudsman's investigation.

Reporting in May by the *New York Times* on the pushback from Lesbos of 12 migrants, including children and an infant, added to mounting evidence of collective expulsions by Greek authorities. The European Commission called for a "proper follow up" by authorities. Prime Minister Kyriakos Mitsotakis called such practices "completely unacceptable" and referred to separate investigations being conducted by Greek prosecutors, the Ombudsman, and the National Transparency Authority (NTA). The European Parliament's LIBE Committee, its PEGA inquiry committee, and nongovernmental groups have raised concerns about the NTA's independence and effectiveness.

In May, Médecins Sans Frontières (Doctors Without Borders, MSF) called on Greek authorities to investigate reports of hundreds of missing migrants and allegations of people being threatened, abducted, and ill-treated on Lesbos. In a November report, MSF highlighted an alarming pattern of violence against individuals reaching Greek shores, adding to the already overwhelming evidence of violence and pushbacks at Greek borders.

A March report by the Greek Council of Refugees found that pushbacks of asylum seekers and migrants to Türkiye are widespread and involve illegal detention, intimidation, physical and sexual violence, and the arbitrary confiscation of personal belongings. Greece's migration minister reported in April that the Greek police prevented 260,000 people from entering the Evros land border in 2022.

At least 20 asylum seekers reportedly died, including two children, during major forest fires in the Evros region in August, highlighting an additional risk to people on the move who are already facing violent pushbacks by authorities and attacks by vigilantes.

The Office of the High Commissioner for Human Rights (OHCHR), after expressing concern about the ongoing criminalization of human rights defenders providing lifesaving assistance to migrants, urged Greece in August to "ensure a transparent and impartial investigation" into alleged violations of nonrefoulement and the right to life involving Greek law enforcement personnel, including the Hellenic Coast Guard.

In September, a Greek court awarded €15,920 in compensation to an Afghan asylum seeker unjustly imprisoned for three years on charges of smuggling and causing a shipwreck. According to lawyers, the case is one of thousands, with people charged or convicted of smuggling making up the second largest prison population in Greece.

Nongovernmental groups PRO ASYL and Refugee Support Aegean in May denounced conditions in the EU-funded Closed Controlled Access Centres in the Aegean islands, calling them prison-like facilities that fail to meet human rights standards. In a May report, INTERSOS Hellas, HIAS, and the Greek Council for Refugees published their findings that refugees and rejected asylum seekers in Greece face widespread food insecurity due to complex and lengthy procedures coupled with discriminatory criteria that, in practice, exclude them from most social benefits in Greece.

The UN working group on the use of mercenaries issued a report in July based on a visit to Greece in December 2022. The report, which examines the role of private security companies and security personnel in the migration context, calls for additional "government efforts to strengthen existing complaint mechanisms and ensure the prevention of human rights violations and protection of vulnerable groups."

In January, the European Commission issued infringement letters against Greece, including over the arbitrary detention of asylum seekers during screening procedures.

In February, the Council of State submitted preliminary questions to the Court of Justice of the European Union (CJEU) regarding Greek legislation designating Türkiye as a safe third country for asylum seekers from Afghanistan, Syria, Somalia, Pakistan, and Bangladesh.

Racism and Intolerance

In April, the Racist Violence Recording Network (RVRN) reported 74 incidents of racist violence in 2022 and noted that underreporting of racist violence continued.

In August, racist violence escalated in Evros against asylum seekers and migrants, whom vigilantes accused, without presenting evidence, of being responsible for forest fires. Numerous reports and videos about vigilante "militias" targeting asylum seekers and migrants emerged as well as a viral video showing a civilian holding 13 migrants against their will in his truck while calling for a pogrom against them. He was arrested along with two alleged accomplices.

Women's Rights

According to a March report by the Mediterranean Institute for Investigative Reporting, Greece recorded the highest annual increase in reported femicides among 20 European countries during the pandemic, with an increase of 187.5 percent in just one year, from 2020 to 2021.

Refugee Support Aegean reported in July that Afghan single mothers seeking asylum in Greece face challenges and protection risks.

In an April ruling concerning the living conditions of a pregnant woman in a reception center for asylum seekers, the European Court of Human Rights found that Greece had violated the prohibition on torture or inhumane or degrading treatment or punishment by forcing the woman to live in conditions that violated her human rights.

Guatemala

Guatemala's democratic backsliding accelerated during 2023 with corruption weakening the country's democracy and justice system. Authorities undermined institutional checks on the abuse of power to prevent accountability. Independent journalists, prosecutors, and judges who had investigated and exposed corruption, human rights violations, and abuse of power faced increased harassment and criminal prosecution.

On August 20, opposition and anti-corruption candidate Bernardo Arévalo won the elections, despite authorities' attempt to make the playing field uneven. Attorney General Consuelo Porras led efforts to overturn the vote, including through politically motivated criminal investigations.

Lack of judicial independence and challenges in protecting the rights of migrants, women and girls, and lesbian, gay, bisexual, and transgender (LGBT) people remain major concerns.

Elections and the Right to Vote

During 2023, Guatemala elected a new president, 160 lawmakers, and more than 300 mayors in a context of deteriorating human rights safeguards. Institutions charged with overseeing the elections had little independence or credibility.

Between February and May, three presidential candidates—left-wing Indigenous leader Telma Cabrera, and right-wing Roberto Arzú and Carlos Pineda, who was then showing in some surveys as the leading presidential candidate—were barred from running for office on dubious grounds. The Attorney General's Office launched an arbitrary criminal investigation against presidential candidate Edmond Mulet because he criticized a judge's decision to investigate nine journalists.

After the first round of presidential elections held on June 25, the Supreme Electoral Tribunal (TSE) announced that Sandra Torres, of the Unidad Nacional de la Esperanza (UNE), and Arévalo, of the progressive Movimiento Semilla, would compete in the August 20 runoff.

On June 30, losing political parties filed suit, claiming fraud. Electoral observers from the European Union and the Organization of American States (OAS) found no evidence of it. However, the Constitutional Court temporarily halted election result announcements and ordered a new process for challenging alleged vote irregularities. When no irregularities were found, the Supreme Court approved the results on July 10.

On July 12, a judge granted a request by the Attorney General's Office to suspend Semilla's registration on the basis of alleged registration-related crimes. The Constitutional Court overruled the decision the next day, allowing the election to proceed.

Arévalo won the August 20 runoff with almost 60 percent of the vote. Although the EU and OAS electoral observation missions found no evidence of serious irregularities, the UNE challenged the results, including through a criminal complaint making unsubstantiated allegations of fraud.

The Attorney General's Office raided Semilla's and the TSE's headquarters, seized electoral material, and asked a court to investigate TSE magistrates.

On August 28, the TSE's Office of Citizen Registry suspended Semilla's legal registration as a result of the Attorney General's Office's investigation. The decision was confirmed on November 2, once the electoral process was officially closed on October 31.

In October, Guatemalans took to the streets to protest efforts to overturn the electoral results. Protests, led by Indigenous groups, demanded the resignation of Attorney General Consuelo Porras. The attorney general and the Constitutional Court urged the government to use force in response to road blockings. At time of writing, security forces had used force in very few incidents. In some cases, individuals attacked protesters, including by firing gunshots. One protester died in mid-October.

In November, the Attorney General's Office requested 27 arrest warrants against activists, students, academics, human rights defenders, and a Semilla member. Prosecutors accused them of participating in, or promoting, a largely peaceful protest in 2022 in Guatemala's largest university. The Attorney General's Office also asked the Supreme Court to lift the immunity of Arévalo and Vice President-elect Karin Herrera so they could be investigated for allegedly promoting the student protest through social media. In December, prosecutors asked the TSE to "annul" the electoral results, alleging irregularities.

Later that month, in a case brought by a group of local lawyers, the Constitutional Court ordered that Congress and other authorities ensured that all elected authorities take office on January 14 and 15, as required under the Guatemalan Constitution. However, the court said its decision was "without prejudice" to the powers of Attorney General's Office to investigate and prosecute alleged crimes..

Corruption

For years, investigations have revealed that businesspeople coordinated with corrupt officials to pack the courts and that money linked to corruption and organized crime is often used to finance electoral campaigns.

Attorney General Porras has weakened the agency responsible for investigating corruption—the Special Prosecutor's Office against Impunity (FECI)—halting the progress of cases. The FECI has pivoted to pursuing spurious criminal investigations against anti-corruption advocates, including judges, prosecutors, and journalists.

Guatemala ranks 13 of 15 Latin American countries in its ability to detect, punish, and prevent corruption, according to the Americas Society and Council of the Americas report. Since 2021, Guatemala has experienced the sharpest decline in the index in the region.

Judicial Independence and Checks on Executive Power

Measures by Congress, the Attorney General's Office, and other authorities have obstructed accountability for corruption, weakening the rule of law and undermining human rights guarantees. Corrupt political, economic, and military elites have co-opted a large part of the country's justice system, allowing them to profit with impunity.

Efforts to undermine institutional safeguards increased since the expulsion of the United Nations-backed International Commission against Impunity in

Guatemala (Comisión Internacional Contra la Impunidad en Guatemala, CICIG) by then-President Jimmy Morales in late 2019.

As of October, Congress had yet to comply with a 2020 Constitutional Court order to appoint judges and magistrates to fill vacant seats on the Supreme Court and appeals courts for the 2019-2024 term. The selection process has been marred by influence-peddling allegations.

On August 28, prosecutors raided the homes of former senior prosecutor Juan Francisco Sandoval, who lives in exile, and arrested Claudia González, a former CICIG commissioner who currently works as the lawyer of many independent prosecutors and judges. Prosecutors cited alleged abuse of authority in the influence-peddling investigation that CICIG started in 2017 against current Supreme Court of Justice Magistrate Blanca Stalling.

As of September, more than 40 judges, prosecutors, and former CICIG officials had been forced into exile.

As of October, Virginia Laparra, an anti-corruption prosecutor, remained in prison, serving a four-year sentence for "abuse of authority" regarding administrative complaints she filed against Judge Lesther Castellanos. In May, the UN Working Group on Arbitrary Detention deemed her case arbitrary and called for her release.

In November, members of Congress whose terms ended in January 2024 swiftly appointed a new Supreme Court after a process marred by irregularities. The 13 magistrates appointed include people who have faced several criminal investigations, including for alleged influence-peddling.

Freedom of Expression

Authorities have created a hostile environment for journalists and media outlets, including through verbal attacks, restrictions, and abusive criminal proceedings.

The Journalists' Observatory, a nongovernmental organization (NGO), documented 120 instances of attacks, harassment, and criminalization of media personnel in the first seven months of 2023, exceeding the total of 117 incidents in 2022. Over 500 such incidents have been reported since the beginning of Alejandro Giammattei's presidential term in 2020. The Office of the UN High Commissioner for Human Rights (OHCHR) registered that at least six journalists fled the country in 2022. The Journalists' Observatory found that the frequency of attacks escalated during election season.

On June 14, a court convicted José Rubén Zamora, a leading investigative journalist and the owner and editor of *El Periodico*, an independent outlet, of alleged money laundering. In October, a higher court annulled the decision, ruling that the case should be tried again. *El Periodico* had ceased operations in May, citing persecution. Zamora remained in prison at the time of writing.

On August 11, unidentified attackers shot and killed journalists Edin Alonso and Hugo Gutiérrez in the southwestern department of Retalhuleu. They managed a Facebook page for local news and had reportedly received threats.

Attacks on Human Rights Defenders

Abuses against human rights defenders and social leaders increased. In 2022, the non-profit Unidad de Protección a Defensoras y Defensores de Derechos Humanos de Guatemala (UDEFEGUA) documented 3,574 instances of aggression—including criminalization, harassment, intimidation, threats, and violence against women—against individuals, organizations, and communities that defend human rights, which is the highest recorded number in 22 years.

Women's and Girls' Rights

By August, the Women's Observatory of the Attorney General's Office had counted more than 22,000 women victims of gender-based violence and another 98 victims of femicide in 2023. OHCHR stated that insufficient public resources were being allocated to prevent violence against women and protect victims.

The Observatory for Sexual and Reproductive Rights (OSAR), an NGO, reported more than 43,000 pregnancies among adolescents and girls, including 1,589 among girls ages 10 to 14, between January and August.

Abortion is legal only when a pregnant person's life is at risk. In 2022, lawmakers tried to broaden the circumstances under which people could be prosecuted for accessing abortion, but Congress shelved the bill after then-President Giammattei threatened to veto it.

Sexual Orientation and Gender Identity

Authorities have historically failed to protect LGBT people from bias-motivated violence and discrimination. Guatemala has no comprehensive civil legislation protecting people from discrimination on the grounds of sexual orientation or gender identity and no legal gender recognition procedure for transgender people.

In June 2023, a court in Guatemala sentenced a man to 16 years' imprisonment for the killing of Andrea González, a transgender woman and leader of OTRANS, a trans rights organization. The court did not consider the crime a femicide, and Guatemala does not have hate crime legislation that covers sexual orientation or gender identity.

A bill that stigmatizes transgender people remains pending in Congress at time of writing.

Guatemalan civil society reported that, from January through June 2023, at least 17 LGBT people had been killed, which has been the deadliest half-year since 2020.

Disability Rights

Guatemala has taken no action to ensure the right to legal capacity of people with disabilities in domestic legislation. This subjects them to violations of the rights to personal integrity, economic opportunity, sexual and reproductive choice, and access to justice.

A disability certification process initiated in 2023 aims to better recognize, identify, and support individuals with disabilities and their families.

Failure to Protect Children

The Women's Observatory estimates that in 2023, more than 8,800 children, including adolescents, were victims of mistreatment and abuse as of August.

Authorities reported over 21,000 cases of severe malnutrition, a 40 percent increase from 2022, and 42 deaths in children under 5, as of September.

Migrants and Asylum Seekers

In cooperation with the administration of United States President Joe Biden, then-President Giammattei increased efforts to prevent non-Guatemalan migrants and asylum seekers from reaching the US by deploying additional police and military forces in the southern border and the country's interior.

Guatemala and the US announced, in June, the implementation of a six-month pilot program establishing "safe mobility offices" to "facilitate access to lawful pathways" for Guatemalans to the US and other countries and for "family reunification" and "access to temporary work visas."

Key International Actors

In January, OHCHR said Guatemala faced "systemic and structural challenges," including regarding "inequality and discrimination, the justice system, the fight against impunity, the democratic space, and the right to promote and protect human rights." Both OHCHR and the UN special rapporteur on the independence of judges and lawyers noted that many investigations against prosecutors and judges violate judicial independence and due process and appear to be in retaliation for their work fighting corruption.

In April, the IACHR included Guatemala, along with Venezuela, Cuba, and Nicaragua, in a chapter of its annual report for countries suffering serious attacks on democratic institutions or grave, massive, or systematic human rights violations.

The OAS, the Inter-American Commission on Human Rights (IACHR), the UN secretary-general, the EU, the US government, European governments, Latin American governments, including Brazil and Chile, and several European embassies in Guatemala expressed concerns about attempts to undermine election results.

The OAS and EU electoral observation missions played a critical role in ensuring Guatemala's right to vote. They spotlighted the "high judicialization" of the election, the weakening of the rule of law, and attacks on freedom of expression, among other issues.

The OAS Permanent Council and the organization's Secretary General Luis Almagro also played an important role. Almagro visited the country in August, September and December, at the government's invitation, and urged all parties to respect the electoral results. His office also conducted efforts to mediate between protesters, the Attorney General's Office, and the government as well as to help promote a smooth transfer of power.

In July, the US Department of State released its *Corrupt and Undemocratic Actors Report*, which imposed sanctions on several current and former Guatemalan officials, including Castellanos, who filed the case against prosecutor Laparra, and Judge Fredy Orellana, who suspended the Semilla political party. In December, the US government sanctioned Luis Miguel Martinez Morales, a close ally to President Giammattei and a former government official, under the Global Magnitsky program. Later that month, it imposed visa restrictions on nearly 300 Guatemalans, including private sector representatives and over 100 members of Congress, for "undermining democracy and the rule of law."

Also in December, the EU High Representative High Representative Josep Borrell said that the EU had "agreed in principle and [was] ready to adopt a framework allowing for targeted restrictive measures" against people responsible for trying to overturn the elections. The European Parliament passed resolutions, in September and December, condemning arbitrary persecution of judges, prosecutors and judges, as well as the attempts to undermine the electoral results.

Responding to stigmatizing messages, intimidation, and murder threats against President-elect Arévalo and Vice President-elect Herrera, the IACHR issued precautionary measures to protect them.

Haiti

In 2023, Haiti's security, justice, political, and humanitarian crises worsened. Killings, kidnappings, and sexual violence by criminal groups increased dramatically. The state response was weak to nonexistent, and the justice system was barely functioning.

More than 40 percent of Haiti's population experienced acute food insecurity. Access to electricity, safe drinking water, sanitation, health care, and education was severely limited.

In October, the United Nations Security Council authorized a Multinational Security Support Mission, led by Kenya, to improve security.

Prime Minister Ariel Henry did not reach a consensus with Haitian politicians and civil society to enable a democratic transition.

Despite the dire conditions in the country, foreign governments returned more than 100,000 people to Haiti from January through August; the Dominican Republic was responsible for 94 percent of the returns.

Political Crisis

Since the assassination of President Jovenel Moïse in July 2021, Prime Minister Henry, who never received parliamentary approval and thus does not have a constitutional mandate, has been ruling by decree. Parliament has been dysfunctional since 2019, when President Moïse refused to organize legislative elections. Since January 2023, the country has had no national elected officials.

In June 2023, Henry and Haitian political and civic leaders met in Jamaica, led by the Caribbean Community (CARICOM) Eminent Persons Group, consisting of three former prime ministers from the region, to seek a political solution to the crisis. They could not reach a consensus. Some political parties and civil society groups signed the Kingston Joint Declaration, calling for a national unity government. Nine major Haitian human rights organizations and a US diaspora group called on the international community to stop propping up those who created Haiti's crisis and instead support the establishment of a transitional government

HUMAN
RIGHTS
WATCH
"Living a Nightmare"
Haiti Needs an Urgent Rights-Based Response to Escalating Crisis

"led by technocrats who would commit to not participating in future elections and who would work ... for the organization of free, fair, and credible elections."

Dysfunctional Criminal Justice System

Haiti's justice system is plagued by insecurity, corruption, strikes, and political interference. Criminal groups have taken over some court buildings, including the Tribunal de Paix in Cité Soleil in July 2020 and the Port-au-Prince Palace of Justice, the main justice complex in the country, in July 2022. They appear to have stolen or destroyed evidence and records that may be impossible to recover, as Haitian courts do not have digital copies of files. The courts have not been relocated.

No progress was made, as of October, in investigations into the massacres in La Saline in 2018, Bel Air in 2019, Plaine du Cul-de-Sac and Cité Soleil in 2022, and Carrefour-Feuilles in 2023.

The Conseil Supérieur du Pouvoir Judiciaire (CSPJ), the judiciary's oversight body, refused to certify 28 judges and prosecutors in January and 12 in June, citing abuse of authority, invalid credentials, and unlawful release of detainees, among other reasons. There is no mechanism to appeal the CSPJ's decisions.

In February 2023, Prime Minister Henry appointed eight judges to the Cour de Cassation, Haiti's Supreme Court, to allow it to function after more than one year during which it did not have enough judges to make up a quorum. Civil society groups argued that Henry did not respect the constitutional procedure for these appointments.

As of September, Haiti's prisons held more than three times their capacity for inmates. Most of the 11,784 detainees—84 percent of whom were awaiting trial—were living in inhumane conditions, without access to adequate food, water, or health care. From January through September, 128 detainees died, most from malnutrition-related diseases.

New penal and criminal procedure codes providing alternatives to pretrial detention are scheduled to come into effect in June 2024.

Investigation of President Moïse's Assassination

President Moïse was assassinated on July 7, 2021. As of May 2023, 45 people were in pretrial detention in Haiti in connection with the case, including 18 former Colombian military officers, whose families complained that they lacked legal assistance and were being mistreated and held in inhumane conditions. In October, police arrested a key suspect.

United States prosecutors allege that conspirators had initially planned to kidnap Moïse but later decided to kill him, hoping to win government contracts under a successor. US judges sentenced a Haitian-Chilean businessman and a former Colombian army colonel to life in prison for their roles in the killing. A former Haitian senator pled guilty; his sentencing was set for December 19. Nine other defendants are awaiting trial in the US.

Violence by Criminal Groups

UN agencies estimate that more than 300 criminal groups controlled 80 percent of Haiti's capital, Port-au-Prince, as of September. Many are alleged to have ties to political and economic elites as well as police officers.

The UN Office of the High Commissioner for Human Rights (OHCHR) recorded the killing of 3,156 people—including 36 police officers—and 1,284 kidnappings by those groups from January through September 2023.

Criminal groups continued to use sexual violence to terrorize the population and demonstrate control. Médecins Sans Frontières (Doctors Without Borders, MSF) reported assisting 1,005 sexual violence survivors at its hospitals in Port-au-Prince between January and May 2023, almost double the number for the same period in 2022.

Human Rights Watch documented abuses committed by criminal groups in four communes in the metropolitan area of Port-au-Prince, including the killing of 67 people—including 11 children and 12 women—and rape of 23 girls and women. Survivors told Human Rights Watch about being dragged off the street, gang raped, and made to watch people getting killed by machete and gunshot.

OHCHR documented dozens of sexual attacks on lesbian, gay, bisexual, and transgender (LGBT) people by gang members between January and June 2022.

Female victims said that criminal groups had subjected them to "corrective rapes" to "cure" them.

The Haitian government has failed to protect people from criminal violence, which has been exacerbated by a continued flow of weapons and ammunition to Haiti, largely from the US state of Florida.

Often in collusion with police, the vigilante justice Bwa Kale movement had reportedly killed more than 420 people suspected of being members of criminal groups from January through September, OHCHR reported. Human Rights Watch verified material posted to social media and news sites confirming four attacks in March and April, three of which took place in the immediate vicinity of police stations.

Criminal groups have formed their own movement in retaliation, Zam Pale. The UN secretary-general warned in July that the Bwa Kale and Zam Kale movements have "sparked a new and alarming cycle of violence" that could lead to further recruitment of children.

Attacks on Journalists

At least three journalists were killed from January through May 2023, the Inter-American Commission on Human Rights said. At least six media workers had been kidnapped in 2023 and others had fled their homes to escape escalating violence, the Committee to Protect Journalists said in September.

Police Conduct

Police killed 407 people from January through September, the UN Integrated Office in Haiti (BINUH) said. According to that office, the prosecutors of Les Cayes and Miragoâne reportedly participated in 7 extrajudicial executions, and individuals wearing police uniforms executed at least 18 people in Tabarre.

The police internal affairs office opened cases of alleged human rights violations against 103 officers from January through September.

Sexual Abuse in Sports

In 2020, the International Federation of Football Association (FIFA) Ethics Committee banned Haitian Football Federation president, Yves Jean-Bart, for life after finding evidence of his systematic sexual abuse of female players. In February 2023, the Court of Arbitration for Sport wrongly annulled FIFA's ban. A criminal case against Jean-Bart is pending in Haiti. More than a dozen male and female survivors and witnesses told Human Rights Watch that he coerced female players into having sex with him.

In July 2022, Evans Lescouflair, a former sports minister, was arrested in Puerto Rico and sent to Haiti in connection with complaints filed by child sexual abuse survivors. He was released, pending trial, in June 2023.

Access to Abortion

Haiti has a total ban on abortion. A criminal code scheduled to take effect in 2024 will legalize it in all circumstances until the 12th week of pregnancy and at any time in cases of rape, of incest, or when the mental or physical health of the pregnant person is in danger.

Disability Rights

Although Haiti ratified the UN Convention on the Rights of Persons with Disabilities, its laws still include offensive terminology, and people with disabilities experience discrimination in access to health, education, and justice. Moreover, stigma places them at a heightened risk of violence.

Local advocates say that people with disabilities face significant obstacles to civic participation, including difficulty obtaining the national identification cards required for voting because the National Identification Office was inaccessible to them.

Economic and Social Rights

The security and political crises compounded a dire humanitarian situation. Heavy flooding in June and July across the country also highlighted Haiti's vulnerability to natural disasters.

According to the World Bank, about 59 percent of Haiti's population of 11.5 million lived on less than US$3.65 per day in 2023. About 5.2 million needed food and shelter assistance, a 20 percent increase from 2022; of these, 4.9 million were acutely food insecure.

As of early 2023, only one-third of Haitians had access to electricity, but only intermittently and at high prices. Only 55 percent of Haitian households had access to safe drinking water and two-thirds of the population had limited or no sanitation services, aggravating the spread of cholera. As of August, the Pan American Health Organization had reported 58,230 suspected cases of cholera, 3,696 confirmed cases, and 823 deaths since the beginning of the ongoing outbreak in October 2022.

International organizations estimate that 75 percent of the country's health facilities have inadequate medical supplies and insufficient trained personnel. Insecurity has triggered an exodus of health workers from Haiti in recent years.

Nearly half of Haitians aged 15 and older are illiterate; in 2020, only 46 percent of children completed primary school. The quality and availability of public education is generally poor, and 85 percent of primary schools and even more secondary schools were private in 2020. High costs, attacks on schools and on children en route, and lack of infrastructure and staff have deprived 4.2 million children of their right to education, UNICEF reported.

Internal Displacement and Migration

Almost 195,000 Haitians were internally displaced by violence from January 2022 through July 2023, the International Organization for Migration (IOM) said. Many others left the country, often on dangerous journeys.

The IOM reported that from January through August 2023, foreign governments returned 103,706 people despite the risk to their lives and physical integrity in Haiti and the UN's calls to stop forced returns there. The Dominican Republic was responsible for 94 percent of returns; the US, the Bahamas, Turks and Caicos, and Cuba were responsible for most of the rest. In April, the UN Committee on the Elimination of Racial Discrimination expressed grave concern about increases in hate speech and racist or xenophobic violence against Haitians abroad and the use of racial profiling by law enforcement in some countries in the Americas.

Humanitarian workers told Human Rights Watch that Dominican authorities routinely rounded up people they suspected were Haitian nationals solely on the basis of skin color. Authorities took them to the border and placed them in cages on flatbed trucks to await processing, in sweltering heat and with little or no access to food or water, before returning them to Haiti.

In September, the Dominican Republic closed its land border with Haiti, as well as all connections by sea and air, in a dispute over a waterway. The UN designated expert on human rights in Haiti warned that this would intensify an already grave crisis, as the country imported at least 25 percent of its food, as well as medical supplies, from its neighbor.

Key International Actors

In late 2022, Prime Minister Henry asked the international community to deploy a specialized armed force, a call echoed by the UN secretary-general. In July, Kenya offered 1,000 police officers to train and assist Haitian police. Human rights groups expressed concern about the Kenyan police's record of human rights abuses.

In October, the UN Security Council authorized the deployment of a Multinational Security Support Mission for an initial period of 12 months to help improve security and build conditions conducive to free and fair elections. The US pledged US$100 million for such a mission in September.

Haitian civil society called for strong accountability measures to avoid repetition of past harms from foreign interventions and urged foreign governments to stop supporting Prime Minister Henry, whom many Haitians see as heading an illegitimate government with links to criminal groups.

In October 2022, the UN Security Council approved sanctions—including asset freezes, travel bans, and arms embargos—against leaders of criminal groups and others involved in violence. As of March 2023, foreign governments had sanctioned 25 individuals. In July, the EU set up its own sanctions regime on Haiti. In October, the council renewed the sanctions measures for one year and broadened the arms embargo, prohibiting all arms sales or transfers by foreign countries to Haiti as a whole, except for the UN-authorized mission and law enforcement.

In April 2023, at Haiti's own initiative, the UN Human Rights Council adopted a resolution by consensus, establishing a UN designated expert on human Rights in Haiti. He completed his second official visit to the country in October.

The UN appealed for US$720 million in aid for Haiti for 2023, almost double the 2022 amount. As of September, it had only raised 26 percent of that amount.

Honduras

President Xiomara Castro has largely failed to deliver on her promise to strengthen human rights and democratic institutions in Honduras.

Honduras continues to face longstanding structural challenges, including systemic corruption, political interference in the justice system, insecurity, a very large percentage of the population living in poverty, and lethal attacks against environmental defenders.

In February, Congress appointed a new Supreme Court. The 15 justices were selected from a list prepared by a committee based on merit, but legislators split vacancies among political parties, as in the past. As of October, selection of a new attorney general was delayed in Congress as parties fought to appoint a person friendly to their interests.

Also as of October, the government continued to negotiate with the United Nations secretary-general to establish a UN-backed international commission against corruption and impunity in Honduras.

Judicial Independence and the Fight against Corruption

The 15 Supreme Court justices appointed by Congress in February will serve for a seven-year period. Legislators retained the partisan practice of allocating selections proportionally among political parties, but this time, they selected from a list prepared by a nominating committee and based on merit, which was an improvement. Legislators also complied with Honduras' legal gender parity requirement and selected the country's first Afro-Honduran justice.

The government and the UN secretary-general are negotiating the establishment of an international commission against corruption and impunity, pursuant to a memorandum signed in December 2022. Between July and October, a group of UN experts visited Honduras three times to assess the viability and legal framework of such a commission.

In July, Congress abrogated Decree 57-2020, which had hampered prosecutors seeking to obtain key documentation in corruption investigations, and modified Decree 93-2021, an obstacle to money laundering prosecutions. In August, Congress abrogated Decree 116-2019, which had effectively barred the Attorney General's Office from investigating the misuse of public funds by legislators for up to seven years, pending an administrative audit.

Gabriela Castellanos, director of the Consejo Nacional Anticorrupción, an independent organization mandated by law in 2005 to fight corruption, left Honduras in June, having received threats after publishing a report on nepotism in the government. Castellanos returned after a month and continued her work denouncing corrupt practices.

Óscar Chinchilla was appointed attorney general in 2018 in violation of a constitutional provision that mandates that the attorney general be selected from a list prepared by a nominating committee. Chinchilla's term ended on August 31, 2023, and a nominating committee selected five candidates to replace him in a process that some civil society organizations said was influenced by political interests. Political jockeying continued in Congress, which, as of October, had not agreed on a new attorney general.

Attacks on Human Rights Defenders

From January through August, 236 human rights defenders were harassed, threatened, or attacked, and at least 13 were killed—compared to 11 killed in all of 2022—the UN Office of the High Commissioner for Human Rights (OHCHR) in Honduras reported. Seventy-five percent of the defenders attacked and more than 90 percent of those killed were environmental or land defenders.

In January, environmental defenders Jairo Bonilla and Aly Domínguez were killed in Guapinol, Colón department. Previously, they had received threats aimed at stopping their activities in defense of the Guapinol and San Pedro rivers. In June, Oquelí Domínguez, Aly's brother and also an environmental defender, was shot dead in Guapinol.

The mechanism Honduras created in 2015 to protect journalists, human rights defenders, and justice officials has serious flaws: It lacks financial autonomy, qualified staff experienced in human rights issues, and trust from defenders, who are afraid to provide personal information that could end up in the hands of those who threaten them.

Economic and Social Rights

Nearly 80 percent of rural Hondurans lived in poverty, having income below US$7 per day. Almost all of them lived in extreme poverty, making less than US$4 per day, according to the latest official data, which is from 2021.

As of March 2023, official data showed 14 percent of Hondurans could not read or write, with the rate reaching 31 percent for those aged 60 and older. Only 56 percent of children between 12 and 14, and 29 percent between 15 and 17, were attending school.

Official data from March 2023 also showed that remittances were almost 8 percent of Hondurans' total source of income. Remittances amount to 27 percent of GDP, the highest rate in Latin America and the Caribbean, according to 2022 World Bank data.

Public Security and Prison Conditions

Honduras is one of the most violent countries in the world, with police reporting 3,661 murders in 2022, a homicide rate of 38 per 100,000 people. According to Insight Crime, a think tank and media organization that reports on crime and security, Honduras has the second highest homicide rate in Latin America and the Caribbean after Jamaica. Preliminary police data shows 2,341 murders from January through September 2023, a 16 percent drop over the same period of 2022.

In December 2022, President Castro declared an ongoing state of emergency in several parts of the country, including the capital district, suspending the rights to freedom of association and assembly and to be informed of the reason for arrest, among others. OHCHR in Honduras expressed concern about the extended use of the emergency without a comprehensive, rights-based public security policy. The government justified the emergency by pointing to a rise in organized crime.

In June, gang violence erupted in a women's prison, resulting in at least 46 deaths. In response, the Castro administration put prisons under military control, a common measure in Honduras that yields no clear results and appears to heighten rights abuses.

As of September, prisons held almost 19,000 detainees, which is 72 percent more than their capacity. Almost half were in pretrial detention, official statistics show.

Women's and Girls' Rights

Based on 2021 data from the UN Economic Commission for Latin America and the Caribbean, Honduras has the highest rate of femicide—defined as "the killing of a woman by a man in the context of unequal power relations between men and women"—in Latin America. The Centro de Derechos de Mujeres, a Honduran nongovernmental organization (NGO) that monitors media, counted 317 femicides from January through September 2023.

Abortion is illegal in Honduras under all circumstances, with prison sentences of up to six years for people who have or perform abortions. In March, the newly appointed Supreme Court justices confirmed a previous ruling rejecting the argument that the ban is unconstitutional.

In March, Congress approved a law mandating comprehensive sexual education to help prevent teenage pregnancies. After fierce backlash from conservative groups, President Castro announced in July that she had vetoed the law.

In March, Castro signed an executive order ending a ban on the sale and use of emergency contraception.

Migration, Asylum, and Internal Displacement

From January through September, Mexico's refugee agency reported 31,055 Hondurans had requested asylum there, second only to Haitians. Many continue on to the United States. Migrants face serious risks—including kidnapping, robbery, and discrimination—throughout their journey.

From January through July, 32,727 Hondurans—12 percent of whom were children—were forcibly returned, the government reported. More than half were from the US, and more than one-third from Mexico.

From January through September, 340,611 migrants entered Honduras without proper documentation or without following established procedures, higher numbers than seen in all of 2022. More than 45 percent of them were Venezuelans, followed by Cubans, Ecuadorians, and Haitians, each representing more than 10 percent.

In March, President Castro signed a law to boost government help for communities and individual victims of internal displacement. Gang violence and human rights violations caused the internal displacement of about 191,000 people between 2004 and 2018, the latest official data shows.

Sexual Orientation and Gender Identity

Lesbian, gay, bisexual, and transgender (LGBT) people in Honduras continue to suffer high levels of violence and discrimination in all areas of life, forcing some to flee the country. Cattrachas, a Honduran organization that monitors media reports, registered 40 homophobic or transphobic killings from January through October 2023.

Honduras has failed to comply with key measures ordered by the Inter-American Court of Human Rights in 2021 in response to the killing of Vicky Hernández, a transgender woman, during the 2009 military coup. Among other requirements, the ruling ordered the creation of a protocol for criminal investigations in cases motivated by anti-LGBT bias and a procedure through which trans people could change their name and gender on official documents to reflect their gender identity. No such protocol or procedure had been established as of October.

Disability Rights

Deficiencies in public infrastructure, difficulties in accessing employment, mistreatment in public transportation services, and poor access to information are part of the barriers people with disabilities face in Honduras, according to a 2022 ombudsperson report, which estimates that 14 percent of Hondurans have some type of physical, sensory, intellectual, or psychosocial disability.

Key International Actors

In March, Honduras broke diplomatic relations with Taiwan and supported the "One China" policy, which holds that Taiwan is an inalienable part of the People's Republic of China. Honduras and China agreed that Honduras would participate in the Belt and Road Initiative, a trillion-dollar project to spur China's investment and advance its foreign policy interests.

As a member of the UN Human Rights Council, Honduras maintained a hesitant stance on human rights throughout 2023. It abstained from voting on a resolution extending the mandate of a group of UN experts investigating systematic rights violations in Nicaragua and on renewing the mandates of the UN special rapporteurs on the human rights situation in Russia and in Belarus. It voted in favor of renewing the mandates of a group of UN experts investigating abuses in Syria and of the special rapporteur on the human rights situation in Iran, among others.

Hungary

The government continued its attacks on rule of law and democratic institutions in 2023. Teacher protests over work conditions and salaries that started in September 2022 culminated in a two-day strike in March, to which the government responded with a new law weakening teachers' professional autonomy. Opposition members throughout the year tried to dismantle police cordons erected around the Prime Minister's Office to obstruct media access that had been ruled unlawful by a court.

The government extended the "state of danger" it originally declared in May 2022 after Russia's full-scale invasion of Ukraine, taking advantage of extraordinary powers to rule by decree and sidestep parliamentary process. Independent journalists and media outlets faced smear campaigns by public officials and pro-government media and obstacles in reporting, including in obtaining public records and meeting with ruling party politicians. Civil society organizations continued to be subjected to smear campaigns by government-aligned media and public officials.

Discrimination and vilification of lesbian, gay, bisexual, and transgender (LGBT) people and Roma persisted. Unlawful pushbacks of migrants and asylum seekers to Serbia continued, and access to the asylum procedure was close to impossible.

The European Union withheld funds to Hungary due to its rule of law abuses and continued its scrutiny of Hungary under the article 7 mechanism designed to hold accountable governments that may be in breach of EU founding values.

Attacks on Rule of Law and Public Institutions

In February and May, the government extended the "state of danger" it had declared a year earlier, which itself had replaced a Covid-19 "state of danger" declared in 2020. The resulting emergency powers enable the government to rule by decree and override any act of parliament. A separate emergency decree has been in force since 2015 over a "state of crisis due to mass migration." The government has misused its excessive powers, among other things, to overrule judicial decisions and restrict teachers' right to strike.

In December 2022, the EU froze delivery of so-called cohesion and Covid-19 recovery funds to Hungary due to rule of law abuses and listed 27 milestones, or prerequisites, the country needs to fulfill to unlock funds. In May 2023, parliament passed a law addressing some concerns about the independence of the judiciary in an effort to unlock EU funds. The law failed to fully comply with the milestones, including to guarantee the integrity of the parliamentary lawmaking process, the independence of the Kuria (Supreme Court), and the effective operations of the National Judicial Council and to remove obstacles currently preventing judges from seeking preliminary rulings from the EU Court of Justice (CJEU). The law also failed to address broader rule of law concerns, including the practice of limitless renewals of states of danger and political capture of the Constitutional Court. On December 13, the European Commission concluded that Hungary had met the conditions linked to judicial independence and announced it was unfreezing €10 billion in EU cohesion funds, while maintaining a freeze on €21 billion in other funds linked to persistent breaches by Hungarian authorities of rule of law principles.

In response to teachers' months-long protests and a two-day strike in March demanding better working conditions and salaries, the government introduced what has been dubbed a "revenge law," increasing teachers' working hours and workloads and allowing the government to relocate them at its discretion. In May, police used tear gas during protests made up largely of high school students, the majority under 18.

In February, the Hungarian parliament, in an expedited procedure, adopted a motion that limits the power of the Hungarian Chamber of Doctors, an independent advocacy body, by abolishing mandatory membership and transferring the power to adjudicate ethical cases to a government body also in charge of creating a new ethical code. The emergency motion was preceded by a dispute between the government and the chamber concerning on-call work and low salaries.

Freedom of Media

Independent journalists and media outlets continued to face obstacles and limited access to public officials and members of government as well as to public information, as authorities largely ignored freedom of information requests.

Between April and August, at least 40 Hungarian news websites, mainly independent outlets, were subjected to repeated cyber attacks, causing websites to crash or slow down due to server overload, leaving readers unable to access information and news for hours at a time.

In late March, four independent weekly papers sued the government, at the national and EU levels, over unequal distribution of state advertising in local media. The media outlets filed a complaint with the European Competition Network, stating that the government places a disproportionate number of ads in pro-government media.

In September, the European Court of Human Rights (ECtHR) ruled that Hungary had violated the right to freedom of expression of the then-independent outlet *Index* when Hungarian courts ruled in favor of then-president Janos Ader, who had sued the outlet for defamation.

In its March 2023 report, the Council of Europe Platform to Promote the Protection of Journalism and Safety of Journalists found Hungary in violation of press freedom for allowing state intelligence to use Pegasus spyware to surveil at least five journalists and media owners. In February, then-Hungarian Justice Minister Judit Varga refused to meet the European Parliament PEGA committee set up to investigate infringement of EU law in relation to Pegasus spyware use.

Independent journalists continue to experience smear campaigns by public officials and pro-government media accusing them of treason, implying they are funded by United States liberal interests or acting on behalf of George Soros.

Attacks on Civil Society

Smear attacks by government officials and pro-government media on civil society organizations continued in 2023. In January, Minister of Regional Development and EU Funds Tibor Navracsics blamed the Hungarian Helsinki Committee and other rights groups for an EU Commission move to stop new grants from the ERASMUS exchange program to Hungarian universities that operate, or are managed by, public trust foundations. The move followed a decision by EU member states to suspend funding to such trusts over concerns about lack of transparency and conflicts of interest.

Sexual Orientation and Gender Identity

The government continued its attacks on LGBT people in 2023.

In July, the government proposed a bill that would exclude transgender women from a women-only pension scheme. The bill was introduced in response to a local court ruling making a transgender woman eligible for a benefit available to women who have worked 40 years but not yet reached the retirement age. At time of writing, the bill was pending before parliament.

Also in July, the Consumer Protection Authority fined Lira, one of the country's largest bookstores, 12 million Hungarian Forints (about US$36,000) for failing to wrap in plastic foil the British webcomic *Heartstopper*, which includes LGBT content. The government body said Lira had breached the 2021 anti-LGBT law prohibiting display of LGBT content to children, a law that the European Commission referred to the CJEU in July 2022 for violating the fundamental rights of LGBT people.

In February 2023, the politically compromised Constitutional Court issued a ruling that continues to block applications by transgender people for legal gender recognition submitted after the 2021 ban on legal gender recognition. The ruling creates two categories of transgender people in Hungary: those who applied early enough to pursue gender recognition and those who did not and are thus ineligible to legally change their gender.

Women's and Girls' Reproductive Rights

Women and girls face increasing and burdensome restrictions on accessing legal abortion, including obligatory counseling sessions prior to an abortion and a requirement to listen to the "fetal heartbeat." Refugee women and girls from Ukraine have also encountered barriers to accessing legal abortion. Curbs on reproductive rights resulted in an increase in women and girls seeking abortion care abroad.

Discrimination against Roma

Discrimination against Roma in education, health care, and employment remained a serious problem in 2023.

In March, the ECtHR found Hungary in violation of the right to non-discrimination in the case of a Roma boy who had been racially segregated in school. The court awarded the applicant €7,000 in damages and ordered the government to develop a policy to end segregation in the school.

Migration and Asylum

Access to the asylum procedure remained virtually impossible following a new 2020 law preventing asylum seekers from lodging protection claims in Hungary. A CJEU decision in June stated that Hungary was violating EU asylum laws by forcing people to lodge protection claims in Serbia and Ukraine.

According to police data cited by the United Nations High Commissioner for Refugees (UNHCR), 436,310 crossings from Ukraine to Hungary took place between February 24, 2022, and September 3, 2023. By July 2023, 37,553 people had registered for Temporary Protection under the EU Temporary Protection Directive triggered by the war in Ukraine.

Pushbacks to Serbia, sometimes violent, continued. According to official police statistics, between January and August 2023, police made over 58,000 "arrests and escorts across the fence," a euphemism for unlawful pushbacks.

In three separate judgments in May, the ECtHR ruled against Hungary for its inhumane migration control and asylum policies. In two cases, the court stated that Hungary had unlawfully and arbitrarily detained asylum seekers. In the third case, the court held that Hungary had unlawfully pushed a 14-year-old unaccompanied Pakistani child back to Serbia without examining his situation or providing him the option of filing an asylum claim. In October, in two other judgments, the court ruled against Hungary concerning its unlawful pushback practices, and in a third judgment, it found that investigations into police violence during a pushback was ineffective. Also in October, the court handed down three judgments ruling that the detention of asylum seekers was unlawful.

India

The Indian government, led by Prime Minister Narendra Modi of the Bharatiya Janata Party (BJP), persisted with policies that discriminate and stigmatize religious and other minorities. This led to increasing incidents of communal violence in many parts of the country, including in Manipur state, where hundreds were killed in ethnic clashes.

The police in BJP-governed states failed to properly investigate crimes against minorities while administrative officials responded by summarily punishing victim communities, including those who protested such abuses. Constitutional authorities like the National Human Rights Commission, and those designed to protect the rights of children, women, religious minorities, tribal groups, and Dalits, did not function independently.

The government promoted the use of a digital public infrastructure to expand the delivery of social and economic services. However, those efforts were harmed by rampant internet shutdowns, lack of privacy and data protection, and uneven access among rural communities.

In September, India, holding the rotating presidency, hosted the summit of the Group of Twenty (G20), the world's largest economies, and pushed to include the African Union as a permanent member and make the group more representative and inclusive.

Jammu and Kashmir

Indian authorities continued to restrict free expression, peaceful assembly, and other rights in Jammu and Kashmir. Reports of extrajudicial killings by security forces continued throughout the year.

Critics and human rights defenders faced arrests and raids based on spurious terrorism allegations. On March 22, prominent Kashmiri human rights activist Khurram Parvez, already detained since November 2021 on accusations of terrorism, was charged on allegations of financing terrorism under the Unlawful Activities (Prevention) Act (UAPA). On March 20, Irfan Mehraj, a journalist formerly associated with Parvez's human rights organization, was also arrested in the same case. UN human rights experts have repeatedly called for Parvez's release and condemned the use of the UAPA to target civil society and human rights defenders.

In April 2023, six UN human rights experts wrote to the Indian government over the alleged arbitrary detention and ill-treatment of human rights defender Muhammad Ahsan Untoo, saying his detention "appears to be part of a strategy to disrupt, intimidate, detain and punish those engaging in journalism and human rights advocacy."

In May, the G20 Tourism Working Group held a meeting in Kashmir, prompting the UN special rapporteur on minority issues to say that "the G20 is unwittingly providing a veneer of support to a facade of normalcy at a time when massive human rights violations" continued to escalate.

Impunity for Security Force Abuses

Allegations of torture and extrajudicial killings persisted, with the National Human Rights Commission registering 126 deaths in police custody, 1,673 deaths in judicial custody, and 55 alleged extrajudicial killings in the first nine months in 2023.

On April 13, 2023, police in Uttar Pradesh state shot and killed an associate and the 19-year-old son of politician Atiq Ahmed, who was serving a life sentence and faced about 100 criminal cases, including for murder. The state's BJP chief minister praised the killings while BJP leaders openly insinuated that Ahmed could also be killed by the police or in an "accident." Two days after his son's killing, Ahmed and his brother were fatally shot at close range on live television as they were being escorted by the police for a routine medical checkup. Two BJP state ministers hailed the murders as "divine justice," renewing concerns about a breakdown in the rule of law in the state.

In April, the Indian government denied permission to prosecute soldiers accused of killing six coal miners in Nagaland state's Mon district in December 2021. In June 2022, the state police had filed charges against 30 soldiers, including a major, after a special investigation team found the military had shot the miners "with a clear intention to kill." But the central government refused to sanction the prosecution, which is required for civilian legal actions to proceed under the colonial-era Armed Forces Special Powers Act (AFSPA). The law has long shielded India's armed forces from being held accountable for grave human rights abuses in Jammu and Kashmir and several states in the northeast.

Religious Minorities, Dalits, and Tribal Groups

On July 31, communal violence broke out in Nuh district in Haryana state during a Hindu procession and swiftly spread to several adjoining districts. Following the violence, as part of a growing pattern, the authorities retaliated against Muslim residents by illegally demolishing hundreds of Muslim properties and detaining scores of Muslim boys and men. The demolitions led the Punjab and Haryana High Court to ask the state whether it was conducting "ethnic cleansing."

On May 3, violence erupted in the northeast Manipur state between the majority Meitei and the minority Kuki Zo communities. By November, more than 200 people were killed, tens of thousands displaced, and hundreds of homes and churches destroyed. The authorities shut down internet access in the state. Prime Minister Modi responded to the violence after nearly three months, only after a video emerged on July 20 showing a Meitei mob stripping and parading two Kuki women on May 4.

Civil society activists alleged that BJP's Chief Minister N. Biren Singh fueled divisiveness in Manipur with political patronage to violent groups in the Hindu-majority Meitei community and by stigmatizing the Kuki by alleging their involvement in drug trafficking and providing sanctuary to refugees from Myanmar. In August, the Supreme Court said the state police had "lost control over the situation," and ordered special teams to investigate the violence, including sexual violence, in Manipur. In September, over a dozen United Nations experts raised concerns about the ongoing violence and abuses in Manipur, saying the government's response had been slow and inadequate.

Counterinsurgency operations against Maoist rebels in central India, home to many tribal communities, led to abuses against villagers. The authorities have often attempted to discredit human rights activists by describing them as Maoists or Maoist supporters.

Despite an official ban on "manual scavenging"—the degrading and dangerous practice of manually cleaning human excrement from private and public dry toi-

"No Internet Means No Work, No Pay, No Food"
Internet Shutdowns Deny Access to Basic Rights in "Digital India"
HUMAN RIGHTS WATCH
INTERNET FREEDOM FOUNDATION

lets, open defecation sites, septic tanks, and open and closed gutters and sewers—continued across the country, leading to deaths and injuries. Mostly Dalits and caste groups customarily relegated to the bottom of the caste hierarchy are forced to do this work.

Freedom of Expression

Authorities intensified efforts to silence civil society activists, independent journalists, and even political opponents through threats and by using politically motivated charges.

In March 2023, a court in Gujarat sentenced prominent opposition leader Rahul Gandhi to two years in prison in a politically motivated defamation case. Gandhi had raised corruption allegations in parliament against billionaire industrialist Gautam Adani, perceived to have close relations with the prime minister. The Supreme Court eventually suspended Gandhi's conviction in August.

In July, Manipur police filed a case of sedition, criminal conspiracy, defamation, promoting enmity, and breach of peace against three women activists who were part of the National Federation of Indian Women's fact-finding team. The team had described the ethnic clashes as a result of "state-sponsored violence" and called for a Supreme Court-monitored investigation.

In September, Manipur police filed criminal cases against the Editors Guild of India after it published a report saying the state leadership had played a partisan role in the ethnic violence.

In October 2023, police raided the office of the news website *NewsClick*, which has been critical of the Modi government, and the homes of several of its journalists and writers on allegations that the website got illegal funds from China, a charge it denies. The police also raided the homes of activists and comedians in Delhi as part of coordinated raids at 30 locations. In Mumbai, the police raided the home of activist Teesta Setalvad, who has been repeatedly targeted for fighting for justice for the Muslim victims of the 2002 riots in Gujarat state and has written articles critical of the government for *NewsClick*.

Soon after the writer Arundhati Roy spoke out at a protest that followed the raids, authorities said they would prosecute her and a Kashmiri academic for allegedly "promoting enmity between different groups," "causing disharmony," and "public mischief" for a speech Roy had made in 2010. A case was also registered under the counterterrorism law, the UAPA, against them.

In February, Indian tax officials raided the BBC offices in an apparent reprisal for a two-part documentary that highlighted Prime Minister Modi's record in failing to protect Muslims. The government had blocked the BBC documentary in India in January, using emergency powers under the Information Technology Rules.

In August 2023, India adopted a personal data protection law granting the government sweeping powers of unchecked state surveillance. In April, the government further expanded its control over online content through the Information Technology (Intermediary Guidelines and Digital Media Ethics Code) Amendment Rules, 2023. The Rules weaken safeguards around encryption and seriously undermine media freedom, privacy rights, and freedom of expression online. They also authorize the government to set up a "fact checking" unit with arbitrary, overbroad, and unchecked censorship powers to identify any online content deemed to be "false" or "misleading" with regard to the Indian government and requires that tech platforms and other intermediaries remove such content. If they do not comply, companies may face legal action.

Indian authorities continued to impose the largest number of internet shutdowns globally in 2022, violating Indian and international human rights standards. The shutdowns disproportionately hurt socially and economically marginalized communities by denying them access to free or subsidized food rations and livelihoods, which requires adequate internet access.

Women's and Girls' Rights

Indian authorities delayed the investigation into allegations of sexual abuse by a member of parliament from the ruling BJP and the president of the Wrestling Federation of India, Brij Bhushan Sharan Singh, despite weeks of protest by athletes. In April, six women and a child filed complaints of sexual abuse with the police against Singh. However, the police only initiated an investigation after the complainants filed a petition in the Supreme Court. In May, police forcibly tackled and temporarily detained protesting athletes, including two Olympic wrestlers. In June, the police finally charged Singh with sexual harassment, assault, and stalking. The case highlighted barriers to justice for sexual assault survivors in India, especially when the accused is powerful.

The authorities did not properly enforce the law to address sexual harassment at work. Women, particularly in the informal sector, remain constrained by stigma, fear of retribution, and institutional barriers to justice. The Indian government has not ratified the International Labour Organization Violence and Harassment Convention (C190), which it voted in favor of in 2019.

In September, the government adopted a law to reserve for women one-third of the seats in the lower house of parliament and state legislative assemblies. The BJP government said that the law, which has been in the works for 27 years, will not be implemented until India completes the next census and redraws the boundaries of constituencies, complicated processes expected to take several years.

Children's Rights

In January 2023, a news outlet reported that for over a year, Diksha, an education app owned and used by the Indian government, had exposed the personal data of nearly 600,000 students, as well as more than 1 million teachers, on the open web for anyone to find. Human Rights Watch found that Diksha transmitted children's data to a third-party company using advertising trackers and also had the capacity to collect children's precise location data, which it failed to disclose in its privacy policy. In February, the government announced a third-party security audit of the app and committed to better protect the data privacy of children and teachers using its app.

Millions of children from socially and economically marginalized communities remained at risk of exclusion from education, child marriage, and child labor.

Disability Rights

Disability rights advocates in India continued to raise concerns about the lack of progress on deinstitutionalization of people with disabilities. In May, Human Rights Watch found arbitrary detention, overcrowding, lack of adequately trained staff, denial of education, and prison-like conditions in a government-run institution for children and adults with disabilities on the outskirts of Delhi. The governing council of the institution has since announced reforms.

Sexual Orientation and Gender Identity

In October, the Supreme Court declined to legalize same-sex marriages, instead accepting the government's offer to set up a panel to consider granting certain benefits associated with marriage to same-sex couples.

Refugee Rights

Indian authorities continued to detain hundreds of Rohingya refugees for immigration-related offenses. On July 24, police in Uttar Pradesh state arrested 74 Rohingya refugees, including women and children, under immigration laws, saying they did not have valid documents. On July 18, when hundreds of Rohingya refugees in Jammu protested their indefinite detention, including through a hunger strike, Indian authorities responded with tear gas and beatings. Two days after the incident, a Rohingya infant died reportedly because of exposure to tear gas.

On August 9, Union Home Minister Amit Shah told parliament that the influx of Kuki refugees from bordering Myanmar had contributed to the unrest and violence in Manipur by creating "insecurities" among the Meitei community. This was one example of BJP leaders making false, prejudicial, and stigmatizing statements against refugees.

Environment and Human Rights

In August, the Indian Parliament passed the Forest Conservation Amendment Act, despite vocal opposition from environmental activists and tribal communities. The law dilutes existing safeguards and could lead to a loss of legal protection for one-quarter of Indian forests—enabling industry, mining, and infrastructure development in formerly protected areas—and threatens encroachment on tribal communities' traditional territories.

Key International Actors

In July, the European Parliament adopted a resolution on the ethnic violence in Manipur, urging Indian authorities to take all necessary measures to protect religious minorities, not to criminalize government critics, to allow independent investigations into the violence, and to end the internet shutdown. The Indian government condemned the resolution, calling it interference in internal affairs and reflective of a "colonial mindset." European Union leaders, and the EU at the UN, remained reluctant to express concerns about human rights abuses in the country.

In June, the United States hosted Modi for a four-day state visit, which included him addressing a joint session of the US Congress. Many Indian diaspora activists and groups protested the Modi administration's poor human rights record, and six Democrats boycotted his speech to Congress. A White House spokesperson also strongly condemned the online harassment faced by a *Wall Street Journal* reporter who questioned Modi on the issue of religious minorities during a joint press conference with US President Joe Biden in Washington.

French President Emmanuel Macron invited Modi as the guest of honor for the July 14 military parade and awarded him the highest rank of France's Legion of Honor. During the visit, India announced a multibillion-dollar arms deal with France, but the two countries failed to discuss human rights.

In April, Australia and India signed a trade deal, after a decade of negotiations. A month later, during Modi's visit to Sydney, Australian Prime Minister Anthony Albanese avoided discussing Modi's human rights record when questioned by the press, instead repeating his refrain that India was the world's largest democracy.

Foreign Policy

In September, India negotiated a resolution at the G20 summit in New Delhi. The statement only mentioned "human suffering and negative added impacts of the war in Ukraine," but it did not condemn Russia's atrocities or its responsibility for disrupting the global grain supply. However, the group agreed to take steps to address challenges, including food insecurity and gender inequality, and to manage global debt vulnerabilities.

India abstained on important UN resolutions, including one condemning Russia's invasion of Ukraine and extending the mandate of the investigation into alleged war crimes in Ukraine and another establishing a probe into serious abuses in the context of the conflict in Sudan, among others.

In September, tensions escalated between India and Canada after Canadian Prime Minister Justin Trudeau announced an investigation into "credible allegations of a potential link between agents of the government of India" and the killing of a Canadian Sikh separatist leader in Canada, allegations that India denied. Earlier in the year, India had raised concerns with Canada about the safety of its diplomats.

Indonesia

Indonesia, a multiparty democracy, continued to fall short in protecting and promoting basic civil and political rights. President Joko "Jokowi" Widodo began the last year of his two terms in office, during which he did little to advance human rights protections in the country. Politically, Jokowi made his son, Gibran Raka, the running mate to presidential candidate Prabowo Subianto after the Constitutional Court—headed by Anwar Usman, Jokowi's brother-in-law—had controversially ruled that 36-year-old Gibran was eligible to join the presidential ticket because he is an elected mayor, despite the statutory age requirement of 40.

Indonesian authorities committed or condoned numerous human rights abuses involving discrimination on religious, ethnic, social, gender, and sexual orientation grounds. Disadvantaged groups—in particular religious minorities, women and girls, and lesbian, gay, bisexual, and transgender (LGBT) people—faced continuing or increasing restrictions on the rights to freedom of expression, belief, religion, and movement. Military and police committed abuses with impunity, especially in West Papua, where authorities continued to restrict travel and access by outside media, diplomats, and human rights monitors.

New Criminal Code

On January 2, 2023, President Jokowi signed into law a new criminal code containing problematic provisions that, if implemented and enforced, would undermine freedoms of speech, belief, and association and imperil the rights of women, religious minorities, and LGBT people. The law comes into effect in January 2026. In late 2022, the government summoned the United Nations' lead representative in Indonesia in response to a critical statement on the law by UN experts, leading the UN to remove the statement from the UN Indonesia website.

In early 2023, the government pledged to consult with stakeholders, embassies, businesses, and civil society groups on implementation regulations, but subsequent consultations were one-sided briefings by officials in which no input was solicited. Many of the law's vague or overbroad provisions remained poorly defined, magnifying concerns about the law's future enforcement.

The new law criminalizes consensual sex outside of marriage and cohabitation of unrelated persons, permitting intrusions into the most intimate decisions of individuals and families. Since same-sex couples cannot marry in Indonesia, the provisions effectively render same-sex sexual conduct illegal. The law also recognizes "any living law" in the country, which could be interpreted as legitimizing hundreds of discriminatory regulations based on Sharia (Islamic law) that local authorities have imposed in jurisdictions across the country, including curfews for women and girls, mandatory hijab dress codes, and provisions that could impact the rights of LGBT people.

The new law maintains provisions criminalizing abortion and expands criminalization to include providing information about obtaining abortions or providing information about contraception to children. The law's blasphemy chapter was expanded to include an article criminalizing apostasy. The law also criminalizes speech insulting or demeaning senior government officials or state institutions and expands articles on criminal defamation and "fake news."

Women's and Girls' Rights

Many provinces, regencies, and cities continued to impose discriminatory dress codes on women and girls. In August, Indonesia's National Commission on Violence Against Women (Komnas Perempuan) held its first-ever hearing on mandatory dress regulations, hearing from female students, teachers, and parents about widespread bullying of those who refuse to wear the jilbab or hijab. Many of those refusing to comply with the rules, including non-Muslims, continued to face expulsion or pressure to withdraw from school. In several cases, female civil servants, including teachers and university lecturers, lost their jobs or resigned for refusing to comply with rules.

The provision in the criminal code banning sex outside of marriage is likely to deter rape victims, who are mostly women and girls, from reporting rapes and could lead to some rape victims being imprisoned if they are suspected of having engaged in consensual sex outside of marriage.

Disability Rights

The Indonesian Mental Health Association had petitioned the Constitutional Court of Indonesia to review article 433 of the Civil Code to ban guardianship of people with psychosocial or intellectual disabilities. In July 2023, in an important step forward, the Constitutional Court partially granted the petitioners' request by altering the nature of guardianship of people with disabilities from being mandatory to being optional.

The UN Committee on the Rights of Persons with Disabilities called on the Indonesian government to eradicate restrictive practices such as *pasung* (shackling). According to a recent media report, seven people with psychosocial disabilities (mental health conditions) who were shackled died on Flores Island between June and September.

Sexual Orientation and Gender Identity

Officials continued to target LGBT people. In July, advocates canceled a regional gathering of LGBT activists in Jakarta in response to harassment and death threats from Muslim conservatives. The ASEAN SOGIE Caucus, a regional organization based in the Philippines, had planned to hold their annual ASEAN Queer Advocacy Week in Jakarta during the Association of Southeast Asian Nations (ASEAN) summit.

On May 28, Pekanbaru police and public security officials arrested 29 women and 28 men in several raided houses in Sukajadi area, accusing them of being "LGBT couples."

Freedom of Religion and Belief

Provisions in a 1965 blasphemy law (already in effect but expanded by the new criminal code), and a 2006 religious harmony regulation, continue to place religious minorities at risk. The 2006 regulation continued to give religious majorities in communities the power to veto religious activities by minority religions or stop them from constructing houses of worship, primarily impacting Christians, Shia Muslims, Hindus, Buddhists, and Confucians. Smaller minorities, including Ahmadiyah, Bah'ai, and Indigenous faiths, continue to face even harsher treatment. As in the previous two decades, the government did too little to stop Islamic groups attacking or harassing religious minorities or to hold those responsible to account. For instance, on September 17, dozens of Muslim militants stopped a religious service held by a Christian group in Depok, arguing it had "no permit" to conduct services.

In March, police arrested a TikTok star, Lina Mukherjee, under the blasphemy law for posting an online video showing her eating pork after saying an Islamic prayer. In September, the Palembang district court sentenced her to two years in prison. Islamic groups have also pressured musical or theater venues to cancel or not host artists deemed to promote un-Islamic values.

Papua Provinces, Ethnic Minorities, and Land Rights

In December 2022, a special court convened in Makassar acquitted an army officer, Isak Sattu, of charges related to an infamous 2014 massacre in West Papua during which soldiers fired on hundreds of protesting Papuans for over 7 minutes, killing 4 teenagers and injuring as many as 21 other people, including women and children.

In April, prominent human rights defenders Haris Azhar and Fatia Maulidiyanti were placed on trial in Jakarta for criminal defamation pursuant to a complaint by Luhut Binsar Pandjaitan, a senior minister in President Jokowi's cabinet, under Indonesia's Electronic Information and Transactions Law (ITE Law), relating to statements they made about Pandjaitan's alleged involvement in a gold mining project in West Papua.

Dozens of Papuans arrested for their participation in widespread anti-racism protests across Papua in 2019, including Malvin Yobe and Victor Yeimo, were released in 2023 after serving sentences. Authorities continue to arrest and prosecute Indigenous Papuans for expressing views in support of peaceful self-determination.

The government's planned evictions of thousands of ethnic Malay people on Rempang Island, south of Singapore, which have been partly enabled by their lack of proper land title, led to massive but largely peaceful protests in September, which authorities met with tear gas and water cannons.

UN experts expressed alarm at reports of increased militarization and intimidation around the Mandalika project on Lombok Island.

Key International Actors

Indonesia chaired ASEAN in 2023, organizing multiple summits, but ASEAN did not press the military junta in Myanmar to implement any provisions of the Five Point Consensus achieved in Jakarta in April 2021 after the military coup in February 2021.

In Johannesburg on August 24, President Jokowi declined to accept an offer to join BRICS (the grouping founded by Brazil, Russia, India, China, and South Africa). The group agreed to add six other countries—Argentina, Egypt, Ethiopia, Iran, Saudi Arabia, and the United Arab Emirates—in an apparent effort to boost influence in the Global South.

At the 52nd session of the UN Human Rights Council in March and April 2023, member states adopted the outcome of the Universal Periodic Review (UPR) of Indonesia, in which the government committed to implement 205 out of the 269 recommendations received, including on ensuring that the new criminal code does not restrict fundamental freedoms, repealing discriminatory laws against LGBT people, and ending discrimination against women and girls.

In October 2023, Indonesia was elected to the Human Rights Council for a three-year term beginning in January 2024. As a previous member, Indonesia had a mixed record, voting to not even discuss a UN High Commissioner for Human Rights' report alleging possible crimes against humanity by China against its Uyghur and other Muslim communities in Xinjiang.

Iran

Iranian authorities brutally cracked down on the "woman, life, freedom" protests sparked after the September 2022 death in morality police custody of Mahsa Jina Amini, an Iranian-Kurdish woman, killing hundreds and arresting thousands of protestors. Scores of activists, including human rights defenders, members of ethnic and religious minorities, and dissidents, remain in prison on vague national security charges or are serving sentences after grossly unfair trials. Security forces' impunity is rampant, with no government investigations into their use of excessive and lethal force, torture, sexual assault, and other serious abuses. Authorities have expanded their efforts in enforcing abusive compulsory hijab laws. Security agencies have also targeted family members of those killed during the protests.

President Ebrahim Raeesi is accused of overseeing the mass extrajudicial executions of political prisoners in 1988.

Excessive and Lethal Force, Torture, and Sexual Assault

Security forces repressed widespread protests that erupted across the country in September 2022 with unlawful killing, torture, sexually assault, and enforced disappearances of protestors, including women and children, as part of a pattern of serious violations. Human rights groups are investigating the reported deaths of approximately 500 protestors, including at least 68 children. In the majority of cases, security forces reportedly shot the victims using various types of bullets.

Cases Human Rights Watch documented included security forces sexually assaulting a 17-year-old boy, security forces pushing a high school student onto a lit gas range during the arrest and beating and whipping her during interrogation, and interrogators torturing a boy by shoving needles under his nails.

Executions

Iran remains one of the world's top practitioners of the death penalty, applying it to individuals convicted of crimes committed as children and under vague national security charges; occasionally, it is also used for non-violent offenses.

Iranian law deems actions like "insulting the prophet," "apostasy," same-sex relations, adultery, alcohol consumption, and certain non-violent drug-related offenses to be punishable by death.

Based on a report from the Iran Human Rights Organization, at least 354 executions took place in Iran during the first half of 2023. This marks a substantial increase compared to the same period in 2022. Among those executed, 122 were charged with "intentional murder," 206 with "drug-related offenses," and 4 with "rape." Furthermore, 10 individuals received death sentences for political or security-related charges or blasphemy, and 1 person was sentenced to death on espionage charges.

Judicial authorities drastically increased the use of vaguely defined national security charges that could carry the death penalty against protestors, including for allegedly injuring others and destroying public property. Following grossly unfair trials where many of defendants did not have access to the lawyer of their choice, authorities issued 25 death sentences in connection to the protests. As of September 20, authorities executed 7 people, and 11 cases were overturned by the supreme court.

On February 21, Branch 15 of Tehran's Revolutionary Court sentenced Jamshid Sharmahd, 67, a German-Iranian citizen with United States residency, to death on the charge of "corruption on earth," according to Mizan news agency. The Iranian authorities allege that he was a leader of an opposition group, the "Kingdom Assembly of Iran"—which was connected to multiple terror attacks, including the 2008 bombing of a mosque in Shiraz— a claim that Sharmahd denies. On May 6, authorities executed Swedish-Iranian national Habibollah Asivad (Chaab) on alleged terrorism charges after abducting him in Turkey.

Freedoms of Assembly and Expression

Iranian authorities severely restricted the freedoms of assembly and expression, arresting hundreds of activists, lawyers, journalists, students, and artists. The authorities also targeted outspoken family members of those killed or families of protesters executed after unfair trials, pressuring them to avoid holding memorial services around the anniversaries of their deaths.

The crackdown extended to universities. Since late July, at least 27 university instructors critical of government policies were dismissed, suspended, or forced to retire or their contracts were not renewed. The actual number is most likely higher. According to the Volunteer Committee tracking detainees, since September, at least 161 students faced disciplinary actions due to protest-related activities. The number of those who were summoned by disciplinary committees was much higher. On August 8, Branch 26 of Tehran's Revolutionary Court sentenced Allameh University student activists Zia Nabavi and Hasti Amiri to one year in prison on the charge of "propaganda against the state," which stemmed from their participation in the protests against the alleged poisoning of schoolgirls in the country.

Artists who vocally supported the protest movement faced reprisals, arrests, and prosecution. Authorities have targeted dozens of high-profile actors supportive of the protests, including Taraneh Alidoosti, who was released from prison on January 4.

On July 12, Isfahan's judiciary chief, Assadolah Jafari, announced that rapper Toumaj Salehi, detained during the protests, received a six-year-and-three-month prison sentence for "corruption on earth." On August 28, authorities arrested a singer and composer, Mehdi Yarahi, after he released a song in support of the protest movement. Mizan News, the judiciary's news outlet, reported that Yarahi was charged with "releasing an illegal song." Kurdish-Iranian rapper Saman Seyedi, known as "Yasin," arrested during the protests, faced "enmity against the state" charges, including weapon possession and conspiracy to threaten national security. He remained imprisoned and reportedly suffered physical and psychological torture, including solitary confinement and severe beatings.

Over the past year, people with disabilities staged several protests over inadequate pension and poor living conditions. On several occasions, security forces attempted to break up their protests, including with tear gas.

Authorities imposed several localized internet shutdowns during protests, particularly in Sistan and Baluchistan province.

Attacks on Human Rights Defenders and Civil Society Activists

Scores of human rights defenders, labor rights activists, and other civil society activists— including Narges Mohammadi, Bahareh Hedayat, Niloufar Bayani, Sepideh Kashani, Houman Jokar, Taher Ghadirian, Keyvan Samimi, Reza Shahabi, Anisha Assadolahi, Mehdi Mahmoudian, and Sepideh Gholian—remain behind bars while authorities continued to harass, arrest, and prosecute those seeking accountability and justice.

In February, Iranian authorities announced a broad amnesty purportedly covering those arrested, charged, or detained during widespread protests. On March 13, Hojatollah Eslam Ejeyi, the head of Iran's judiciary, stated that 22,000 people were included in the amnesty orders related to the protests.

However, the amnesty excluded many human rights defenders with lengthy sentences and protesters facing capital charges. Since April, the authorities arrested, sentenced, or summoned dozens of activists, some of whom had been recently released and granted amnesty.

On April 28, Iran's security forces raided the house of Mohammad Habibi, the imprisoned spokesman of the Tehran Teachers' Union, and arrested nine activists visiting his family. Most of these activists had previously been wrongfully imprisoned.

In July, the Kurdistan Human Rights Network reported that 55 lawyers were summoned to the Prosecutor's Office in Bukan, Kurdistan province. They were accused of supporting Mahsa Jina Amini's family by signing a statement offering legal assistance. On August 30, Saleh Nikbakht, the lawyer who represents Amini's family, appeared before Branch 28 of Tehran's Revolutionary Court on charges of "propaganda against the state," which stemmed from his media interviews about Amini's case.

On August 16, authorities in Gilan province raided homes and detained 12 individuals, including 11 women's rights defenders and a political activist.

Niloofar Hamedi and Elaheh Mohammadi, two journalists from the *Shargh* and *Ham-Mihan* Iranian newspapers who were among the first journalists who reported on Amini's death, were arrested in September 2022. In October, authorities charged them with "collaborating with the hostile American government," "colluding against national security," and "engaging in propaganda activity against the regime."

Due Process Rights, Fair Trial Standards, and Prison Conditions

Iranian courts, particularly revolutionary courts, regularly fall far short of providing fair trials and use confessions likely obtained under torture as evidence in court. Authorities have failed to meaningfully investigate numerous allegations of torture against detainees and routinely restrict detainees' access to legal counsel, particularly during the initial investigation period.

Iranian authorities' violations of due process rights and fair trial standards as well as torture and ill-treatment of detainees have been systemic features of the government's crackdown on anti-government protests. Revolutionary court judges have persistently failed to consider allegations of torture and ill-treatment, including in trials where defendants were sentenced to the death penalty.

On August 31, Javad Rouhi, a 31-year-old imprisoned Iranian protester, died under suspicious circumstances in northern Iran, sparking concerns about his treatment. Rouhi had endured severe torture after his arrest during the September 2022 protests and was subsequently convicted after an unfair trial. Nowshahr prison in Mazandaran province announced that he had been transferred to a hospital due to a "concussion" and died there despite medical assistance. His death is under investigation by the Prosecutor's Office, as confirmed by his lawyer.

In recent years, Iran's security apparatus has escalated its targeting of dual citizens and foreign nationals whom they perceive have links to Western academic, economic, and cultural institutions, using them as bargaining chips in disputes with western states.

Women's and Girls' Rights

Women face discrimination in personal status matters related to marriage, divorce, inheritance, and decisions relating to children. Under the civil code, a husband has the right to choose the place of living and can prevent his wife from having certain occupations if he deems them against "family values." Under the Passports Law, a married woman may not obtain a passport or travel outside the country without the written permission of her husband, who can revoke such permission at any time.

The civil code allows girls to marry at age 13 and boys at age 15 and at younger ages if authorized by a judge.

Cases of femicide are increasingly reported in media and social media, but Iran has no law on domestic violence to prevent abuse and protect survivors. As reported by *Shargh* newspaper, based on official statistics, at least 165 women in Iran were killed by male family members between March 2021 and the end of June 2023, an average of 1 such killing every 4 days. From mid-March to mid-May 2023 alone, 27 women were reported murdered in so-called "honor killings," which are killings of women and girls perpetrated by family members.

In March, Iranian media outlets reported on the apparently deliberate poisoning of girls at least 58 schools in 10 provinces across the country since January 2023. Authorities promised to investigate but have yet to provide any concrete explanation for the incidents.

Since August, the authorities have allowed a limited number of tickets to be sold to women and girls to attend the national football league's games in some cities, including Tehran and Isfahan.

On October 28, Armita Garavand, a 17-year-old student, died after 28 days in a coma. Media reports indicated that she fell unconscious after she was assaulted by an enforcer of compulsory hijab law at the metro station. Authorities said she fell due to a "sudden drop in blood pressure" and have severely restricted the independent media's access to her family and friends.

Iranian authorities have intensified efforts to enforce compulsory hijab laws. They prosecute women and girls, including celebrities, for not wearing the hijab in public; issue traffic citations to passengers without the hijab; and close businesses that do not comply with hijab laws. In recent cases, the judiciary has mandated psychological treatment for at least two actresses convicted of hijab non-compliance, a move protested by Iranian mental health associations.

On September 21, the Iranian parliament approved a draft Hijab and Chastity Bill with 70 articles proposing additional penalties, such as fines, increased prison terms up to 10 years for expressing opposition to hijab regulations, and restrictions on job and educational opportunities for hijab violations. The law also expands the authority of intelligence and law enforcement agencies in enforcing compulsory hijab laws.

Iran's strict anti-abortion laws have introduced additional measures to limit women's access to abortion. The Ministry of Health has halted the issuance of licenses for the production and import of first-trimester prenatal screening kits.

Pregnant people who choose to undergo prenatal genetic screening tests must cover the associated costs themselves.

Sexual Orientation and Gender Identity

Under Iranian law, same-sex conduct is punishable by flogging and, for men, the death penalty. Although Iran permits and subsidizes sex reassignment surgery for transgender people, no law prohibits discrimination against them.

Treatment of Minorities

Iranian law denies freedom of religion to Baha'is and discriminates against them. Authorities continue to arrest and prosecute members of the Baha'i faith on vague national security charges and to close businesses owned by them. Iranian authorities also systematically refuse to allow Baha'is to register at public universities because of their faith.

The government also discriminates against other religious minorities, including Sunni Muslims, and restricts cultural and political activities among the country's Azeri, Kurdish, Arab, and Baluch ethnic minorities. Minority activists are regularly arrested and prosecuted on vaguely defined national security charges in trials that fall grossly short of international standards.

On August 28, the Kurdistan Human Rights Network reported that in July alone, at least 100 individuals had been apprehended for political reasons by security forces in Kurdish areas. A larger number of citizens have been summoned to security and judicial authorities in various cities, including West Azerbaijan, Kurdistan, Kermanshah, Ilam, and Tehran.

On the anniversary of the death in custody of Mahsa Jina Amini, Iran's authorities dispatched thousands of its military-security personnel, along with vehicles and equipment, to Kurdish-majority areas in the western provinces, where protests had been widespread over the past year.

Climate Change Policies and Impacts

As one of the world's top 10 greenhouse gas emitters, Iran's significant contribution to the climate crisis has global human rights implications. The majority of its emissions originate from the energy sector, with 94 percent of electricity generated from fossil fuels. Iran ranks eighth in world crude oil production and third in natural gas production, yet it also possesses substantial renewable energy potential. Energy is heavily subsidized, resulting in high per capita energy consumption. Iran has made limited efforts to reduce fossil fuel dependency, often citing international sanctions as a hindrance to adopting cleaner energy solutions. Notably, Iran remains one of three countries that have yet to ratify the Paris Agreement.

There are longstanding concerns across Iran, particularly Khuzestan province, about the mismanagement of water resources and pollution from oil development.

Key International Actors

The Norwegian Nobel Committee awarded the 2023 Nobel Peace Prize to Narges Mohammadi for "her fight against the oppression of women in Iran and her fight to promote human rights and freedom for all."

The European Parliament awarded the 2023 Sakharov Prize for Freedom of Thought to Mahsa Jina Amini and the Woman, Life, Freedom Movement in Iran.

A Special Session of the UN Human Rights Council in November 2022 created an international fact-finding mission on Iran, mandated to "thoroughly and independently investigate alleged human rights violations in the Islamic Republic of Iran related to the protests that began on 16 September 2022, especially with respect to women and children." The fact-finding mission presented an oral update in June 2023 and is scheduled to present its final report in March 2024.

Iraq

Following decades of armed conflict, Iraq enjoyed its most stable period since before the US-led invasion of 2003. However, the country remained fragile and deeply divided, and grievances driving the 2019 mass protests remained unresolved, including discontent with the current political system, failing public services, deteriorating infrastructure, and rampant corruption. Violent repression of protesters and arrests of journalists covering protests continued in 2023.

In October 2022, just over a year after the 2021 federal elections, political elites finally agreed on the appointment of Mohammed Shia al-Sudani as prime minister. Since Prime Minister al-Sudani took office, he attempted to capitalize on the period of relative calm and stability, centering his agenda around five key issues: combatting corruption, addressing unemployment, reducing poverty, reforming the economy and finances, and improving government services. In June 2023, Iraq's parliament approved an annual budget of 198.9 trillion Iraqi dinars (US$153 billion) for three years (2023 to 2025), the largest in the country's history and the first multiyear budget to be approved.

Iraq made several positive strides in respecting and upholding human rights, such as taking further steps toward implementing the Yazidi Survivors Law and enacting a Civilian Protection Policy. In June 2023, Kurdistan Regional Government (KRG) authorities published an update highlighting positive achievements it had made under its five-year plan to address human rights issues in the Kurdistan Region of Iraq (KRI), published in May 2022.

However, political infighting blocked the passage of key legislation that could protect Iraqis' rights, such as draft laws on child protection and domestic violence. Enacting structural reforms that address the grievances of Iraqi citizens became even more urgent in the context of a worsening climate crisis, stressing the need for Iraq to transition its economy and primary source of government revenue away from fossil fuels.

Women's and Girls' Rights

After playing a central role in the 2019-2020 protest movement, women continued to struggle against patriarchal norms embedded in Iraq's legal system.

Iraq's penal code enables impunity for male violence against women, including provisions that allow the husband to punish his wife, parents to discipline their children, and mitigated sentences for violent acts including murder for so-called "honorable motives." The penal code also allows perpetrators of rape or sexual assault to escape prosecution or have their sentences quashed if they marry their victim.

Women's rights groups continued to advocate for an anti-domestic violence law, but efforts in parliament stalled. Survivors of gender-based violence had limited access to shelter or justice, and some survivors of human trafficking were tried and convicted for prostitution. The few government shelters in the KRI only allowed women to enter or leave with court orders. While there were a small number of underground shelters for women in federal Iraq, run by local nongovernmental organizations (NGOs), they were not widely supported, but often criticized, and sometimes attacked by families and raided by authorities.

Women in unregistered marriages (marriages conducted by religious leaders but not registered with the Personal Status Court) faced severe challenges in accessing government services and social protection if their marriage was not legalized. Unregistered marriages are often done as a way to circumvent legal restrictions on child marriage, polygamy, and forced marriage and to evade having to pay spousal maintenance in case of divorce. Without a civil marriage certificate, women are unable to give birth in government hospitals, access social protection schemes contingent on one's marital status, obtain birth certificates for their children, or have legal recourse to claim spousal maintenance or child support in the event of divorce.

Civil Documentation

In September 2022, seven aid groups found that nearly five years after the government declared victory over Islamic State (ISIS), up to 1 million Iraqis, displaced by the armed group's seizure of swaths of Iraqi territory and the battle to recapture them, remained unable to obtain basic civil documentation. The documents they cannot obtain include certificates of birth, marriage, and death as well as Iraq's relatively new unified national identification card. Such documents are essential for accessing vital public services, including monthly food disbursements and children's access to education.

Women who fled abusive families without their legal identification documents struggled to have them replaced. Without a civil ID, women also face challenges freely moving around and registering for their residence card, which is required to rent housing or secure employment.

Children born of unregistered marriages or born out of wedlock, including those born of rape, may be unable to obtain birth certificates and thus other key civil documents, limiting their access to government services and social protection. If the paperwork is left unresolved, those affected cannot enroll in school, access employment opportunities, and may be forced to enter into unregistered marriages later in life.

Children's Rights

In June 2023, the Iraqi parliament introduced a draft child protection law, the first of its kind for the country and a vital step in safeguarding children's rights in Iraq. If passed, the law would address crucial issues like child labor, exploitation, and abuse. It would also explicitly enshrine children's fundamental rights into law, including the rights to life, health, education, and citizenship.

Over the last 20 years, rates of child marriage in Iraq have been steadily increasing. A study conducted in 2021 by the Ministry of Planning and the Central Statistical Organization found that 25.5 percent of married women in Iraq were married before they were 18, and 5.2 percent of women were married before 15. Poverty, insecurity, and lower educational outcomes for girls have all been associated with increased child marriage rates in Iraq. Child marriage and adolescent pregnancy can have serious adverse health impacts, limit access to education and employment, and exacerbate risks of sexual and domestic violence.

Freedom of Expression

In January 2023, the Iraqi government launched a campaign to target "indecent content" online. The same month, the Ministry of Interior launched a platform that allows Iraqis to denounce or report any social media content that "violates public morals, contains negative and indecent messages, and undermines social stability." Over 96,000 complaints were received in a month. As a result, six people were sentenced to prison terms but have since been released.

The campaign uses article 403 of the Iraqi penal code, which criminalizes published material that "violates public integrity or decency." While Iraq's constitution provides for freedom of expression, including for members of the press and other media, it also includes restrictions on expression assessed by authorities to violate public order and morality.

Vaguely worded laws have been used to target and silence journalists, activists, and rival politicians, including in the KRI. In many cases, spurious anti-defamation lawsuits are less about proving the individual committed a crime, but rather about using the legal proceedings themselves as a punishment or way to control the activities of the person being charged.

Climate Change and Environmental Degradation

The UN ranked Iraq as the fifth most vulnerable country to global warming and climate change, and the environmental crisis in Iraq was steadily increasing in scope and severity. Droughts, desertification, increased frequency and severity of sandstorms, pollution, and rising temperatures are symptomatic of this crisis. Large swaths of Iraq are expected to become uninhabitable in the coming years or decades. Weak environmental protection legislation and dirty industrial practices such as gas flaring have contributed to rising cancer rates among local populations.

A growing environmental movement in Iraq seeks to address the environmental degradation caused by conflict and resource mismanagement, prepare Iraq to adapt to the new realities of climate change, and promote Iraq's transition away from a fossil fuels-based economy. Like activists across the civil society space, their efforts have been met with harassment, intimidation, and threats. In February 2023, a prominent environmental activist was abducted, tortured, and held for two weeks by an unidentified armed group. In March 2023, Prime Minister al-Sudani promised sweeping measures to tackle climate change, including plans to meet one-third of its electricity demands using renewable energy.

Returns of Displaced People

Six years after the last territory controlled by ISIS was retaken by forces from Iraq and a United States-led international military coalition, about 1.16 million Iraqis remain internally displaced, mostly across the KRI. In April 2023, the Ministry of Migration and Displacement hastily closed Jeddah 5, the last official camp for internally displaced people in federal Iraq, with little advance notice and despite concerns about camp residents' safety in their areas of origin.

Since January 2021, Iraqi authorities have repatriated about 10,000 Iraqis unlawfully detained as ISIS suspects and family members in northeast Syria – nearly 7,000 from al-Hol camp, mostly women and children, and about 3,000 men held in prisons whom Iraq said it was prosecuting. Most returnees are sent to Jeddah 1, a temporary "rehabilitation camp" near Mosul, before returning to their places of origin. United Nations Secretary General Antonio Guterres and US officials have lauded the returns, though some NGOs and UN staff have questioned whether the repatriations met UN principles for safe and voluntary returns and expressed concerns about families leaving the camp without essential documentation, which may limit their ability to access government services in their places of origin.

Sixty percent of the population of Sinjar remain displaced in camps and homes since 2014, when they fled ISIS attacks and Iraqi counterattacks. Continued insecurity in Sinjar resulting from Turkish airstrikes and competition between armed groups for control of the area, lagging reconstruction of essential services and infrastructure, and the Iraqi government's failure to provide compensation for homes and businesses lost during military operations were the main barriers to their return.

Sexual Orientation and Gender Identity

In 2023, the political climate toward lesbian, gay, bisexual, and transgender (LGBT) people in Iraq became markedly more hostile. On August 15, Raad Al-Maliki, an independent member of parliament, introduced a bill that would impose the death penalty or life in prison for same-sex conduct and imprisonment for transgender expression. Earlier that month, the Iraqi Communications and Media Commission issued a directive ordering all media outlets to replace the term "homosexuality" with "sexual deviance" in their published and broadcasted language and banning use of the term "gender."

In the KRI, on May 31, a court ordered the closure of Rasan Organization, a human rights organization, over "its activities in the field of homosexuality." In September 2022, members of the Kurdistan regional parliament introduced a bill that would punish any individual or group that advocates for the rights of LGBT people.

The targeting of LGBT people online and violence against LGBT people, including killings, abductions, torture, and sexual violence by armed groups in Iraq continued to be met with impunity. Iraqi authorities have also targeted LGBT people using a range of vague provisions in Iraq's penal code aimed at policing morals and public indecency and limiting freedom of expression.

Key International Actors

Twenty years after the US-led invasion of Iraq, the US government has failed to provide compensation or other redress to Iraqis who suffered torture and other abuses at US-run prisons in the country. Survivors still have no clear path to raise a claim with the US government or apply for compensation or recognition, even though the effects of torture are a daily reality for many Iraqi survivors and their families.

Türkiye continues regularly conducting airstrikes and targeted assassinations in northern Iraq, primarily targeting the Kurdistan Workers Party (PKK) and Sinjar Resistance Units (YBS), sometimes killing civilians. In July 2023, four claimants who survived or witnessed a Turkish airstrike that allegedly targeted a civilian hospital in Sinjar, killing eight people, issued a formal complaint to the UN Human Rights Council. Iraq has repeatedly condemned the attacks as a violation of its sovereignty but has largely refrained from investigating the attacks or providing compensation to victims.

Israel and Palestine

In 2023, civilians were targeted, attacked, and killed at a unprecedented scale in the recent history of Israel and Palestine.

On October 7, Hamas-led gunmen from the Gaza Strip launched an attack in southern Israel, deliberately killing civilians, firing into crowds, gunning people down in their homes, and taking hostages back to Gaza, including older people and children, acts that amount to war crimes. According to Israeli authorities, more than 1,200 people, most of them civilians, have been killed since October 7 and 133 remained held hostage, as of December 15.

Shortly thereafter, Israeli authorities cut off essential services, including water and electricity, to Gaza's population and blocked the entry of all but a trickle of fuel and critical humanitarian aid, acts of collective punishment that amount to war crimes and were ongoing at time of writing. Israeli air strikes incessantly pounded Gaza, hitting schools and hospitals and reducing large parts of neighborhoods to rubble, including in attacks that were apparently unlawful. Israeli forces also unlawfully used white phosphorous in densely populated areas. They ordered the evacuation of all people from northern Gaza and displaced an estimated 85 percent of Gaza's population—1.9 million people—as of December 11. More than 18,700 Palestinians, most of them civilians, including more than 7,800 children, were killed between October 7 and December 12, according to Gaza authorities.

The blockade exacerbated the humanitarian situation stemming from Israel's 16-year-long sweeping restrictions on the movement of people and goods into and out of Gaza. The prolonged closure, as well as Egyptian restrictions on its border with Gaza, has deprived the 2.2 million Palestinians in Gaza, with rare exceptions, of their right to freedom of movement and opportunities to better their lives; severely limited their access to electricity, health care, and water; and devastated the economy.

In the West Bank, between the start of 2023 and December 12, Israeli forces had killed 464 Palestinians, including 109 children, according to the United Nations Office for the Coordination of Humanitarian Affairs (OCHA), more than twice as many as in any other year since 2005, when the UN began systematically recording fatalities. This included unlawful killings stemming from Israel's regular use of excessive lethal force and some cases of extrajudicial executions.

Israeli authorities also held 2,873 Palestinians in administrative detention, without charge or trial based on secret information, as of December 1, according to Israeli Prison Services figures. This figure marks a three-decade high, according to the Israeli human rights group HaMoked.

During the first half of 2023, the Israeli government approved building 12,855 new housing units in settlements in the occupied West Bank. This is the highest number the Israeli group Peace Now, which has systematically tracked plans since 2012, has ever recorded. The transfer of civilians into occupied territory is a war crime.

During the first eight months of 2023, incidents of settler violence against Palestinians and their property reached their highest daily average since the UN started recording this data in 2006: an average of three incidents per day as compared to two per day in 2022 and one in 2021. This included rampages by mobs of settler in Huwara and Turmus Ayya. That rate increased to over five incidents per day after October 7.

Prominent Palestinian civil society organizations remain outlawed as "terrorist" and "illegal" organizations. Israeli forces raided their offices in August 2022.

Israeli authorities' repression of Palestinians, undertaken as part of a policy to maintain the domination of Jewish Israelis over Palestinians, amount to the crimes against humanity of apartheid and persecution.

Gaza Strip

Amid Israeli intense military operations since October 7, more than 46,000 housing units have been destroyed and 234,000 others damaged, accounting for 60 percent of the housing stock in Gaza, as of November 24, according to aid organizations. At least 342 schools have been damaged, according to OCHA, and 187 "attacks on health care" were carried out, damaging 24 hospitals, according to the World Health Organization (WHO).

Israeli air strikes and the blockade caused the majority of hospitals to cease operating. The lack of electricity and fuel forced wastewater, desalination facilities, and bakeries to shut down and contributed to telecommunications blackouts. The lack of water created a public health crisis. While some aid trucks began entering Gaza on October 21, with even more entering during a multiday ceasefire that began on November 24, the aid fell short of meeting the needs of Gaza's population.

Israel's order to evacuate northern Gaza did not take into the account the needs of older people, people with disabilities, and patients, many of whom are unable to leave. The move risks forced displacement, a war crime.

A prior round of hostilities in May, featuring Israeli strikes on Gaza and rocket attacks on Israel by Palestinian armed groups in Gaza, left at least 33 Palestinians in Gaza, including at least 12 civilians, and 2 civilians in Israel dead, according to OCHA.

Israeli Closure Policy

Since 2007, Israeli authorities have blocked most of Gaza's population from traveling through the Erez Crossing, the only passenger crossing from Gaza into Israel through which Palestinians can travel to the West Bank and abroad. Israeli authorities often justify the closure, which came after Hamas seized political control over Gaza from the Fatah-led Palestinian Authority (PA) in June 2007, on security grounds. However, the closure policy is not based on an individualized assessment of security risk; a generalized travel ban applies to all except those whom Israeli authorities deem as presenting "exceptional humanitarian circumstances," mostly people needing vital medical treatment and their companions, as well as prominent businesspeople.

Even those seeking urgent medical care outside of Gaza at times face denials or delays in approvals. WHO reported that 839 Palestinians in Gaza died between 2008 and 2021 while waiting for a response to their permit requests.

During the first eight months of 2023, an average of 1,653 Palestinians in Gaza exited via Erez daily, according to the Israeli rights group Gisha. This marked an increase over previous years, largely driven by work permits, but remains less than 7 percent of the daily average of more than 24,000 before the beginning of the Second Intifada, or Palestinian uprising, in September 2000.

Gaza's exports during the first eight months of 2023, mostly produce destined for the West Bank and Israel, averaged 607 truckloads per month, less than the monthly average of 1,064 truckloads prior to the June 2007 tightening of the closure, according to Gisha. Authorities severely restricted the entry of construction materials and other items they deemed "dual-use" materials that could also be used for military purposes. The list of such items also includes X-ray and communications equipment, spare parts and batteries for assistive devices for people with disabilities, and other vital civilian items.

Since October 7 and until time of writing, Israeli authorities sealed its crossings into Gaza, blocking the entry of people and goods, including residents in need of urgent medical care, from leaving Gaza via Erez. Israeli authorities have regularly resorted to such measures, which target civilians and amount to unlawful collective punishment.

The closure limits access to basic services. Between January and September 2023, families in Gaza were without centrally provided electricity for an average of 13 hours per day, according to OCHA. Chronic prolonged power outages encumber many aspects of everyday life, including heating, cooling, sewage treatment, health care, and business. The outages imposed particular hardships on people with disabilities, who rely on light to communicate using sign language or equipment powered by electricity to move, such as elevators or electric wheelchairs. More than 96 percent of groundwater in Gaza, its only remaining natural water source, is "unfit for human consumption," according to the Palestinian Water Authority and OCHA. This leaves most Gaza residents reliant on desalination and water coming via Israel, which have been disrupted amid the hostilities. Before October 7, about 80 percent of Gaza's residents relied on humanitarian aid, according to the UN Relief and Works Agency for Palestine Refugees in the Near East (UNRWA).

Egypt also restricts the movement of people and goods via its Rafah crossing with Gaza, at times fully sealing the crossing. In the first eight months of 2023, an average of 27,975 Palestinians crossed monthly in both directions, less than the monthly average of over 40,000 before the 2013 military coup in Egypt, according to Gisha.

Abuses by Hamas and Palestinian Armed Groups

Hamas and other Palestinian armed groups on October 7 deliberately killed civilians and committed a range of other abuses, including taking civilians hostage, and launched thousands of indiscriminate rockets at Israeli communities, all of which are war crimes. During the October 7 attacks, Hamas-led fighters attacked the "Supernova Sukkot Gathering" outdoor music festival, killing at least 260 people, according to the Israeli rescue service, and invaded homes. Armed groups threatened to execute hostages. They released some of the hostages in late November in exchange for the release by Israel of Palestinian prisoners, as part of a short-term ceasefire agreement.

Human Rights Watch investigated an October 17 explosion at the al-Ahli Hospital in Gaza City, which caused scores of casualties, and found that it resulted from an apparent rocket-propelled munition, such as those commonly used by Palestinian armed groups.

In June 2022 and January 2023, Hamas authorities published footage that appeared to show Avera Mangistu and Hisham al-Sayed, Israeli civilians with psychosocial disabilities that they have apparently held for more than eight years after the two men entered Gaza. Their incommunicado detention is unlawful.

Courts in Gaza had sentenced 203 people to death since June 2007 when Hamas authorities took control in Gaza, including 14 people between January and September 2023, according to Gaza-based organizations Palestinian Center for Human Rights (PCHR) and al-Mezan. Hamas authorities have carried out 33 executions since June 2007 for common criminal offenses and "collaboration" with Israel; none occurred during the first nine months of 2023.

Hamas authorities forcibly dispersed protesters during the summer "We Want to Live" demonstrations against difficult living conditions, roughing up and detaining some demonstrators and journalists, according to PCHR and al-Mezan. The Palestinian statutory watchdog, the Independent Commission for Human Rights (ICHR), received 56 complaints of arbitrary arrests and 81 complaints of torture and ill-treatment against Hamas authorities between January and August 2023.

Hamas authorities have blocked some women from traveling pursuant to regulations issued in February 2021 that allow male guardians to apply to courts to block unmarried women from leaving Gaza when such travel will cause "absolute harm," a broad term that allows men to restrict women's travel at will. In January, Hamas authorities tracked down and forcibly returned two women, Wisam and Fatma al-Tawil, to their father, whom they had previously fled from after reporting severe domestic violence, including death threats.

West Bank

Israel's repression of Palestinians in the West Bank intensified during 2023, especially after October 7.

Israeli Use of Force

Israeli forces carried out several large-scale raids in 2023, particularly targeting the city of Nablus and Jenin refugee camp. The latter on July 3-4 was the scene of the largest and deadliest operation in the West Bank since 2005, resulting in the killing of 12 Palestinians, including 4 children, the temporary displacement of 3,500 people, and damage to 460 housing units, according to OCHA.

The more than 460 killed in 2023—at least an 18-year-high—included Palestinians who attacked Israelis or threw Molotov cocktails or stones at Israeli forces, bystanders, those helping the wounded, and others uninvolved in the fighting. OCHA reported that more than half the fatalities since October 7 took place during Israeli operations that did not involve armed clashes.

Israeli settlers killed 15 Palestinians, as of December 7, according to OCHA. Between October 7 and November 28, settlers attacked 93 Palestinian communities, the Israeli human rights group Yesh Din found.

Israeli authorities have rarely held accountable security forces who used excessive force or settlers who attacked Palestinians. Less than 1 percent of complaints of abuses by Israeli forces filed by Palestinians in the West Bank between 2017 and 2021 and 7 percent of complaints of settler violence between 2005 and 2022 led to indictments, according to Yesh Din. Even in the settler rampage of Huwara, Israeli authorities released most of the 17 men arrested on suspicion of involvement within days of their arrest. In July, the Jerusalem District Court acquitted the officer who in Jerusalem in 2020 killed Eyad al-Hallaq, a 32-year-old unarmed Palestinian man with autism who had threatened no one. The court called the fatal shooting an "honest mistake."

Unchecked settler violence and intimidation continues. According to OCHA, 1,105 Palestinians, including 4 entire communities, displaced since the beginning of 2022 cite settler violence and the prevention of access to grazing lands by settlers as the primary reason that they were forced to leave their homes. Between October 7 and December 13, 1,257 people have been displaced.

Palestinian Attacks

As of November 30, Palestinians killed 24 Israeli civilians during fatal attacks in the West Bank, a more than 15-year-high, according to OCHA. This included an incident in January in which a Palestinian killed seven civilians, including a child, in the Israeli settlement of Neve Yaakov in occupied East Jerusalem. Hamas praised many of the attacks.

Israeli Detention, Torture, and Ill-Treatment of Palestinians

Israeli authorities apply Israeli civil law to settlers but govern West Bank Palestinians under harsh military law. In so doing, they deny them basic due process and try them in military courts with a nearly 100 percent conviction rate against Palestinians.

As of December 1, Israel held 7,677 Palestinians in custody for "security" offenses, according to Israeli Prison Services figures. This includes 200 Palestinian children, as of November 6, according to the Palestinian prisoner rights group Addameer. Israel incarcerates many Palestinians from the Occupied Palestinian Territory (OPT) inside Israel, complicating family visits and violating international humanitarian law's prohibition against their transfer outside occupied territory.

In May, Khader Adnan, 45, died in his prison cell on the 86th day of his hunger strike against Israeli detention practices. Adnan spent about eight years detained, much of it in administrative detention, and launched previous months-long hunger strikes to challenge Israeli repression.

More than 1,400 complaints of torture, including painful shackling, sleep deprivation, and exposure to extreme temperatures, committed by the Shabak (the Israel Security Agency) in Israel and the OPT have been filed with Israel's Justice Ministry since 2001, resulting in three criminal investigations and no indictments, according to the Israeli rights group the Public Committee Against Torture in Israel. The group Military Court Watch reported that in 26 cases of detention of Palestinian children they documented in 2023, 69 percent said they were physically abused in detention by Israeli forces and 73 percent were strip searched.

Palestinian rights groups have also reported a deterioration in the conditions of Palestinian prisoners, including violent raids, retaliatory prison transfers and isolation of prisoners, less access to running water and bread, and fewer family visits. Conditions worsened after October 7.

Settlements and Home Demolitions

Israeli authorities provide security, infrastructure, and services to more than 710,000 settlers in the West Bank, including East Jerusalem.

According to OCHA, Israeli authorities demolished 1,004 Palestinian homes and other structures in the West Bank, including East Jerusalem, in 2023 as of December 11, displacing 1,870 people, which surpasses 2022 figures. Most buildings were demolished for lacking building permits, which authorities make nearly impossible for Palestinians to obtain in these areas.

The difficulty in obtaining Israeli building permits in East Jerusalem and the 60 percent of the West Bank under Israel's exclusive control (Area C) has driven Palestinians to build structures that are at constant risk of demolition or confiscation for being unauthorized, including dozens of schools. Entire Palestinian communities in areas like the South Hebron Hills find themselves at high risk of displacement. International law prohibits an occupying power from destroying property unless "absolutely necessary" for "military operations."

Authorities also sealed the family homes of Palestinians suspected of attacking Israelis, acts of unlawful collective punishment.

In July, Israeli police forcibly evicted two older Palestinians, Nora Ghaith, 68, and Mustafa Sub-Laban, 72, from their long-time family home in the Old City of occupied East Jerusalem to make way for Israeli settlers after the Israeli Supreme Court in March denied their final appeal after a decades-long legal battle. They did so under a discriminatory law that allows settler organizations to pursue claims for land they claim Jews owned in East Jerusalem before 1948, a strategy they have particularly used in Sheikh Jarrah and Silwan. Palestinians are meanwhile barred under Israeli law from reclaiming property they owned in what became Israel and from which they fled or were expelled in 1948.

Freedom of Movement

Israeli authorities continued to require Palestinian ID holders, with rare exceptions, to hold difficult-to-obtain, time-limited permits to enter Israel and large parts of the West Bank, including East Jerusalem. B'Tselem describes this as "an arbitrary, entirely non-transparent bureaucratic system" where "many applications are denied without explanation, with no real avenue for appeal."

As of early this year, Israeli authorities maintained 645 checkpoints and other permanent obstacles within the West Bank, according to OCHA, in addition to ad hoc "flying" checkpoints. Israeli forces routinely turn back or delay and humiliate Palestinians at checkpoints without explanation while permitting largely unfettered movement to Israeli settlers.

Israel continued construction of the separation barrier. Authorities began building the barrier more than two decades ago, ostensibly for security reasons, but 85 percent of it, according to OCHA, falls within the West Bank rather than along the Green Line separating Israeli from Palestinian territory. The barrier cuts off thousands of Palestinians from their agricultural lands, isolates 11,000 Palestinians who live on the western side of the barrier but are not allowed to travel to Israel and whose ability to cross the barrier to access their property and basic services are highly restricted. When complete, 9 percent of the West Bank will be isolated beyond the separation barrier.

Abuses by the Palestinian Authority

The State of Palestine published the Convention against Torture and its Optional Protocol in the Palestinian Official Gazette in September, effectively making it Palestinian law. Also in September, the UN Subcommittee on Prevention of Torture visited places of detention in the West Bank. However, the PA continued its systematic practice of arbitrarily detaining opponents and critics, including students. Lawyers for Justice, a group that represents Palestinians detained by the PA, documented 726 Palestinians they determined were detained arbitrarily between January and August 17, generally for periods of days or a few weeks. Between January and August 2023, the Palestinian statutory watchdog ICHR received 162 complaints of arbitrary arrests, 86 complaints of torture and ill-treatment, and 13 complaints of detention without trial or charge pursuant to orders from a regional governor against the PA.

In August, the PA registered Lawyers for Justice after blocking its registration for months.

Personal status laws for both Muslims and Christians discriminate against women, including in relation to marriage, divorce, custody of children, and inheritance. Palestine has no comprehensive domestic violence law. The PA has long been considering a draft family protection law, but women's rights groups have raised concerns that it does not go far enough to prevent abuse and protect survivors.

Israel

For much of the year, Israelis took to the streets in unprecedented weekly protests across the country to oppose the government's plan to weaken judicial independence. In July, the government implemented part of its plan when the Knesset passed a law that bars the Supreme Court from assessing the "reasonableness" of government decisions. The Supreme Court is reviewing the law in response to petitions challenging it.

The Knesset renewed in March a temporary order that bars, with few exceptions, the granting of long-term legal status inside Israel to Palestinians from the West Bank and Gaza who marry Israeli citizens or residents. Such a restriction, which has been in place since 2003, does not exist for individuals of virtually any other nationality who marry Israeli citizens or residents.

In February, the Knesset passed a law, now in effect, that authorizes the revocation of citizenship or permanent residency of Palestinians who commit a "terrorist act" and receive compensation from the PA for that act and their consequent deportation to the West Bank.

In September, Netanyahu called for deporting African asylum seekers involved in violent clashes in Tel Aviv. Israeli authorities continued to systematically deny the asylum claims of African—largely Eritrean, Ethiopian and Sudanese—asylum seekers in the country, estimated by the Hotline for Refugees and Migrants to number 34,500, while allowing in tens of thousands of Ukrainian refugees. Over the years, the government has imposed restrictions on African asylum seekers' movement, work permits, and access to health care and to education to pressure asylum seekers to leave.

Key International Actors

Many states condemned the Hamas-led October 7 attacks. Far fewer, though, condemned Israeli authorities' grave abuses. The United States and other Western countries provided arms or military support to Israel, while other countries have provided military aid to Palestinian armed groups, which, in the face of ongoing grave abuses, risk making them complicit in war crimes.

President Joe Biden and other US officials traveled to Israel several times to urge civilian protection and to lobby Israeli officials to allow aid into Gaza, although at time of writing, the United States had not conditioned its military support to Israel on abiding by those requests. After October 7, the Biden administration requested US$14.3 billion for further arms to Israel in addition to the $3.8 billion in US military aid Israel receives annually. The US also either transferred or announced it is planning to transfer Small Diameter Bombs, Joint Direct Attack Munition (JDAM) guidance kits, 155mm artillery shells, and 1 million rounds of ammunition, among other weapons. However, the US halted small arms shipments out of concern that they could be transferred to settlers.

In September, the US admitted Israel into its visa-waiver program, allowing Israeli citizens visa-free entry, despite Israel not fully eliminating discrimination against US nationals of Palestinian, Arab, or Muslim origin when they travel to Israel and the OPT.

In December, the US and the United Kingdom issued travel bans against violent settlers in the West Bank.

In mid-October, the US vetoed a resolution calling for humanitarian pauses in Gaza, but it abstained on a similar resolution in November. Like the resolution the US vetoed, the one the UN Security Council adopted called for Israel and Palestinian armed groups to protect civilians and respect international humanitarian law. It was the council's first adopted resolution on Israel and Palestine since 2016. But again in December, the US vetoed a Security Council resolution calling for a ceasefire between Israeli forces and Palestinian armed groups. The General Assembly passed two resolutions calling for a ceasefire, one in October and the other in December.

Divisions among European Union member states prevented the bloc from reaching the unanimity necessary to adopt strong positions and concrete measures in response to Israeli abuses. This was particularly visible after October 7, including through EU member states' diverging votes at the UN. While condemning Hamas, EU states could not unanimously agree on calling out Israel's war crimes. The EU high representative, Josep Borrell, proposed a package of targeted sanctions for settlers' abuses in the West Bank, but prospects for its adoption remained slim in light of the unanimity requirement.

The UN high commissioner for human rights in June updated the database of businesses operating in settlements. In July, the UN Human Rights Council passed a resolution to ensure funding for the continued updating of the database.

The International Criminal Court (ICC) prosecutor's Palestine investigation remained ongoing. The prosecutor spoke from the Rafah Crossing and visited Israel and Palestine amid the hostilities. He signaled the ICC's ongoing mandate to the parties and made clear that any serious crimes committed in the current hostilities fall within the court's mandate.

In July, 54 states and 3 intergovernmental organizations made submissions to the International Court of Justice (ICJ) on the advisory opinion the UN General Assembly requested in December 2022 on the legal status of Israel's prolonged occupation and legal consequences of its abuses against Palestinians. Public hearings on the request for an advisory opinion are scheduled to open at the ICJ on February 19, 2024.

Italy

In 2023, the government intensified its efforts to deter migration through obstruction of nongovernmental rescue groups, migration cooperation with rights-abusing countries, and regressive asylum practices.

Authorities undermined the rights of same-sex parents. Gender-based violence and an inadequate state response remained serious concerns.

With one-fourth of the population at risk of poverty or social exclusion, the government eliminated an important income support program.

International human rights bodies highlighted pressure on civil society organizations aiding migrants, racism and discrimination targeting Roma and people of African descent, and rule of law concerns.

Migrants and Asylum Seekers

According to government statistics, by mid-September, more than 127,200 people, including 11,630 unaccompanied children, reached Italy by sea, almost double the number in the same period in 2022. The government's failure to ensure adequate facilities and swift transfers to the mainland meant the reception center on Lampedusa island was at times severely overcrowded.

The government obstructed rescues in the Mediterranean Sea by nongovernmental organizations (NGOs). A government decree, converted into law in February 2023, imposes new requirements, including an obligation on NGO vessels to go to an assigned port immediately following a rescue, effectively prohibiting multiple rescues on the same voyage. As of September, the government had detained at port NGO vessels 8 times for 20 days for violating the decree. The United Nations High Commissioner for Human Rights and the Expert Council on NGO Law of the Council of Europe expressed serious concerns about the law. In July, five NGOs filed a complaint with the European Commission against Italy, alleging the law is incompatible with European Union and international law.

A new policy of assigning disembarkation ports in central and northern Italy rather than the closer ports of Sicily has meant that rescue organizations have less time and resources for rescue operations in the Mediterranean Sea. In June, an administrative court upheld the government's distant port policy when it rejected a complaint lodged by Médécins Sans Frontières (Doctors Without Borders, MSF).

A government decree converted into law—the "Cutro decree"—in May made it more difficult for people to obtain special protection—a temporary right to remain on humanitarian grounds—and increased the scope for detention under accelerated border asylum procedures, among other changes that undermine the rights of asylum seekers and migrants. In September, the government increased detention pending deportation from 3 to 18 months in certain cases. In October, judges in Sicily ruled in separate cases that the detention of Tunisian asylum seekers under provisions of the Cutro decree violated EU and national law and ordered their release; a court in Florence blocked the deportation of a Tunisian saying the government should revisit its determination of Tunisia as a safe country of origin. Positively, the government approved significantly higher quotas for work visas in various sectors of the economy for 2023-2025 compared to previous years.

The government intensified cooperation on migration with other countries without regard for human rights. On the heels of an EU-Tunisia deal to limit boat departures from that North African country, which Italian Prime Minister Giorgia Meloni helped broker, the Italian government hosted leaders from the Middle East and North Africa for an anti-migration summit in July. Italy's "Memorandum of Understanding" with Libya—the basis of bilateral migration cooperation—automatically renewed in February 2023 for three years. In November, Italy announced an agreement with Albania to detain in that country people, including asylum seekers, rescued at sea by Italian ships. The plan, which raises concerns about respect for the right to asylum, freedom from arbitrary detention, and the offshoring of responsibility, was awaiting parliamentary approval in both countries at time of writing.

In a joint communication sent to the government in February, three UN special rapporteurs expressed serious concern about due process violations and the criminalization of sea rescues in the ongoing trial of 21 people charged with facilitating unauthorized immigration in relation to rescues in 2016 and 2017. The accused, who face up to 20 years in prison, include four members of Iuventa, a rescue ship seized in 2017 by the Italian authorities, staff of two NGOs, and a shipping company.

The European Court of Human Rights condemned Italy in November for arbitrarily detaining unaccompanied children in inhuman and degrading conditions in 2017. The same month, parliament rolled back safeguards for unaccompanied children with respect to age determination, accommodation, and asylum.

Discrimination and Intolerance

In August, the UN Committee on the Elimination of Racial Discrimination criticized Italy for its failure to collect disaggregated data, an incomplete definition in domestic law of racial discrimination, the lack of a fully independent national equality body, the use of racist political discourse by politicians and reports of racist hate incidents, persistent and widespread structural discrimination against Roma, Sinti, and Camminanti communities, and acts of violence, stigmatization, and harassment of people of African descent. Five Verona police officers were arrested in June on charges of torturing non-Italians, unhoused people, and other vulnerable people in the street; two of them were charged with the aggravating circumstance of racial bias.

Poverty and Inequality

According to data published by the national statistical institute ISTAT in 2023, almost 10 percent of the Italian population lived in absolute poverty in 2022, an increase from 2021 attributed to the impact of inflation. Foreigners living in Italy were more than four times more likely to experience absolute poverty.

The government eliminated the "citizen income" anti-poverty measure in May and replaced it with more limited programs for different categories of individuals. Individuals defined as "employable" will receive lower monthly payments for a maximum of 12 months linked to a job training requirement, while those living in a family with children, anyone over 60 years old, and people with disabilities may apply to receive slightly higher monthly payments for up to 30 months. The government maintained its opposition to the introduction of a statutory minimum wage.

An estimated 2.2 million households, including almost 1 million children, were unable to maintain adequate energy services at affordable costs, with a higher incidence in the south and among immigrant families. The government extended measures to counter rising energy costs, including income-based subsidies for domestic gas and electricity and reduced costs for households using electricity for medical equipment.

Women's Rights

The Interior Ministry reported that 61 women were killed by relatives or people they knew in the first 8 months of the year, 38 of them by a partner or ex-partner, a slight decrease from the same period last year.

In March, a Florence court absolved two men of rape, arguing that they were not fully aware of the survivor's lack of consent and stating that previous behavior by the victim justified the "misunderstanding." There was sensationalist media coverage of a gang-rape by six men and one boy of a young woman in Palermo in July, including the circulation of videos and the publication of her name.

The government proposed new measures to counter gender-based violence following the June stabbing murder of a 29-year-old woman—seven months pregnant at the time—by her boyfriend. The draft law creates teams of specialized prosecutors, increases the use of electronic bracelets, increases prison sentences for recidivists, and allows for arrests based solely on video or photographic evidence within 48 hours of stalking, domestic violence, or violation of protection orders. Women's rights groups criticized the bill for failing to include more preventive measures and sufficient financing. Following a June visit, the Council of Europe's Commissioner for Human Rights expressed deep concern over the shortage of shelters and support services for women victims of gender-based violence.

In January, a senator from Prime Minister Meloni's Brothers of Italy party tabled a bill to grant legal personhood from the moment of conception, which would effectively ban abortion. The bill had not yet been debated at time of writing.

Sexual Orientation and Gender Identity

In March, a Senate committee voted against government support for a European Commission proposal for an EU directive to ensure cross-border recognition of same-sex parents. In January, the interior minister ordered all prefects to annul transcriptions of births identifying two gay or two lesbian parents, citing a December 2022 Supreme Court judgment and arguing that these couples must follow a particular adoption process. In June, a prosecutor in a city in northern Italy ordered the cancellation of 33 birth certificates of lesbian couples' children. In July, the lower house of parliament approved a bill to make it a crime to have a child via surrogacy abroad (the practice is already illegal in Italy), punishable by up to two years in prison and up to a €1 million fine. At time of writing, the Senate had not yet voted on the bill.

An online government survey found that one-third of LGBT respondents reported experiencing a hostile working environment and 44 percent said they had been discriminated against. Italy remained 22nd out of 27 EU countries in ILGA-Europe's annual ranking of respect for a range of rights of LGBT people. No official statistics on hate crimes against LGBT people were available.

Rule of Law

In a report published in April, following a visit in 2022, the Council of Europe Committee for the Prevention of Torture expressed concern about overcrowding and conditions in Italian prisons (at 114 percent of official capacity when the committee visited), isolation regimes and the use of mechanical and chemical restraints in psychiatric facilities, and the de facto deprivation of liberty of older people in two social care establishments due to restrictions and lack of alternatives in the community. In its yearly rule of law report, the European Commission noted an increase in lawsuits targeting journalists and narrowing of civic space and called on Italy to establish an independent human rights institution.

Japan

Japan is a liberal democracy with an active civil society.

The Diet, Japan's parliament, passed a bill that amends immigration law to allow the government to deport asylum seekers under certain conditions. Child sexual exploitation also received renewed scrutiny after the BBC reported in March on Japanese pop mogul Johnny Kitagawa's history of child sexual abuse, prompting several hundred survivors to come forward.

Japan has no laws prohibiting racial, ethnic, or religious discrimination or discrimination based on sexual orientation or gender identity. Japan does not have a national human rights institution.

Asylum Seekers and Refugees

Japan's asylum and refugee determination system remains strongly oriented against granting refugee status. In 2022, the Justice Ministry received 3,772 applications for refugee status but recognized only 202 people as refugees, many of whom were Afghan staff of the Japanese embassy in Kabul and their family members. Japan also categorized 1,760 people, of whom 1,682 were from Myanmar, as needing humanitarian considerations, allowing them to stay in Japan.

In June, the Diet passed a bill to amend the Immigration Control and Refugee Recognition Act. The new law allows Japan to deport asylum seekers who apply for refugee status more than twice.

Migrant Workers

The government continued the foreign technical intern training program, which binds workers to their sponsoring employers without the option of changing them, to recruit more foreign workers, many from Southeast Asia. The program has drawn criticism for human rights violations, including payment of sub-minimum wages, illegal overtime, forced return of whistleblowers to their home countries, and dangerous or unhygienic working conditions. In May, a panel of experts mandated by the government to evaluate the program recommended Japan abolish it.

HUMAN
RIGHTS
WATCH
Japan's "Hostage Justice" System
Denial of Bail, Coerced Confessions, and Lack of Access to Lawyers

Death Penalty

There had been no executions in Japan in 2023 at time of writing. As of December 2022, 107 people were on death row. Concerns have long been raised about death row inmates, including their inadequate access to legal counsel and that they are notified of their execution only on the day it takes place.

In late October, a retrial for Iwao Hakamada, an 87-year-old former professional boxer arrested in 1966 and sentenced to death for the murder of a family of four, began after decades of retrial request processes. This is the fifth time a death penalty case will be retried in Japan. In earlier cases, the defendants were all acquitted.

Criminal Justice System

A Human Rights Watch report in May found that Japan's system of "hostage justice" is rife with human rights abuses, including coercing suspects to confess through repeated arrests and denial of bail and questioning them without a lawyer.

In the same month, the Diet revised the Criminal Procedure Code to introduce some alternative measures to pretrial detention, including the use of GPS devices to track suspects who are released on bail. The Japan Federation of Bar Associations called on Japan to address its abusive bail practice, including by using such alternative measures.

Disability Rights

Japan's psychiatric care sector uses arbitrary detention, abusive physical restraints, and forced treatment in violation of basic rights and in need of major reform. Local activists have raised concerns about the increasing number of people with psychosocial disabilities who are detained in psychiatric facilities against their will. The current psychiatric system incentivizes involuntary hospitalization.

施錠確認
HUMAN
RIGHTS
WATCH
“They Don’t Treat Us Like
Human Beings”
Abuse of Imprisoned Women in Japan

Women's and Girls' Rights

Women's rights activists in Japan achieved several milestones in their campaign for women's rights.

In April, Japan approved medical abortion, which the World Health Organization has approved of as a safe method to terminate a pregnancy. For years, only procedural abortions were available in Japan. In general, however, spousal authorization remains a requirement.

In June, the Diet revised the penal code's definition of rape to include "nonconsensual sexual intercourse" laid out in eight scenarios and removed the requirement of "violence or intimidation." The statute of limitations for reporting rape was also increased from 10 to 15 years and the age of consent raised from 13 to 16 years, without criminalizing consensual sexual behavior by adolescents close in age, in addition to several other revisions.

Corporal Punishment Against Children

In December 2022, after decades of criticism by children's rights groups, the Diet scrapped article 822 of the Civil Code, which authorized a person with parental authority to "discipline" a child, and introduced a new article that prohibits corporal punishment.

Sexual Orientation and Gender Identity

In June, after years of campaigning by LGBT and human rights groups, including Human Rights Watch, the Diet passed its first law on sexual orientation and gender identity. The law seeks to "promote understanding" for the respect of all citizens regardless of their sexual orientation or gender identity and to avoid "unfair discrimination." While it is a good start, the law falls short of comprehensive nondiscrimination legislation.

In July, the Supreme Court issued a landmark decision that the trade ministry's ban against a transgender woman employee who had not undergone surgery from using the women's bathroom was illegal.

Following years of litigation and advocacy, including by Human Rights Watch, in October, the Supreme Court ruled as unconstitutional the country's law mandating sterilization surgery for transgender people as a requirement for legal gender recognition.

Enforced Disappearances by North Korea

In a landmark ruling in October, a Tokyo High Court found the North Korean government liable for human rights violations against Koreans and Japanese citizens it had enticed to relocate to North Korea through its "Paradise on Earth" campaign. Under the campaign, approximately 93,000 ethnic Koreans (Zainichi) and Japanese migrated to North Korea between 1959 and 1984 with the false promise of a better life. The ruling overturned the Tokyo district court's decision that denied the plaintiffs' demand because of a lack of jurisdiction and the statute of limitations.

Climate Change and Policy Impacts

Japan is among the top 10 emitters of greenhouse gases responsible for the climate crisis. In February, Japan adopted their new decarbonization strategy, the Green Transformation (GX) Basic Policy. Critics of the plan underscore its focus on energy security, economic growth, and the use of "clean coal technologies" at the expense of meaningful and ambitious emissions reductions.

Japan hosted the G7 Summit in May. The summit communiqué represents a significant increase in the G7's ambition for phasing out unabated fossil fuels. However, Japan itself remains the only G7 country planning to build new coal-fired power plants.

In 2023, Japan again experienced its hottest summer on record with serious health impacts on older people and pregnant people.

Foreign Policy

The Japanese government officially states that "the promotion and protection of all human rights is a legitimate interest of the international community" and "grave violations of human rights need to be addressed in cooperation with the international community." However, Japan's diplomatic response to rights abuses often contradicted or failed to fulfill its commitment, partly as it downplays concerns for human rights to compete against China for political and economic influence.

In December 2022, in a rare move, Japan's House of Councilors approved a resolution, nearly identical to one passed by the House of Representatives in early 2022, highlighting human rights abuses in different areas, including Xinjiang, Tibet, Inner Mongolia, and Hong Kong, without naming the Chinese government.

In January, Human Rights Watch found that Japan's Yokogawa Bridge Corp. apparently transferred about US$2 million to a conglomerate owned by the Myanmar military for the Bago River Bridge Construction Project, with US government approval. In April, Japan said the Myanmar military had confirmed that it had misused two Japan-funded civilian vessels to transport soldiers and weapons in Rakhine State in September 2022.

Jordan

Jordanian authorities continued to limit civic space in 2023, quashing dissent by arresting and harassing peaceful dissidents and journalists and using vague and abusive laws to limit free speech and peaceful activism in violation of international legal protections.

In August, Jordanian authorities promulgated a new repressive cybercrime law that further undermines free speech online, threatens internet users' right to anonymity, and introduces a new authority to control social media that could pave the way for a surge in online censorship.

In May, authorities finally rescinded a state of emergency declared in March 2020 in response to the Covid-19 pandemic that had granted the prime minister sweeping powers to rule by decree.

Freedom of Expression

Jordanian law criminalizes speech deemed critical of the king, foreign countries, government officials and institutions, Islam, and Christianity and defamatory speech.

In August, Jordan's parliament hastily overhauled the country's cybercrime law, circumventing public discourse and input. The law uses imprecise, vague, and undefined terminology like "fake news," "inciting immorality," and "online assassination of character." Such language falls short of meeting international legal standards for clear and precise legislation, making it difficult for individuals to understand and adhere to the law.

Notably, authorities dramatically increased penalties for online defamation or "character assassination" to a minimum three-month jail sentence or a fine of up to 20,000 Jordanian dinars (about US$28,000). In 2021, the number of cases relating to online defamation under the 2015 cybercrime law reached 4,030, nearly double the number from the previous year, according to the annual reports from the National Center for Human Rights (NCHR).

In May, the trial of political activist Sufyan al-Tal and two other men, Abed Tawahiya and Omar Abu Rasaa, on charges related to free expression began.

While al-Tal was released on bail soon after his arrest, Abu Rasaa and Tawahiya remain detained. In August, authorities briefly detained journalist Heba Abu Taha after she was sentenced to three months in prison for criticizing normalization with Israel in a Facebook post. She was released pending appeal. Also in August, a court sentenced commentator Ahmed Hassan al-Zoubi to one year in prison for a 2022 Facebook post criticizing the government's response to fuel price protests. Following a lengthy hunger strike to protest his own detention, the health of activist Hamad al-Kharsha had deteriorated by September. Authorities had arrested him in January 2022, and he is facing charges based on a coerced confession, according to his lawyer.

Freedoms of Assembly and Association

Under the Public Gatherings Law amended in March 2011, Jordan did not require government permission to hold public meetings or demonstrations, but authorities continued to require organizations and venues to obtain permission from the Interior Ministry or General Intelligence Department to host events.

Several Jordanian laws restrict freedom of association, including the Labor Law of 1996, which limits the ability to freely form trade unions, and the Associations Law of 2008, which regulates the formation and operation of nongovernmental groups (NGOs). Jordanian authorities impose onerous pre-approval restrictions on the receipt of foreign funding by NGOs.

In late 2019, Jordanian authorities created a centralized committee under the Prime Minister's Office to study and decide on foreign funding approval requests. However, representatives of donor states and local NGOs told Human Rights Watch in 2023 that the committee has done little if anything to ease restrictions.

Refugees and Migrants

By late 2023, over 655,000 people from Syria had sought refuge in Jordan, according to the United Nations High Commissioner for Refugees (UNHCR). Over 85 percent of Syrians lived outside refugee camps in rented accommodations.

HUMAN
RIGHTS
WATCH
Automated Neglect
How The World Bank's Push to Allocate Cash Assistance
Using Algorithms Threatens Rights

According to UNHCR, Jordan also hosted asylum seekers and refugees from other countries in 2023, including 61,081 Iraqis, 12,772 Yemenis, 5,163 Sudanese, 593 Somalis, and 1,195 people from other countries. Authorities continued to enforce a January 2019 decision banning UNHCR from registering as asylum seekers non-Syrians who officially entered the country for the purposes of medical treatment, study, tourism, or work, effectively barring their recognition as refugees and leaving many without UNHCR documentation or access to services.

Authorities continued to implement the Jordan Compact, the 2016 agreement between the Jordanian government and donor countries, which aimed to improve the livelihoods of Syrian refugees by granting new legal work opportunities and improving the education sector. By July 2023, labor authorities stated that they had issued or renewed at least 373,000 work permits for Syrians since 2016, although many of these were renewals. Most professions remained closed to non-Jordanians, and many Syrians continued to work in the informal sector without labor protections.

The roughly 230,000 school-age Syrian refugees in Jordan face multiple obstacles to education that are most acute for children ages 12 and older. Only one-quarter of secondary-school-age Syrian refugee children in Jordan were enrolled in school.

Jordan hosted an estimated 49,000 documented migrant domestic workers in 2023, according to Labor Ministry statistics, mostly from the Philippines, Sri Lanka, and Indonesia. NGOs repeatedly referred domestic workers who had suffered multiple abuses to Labor Ministry investigators. Abuses included wage theft, unsafe working conditions, long working hours without rest, passport and document confiscation, and physical, verbal, and sexual abuse.

Women's and Girls' Rights

Despite amendments in 2019, Jordan's personal status code remains discriminatory. Women and girls over 15 need the permission of a male guardian to marry for the first time, and marriages between Muslim women and non-Muslim men are not recognized. Women cannot travel abroad with their children without male guardian or judicial consent.

Article 98 of Jordan's penal code, amended in 2017, states that the "fit of fury" defense does not allow mitigated sentences for perpetrators of crimes "against women," but judges continued to impose mitigated sentences under article 99 if family members of victims did not support prosecutions of their male family members. Article 340 of the penal code also allows a man to receive a reduced sentence if he kills or attacks his wife or any of his female relatives in the act of committing adultery or in an "unlawful bed."

Such discriminatory laws leave women exposed to violence. Similarly, the penal code and Juveniles Act do not prohibit corporal punishment and allow parents to punish children in accordance with "general norms."

Article 9 of Jordan's Nationality Law does not allow Jordanian women married to non-Jordanians to pass on nationality. And while non-citizen children of Jordanian women no longer need work permits, many professions remain closed to them.

Sexual Orientation and Gender Identity

Jordan has no laws that explicitly criminalize same-sex relations. The penal code includes vague "immorality" provisions that are used to target sexual and gender minorities. Jordanian law does not prohibit discrimination based on sexual orientation and gender identity.

Lesbian, gay, bisexual, and transgender (LGBT) activists in Jordan reported facing increased harassment by authorities in 2023, which included the detention of two activists and freezing of their bank accounts, the closure of two LGBT rights organizations, and threats by security forces to expose LGBT people to their family members.

In a 2023 report, Human Rights Watch documented the far-reaching offline consequences of online targeting against LGBT people in Jordan, including entrapment, online extortion, online harassment, and reliance on illegitimately obtained digital information based on arbitrary phone searches in prosecutions. As a result of digital targeting, LGBT people said they felt unable to safely express their sexual orientation or gender identity online and that LGBT rights activism has subsequently suffered.

Social Protection and Economic Rights

Jordan continues to grapple with high unemployment, particularly for youth and women, coupled with a sharp rise in poverty following the Covid-19 pandemic and an increase in the cost of living that makes it difficult for many people to afford necessities. A decade of International Monetary Fund (IMF) loan programs has both failed to bring down Jordan's high debt levels and introduced economic reforms that further increased prices, including for fuel and electricity. Human Rights Watch reported in June that Jordan's automated cash transfer program for workers on low incomes, developed with significant financing from the World Bank, is undermined by errors, discriminatory policies, and stereotypes about poverty. The program is part of a social protection system that is failing to provide support to many people even as they go hungry, fall behind on rent, and take on crippling debt.

Jordan remains one of the few countries in the world that still allows imprisoning people for debt, which is prohibited under international law. In 2023, authorities lifted the pandemic-related state of emergency, ending a moratorium on debt-related imprisonment for sums exceeding 5,000 Jordanian dinars (about US$7,000). Human Rights Watch documented how, in the absence of an adequate social security net, tens of thousands of Jordanians took out loans to cover basic necessities, only to end up in prison or wanted for failure to repay.

Criminal Justice System

Local governors continued to use provisions of the Crime Prevention Law of 1954 to place individuals in administrative detention for up to one year, in circumvention of the Criminal Procedure Law. Jordan's NCHR reported in 2023 that only 2,258 people were administratively detained in 2021, marking a dramatic decrease from the 21,322 administrative detentions in 2020.

Kazakhstan

Authorities in Kazakhstan did not meaningfully address persistent human rights violations in 2023 or ensure accountability for past abuses. Two years after large-scale anti-government protests rocked Kazakhstan in January 2022, few officials have been held accountable for their part in disproportionate use of force against protesters, arbitrary arrests and imprisonment, and torture and ill-treatment of detainees.

Violent attacks on journalists increased in early 2023 and authorities persisted in using overbroad criminal charges against government critics and activists. Heavy restrictions in law and practice on the right to peaceful protest and freedom of speech and religion continued. New legislation strengthening protections for women fell short of criminalizing domestic violence as a stand-alone offense.

In February 2023, Kazakhstan signed the Third Optional Protocol to the Convention on the Rights of the Child.

Parliamentary Elections

On March 19, Kazakhstan held parliamentary elections that fell short of democratic standards. The Organization for Security and Co-operation in Europe (OSCE) Office for Democratic Institutions and Human Rights (ODIHR) election monitoring mission noted that Kazakhstan had adopted legal amendments leading to increased competition, but "significant procedural irregularities were observed." Opposition groups continued to face serious obstacles to registration.

Accountability and Justice

Kazakhstan's investigations into the January 2022 events have been one-sided, leading to over 1,200 convictions of protesters and others, with only a few dozen law enforcement officers "brought to criminal responsibility," according to the Prosecutor General's office. Authorities in Taraz, Kyzylorda, and Shymkent closed investigations into the deaths of dozens of people killed in those cities during the events on the grounds that the officers' actions did not constitute a crime.

Authorities have also posthumously prosecuted at least 15 people, in violation of their right to a fair trial.

Torture and Ill-Treatment

A serious lack of accountability for torture and ill-treatment persists. In January 2023, human rights groups documented how authorities tortured and ill-treated detainees in the aftermath of the January 2022 events, including by beating and burning them, administering electric shocks, and using sexual violence, including rape and threats of rape, against both male and female detainees. The groups registered 13 cases of torture and ill-treatment of children. At least 23 police officers had been convicted for torture in trials connected to the January 2022 events at time of writing, but dozens of other torture investigations have been closed on the grounds that the allegations were "unsubstantiated."

In September, a video emerged of police beating prisoners, including Timur Danebaev, an activist who was sentenced to three years in prison in June on overbroad criminal charges of "inciting ethnic discord."

In its June concluding observations, the United Nations Committee Against Torture (CAT) was concerned about the "many consistent reports" of torture and urged Kazakhstan to ensure accountability for "all acts of torture and ill-treatment, including excessive use of force."

Government Opponents and Other Critics

On April 10, an Almaty court convicted Zhanbolat Mamay, the head of the unregistered Democratic Party of Kazakhstan, on charges of organizing mass riots, insulting law enforcement officers, and disseminating knowingly false information. He was sentenced to a suspended six-year prison term. In June, his conviction was upheld on appeal.

On July 11, an Almaty court sentenced Aigerim Tleuzhanova, an activist and journalist who was tried along with four others, to four years in prison for allegedly attempting to seize Almaty airport during the January 2022 events. Tleuzhanova admitted she was at the airport but denied any wrongdoing.

Kazakh authorities continue to target peaceful political opposition activists with criminal charges of membership in banned "extremist" groups (article 405 of the Criminal Code). In May, police arrested Marat Zhylanbaev, the head of the unregistered political opposition group "Alga, Kazakhstan," on this charge and for allegedly financing "extremist" activities, immediately after Zhylanbaev finished serving 20 days' administrative arrest for staging an unsanctioned protest in Astana.

Freedom of Assembly

The right to peaceful assembly remains heavily restricted and policed. People who try to peacefully protest are detained, fined, or given short-term custodial sentences. On August 1, police detained relatives of people killed during the January 2022 events who were protesting outside the Shymkent city administration. A Shymkent court sentenced one protester to 5 days and another to 10 days of administrative arrest. Ethnic Kazakhs in Almaty who intermittently protest the Chinese government's abuses of Uyghurs in Xinjiang also face arrest.

Freedom of Expression

There was a notable increase in harassment, threats, and assaults on journalists in Kazakhstan in early 2023. In January and February, media offices were vandalized and journalists' cars and apartments were attacked or set on fire. On January 20, the European Union, United States, and British embassies in Astana expressed concern and called for accountability. Authorities opened an investigation.

On July 3, a Turkestan regional court sentenced journalist Amangeldy Batyrbaev to 20 days' administrative detention on charges of defamation for a Facebook post about a deputy in parliament. On February 3, an Astana court sentenced Makhambet Abzhan, a blogger, to nine years in prison on charges of "distributing deliberately false information" and "extortion," after a closed trial.

On August 11, Zhetysu police subjected journalist Sandugash Duysenova to a filmed strip search after detaining her on charges of violating privacy. Authorities later dropped the case. On August 18, KazTAG journalist Diana Saparkyzy was attacked by five unidentified men while trying to report on mining deaths outside Karaganda.

In late July, Kazakhstan adopted new media legislation that introduces penalties for "placing, disseminating false information," an overbroad provision that poses a risk to free speech.

Labor Rights

Authorities continue to obstruct workers' efforts to organize and register independent trade unions. Between January and April 2023, there was industrial unrest in western Kazakhstan as oil workers variously demanded jobs, better pay, and improved working conditions. On September 1, the sectoral Trade Union of Fuel and Energy Industry Workers successfully registered a local-level trade union in Almaty, a step toward the sectoral union being able to reregister after a court suspended its activities in 2021.

Authorities continued to ignore a May 2021 UN Working Group on Arbitrary Detention decision calling for the immediate release of imprisoned labor activist Erzhan Elshibaev.

Violence against Women and Girls

In April 2023, Kazakhstan strengthened legal protections for women, including by eliminating the possibility of reconciliation after repeated acts of family abuse (a provision that had empowered abusers), enabling police to impose administrative penalties on aggressors without a survivor's complaint, and increasing administrative arrest to up to 10 days for breaching a protection order. Kazakhstan still has not criminalized domestic violence, a widespread and underreported problem, as a stand-alone offense. Almaty city authorities continued to interfere in activists' efforts to protest on March 8, International Women's Day.

Disability Rights

An obligatory medical exam and other barriers continue to obstruct children's access to inclusive education. Children with disabilities face isolation, violence, neglect, physical restraint, and overmedication in segregated special schools or residential institutions. In August, the media reported that 14 children in a state residential institution in Karaganda were hospitalized with poisoning and that one of the children later died. Police opened an investigation.

In June, CAT expressed concern about the treatment of people with disabilities and laws that allow for "the forced hospitalization of persons with disabilities, including children, either for monitoring or treatment."

Sexual Orientation and Gender Identity

Kazakhstan does not provide legal protection against discrimination based on sexual orientation or gender identity. In June, CAT called on Kazakhstan to "revoke the requirement of mandatory reassignment surgery," part of the invasive, humiliating process for changing one's legally recognized gender in the country.

Freedom of Religion

Religious groups face mandatory registration requirements and strict restrictions on the dissemination and sale of religious literature. International religious freedom watchdogs reported that from January to June 2023, 10 individuals and organizations had been prosecuted for "maintaining and using places to pray without state permission" and at least 9 Muslims were serving prison sentences related to their social media posts on Islam.

Poverty and Inequality

Poverty is on the rise in Kazakhstan, and marginalized populations are far from enjoying their economic, social, and cultural rights. Kazakhstan has committed to uphold the right to social security, but rigid eligibility criteria and means tests for Kazakhstan's main social assistance program, Targeted Social Assistance, have excluded many people who need support. Low-income families also face stigma and discrimination when trying to access these benefits.

Asylum Seekers and Refugees

After holding five activists from Karakalpakstan, Uzbekistan's autonomous region, under extradition arrest for 12 months, Kazakh authorities released them between September and November 2023. Their applications for refugee status were denied.

Key International Actors

Several high-level European and US officials visited Kazakhstan in 2023, including US Secretary of State Antony Blinken in late February, United Kingdom Foreign Secretary James Cleverly in March, and German President Frank Steinmeier in June. Also in June, European Council President Charles Michel met with President Kassym-Jomart Tokayev on the sidelines of the EU's second high-level meeting with Central Asia's presidents in Kyrgyzstan.

At the EU-Kazakhstan Human Rights Dialogue and Subcommittee on Justice and Home Affairs meeting in March in Brussels and at the Cooperation Committee meeting in Astana in May, EU officials renewed their calls for an independent investigation into the January 2022 events.

The UN High Commissioner for Human Rights Volker Turk, after his visit to Kazakhstan in March, called for an "after action" review of the January 2022 events and "justice, reparations, and truth" for all victims. He also called for the explicit criminalization of domestic violence in Kazakhstan's criminal code and action by authorities on "protection of journalists" and "freedom of expression."

On the sidelines of the UN General Assembly on September 19, President Tokayev met with President Joe Biden during the first US-Central Asia presidential summit; human rights concerns did not feature prominently in the discussions.

Kenya

In August 2022, Kenya held a disputed presidential election that, after an unsuccessful court challenge by the main opposition candidate, Raila Odinga, resulted in the declared winner, William Samoei Ruto, forming a new government. The opposition rejected the court decision and resorted to organizing street protests. Despite promises made by President Ruto during campaigns to respect human rights, the human rights trajectory in Kenya has further deteriorated over the past year.

Kenyan and international groups have continued to implicate police and other security agencies in serious human rights abuses, including extrajudicial killings. The authorities have failed to ensure accountability for these abuses, including by failing to investigate and prosecute police officers implicated in the abuses during opposition protests in 2023. The Director of Public Prosecutions (DPP) announced the withdrawal of charges against senior government officials, including those accused of involvement in human rights abuses, which could have serious long-term implications for Kenya's efforts to address the long-standing challenge of impunity.

Abuses by Police

Kenyan police responded with excessive force to protests organized between March and July by the leading opposition coalition, *Azimio la Umoja*, Swahili for Resolution for Unity. The protesters demanded that the government address the rising cost of living and alleged fraud in the 2022 elections. Human Rights Watch and Amnesty International documented the killing of at least 16 people and the maiming of scores of protesters, bystanders, and people shot in their homes by police and armed pro-government gangs.

During the March protests, armed gangs raided and looted businesses owned by opposition leader Odinga and the immediate past president, Uhuru Kenyatta, in the capital, Nairobi. The government accused Kenyatta of sponsoring the protests. In July, armed gangs, alongside police, beat and shot at peaceful protesters on the streets of Kisumu, western Kenya, and Nairobi, notably in the informal settlements of Kibera and Mathare. There were also concerns regarding an increase in sexual violence perpetrated by police and private actors. Sexual violence has often accompanied political unrest in the country.

At time of writing, the Independent Policing Oversight Authority (IPOA) has yet to conclude its investigations into the deaths and alleged unjustified use of force by the police. Kenya has a long history of impunity for police use of excessive force against protesters in the aftermath of election disputes. Little has been done to ensure accountability for similar abuses by police during election related protests in 2017, 2013, and 2007.

Starvation Cult and Malindi Mass Graves

In April, the government discovered secret mass graves of the followers of a "starvation cult" in a forest in Shakahola area in the coastal town of Malindi. The authorities said they had, as of September 2023, dug up several mass graves in the forest with a total of more than 400 bodies of suspected followers of the cult, most of whom had either been strangled or clobbered to death as opposed to starving to death. However, investigations by Human Rights Watch found that only 12 bodies had been positively identified and none had been released to their families for burial.

Police said they had arrested the pastor behind the cult, Paul Mackenzie, and at least 37 of his followers. Lawyers and Kenyan human rights groups have expressed concerns over the violation of the rights of accused persons, with Pastor Mackenzie being held in solitary confinement for several months despite not being formally charged and his co-accused being denied access to family and lawyers.

Challenges for Accountability

Since September 2022, the DPP has dropped several cases of corruption and human rights abuses against Ruto's close allies, some of whom he has since appointed to his cabinet. These unprocedural withdrawals of cases could undermine Kenya's fight against corruption and other human rights concerns. Some legal experts have suggested that the authorities have withdrawn about 30 high profile cases from the courts within the first seven months of Ruto's presidency.

The withdrawn cases included those relating to the theft of public resources, sexual assault, and murder by defendants later appointed to senior government positions.

Soon after Ruto's inauguration in September 2022, the DPP announced an out-of-court settlement between a former member of parliament and a woman who accused him of attempted rape. Soon after the survivor withdrew the case from court, Ruto appointed this politician as a cabinet minister. The DPP also withdrew other cases against him, including those relating to corruption, incitement, and abuse of office.

In October, the DPP withdrew corruption charges against a former Malindi member of parliament, whom the president later appointed as a minister, for embezzling 19 million Kenyan shillings (about US$155,700) from the Malindi National Government Constituency Development Fund. She also faced other charges of conflict of interest, acquisition of proceeds of crime, and money laundering. The case proceeded against the eight other co-defendants.

On November 10, the DPP dropped the corruption case against a senior political figure and nine others for lack of evidence. In 2021, he was charged with fraudulently acquiring more than 7.3 billion Kenyan shillings (about $62.8 million) from the government. He alleged that the charges had been politically motivated by the former administration because of his support for Ruto's presidential bid. The DPP soon after halted extradition proceedings against two other political figures. These two were to face prosecution in the United Kingdom for corruption and money laundering. The authorities have ignored concerns raised by human rights and anti-corruption groups and, instead, announced plans to amend the Leadership and Integrity Act to allow even those convicted of corruption and other criminal offences to hold public office.

Sexual Orientation and Gender Identity

In February, the Supreme Court of Kenya upheld high court and court of appeal decisions directing the government to register the National Gay and Lesbian Human Rights Commission (NGLHRC) as a nongovernmental organization (NGO). In 2013, NGLHRC challenged the decision of the NGO Coordination Board to deny it registration. The courts described the government's decision not to register

NGLHRC based on the applicants' sexual orientation as unconstitutional. In September 2023, the court rejected a challenge to the earlier ruling.

President Ruto condemned the Supreme Court decision—which sparked pockets of public protest—stating that the country would not endorse same-sex conduct. Capitalizing on negative public sentiment for political gain, at least three political leaders threatened to introduce legislation that would further criminalize same-sex conduct. Article 162 of the penal code punishes "carnal knowledge against the order of nature" with up to 14 years in prison, while article 165 punishes "indecent practices between males" with up to five years in prison.

Women's and Girls' Rights

Violence and harassment against women at work remains highly prevalent in Kenya, particularly for those in the informal sector. About 83 percent of the workforce is in the informal sector, and 89 percent of women in the country work in the informal sector. Section 6 of the Kenyan Employment Act (2007) prohibits sexual harassment in the workplace, but it only obligates employers with more than 20 employees to have a sexual harassment policy. Kenya voted in favor of but has yet to ratify the International Labour Organization Violence and Harassment Convention (C190), which requires comprehensive protections to end violence and harassment, including gender-based violence, at work.

In January 2023, the Kenya National Bureau of Statistics released the key indicators report from the 2022 Kenya Demographic and Health Survey. The report confirmed the continued lack of equity in access to maternal healthcare. For example, only 69 percent of women and girls with low income have access to skilled attendants during birth as compared to 99 percent of women and girls with high income. At time of writing, the government has not released the full report.

In July 2023, the government launched the End Triple Threat Campaign, geared toward addressing the three key threats to adolescent health in the country: teenage pregnancy, new HIV/AIDS infections, and sexual and gender-based violence. Unfortunately, this campaign has not triggered any review of laws and policies that hinder adolescents' access to sexual and reproductive health services, specifically the Reproductive Health Policy (2022-2032) and the 2022 Children's Act. The Campaign also has not catalyzed the review of the education curriculum to ensure that it provides adolescents with the comprehensive sexuality education they need to protect themselves against these threats. Finally, it has not pushed the government to ensure the meaningful participation of adolescents and civil society in the ongoing review of the country's adolescent sexual and reproductive health policy.

Further, the government has failed to ensure that women and girl survivors of sexual violence can access safe, legal abortion care in line with the country's constitution. As a result, survivors of sexual violence who become pregnant are still forced to resort to unsafe abortion.

Refugee Rights

In mid-2023, the Kenyan government announced the rollout of its multi-year "Shirika Plan" to promote the socioeconomic inclusion of refugees. The plan will transform Dadaab and Kakuma refugee camps into integrated settlements where refugees will live alongside local communities, contribute to local economies, and have access to government services. This shift away from Kenya's prior policy—which had focused on encampment and repatriation, with multiple threats to close the camps—marked a step forward for refugee rights. Kenya hosted 636,000 refugees as of July 2023.

Key International Actors

Kenya remains a strategic player and regional hub on key African and global issues. Kenya contributes troops to the peace missions in Somalia and the Democratic Republic of Congo. The government is a leading actor in negotiations for peace and the cessation of hostilities in the conflicts in Ethiopia, Sudan, South Sudan, and Congo. Although one of the warring parties publicly rejected President Ruto as the head of the peace talks in Sudan based on allegations that he supports the other side, he continues to spearhead mediation efforts of the Inter-Governmental Authority on Development (IGAD), which is acting on behalf of the African Union.

Key regional actors have been involved in efforts to settle the differences between President Ruto and Odinga, who has led several protests against Ruto's administration. Tanzanian President Samia Suluhu and South African President Cyril Ramaphosa initiated preliminary negotiations. The protests eventually ended and ongoing talks between the government and the opposition began after former Nigerian president, Olusegun Obasanjo, held several meetings with Ruto and Odinga in Nairobi.

In June, the European Union Commission and Kenya concluded the negotiations of an Economic Partnership Agreement that includes commitments by both parties on climate change, labor rights, and women's rights.

Kosovo

Accountability for serious crimes and media freedom continue to be pressing concerns.

Tensions flared up in the north in May when ethnic Albanian mayors took office in municipalities following local elections that were largely boycotted by the ethnic Serb majority. Ensuing protests resulted in NATO forces clashing with protesting ethnic Serbs in the north, injuring at least 50 Serbs and 25 NATO soldiers. In September, a Kosovo police officer was killed by a group of heavily armed Serb gunmen in Banjska who then took shelter inside an Orthodox church. Kosovo security forces shot three of the group dead and arrested at least eight others, and Serbia increased military deployments at its border with Kosovo.

The United Nations failed to apologize and pay individual compensation to Roma, Ashkali, and Balkan Egyptian victims of lead poisoning in contaminated camps for displaced people run by the UN Mission in Kosovo (UNMIK) in 1999. A 2016 report by the Human Rights Advisory Panel (HRAP), an independent body established to investigate complaints of abuses by UNMIK, found that the UN should pay individual compensation and apologize to victims.

Accountability for War Crimes

In April, the trial of former Kosovo President and Prime Minister Hashim Thaci and three other former senior Kosovo Liberation Army (KLA) officials began in The Hague before the Kosovo Specialist Chambers. The accused, who spent almost 2.5 years in pretrial detention, are charged with war crimes and crimes against humanity allegedly committed in 1998 and 1999. All four men pled not guilty.

In December 2022, the Specialist Chambers sentenced KLA commander Salih Mustafa to 26 years in prison for war crimes and ordered him to pay €207,000 in reparations to victims. His case was under appeal at time of writing. In February, the Specialist Chambers began the trial of KLA member Pjeter Shala, who is accused of abusing detainees at a metal factory in Kukes, northern Albania, in 1999. Also in February, appeals judges upheld a May 2022 verdict on all but one charge against two members of the KLA War Veterans Association, Hysni Gucati and Nasim Haradinaj, over revealing the names of potential witnesses in the Thaci et al. trial, reducing their prison sentences of 4.5 years by 3 months. In August, former KLA member Dritan Goxhaj was arrested in Tirana, Albania, for revealing the names of five potential witnesses testifying before the Specialist Chambers. Goxhaj was awaiting extradition to the Netherlands at time of writing.

In June, in a retrial, the basic court in Prizren convicted former KLA fighter Remzi Shala of the 1998 kidnapping of a suspected ethnic Albanian collaborator and sentenced him to 9.5 years in prison.

In July, Kosovo's Special Prosecution filed two separate indictments regarding war crimes. The first indictment charged a former member of the Serbian armed forces with expelling ethnic Albanians and looting and burning their property during the 1998-1999 war. The second charged a former member of the Serbian armed forces with crimes against humanity for his involvement in murder, raids, beatings, mistreatment, torture, and the deportation of thousands of ethnic Albanians from Reznik during the war.

In June, Kosovo's Special Prosecution charged a former Serbian policeman with war crimes against civilians for his participation in the May 1999 shooting of 19 ethnic Albanians in the village of Ozdrim.

Freedom of Media

Journalists continued to be subjected to physical attacks, threats, and obstructions in their work. Between January and September 2023, the Association of Journalists of Kosovo (AGK), recorded 60 incidents against journalists, including 16 attacks and 22 threats.

In early June, AGK recorded six separate attacks by protesters on ethnic Albanian journalists on the same day in the ethnic Serb majority town Leposavic in north Kosovo. The Journalists were in Leposavic to report on increased tensions and protests by ethnic Serbs following local municipal elections in the north in May. One journalist suffered a broken arm and others were hit by stones to the head and legs. Police were investigating the attacks at time of writing.

In May, journalist Burim Zarici was attacked in Zvecan while filming an attack on a Kosovo Police car. The perpetrator was convicted.

Also in May, RTV21 cameraman Berat Bahtiri and journalist Lirie Dibrani were attacked by protesters in North Mitrovica while covering tensions between Kosovo Serbs and Albanians in the north. Bahtiri lost his equipment. Police were investigating the case at time of writing.

In March, RTV editor and journalist Alban Selimi's garage was set on fire. A suspect was arrested, tried, and convicted of arson. Selimi believes the attack is linked to a 2021 story he wrote alleging the perpetrator's relatives were involved in usurping land.

Sexual Orientation and Gender Identity

Threats and acts of discrimination against lesbian, gay, bisexual, and transgender people (LGBT) continue. According to the local LGBT organization CEL, many LGBT people faced threats, intimidation, and violence from family members in 2023, with poor responses from state authorities when they reported any abuse. CEL itself regularly receives threats and hateful comments on its social media accounts.

Women's and Girls' Rights

The government in January decided to extend the deadline for survivors of sexual violence during the Kosovo war to register and receive special welfare benefits. The special commission to recognize and verify such survivors was set up in 2018 and was set to finish registrations in February. Of an estimated 20,000 wartime rape victims, fewer than 2,000 have applied to the commission.

The Kosovo Agency of Statistics showed that only 20 percent of women participated in the labor force and called for more reforms for women to contribute toward the economy and prosperity.

Survivors of domestic violence continue to face obstacles accessing justice and support when leaving abusive environments.

Asylum Seekers and Displaced Persons

Between January and August, the Kosovo Ministry of Internal Affairs registered 292 forced returns to Kosovo, the majority from Germany. Sixteen were children. Of those forcibly returned, nine were Roma, two Ashkali, one Serb, and rest ethnic Albanian. During the same reporting period, the ministry registered 28 voluntary returns to Kosovo. The ministry claimed to have no data on the ethnicity of those who voluntarily returned. By mid-August, Kosovo had registered six asylum seekers from Ukraine.

Accountability of International Institutions

In a July report, the UN special rapporteur on the promotion of truth, justice, reparation and guarantees of non-recurrence recommended that the UN provide full and effective reparations, including a fully funded reparation program, to Roma, Ashkali, and Balkan Egyptian victims of lead poisoning who had resided in contaminated camps for displaced people run by UNMIK. A 2016 report by the Human Rights Advisory Panel (HRAP), an independent body established to investigate complaints of abuses by UNMIK, recommended the UN pay individual compensation and apologize to victims. The UN has yet to comply with the recommendations at time of writing.

Key International Actors

Concluding that Kosovo had failed to reduce tensions in the north, as asked on June 3 by 27 European Union member states, the EU implemented a range of punitive measures later that month. These included Kosovo's exclusion from high-level meetings and the suspension until 2024 of pre-accession funds to Kosovo. At time of writing, the measures were still in place.

In May, the United States Ambassador called on Prime Minister Albin Kurti to take concrete steps to de-escalate the situation in the north.

The November European Commission's enlargement report on Kosovo said that while some legislative achievements were made, more needed to be done on justice reforms and the rule of law, stressing the strengthening of the integrity, accountability, independence, and efficiency of the justice system. The Commission also noted the lack of progress on freedom of expression and remained concerned about physical attacks and threats against journalists, public smear campaigns, and hate speech.

Kuwait

On June 6, Kuwait held its third general elections in three years.

Kuwaiti authorities used provisions in the penal code and national security and cybercrime laws to restrict free speech and prosecute Kuwaitis and non-nationals, particularly for comments made on social media. On July 23, authorities executed five people convicted of drug-related offenses and murder. This is the second time Kuwait has carried out multiple executions in the past two years, which had not previously occurred since 2017.

Authorities did not make progress in protecting the rights of the Bidun, a community of stateless people who claim Kuwaiti nationality, whose status remains in legal limbo while the government suppresses and penalizes their peaceful activism.

Freedoms of Expression and Assembly

Several penal code provisions, as well as the cybercrime law, criminalize speech deemed insulting to religion, the emir, or foreign leaders.

According to the Gulf Center for Human Rights, on May 15, 2023, the Criminal Court in Kuwait convicted Salman Al-Khalidi to a five-year prison sentence with hard labor on charges that included "intentionally spreading false and malicious rumors abroad about the country's internal conditions, publishing what would harm relations of Kuwait with other countries," through his account on the social media platform X, formerly known as Twitter. Al-Khalidi had previously been sentenced to five years' imprisonment, but he was pardoned by the authorities.

On August 23, *al-Qabas* paper reported that the Ministry of Information had finished preparing a new draft law to regulate the media. According to the outlet, the draft law includes fines of at least 10,000 Kuwaiti dinars (about US$3,200), imprisonment of up to three years for insulting the emir, and a ban on publishing his statements without permission, and it extends the same prohibitions to the crown prince. The draft law also includes prohibitions on criticizing religion or Kuwait's constitution, "violating public morals," and "revealing information about confidential official communications" without regard for the public interest.

Article 12 of the 1979 Public Gatherings Law bars non-Kuwaitis from participating in public gatherings. Authorities continued to prosecute and target outspoken members of the Bidun community. In January, authorities denied entry to Mona Kareem, an academic from the Bidun community, who resides in the United States and was traveling to visit her family.

Women's Rights

Kuwait's personal status laws discriminate against women in matters of marriage, divorce, and child custody, including by requiring women to have male guardian permission to marry. Women can only apply to the courts for divorce on limited grounds, while men can divorce without any restrictions. Kuwaiti women married to non-Kuwaitis cannot pass Kuwaiti citizenship to their children or spouses on an equal basis with Kuwaiti men.

Article 153 of the penal code allows men who kill their wives, daughters, sisters, or mothers upon finding them in the act of extramarital sex to receive a reduced sentence of a maximum of three years in prison or a fine. Article 182 allows an abductor who uses force, threats, or deception with the intention to kill, harm, rape, prostitute, or extort the victim to avoid punishment if he marries the victim with the permission of her guardian.

Women do not require guardian permission to travel abroad alone, but a woman may lose her right to spousal maintenance if her travel abroad is deemed by a court to be disobedient to her husband.

In recent years, legislative and policy initiatives have targeted women's rights and gender equality. In September 2023, a few days before the start of classes at Kuwait University, the College of Law canceled mixed-gender classes for the academic year.

On September 17, the National Assembly passed the implementation law for the 2020 domestic violence law. The 2020 law includes some penalties to combat domestic violence and provides some assistance for survivors, but due to a lack of implementation, shelters remained closed.

Sexual Orientation and Gender Identity

The penal code criminalizes adultery with up to five years in prison and a fine, and article 193 punishes consensual same-sex relations between men by up to seven years in prison. In a positive step, in February 2022, the Constitutional Court ruled unconstitutional a 2007 penal code provision, article 198, which prohibited "imitating the opposite sex." However, transgender people continue to face threats and harassment. In December 2022, the *Kuwait Times* reported that local security forces deported around 3,000 gay and transgender people during "extensive security campaigns" over the past 11 months.

Stateless People and Migrants' Rights

Authorities have discriminated against the Bidun, a group of about 100,000 stateless people who claim Kuwaiti nationality, since Kuwait's independence in 1961. The government rejects their claims and refers to them as "illegal residents." The government has failed to create a transparent process to determine their citizenship claims or provide them with a path to nationality while creating obstacles for Bidun to obtain civil documentation, receive social services, and access their rights to health, education, and work.

The Central System for the Remedy of Situations of Illegal Residents, the administrative body in charge of Bidun affairs, has been issuing temporary ID cards that often state the cardholder possesses Iraqi, Saudi, Iranian, or other citizenship. It is unclear how the agency determined this, and no due process procedures appear to be available for Bidun to challenge the determinations

Unless their fathers or grandfathers occupy certain public sector jobs, such as in the military or the Ministries of Health or Education, or their mothers have Kuwaiti nationality, Bidun children are barred from free public schools. On September 12, Kuwaiti media reported that the Minister of Education and Higher Education and Scientific Research Adel Al-Mana announced Bidun students with expired ID cards are allowed to register in public and private school for the coming academic year. It is unclear how this will be implemented.

Two-thirds of Kuwait's population are migrant workers, who remain vulnerable to abuse, largely due to the *kafala* (sponsorship) system, which ties migrants' visas to their employers and requires that migrants get their employers' consent to leave employment or change jobs. Over the last year, no additional legal reforms were introduced to end the abusive kafala system.

Migrant domestic workers face additional forms of abuse, including being forcibly confined in their employers' homes and verbal, physical, and sexual abuse. While government shelters and complaint procedures exist for victims, there are serious barriers to accessing them, particularly for abuses like wage theft.

Climate Change Policies and Impacts

As one of the world's hottest and most water-stressed countries, Kuwait is acutely vulnerable to the impacts of climate change. As the world's seventh largest exporter of crude oil, the country has the sixth highest greenhouse gas emissions per capita globally.

The increasing frequency and intensity of heat waves, decreasing precipitation, and rising sea levels pose risks to the rights to health, life, water, and housing, especially of low-income migrant workers and the Bidun who are already marginalized.

Kuwait implements a summer midday ban that prohibits outdoor work during pre-defined times and months despite strong evidence of its ineffectiveness. Certain outdoor workers like bike delivery riders and street vendors continue to work under unbearable conditions. According to a study published in 2023, there is a need for stronger risk-based heat standards to effectively protect outdoor workers.

Kyrgyzstan

Human rights protections and civil liberties in Kyrgyzstan continued to decline in 2023, with systematic stifling of critical voices by the authorities. Civil society and media freedom came under severe threat, with criminal cases against leading media outlets and draft laws that would allow the expansion of state control over the work of nongovernmental organizations (NGOs) and censorship of information. A law was adopted banning "propaganda of non-traditional relations and same-sex partnerships."

A blanket ban on protests, initially introduced in March 2022, was extended through October 2023. At time of writing, activists, journalists, human rights defenders, and politicians detained in October 2022 remained in pretrial detention, and an effective and independent investigation into the death in custody of human rights defender Azimjon Askarov in 2020 had yet to be completed.

Despite measures implemented to combat domestic violence, impunity for such crimes persists.

In February 2023, Kyrgyzstan started a three-year term as a member of the United Nations Human Rights Council.

Civil Society

In May, the Kyrgyz parliament proposed the "Foreign Representatives" draft law, which would require NGOs receiving foreign funding and engaging in political activities to register with the Justice Ministry as "foreign representatives." Non-compliance could result in the suspension of activities, including banking operations, for up to six months. At time of writing, parliament had not adopted the draft law.

In May 2023, Kyrgyzstan Ombudsperson Atyr Abdrakhmatova's term was ended, when a majority of members of parliament voted in favor of a dismissal motion after she presented her annual report to the Kyrgyz parliament. Commentators linked the move to her independent approach to human rights in the country since taking office in 2022.

In January 2023, Kyrgyzstan's Supreme Court acquitted Kamil Ruziev, head of the human rights NGO Ventus, of charges of forgery brought against him in 2020 by the State Committee on National Security (GKNB) in apparent retaliation for his efforts to bring to justice security service officers allegedly engaged in torture of detainees.

Freedom of Expression

In May, a draft mass media law, which would significantly restrict the ability of civil society organizations and media to operate independently, was registered for consideration in the Kyrgyz parliament. The draft law establishes vague and broadly worded prohibitions for media, and failure to respect them can lead to forced suspension and termination of media outlets and closure of websites. At time of writing, the bill was still pending before parliament.

In July, the Bishkek City Court overturned an earlier court decision to shut down Radio Free Europe/Radio Liberty's (RFE/RL) Kyrgyz Service, known as Radio Azattyk, in response to the broadcaster's refusal to remove a video covering the border conflict between Kyrgyzstan and Tajikistan in September 2022. Kyrgyz authorities had previously blocked Radio Azattyk's websites and froze its bank account.

On August 28, 2023, Kyrgyz authorities initiated a lawsuit to close down Kloop Media Public Foundation, an independent online news outlet, accusing it of failing to register as a mass media outlet. The lawsuit claims the outlet publishes criticism only of the government and it refers to a pretrial criminal investigation into alleged Kloop involvement in "public calls for the violent seizure of power online."

Throughout 2023, Kyrgyz security services targeted bloggers for their social media posts, often using vague provisions of the Criminal Code such as incitement to ethnic or national hatred (article 330) and calls for disobedience to authorities and riots (article 278). One case involves 20-year-old Facebook blogger Yrys Zhekshenaliev, who was detained in August 2022 and placed under house arrest. He could face a six-year prison sentence if found guilty.

In September, Kyrgyzstan's Supreme Court upheld a previous court decision that expelled investigative journalist Bolot Temirov from the country in November

2022. This decision followed Temirov's earlier acquittal on drug possession charges, which had stemmed from a controversial police raid on his independent journalism outlet, Temirov Live, in January 2022.

Access to Justice

More than 20 individuals who opposed transferring the Kempir-Abad dam to Uzbekistan as part of a border demarcation agreement were detained in October 2022. Over a year later, they remained in detention, including under house arrest, awaiting trial. They include activists, human rights defenders, bloggers, and politicians who face charges of preparing to incite riots, punishable by up to 10 years in prison. Some have spent all their time in detention facilities with poor conditions that violate international standards. In January 2023, the Kempir-Abad case was classified, which made investigation materials unavailable to the defense lawyers. Court hearings started on June 22, 2023, but were held behind closed doors. Detainees have reported ill-treatment and being denied medical assistance.

In October, Kyrgyzstan's president signed into law amendments previously approved by the parliament, which allow the president or the court's chairperson to review Constitutional Court decisions in specific categories of cases, including those deemed contrary to "moral values" or "public consciousness," or cases in which "new circumstances" warrant review. These changes followed a controversial Constitutional Court decision in June permitting matronymic alongside patronymic family names. The amendments would be a departure from the previous understanding that Constitutional Court decisions are final and non-appealable.

Freedom of Assembly

On June 6, Kyrgyzstan's security services detained approximately 30 individuals, members of the "Eldik Kenesh" political party, on suspicion of plotting to overthrow the government. The GKNB alleged that the group intended to incite unrest and exploit the turmoil to seize power and had recruited over 100 dissatisfied citizens over the past year, possibly with overseas involvement, to provoke street unrest.

HUMAN
RIGHTS
WATCH
Abused by Relatives,
Ignored by the State
Domestic Violence Against and Neglect of Women and Girls
with Disabilities in Kyrgyzstan

In May, civil society activist Ondurush Toktonasyrov, who had previously been detained numerous times for his peaceful protests, was arbitrarily detained by law enforcement and questioned as part of a criminal case against him on trumped up charges. Toktonasyrov is accused of inciting racial, ethnic, national, religious, or interregional hatred for Facebook posts on the Russian invasion of Ukraine and on internal political events of Kyrgyzstan. In August, the investigation was completed, and his trial was pending at time of writing.

Violence against Women and Girls

Cases of violence against women and girls remain underreported, and survivors face multiple barriers to accessing services and justice. These include insufficient shelter space and other essential services, dismissive responses by authorities, stigma, and attitudes that perpetuate harmful stereotypes and practices, including by police, judicial officials, and government and religious leaders. In the first eight months of 2023, the Interior Ministry registered 8,502 domestic violence complaints.

In January, Miss Universe contestant Altynai Botoyarova was shamed and pressured into making an apology on social media after using the platform to call attention to gender-based violence in Kyrgyzstan. On International Women's Day in March, protesters in Bishkek demanded more action by police and courts on gender-based violence. In September, parliamentarians called for harsher measures on domestic violence after a woman's ex-husband brutally attacked her with a knife, despite her having reported him to police numerous times for rape, physical violence, and threats.

Sexual Orientation and Gender Identity

In August 2023, President Sadyr Japarov signed into law a bill on the "protection of children from harmful information" that deems information about "non-traditional sexual relationships" harmful to children's health and development, effectively criminalizing any discussion of LGBT people. Distribution of such information is subject to fines ranging from the equivalent of US$25 to $250.

In July, members of parliament submitted for public consideration a new anti-discrimination law aimed at preventing, stopping, and eliminating all forms of discrimination by state bodies and private companies against citizens on the basis of race, language, disability, ethnicity, and age. However, the draft law excludes sexual orientation and gender identity as protected categories.

In early May, Kyrgyzstan dissolved the Country Coordinating Mechanism (CCM), the national committee responsible for HIV strategy and UN Global Fund allocation. Parliament members objected to the allocation of funds for HIV prevention among men who have sex with men (MSM) and transgender individuals, citing cultural norms and fears the projects would lead to advocacy for same-sex marriage. The decision affects HIV prevention programs, endangering the health of members of affected communities.

Disability Rights

Starting in January 2023, Kyrgyz authorities increased monthly social benefit payments to adults and children with disabilities by anywhere from 50 to 100 percent depending on the degree of disability. The services of personal assistants have also been extended to adults with first-degree disabilities from childhood.

In August, the Ministry of Labor and Social Protection presented a draft resolution that seeks to align sociomedical examinations used for disability assessments with standards in the UN Convention on the Rights of Persons with Disabilities, marking the state's further transition from a medical model of disability support to a social one. However, despite this progress, there are still few accessible rehabilitation centers available for girls and women with disabilities and few shelters available for survivors of family abuse and domestic violence.

Conflict at the Kyrgyzstan-Tajikistan Border

Following the armed conflict in September 2022 between Tajikistan and Kyrgyzstan forces, in which at least 37 people, including 5 children, were killed, bilateral relations remained tense, although negotiations continued in 2023 on demarcation and other border-related issues. Both countries committed apparent war crimes in the conflict, leading to the deaths of civilians and the destruction of civilian property, including schools, according to a research report by Human Rights Watch published in May. Also in May, both governments committed to end the use of military drones to patrol the border. The use of such drones in the conflict led to civilian deaths, according to the Human Rights Watch report.

Key International Actors

On July 13, the European Parliament adopted a resolution expressing concern over the decline in democratic standards and human rights in Kyrgyzstan and urging Kyrgyz authorities to repeal the "false information" law and review draft legislation concerning "foreign representatives," "mass media," and "protecting children from harmful information."

A delegation of the European Parliament Foreign Affairs Committee visited Kyrgyzstan in August 2023 in the context of intensifying relations with Central Asian states following Russia's invasion of Ukraine and ahead of the expected signature of an EU-Kyrgyzstan Enhanced Partnership and Cooperation Agreement.

President Japarov met with European Council President Charles Michel on the sidelines of the second high-level EU-Central Asia dialogue at level of heads of state in Kyrgyzstan in June 2023.

United States President Joe Biden met President Japarov on the sidelines of the UN General Assembly in New York on September 19, part of the first-ever US summit with presidents of the five Central Asian countries.

On May 5, the European Union noted the dismissal of the Kyrgyz Ombudswoman Atyr Abdrakhmatova as a negative development and encouraged Kyrgyz authorities to abide by the country's international human rights commitments.

In November, during its annual Human Rights Dialogue with Kyrgyzstan, the EU expressed concern about growing restrictions on the freedom of expression and the continuously shrinking space for civil society. The EU noted that legislation aimed at controlling so-called foreign representatives could impact cooperation activities supported by the EU and other international donors in Kyrgyzstan.

In September, the education ministry submitted for public discussion a draft resolution to endorse the Safe Schools Declaration.

HUMAN
RIGHTS
WATCH
"Cut Off From Life Itself"
Lebanon's Failure on the Right to Electricity

Lebanon

Lebanon continued to grapple with an acute economic and financial crisis that has impoverished most of the population since 2019. Human rights conditions in the country deteriorated in 2023, with a noticeable uptick in prosecutions for critical speech, growing restrictions against refugees and lesbian, gay, bisexual, and transgender (LGBT) people, and continued impunity for previous abuses.

Tensions have increased along the Lebanon-Israel border, where armed clashes between the Israeli army and various Lebanese and Palestinian armed groups have been ongoing since October 8. As of November 23, Israeli attacks in Lebanon have reportedly killed at least 14 civilians, in addition to at least 85 Hezbollah fighters. Rocket strikes and other attacks into Israel by Hezbollah and Palestinian groups have reportedly killed at least three civilians and six soldiers.

No official has been held accountable for the catastrophic Beirut port explosion in August 2020, and implicated officials have successfully obstructed the domestic investigation since December 2021. The authorities failed to implement crucial economic and financial reforms needed to alleviate the consequences and address the root causes of the economic crisis while they stepped up harassment of lawyers, activists, journalists, and comedians in response to their public criticisms of the government and public officials. In April and May, the Lebanese army summarily deported thousands of Syrians back to Syria.

In February 2023, a United Kingdom court ruled in favor of three families whose relatives were victims of the 2020 port explosion in a lawsuit brought against the company that owned the 2,750 tons of ammonium nitrate that was stored in hazardous conditions in port and is believed to have led to the explosion. In March, 38 countries expressed concern about obstruction of and interference with the domestic investigation into the explosion while the UN expert on judicial independence, Margaret Satterthwaite, criticized obstruction of the investigation by implicated actors. On March 28, nine members of parliament introduced two draft laws that would strengthen the independence of judicial investigations and prevent political interference with the judiciary, but all legislation remained stalled at time of writing because of the ongoing presidential vacuum.

Parliament has repeatedly failed to elect a president since October 2022 or put in motion legislative reforms demanded by International Monetary Fund (IMF) that would unlock billions of dollars in aid. Thousands of prisoners, many held in pretrial detention, continued to languish in overcrowded detention centers across the country without adequate access to health care, medicine, or food.

Accountability and Justice

August 4, 2023 marked three years since the Beirut port explosion that killed at least 220 people, wounded over 7,000, and caused extensive property damage. The domestic investigation into the blast remained frozen and politicians continued to interfere to disrupt the lead investigator, Judge Tarek Bitar. On January 23, Judge Bitar took steps to overcome legal barriers preventing him from resuming his work, ordered the release of five suspects, and charged and summoned others for interrogation, including the top public prosecutor, Ghassan Oueidat. In response, Oueidat ordered law enforcement agencies not to execute Bitar's "null" orders, charged Bitar with several crimes, including "usurping power," and ordered the release of all the detainees in the case.

Families of the victims and several local and international rights groups continued to call for an international, independent, and impartial investigation into the blast, including a fact-finding mission to be established by the United Nations Human Rights Council. On March 7, 2023, 38 countries expressed concern about the systemic obstruction and interference with the domestic investigation in a joint statement delivered by Australia before the UN Human Rights Council. During the September 2023 Human Rights Council session, the UN high commissioner for human rights called for an international fact-finding mission into the blast.

Economic Crisis and Rights

Most people in Lebanon were unable to secure their economic and social rights amid the deepening economic crisis, with low-income households bearing the brunt of the crisis. Existing social assistance programs, funded in part by the World Bank, extended minimal coverage and very narrowly targeted households in extreme poverty, leaving large segments of the population who did not qualify vulnerable to hunger, unable to obtain medicines, and subject to other deprivations that undermine their rights.

By mismanaging the electricity sector for decades, Lebanese authorities massively failed to uphold the right to electricity, which Human Rights Watch found is essential to the right to an adequate standard of living. Lebanon's failure to provide electricity beyond a few hours per day left people in the dark and dramatically reduced their access to critical rights, such as food, water, education, and health care.

The economic crisis also threatened the education sector, leaving public school students at risk of losing another year of school due to a budget shortfall and years of mismanagement at the Ministry of Education.

Prison conditions dangerously deteriorated amid the economic crisis, with a majority of prisoners, some held in pretrial detention, subjected to unprecedented overcrowding, subpar health care, disruptions in food supply, and a drop in food quality.

In April 2022, the Lebanese government and the IMF reached a staff-level agreement that would unlock US$3 billion over 46 months, provided the adoption of key reforms, including the adoption of a bank secrecy and capital controls law and the restructuring of the Lebanese banking sector. More than 1.5 years later, the reform process remained stalled, and in September 2023, the IMF criticized the government's "lack of action on urgently needed reforms." Caretaker Economy Minister Amin Salam stated in August that "a growing number" of officials in the country believed that an IMF loan agreement with Lebanon was no longer needed.

Freedom of Expression

Lebanese authorities increasingly instrumentalized criminal defamation laws to intimidate and harass critics of the government and public officials amid the economic crisis.

In April, the Beirut Bar Association summoned Nizar Saghieh, a prominent lawyer and head of the research and advocacy organization Legal Agenda, to appear before the Bar Association for publicly protesting amendments to the Bar's

Legal Code of Ethics that limit the ability of lawyers to make public statements without prior approval. In March 2023, State Security summoned Jean Kassir, co-founder of the independent media outlet *Megaphone*, after it published online posts stating that "Lebanon [is] ruled by fugitives from justice." Lara Bitar, editor-in-chief of the Public Source site, was also summoned for interrogation on March 31 by the Cybercrimes Bureau of the Internal Security Forces (ISF) for an article she had written about a local political party. In July, a Lebanese court sentenced journalist Dima Saddek to one year in prison following a defamation claim filed against her by Gebran Bassil, a member of parliament and the head of the Free Patriotic Movement (FPM), after she criticized the actions of FPM supporters. In August, Lebanese authorities, including the Lebanese military prosecution and the ISF's Criminal Investigations Division, summoned for investigation and subsequently arrested prominent comedian Nour Hajjar in retaliation for jokes he had made on stage. In September, journalist Majdoline Lahham was also summoned for investigation by the ISF's Criminal Investigations Division following a defamation claim filed against her in response to a post she shared on social media highlighting corrupt practices by the head of the Sunni Sharia Court of Beirut, Judge Mohammad Ahmad Assaf.

Women's Rights

Various religion-based personal status laws are discriminatory against women and allow religious courts to control matters related to marriage, divorce, and children. Under all personal status laws, a woman can be found legally recalcitrant (disobedient) if she leaves the marital home and refuses to cohabit with her husband without a reason that the religious courts consider legitimate. A woman found to be legally recalcitrant is not entitled to spousal maintenance (financial support) from her husband.

Lebanon's nationality law bars Lebanese women, but not men, from passing citizenship to their children and foreign spouses. Cases of domestic violence, including killings, are on the rise.

In September 2022, the General Directorate of Personal Status stopped recognizing foreign civil marriages and began to deregister ones it had previously recognized, including for some married couples expecting children.

Migrant Workers

The legal status of thousands of migrant domestic workers in Lebanon, including workers from Ethiopia, the Philippines, Bangladesh, and Sri Lanka, was regulated by a restrictive and abusive regime of laws, regulations, and customary practices known as the *kafala* (sponsorship) system.

Recruitment agencies were accused of subjecting workers to abuse, labor violations, and human trafficking and in 2020, they successfully lobbied to block a new standard unified contract adopted by the Ministry of Labor that would have introduced vital safeguards for workers. Lebanon's top administrative court blocked the implementation of the contract, just a little over a month after its adoption, on the basis that it dealt "severe damage" to the interests of recruitment agencies.

Sexual Orientation and Gender Identity

LGBT people continue to face systemic discrimination in Lebanon. Article 534 of the penal code punishes "any sexual intercourse contrary to the order of nature" with up to one year in prison, despite a series of court rulings between 2007 and 2018 that consensual same-sex relations are not illegal.

In August, Caretaker Minister of Culture Mohammed Mortada and member of parliament Ashraf Rifi introduced separate bills that would explicitly criminalize same-sex relations between consenting adults and punish anyone who "promotes homosexuality" with up to three years in prison.

Also in August, men belonging to the "Soldiers of God," a group openly hostile to LGBT people, attacked a bar where a drag event was being held in Beirut and assaulted attendees. Agents of the ISF who arrived at the site failed to intervene and protect the bar's attendees.

In July, Hezbollah's leader, Hassan Nasrallah, incited violence against gay and lesbian people by calling for their killing, sparking terror among LGBT people, with many receiving death threats and online harassment.

A 2023 Human Rights Watch report described the far-reaching offline consequences of online targeting of LGBT people, including blackmail and being outed, family violence, and arbitrary arrests by Lebanon's ISF.

Refugees

Lebanese authorities continued to pursue policies and deploy tactics designed to coerce Syrian refugees to return to Syria.

Between April and May 2023, the Lebanese Armed Forces (LAF) arbitrarily arrested and summarily deported thousands of Syrians, including unaccompanied children, to Syria, and it intensified raids on houses of refugees in neighborhoods across the country, including Mount Lebanon, Jounieh, Qob Elias, and Bourj Hammoud. Many of those forcibly returned were registered or known to the UN Refugee Agency (UNHCR).

According to the UN, there were nearly 520,000 Palestinian refugees, including over 31,000 from Syria, living in Lebanon, where they continued to face restrictions, including on their right to work and own property.

In July, armed clashes erupted in the Ain El Hilweh Palestinian refugee camp near Saida after militants ambushed and killed a Fatah commander alongside his bodyguards. About 20,000 people, including 12,000 children, were displaced as a result of the deadly fighting, according to Save the Children. More than 30 people, including civilians, were killed in the clashes.

Legacy of Past Wars and Conflicts

An estimated 17,000 Lebanese were kidnapped or "disappeared" during the 1975-1990 civil war and authorities took no recent steps to uncover their fate.

In January, the UN extended the mandate of the Special Tribunal for Lebanon until the end of December to allow it to finalize its work. The tribunal had convicted Hezbollah agents in absentia in 2022 for planning and executing the assassination of the late Prime Minister Rafik El Hariri in 2005.

Key International Actors

France, Syria, Iran, Saudi Arabia, and other regional powers exert their influence in Lebanon through their local political allies.

Human Rights Watched verified the use of white phosphorous in south Lebanon by Israeli forces, in addition to indiscriminate attacks on civilians and the apparent deliberate targeting of journalists, amounting to possible war crimes.

In July, the European Union extended its targeted sanctions framework for Lebanon for another year, which allows for targeted sanctions against individuals or entities for undermining democracy and the rule of law, but the EU has yet to target any individual or entity.

Also in July, the European Parliament adopted a resolution on Lebanon calling for targeted sanctions against those obstructing justice for the 2020 Beirut blast and urging the UN Human Rights Council to establish an independent investigation to ascertain responsibility for the blast. At the council, the EU repeatedly called for a swift, transparent, and credible investigation.

In July, the United States, the UK, and Canada imposed coordinated targeted sanctions on Lebanon's former Central Bank governor, Riad Salameh, and his associates, after the end of his 30-year tenure, for their alleged role in an extensive corruption and money laundering scheme. In May, France issued an arrest warrant against Salameh and Interpol issued a red notice in his name. Salameh's first deputy, Wassim Mansouri, assumed the role of acting governor in August.

Libya

Human rights violations and abuses by armed groups and militias remain pervasive, as political elites and myriad quasi-authorities compete for legitimacy and control of territory, nearly 12 years into Libya's political transition away from Muammar Gaddafi's strong-man rule.

Authorities in both east and west Libya are cracking down on the activities of civic groups, harassing and sometimes detaining and prosecuting local staff members of nongovernmental organizations (NGOs), and imposing obstacles for non-Libyans to obtain entry visas. In March, the Tripoli-based prime minister declared that NGOs that fail to overcome the nearly insurmountable conditions for registration, administration, and operations would be ruled unlawful.

On September 10, a massive storm (Storm Daniel) hit eastern Libya, mostly affecting the city of Derna, and led to the confirmed deaths of 4,352 people as of October 31, with 8,500 reported missing and 43,400 displaced, according to the United Nations. The direct cause of many of the casualties and much of the damage was the torrent of water after two dams collapsed, which washed neighborhoods into the Mediterranean Sea. Libyan groups have called for an independent international investigation into the alleged failure by authorities to conduct preventive maintenance of infrastructure and to evacuate communities at risk.

Political Process and Elections

Two rival administrations continue to compete for control in Libya: the Tripoli-based Government of National Unity (GNU), headed by Abdelhamid Dabeiba, and a parallel body in eastern Libya, the Government of National Stability (GNS), established by the eastern, Tobruk-based parliament, the House of Representatives (HoR).

Elections remain elusive as competing authorities disagree over amendments to the 2011 constitutional declaration regarding elections.

Libyans have not voted in presidential or parliamentary elections since 2014, when a contested vote led to divided rule and conflict. At time of writing, there was no confirmed date to hold elections.

Libya's 2011 interim constitution remains the only one in place. A draft constitution submitted by the elected Libyan Constitution Drafting Assembly in July 2017 has yet to be put to a national referendum.

Armed Conflict and War Crimes

Fighting in Tripoli on August 14 and 15 between two major armed groups, one linked to the GNU Interior Ministry and the other to the Defense Ministry, resulted in at least 55 people killed and over 100 injured, including an undisclosed number of civilians, according to the UN. Clashes in April between rival armed groups in Zawiya resulted in at least four civilians killed, and in May, renewed clashes there reportedly killed two people.

As of March, the Tarek Ben Ziyad Brigade and Brigade 20/20 of the Libyan Arab Armed Forces (LAAF), the armed group controlling eastern and much of southern Libya, forcibly evicted on short notice more than 20,000 residents of Benghazi and forced them to rescind their property or ownership documents without an appropriate compensation scheme for residents, according to 6 UN experts and the UN Working Group on Arbitrary Detention. The Brigades' members demolished scores of residential units, including historic neighborhoods and protected heritage sites in the Benghazi center to make way for new residential and commercial building developments, and briefly arrested several residents and at least two activists protesting the evictions, the experts said.

In Tarhouna, where hundreds went missing between 2014 and 2020 when the al-Kaniyat militia under the leadership of al-Kani family members controlled the town, the General Authority for the Search and Identification of Missing Persons continued to identify the remains of hundreds found in mass graves in the area. As of October 31, no trials of those allegedly involved in the killings and disappearances had commenced.

Antipersonnel landmines and unexploded ordnance (UXO), including cluster munition remnants, continued to pose a risk, especially in Tripoli and its surroundings, where they killed or injured scores of civilians, including deminers, during and after the 2019-2020 Tripoli conflict. There are remnants from previous conflicts in 2011, 2014, and some that date back to World War II. Libya has not ratified the international Mine Ban Treaty or the Convention on Cluster Munitions, which respectively prohibit antipersonnel mines and cluster munitions. In September, an official from the International Committee of the Red Cross warned that the flooding in Derna "shifted unexploded ordnance into areas previously free of weapon contamination," increasing the risk for residents and aid workers.

Three years after a ceasefire agreement ended the 2019-2020 Tripoli conflict, Turkish and other military forces; thousands of foreign fighters from Chad, Sudan, and elsewhere; and members of private security companies, including the Wagner Group, remained present in Libya.

Libya has not endorsed the Safe Schools Declaration to protect education during armed conflict.

Judicial System and Detainees

Libya's criminal justice system remained weak with serious due process concerns. Judges, prosecutors, and lawyers remained at risk of harassment and attack by armed groups. Military courts continued to try civilians.

On December 6, the HoR voted to establish a constitutional court in Benghazi, despite the lack of a permanent constitution and without the buy-in of key stakeholders, including the High State Council (HSC), an advisory body to the GNU. In June, the Supreme Court of Libya ruled it unconstitutional.

Twenty-eight official prisons under the supervision of the justice ministry held 19,103 people, including 216 women, as of May 5, according to the UN Support Mission in Libya (UNSMIL). Many others are held in prolonged detention without trial, in prisons run by militias and only under the nominal control of authorities. Inhumane conditions, including severe overcrowding, torture, and ill-treatment, are prevalent at these facilities.

International Justice

The prosecutor of the International Criminal Court (ICC), Karim Khan, continued the investigation in Libya.

In May, Khan announced to the UN Security Council that ICC judges had issued four new arrest warrants against individuals for serious crimes in Libya that remained sealed and that he had applied for two more.

Saif al-Islam Gaddafi, a son of Muammar Gaddafi, who is wanted by the ICC since 2011 for serious crimes he allegedly committed during the Libyan revolution of that year, remains a fugitive, and Libya is under a legal obligation to surrender him to the Hague.

Ending its mandate in March, the UN Independent Fact-Finding Mission (FFM) on Libya found in its final report "reasonable grounds to believe that crimes against humanity were committed against Libyans and migrants throughout Libya, in the context of deprivation of liberty." The mission also found that arbitrary detentions, murders, torture, rapes, enslavement, sexual slavery, extrajudicial killings, and enforced disappearances were widespread. Libyan authorities pledged in 2022 at the Human Rights Council to use the FFM's findings and recommendations as a baseline for future reports to the council and treaty bodies, according to the FFM's final report.

Death Penalty

The death penalty is stipulated in over 30 articles in Libya's penal code, including for acts of speech and association. While military and civilian courts continued to impose the death penalty, no executions have been carried out since 2010.

Six Libyan women and men, arrested separately in March, are reportedly facing the death penalty for allegedly converting to Christianity and for proselytizing. They have reportedly been charged under article 207 of the penal code for "promoting theories or principles" that aim to overthrow the political, social, or economic system and for possessing "books, publications, illustrations, slogans, or any other material with the intent to endorse the aforementioned acts or advocate them in any other way." A lawyer representing one of them said his client was tortured during interrogation.

In a mass trial, a Misrata criminal court in May sentenced 23 defendants to death, 14 to life in prison, and another 14 to varying prison terms for their alleged links to Islamic State (ISIS) in 2015 in Sirte, including the killing of 21 mostly Egyptian Copts. Five were acquitted.

Freedoms of Assembly and Association

Libya's penal code stipulates severe punishments, including the death penalty, for establishing "unlawful" associations and prohibits Libyans from joining or establishing international organizations without government permission.

After months of increasing restrictions on civic groups and NGOs, including harassment, detention, and prosecution of local staff members, and after a March 8 edict by the Supreme Judicial Council declaring null and void any organizations not established according to a draconian 2001 Gaddafi-era law, the GNU prime minister in a March 21 circular gave NGOs provisional legal standing until they "correct their legal status" in line with the 2001 law.

Freedom of Expression

In the aftermath of the flooding, and after a demonstration on September 18 by Derna residents calling for an international investigation into the causes of the flooding and accountability for negligent officials, armed groups affiliated with the eastern Internal Security Agency seized and detained at least five Derna residents who had demonstrated, according to activists. On September 19, the LAAF ordered most media organizations and journalists to leave Derna, sparking concerns about a media blackout on the relief operation.

On October 2, the Benghazi Internal Security Agency arrested Fathi al-Baaja, a university professor and former member of the 2011 National Transitional Council, together with two political activists, Seraj Doghman and Tarek al-Bishari, after discussions at a symposium on repercussions of the Derna dams collapse. As of November 1, they remained in detention without any formal charges.

Eastern-based authorities on February 16, 2023, announced that they would start enforcing an anti-cybercrime law passed by the HoR in September 2022. Four UN experts criticized the law as infringing on the rights of free expression, privacy, and free association and called for its revocation. On February 17, eastern Libyan authorities arrested two women—a singer and an online content creator— for allegedly violating "honor and public morals." Both women have been released since.

In December 2022, a Tripoli court sentenced four men to three years in prison with hard labor for their involvement with the Tanweer movement and for being "atheist, areligious, secular and feminist." The FFM said that evidence "was extracted under coercive circumstances without lawyers present" and was concerned that "the legal provisions relied upon are inconsistent with the principle of legality and international human rights law."

Women's Rights, Sexual Orientation, and Gender Identity

In May, the Tripoli Internal Security Agency, a body linked to the GNU, began requiring Libyan women traveling without a male escort to complete a detailed form about the reasons for their travel and past travel, which is not a requirement under Libyan law and violates women's rights to equality and freedom of movement.

Libya lacks a domestic violence law that sets out measures to prevent domestic violence, punish abusers, and protect survivors. The penal code allows for a reduced sentence for a man who kills or injures his wife or another female relative because he suspects her of extramarital sexual relations. It also allows perpetrators of rape to escape prosecution if they marry their victims.

Libya's Family Code discriminates against women with respect to marriage, divorce, and inheritance. The 2010 nationality law also discriminates by allowing only Libyan men to pass on Libyan nationality to their children and requiring women to get the authorities' permission before marrying a non-Libyan man.

The penal code prohibits all sexual acts outside marriage, including consensual same-sex relations, and punishes them with flogging and up to five years in prison.

Internally Displaced People

As of August, there were about 125,802 internally displaced people in Libya, according to the UN Refugee Agency (UNHCR). These include thousands of former residents of the town of Tawergha, who were driven out by anti-Gaddafi groups from Misrata in 2011 and have been unable to return due to the deliberate destruction of the town and the scarcity of public services. They also include thousands of families forcibly displaced by the LAAF from Benghazi, Ajdabiya, and Derna since 2014.

As of October 31, an additional 43,421 remain displaced, including 16,000 children, because of Storm Daniel's impact on northeastern Libya.

Migrants, Refugees, and Asylum Seekers

According to the International Organization for Migration (IOM), 947 people were found dead and 1,256 went missing at sea along the central Mediterranean migration route after departing from Libya between January 1 and November 25.

According to IOM and UNHCR, as of April, there were 705,746 migrants and as of October, there were 50,986 registered asylum seekers and refugees.

As of July, Tunisian security forces collectively expelled over 900 African migrants and asylum seekers to a remote, militarized buffer zone at the Tunisia-Libya border. Over 150 people were transferred to Libya, where they faced arbitrary detention and deportation. In August, Libyan authorities said they had recovered at least 27 bodies in the border area since the start of the expulsions.

Between January and November 25, Libyan forces intercepted or rescued 15,057 migrants and asylum seekers attempting to cross the Mediterranean and returned them to Libya, according to the IOM. In Libya, they faced arbitrary and indefinite detention in inhumane conditions in facilities run by the GNU's Interior Ministry and were held with smugglers and traffickers, where they were subjected to forced labor, torture, ill-treatment, extortion, and sexual assault, according to the FFM.

Key International Actors

United States authorities announced on December 12, 2022 that they took custody of Abu Agela Masud Kheir Al-Marimi, a former official of Gaddafi's government, accusing him of complicity in the downing of Pan Am flight 103 in 1988 over the Scottish town of Lockerbie, killing 270 people. On January 25, a US court appointed a Federal Public Defender as al-Marimi's counsel, and on February 8, he pleaded not guilty to the formal charges of destruction of aircraft resulting in death. As of October 31, the trial had not started.

The Libyan General Prosecutor announced an investigation into the transfer to US custody of al-Marimi, who had no outstanding arrest warrant in Libya.

The European Union continued to cooperate with abusive Libyan Coast Guard forces, providing material and technical support and aerial surveillance to help them intercept Europe-bound migrants at sea and return them to Libya. In February, Italy handed over to the Coast Guard a search-and-rescue vessel paid for by the EU, and promised four more, deepening the EU's complicity in that agency's human rights abuses.

Malawi

In 2023, the authorities in Malawi began a process of detaining and forcibly relocating refugees and asylum seekers from across the country to Dzaleka refugee camp. The police and military used excessive force during the roundups and detained children in prisons with adults.

According to the World Bank, Malawi is the fourth poorest country in the world. Over half the population lives in poverty, and one-fifth in extreme poverty. For those living in poverty, many basic needs are out of reach including access to education, health services, safe drinking water, and basic sanitation. A cholera outbreak killed thousands of people, including hundreds of children.

In July, led by leaders of the country's major religions, many people took to the streets to protest same-sex relations, ahead of a court challenge to laws that criminalize sexual relations that are "against the order of nature."

Ongoing Cholera Outbreak

Since early 2022, Malawi has been battling a cholera outbreak, which the World Health Organization (WHO) said was the deadliest outbreak of cholera in the country's history. As of August, there were reportedly a total of 58,982 cholera cases including 1,768 deaths. In July, the United Nations Children's Fund (UNICEF) reported that over 14,000 children had contracted cholera, and over 220 had died. The authorities took some positive steps to address the crisis, including by securing 1.4 million doses of Oral Cholera Vaccine and working with WHO, which deployed international experts to provide emergency support to Malawi's health authorities in improving disease surveillance, prevention, and treatment measures.

Severe Tropical Cyclone Freddy

In March, Severe Tropical Cyclone Freddy hit Malawi, devastating 15 districts in the south of the country. By the end of March, over 500,000 people had been internally displaced by the storm, with over 1,000 dead or missing. Public infrastructure, including schools, health facilities, and roads, was extensively damaged in the 15 districts. Women and girls were at particular risk due to sexual harassment and violence in camps set up for people displaced by the cyclone. People with disabilities lost assistive devices, including wheelchairs, clutches, white canes, and hearing aids.

Malawi is one of the poorest countries in the world, with over 80 percent of the population dependent on agriculture. The economy is extremely vulnerable to climate change and natural disasters. President Lazarus Chakwera told the media in May that the country had lost US$500 million to Severe Tropical Cyclone Freddy, affecting the government's ability to provide shelter, sanitation, food, and other essential services to the hundreds of thousands affected by the storms.

Right to Education

Schools were closed for at least four weeks, as more than 490,000 primary- and secondary school-aged children were unable to attend school due to damage to school buildings caused by Cyclone Freddy. Many of the children in the southern parts of the country were directly impacted by the floods triggered by the cyclone and were forced to move into temporary shelters, impacting their right to access education. The suspension of schools was a particular concern for girls, because lack of access to education is linked to a heightened risk of child marriage. Malawi has very high rates of child marriage, with 42 percent of girls and 7 percent of boys married before age 18.

United Nations experts also raised concerns about the large numbers of children working on tobacco farms in Malawi and remaining out of school.

Older People's Rights

Section 13(j) of the Constitution of the Republic of Malawi provides that the government shall respect and support older people through the provision of community services and encourage their participation in the life of the community.

Media reports in July indicated that there was an increase in the attacks on older people in both rural and urban areas of the country. Most of the attacks were based on accusations of witchcraft. An Afrobarometer survey found that three in four Malawians (74 percent) believe "a lot" in the existence of witchcraft, and that most Malawians associate witchcraft with using magic to kill people, make them sick, or bring them misfortune. The survey also showed that older people, especially older women, are at greatest risk of being victims of witchcraft accusations. Malawi's laws do not recognize the existence of witchcraft, and it is a crime to accuse someone of witchcraft.

Twenty-two older people were killed between January and August 2023, according to the Malawi Network of Older Persons Organisations (MANEPO), for allegedly engaging in witchcraft. In March, MANEPO stated that 72 older people had been killed in the past two years over witchcraft accusations, but "none of the 72 cases has been tried and concluded."

Malawi has no specific legislation protecting the rights of older people, although the 2016 National Policy for Older Persons recognizes the state's duty to do so. The government is currently developing an Older Persons' Bill to improve the implementation of the National Policy for Older Persons. In January, officials from Centre for Human Rights and Rehabilitation (CHRR), a leading human rights nongovernmental organization (NGO) in Malawi, called on the government to fast-track the bill in parliament so that the law can be used to protect older people from attacks related to witchcraft accusations. In February, the government reported that the Ministry of Justice was reviewing the bill before handing it over to the relevant parliamentary committee. In September during the UN Human Rights Council session, Malawi supported a "comprehensive international legally binding instrument on the rights of older persons."

The Malawi Law Society and the Network for Older Persons' Organizations also called on the Malawi Police Service (MPS) to swiftly investigate and prosecute those involved in the abuse, torture, or killing of older people or any person over allegations of witchcraft.

Refugee Rights

Malawi hosted over 50,600 refugees and asylum seekers as of May 2023, according to the United Nations High Commissioner for Refugees (UNHCR). In May, the authorities started detaining and forcibly relocating refugees and asylum seekers from across the country. The police, aided by the military, arrested men, women, and children living in rural and urban districts, shut down their businesses, temporarily detained them in prisons, and later left them empty-handed at Dzaleka refugee camp. Some of those arrested reported beatings and destruction or theft of their property.

Children were among those caught up in the sweeps and taken to Maula Central Prison, a maximum-security prison in Lilongwe. This was in violation of international human rights standards, which prohibit detaining children solely for immigration reasons and in adult prisons.

The roundups of refugees and asylum seekers follow a March 27 government directive to enforce its encampment policy, which restricts refugees' freedom of movement by requiring them to live in Dzaleka camp. The government ordered all refugees and asylum seekers living in urban and rural areas to return to the camp by April 15 or face enforced relocation.

Government officials have also accused refugees of creating economic problems for Malawians, rhetoric that fosters xenophobia.

UNHCR in May called on Malawi's government to rescind its refugee relocation decision, warning that Dzaleka camp was already severely overcrowded and unable to meet the food, health, water, shelter, and sanitation needs of its existing population.

Malawi is party to the 1951 UN Refugee Convention and the 1969 African Refugee Convention, as well as the Convention on the Rights of the Child, which applies to refugee children (art. 22). The 1951 Refugee Convention recognizes the right of freedom of movement and choice of residence for refugees lawfully within a country (art. 26) and prohibits restrictions on the freedom of movement of asylum seekers unless such restrictions are deemed "necessary" (art. 31.2). However, Malawi entered reservations when it ratified the 1951 Convention, stating that it considered certain provisions "not legally binding," including refugees' rights to freedom of movement, employment, property, and public education.

Malawi's Refugee Act of 1989 provides for procedures to determine refugee status but does not address the rights of refugees.

Sexual Orientation and Gender Identity

Malawi's Penal Code contains several provisions that criminalize adult consensual same-sex conduct, with punishment of up to 14 years in prison. The government enacted a new anti-homosexuality law in January 2011, amending the Penal Code to extend the crime of "gross indecency" to women, with up to five years in prison. In 2012 and again in 2015, the Ministry of Justice announced a moratorium on enforcing these laws. But in 2016 the Mzuzu High Court issued an order suspending the moratorium pending judicial review. This has led to legal ambiguity.

In July, Malawi's High Court, sitting as a constitutional court, heard a case involving Jan Willem Akstar, a Dutch citizen, and Jana Gonani, a transgender Malawian woman. Akstar, was arrested in 2020 and charged with nine offenses of sexual abuse and sodomy. In December 2021, a magistrate court convicted Gonani of an offense contrary to section 153(c) of the Penal Code for having "willfully and unlawfully permitted a male person to have sexual intercourse of him against the order of nature," which carries a prison sentence of up to 14 years. Gonani appealed to the Constitutional Court to declare the legislation unconstitutional, arguing that the laws violate citizens' rights to privacy and dignity.

Key International Actors

President Lazarus Chakwera was expected to attend the September inauguration of Zimbabwean president, Emmerson Mnangagwa, who was re-elected in the disputed August 23 presidential election, but did not. The minister of homeland security represented him.

On January 31, the government interdicted and suspended from work the director general of the Anti-Corruption Bureau on the basis that she was facing criminal defamation charges for sharing inside information on an investigation with a third party. The United States ambassador to Malawi, David Young, said that the United States was deeply concerned as "these recent actions undermine the credibility of the government of Malawi's stated commitment to the fight against corruption." The US is Malawi's biggest financial supporter, providing more than US$350 million annually in bilateral assistance.

In January, the British High Commissioner to Malawi, Sophia Willitts-King, met with Malawi's justice minister over concerns about rising corruption, stressing that local taxpayers and donors could not keep "putting money in a leaking bucket."

After a first three-year term (2021-2023), Malawi was in October re-elected by the UN General Assembly as a member of the UN Human Rights Council until 2026.

Malaysia

In his first year as prime minister, Anwar Ibrahim, a former political prisoner, largely failed to uphold his pledges to address repression and corruption. The government's abolition of the mandatory death penalty was a significant step, although capital punishment remains a sentencing option for some criminal offenses. Authorities continued to use broad and vaguely worded laws to criminalize free speech. Officials have targeted refugees and migrants as well as lesbian, gay, bisexual, and transgender (LGBT) people with hateful rhetoric and crackdowns.

Freedoms of Expression and Assembly

The new government continued to use repressive laws it had pledged to reform, including the Sedition Act 1948 and the Communications and Multimedia Act (CMA) 1998.

In February, police arrested two teenagers under CMA section 233, on the "improper use of network facilities or network service," and the Minor Offences Act 1995 over a TikTok video in which they criticized a history exam using "abusive words." William Khor Wai Loon was charged in March under the Sedition Act section 4 and CMA section 233 for an Instagram post calling for a demonstration against the king. Reymi Abdul Rahim was charged in July under CMA section 233 for Twitter posts allegedly insulting the Johor sultan and royal family.

In July, opposition politician and Kedah state's chief minister, Muhammad Sanusi Md Nor, was charged under the Sedition Act for remarks regarding the country's sultans. Prime Minister Anwar defended the charges, claiming that using the Sedition Act is unavoidable "when it comes to matters concerning the position and dignity of the rulers."

In September, the Court of Appeal dismissed his appeal and ordered preacher Wan Ji to begin his nine-month sentence on sedition charges for Facebook posts he made regarding the Selangor sultan.

Police arrested political activist Badrul Hisham Shaharin, also known as Chegubard, on September 14, reportedly due to a TikTok video critical of the prime minister. Police again summoned Chegubard and others for questioning under the Peaceful Assembly Act 2012 following a rally on Malaysia Day (September 16) protesting the dismissal of corruption charges against Deputy Prime Minister Ahmad Zahid Hamidi.

The regulatory Malaysian Communications and Multimedia Commission (MCMC), overseen by the Communications and Digital Ministry, implemented access bans on online news portals to censor critical speech. Between June and August, the commission blocked sites including MalaysiaNow, UtusanTV, Malaysia Today, and TV Pertiwi. MCMC defended the bans as tackling "the spread of false information, offensive content, and defamation."

In June, the commission announced plans to take legal action against the company Meta for its alleged failure to remove from Facebook "undesirable contents relating to the aspects of Race, Royalty, Religion (3R), defamation, impersonation, online gambling as well as scam advertisements." The government considered an amendment to the CMA that would expand the powers of the MCMC and increase penalties under section 233.

In September, the government banned the film "Mentega Terbang," which deals with themes of religion and grief, under the Film Censorship Act. The film had been pulled from streaming services in March following widespread threats and condemnation from religious conservatives.

Refugees, Asylum Seekers, and Migrants

Malaysia is not a party to the 1951 Refugee Convention and lacks domestic asylum procedures. About 180,000 refugees and asylum seekers—the majority from Myanmar, including over 100,000 ethnic Rohingya Muslims—are registered with the United Nations Refugee Agency (UNHCR) but are not granted legal status, leaving them unable to formally work or enroll in government schools.

The new government has continued to deny UNHCR access to immigration detention centers. The agency has been barred from assessing whether detainees are entitled to protection since August 2019. Between 10,000 and 18,000 migrants and refugees are held in immigration detention centers nationwide at any one time, including more than 1,000 children, according to parliamentary reports.

Immigration detainees spend months or years in overcrowded, unhygienic conditions, routinely subjected to degrading treatment and physical and psychological abuse, without judicial oversight. The home affairs minister made statements in February and April regarding plans to release children from immigration detention, yet no further progress has been announced.

From January to May, authorities deported more than 18,000 undocumented migrants and asylum seekers from immigration detention centers, according to the government.

In January, authorities deported 114 Myanmar nationals, including children, without giving them a chance to file asylum claims, in an apparent violation of international customary law's prohibition on refoulement, the forcible return of refugees to a country where their life or freedom would be threatened. The High Court had issued a temporary stay of deportation in February 2021, after the military launched a coup in Myanmar, but it lifted the order in December 2022.

In August and early September 2023, officers detained hundreds of undocumented migrants, including children, in raids.

On July 4, Myanmar refugee activist Thuzar Maung and her family were abducted by unidentified men from their home in Kuala Lumpur. Their whereabouts remain unknown.

Criminal Justice System

Parliament adopted two bills in April that abolished the mandatory death penalty. The Abolition of Mandatory Death Penalty Act 2023, which came into force in July, removed the mandatory death penalty for the 12 offenses that carried it and removed the death penalty as an option for 7 offenses. However, the new law retains the death sentence for drug trafficking under the Dangerous Drugs Act 1952, the most common conviction for death row prisoners.

Malaysia detains individuals without trial under restrictive laws. The Security Offenses (Special Measures) Act 2012 (SOSMA) allows for preventive detention of up to 28 days without judicial review for a broadly defined range of "security offenses." Different rules of evidence and trial procedure apply for SOSMA offenses, which are non-bailable. Beginning in July, family members of 69 detainees being held under SOSMA staged a hunger strike outside Sungai Buloh

Prison. Police investigated the protest under the Peaceful Assembly Act and Child Act 2001.

Both the Prevention of Crime Act (POCA) 1959 and the Prevention of Terrorism Act 2015 allow government-appointed boards to impose detention without trial for up to two years, renewable indefinitely.

The Independent Police Complaints Commission (IPCC), which came into force on July 1, is a toothless commission with no powers of search and seizure, limited powers to compel the production of evidence, and no ability to hold hearings.

Freedom of Religion

Malaysia restricts the rights of followers of any branches of Islam other than Sunni, with those following Shia or other branches subject to arrest for deviancy. In March, the Court of Appeal dismissed a challenge by Sisters in Islam, a civil society group working to promote the rights of Muslim women, against a 2014 fatwa declaring the group as deviant from Islamic teachings. The group appealed the dismissal at the Federal Court.

In April, Siti Nuramira Abdullah was fined 8,000 Malaysian ringgit (US$1,800) under penal code section 298 for a 2022 open mic comedy performance during which she had removed her headscarf and *baju kurung*, a traditional dress.

Sexual Orientation and Gender Identity

State-sponsored discrimination against LGBT people remains pervasive in Malaysia, including the funding of conversion practices. Federal law punishes "carnal intercourse against the order of nature," interpreted as adult consensual same-sex conduct, with up to 20 years in prison and mandatory caning. State and federal territory Sharia (Islamic law) criminalize both same-sex activity and gender nonconformity.

In January, Anwar rejected the idea that LGBT Malaysians would be recognized and protected under his government, saying: "These politicians will say that if Anwar becomes prime minister ... LGBT will be recognized. This is a delusion. Of course, it will not happen."

In August, the Ministry of Home Affairs issued a ban on all Swatch products with LGBT, queer, and plus (LGBTQ+) branding under the draconian Printing Presses and Publications Act 1984, criminalizing the production, import, sale, distribution, or possession of the watches and any related materials with up to three years in prison. Authorities had confiscated the watches from stores in May.

The Ministry of Communications and Digital issued a directive canceling the last two days of the Good Vibes Festival in July following an onstage kiss between The 1975 bandmembers to protest Malaysia's anti-LGBT laws.

Women's Rights

The Cabinet announced in February plans to amend the Federal Constitution to grant Malaysian citizenship to children born overseas to Malaysian mothers and foreign fathers. However, the citizenship amendments also contain provisions that will perpetuate child statelessness. At time of writing, the amendments had been discussed in the cabinet and presented to the Conference of Rulers.

In March, police launched an investigation into an International Women's Day rally in Kuala Lumpur under the Peaceful Assembly Act and Minor Offences Act.

Environment and Indigenous Peoples' Rights

Indigenous communities continue to be displaced by business activities carried out without adequate consultation or compensation.

In January, the Court of Appeal ordered the Johor state government to support the resettlement of 135 Orang Asli Seletar families whose land had been sold to developers.

On July 4, police arrested an Orang Asli man for protesting logging surveyors in Pahang. The company was reportedly launching a logging project in a protected water catchment area on native customary land within the Bukit Ibam Forest Reserve.

A group of Orang Asli lodged a police report in September on behalf of 1,000 people in Gua Musang who complained that logging and farming projects had encroached on their land in recent months.

In September, Samling Group, a Malaysian timber and palm oil multinational company, withdrew a defamation lawsuit against the Indigenous organization SAVE Rivers following a settlement. The suit, filed in 2021, claimed that SAVE Rivers' publication of articles alleging that Samling failed to gain the free, prior, and informed consent of Indigenous communities prior to logging in their native customary land was defamatory.

The government has criticized the European Union's adoption of the EU Deforestation-Free Products Regulation (EUDR), which entered into force in June, requiring EU-based companies to ensure their imports and exports are "deforestation-free" and uphold human rights. Malaysia, Indonesia, and the EU established a joint task force to negotiate palm oil trade under the EUDR.

The government is taking steps to scale up the development of carbon offsetting projects, particularly in forested areas, yet state authorities lack adequate policies to protect human rights and mitigate risks to communities. The government also has not recognized Indigenous peoples' ownership of the carbon stored in their native customary lands.

HUMAN
RIGHTS
WATCH
"We Still Haven't Recovered"
Local Communities Harmed by Reclamation Projects in the Maldives

Maldives

Respect for freedom of expression and peaceful assembly in the Maldives deteriorated in the lead-up to the September presidential elections. The police used excessive force against protesters and journalists covering demonstrations. The government continued to approve land reclamation projects without adequately mitigating the environmental impact, leaving island communities at risk of flooding and loss of livelihoods.

In August, the government ratified the United Nations International Convention for the Protection of All Persons from Enforced Disappearance. However, it failed to enact crucial reforms to deliver accountability for these abuses.

The Maldives election went to a runoff on September 30, with Mohamed Muizzu of the Progressive Party winning. Shortly after the election, president-elect Muizzu secured the release from prison of the former president, Abdulla Yameen, who had been convicted of corruption and sentenced to 11 years in prison in 2022.

On November 22, the Criminal Court acquitted the last two suspects in an investigation into past attacks on journalists. Civil society groups had criticized the trials for delays and alleged political interference.

Freedoms of Expression and Assembly

The government ignored calls from civil society organizations to amend the Freedom of Assembly Act, which the government used to block protests in the lead-up to the presidential elections. On June 19, police used excessive force against protesters and opposition party members at campaign rallies. In August, during President Ibrahim Mohamed Solih's campaign trip to the southern island of Madaveli, the police arrested four protesters who had accused Solih of failing to deliver on campaign promises.

Human rights defenders, LGBT rights activists, and civil society organizations faced intimidation and threats on social media, often from Islamist extremist groups. On March 28, the Maldives civil court upheld a December 2019 decision to deregister the Maldivian Democracy Network (MDN), a human rights organization, following attempts by the group's executive director to reverse the ban. The initial deregistration of MDN appeared to be a politically motivated move to appease powerful Islamist groups in the Maldives, which had long threatened and incited violence against MDN.

In her March report, Fionnuala Ní Aoláin, the UN special rapporteur on counterterrorism and human rights, expressed deep concern about the "level of impunity" in the Maldives for abuses, including enforced disappearances. She highlighted the closing down of civic space in the Maldives and the lack of protection for civil society actors and human rights defenders. On July 11, Family Legal Clinic, a nongovernmental organization (NGO) providing pro bono legal services in the Maldives, released a statement detailing threats its staff had received and vandalism to its property.

The authorities seldom investigate and prosecute the perpetrators of threats, intimidation, and violence against civil society groups and critical voices in the Maldives. The families of Ahmed Rilwan, a prominent outspoken journalist who was forcibly disappeared in 2014, and Yameen Rasheed, a blogger and government critic who was murdered in 2017, still await justice.

Freedom of Media

The use of excessive force against journalists intensified, particularly against those covering the elections and opposition protests. In February, police assaulted journalists Hassan Shaheed and Ahmed Misbaah while they were covering protests held by an opposition party in the capital city of Malé. In March, police assaulted and arrested journalist Hussain Juman while he was covering an opposition rally in Malé. In July, police assaulted a media worker, Misbah, and a journalist, Maathu Hussain, who were also covering an opposition protest.

The Evidence Act, under which courts can compel journalists to reveal their sources, is still in effect in the Maldives, despite promises that it would be amended. In March, the authorities proposed an amendment to the Elections Act that would prevent freelance and foreign journalists from reporting on the voting process.

The Maldives dropped significantly in the World Press Freedom Index in 2023, ranking 100th out of 180 countries, down from 72nd place two years ago. Reporters Without Borders cited the Evidence Act in particular as a reason for the drop.

Women's and Girls' Rights

Despite calls from UN experts in 2022, the government failed to take concrete steps to address gender-based discrimination and violence in the Maldives. At the UN Human Rights Council in March, Special Rapporteur Ní Aoláin warned that Maldivian women human rights defenders were increasingly vulnerable to online harassment and intimidation.

Women and girls in the Maldives continue to suffer from structural discrimination rooted in pervasive societal norms, gender-stereotyping, and religious conservatism, contributing to the significant barriers that women face to equal participation in the labor force.

In 2021, the Maldivian government outlined plans to criminalize female genital mutilation (FGM) following recommendations from the UN Committee on the Elimination of Discrimination against Women. Nevertheless, two years on, and despite relentless campaigning from women's rights groups, the practice remains legal in the Maldives.

Sexual Orientation and Gender Identity

Adult consensual same-sex sexual conduct remains a criminal offense under the Maldivian penal code. Punishment can include prison sentences of up to eight years and lashes, which applies to both men and women. Same-sex marriage is also illegal and punishable by up to one year in prison.

In March, the Maldivian High Court commuted the sentence of police officer Abdul Rahman Rafeeu, who was convicted of engaging in same-sex relations with a Bangladeshi man in September 2022 and sentenced to over 14 months in prison. The sentence was reduced by 2 months and 12 days. The police officer was initially arrested along with two other men for engaging in same-sex sexual acts; the Bangladeshi national was also sentenced to jail time.

Climate Change and Environmental Harm

Low-lying Maldives is acutely vulnerable to the impacts of climate change, with over 80 percent of the country less than one meter above sea level. The Maldives has maintained a strong voice on climate-related issues in international forums, including at the UN. Domestically, the government has yet to live up to its standards by failing to enforce its own environmental laws, consult local communities ahead of reclamation projects, heed environmental impact assessment recommendations, and provide resources for the ongoing monitoring of development projects.

Key International Actors

Due to the Maldives' historical ties and geostrategic location, both India and China vie for influence by granting development loans and building bridges and other infrastructure. India has also strengthened its military relations with the Maldives.

In recent years, the US, Australia, and the United Arab Emirates have also taken steps to increase their diplomatic presence in the country and strengthen bilateral cooperation, particularly in the realms of security and climate change.

In September, the United States government established its first-ever diplomatic embassy in the Maldives, having previously managed relations from its embassy in Sri Lanka. At a meeting with the Maldivian ambassador, US President Joe Biden praised the Maldives for its efforts to mitigate the impacts of climate change.

The Maldives retains strong bilateral ties with the European Union. At a meeting between EU and Maldives officials, the EU emphasized the importance of maintaining a commitment toward "the protection of human rights" and "implementing reforms in the justice sector."

Mali

The human rights situation in Mali significantly deteriorated in 2023, as attacks against civilians by Islamist armed groups linked to Al-Qaeda and the Islamic State in the Greater Sahara (ISGS) and large-scale abusive counterterrorism operations by Malian armed forces and associated foreign fighters surged. Clashes between the Malian armed forces and a coalition of armed groups called the Coordination of Azawad Movements (*Coordination des mouvements de l'Azawad*, CMA)—an alliance of mostly ethnic Tuareg rebel groups that have sought independence for the Malian northern desert region they call Azawad—put a 2015 peace deal between the two parties at risk.

The violence exacerbated an already dire humanitarian crisis, with 8.8 million people requiring assistance and over 575,000 forced from their homes, including 375,000 internally displaced people and 205,000 refugees in neighboring countries as of August 2023.

The government dealt a severe blow to human rights monitoring and civilian protection by requesting the United Nations Security Council withdraw the UN peacekeeping mission to Mali, the UN Multidimensional Integrated Stabilization Mission in Mali (MINUSMA). The departure of MINUSMA, set for December, has raised concerns about exposure to heightened risk of violence for communities in northern and central Mali.

Authorities cracked down on the media and opposition voices, narrowing civic space.

The mounting abuses occurred amid a background of an ongoing political crisis. A referendum in June approved amendments to the constitution, including changes granting more powers to the president. The transitional military authorities said the referendum will pave the way to elections in 2024 and a return to civilian rule, but only 39 percent of eligible voters cast a ballot, with some regions, including Kidal, not holding the referendum at all, raising concerns about its fairness and validity. In September, government spokesman Abdoulaye Maiga announced that the presidential election scheduled for February 2024 would be postponed for "technical reasons," including the adoption of a new constitution and a review of the electoral lists.

The transitional government, which came to power in a 2021 coup, undermined efforts to investigate the mounting allegations of atrocities by state actors. Impunity for past and ongoing abuses by all armed groups persisted.

The engagement of the Russia-linked Wagner Group, and the mounting allegations of summary executions and other abuses by them, intensified tensions between Mali and its regional and international partners—including France, the UN, and neighboring West African countries—increasing Mali's political isolation.

Atrocities by Islamist Armed Groups

During 2023, Islamist armed groups aligned with the ISGS and Al-Qaeda carried out numerous unlawful attacks that killed hundreds of civilians as well as attacks killing scores of government security force personnel.

In areas under their control, Islamist armed groups raped women and girls, imposed *zakat* (religious tax), and implemented Sharia (Islamic law) and punishments via courts that did not adhere to fair trial standards. These groups also contributed to food insecurity by attacking those who did not conform to their vision of Islamic law, including by looting livestock and besieging cities and villages.

From January to April in Ménaka and Gao regions, clashes between the ISGS and the rival Al-Qaeda-linked Group for the Support of Islam and Muslims (*Jama'at Nusrat al-Islam wa al-Muslimeen*, JNIM), both seeking to control supply routes and increase their areas of influence, led to a sharp deterioration of the security situation, with hundreds of civilians killed.

In January, an armed clash between ISGS and JNIM fighters near the village of Teguerert, Ménaka region, largely populated by ethnic Dawsahak people, resulted in the burning of houses and massive displacement of the local population. More than 40 fighters from both groups were killed and dozens of civilians were wounded.

In February, ISGS fighters came to Konga, a settlement in the village of Kounsoum, Gao region, searching for a man they accused of collaborating with the Malian army. They did not find him and in retaliation killed his two wives.

In March, ISGS fighters threatened the population of Essaylal, Ménaka region, issuing an ultimatum for people to leave the area within three days. The majority of Essaylal residents then fled to seek refuge in Ménaka city.

On April 21, JNIM claimed responsibility for an April 18 attack in Nara, Koulikoro region, during which the chief of staff of Mali's interim president, Oumar Traoré, was killed. Three other men, including a security guard, a contractor, and a driver, were also killed. On April 22, an attack in Sevaré, Mopti region, also claimed by JNIM, left at least 10 civilians dead and 60 injured as well as more than 20 buildings destroyed.

On April 23, ISGS fighters entered the village of Tannal Koyratadji, Gao region, killed two older men, injured at least seven men, and looted food and livestock.

In early May, ISGS fighters led two consecutive attacks on the village of Labezzanga, a coastal village along the Niger River, Gao region, where they killed four men, injured another, and looted livestock.

On May 20 and 23, ISGS fighters attacked the village of Seyna Gourma, Gao region. On May 20, they looted livestock. Three days later, they went door-to-door, searched homes, beat villagers, and again looted livestock.

On June 27, scores of ISGS fighters attacked Dangabari, Gaina, and other villages in Gabero municipality, Gao region, killing at least nine men and two boys in Dangabari, four men in Gaina, and looting livestock.

On August 6, JNIM fighters led a deadly attack in Bodio, killing 15 people, including 4 men, including an 18-year-old. They also looted livestock and civilian property and burned at least 10 homes.

On September 7, Islamist fighters attacked a boat traveling on the Niger River from Gao to Mopti. Human Rights Watch found that over 120 died in the boat attack.

Abuses by State Security Forces

Malian and allied foreign fighters apparently associated with the Russia-linked Wagner Group were implicated in hundreds of unlawful killings of civilians, mostly during large counterterrorism operations in central Mali.

On February 3, scores of "white" fighters in military uniforms and at least one Malian soldier carried out an operation in Séguéla village, Ségou region, searching for Islamist fighters. During the operation, they looted homes and shops, beat people, and arrested 17 men. On February 21, near Doura, Ségou region, villagers found the bodies of eight of the arrested men. The whereabouts of the remaining nine remain unknown.

On March 6, members of the Malian armed forces along with "white" fighters conducted an airborne operation in Sossobé village, Mopti region, during which they killed five civilian men, beat villagers, and looted property. They also arrested 21 men and took them away in helicopters. The whereabouts of those taken remain unknown.

On March 23 and 24, scores of Malian and "white" foreign soldiers accompanied by pro-government militiamen carried out an operation in Ouenkoro village, Mopti region, in which they killed at least 20 civilians, including a woman and a 6-year-old. They also beat people, looted property, and arrested 12 men, whom they took to an army camp in the town of Sofara, Mopti region, torturing them to force confessions regarding their affiliation or complicity with Islamist armed groups.

On April 22, scores of Malian soldiers carried out an operation in Trabakoro village, Nara region, searching for Islamist fighters, during which the soldiers killed 18 people: 14 children and 4 women.

Media reported that on June 15, a convoy of "white" fighters hit an improvised explosive device near the village of Keibané, Nara region, killing 2 and wounding 11. The fighters carried out a reprisal attack against local villagers, killing at least five.

On July 27, Malian soldiers executed four men and a child in Gadougou, an ethnic Fulani settlement in Nara region. Witnesses said the soldiers were searching for Islamist fighters.

On August 6, Malian soldiers and associated "white" fighters arrested 16 men and 1 boy in Sambani, Timbuktu region, suspecting them of collaborating with Islamist groups. The following day, villagers found the bodies of those arrested about one kilometer from Sambani.

Abuses of Civil and Political Rights

Threats, harassment, intimidation, and enforced disappearances of journalists, bloggers, and civil society activists continued.

On February 20, in Bamako, Mali's capital, thugs broke into the office of the Press House (*Maison de la presse*), an umbrella organization bringing together several media groups, ransacked it, and disrupted a news conference held by members of a political opposition platform that had opposed the constitutional reform referendum.

On March 13, security forces arrested Mohamed Youssouf Bathily, a radio and television host, better known by the pseudonym Ras Bath, in Bamako for saying that former Prime Minister Soumeylou Boubèye Maïga, who died in detention in 2022, had been assassinated. On June 13, a Bamako court sentenced him to three years in prison.

On March 15, security forces in Bamako arrested Malian social media influencer Rokia Doumbia, known as "Rose vie chère," for denouncing the transitional government's "failure" to tackle inflation and insecurity in a TikTok video. Charged with "inciting riot" and "disrupting public order," she was sentenced to one year in jail on August 2.

On April 6, masked gunmen abducted journalist Aliou Touré in Bamako after he attended a press conference calling for the release of Ras Bath. He was found unharmed four days later.

Accountability for Abuses

There was little progress in government investigations into several incidents of reported abuse.

On June 26, Human Rights Watch sent letters to Mali's justice and defense ministers detailing its findings about abuses by members of the Malian armed forces during military operations in the villages of Ouenkoro, Séguéla, Sossobé, and Thioffol, in Mopti and Ségou regions, between December 2022 and March 2023. In its July 20 response, through the Minister of Foreign Affairs and International Cooperation, the government said it was not aware of any human rights violations, but "the public prosecutor in charge of the Specialized Judicial Unit, on the instructions of the Minister of Justice and Human Rights, opened a judicial investigation for war crimes and crimes against humanity against X" and "the findings of various investigations will be brought to the attention of national and international opinion in due course." As of September 2023, Human Rights Watch was not aware of any progress in any of the promised inquiries.

On June 19, Malian authorities announced they would open an espionage prosecution against those responsible for a May 12 UN report accusing Malian troops and Wagner Group fighters of killing over 500 people, of whom most were summarily executed during a military operation in Moura, in central Mali, in March 2022. The public prosecutor, Ladji Sara, said in a statement that those behind the report are "all co-perpetrators or accomplices in the crimes of espionage, undermining the morale of the army or air force."

On June 21, 2023, the International Basketball Federation (FIBA) issued a lifetime ban on Amadou Bamba, the former Malian women's national basketball team coach, and sanctions on four other top officials. Sanctioned officials include the former national federation president, Harouna Maiga. In June 2021, Human Rights Watch issued a report about the sexual extortion of children and coverups of abuse in the Mali Basketball Federation. In July 2021, Malian authorities arrested and indicted Bamba, then the head coach of Mali's under-18 girls' national basketball team, who is awaiting trial for "pedophilia, attempted rape, and molestation." However, more than two years after the widespread sexual abuse came to light, survivors and whistleblowers still live under threat and cannot safely play. A teenage whistleblower faced threats and lost career opportunities after reporting her sexual abuse and subsequently sued the federation for failing to protect her from retaliation.

The International Criminal Court concluded the trial of Al Hassan Ag Abdoul Aziz Ag Mohamed Ag Mahmoud, a former Islamist group commander, on charges of war crimes and crimes against humanity, including rape and sexual slavery committed in 2012-2013. A verdict is pending at time of writing.

Key International Actors

The deployment in late 2021 of the Russian Wagner Group, described by the Malian government as "military trainers," and subsequent allegations of atrocities against them and Malian security forces, brought sharp condemnation from

Mali's bilateral and multilateral partners, including the United States, France, the European Union, the UN, and the Economic Community of West African States. In February, the EU sanctioned the head of the Wagner Group in Mali.

Also in February, the Malian authorities ordered MINUSMA's human rights chief, Guillaume Ngefa-Atondoko Andali, to leave the country, accusing him of "destabilizing and subversive actions."

On June 16, the foreign minister, Abdoulaye Diop, told the UN Security Council to withdraw MINUSMA "without delay" and rejected the UN report on the Moura massacre. The government denounced what it considered to be the "instrumentalization and politicization of the human rights issue."

On August 30, Russia vetoed a UN Security Council resolution that would have extended sanctions against eight people suspected of sabotaging the 2015 peace deal and the work of a panel of experts tracking abuses by armed groups and Malian security forces. The cessation of the panel's activities could harm efforts toward accountability for conflict-related abuses in a country already marked by shrinking civic space and an increased crackdown on dissent and independent media.

Mexico

President Andrés Manuel López Obrador, who took office in 2018, has made little progress in addressing Mexico's serious human rights challenges, including extreme criminal violence, abuses against migrants, gender-based violence, attacks on independent journalists and human rights defenders, torture, disappearances, and extrajudicial killings.

The poverty rate has fallen under López Obrador's presidency, from 41.9 percent in 2018 to 36.3 percent in 2022, according to the official poverty analysis agency. However, extreme poverty has remained unchanged and the number of people without access to health care has more than doubled. Analysts have pointed to a major increase in the minimum wage and a near-doubling of remittances from Mexicans abroad as possible contributors to the drop in poverty.

Security and Access to Justice

Rates of violent crime have skyrocketed in Mexico since the beginning of the "war" on organized crime in 2006. The homicide rate fell from 28 homicides per 100,000 people in 2021 to 25.9 in 2022 but remains among the highest in the world. Two-thirds of homicides in 2022 were committed with firearms. Authorities estimate that about 70 percent of firearms used in crimes are smuggled into Mexico from the United States.

The justice system regularly fails to provide accountability for violent crimes and human rights violations. About 90 percent of crimes are never reported, one-third of reported crimes are never investigated, and just under 16 percent of investigations are resolved (either in court, through mediation, or through some form of compensation), meaning authorities resolved just over 1 percent of all crimes committed in 2022.

Torture

Torture is widely practiced by police, prosecutors, and soldiers to obtain confessions and extract information. In the most recent survey of incarcerated people conducted by Mexico's national statistics office in July 2021, nearly half of respondents said that police or soldiers had subjected them to physical abuse after they were detained. Among those who had confessed to a crime, 38 percent said they did so only because authorities had beaten or threatened them.

Authorities received at least 15,904 criminal complaints of torture between January 1, 2018, and March 31, 2023, according to a national registry created by the Attorney General's Office.

Arbitrary Detention

The United Nations Working Group on Arbitrary Detention visited Mexico in September and expressed concern that "arbitrary detention remains a widespread practice in Mexico and is too often the catalyst for ill-treatment, torture, enforced disappearance and arbitrary executions."

Judges are legally required to order pretrial detention for those accused of many offenses, without evaluating the circumstances of the case, violating international human rights standards. More than 40 percent of imprisoned people in 2021 had not been convicted of any crime. Prosecutors continue to use *arraigo* detention, a mechanism allowing them to obtain judicial authorization to detain anyone for up to 40 days without charge.

The Inter-American Court of Human Rights ruled in November 2022 and January 2023 that Mexico's use of mandatory pretrial detention and arraigo detention violates human rights standards and ordered it to reform its laws and constitution. In July, a regional federal appeals court ruled that, following the Inter-American Court's decision, judges may hear appeals from people placed in mandatory pretrial detention and may order their conditional release pending trial. The ruling applies in 18 states in central and northern Mexico.

Law enforcement agencies are legally required to record detentions they conduct in the National Detention Registry, created in 2019. Both the army and the navy continue to detain civilians without reporting these detentions in the registry.

Military Abuses

Like his predecessors, President López Obrador has relied heavily on the military for public security. Congress, controlled by López Obrador's party, disbanded the Federal Police in 2019 and replaced it with the National Guard, a military force.

As of August 2023, there were more than 266,000 soldiers, marines, and national guard members deployed domestically.

From 2007 through July 2023, the army killed 5,488 civilians, according to government data. These killings are rarely independently investigated. In 2022, the National Human Rights Commission received 1,005 complaints against the army and National Guard, the highest number in nine years.

There is strong evidence that the military has used the spyware Pegasus during the López Obrador administration to illegally spy on human rights defenders, journalists, opposition party politicians, and senior government officials.

The military has obstructed the investigation and prosecution of past human rights abuses. In July, the group of independent international experts investigating the 2014 Ayotzinapa mass kidnapping and disappearance closed their investigation and left the country, saying military obstruction and lies prevented them from determining the truth. Leaked emails suggest senior military officials had pressured the government to drop charges against soldiers implicated in the case. In August, the truth commission investigating military abuses against leftist activists during the Cold War said the military and intelligence services had refused to give them access to key documents.

Disappearances

Thousands of people go missing every year in Mexico. Authorities regularly fail to take basic steps to search for missing people.

Lack of forensic capacity contributes to disappearances and hinders their resolution. Authorities failed to identify roughly 10,000 human remains in 2021, which is about 12 percent of those processed by morgues that year. Most unidentified remains were placed in storage or buried in municipal graves. Many other missing people were likely killed and buried in hidden graves by criminal groups, the military, or the police. From 2006 to 2023, authorities and activists found more than 5,600 such graves across the country.

In September, Mexican officials appeared before the UN Committee on Enforced Disappearances (CED) in Geneva following the CED's 2021 visit to Mexico. CED members expressed concerns about continuing "near-total impunity" for disappearances and the growing number of threats, attacks, and killings of those searching for disappeared relatives. In May, the CED issued its first decision on an individual complaint from Mexico, finding that the state had violated its international legal obligations to conduct a prompt, exhaustive, and impartial investigation of the enforced disappearance of a young man who was removed from his home by armed men in police uniforms in 2013.

President López Obrador has claimed the official number of missing people, which surpassed 110,000 in 2023, has been deliberately inflated to hurt him politically. In June, he announced a new "search program" in which officials contact the families of those reported missing to ask if they have returned home on their own. In August, the head of the National Search Commission, which manages the missing persons registry, resigned after the government reportedly asked her to manipulate the data to "reduce" the number of people reported missing. In October, the government named an official from the Education Ministry as the new search commission head. The UN Office of the High Commissioner for Human Rights in Mexico and many victims' collectives expressed concern about the lack of transparency in the nomination process. In December, the government announced it had reviewed the missing person's registry and claimed only around 12,000 people on it were "confirmed disappeared".

Privacy and Access to Information

President López Obrador has transferred hundreds of government tasks to the military, limiting access to public information because the military often refuses to comply with transparency requests. In May, the Supreme Court overturned an executive order that had exempted the government from complying with transparency requests regarding infrastructure projects. Hours after—and despite—the ruling, the president issued a similar executive order.

In March and April, López Obrador and legislators from his party blocked nominations to fill vacant seats on the board of the transparency and data protection agency, leaving it without enough members legally required to review cases or issue decisions. In August, the Supreme Court ruled the remaining board members could resume reviewing cases until the Senate fills the vacant seats.

Attacks on Journalists and Human Rights Defenders

Mexico is one of the most dangerous countries in the world for journalists. From January to September 2023, eight journalists were killed. In the first half of 2023, Article 19 recorded 272 threats, attacks, or other forms of aggression against journalists. Many journalists self-censor.

Authorities routinely fail to adequately investigate crimes against journalists. From its creation in 2010 through July 2023, the federal special prosecutor's office to investigate crimes against journalists had opened 1,654 investigations and obtained 35 convictions, including 7 for homicide, and 120 settlements. The vast majority of convictions have been obtained since the current special prosecutor was appointed in 2017.

Mexico is also one of the most dangerous countries in the world for human rights defenders. Twenty-two human rights defenders were killed in 2022, according to the human rights group Comité Cerezo.

A federal government program provides bodyguards and panic buttons to at-risk journalists and human rights defenders. The mechanism lacks sufficient staff and funding and struggles to coordinate with state and local officials. Eight journalists and two human rights defenders have been killed while under the program's protection.

Women's and Girls' Rights

A wave of states legalized abortion in recent years. As of September, 12 states allowed abortion for any reason up to at least 12 weeks of pregnancy. All states allow abortion in cases of rape. Despite legalization, women, girls, and other pregnant people continue to face many barriers when trying to access abortion.

The Supreme Court ruled in 2021 that the absolute criminalization of abortion is unconstitutional and that people should not be criminally prosecuted for undergoing the procedure. It also established that state governments do not have the authority to legislate that life begins at conception and that medical personnel's right to conscientiously object to performing abortions is subject to limits.

In 2022, the government reported about 3,757 killings of women, one-quarter of which were considered femicides, killings of women because of their gender. Women's rights groups say femicide is likely under-reported.

Mexico officially ratified the International Labour Organization Violence and Harassment Convention (C190) in July 2022. The treaty obligates Mexico to provide comprehensive protections to ensure a world of work free from violence and harassment, including gender-based violence.

Migrants and Asylum Seekers

Criminals and government officials often prey upon people migrating through Mexico. Crimes against migrants are rarely reported, investigated, or punished.

President López Obrador has intensified efforts to prevent migrants from traveling through Mexico to reach the US, including by deploying more than 31,000 soldiers for immigration enforcement. Authorities detained 444,000 migrants in 2022, the highest number ever.

Immigration detention centers are notoriously overcrowded, unsanitary, and dangerous. In April, 40 people died in a fire at an immigration detention center in Ciudad Juárez after staff did not release them from their shared cell.

Soldiers and immigration agents operate immigration checkpoints throughout the country. In May 2022, the Supreme Court ruled these checkpoints unconstitutional, saying they disproportionately affect Indigenous and Afro-Mexican people. However, the checkpoints continue to operate.

Since 2019, Mexico has allowed the US to expel certain non-Mexican migrants and asylum seekers to Mexico, where they are routinely targeted for serious abuses, including sexual assault, armed robbery, kidnapping, and extortion.

The government has greatly expanded the capacity of the asylum system, with significant assistance from the UN Refugee Agency (UNHCR), which provides the majority of funding for staff and other operating expenses. However, the system remains severely overstretched. From January through August 2023, nearly 100,000 people applied for refugee status in Mexico, but the government resolved just over 18,000 cases; in 71 percent of those, the government granted refugee status or complementary protection.

Sexual Orientation and Gender Identity

Same-sex marriage is available in all 32 states. Twenty-one states allow transgender people to change their names and gender markers on birth certificates through a simple administrative process. In 2019, the Mexican Supreme Court issued a landmark ruling with clear guidelines on legal gender recognition, holding that it must be an administrative process that "meets the standards of privacy, simplicity, expeditiousness, and adequate protection of gender identity" set by the Inter-American Court of Human Rights. In March 2022, the court expanded the right to legal gender recognition to include adolescents and other children.

Disability Rights

People with disabilities lack access to justice, education, legal standing, and other fundamental rights. In 2019, Human Rights Watch documented cases of state-run hospitals and private individuals who shackled people with disabilities. Women with disabilities suffer disproportionate violence.

In many states, people with disabilities have no choice but to depend on their families for assistance or to live in institutions, which is inconsistent with their right to live independently and be included in the community under the Convention on the Rights of Persons with Disabilities (CRPD).

In May and June, Congress approved reforms requiring domestic violence shelters to be accessible for women with disabilities and establishing that everyone over 18 has full legal capacity and the right to supported decision-making.

In 2022, Congress prohibited forced psychiatric treatment and restraints, including shackling. The reform mandates community-based services and the conversion of psychiatric hospitals to general hospitals.

Older People's Rights

In March, Mexico ratified the Inter-American Convention on Protecting the Human Rights of Older Persons.

Climate Policy and Impacts

As one of the world's top 15 emitters of greenhouse gases, Mexico is contributing to the climate crisis that is taking a growing toll on human rights around the globe. In 2021, a judge annulled the López Obrador administration's climate action plan because it did not increase emissions reduction targets in violation of Mexican law. In November 2022, the government updated its plan but still allowed higher emissions than what it had pledged. This contravenes its obligation under the Paris Agreement to establish progressively ambitious targets. The new climate action plan also fails to commit to a net-zero target.

The Climate Action Tracker, which provides independent scientific analysis, rated Mexico's 2022 climate action plan as "critically insufficient" to meet the Paris Agreement goal to limit global warming to 1.5 degrees Celsius above pre-industrial levels.

The López Obrador administration has pursued a policy of investment in fossil fuels, acquiring an oil refinery in the US and fast-tracking the construction of another in Dos Bocas, Tabasco state. President López Obrador has bet on the oil industry as a pathway to energy self-sufficiency.

Key International Actors

As a member of the UN Human Rights Council in 2023, Mexico supported a number of important initiatives to ensure scrutiny and advance accountability on several pressing human rights crises, including on Belarus, Burundi, Eritrea, Israel and Palestine, Nicaragua, Sudan, and South Sudan. They did not, however, support continued scrutiny of Russia's human rights abuses. Mexico continued to lead on important thematic resolutions on a range of important issues, including on the rights of migrants, the death penalty, and the rights of people with disabilities.

Morocco and Western Sahara

The crackdown on freedom of expression and association in Morocco continued with several high-profile journalists, activists, and protest leaders imprisoned in apparent retaliation for their criticism of the ruling monarchy. Authorities constrain human rights and independence activists in Western Sahara via harassment, surveillance, and in some cases lengthy imprisonment after unfair trials.

Freedom of Speech

The Court of Cassation in May confirmed a three-year prison sentence for Mohamed Ziane, an 80-year-old lawyer and Morocco's human rights minister between 1995 and 1996, on 11 charges including "defamation and contempt of public officials, adultery, and sexual harassment." Amnesty International reported that at least six of the charges against Ziane violated his right to freedom of speech. He has been held since November 2022 in solitary confinement at El Arjat prison, near Rabat, and was denied reading or writing materials for about six months, according to his lawyer.

Independent journalists Omar Radi, Soulaiman Raissouni, and Taoufik Bouachrine continue to serve prison sentences handed down to them after flawed court proceedings on various charges, including some relating to sexual assault and sexual harassment. Human Rights Watch documented multiple underhanded tactics used by Moroccan authorities against each of the three, and more generally to crush dissent and dissenters. Criminal charges of a sexual nature, unfair trials, and long prison terms are among these tactics, part of an "ecosystem of repression" that includes harassment and smear campaigns in state-aligned media, targeting of relatives, video and digital surveillance, and sometimes physical intimidation and assault. In July, the Court of Cassation definitively upheld Radi's six-year prison term and Raissouni's five-year conviction, while Bouachrine continues serving his 15-year prison sentence, which the Court of Cassation upheld in 2021. A royal pardon is their last hope for early release.

On July 31, a Moroccan first instance court sentenced Saïd Boukioud, 48, to five years in prison under article 267 of the penal code for criticism on Facebook in 2020 of the king's decision to normalize ties with Israel. Under article 267, acts deemed to "undermine the monarchy" carry a six-month to two-year prison sentence, which can be increased to five years if the act is committed online.

Human Rights Watch has previously documented the cases of dozens of journalists and social media activists convicted by Moroccan courts on charges of libel, publishing "false news," "insulting" or "defaming" local officials, state bodies or foreign heads of state, and "undermining" state security or the institution of the monarchy.

In September, Moroccan police deported journalists Quentin Müller and Thérèse Di Campo of *Marianne*, a French news magazine, after arresting them at their hotel in Casablanca. The government's spokesperson stated that they were expelled for operating in Morocco as journalists without official authorization. Their expulsion was the latest of many such expulsions of foreign journalists justified by authorities on similar grounds.

Freedom of Assembly

Authorities continued to impede the work of the Moroccan Association for Human Rights (AMDH), the country's largest independent human rights group. Authorities have historically declined to process the administrative formalities for dozens of AMDH local branches, impeding their ability to open new bank accounts or rent spaces, according to the AMDH. The AMDH has reported that other civic groups are also affected by authorities' denial of legal status or refusal to complete administrative procedures, including groups that work on violence against women and youth groups.

Women's and Girls' Rights

In September, King Mohammed VI formally instructed the head of government to begin revising the 2004 Family Code, also known as the Moudawana. Justice Minister Abdellatif Ouahbi emphasized the government's intention to address existing gender inequalities in the law relating to marriage, divorce, and guardianship of children.

The Code currently provides that a child's default legal representative is the child's father, even if a mother has court-ordered custody of the child after divorce. It also stipulates that women and girls inherit just half of what their male relatives receive. The Code sets 18 as the minimum age of marriage but allows judges to grant "exemptions" for girls ages 15 to 18 to marry at the request of their families.

Morocco's law does not explicitly criminalize marital rape. Women who report rape can find themselves prosecuted instead for engaging in illegal sexual intercourse outside of marriage. A 2018 law on violence against women criminalized some forms of domestic violence, established prevention measures, and provided new protections for survivors. However, the law also created barriers for survivors to access these protections, failed to delineate the duty of care for police, prosecutors, and investigative judges in domestic violence cases, and did not stipulate funding for women's shelters.

Penal Code

The Penal Code criminalizes several aspects of private life. Abortion remains criminalized under article 453 except when the mother's health is at risk and in limited other cases such as rape or incest. However, the article stipulates that the procedure requires consent from the partner and/or a physician. Otherwise, a person who "intentionally obtains an abortion" can face up to two years in prison, and those who perform it can face up to five years.

Article 490 punishes sex outside of marriage with at least one year of imprisonment. Article 491 provides for a prison term of one to two years for adultery, which can be prosecuted if the spouse of one of the parties files a complaint or, in case their spouse is abroad, a prosecutor initiates a criminal case against the individual suspected of adultery and their accomplice.

Article 489 of the penal code criminalizes same-sex relations and stipulates six months to three years in prison. Morocco has over the years used this provision to prosecute and imprison men, even when there was no evidence of them engaging in same-sex sexual acts.

Western Sahara

Steffan de Mistura, the personal envoy of the United Nations secretary-general for Western Sahara, visited the region in September for the first time since his appointment in 2021. In March the UN high commissioner for human rights declared his desire to undertake meaningful missions to the region, noting it had been almost 8 years since OHCHR last visited.

Most of Western Sahara has been under Moroccan control since Spain, the territory's former colonial administrator, withdrew in 1975. In 1991, both Morocco and the Polisario Front, a liberation movement that seeks self-determination for Western Sahara, agreed to a UN-brokered ceasefire to prepare for a referendum on self-determination. That referendum never took place. Morocco rejects holding a vote on self-determination that would include independence as an option; it considers Western Sahara to be an integral part of the kingdom.

In December 2020, former United States President Donald Trump rejected the UN-sponsored process for self-determination of the Sahrawis by recognizing Morocco's sovereignty over Western Sahara. Since then, Morocco has been pressuring Western allies, including Spain and France, to do the same. In July, Israel recognized Morocco's sovereignty over the Western Sahara.

Nineteen Sahrawi men remained in prison after they were convicted in unfair trials in 2013 and 2017 for the killing of 11 Moroccan security force members, during clashes that erupted after authorities forcibly dismantled a large protest encampment in Gdeim Izik, near El-Ayun, in 2010. Both courts relied almost entirely on confessions to convict them without seriously investigating claims the defendants signed their confessions under police torture. The Cassation court, Morocco's highest judicial instance, upheld the verdicts on appeal on November 25, 2020.

Rif Region

A group of 40 protesters associated with the Hirak, a movement from Morocco's northern Rif region, which in 2016 and 2017 protested against local socioeconomic conditions, remain imprisoned, some serving decades-long sentences. An appeals court in 2019 upheld the convictions, despite credible allegations of confessions obtained under torture. Among them are the Hirak's leaders Nasser Zefzafi and Nabil Ahamjik.

Refugees and Asylum Seekers

Morocco's parliament has yet to approve a 2013 draft law on the right to asylum. A 2003 migration law that criminalizes irregular entry into the country without providing exceptions for refugees and asylum seekers remains in effect.

As of September 2023, there were over 19,000 refugees and asylum seekers in Morocco registered with the UN refugee agency, UNHCR. Over half were from west, central, and northeast African countries, and around 30 percent were Syrians. The Moroccan delegation said in a statement made in March to the Committee on the Protection of the Rights of All Migrant Workers that Morocco had regularized the status of 58,000 migrants via three-year visas in 2022.

Moroccan authorities failed to carry out a credible independent investigation or offer appropriate compensation to survivors and families of victims of a June 24, 2022, incident in which Moroccan and Spanish border police used excessive force in response to an attempt by 1,300 to 2,000 men—most from Sudan, South Sudan, and Chad—to scale the chain-link fences around the Spanish enclave of Melilla. At least 23 migrants or asylum seekers died that day, and dozens remained missing as of mid-2023. Spain and Morocco deny responsibility for the deaths and disappearances.

In February, Spain and Morocco announced "intensified" cooperation, including in "the fight against irregular migration, border control."

After his arrest in January at the Marrakesh airport, Moroccan authorities on February 6 extradited Saudi national Hassan al-Rabea to Saudi Arabia in violation of the principle of non-refoulement under international human rights and refugee law. Al-Rabea, from the Shia minority in Saudi and whose family has been targeted with arrests and executions, including for protest related offenses, was wanted for his alleged collaboration with "terrorists" to help him leave Saudi Arabia "in an irregular fashion," a charge that carries a prison sentence of 10 to 20 years.

Yidiresi Aishan (also known as Idris Hasan), a Uyghur activist, remained under threat of extradition from Morocco to China. Aishan has been detained since his July 2021 arrest upon arrival in Morocco from Turkey based on an Interpol red notice, which the Interpol has since cancelled. Aishan remained in Tiflet prison, east of Rabat, since then, pending an extradition that has been cleared by Morocco's Court of Cassation, but not yet executed. China's abusive policies targeting Uyghurs, which amount to crimes against humanity, include coercing Uyghurs abroad to return to Xinjiang where they face arbitrary imprisonment.

Mozambique

The security situation in northern Mozambique improved significantly, with many displaced people returning to their areas of origin in the districts most affected by the armed conflict between an armed group linked to Islamic State (ISIS), known locally as Al-Shabab or "Mashababos," and joint Mozambican, Rwandan, and Southern African forces. Authorities announced the killing of the alleged Al-Shabab leader Bonomade Machude Omar, but the group continued to operate in Macomia and Mocimboa da Praia districts.

Members of the Southern African Development Community Mission in Mozambique (SAMIM) were implicated in the mutilation and other mistreatment of the dead in Cabo Delgado. State security forces continued to use lethal force and arbitrary arrest and detention to limit people's right to peaceful protest across the country. Parliament ordered the government to review a draft law that would permit excessive government interference in nongovernmental organizations (NGOs), including the authority to shut down an organization. Mozambique began a two-year mandate as a non-permanent member of the UN Security Council.

Violence in Northern Mozambique

The security situation in northern Mozambique improved significantly during the year, with many people returning to Palma and Mocimboa da Praia districts, which had been most affected by the armed conflict. The United Nations High Commissioner for Refugees (UNHCR) reported that 420,000 internally displaced people returned to their areas of origin, but many more remained displaced due to continued violence. Access to basic needs, including food, water, shelter, health care, and education, remained a challenge for many returnees who were confronted with massive destruction in their areas of origin. According to Médecins San Frontières (Doctors Without Borders, MSF), in Mocimboa da Praia, which has the largest number of returnees, most public buildings, including schools, hospitals, and health centers, and water infrastructure were destroyed.

Fighting between Al-Shabab and the Mozambican defense and security forces, with support from Rwanda and SAMIM, intensified in Macomia district, with militants reportedly killing several soldiers in July and August.

In August, the Mozambican armed forces announced the killing of the alleged Al-Shabab leader Bonomade Machude Omar, also known as Abu Sulayfa Muhammad and Ibn Omar. In September, a month after his death, militants reportedly returned to Mucojo town, Macomia district, where they allegedly beat three people. Also in September, in an ISIS attack in Naquitengue village, Mocimboa da Praia, armed men executed at least 11 people believed to be Christians.

Conduct of Security Forces in Cabo Delgado

SAMIM members were implicated in abuses during their military operations in Cabo Delgado province. In January, a video appeared on social media showing South African soldiers, who are part of the SAMIM forces, throwing corpses onto a pile of burning rubble. International humanitarian law prohibits the mutilation and other mistreatment of the dead. The Southern African Development Community (SADC) condemned the acts in the video and announced an investigation, but it has yet to provide any updates on the investigation.

In April, the Mozambican government gave legal authority to an abusive militia to fight Al-Shabab in the north of the country. The militia, largely consisting of demobilized soldiers, has operated without oversight, accountability, or a legal mandate since 2018, when former soldiers first offered to fight the insurgency. Their activities have often been associated with unlawful killings and other human rights abuses.

Election-Related Violence

The October 11 municipal elections were marred by violence and serious irregularities, leading district courts to order a rerun of the voting or a recount of votes in many municipalities.

Following the elections, police clashed with opposition party members across the country. They used excessive force and fired tear gas at crowds of opposition supporters backing the political party RENAMO, who were in the streets to either contest the results or to peacefully celebrate non-official results in Nampula, Cuamba, Moatize, and Vilankulos municipalities.

Police were also implicated in arbitrary detentions of opposition members throughout the election process. On October 12, one day after the voting, police detained the RENAMO candidate and mayor of Quelimane city, Manuel de Araujo, allegedly because he was visiting polling stations, which police said was "disturbing" the vote-counting process. Earlier in the month, police in Beira city arrested three members of the Democratic Movement of Mozambique (MDM), a national opposition party in power in that city. They were released after a judge found no legal basis for their arrests.

Freedom of Assembly and Association

Freedom of peaceful assembly and association was under pressure as the government submitted for parliamentary approval a draft law on nonprofit organizations that would permit excessive government interference in NGOs, including the authority to shut down an organization. The government said the law intended to counter money laundering and terrorist financing, after the Financial Activities Task Force (FATF), an influential intergovernmental organization that monitors countries' efforts to counter money laundering and terrorist financing, placed Mozambique under increased monitoring in 2021. In August, following months of advocacy by rights organizations, parliamentarians approved a revised draft and warned the government that preventing and combating money laundering and terrorist financing should not be done at the expense of fundamental rights.

Right to Peaceful Protest

State security forces used lethal force and arbitrary arrests and detentions to limit people's right to peaceful protest across the country.

In March, police used tear gas on the funeral procession of a famous Mozambican rap star, Edson da Luz, known as "Azagaia," who died from a sudden illness. As the funeral convoy and thousands of people approached an area containing the president's official residence in Maputo city, which is off-limits to pedestrian traffic, armored vehicles and dozens of heavily armed riot police blocked the road. The police ordered people to change course and then, without warning, used tear gas to disperse the crowd, causing mass flight.

Also in March, police detained at least three people in Beira city for participating in a tribute march to Azagaia. Police blocked the march halfway through, despite authorization for it to take place. A police source told journalists that the police had received orders for the march not to take place.

In May, four people were shot dead when police fired bullets against a group attacking homes and property belonging to local officials, following false claims about the spread of a cholera outbreak in Nacala-Porto, in the northern province of Nampula.

In August, police prevented a group of medical doctors from hosting a public health fair in Maputo, organized by the Mozambican Medical Association as part of activities linked to their nationwide strike. Police claimed the group did not have the authorization to hold the event and dispersed the doctors and their patients. A spokesman for the doctors told local media that they had requested and obtained authorization from the city council and were even allowed to borrow some municipal furniture for the event.

Unresolved Kidnappings

Kidnappings for ransom continued across the country, with police failing to properly investigate the cases. Attorney-General Beatriz Buchili denounced police complicity in kidnapping cases in Mozambique, claiming the involvement of some "members of the police, lawyers, magistrates, and other figures in the judiciary creates fragilities in investigating these cases."

In January, a Mozambican businessman who had been kidnapped in Matola in December 2022 was found dead, after the kidnappers told his family members to pick him up at a location because his health condition was "very bad."

In July, an owner of a liquor shop in Maputo was kidnapped in front of his shop in one of the busiest streets in the city. According to local press, members of his family had also been kidnapping victims in the past.

In September, residents prevented an attempted kidnapping of a businessman at his shop near two police stations in a busy Maputo neighborhood.

Following all these cases, police pledged to investigate, but at time of writing, they had not announced updates on any investigations.

Key International Partners

Mozambique started a two-year mandate as a non-permanent member of the UN Security Council. In March, as it took over the rotating month-long presidency of the council for the first time, President Filipe Nyusi called for greater coordination between the Security Council and the African Union (AU) to control the spread of terrorism in Africa and the Middle East.

The European Council approved €20 million to support the deployment of the Rwanda Defense Force in Cabo Delgado province. Additionally, the European Union has supported the Mozambican Armed Forces with €89 million and a Training Mission (EUTM).

In January, United States Ambassador to the UN Linda Thomas-Greenfield visited Mozambique, where she focused on "regional security issues, food insecurity, humanitarian issues, and supporting African efforts to mitigate climate change."

In June, the chairperson of the AU Commission, Moussa Faki Mahamat, welcomed the closure of the last military base of the former rebel group and main opposition party RENAMO as "a tremendous contribution towards silencing the guns in Africa."

In July, SADC leaders meeting in the Angolan capital of Luanda agreed to extend the organization's military mission in Mozambique for another year to consolidate what they called "gains achieved."

Myanmar

Since the February 2021 military coup in Myanmar, the junta has driven the country further into a human rights and humanitarian catastrophe. At least 55 townships are under martial law. Faced with opposition from the general population and pro-democracy armed groups, the military has struggled to maintain control over the country. The junta's widespread and systematic abuses against the population—including arbitrary arrests, torture, extrajudicial killings, and indiscriminate attacks on civilians—amount to crimes against humanity and war crimes.

Citing ongoing violence, Myanmar's junta postponed a planned so-called election slated for August after extending a "state of emergency" for the fourth time since the coup. The junta announced slightly reduced sentences for National League for Democracy (NLD) party leader Aung San Suu Kyi and President Win Myint, who are serving lengthy sentences on multiple bogus charges.

Some countries have imposed targeted sanctions, but the international response to the crisis has been uncoordinated. The Myanmar military has yet to face real consequences for the abuses it has committed, both before and since the coup.

Shrinking Civic Space and Junta's Sham "Elections"

In March, the junta announced that the NLD was among 40 political parties and other groups dissolved for failing to register according to the new Political Party Registration Law. The law's provisions appear intended to delay indefinitely, rather than facilitate, Myanmar's return to civilian democratic rule. Many parties, including the NLD, refused to comply with the requirement that they register within 60 days of the law's promulgation because they believe the military's proposed "elections" will not be credible.

Under the new law and earlier martial law orders, any election would be dominated by junta-backed political parties and the military itself, which already holds 25 percent of seats in the national and local legislatures under the 2008 Constitution. In the face of widespread political oppression, free and fair elections are not possible in Myanmar for the foreseeable future.

Free Myanmar
Free
Aung San Suu Kyi
HUMAN RIGHTS WATCH
"Our Numbers are Dwindling"
Myanmar's Post-Coup Crackdown on Lawyers

The junta claims it has digitized early census data of up to 51 million individuals and had collected the biometric data of up to 700,000 individuals by August. The junta's Ministry of Immigration and Population is collecting fingerprints, iris scans, face scans, and other personal details to link this data to citizenship documents, passports, bank details, and purchases, such as for SIM cards and mobile phones. These efforts may increase digital surveillance of activists, human rights defenders, and opposition members and be used to further scrutinize citizenship rights of ethnic and minority groups.

Targeted Arrests and Denial of Fair Trial Rights

The targeting of activists and rights defenders has escalated over the past year. At least 24,000 anti-coup protesters have been arrested since the coup and 4,000 killed, according to the Assistance Association for Political Prisoners. The Peace Research Institute of Oslo estimates actual figures are much higher.

In the face of mass arrests, dozens of lawyers in Myanmar have attempted to represent those arrested and provide them a legal defense. At every turn, however, lawyers have faced systematic obstacles imposed by military authorities and restrictions impeding their work. They themselves have faced threats, arbitrary arrests and detention, and politically motivated prosecution, and in some instances, torture and ill-treatment.

The junta has created "special courts," closed courts inside prisons to fast-track politically sensitive cases. As a result, many cases that would have been heard before regular criminal courts before the coup are now under the jurisdiction of these junta-controlled special courts. Restrictions on lawyers inside special courts have denied suspects their rights to due process and a fair trial.

In parallel, military tribunals that are in operation in townships under martial law determine cases for civilians but are entirely opaque and closed to public scrutiny.

In August, the junta announced the release of thousands of prisoners in an amnesty that coincided with the reduction of Aung San Suu Kyi's and Win Myint's sentences. However, as in the past, few of those released were political prisoners, and many of those released had already served most of their sentences and were soon due for release. Myanmar's military authorities have long used amnesties as a tool to gain credibility and deflect international pressure.

In September, a court sentenced photojournalist Saw Zaw Thaike, of the banned independent publication *Myanmar Now*, to 20 years in prison with hard labor, in a trial carried out inside Insein prison where he had no legal representation. His sentence is the longest given to any journalist since the coup.

Military Attacks on Civilian Populations

On April 11, the military used a thermobaric bomb during an attack on an opposition building in the village of Pa Zi Gyi in Sagaing Region, killing more than 160 people, including many children. This enhanced-blast type munition caused indiscriminate and disproportionate civilian casualties in violation of international humanitarian law and was an apparent war crime.

Other attacks in which Myanmar's military may be responsible for laws-of-war violations include airstrikes on April 10 in Chin State that killed nine civilians and in Bago Region on May 2 that killed three civilians. An air and ground assault in Magway Region on April 21 burned a Japan-funded hospital. And in March, after the military captured a town in Shan State, 22 people were summarily executed, with many of the victims bearing marks of torture.

On October 9, the Myanmar military attacked a village hosting hundreds of displaced civilians in Kachin State, killing 28 civilians, including 11 children, committing an apparent war crime.

Across the country, including in other areas such as in Chin, Kachin, Karen, and Karenni States, airstrikes by the military have increased significantly in 2023. Airstrikes in some regions have increased more than 300 percent in the past year. The military has also continued using domestically produced cluster munitions; their use was first recorded in Myanmar after the coup. Cluster munitions are prohibited under a 2008 convention signed by 123 countries; Myanmar has not signed it.

Non-state armed groups have also committed crimes against civilians, including sexual violence and grave violations against children.

Displacement and Humanitarian Aid

Nearly 2 million people have been internally displaced and 94,000 refugees have fled to neighboring countries. On October 27, fighting between the military and a coalition of ethnic armed groups and People's Defense Forces caused about 500,000 people across the country to be newly displaced. Many internally displaced people have fled air and ground attacks multiple times. The United Nations Office for the Coordination of Humanitarian Affairs (OCHA) said 18 million people required humanitarian aid.

Junta restrictions on humanitarian aid have threatened millions in conflict areas. The Myanmar military has deliberately blocked aid as a form of collective punishment. The blockages sustain the military's longstanding "four cuts" strategy, in which the armed forces maintain control of an area by isolating and terrorizing the civilian population.

On May 14, Cyclone Mocha—which is tied with another for strongest tropical cyclone ever recorded in the northern Indian Ocean—made landfall, leaving a trail of destruction and affecting at least 7.9 million people across Chin, Kachin, and Rakhine States and Sagaing and Magway Regions, according to OCHA figures. "The impact of climate change on children and families is clear for all to see," UNICEF noted following the cyclone. Junta authorities refused to authorize travel and visas for aid workers, release urgent supplies from customs and warehouses, or relax onerous and unnecessary restrictions on lifesaving assistance.

The junta's restrictions disregarded many international calls regarding humanitarian aid, most notably the five-point consensus from the Association of Southeast Asian Nations (ASEAN) and the December 2022 UN Security Council resolution, which urged "full, safe and unhindered humanitarian access."

Conflict and reduced agricultural production are contributing to significant food insecurity, according to the UN Food and Agriculture Organization. In addition, a severe devaluation of the Myanmar currency led to dire banking and supply chain crises and shortages of food, medicine, and other essentials.

Rohingya Apartheid

More than 600,000 Rohingya in Myanmar continue to live under apartheid conditions, facing persecution and effective imprisonment from the junta authorities. Of this population, roughly 140,000 Rohingya have been confined to camps in central Rakhine State since 2012, denied the right to return to their homes.

The junta continued carrying out the problematic "camp closure" process, which entails replacing temporary longhouses with permanent structures built on top of or near the existing sites, further entrenching segregation. Across the camps in central Rakhine State, fewer than half of all camp shelters have received any repairs over the past two years.

When Cyclone Mocha hit, local junta authorities failed to adequately communicate the storm's risks, assist Rohingya in finding shelter or transportation, or support search-and-rescue operations following the storm.

Bangladesh authorities and the Myanmar junta took steps toward a pilot repatriation process, which has been marked by coercion and deceit. Conditions for the safe, sustainable, and dignified return of Rohingya did not exist throughout the year.

Sexual Orientation and Gender Identity

Myanmar's penal code punishes "carnal intercourse against the order of nature" with up to 10 years in prison and a fine. Under the military junta, lesbian, gay, bisexual, and transgender (LGBT) people have been particularly likely to be targeted with sexual violence in custody.

Women's and Girls' Rights

Since the coup, there has been an uptick in reports of sexual violence and other forms of gendered harassment by both military and non-state perpetrators. In addition, women and girls remain extremely vulnerable to gender-based violence, particularly in the context of ongoing conflict. Women also reported a significant decline in their ability to participate in politics and education. Sixteen percent of girls and 5 percent of boys are married before age 18, and women and girls are at risk of trafficking for sexual exploitation inside and outside the country.

Key International Actors

Since passing a resolution on Myanmar in December 2022, the UN Security Council has done little more than issue a few statements. The Myanmar military has continued to ignore the resolution, and the council has taken no further concrete, meaningful actions: it has not instituted a global arms embargo, referred the country situation to the International Criminal Court (ICC), or imposed binding targeted sanctions on junta leadership and military-owned companies.

The European Union passed a sixth and then a seventh tranche of restrictions on Myanmar in February and July, imposing sanctions on a total of 99 individuals and 19 entities.

In May, the UN special rapporteur on human rights in Myanmar, Tom Andrews, released a report on the US$1 billion trade in arms and raw materials for weapons since the coup. It traced the flow of weapons and materiel to entities based in Russia, China, Singapore, Thailand, and India. The report described how arms dealers have relied on lax enforcement and avoided sanctions by using "front companies."

In June, the United States imposed sanctions on Myanmar's defense ministry and two banks, Myanmar Foreign Trade Bank (MFTB) and Myanmar Investment and Commercial Bank (MICB), used by the junta to purchase weapons and other dual-use goods. In response, Singapore's United Overseas Bank, the foreign bank of choice for Myanmar's military, suspended all bank-to-bank transfers. Bangladesh's Sonali bank has also frozen transfers and accounts of MFTB and MICB.

On August 23, the US extended targeted sanctions to include aviation fuel, citing the Myanmar military's increased attacks on civilians. The US Department of the Treasury's Office of Foreign Assets Control (OFAC) determined sanctions "to be imposed on any foreign individual or entity that operates in the jet fuel sector" of the Myanmar economy. OFAC also designated sanctions on two individuals and one entity involved in the procurement and distribution of jet fuel as well as two other entities owned by the two individuals.

On October 31, the US imposed a ban on financial transactions involving the Myanma Oil and Gas Enterprise (MOGE), which goes into effect on December 15. The directive prohibits persons and companies under US jurisdiction from directly or indirectly providing financial services to MOGE, including deposits, transfers, loans, insurance, investments, foreign exchange, and other services. The US, Canada, and the United Kingdom also coordinated on additional sanctions on individuals and entities.

Earlier in the year, Canada, the UK, and the EU had imposed targeted sanctions on specific individuals and entities involved in supplying aviation fuel to the Myanmar military. However, at least five British insurance companies are still providing coverage for aviation fuel deliveries to Myanmar.

In September, ASEAN decided at its annual summit that Myanmar would not be allowed to chair the bloc, whose chair rotates every year in alphabetical order, in 2026. ASEAN member states decided that a "troika," comprising the immediate past, present, and incoming future chairs of ASEAN, would handle Myanmar issues going forward.

At the ICC, the prosecutor continued his office's investigation into alleged crimes against humanity following the 2017 ethnic cleansing campaign against the Rohingya based on the completion of these crimes in Bangladesh, an ICC member country. The Independent Investigative Mechanism for Myanmar continued gathering evidence for future prosecutions.

The Gambia's case alleging Myanmar's violation of the Genocide Convention is ongoing before the International Court of Justice, with Myanmar filing its counter-memorial in August. On November 15, Canada, Denmark, France, Germany, the Netherlands, and the UK filed a joint declaration to intervene in support of The Gambia's case.

Nepal

A new governing coalition led by Prime Minister Pushpa Kamal Dahal took office following elections in late 2022, but it was affected by instability in its early months.

The government publicly committed to advance the transitional justice process, including to provide reparations to victims and seek accountability for crimes committed during Nepal's 1996-2006 internal armed conflict. Although a draft bill proposed some positive steps, it falls short of meeting Nepal's international legal obligations.

Police officers accused of recent rights violations were not held accountable, while investigations into corruption allegations were met with political interference.

Thousands received official documentation that had previously been denied after amendments to the citizenship law. But the amendments did not address provisions that discriminate against women by limiting their right to pass citizenship to their children.

Although 40 percent of the population is under 18, children receive only a small share of social protection spending. Despite earlier pledges to do so, the successful Child Grant program was not extended in the 2023 budget. Cuts to the health budget threatened services, including for maternal health and child malnutrition.

In June, in a significant ruling, the Supreme Court ordered the government to immediately begin registering same-sex marriages, but lower courts refused to implement the ruling.

Transitional Justice

Victims of abuses during the armed conflict and United Nations human rights experts raised concerns after an amended transitional justice bill was presented to parliament in March. The bill was in response to a 2015 Supreme Court ruling that Nepal's existing legislation is unlawful, particularly because it allows amnesties for serious crimes under international law. In late 2023, a parliamentary committee proposed further amendments.

Some aspects of the bill can be the basis for progress. It guarantees the right to reparation and interim relief for some victims who were left out of earlier relief packages. It also mandates Nepal's Truth and Reconciliation Commission to study the root causes of the conflict and recommend institutional reforms to guarantee the non-recurrence of abuses. Dahal said his government wants to create enabling circumstances for perpetrators in "revealing the truth, providing reparation to the victim and apologizing for his or her wrongdoing."

However, unless it is appropriately amended, the bill will enable amnesties for murder, sexual violence not amounting to rape, "beating and mutilation," and "any inhuman act[s] that are against international human rights and humanitarian law." The bill fails to establish a special investigation unit to collect evidence of these crimes, and it includes a statute of limitations that severely limits access to justice for survivors of sexual violence.

Rule of Law

The impunity given to alleged perpetrators of conflict-era violations also extends to members of the police and security forces for violations committed since the 2006 peace agreement. Frequently, the government appoints committees to investigate alleged abuses, such as killings in police custody, and pays compensation to the victim's family. Even when cases are initially registered, alleged perpetrators are not prosecuted.

On August 16, Vinod Tolangi and Akash Balami died, reportedly as a result of beatings at a prison in Sankhuwasabha district. Police initially refused to accept a complaint, saying they died in a prison fight. However, the government later appointed three committees to investigate, and a case was subsequently registered against 12 people, including 2 police officers.

Advocacy Forum, a Nepali human rights organization, documented 39 custodial deaths between 2018 and 2022. While the authorities blamed suicide in many instances, activists fear many died after torture in custody.

In 2020, the National Human Rights Commission published 20 years of data, naming 286 people, including military personnel and former Maoist insurgents, as suspects in serious crimes that authorities had failed to prosecute. No prosecution is known to have occurred in any of these cases since the report was published. On July 16, the government proposed new legislation that would allow the government to withdraw criminal cases against political leaders and party activists if they were of a "political nature."

In May, the police took an unusual step of arresting senior politicians and officials allegedly involved in a corrupt scheme to help people fraudulently emigrate to the United States. At least 30 people face charges. However, in August, senior police officers leading the investigation were transferred, reportedly due to political pressure.

In March, the government appointed an officer implicated in a 2009 torture case as the country's most senior police officer.

Women's and Girls' Rights

Nepal's citizenship law still discriminates against women, even after being amended in 2023 to recognize the citizenship of many who had previously been denied documentation. The children of single Nepali mothers can receive citizenship only if the mother declares that the father cannot be identified. If the declaration is alleged to be false, she can be criminally prosecuted. Children of a Nepali woman and a foreign father can only receive a category of citizenship that excludes them from holding high office. These restrictions do not apply to Nepali fathers.

Although it had fallen steadily before 2020, the maternal mortality rate in Nepal remains high and increased because of lockdowns during the Covid-19 pandemic. The government announced health budget cuts that officials said would impact services, most affecting women from disadvantaged social groups.

Nepal continues to have a high rate of child marriage, although the law requires both men and women to be at least 20 when they marry. According to UNICEF, 33 percent of girls and 9 percent of boys are married before the age of 18. The rate of child marriage is believed to have increased during the pandemic.

Although the statute of limitations for prosecuting rape allegations was extended in 2022 to two years (or three years if the victim is a child), it remains too short and an obstacle to justice.

Women from disadvantaged social groups, particularly Dalits, are at heightened at risk of sexual violence and face greater barriers to justice.

Children's Rights

Around 40 percent of Nepal's population is under 18, but children receive only around 4 percent of the government's social protection budget. Nepal has a proven social protection program for children, the Child Grant, but in 2022, it covered just 9.5 percent of all children.

The absence of social protection further exposes children to the harmful effects of economic and climate-related shocks and unpredictable crises like the Covid-19 pandemic, which drove many families into poverty and children into child labor. In April 2023, 16 Nepali and international civil society organizations wrote to Nepal's finance minister urging an expansion of the Child Grant.

Government officials warned that services for children suffering malnutrition would be harmed due to health budget cuts.

Sexual Orientation and Gender Identity

In a historic ruling, on June 28, the Supreme Court ordered the government to register same-sex marriages. Although Nepal's civil code currently describes marriage as between a man and a woman, Nepal's 2015 constitution prohibits gender discrimination and upholds the rights of sexual minorities. Lower courts, which register marriages, have refused to do so for same-sex couples; court cases challenging their refusal remain pending.

In principle, transgender people in Nepal can change their legal gender through a self-declaration process, but the gender markers are limited to a third, "other" category, and in the absence of an official protocol, transgender people often face demands for medical verification, which can be rife with abuse.

Key International Actors

Nepal is part of the Chinese government's Belt and Road Initiative, although there have been delays in implementing any projects. The government restricts free assembly and expression rights of the Tibetan community under pressure from Chinese authorities.

Nepal is a participant in the United States government's Millennium Challenge Corporation, which some see as an attempt to counter the country's ties with China.

Nepal has an Extended Credit Facility with the International Monetary Fund (IMF). Human Rights Watch has called on the IMF to make the expansion of the Child Grant a "performance criterion" for Nepal's IMF program.

Nepal's donors, including European bilateral donors and UN agencies, have continued to fund programs to support police reform and access to justice, but they have not been able to strengthen accountability.

UN special rapporteurs warned that without amendments, the transitional justice bill would "place Nepal in contravention of its international human rights obligation to investigate and punish serious human rights violations."

Nicaragua

The government of President Daniel Ortega and his wife, Vice President Rosario Murillo, continued to repress all forms of dissent and isolate Nicaragua.

The government has tightened its grip on power by cracking down on critics, including members of the Catholic Church, and dismantling civic space. It has massively closed media outlets, NGOs, and universities, violating freedoms of expression and association and restricting the right to education.

Other persistent problems include a total abortion ban, attacks on Indigenous and Afro-descendent communities, and widespread impunity for human rights violations.

Persecution of Critics

As of October, 81 people perceived as government critics remained in detention, a Nicaraguan rights group reported, most charged with "undermining national integrity" and "propagating fake news."

In February, the government stripped 317 people of their nationality, including 222 political prisoners the government expelled to the US, labeling them as "traitors" and confiscating their assets. The decision, which violated international human rights law, left many stateless.

Authorities removed birth certificates and academic records of some of those expelled from the civil registry, impeding the right to access personal information. They also erased critics' personal data from the Nicaraguan Institute of Social Security, depriving many of their pensions. In May, the Supreme Court permanently suspended the licenses of 25 lawyers and notaries, ruling that because they were now considered "foreigners," they could no longer exercise their profession in Nicaragua.

Freedom of Religion

Attacks on the Catholic Church, which began in 2018, have escalated.

In August 2022, police officers detained Bishop Rolando Álvarez, an outspoken government critic, and charged him with "undermining national integrity" and "propagating fake news." In February, Álvarez refused to be expelled and a judge sentenced him to 26 years in prison. The UN Office of the High Commissioner for Human Rights (OHCHR) reported in June that Álvarez was being held incommunicado.

In May, the police announced that authorities were investigating the Catholic Church for alleged money laundering and had frozen several dioceses' bank accounts.

In August, authorities canceled the legal registration of the Jesuit-run Universidad Centroamericana (UCA), seizing its assets and leaving thousands of students in limbo. The closure brings the number of universities shut down since December 2021 to 28.

In October, the government released 12 Catholic priests and sent them to Rome, following what it described as an "agreement with the Vatican."

Authorities also banned the 2023 Easter processions and closed the Jesuit religious order in August, confiscating its properties. They also continued to expel foreign priests and nuns.

Freedoms of Expression and Association

Human rights defenders, journalists, and critics are targets of death threats, assaults, intimidation, harassment, surveillance, online defamation campaigns, and, as discussed above, arbitrary detention, prosecution, and deprivation of nationality.

Authorities had closed over 3,500 NGOs as of November 2023, including women's, religious, international aid, and medical groups. This represents roughly 50 percent of NGOs officially operative in Nicaragua before April 2018. The closures have cut off essential services to many beneficiaries.

Between 2018 and 2022, the government closed at least 57 media outlets, 30 in 2022 and 2 in 2023, the Nicaraguan Platform of NGO Networks reported.

Abusive legislation enabled many of the closures. A 2020 “foreign agents” law, for example, allows the cancelation of legal status of organizations that obtain foreign funds for activities that “interfere in Nicaragua’s internal affairs.”

Between April and June, 23 journalists fled the country, civil society groups reported, bringing the total of media workers who fled Nicaragua since 2018 to 208.

Authorities have imposed restrictions to hinder several outlets’ operations, including censorship and blocking access to printing materials. Police have raided and seized assets from *Confidencial*, *100% Noticias*, and *La Prensa*.

In August, a court sentenced journalist Victor Ticay to eight years in prison on charges of undermining national integrity and disseminating false news.

Indigenous Peoples’ Rights

Indigenous and Afro-descendant peoples face discrimination, reflected in disproportionate poverty rates, illegal encroachment on their traditional territories, and persistent violence.

In October, the Supreme Electoral Council stripped the legal status of the Indigenous political party YATAMA, accusing the party of “undermining Nicaragua’s national integrity.” Police had detained two of YATAMA’s main leaders, Brooklyn Rivera and Nancy Henríquez, in late September. The whereabouts of Rivera, YATAMA’s only representative in Congress, remained unknown at time of writing, according to family members.

Between August 2022 and June 2023, OHCHR recorded eight violent attacks on Indigenous peoples, especially in the Mayangna Sauni As territory of the Bosawás Biosphere Reserve.

In March, settlers attacked the Wilú community in the Mayangna Sauni As territory, killing 5 people, displacing 28 families, and setting fire to all buildings.

Settlers have taken approximately 21,000 hectares from the Miskitu people and forcibly displaced around 1,000, presumably serving forestry and mining interests. Death threats have forced some Indigenous authorities into exile, and the government has prevented some from returning to Nicaragua.

The Rama Kriol autonomous territory, which makes up two-thirds of the Indio Maiz biological reserve and is home to the Rama Indigenous people and Kriol Afro-descendant people, is also under heavy pressure from illegal cattle ranchers.

Impunity for 2018 Crackdown

Police, in coordination with armed pro-government groups, repressed massive anti-government protests in 2018, killing at least 328 people, injuring some 2,000, and detaining hundreds. Authorities reported that 21 police officers were killed in the context of demonstrations.

Many protesters were detained for months, subjected to torture and ill-treatment, including electric shocks, severe beatings, fingernail removal, asphyxiation, and rapes. Serious violations of due process and other rights marred prosecutions against protesters.

No police officer has been convicted in connection with abuses related to the crackdown.

Women's and Girls' Rights

Nicaragua has, since 2006, prohibited abortion under all circumstances. Those who have abortions face prison sentences of up to two years; medical professionals who perform them face up to six years. The ban forces women and girls to continue unwanted pregnancies, putting their health and lives at risk.

Restrictive abortion laws, compounded by the lack of information and comprehensive sexuality education, impose barriers to identifying sexual violence. In May 2019, NGOs submitted the cases of "Susana" and "Lucía," two girls who survived sexual violence and were forced to become mothers, to the UN Human Rights Committee.

Rates of domestic abuse, violence against women, and femicide—legally defined in Nicaragua as "the murder of a woman in the public or private sphere"—increased from August 2019 to December 2020, OHCHR reported.

The government did not publish figures on femicides and other forms of violence against women in 2022 and 2023. OHCHR reported 36 femicides between January and June 2023, including the 4 murders of girls under age 16.

Disability Rights

Discrimination against people with disabilities in Nicaragua is widespread. People with disabilities face severe problems in accessing schools, public health facilities, and other institutions. Under Nicaraguan law, 2 percent of public officials should be people with disabilities, but the quota is not respected, and there are few employment opportunities for people with disabilities.

Nicaraguan Asylum Seekers and Migrants

Between 2018 and June 2022, more than 260,000 Nicaraguans, over 4 percent of the estimated population, fled, mostly to Costa Rica and the United States.

Many have been forced to leave their country due to political persecution and the lack of opportunities.

Key International Actors

In April, the United Nations Human Rights Council renewed for two years the mandates of the Group of Human Rights Experts on Nicaragua and the reporting mandate of the OHCHR. Previously, the Group of Experts had released a report in March finding reasonable grounds to believe that the authorities had committed crimes against humanity, including murder, imprisonment, torture, sexual violence, forced deportation, and persecution on political grounds.

Pope Francis called Ortega's government a "grotesque dictatorship" in March. The Vatican closed its embassy in Nicaragua in April after the government suggested suspending diplomatic relations.

In September, UN High Commissioner for Human Rights Volker Türk reported a "continued and widespread deterioration of human rights" and that the government keeps "punishing and locking out those who voice their views" and "intensifying the country's isolation."

No international monitoring bodies have been allowed to enter Nicaragua since 2018, when the authorities expelled the Inter-American Commission on Human Rights (IACHR) Special Monitoring Mechanism for Nicaragua, the IACHR-appointed Interdisciplinary Group of Independent Experts, and OHCHR.

In July, Nicaragua participated in the European Union-Community of Latin American and Caribbean States (EU-CELAC) summit. It was the only country that did not support a paragraph in the summit's final resolution expressing concern about the war in Ukraine. Russia has supplied Nicaragua with military equipment and security infrastructure in the past years.

In September, the board of the UN Green Climate Fund (GCF) temporarily suspended disbursements for Bio-CLIMA, an environmental project, citing "instances of policy non-compliance." Bio-CLIMA had the stated objective of reducing deforestation and strengthening resilience in Bosawás and Río San Juan Biospheres, but the Nicaraguan NGO Fundación del Río reported a lack of free, prior, and informed consent from Indigenous and Afro-descendant communities. A final decision regarding the suspension of funds is expected earlier in 2024.

The US State Department's *Corrupt and Undemocratic Actors Report*, released in July, imposed sanctions on the attorney general and parliamentary leaders. As of March 2023, the US Treasury Department had imposed asset-blocking sanctions on 11 entities and 43 people, including members of the government, legislature, and judiciary. In April, the US State Department sanctioned three judges who had helped strip the aforementioned 317 Nicaraguans of their citizenship; between August and September, it sanctioned 200 municipal officials accused of human rights violations in connection with the closures of UCA and the Central American Institute of Business Administration (INCAE).

The EU renewed sanctions on 21 individuals and 3 state-linked entities in October. In June, the European Parliament strongly condemned "the Nicaraguan regime's widespread perpetration of systematic and deliberate human rights violations against its population for purely political reasons" and called for the release of all arbitrarily detained political prisoners.

The United Kingdom and Canada have respectively sanctioned 13 and 35 individuals implicated in human rights violations.

In November 2021, Nicaragua announced its withdrawal from the Organization of American States (OAS). Nicaragua withdrew from the OAS in 2021. The decision took effect in November 2023. The OAS Permanent Council said in a resolution adopted in November that it will continue "paying special attention to the situation in Nicaragua."

Niger

The July 26 military coup drew global attention to the human rights situation in Niger, including restrictions on freedom of expression and the erosion of civic space. On that day, army officers of the self-proclaimed National Council for the Safeguard of the Homeland (Conseil national pour la sauvegarde de la patrie, CNSP) announced on national television the overthrow of the government of President Mohamed Bazoum. They dissolved the constitution, suspended all institutions, and closed the country's borders. They arrested Bazoum, his wife and son, and several other state officials, arguing that they were taking action because of Niger's deteriorating security situation. On July 27, Gen. Abdourahamane "Omar" Tiani, head of Niger's presidential guard, appointed himself head of the country's new military government.

In response to the coup, on July 30, the Economic Community of West African States (ECOWAS) suspended all ties with Niger and threatened military action if the CNSP did not release Bazoum, return him to power, and restore constitutional order. On August 10, ECOWAS further condemned the coup and imposed sanctions on the country and the coup leaders, including travel bans and asset freezes.

On August 19, following talks with an ECOWAS delegation, Tiani announced a three-year transition to democratic rule, a plan rejected by ECOWAS.

Since the coup, freedom of expression has been curtailed and independent journalists have faced arrests, threats, and harassment. Political space shrank, with the junta banning the activities of all political parties and arresting several members of the ousted government and its supporters.

Niger continued to battle Islamist armed groups, including the Islamic State in the Greater Sahara (ISGS) and the rival Al-Qaeda-linked Group for the Support of Islam and Muslims (Jama'at Nusrat al-Islam wa al-Muslimeen, JNIM), as well as Boko Haram and the Islamic State in West Africa Province (ISWAP) in its western and southeastern regions.

Flooding and torrential rains in July destroyed tens of thousands of homes and crops and led to at least 41 deaths across the country as well as mass displacement.

The humanitarian situation remained critical, with 4.3 million people, about 17 percent of the population, in need of humanitarian assistance and over 370,000 people internally displaced. Niger also hosted over 320,000 refugees and asylum seekers as of August, and continued to receive new arrivals, primarily from Nigeria, Mali, and Burkina Faso, as well as over 20,000 migrants expelled from Algeria to Niger's Agadez region during 2023.

Post-Coup Violence

After the coup, supporters of the CNSP, at times organized in vigilante committees, have committed several acts of violence against members of Bazoum's party, the Nigerien Party for Democracy and Socialism (Parti Nigérien pour la Démocratie et le Socialisme, PNDS-Tarayya). CNSP supporters are believed to have perpetrated the violence as a result of political tensions over a possible ECOWAS military intervention.

On July 27, supporters of the junta ransacked and set fire to the PNDS headquarters in the capital, Niamey. They also burned scores of vehicles and physically assaulted several PNDS members who had gathered at the party's headquarters for a meeting. The security forces did not take adequate measures to prevent the violence. In August, youth vigilantes supporting the CNSP sexually assaulted several women during unlawful patrols at Niamey's main roundabouts, according to the police and the Nigerien League for Women's Rights. At least four of the victims filed complaints with the Nigerien police against their abusers, but so far, none of the perpetrators has been charged with these offenses.

Post-Coup Arbitrary Arrests

Since the coup, the junta has arbitrarily arrested several officials from the ousted government, including Sani Mahamadou Issoufou, former minister of petroleum; Hamadou Adamou Souley, former minister of home affairs; Kalla Moutari, former defense minister; and Ahmad Jidoud, former minister of finance. In September, they were transferred to prisons in Filingué, Say, and Kollo in Tillabéri region and in Niamey and charged with "threatening state security" by a military court despite being civilians, in violation of due process.

Bazoum, his wife, and his son have remained in detention since July 26 at the presidential palace in Niamey. On August 13, the military authorities announced plans to prosecute Bazoum for "high treason" and undermining national security, but he had not been brought before a judge at time of writing. On September 18, Bazoum filed a petition with the ECOWAS Court of Justice in Abuja, Nigeria, citing human rights violations against him and his family in detention. He also called for his immediate reinstatement as president. At time of writing, the court was due to issue its verdict on November 30. On October 3, Salem Mohamed Bazoum, the former president's son, contested the legality of his detention before a Niamey high court and on October 6, the court ordered his release. However, the CNSP has yet to comply with the ruling. In an October 20 press release, lawyers representing Bazoum said that he, his wife, and his son were being detained in a secret location and rejected the military authorities' claim that he had attempted to escape.

Post-Coup Attacks on Freedom of Expression

Since the coup, the junta has restricted freedom of expression and shut down media. Local and international journalists have been physically attacked, threatened, verbally harassed, and cyber-harassed.

On July 28, Soufiane Mana Hassan, editor of the newspaper *Le Témoin de l'Histoire*, was threatened on the street about his newspaper's coverage and his social media posts.

On July 30, demonstrators at a CNSP march threatened French journalists Anne-Fleur Lespiaut and Stanislas Poyet. In early August, Lespiaut was cyber-harassed by CNSP supporters.

On August 3, the CNSP indefinitely suspended local retransmissions of international news broadcasters Radio France Internationale (RFI) and France 24, a violation of the right to free and independent information. The blocking created an information gap, as local media outlets lost access to reliable and independent international news sources. Nigerien outlets were also stopped from reporting freely.

On August 19, Amaury Hauchard and Poyet were verbally and physically attacked while covering an event of Volunteers of the Homeland, civilian auxiliaries of the army. Poyet's passport was stolen, and his media equipment was broken. Hauchard required stitches.

On September 30, men who identified themselves as security force members arrested and took away Samira Sabou, a blogger and journalist, from her mother's home in Niamey. Sabou's whereabouts remained unknown for seven days. The Niamey judicial police initially denied arresting her, but on October 7, she was transferred to the criminal investigations unit of the Niamey police, where her lawyer and husband visited her. On October 11, she was charged with "production and dissemination of data likely to disturb public order" and released pending trial.

Sabou had already been arrested previously for her journalism. In 2022, she was sentenced to a one-month suspended prison sentence for reporting on drug trafficking in Niger. In 2020, she was subjected to 48 days of arbitrary detention and cybercrime charges.

The junta has silenced dissenting voices. In an August 22 decree, Niger's new leader Gen. Tiani announced the removal from office of six academics and state officials, without any explanation. The day before, those removed had signed a petition, along with other academics, distancing themselves from an August 1 statement by the National Union of Teachers and Researchers in support of the CNSP.

On October 3, Samira Ibrahim, a social media user known as "Precious Mimi," was convicted and given a six-month suspended sentence and a fine of XOF 300,000 (about US$479) for "producing data that could disturb public order." The charge related to a Facebook post, in which she referred to Algeria's refusal to recognize the new Nigerien junta.

Attacks by Islamist Armed Groups

An Islamist insurgency, which broke out in northern Mali in 2012 before spreading to neighboring Niger and Burkina Faso in 2015, has resulted in widespread abuses in Niger for more than a decade. The so-called three borders area, in southwest Niger's Tillabéri region, between Burkina Faso, Mali, and Niger, has regularly suffered attacks by armed groups linked to Islamic State (ISIS) and Al-Qaeda.

On July 14, suspected members of an Islamist group killed four civilians and injured seven others in an attack in Tillabéri region. An October 2 attack by suspected members of an Islamist armed group using improvised explosive devices in vehicles killed at least 29 soldiers in Niger's western Tahoua region. The junta declared three days of national mourning.

Intercommunal Violence

In April, violent clashes between sedentary ethnic Djerma communities and nomadic ethnic Fulani communities in the Tillabéri region led to several deaths and injuries and the displacement of about 18,000 people. Between August 15 and 16 in the same area, clashes between the two communities led to the killing of 25 civilians.

Migrants' Rights

Between January and August, Algeria deported more than 20,000 migrants of multiple nationalities, including children, in multiple collective expulsions to its border with Niger, according to the Niger-based nongovernmental organization (NGO) Alarme Phone Sahara. An estimated 8,000 to 11,000 expelled people arrived between January and April alone in the village of Assamaka, 15 kilometers from the Algerian border, in Niger's Agadez region. Médecins Sans Frontières (Doctors Without Borders, MSF) called the numbers "unprecedented." MSF, Alarme Phone Sahara, and the International Organization for Migration (IOM) raised the alarm in March and April as thousands of migrants remained stranded in Assamaka without access to shelter, health care, protection, or basic necessities, also straining resources for members of the host community.

With Niger's borders closed following the July coup, thousands of migrants, refugees, and asylum seekers remained trapped in Niger in deteriorating humanitarian conditions, some in Assamaka and others in overcrowded IOM transit centers. In September, the IOM called on Nigerien authorities to establish a humanitarian corridor to enable voluntary returns of stranded migrants to their countries of origin.

Child Marriage and the Denial of the Right to Education

Niger has the highest prevalence of child marriage of any country in the world, according to UNICEF, with 76 percent of girls marrying before their 18th birthday.

In 2018, the latest year for which data is available, about 26 percent of children completed primary education and less than 5 percent completed lower secondary school; about 20 percent of girls completed primary education and less than 5 percent completed lower secondary school. In 2019, the government issued an order specifically requiring that married and pregnant students and adolescent mothers stay in school but has done little to implement it.

Key International Actors

On July 29, European Union foreign policy chief Josep Borrell announced the immediate suspension of budget support to Niger and of all security cooperation activities with it.

On August 3, Amadou Abdramane, CNSP's spokesperson, announced that five military cooperation agreements with France, Niger's former colonial power, were being revoked.

On August 22, the African Union (AU) suspended Niger from its organs, institutions, and actions. Divisions among AU member states over the use of force led to the body calling for a peaceful approach to restoring constitutional order in Niger, rather than a military intervention by West African states.

On August 25, Niger coup leaders gave French ambassador Sylvain Itte 48 hours to leave the country. France initially ignored the directive, declaring the CNSP illegitimate, but changed course on September 24, when French President Emmanuel Macron withdrew the ambassador and announced the withdrawal of all 1,500 French troops stationed in Niger by the end of 2023.

In September, the United Nations and local and international relief organizations warned about the negative impact of ECOWAS sanctions on the population of Niger, with food prices rising and limited accessibility to imported food items and other goods. They called on ECOWAS to introduce humanitarian exemptions to the collective sanctions to ensure access to humanitarian assistance services for vulnerable populations. Niger is one of the poorest countries in the world ranking 189 out of 191 in the 2022 UN Human Development Index.

On October 30, the United States announced that Niger will lose privileged access to the US market offered under the African Growth and Opportunity Act (AGOA).

Nigeria

Former Governor of Lagos State Bola Ahmed Tinubu emerged as the winner of Nigeria's closely watched February 2023 presidential election. Despite repeated calls to Nigerian authorities to prioritize accountability for past elections-related abuses and address widespread insecurity, the February elections were blighted by incidents of logistical failures and violence at the polls.

Multiple armed groups continue to kill and jeopardize the livelihood of millions across the country. In the Northwest, gangs of so-called bandits carry out widespread killings, kidnappings, sexual violence, and lootings, while in the Northeast, there has been a resurgence of attacks by the Islamic State West Africa Province (ISWAP), a breakout faction of Boko Haram.

Decades long intercommunal conflict between farmers and herders in the Middle Belt and Northcentral region continue to claim lives, while the authorities struggle to contain the clashes around land and other resources, which are exacerbated by ethnic and religious tensions.

In their responses to the security crisis across the country, security forces continue to be implicated in gross human rights abuses, including indiscriminate airstrikes, while the authorities have repeatedly failed to hold officers responsible for the abuses accountable through the justice system.

High rates of inflation due to the removal of a subsidy on petrol, among other factors, gave rise to an increase in multidimensional poverty and economic inequality. The high inflation rate undermined access to food and other necessities in a country where millions live in extreme poverty without a functional social protection system.

Election-Related Violence

According to the Center for Democracy and Development, a nongovernmental organization (NGO), a total of 109 election-related deaths were recorded across Nigeria in the build-up to the 2023 general elections.

The presidential and federal legislative elections recorded several incidences of violence at the polls, especially in battleground states like Lagos. Voters were exposed to violence by people referred to as "thugs" acting for, or on, behalf of politicians and political parties.

In some cases, voters were injured and stripped of their right to vote without any intervention from security forces.

Violence in the Northwest and Northcentral Regions

In the Northwest, armed gangs of "bandits" continue to carry out widespread killings, kidnappings, sexual violence, and lootings. In February, a bloody confrontation between local vigilantes and bandits led to the killing of over 100 people in Katsina State. In April, at least 80 people, mostly women and children, were kidnapped by bandit gangs in Zamfara State. In July, a video surfaced online where four female college students, whom they had abducted six months earlier, begged the government to pay their ransom so they would not be married off by the bandits.

Intercommunal violence between farmers and herders in the Northcentral region also recorded a high number of deaths. In May, over 100 people were killed in Plateau State. The violence was reportedly in reprisal for farmers killing a herder after he and his cattle had encroached on their land.

A March report by the International Organization for Migration (IOM) documented a total of 1,190,293 internally displaced people in 191,688 households across the 8 states in the Northcentral and Northwest regions because of violence.

Separatist Agitations in the Southeast Region

An ad hoc committee of the House of Representatives investigating communal clashes in Abia State called for the release of Nnamdi Kanu, the leader of the Indigenous People of Biafra (IPOB), a group agitating for the secession of the Southeast region. Kanu was discharged and acquitted of treason and terrorism-related charges by Nigeria's Court of Appeal, but he remains in custody following a further appeal to the Supreme Court by the federal government to challenge this decision.

States in the Southeast sought to put an end to the "sit at home order," introduced by IPOB in 2021, which required citizens in the region to stay at home and for public places to stay closed on Mondays and any other day that is announced, including days Kanu is set to appear in court. Although IPOB says it has suspended the order, gunmen seeking to enforce it continue to kill, maim, and destroy properties of citizens in the region who defy it.

In Enugu, the state government sealed some commercial banks and shops for allegedly observing the Monday sit-at-home order.

Boko Haram Conflict

Communities in Borno State, the epicenter of the Boko Haram conflict, witnessed a resurgence in attacks and kidnappings by armed groups. In March, over 30 fishermen and farmers were gruesomely killed in an attack in Ngala Local Government Area. In June, about 36 people, including farmers, were killed in Dambo, Jere, and Mafa Local Government Areas.

According to a media report, ISWAP, a prominent breakout faction of Boko Haram, imposed a ban on farming, fishing, and herding activities in Marte Local Government Area. The move to halt agricultural activities was apparently to punish the farming communities for spying on them for the military, which carried out aerial bombardment against ISWAP.

Abuses by Security Forces

In January, an erroneous military airstrike in Nasarawa State killed 39 people and injured 6 others. Since 2017, over 300 people are reported to have been killed by airstrikes that the Nigerian air force claimed were intended for bandits or members of Boko Haram and its breakout factions but instead hit civilians. In 2022, the Nigerian air force announced an investigation into accidental airstrikes on civilians but provided no further details.

In July, anti-police brutality protests erupted in Anambra State, following the death of Chidubem Ezenwa in police custody, after allegedly being beaten by police operatives and other inmates. Police said the inmates who beat him up have been arraigned for murder.

Accountability for Serious Crimes

In February, the National Human Rights Commission began an investigation into allegations of forced abortions and infanticide in the Northeast Boko Haram conflict, but it has yet to produce its findings.

Domestic trials for hundreds of Boko Haram suspects have remained postponed since 2018.

The International Criminal Court (ICC) Office of the Prosecutor continued to consider whether to open an investigation into serious crimes committed in Nigeria and indicated plans to decide in 2024.

Freedom of Expression and Media

In May, a Nigerian Court found that the National Broadcasting Commission (NBC), the country's broadcast regulator, has no power to impose fines on broadcast stations. In April, NBC had fined Channels Television 5 million Nigerian naira (about US$6,500) for allegedly violating the NBC code in a program during which a vice presidential candidate called on the authorities not to swear in Bola Tinubu.

Although the Nigerian Constitution guarantees the right to freedom of expression, thought, and conscience, insult to religion remains a criminal offense and Sharia (Islamic law), applicable in 12 northern states, criminalizes blasphemy.

Blasphemy-related accusations and killings remain a concern in northern Nigeria. In June, Usman Buda was attacked and killed by a mob in Sokoto State for alleged blasphemy against the Prophet Mohammed.

Poverty and Inequality

President Tinubu announced the removal of an existing subsidy on fuel during his inauguration in May, resulting in increases in the price of food and other basic necessities. The authorities did not put in any measures to cushion the impact of the petrol subsidy removal, leaving many Nigerians struggling to meet the basic needs of themselves and their families.

The ability of communities to fish and farm continues to be stunted by rampant oil spills while the costs to public health is worsened by oil pollution and the ongoing practice of excessive gas flaring.

In August, President Tinubu announced a $650 million package that included funds to allow for a review of the minimum wage; support for small and medium businesses; and the purchase of gas-powered buses to reduce the cost of transportation, among other things.

Sexual Orientation and Gender Identity

In August, police in Delta State arrested dozens for allegedly participating in a gay wedding at a hotel. The police streamed on Facebook a public parade of the detainees in front of journalists, where they were interrogated regarding the accusations in violation of their rights to fair trial, dignity, and privacy.

A total of 69 people were remanded to prison in connection with the incident and later released on bail pending trial.

In October, 76 people were arrested in Gombe State for allegedly attending a birthday party for gay people. The arrests were conducted by the Nigerian Security and Civil Defense Corps, the country's paramilitary agency, which also alleged that the organizers of the party planned to hold a same-sex wedding.

The Same Sex Marriage Prohibition Act, 2013, punishes same-sex marriage and public displays of same-sex relationships with 14 and 10 years' imprisonment, respectively. It also punishes establishing, supporting, and participating in gay organizations with 10 years in prison.

A 2016 Human Rights Watch report found that, despite no evidence that anyone had been prosecuted or sentenced under the law by that time, the law had served to legitimize abuses against lesbian, gay, bisexual, and transgender (LGBT) people in Nigeria, including extortion, arbitrary arrest, torture, and physical and sexual violence.

The police used the law for the first time in 2019 to prosecute 47 men accused of same-sex public displays of affection in Lagos State. A court dismissed the case because the police failed to appear and present witnesses.

Women's and Girl's Rights

The outcomes of the 2023 elections in Nigeria have continued to raise concerns about the participation and representation of women in politics. Women were elected to only 20 out of 469 federal legislative seats in the National Assembly, which comprises the Senate and the House of Representatives. This is a decline from the already abysmal number of 21 in the previous national elections.

A 2022 report by Gender Strategy Advancement International, a Nigerian NGO, highlights that although women make up 49 percent of Nigeria's population, only 6.7 percent hold positions in government, as women continue to suffer injustices and marginalization resulting from laws, religious and cultural norms, gender stereotypes, and low levels of education, among other things.

The government has yet to adopt proposed amendments to the country's constitution, aimed at fostering women's equality and participation in politics and government leadership, including through affirmative action.

Nigeria continued to have one of the highest rates of maternal mortality in the world, attributable to inadequate and unequitable access to maternal health care and a lack of access to safe and legal abortion. Nigeria also has one of the world's highest rates of child marriage because of poor enforcement of national and state laws.

Disability Rights

In January, then-President Muhammadu Buhari signed the Mental Health Bill into law, replacing the 1958 Lunacy Act. The new bill established some protections for people with mental health conditions, including the right to participate in their treatment plans. It also imposes a ban on chaining people with mental health conditions and aims to expand community-based coverage so more people can access mental health services. Contrary to international human rights standards, the law continues to permit involuntary treatment and allows coercion in other forms, including restraints and seclusion.

Thousands of people with mental health conditions or psychosocial disabilities in Nigeria continue to be shackled, chained, and locked in confined spaces in various facilities across the country, including in some traditional and religious healing centers, state-run rehabilitation centers, and even in some psychiatric hospitals.

Older People's Rights

Following a visit to Nigeria, the United Nations independent expert on the enjoyment of all human rights by older persons said in a July report that ageism and age discrimination are pervasive; poverty in older age is rampant; older people's access to health care is limited; violence against older people is a serious concern, particularly for women and LGBT people; and large numbers of older people are without appropriate care and support in the country.

Foreign Policy

Nigeria condemned the July military coup d'état in neighboring Niger and called for a restoration of democracy in the country. President Tinubu led the Economic Community of West African States (ECOWAS). Although the junta in Niger defied the ultimatum, ECOWAS did not follow up on its threat of military intervention.

North Korea

The Democratic People's Republic of Korea (DPRK, North Korea) remains one of the most repressive countries in the world. A 2014 United Nations Commission of Inquiry (COI) report found that the government committed systematic, widespread, and gross human rights violations that constitute crimes against humanity. Ruled by third-generation totalitarian leader Kim Jong Un, the government maintains fearful obedience by using threats of torture, executions, imprisonment, enforced disappearances, and forced labor. It systematically denies basic liberties, including freedom of expression, association, and religion. It does not tolerate pluralism, and it bans independent media, civil society organizations, and trade unions.

In 2023, the government continued to maintain extreme and unnecessary measures under the pretext of protecting against the Covid-19 pandemic, with deepened isolation and repression; border, trade, and travel restrictions; and strong ideological control. These restrictions severely aggravated the existing food crisis and exacerbated the country's chronic lack of access to medicines, medical supplies, and other necessities. They hurt market activities the population relied on to survive and severely undermined people's ability to make a living in 2023. The impact of the nearly four-year-long Covid-19 nation-wide country lockdown intensified as the country was hit by major droughts in March and April and flooding in August.

The government continued to prioritize weapons development, conducting over 30 missile tests between January and September, including three long-range intercontinental ballistic missiles.

Freedom of Expression and Information

The government does not permit freedom of thought, expression, or information. All media is strictly controlled. Accessing phones, computers, televisions, radios, or media content that is not sanctioned by the government is illegal and considered "anti-socialist behavior" that is punished, including through the use of torture and forced labor. The government regularly cracks down on those accessing unsanctioned media. It also jams Chinese mobile phone services at the border and targets for arrest people for communicating with contacts outside the country.

In January 2023, the government enacted the Pyongyang Cultural Language Protection Act, banning the use of language that is South Korean in style or appears to have foreign influence. The law criminalized communications "in the puppet language," a reference to the South Korean language style, setting punishments of six years or more of forced labor and even the death penalty in some cases. It also encourages the authorities to use public trials and executions to "awaken the masses."

In March and April, authorities reportedly conducted public trials in Ryanggang province under the law. One trial targeted 17 young people for watching unsanctioned videos and using South Korean language. One leader of the group was sentenced to 10 years of forced labor. In another trial, 20 youth athletes were sentenced to three to five years of forced labor for using South Korean vocabulary.

Freedom of Movement

Moving from one province to another, or traveling abroad without prior approval, continued to be illegal. The government maintained heightened enforcement of a ban on "illegal" travel to China through border buffer zones on the northern border to protect against Covid-19. Border guards remained under orders to "unconditionally shoot" anyone entering or leaving without permission. Authorities' strict enforcement of these restrictions severely impacted people's livelihoods and ability to access food, medicines, and other essential goods.

In August, North Korean state media officially announced the reopening of its borders to citizens residing abroad after they were closed in January 2020. North Korea's national airline restarted international flights, and the former North Korean ambassador to China returned to North Korea. In March, authorities allowed some Chinese diplomats to enter the country. However, humanitarian organizations and most diplomats remained unable to return. Informal trade activities stayed banned. Official trade by rail and waterways increased but remained lower than before the Covid-19 pandemic.

Activist networks in China and South Korea that help North Koreans flee their country and transit through China to a safe third country were able to resume activities, but they faced major obstacles due to increased security enforcement and mass surveillance in China. Many North Koreans in China remained hidden in safe houses. The Chinese government continued to seek to detain North Korean asylum seekers and return them to North Korea, violating China's obligations as a state party to the UN Refugee Convention. Many North Koreans detained in China were forcibly returned to North Korea—80 in August, 40 in September, and at least 500 in October—where they almost certainly faced grave abuses for their attempted escape. North Korean law states that leaving the country without permission is a crime of "treachery against the nation," punishable by death.

In 2019, over 1,000 North Korean asylum seekers were resettled in South Korea, but this number declined to 67 in 2022 and only 139 between January and September 2023.

Right to Health

North Korea is one of the poorest countries in the world. The government has constantly struggled with chronic food insecurity. Insufficient domestic food production and the government's prioritization of military and security development made the ability of the North Korean people to get food, medicine, and other necessities almost totally reliant on both official and unofficial trade with China and private product distribution across the country and market activity.

The excessive and unnecessary Covid-19 related restrictions blocked most sources of income for a large majority of the population, reducing their ability to buy any already limited food and basic necessities available in the markets. They adversely impacted the ability of ordinary North Koreans to conduct basic economic activities, generally worsening their rights to food, health, and an adequate standard of living.

There were reports of a mass vaccination campaign and a second round of vaccinations for Covid-19 in North Pyongan province, Nampo port, and Pyongyang in September 2022. However, there are no official numbers of vaccinated people available.

Forced Labor

The North Korean government routinely and systematically requires forced, uncompensated labor from much of its population to sustain its economy. The government's forced labor demands target women through the Women's Union, children at schools, workers at state-owned enterprises or deployed abroad, detainees in short-term hard labor detention centers (*rodong dallyeondae*), and prisoners at long-term ordinary prison camps (*kyohwaso*) and political prison camps.

At some point in their lives, a significant majority of North Koreans must perform unpaid hard labor, often justified by the state as "portrayals of loyalty" to the government. Since punishment for crimes in North Korea is arbitrary and dependent on a person's record of loyalty, personal connections, and ability to pay bribes, the refusal of a government order to work as a "volunteer" can result in severe punishment, including torture and imprisonment. North Korea remains one of only seven UN member states that has not joined the International Labour Organization.

At-Risk Groups under Songbun

North Korea uses *songbun*, a sociopolitical classification system that, in its creation, grouped people into "loyal," "wavering," or "hostile" classes and discriminates against those placed in the lower classes in employment, housing, and education.

Women's and Girls' Rights

In February 2023, Elizabeth Salmon, the UN special rapporteur on North Korea, raised concerns about the disproportionate impact of the Covid-19 restrictions on women and girls, the declining economic participation of women, and the impact on livelihoods since women are the main breadwinners in most families. She also flagged possible increases in domestic violence and economic pressures linked to the pandemic. The government has failed to take any meaningful action to address the country's intense and pervasive women's rights violations, including sexual and gender-based violence, widespread discrimination, and enforcement of rigid gender stereotypes.

Key International Actors

The 2014 COI report recommended the UN Security Council refer the situation in North Korea to the International Criminal Court. In August 2023, the UN High Commissioner of Human Rights restated this recommendation to the UN Security Council, noting its ongoing documentation of crimes and abuses, including crimes against humanity against people held in long-term prison camps (kyohwaso) and short-term detention facilities.

The UN Security Council held an Arria-formula meeting on human rights issues in March 2023 and a formal debate in August, its first discussions on human rights in North Korea since 2017. (The council regularly debates and passes resolutions to address North Korea's weapons proliferation activities.) Due to opposition by China and Russia, the council remained unable to adopt any resolution addressing the situation. The council's separate debates on weapons proliferation in March, May, and June featured minimal discussion of human rights issues.

The UN General Assembly was expected to pass a resolution on North Korea's human rights record in December, as it has repeatedly done since 2007.

South Korea strengthened its commitment to promote human rights in North Korea. The United States government maintained human rights-related sanctions on the North Korean government and on Kim Jong Un and several other officials. In December 2022, the European Union extended human rights-related sanctions on two top government officials and the country's public prosecutor's office. The EU continued to lead on bringing resolutions on North Korea at the UN General Assembly and UN Human Rights Council. Japan continued to demand the return of Japanese citizens whom North Korea abducted in the 1970s and 1980s. Some Japanese civil society groups allege the number of abductees is much higher than reported.

CENTRAL PRISON & CORRECTIONAL
FACILITY KARACHI
NELSON
HUMAN
RIGHTS
WATCH
"A Nightmare for Everyone"
The Health Crisis in Pakistan's Prisons

Pakistan

Pakistan's political and economic crises deepened in 2023. Following a similar playbook as its predecessors, the government of Prime Minister Shehbaz Sharif clamped down on the media, nongovernmental organizations (NGOs), and political opposition. The authorities used draconian counterterrorism and sedition laws to intimidate peaceful critics. The government's term ended in August, and an interim government headed by Caretaker Prime Minister Anwar Kakar took over. Elections previously scheduled for November were delayed due to an incomplete census and constituency delimitation process.

Blasphemy-related violence against religious minorities, fostered in part by government persecution and discriminatory laws, intensified. Attacks by Islamist militants, notably the Tehrik-i-Taliban Pakistan (TTP) and Islamic State of Khorasan Province (ISKP), targeting law enforcement officials and religious minorities, killed dozens of people in 2023.

With poverty, inflation, and unemployment soaring, Pakistan faced one of the worst economic crises in its history, jeopardizing millions of people's rights to health, food, and an adequate standard of living. The insistence of the International Monetary Fund (IMF) on austerity and the removal of subsidies without adequate compensatory measures resulted in additional hardship for low-income groups. Pakistan remained exceedingly vulnerable to climate change and faced rates of warming considerably above the global average, making extreme climate events more frequent and intense.

In a positive development, the Sindh government attempted to rehabilitate those who suffered catastrophic losses in the 2022 floods by providing land titles and funds to construct houses for people who were previously landless. As of early August, there were 2.1 million eligible beneficiaries of this program.

Freedom of Expression and Attacks on Civil Society Groups

Government threats and attacks on the media created a climate of fear among journalists and civil society groups, with many resorting to self-censorship. Authorities pressured or threatened media outlets not to criticize government institutions or the judiciary.

In the violence following the arrest of former Prime Minister Imran Khan, members of his political party, Pakistan Tehrik-i-Insaaf (PTI), attacked the offices of public broadcaster Radio Pakistan and the state-owned news agency Associated Press of Pakistan in Peshawar.

On May 11, journalist Imran Riaz Khan was arrested as he was attempting to take a flight to Oman. Khan returned home on September 25; he has not been presented in court at any time since his arrest.

Pakistan's sedition law, based on a colonial-era British provision, is vague and overly broad and has often been used against political opponents and journalists. In March, the Lahore High Court declared the sedition law unconstitutional. The government filed an appeal in the Supreme Court against the decision and the appeal remains pending. However, the authorities continued to use sedition prosecutions. In August, Imaan Mazari-Hazir, a lawyer, and Ali Wazir, a political activist, were charged with sedition for a speech made in Islamabad. Hazir and Wazir were subsequently granted bail.

In August, the police arrested Fayaz Zafar, a reporter for the Pashto-language broadcaster Voice of America Deewa (VOA Deewa), following a magistrate's order accusing him of using social media to spread "fake, offensive and hatred contents to defame and incite the public" against the government and law enforcement agencies. Zafar was later released.

NGOs reported intimidation, harassment, and surveillance of various groups by government authorities. The government used its regulation of INGOs in Pakistan policy to impede the registration and functioning of international humanitarian and human rights groups.

Freedom of Religion and Belief

The Pakistani government did not amend or repeal blasphemy law provisions that have provided a pretext for violence against religious minorities and left them vulnerable to arbitrary arrest and prosecution. The death penalty is mandatory for blasphemy, and dozens of people remained on death row as of late 2023. Since 1990, at least 65 people have reportedly been killed in Pakistan over claims of blasphemy.

Members of the Ahmadiyya religious community continue to be a major target for prosecutions under blasphemy laws and specific anti-Ahmadi laws. Militant groups and the Islamist political party Tehreek-e-Labbaik (TLP) accuse Ahmadis of "posing as Muslims." Pakistan's penal code also treats "posing as Muslims" as a criminal offense. On July 25, a mob vandalized an Ahmadiyya place of worship in Karachi, Sindh province. On August 18, a mob attacked a factory owned by an Ahmadi in Lahore, accusing him of blasphemy. Instead of prosecuting the attackers, the authorities charged eight members of Ahmadi community with blasphemy.

On August 16, 2023, several hundred people attacked a Christian settlement in Faisalabad district, Punjab province, after two members of the community were accused of committing "blasphemy." The mob, armed with stones and sticks, vandalized several churches, dozens of houses, and a cemetery. While the police arrested 130 people alleged to have been involved in the attacks, residents told local rights activists that hours before the attack, the police warned them a mob was coming but claimed they could do nothing to stop it.

Violence against Women and Girls

Violence against women and girls—including rape, murder, acid attacks, domestic violence, denial of education, sexual harassment at work, and child and forced marriage—is a serious problem throughout Pakistan. Human rights defenders estimate that roughly 1,000 women are murdered in so-called "honor killings" every year.

The United Nations Children's Fund (UNICEF) estimates that 18.9 million girls in Pakistan are married before the age of 18 and 4.6 million before 15. Many married girls are forced into dangerous pregnancies at a young age and pregnancies that are too closely spaced. Women from religious minority communities remain particularly vulnerable to forced marriage. The government did little to stop such early and forced marriages.

There was nationwide outrage after a woman was raped at gunpoint in a park in Islamabad on February 2. Two weeks later, the Islamabad police claimed that both alleged perpetrators were killed in an exchange of gunfire while the police attempted to arrest them.

In Punjab province, 10,365 cases of violence against women were reported to the police in the first four months of 2023, according to a local NGO. The actual number of incidents is likely to be much higher given barriers to reporting, harmful social norms, and ineffective and harmful responses by the police. Pakistan's conviction rate for rape is less than 3 percent.

Children's Rights

Over 6 million primary school-age children and 13 million secondary school-age children in Pakistan were out of school, most of them girls. Human Rights Watch found that girls miss school for reasons including lack of schools, costs associated with studying, child marriage, harmful child labor, and gender discrimination.

Employment of child domestic workers remains prevalent despite attempts to prohibit it. In July, the case of Rizwana, a 14-year-old child brutally tortured for months while employed by a judge's family, spotlighted the issue of abuse and mistreatment of child domestic workers. In February, an 11-year-old child domestic worker, Qabool, was beaten to death by his employer in Karachi.

Child sexual abuse remains common. The children's rights organization Sahil reported an average of over 12 cases daily of child sexual abuse across Pakistan for the first 6 months of 2023.

Disability Rights

A lack of awareness about mental health in Pakistani society contributes to the abuse of those with psychosocial disabilities (mental health conditions. Prisoners who ask for mental health support are often mocked and denied services. The prison system lacks mental health professionals, and prison authorities tend to view any report of a mental health condition with suspicion. Psychological assessments for new prisoners are either perfunctory or not done at all. The prevalence of the use of solitary confinement in Pakistani prisons poses additional risks for people with psychosocial disabilities.

Terrorism, Counterterrorism, and Law Enforcement Abuses

The TTP, Al-Qaeda, the Balochistan Liberation Army (BLA), the ISKP, and their affiliates carried out suicide bombings and other indiscriminate attacks against security personnel that caused hundreds of civilian deaths and injuries during the year. According to a Pakistani think tank, Pakistan Institute for Conflict and Security Studies (PICSS), there were 99 militant attacks in August, the highest number of attacks in month since 2014.

Violence swept across Pakistan on May 9, 2023, after the police arrested former Prime Minister Imran Khan on corruption charges. Many of Khan's supporters attacked police officers and set fire to ambulances, police vehicles, and schools. Among the places targeted were the military headquarters in Rawalpindi and houses of senior military officials. Following the clashes, the police arrested thousands of members of Khan's political party, PTI, on charges of criminal intimidation, rioting, and assault on government officials. Many were charged under vague and overbroad laws prohibiting rioting and creating threats to public order; those accused of breaking and entering into restricted access military installations were tried in military courts violating principles of due process and fair trial.

Sexual Orientation and Gender Identity

Same-sex sexual conduct between men remains a criminal offense under Pakistan's criminal code, placing men who have sex with men and transgender women at a higher risk of police abuse and other forms of violence and discrimination.

Transgender women in Pakistan, particularly in Khyber-Pakhtunkhwa province, remained under attack. In May, the Federal Shariat Court ruled that provisions of the Transgender Act 2018 relating the right to being legally recognized by their self-perceived gender identity and the right of inheritance for transgender people were "un-Islamic." This ruling caused great apprehension in the transgender community. The appeal against the Federal Shariat Court decision remained pending in the Supreme Court by the end of the year.

The Sindh Human Rights Commission, an independent statutory body, issued guidance to police to stop harassing and arresting transgender people. The guidance said that offenses related to poverty and homelessness should be decriminalized, an important step toward changing discriminatory laws, policies, and public attitudes in Sindh province.

Refugees

In October, the government gave a 28-day deadline for "illegal immigrants" to leave the country, warning that law enforcement agencies would forcibly deport them. According to the Pakistani authorities, there are 1.73 million unregistered Afghans living in the country. The government justified the decision to forcibly deport Afghans by claiming that Afghan nationals were involved in most of the suicide bombing attacks in Pakistan in 2023. The UN High Commissioner for Refugees (UNHCR) responded to this in a statement saying, "any refugee return must be voluntary and without any pressure to ensure protection for those seeking safety." The UN High Commissioner for Human Rights and UN independent human rights experts also raised concerns that Afghans in Pakistan have been subjected to arrests, exploitation, and undignified treatment.

In 2023, Pakistani authorities continued to intimidate and harass Afghans living in Pakistan. Undocumented Afghans remained vulnerable to abuse by police and district administrations and faced difficulties in accessing employment and education.

Economic and Social Rights

In 2023, depreciating local currency, skyrocketing inflation, and the removal of subsidies for electricity and fuel without adequate compensatory measures made it difficult for many people in Pakistan to realize their economic and social rights. Pakistan's central bank's foreign exchange reserves decreased to a historic low of US$3 billion in January, an amount covering fewer than three weeks of imports. In July, Pakistan reached an agreement with the IMF for $3 billion that mandated the government remove energy and fuel subsidies, move to a market-based exchange rate, and increase taxes. This resulted in widespread protests against higher electricity bills, inflation, and food shortages.

The economic crisis came amid the devastating economic cost of the 2022 floods.

Nearly 37 percent of Pakistan's 230 million people faced food insecurity as of 2018, yet only 8.9 million families received assistance to mitigate the impact of rampant inflation.

Following the release of a Human Rights Watch report documenting the barriers to accessing health care in Pakistani prisons, including for prisoners with disabilities, Prime Minister Shehbaz Sharif ordered measures to improve sanitation and access to health care in Lahore central prison, including a dedicated hospital. He also vowed to initiate prison reforms throughout the country.

According to the Federal Ombudsman Secretariat for Protection Against Harassment, statistics show that rates of sexual harassment at work have increased, with women disproportionately impacted. Despite the prevalence of sexual harassment at work, the government has not ratified the International Labour Organization Violence and Harassment Convention (C190), which requires comprehensive protections to end violence and harassment, including gender-based violence, at work.

Key International Actors

In July, the European Union proposed extending Pakistan's Generalised Scheme of Preferences Plus (GSP+) status by another four years, enabling Pakistan to enjoy trade preferences and access to the European market.

In July, United States Secretary of State Antony Blinken and Pakistani Foreign Minister Bilawal Bhutto met, noting "positive momentum" in Pakistani-US relations and agreeing to remain "constructively engaged to promote peace, security and development."

Also in July, Human Rights Watch urged Pakistan to make a submission to the International Court of Justice (ICJ) on the legal consequences of Israel's prolonged occupation of the West Bank and Gaza. In August, Pakistan made a formal submission on the subject to the ICJ.

Pakistan and China deepened their extensive economic and political ties in 2023, and work continued on the China-Pakistan Economic Corridor, a project consisting of the construction of roads, railways, and energy pipelines.

Papua New Guinea

Although a resource-rich country, the World Bank estimates that almost 40 percent of the population of Papua New Guinea (PNG) lives in poverty, with only 20.9 percent having access to electricity. Most people in PNG live without consistent access to clean water. James Marape is now into his second term as prime minister, and despite promising to address rampant corruption and discrimination against women, PNG's human rights record has not improved.

Violence that started during the 2022 general elections persisted in the Highland regions in 2023. Since the elections, conflict over resources in other regions has resulted in more than 400 deaths and displaced over 20,000 people. The increase in violence in recent years has been attributed to the widespread trade of guns and other weapons as well as the weak rule of law in the country. Gunmen are available for hire to carry out violent, lethal attacks. In August, a video went viral showing the naked corpses of three mercenaries being dragged behind a truck as people cheered.

On September 27, the National Parliament of PNG took a positive step forward in addressing gender-based violence at work by ratifying the International Labour Organization (ILO) Violence and Harassment Convention (C190), which requires comprehensive protections to end violence and harassment, including gender-based violence, at work.

Women's and Girls' Rights

PNG remains a dangerous place to be a woman or girl. Over 1.5 million people experience gender-based violence each year. PNG laws designed to protect women and children, including the Family Protection Act 2013 and the Lukautim Pikinini (Child Welfare) Act 2015, are rarely enforced. Initiatives such as Family Sexual and Violence Units within the police force remain limited in number and capacity, a problem compounded by a dire lack of services in communities for gender-based violence survivors.

Violence and lawlessness have exacerbated pervasive sexual and gender-based violence in PNG. In June, in the village of Walagu in Hela Province, women and girls as young as 12 were kidnapped and sexually assaulted en masse by a gang thought to be retaliating for the police's response to another kidnapping in February. Addressing these abuses is complicated by the geography of the highlands and limited phone reception, and at time of writing, no arrests had been made.

PNG has one of the highest maternal mortality rates in the region. The risk of maternal death is increased by limited access to hospitals, with over 80 percent of the population living outside of urban centers. Current data reported by health centers indicates that 171 out of every 100,000 women die giving birth, but the number could be up to three times higher. The government has failed to take effective action to end child marriage; 27 percent of girls and 4 percent of boys are married before age 18.

In May, it was discovered that the Department for Community Development and Religion had used 2.5 million Kina (about US$678,000) earmarked for measures to combat gender-based violence for travel and other miscellaneous expenses.

Also in May, the Parliamentary Committee on Gender Equality and Women's Empowerment (GEWE) heard testimonies from civil society groups and discussed efforts to combat gender-based violence and violence based on accusations of sorcery, though it remains to be seen whether its findings will have any effect on the status of women and girls in the country.

Police Abuse and Corruption

PNG police are severely understaffed, chronically underfunded, and often lack resources such as petrol, stationery, and vehicles. There is about 1 police officer per 1,845 people, which is far lower than the ratio of 1 officer to every 450 people that the United Nations recommends.

In August, police in Enga Province were authorized to use lethal force to quell violence that killed up to 70 people in July and August. This raised concerns that the unit that had been mobilized on "shoot-to-kill" orders would aggravate the situation, especially given the PNG police's long record of violence with impunity.

Sexual Orientation and Gender Identity

Male same-sex relations are punishable by up to 14 years' imprisonment under PNG's criminal code. While there is little information on actual convictions, the law is sometimes used as a pretext by officials and employers to harass or extort money from lesbian, gay, bisexual, and transgender (LGBT) people in PNG.

In June, Prime Minister Marape confirmed that his administration does not intend to repeal the laws criminalizing male homosexuality, maintaining that PNG's current legal framework is enough to protect the rights of its citizens. The same month, the United States embassy flew a pride flag, prompting outrage from the general public. In response, Marape sent a letter to the embassy reminding it of what he called PNG's values surrounding homosexuality as a majority Christian country.

Children's Rights to Health and Education

PNG has an underfunded health system, and 1 in 13 children die each year, mostly from preventable diseases. Rural children are twice as likely to die before their fifth birthday compared to their urban counterparts.

In 2020 (the latest year for which data is available), the completion rate was only 59 percent for primary education and 30 percent for lower secondary. One-third of the schools in Porgera, Enga Province, remain closed due to the violence persisting in the region since the 2022 elections.

Freedom of Speech

In February, PNG's Department of Information and Communications Technology released a draft of a new National Media Development Policy that could threaten press freedom if passed. There are concerns about the draft law's inclusion of a clause that would allow the government to punish journalists and media organizations that create content that is against the country's development objectives, which have been exacerbated by Prime Minister Marape's ongoing criticism of the press since his re-election last year.

Disability Rights

People with disabilities are often unable to participate in community life or work because of lack of accessibility, stigma, and other barriers. Children with disabilities in PNG face abuse, discrimination, and a wide range of barriers to education. Access to mental health services and other support services are limited, and many people with psychosocial disabilities and their families often consider traditional healers to be their only option. Although PNG has developed a national disability policy, the government has yet to pass comprehensive disability legislation.

Asylum Seekers and Refugees

While the Australian government formally withdrew from offshore processing in PNG, over 75 people remain in Port Moresby, waiting to be resettled. In July, parliamentary documents revealed that Australia agreed to pay PNG to provide welfare to the refugees. The Australian government has refused to disclose the terms of the agreement, including how much money it is paying PNG.

Refugees and asylum seekers in PNG endure violence and harassment, with little protection from authorities. Medical facilities have proven unable to cope with the complex medical needs of asylum seekers, particularly their mental health needs.

Key International Actors

US Secretary of State Antony Blinken visited PNG in May to sign two cooperation agreements that would allow the US to deploy troops to PNG in an emergency and board PNG ships to help patrol the waters for trafficking and unregulated fishing activities. The same month, Indian Prime Minister Narendra Modi also visited PNG for the third Forum for India-Pacific Islands Cooperation. Following the first Korea-Pacific Islands Summit at the end of May, South Korean President Yoon Suk-yeol agreed to expand cooperation with 17 Pacific countries, including PNG.

PNG is Australia's closest neighbor and biggest aid recipient. In the 2024 fiscal year, it will receive 500 million Australian dollars (or approximately US$323 million) from Australia. At time of writing, PNG and Australia were still negotiating the terms of their defense agreement.

In September, PNG became the fifth country to open an embassy to Israel in West Jerusalem.

Peru

Years of political instability worsened in December 2022 when then-President Pedro Castillo attempted to close Congress, take over the judiciary, and rule by decree in what amounted to a failed coup. Congress removed him, and Vice President Dina Boluarte became president. Protests erupted throughout the country, mainly calling for early elections. Security forces responded with disproportionate force. From December 2022 through March 2023, 50 protesters and bystanders were killed and more than 1,300 people were injured, including hundreds of police officers.

Human Rights Watch identified serious flaws in the initial investigations of the killings. The Boluarte administration has failed to take measures to reform law enforcement so that abuses do not happen again.

Members of Congress eliminated checks on Congress' power, undermining independent institutions and rights protections. Congress arbitrarily removed a top prosecutor from office and initiated a "summary" process to replace the National Board of Justice. It named an ombudsperson without human rights expertise and sought to erode the independence of the National Electoral Tribunal.

Groups involved in illegal mining, logging, land grabbing, and drug trafficking continue to destroy Peru's Amazon and to threaten and attack its defenders.

Protest-Related Violence and Abuses

After Castillo's failed coup, thousands of people took to the streets, mostly rural workers and Indigenous people in the south. While most protests were peaceful, there were incidents of grave violence. Roadblocks set up by protesters contributed to the deaths of 11 people, including 2 children, who could not reach hospitals or who had car accidents, the Ombudsperson's Office reported.

The response by the military and police was indiscriminate, disproportionate, and brutal. Security forces fired assault rifles and handguns at unarmed protesters and bystanders. Fifty people, including eight children, were killed, the vast majority by gunshot wounds. One police officer was killed in unclear circumstances.

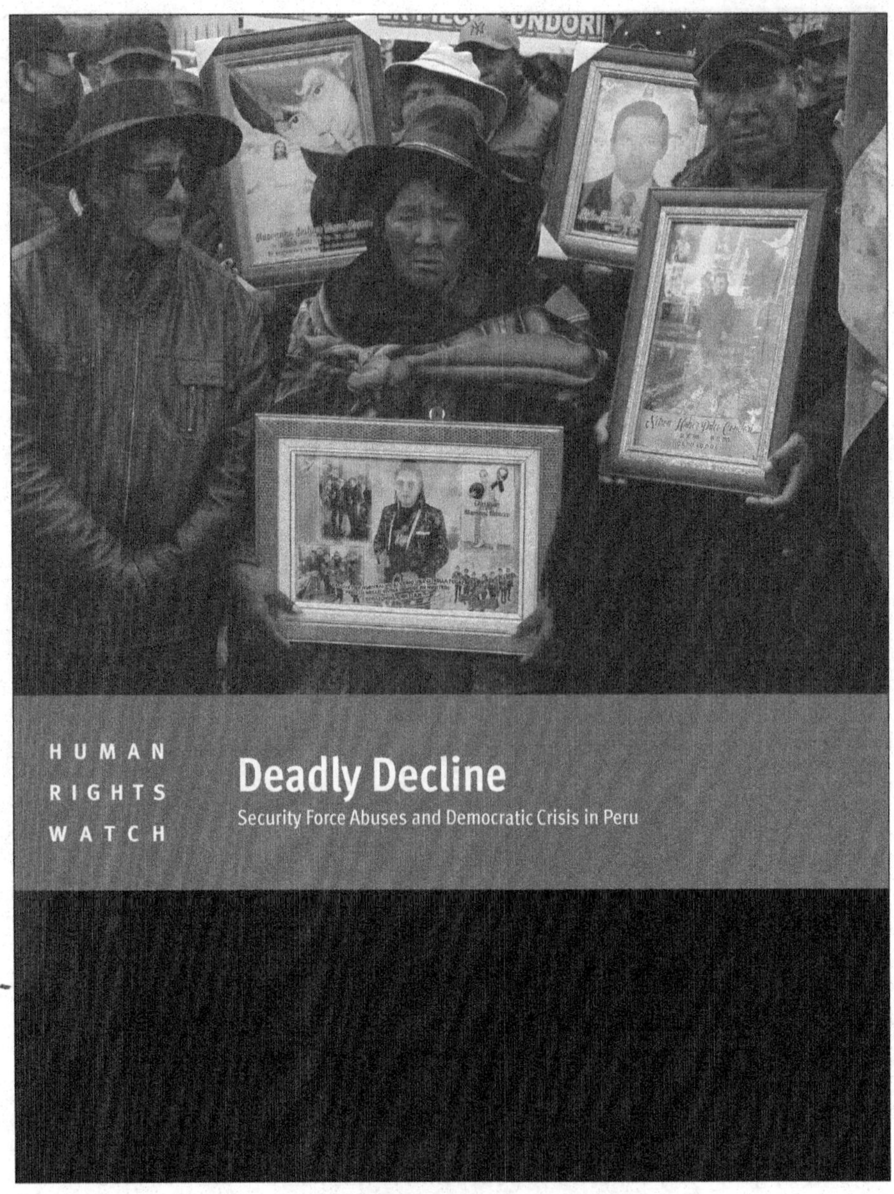
HUMAN
RIGHTS
WATCH
Deadly Decline
Security Force Abuses and Democratic Crisis in Peru

Government officials insinuated the protesters were "terrorists" and dismissed or denied the abuses, failing to take action to prevent them.

Prosecutors failed to collect key initial evidence of human rights violations. In March, the attorney general created a special group of prosecutors to investigate the cases based in the capital, Lima.

In June, the minister of defense said that 32 military officers had been disciplined for their actions in Ayacucho, where 10 people were killed in the December protests, but he did not disclose the measures taken. In July, the Interior Ministry told Human Rights Watch that police had been disciplined in just one case, for violence against Indigenous women in Lima.

As of October, the investigation into the killing of two protesters during protests in Lima in 2020, in which police also used excessive force, appeared stalled.

Threats to Democratic Institutions

Congress has repeatedly taken actions to undermine other democratic institutions and to limit lawmakers' accountability.

In 2022, Congress appointed six of the seven members of the Constitutional Tribunal in a process that lacked transparency and clear criteria. In February 2023, the tribunal issued a ruling shielding Congress from almost any judicial oversight.

The tribunal allowed the selection of a new ombudsperson to go forward despite procedural concerns. In May, Congress elected Josué Gutiérrez, a former congressman without any human rights expertise who had made homophobic statements during the selection process.

The Constitutional Tribunal also opened the door for Congress, many of whose members had falsely claimed that the 2021 elections were fraudulent, to coopt the National Elections Tribunal by asking lawmakers to approve a constitutional amendment to grant them the power to impeach members of the elections tribunal. As of September, there were four proceedings in Congress to try to remove Jorge Luis Salas Arenas, president of the National Elections Tribunal. In September, the Inter-American Court of Human Rights granted Salas Arenas provisional measures, citing risks to his life and personal integrity, and ordered the government to strengthen measures taken to protect Salas and investigate the threats against him.

In a serious blow to judicial independence, in June, Congress removed Zoraida Ávalos, a former attorney general, from her job as a prosecutor for five years for not charging former President Castillo with corruption. Ávalos had opened the first corruption investigations against sitting presidents ever—Martín Vizcarra and Castillo—but did not charge them because she concluded a constitutional provision barred it. The National Board of Justice, the body in charge of appointing and removing prosecutors and judges, said Ávalos' decision was based on her legal analysis of the case as part of her autonomy as a prosecutor.

In September, Congress approved a "summary" process to investigate and remove the members of the National Board of Justice, claiming that the board's statement in defense of judicial independence in the Ávalos case interfered with Congress' powers, among other accusations. If members of Congress take control of the board, they can appoint new heads of the agencies that manage elections and the electoral registry in early 2024.

The board also came under attack from the attorney general, Patricia Benavides, who obtained judicial injunctions to block the board from investigating her for allegedly shielding her sister, a judge, in a corruption investigation; irregularities in transfers of prosecutors; and failure to produce her Ph.D. and master's theses.

Corruption

Corruption is a major factor in the deterioration of public institutions, deficient public services, and environmental destruction in Peru. Five former presidents have been charged with corruption. President Boluarte is under investigation for having allegedly received illicit contributions to her political campaign. As of March 2023, at least 37 of the 130 members of Congress were under criminal investigation for corruption and other offenses.

In October, the authority in charge of prosecutors' disciplinary matters suspended a top anti-corruption prosecutor for eight months for statements he had made to the press.

Economic and Social Rights

As of 2022, 27 percent of the population lived in poverty, a sharp increase from 20 percent in 2019 (pre-pandemic), official data showed. People living in extreme poverty—unable to afford their most basic food needs—amounted to 5 percent of the population in 2022, compared to 3 percent in 2019. Children, people living in rural areas, and those who self-report as Black or Indigenous are disproportionately affected.

One out of five rural children between 12 and 16 years old did not attend school as of 2022, official data showed. In urban areas, the ratio falls to one out of seven.

As of March, official data showed that 68 percent of workers in cities and 95 percent in rural areas worked in the informal labor market, where they lacked formal labor and social protections, such as employer-based social insurance including for unemployment, disability, and pension.

Women's and Girls' Rights

Gender-based violence is a significant problem. The Ombudsperson's Office reported 112 femicides—defined as the killing of a woman or girl in certain contexts, including domestic violence—from January through August 2023. There were 137 femicides in 2022 and 146 in 2021.

Women, girls, and other pregnant people can legally access abortions only when a pregnancy threatens their life or health; even then, many face barriers. In June, the UN Committee on the Rights of the Child found Peru responsible for violating the rights of an Indigenous girl who had become forcibly pregnant at 13, after years of sexual abuse by her father. Authorities denied her an abortion and, after she miscarried, filed abortion charges against her.

In March, the Constitutional Tribunal ordered the free distribution of emergency contraception pills after a yearslong fight by women's rights groups.

Environment and Indigenous Peoples' Rights

Peru lost 161,000 hectares of primary forest in 2022, according to the latest data available and compiled by Global Forest Watch. Illegal logging and mining, land grabbing, and coca cultivation for drug trafficking are driving the destruction of the Amazon. Illegal use of mercury for gold mining, often smuggled in across the border from Bolivia, is contaminating waterways, likely impacting human health, and making it harder for children to learn at school, officials told Human Rights Watch.

Groups involved in those illegal activities routinely threaten and attack forest defenders. In April, Indigenous leader Santiago Contoricón Antúnez was murdered in Junín department. His community attributed the killing to his opposition to drug cartels that move cocaine through their territory. In May, Percy García Serpa was shot in the back and killed in a rural community near Lima. He opposed land grabbing and had received death threats, his relatives and colleagues said.

In 2021, the government created an inter-ministerial mechanism for the protection of human rights defenders, but as of August 2023, it was only staffed by six people. The mechanism has no funding of its own; ministries have to cover the cost of protection measures within their purview. As of August, the Interior Ministry, which is in charge of police, had yet to develop a protocol for coordination with the mechanism. Environmental defenders told Human Rights Watch that protection measures were very insufficient.

Lawmakers have voted twice—in 2020 and 2022—not to ratify the Escazú Agreement, a Latin American treaty promoting access to information, justice, and public participation in environmental matters and the protection of environmental defenders.

Attacks on Journalists

The right-wing group La Resistencia publicized addresses and met outside the homes of journalists and the offices of human rights defenders. The group's members have insulted, harassed, and physically attacked journalists.

Charges of defamation have repeatedly been used to stifle reporting in the public interest in Peru, the Committee to Protect Journalists said. For instance, since late 2018, journalists Paola Ugaz and Pedro Salinas have faced prosecution on charges of defamation and other offenses in cases connected to their reporting on sexual abuse scandals involving a Catholic lay organization.

Sexual Orientation and Gender Identity

In a ruling published in April, the Inter-American Court of Human Rights found Peru responsible for violating a gay man's rights after he faced discrimination by a commercial establishment and Peruvian authorities. The court ordered Peru to create a guide on lesbian, gay, bisexual, and transgender (LGBT) rights in the provision of services and to use it to train authorities and to monitor companies' compliance with principles of equality and nondiscrimination.

There is no simple administrative process for legal gender recognition for transgender people in Peru.

Refugees, Asylum Seekers, and Migrants

In January, Congress modified Peru's immigration law, making it easier for authorities to deny migrants entry and transit; adding vague obligations for foreigners, such as to "respect Peru's historic and cultural legacy"; and erecting obstacles to migrants' access to housing. The Ombudsperson's Office filed a lawsuit opposing the changes, as they "criminalize migration, validate discrimination, and affect foreigners' fundamental rights."

In January, roadblocks set up by protesters contributed to the deaths, from respiratory ailments, of six Haitian adults and a child, the International Organization for Migration (IOM) said. The roadblocks forced the Haitians to stay in a high-altitude border town with low nighttime temperatures and a scarcity of food.

In April, hundreds of migrants from Venezuela and other countries were stuck at the border between Chile and Peru, after Peruvian guards blocked them from entering, allegedly due to their lack of proper documentation. Problems continued in August and September.

As of May, more than 1.52 million Venezuelan refugees, asylum seekers, and migrants were staying in Peru, according to UN agencies and the Inter-American Commission of Human Rights. From 2016 to July 2023, Peru received 608,816 asylum requests from Venezuelans and had granted asylum to 4,903 people—fewer than 1 percent of asylum seekers—according to data the Ministry of Foreign Affairs provided to Human Rights Watch.

Confronting Past Abuses

After the Truth and Reconciliation Commission's 2003 final report, which estimated that almost 70,000 people were killed or disappeared during the conflict, the Attorney General's Office opened 53 cases concerning human rights abuses during the armed conflict between the government and armed groups, including Shining Path, from 1980 through 2000. In August, the Ombudsperson's Office said that 23 cases ended with at least one conviction, 8 with acquittals, and 22 remained in process.

Disability Rights

In June, Congress passed a law—without consulting organizations of people with disabilities—that recognizes the need to regulate personal assistance services for people with disabilities. The law does not create a clear obligation on the part of the state to ensure personal assistant services and conflates support for independent living with care.

Key International Actors

International responses to former President Castillo's failed coup were inconsistent. Chile, Ecuador, the United States, the European Union, Canada, and others spoke up for the rule of law. But Argentina, Bolivia, Colombia, and Mexico issued a joint statement defending the former president and made no reference to his illegal attempt to dissolve Congress and take over the judiciary.

The EU and Chile publicly condemned abuses by security forces during the protests. It was not until March that the US, in its annual country report, included a reference to "arbitrary or unlawful killings" by security forces.

Philippines

The human rights situation in the Philippines remains dire amid extrajudicial killings, attacks against political activists and journalists, and abuses committed during the armed conflict with the 54-year-old communist insurgency. The government has increasingly constricted democratic space by using the justice system to target leftist activist groups.

Nonetheless, President Ferdinand Marcos Jr.'s measured rhetoric about human rights is a stark contrast to the unabashedly anti-rights positions of his predecessor, Rodrigo Duterte, whose catastrophic "war on drugs" killed thousands. In several international forums, Marcos has affirmed his administration's commitment to human rights. The government has likewise begun engaging more openly with international actors, for example, by inviting UN human rights experts to the country.

The Philippine government still refuses to cooperate with the investigation of the International Criminal Court (ICC) into possible crimes against humanity committed in the context of Duterte's "drug war" and when Duterte was mayor of Davao City. In January 2023, the ICC's pre-trial chamber authorized the Office of the Prosecutor to resume its investigation following a request by the Philippine government to defer the inquiry to national authorities. The government appealed, contending that the ICC judges erred by dismissing Manila's position that the court no longer has jurisdiction over the situation in the Philippines after its withdrawal from the court's founding treaty took effect in March 2019. In July 2023, the ICC appeals chamber confirmed the prosecutor's resumption of the investigation, paving the way for the next step toward justice for the thousands of victims of extrajudicial killings and their families in the government's "war on drugs."

Extrajudicial Killings

Marcos has not ended Duterte's "drug war." Law enforcement officers and their agents continue to conduct raids using the former president's orders as justification. The official "drug war" death toll from July 1, 2016, to May 31, 2022, is

6,252; unidentified gunmen murdered thousands more. The Philippine government has not updated its statistics since May 2022.

While the killings have significantly dropped overall since Marcos took office on June 30, 2022, they have continued. According to monitoring by the University of the Philippines Third World Studies Center, more drug-related killings occurred in the first year of the Marcos administration than in the Duterte administration's final year. As of November 15, 471 people have been killed in drug-related violence under Marcos, perpetrated both by law enforcers and unidentified assailants. Most of these cases, as with the previous ones, remain uninvestigated. In Davao City, a hotspot of drug-related killings according to the University of the Philippines' data, police have perpetrated most killings.

Many extrajudicial killings have taken place in the context of political violence, particularly linked to elections. On March 4, ex-military men stormed the residence of Negros Oriental governor Roel Degamo and killed him and nine others. A political rival has been implicated in the massacre, which is the worst incident of political violence in the Philippines since the Maguindanao Massacre in 2009.

Journalists have also been targeted, with 4 killed so far under Marcos, bringing the death toll since 1986, when democracy was restored, up to 177. The latest fatality reported was Cresenciano Bunduquin, a broadcaster in Oriental Mindoro province who was gunned down on May 31. The killing in October 2022 of popular radio commentator Percy Mabasa remains unsolved.

Insurgency-related killings have noticeably worsened, particularly on the island of Negros, which has long been a hotbed of the communist movement. In June, a couple and their two children were killed by gunmen in Negros Occidental; relatives and witnesses said the military had earlier accused the couple of working for the communist New People's Army (NPA).

The security forces have also killed children during operations. In August, police shot dead Jemboy Baltazar, 17; witnesses alleged the police claimed Baltazar had illegal drugs to justify the shooting. Also in August, a police officer shot dead John Frances Ompad, also 17.

Attacks on Activists, Unionists, and Journalists

Incidents of "red-tagging" by the authorities and government supporters and pro-government media continued. Getting red-tagged is often a prelude to physical attack, raising fears among activists and constricting democratic space. Government actors have red-tagged activists, unionists, environment defenders, Indigenous leaders, teachers, students, and journalists.

In May, the hosts of a pro-government TV program accused the National Union of Journalists of the Philippines and its chair, Jonathan de Santos, of working with communist insurgents. In June, several activists and environmental defenders in the northern Philippines sought protection from the Supreme Court after they were red-tagged by the military and the police. Some victims of red-tagging are bringing lawsuits in response: In July, Carol Araullo, a longtime leftist activist, sued the hosts of a pro-government TV show for red-tagging her and her family. In September, her son, journalist Atom Araullo, also brought a case.

In some cases, the red-tagging has turned into "terrorist"-tagging, with the government using the country's harsh and overbroad Anti-Terror Act to target civil society organizations, accusing them of terrorist financing. In September, the military filed a complaint against CERNET, a nongovernmental organization (NGO) in the central Philippines, for allegedly providing funds to the New People's Army, a charge the group denied.

The targeting of unions and labor activists was the focus of a high-level mission of the International Labour Organization in January. The mission denounced red-tagging and other forms of harassment against trade unionists. In April, President Marcos signed Executive Order 23, which promises protection to workers and respect for their right to organize.

There was some good news, however. Former senator Leila de Lima, a prominent political prisoner and staunch human rights activist, was released in November after a court granted her bail in the last drug case filed against her by the Duterte administration. She was arrested and detained nearly seven years ago on bogus drug charges. In September, a Manila court acquitted Nobel Peace Prize laureate and Rappler CEO Maria Ressa of tax evasion charges, leaving two cases pending in courts against her and her colleagues.

Enforced Disappearances

Enforced disappearances remain a persistent human rights violation in the Philippines. Two infamous enforced disappearance cases—of peasant activist Jonas Burgos in 2007 and two University of the Philippines students, Karen Empeno and Sherlyn Cadapan, in 2006—remain unresolved.

In January, labor rights activists Dyan Gumanao and Armand Dayoha were abducted in broad daylight at a port in Cebu City. They surfaced a few days later and accused the police of kidnapping them and mistreating them.

In April, activists Gene Roz Jamil "Bazoo" de Jesus and Dexter Capuyan were allegedly abducted by government operatives in Taytay, just southeast of Manila. They remain missing.

In September, two environmental activists, Jonila Castro and Jhed Tamano, went missing. The government later publicly presented them and claimed that they were NPA fighters who had surrendered. But the two activists, during a government-organized press conference, said that the military had abducted them.

Key International Actors

Despite ongoing serious abuses and the lack of accountability, the Philippines continue to benefit from the European Union's Generalised Scheme of Preferences Plus (GSP+), which grants tariff preferences for exports to the EU market conditioned on the country's compliance with 27 rights conventions.

In an April visit to Manila, EU Special Representative for Human Rights Eamon Gilmore highlighted shortcomings in the Philippines' compliance with its GSP+ human rights obligations and stressed that "doing business with the EU means addressing human rights issues." Members of the European Parliament also remained highly critical of the Philippines' rights record and questioned its eligibility for the GSP+ program.

In August, EU Commission President Ursula von der Leyen visited Manila and praised the Marcos administration for "improving" the human rights situation in the country. Von der Leyen announced the resumption of negotiations for a bilateral free trade agreement, which had been frozen under Duterte due to human rights abuses. In November, the EU released a report on the human rights situation in the Philippines, as required under the GSP+ program, which highlighted major rights shortcomings and emphasized the need for progress.

The UN Joint Program (UNJP), created in 2020, has continued to build the capacity of accountability mechanisms in the country. Although it has trained law enforcement officers on proper methods to investigate rights abuses, particularly extrajudicial killings, the UNJP has had little impact because of the Covid-19 pandemic and initial lack of cooperation from the Philippine government.

The UNJP's mandate will end in July 2024. If extended, the program needs monitoring and reporting mechanisms.

After eight years of negotiations, in April, the United States Biden administration signed an enhanced cooperation agreement with the Philippines to fund and provide rapid support to respond to humanitarian, climate, and "other shared challenges." In October, the US and the Philippines held two weeks of military exercises amid rising tensions with China over the territory of the South China Sea.

Poland

A new coalition government came to power in December following national elections in October, offering the prospect of improvement regarding the rule of law, women's rights, and lesbian, gay, bisexual, and transgender (LGBT) rights.

The outgoing Law and Justice party (PiS) government undermined the rule of law during the year through attacks on judicial independence, independent media, and critical civil society and activist voices. Discrimination against LGBT people and attacks on women's rights, particularly reproductive rights, continued and these groups remained targets of hateful public rhetoric by government officials.

While the Polish government and people generally maintained their welcome to nearly 1 million Ukrainian refugees, Polish authorities at the border with Belarus persisted in unlawful pushbacks of migrants and asylum seekers. Polish officials harassed volunteers helping non-Ukrainian migrants and asylum seekers, including by prosecuting humanitarian volunteers for human smuggling.

Judicial Independence and Rule of Law

The outgoing government weakened the independence of the justice system and attacked independent judges. Poland's Covid-19 recovery funds remained blocked by the EU as Poland did not meet core benchmarks related to reform of the judiciary.

In December, the Constitutional Tribunal, on request by the president, ruled unconstitutional a law that would have transferred powers to adjudicate disciplinary cases against judges from a chamber in the Supreme Court to the Supreme Administrative Court. The Organization for Security and Co-operation in Europe (OSCE) Office for Democratic Institutions and Human Rights (ODIHR) stated in January that the bill failed to address outstanding concerns about the disciplinary regime in the Polish judiciary, noting that the Supreme Administrative Court is largely composed of judges appointed by the politically compromised National Judicial Council.

In February, the European Commission referred Poland to the Court of Justice of the European Union (CJEU) for violations of EU law by the compromised Polish Constitutional Tribunal, particularly for its July 2021 and October 2021 rulings stating that provisions in EU treaties were incompatible with the Polish constitution.

In May, and with subsequent amendments in July, Poland passed a controversial law creating a commission to investigate "Russian influence" in the country between 2007 and 2022 and giving the commission power to ban opposition party members from public office without judicial oversight. Critics dubbed the law "lex Tusk" because of concerns it would be used to discredit former and potential future Prime Minister Donald Tusk. Proposed in May, the law met with criticism from the United States and EU, including infringement proceedings launched by the European Commission. Amendments introduced by President Andrzej Duda fell short of addressing concerns about the possible targeting of opposition party members and others suspected of being under "Russian influence."

In February, Poland informed the European Court of Human Rights (ECtHR) that it would not respect a December 2022 ECtHR interim measure ordering the suspension of decisions to transfer three Polish judges to other court departments.

Judges continued to be vilified and subjected to disciplinary proceedings for standing up for the rule of law. In March, a deputy disciplinary commissioner started disciplinary proceedings against a Krakow judge for applying EU law. Four other judges faced disciplinary proceedings for being critical of appointments of judges by the politicized National Judicial Council and for applying EU law. Judges were charged under the so-called Muzzle Law, which the CJEU ruled contrary to EU law in June 2023. The battle between "old" and "neo" judges at the Supreme Court continued throughout the year. Three "old" judges appointed by the pre-2015 National Judicial Council assigned to the Supreme Court's criminal chamber resigned after a "neo" judge was appointed by the now politicized National Judicial Council to head the chamber.

In July, the ECtHR ruled that Judge Igor Tuleya's suspension in 2020 violated EU law and that he should be reinstated to the bench with full pay. Tuleya was openly critical of the government's overhaul of the judiciary. Also in July, the ECtHR ruled that Tuleya's suspension lacked a legal basis and reiterated that the Disciplinary Chamber that suspended him is "not an independent and impartial tribunal established by law." The court's judgment stated there were 397 similar cases from Polish judges pending before the ECtHR.

In September, PiS revealed its plan for further overhauling the court system in its election program, outlining the transformation of current courts and the establishment of new courts where, critics fear, judges would be vetted and appointed by party loyalists.

The European Commission's *Rule of Law Report* on Poland, published in July, raised serious concerns about the independence of the Polish judiciary, including disciplinary investigations and proceedings against judges and failures to implement judgments and interim measures issued by the ECtHR.

Freedom of Media

Independent media outlets and journalists faced continued difficulties operating freely and without interference. While Poland's ranking rose from 66 in 2022 to 57 in the Reporters Without Borders' 2023 World Press Freedom Index, the group noted concerns that public media was becoming a government "mouthpiece" and that ruling party politicians were verbally attacking critical journalists and filing strategic lawsuits against public participation (SLAPPs) to try to silence them.

A July report by the Helsinki Foundation for Human Rights showed the detrimental effects on media freedom of the 2020 acquisition of *Polska Press* by state-controlled oil company PKN Orlen. Former and current journalists at *Polska Press* quoted in the report expressed concerns about political interference in the editorial process, being hindered from reporting on certain issues, including LGBT and migrant issues, and a clear shift to favorable reporting on the ruling party.

In July, freelance photojournalist Maciej Piasecki was forcibly removed by police from documenting an environmental protest in Warsaw. Piasecki was pushed to the ground by seven or eight policemen, handcuffed, brought to a police station, detained, and questioned for six hours. He was released without charge.

At time of writing, Spanish freelance journalist Pablo González remained in pre-trial detention, accused of being a Russian spy. Gonzalez was arrested in February 2022 by the Polish Security Services in Rzeszow, close to the border with

Ukraine, where he was reporting on the refugee crisis caused by Russia's full-scale invasion of Ukraine. Press freedom organizations raised concerns that no evidence or allegations against Gonzales had been made public.

Sexual Orientation and Gender Identity

Smear campaigns against LGBT people continued during the year. In August, in a third attempt to ban inclusive sexual education, a bill was passed by the Sejm that would restrict access to schools for nongovernmental organizations providing sexuality education. The bill, following two previous attempts championed by PiS Education Minister Czarnek, was dubbed "Lex Czarnek 3.0." President Duda vetoed the two previous versions of the bill due to failure by the government to gain "social acceptance." Following a senate resolution to reject the bill, it was pending before the Sejm at time of writing.

During the year, Czarnek made several statements attacking LGBT people and sexuality education, including trying to blame an increase in youth suicide on "LGBT ideology" and claiming that the new law would prevent the "moral corruption" and "sexualization of children" in schools and preschools.

In May, the country's children's rights commissioner—referring to a nongovernmental study listing some 2,500 schools in Poland as LGBT-friendly, a list intended to help young people choose open, tolerant, and safe schools—ordered an inspection of some of these schools, justifying his decision by stating that "children must be protected from criminals."

Also in May, the Warsaw district court found three LGBT activists guilty of vandalizing a van displaying and broadcasting anti-LGBT messages in June 2020 and sentenced them to between 6 and 12 months of community service. The decision was under appeal at time of writing. In July, an appellate court overturned the April conviction of an anti-LGBT van driver, acquitting him of defamation on the perverse basis that the driver's anti-LGBT slogans were "true." The incident took place in 2019.

A first instance court in April convicted two women of "offending religious feelings" by displaying Virgin Mary and Jesus with rainbow halos during a LGBT rights march in 2021, sentencing one to five months of community service, and the other to a 2,000 zloty fine. The decision was under appeal at time of writing.

In January, the European Commission quietly and without explanation dropped legal action against Poland over local authorities' adoption of anti-LGBT resolutions establishing so-called LGBT Ideology-free zones. Fifteen local anti-LGBT resolutions remained in force at time of writing.

Access to Abortion

The situation for women's rights remained precarious for most of the year, with an abortion activist sentenced to jail time, criminal investigations opened in abortion cases, and authorities targeting women and girls seeking urgent health care and the doctors providing it.

In March, a Warsaw court convicted Justyna Wydrzynska, cofounder of the activist group Abortion Dream Team, for helping a woman procure pills for a medication abortion and sentenced her to eight months of community service. Wydrzynska appealed the ruling, and her case was pending at time of writing.

The outgoing government's dubious use of its powers to chase down alleged abortion-related activity led to sweeping and speculative investigations and overbroad searches, including of women and girls seeking urgent health care and doctors. Following a Constitutional Tribunal ruling in October 2020 that virtually banned access to legal abortion, six women are known to have died after being denied abortion care despite pregnancy complications that threatened their health or lives, including a 33-year-old woman who died in May 2023. People fleeing the war in Ukraine are also denied access to safe and legal abortion.

In June, the European Court of Human Rights declared eight cases challenging Poland's extremely restrictive abortion law were inadmissible. About 1,000 abortion rights-related cases submitted to the court since 2021 are ongoing.

Migration and Asylum

By the end of September, Poland had provided temporary protection to more than 950,000 Ukrainian refugees since Russia's February 2022 invasion of Ukraine.

While accepting refugees from Ukraine, Polish authorities engaged in unlawful and sometimes violent pushbacks of migrants and asylum seekers, including women and children, arriving from Belarus.

Volunteers aiding stranded migrants and asylum seekers in the border area continued to face criminal charges, harassment, and intimidation by border officials. In February, an Ethiopian woman died in a wooded border area after her husband and traveling companions were pushed back to Belarus. A Somalian woman died in September in Minsk, Belarus, after being stranded in the border area for 40 days, pushed back several times by both countries' border guards. The authorities detained one volunteer in September and accused her of leading a criminal group because of her activities in support of migrants and asylum seekers crossing from Belarus to Poland. She was later released on bail. Justice Minister Zbigniew Ziobro made prejudicial public comments about the volunteer's alleged guilt.

The government continued to deny border abuses and smear critics of its border policies. Polish director Agnieszka Holland's movie "The Green Border," which depicts the abuse of migrants and asylum seekers on Poland's border with Belarus, premiered in September and was attacked by Minister Ziobro, who described the movie as "anti-Polish Nazi propaganda." The Ministry of Interior announced it would broadcast a clip prior to screenings of the movie to inform viewers of "untruths and distortions."

Qatar

Qatar hosted the 2022 Fédération Internationale de Football Association (FIFA) World Cup between November and December 2022. Qatari authorities and FIFA failed to provide compensation to migrant workers for widespread abuses, including wage theft and the unexplained deaths of workers who prepared and delivered the tournament. Migrant workers faced new forms of exploitation, highlighting the inadequacies of Qatar's labor reforms and the shameful human rights legacy of the 2022 World Cup. Qatari laws also continue to discriminate against women due to abusive male guardianship policies and against lesbian, gay, bisexual, and transgender (LGBT) individuals.

Migrant Workers

The 2022 FIFA World Cup failed to achieve significant migrant labor reforms in Qatar, with workers who built tournament infrastructure and their families uncompensated for widespread wage theft, illegal recruitment fees, and unexplained deaths. The post-tournament economic slowdown created new vulnerabilities for the migrant workforce, with some workers being unpaid for months or paid far less than their contracts stipulated. Workers still struggle to change jobs easily. Many workers were compelled to wait in Qatar despite unpaid wages or end-of-service benefits, because they risked losing their wages if they left the country.

Qatar announced in 2020 that it allowed migrant workers to change jobs or exit the country without employer permission, initiated wage protection measures such as the Wage Protection System and the Workers' Support and Insurance Fund, and set a higher minimum wage for all workers. Yet, Human Rights Watch found that the benefits of these initiatives were limited due to their late introduction, narrow scope, or weak enforcement. Public scrutiny in the lead-up to the World Cup also highlighted the thousands of unexplained migrant worker deaths in Qatar. But Qatar failed to make public any data on these deaths or investigate their causes. A majority of deaths are attributed to "natural causes," and under Qatari labor law, only deaths considered work-related are compensated. Just a few companies adopted good practices, like life insurance for migrant workers that covers injuries and deaths and recruitment cost reimbursement schemes.

Qatari authorities deflected widespread calls for remedy for these widespread abuses—including by 14 national football associations, political representatives, and current and former players—claiming the criticism was racist and falsely insisting that existing compensation mechanisms to address the longstanding abuses were adequate, claims repeated by FIFA.

Women's Rights

Human Rights Watch documented how the discriminatory male guardianship system, which is incorporated into Qatari law, regulations, and practices, puts extensive restrictions on women's abilities to make autonomous decisions about their lives.

Women in Qatar must obtain permission from their male guardians to marry, study abroad on government scholarships, work in many government jobs, travel abroad until certain ages, and receive some forms of reproductive health care.

Single Qatari women below 25 require their guardian's permission to travel outside Qatar. Married women at any age can travel without permission, but men can petition a court to prohibit their wives' travel. Qatari women are prohibited from being at events and bars serving alcohol, and unmarried Qatari women under 30 cannot check into hotels without a male guardian. Women face discrimination in practice while trying to rent apartments without a male guardian's permission.

Guardian permission is required to work for government institutions, and women attending Qatar University face restrictions on their movements. Male guardians and other family members can report women to the police for being "absent" from their homes, which can lead to their arrest and forcible return home or to administrative detention.

Qatar's Family Law also discriminates against women in marriage, divorce, child custody, and inheritance. Women require a male guardian's permission to marry, and married women are required to obey their husbands and can lose their husband's financial support if they work or travel against their husband's wishes. Men have a unilateral right to divorce, while women must apply to the courts for divorce on limited grounds. Under inheritance provisions, female siblings receive half the amount their brothers get.

The Family Law forbids husbands from hurting their wives, but Qatar does not have a law on domestic violence or measures to protect survivors and prosecute their abusers.

Women are denied the authority to act as their children's primary guardian, even when they are divorced and have legal custody. While Qatari men can pass citizenship to their spouses and children, children of Qatari women and non-citizen men can only do so under narrow, discriminatory conditions. Qatar passed a permanent residency law permitting children of Qatari women married to non-Qatari men, among others, to apply for permanent residency, own real estate, and receive government health and education services.

Sexual Orientation and Gender Identity

Human Rights Watch documented cases of LGBT people in Qatar who were arbitrarily arrested and treated poorly in detention, including cases of severe and repeated beatings, verbal abuse, and sexual harassment in police custody. Security officers also inflicted verbal abuse, extracted forced confessions, forced detainees to sign pledges that they would "cease immoral activity," and denied detainees access to legal counsel, family, and medical care. Security forces mandated that transgender women detainees attend conversion therapy sessions at a government-sponsored "behavioral support" center.

Qatar's penal code, under article 285, criminalizes extramarital sex, including consensual same-sex relations, with up to seven years in prison. It provides penalties between one and three years (article 296) for any male who "instigates" or "entices" another male to "commit an act of sodomy or immorality." A penalty of 10 years' imprisonment (article 288) is imposed on anyone who engages in consensual sexual relations with a person above 16, outside marriage, which could apply to consensual same-sex relations between women, men, or heterosexual partners.

Qatar surveils and arrests LGBT people based on their online activity and censors traditional media related to sexual orientation and gender identity, including ones that support LGBT individuals.

Freedom of Expression

Qatar's penal code criminalizes criticizing the emir, insulting Qatar's flag, defaming religion, including blasphemy, and inciting "to overthrow the regime." Qatar's 2014 cybercrimes law provided for a maximum of three years in prison and/or a fine of 500,000 Qatari riyal (about US$137,325) for anyone convicted of spreading "false news" (an undefined term) on the internet or for posting online content that "violates social values or principles" or "insults or slanders others." In January 2020, Qatar amended its penal code to impose up to five years in prison for spreading rumors or false news (undefined terms) with ill-intent and/or a fine of 100,000 Qatari riyal (about $27,465).

Former Supreme Committee for Delivery and Legacy media and communications director Abdul Ibhais, who was arrested in November 2019, is serving a three-year jail sentence for bribery. He claims being subjected to a malicious prosecution in retaliation for his criticism of the handling of a 2019 migrant workers' strike in Qatar. His trial, based on coerced confessions, was unfair.

Statelessness

Qatar's decision to arbitrarily strip families from the Ghufran clan of their citizenship since 1996 has left some members stateless and deprived them of basic human rights. Stateless members of the Ghufran clan are deprived of their rights to work, education, healthcare, marriage and starting a family, own property, and freedom of movement. Without valid identity documents, they face restrictions in accessing basic services and risk arbitrary detention. Those living in Qatar are denied the government benefits provided to Qatari citizens, including state jobs, food and energy subsidies, and free basic healthcare.

Climate Change Policy and Actions

Qatar is contributing significantly to the global climate crisis. It has the highest greenhouse gas emissions per capita globally. It has the world's third largest reserves of natural gas and until recently was the world's largest exporter of liquified natural gas (LNG).

In its updated Nationally Determined Contribution (NDC), a Paris Agreement-mandated five-year national climate change action plan, Qatar set a target of reducing emissions by 25 percent from the baseline scenario, without specifying what the baseline scenario is. Qatar has taken few steps to move away from the production and use of fossil fuels; instead, it is doubling down on producing LNG for export.

Qatar is itself vulnerable to the impacts of climate change. 97 percent of Qatar's population lives along an exposed coastline, making them particularly vulnerable to both sea level rise and extreme weather events. Migrant workers, especially in outdoor sectors like construction, are disproportionately exposed to Qatar's extreme heat and already face severe health risks.

Human Rights Watch documented the inadequacies of current heat protection measures like midday bans. While Qatar expanded heat protection measures, including the prohibition of work when the wet-bulb globe temperature (WBGT) exceeds 32.1 degrees Celsius (about 90 degrees Fahrenheit), the threshold temperature is set too high to effectively protect workers and serious enforcement gaps remain.

Key International Actors

Qatar's geopolitical standing has strengthened due to Russia's full-scale invasion of Ukraine, especially in Europe, where Qatar's LNG serves as an alternate to Russian energy. Qatar is an increasingly important LNG exporter.

Members of the International Labour Organization elected Qatar as president of the 111th session (June 5-16) of the International Labour Conference, despite Qatari authorities' patent failures to protect labor rights, including migrant workers' right to unionize.

Qatar's selection for the 2022 World Cup came amid investigations by Belgian authorities into allegations of corruption of European Parliament members, a scandal known as "Qatargate" that has highlighted the country's alleged role, along with that of other states, to bribe European parliamentarians to launder its image. The scandal led to consideration of stronger transparency and integrity rules for EU institutions, but it was also instrumentalized by some political groups to attack NGOs.

In September, the EU held a human rights dialogue with Qatar. No tangible deliverables were disclosed.

Russia

In the second year of Russia's full-scale invasion of Ukraine, Russian authorities have further intensified efforts at home to eradicate any dissent about the war or the Kremlin's domestic policies. They adopted and enforced new, repressive legislation, issued punitively long prison sentences for peaceful anti-war speech, and forcibly closed several prominent human rights groups.

Russia remained the most sanctioned country in the world.

The failed mutiny by the Wagner mercenary group prompted President Vladimir Putin to admit that the group, known for serious human rights abuses in its overseas operations and for recruiting Russian convicts to fight in Ukraine in exchange for amnesty, was fully funded from Russia's budget.

In March, the International Criminal Court issued arrest warrants for Putin and Russian children's rights commissioner Maria Lvova-Belova for the forcible transfer of Ukrainian children from occupied areas of Ukraine and their unlawful deportation to Russia. In response, in April, Russia adopted a law criminalizing assistance to foreign and international bodies "to which Russia is not a party." For more information on Russian forces' violations of the laws of war in Ukraine, including potential war crimes and crimes against humanity, see Ukraine chapter.

New laws imposed extensive limitations on rights and access to state services for perceived draft evaders.

Freedom of Expression

Russian authorities continued to use administrative and criminal charges of "discreditation" and "false information" about Russia's armed forces to suppress anti-war speech and prosecute and imprison individuals for their lawful, peaceful expression. According to the human rights group OVD-info, in 2023, at least 77 people were convicted and sentenced on "false information" and 52 on "discreditation" charges; as of October 2023, criminal cases have been opened against over 350 people on these charges. Among them were both prominent opposition figures and people with no background in activism.

In December 2022, a Moscow court sentenced political opposition figure Ilya Yashin to eight-and-a-half years in prison on "false information" charges. In April 2023, after a year in pretrial detention, another prominent opposition figure, Vladimir Kara-Murza, received a 25-year sentence in a maximum-security prison on combined charges of treason, "false information," and involvement with an "undesirable organization."

In March, a new law extended "discreditation" and "false information" provisions to cover "volunteers" taking part or "assisting" in armed conflicts.

An April law allowed the authorities to strip naturalized Russian nationals of their citizenship, even if this rendered them stateless, and deport them for committing "discreditation" and "false information" offenses.

Authorities increasingly used Russia's "undesirable organizations" legislation to outlaw exiled independent Russian media, including TV Rain, Meduza, The Project, and Novaya Gazeta Europe. Between 2022 and 2023, at least five people were convicted for reposting publications by "undesirable" media.

Russian authorities also increasingly prosecuted people on bogus treason, confidential cooperation, and espionage charges. In March, the Russian Federal Security Service (FSB) arrested *Wall Street Journal* reporter Evan Gershkovich on espionage charges. At time of writing, he remained in pretrial detention.

In the first half of 2023 alone, the FSB opened more new treason cases, against a variety of individuals, than in all of 2022. An April law increased the penalties for treason and other crimes.

According to Russian human rights group First Department, in 2023, authorities opened at least 21 criminal cases against people who allegedly engaged in "confidential cooperation" with non-Russian nationals under a law reminiscent of the Soviet-era ban on contact with foreigners.

In October, a journalist with Radio Free Europe/Radio Liberty (RFE/RL) (a US government-funded media organization), Alsu Kurmasheva, was arrested for failing to register as a foreign agent while allegedly gathering information on the Russian military for foreign sources. This is the first known application of such charges. She faces up to five years in prison. At time of writing, she remained in pretrial detention.

Russian authorities also used legislation against the rehabilitation of Nazism to suppress legitimate free expression. In January, a Russian publishing house censored sections of a book by an American author that compared the Soviet army's conduct in Poland during World War II to that of Nazi Germany.

In November, Russian authorities opened a criminal case against the local head of an opposition party in Russia's Kamchatka region for social media posts comparing images of "patriotic" singer Shaman (Yaroslav Dronov) with images of a Nazi youth from the 1972 movie *Cabaret*. He faces up to four years' imprisonment for display of Nazi symbols. In June, a court in Blagoveschensk, in Russia's Far East, fined a former deputy of the local legislative assembly on similar administrative charges for reposting on social media a parody video showing clips from a video by Shaman side by side with a clip from *Cabaret*. Shaman shot to fame after the start of the full-scale invasion of Ukraine with a number of "patriotic" music video releases.

Freedom of Assembly

Freedom of assembly remained effectively defunct. Since 2020 Russian authorities have repeatedly used Covid-19 restrictions as a pretext to ban opposition and anti-war protests in the country, despite lifting all other Covid-19 related restrictions and organizing large crowds not adhering to quarantine requirements for pro-Kremlin events, including concerts in support of Russia's full-scale invasion of Ukraine. In February, authorities in various regions detained and prosecuted individuals who participated in sparse protests on the anniversary of Russia's full-scale invasion of Ukraine.

Freedom of Association

Russian authorities again expanded legislation on "foreign agents" and "undesirable organizations." They added at least 192 individuals and organizations to the "foreign agents" registry, with the total count reaching 707 as of November 3. At least 44 organizations were banned as "undesirable" in 2023; according to a Russian governmental website, which in some countries outside Russia can be accessed only with certain types of VPNs, the cumulative count was 116 organizations as of early November.

A December 2022 law streamlined criminal prosecutions for noncompliance with the "foreign agents" law and drastically increased penalties for creating or participating in "destructive" nongovernmental organizations (NGOs), further increasing avenues for authorities to penalize civic activists. In February, Artiom Vajenkov, coordinator of Russia's leading independent election watchdog Golos, became the first person accused of revised "foreign agent" charges.

Laws adopted in July and August further harshened the "foreign agents" legislation, outlawed foreign organizations without legal presence in Russia, and criminalized participation in their activities.

In March and April, authorities respectively banned Transparency International and the EU-Russian Civil Society Forum as "undesirable."

In August, police detained Grigoriy Melkonyants, the chair of Golos, and raided the apartments of several members and perceived affiliates on allegations of continued participation in the European Network of Election Monitoring Organizations despite Golos' departure from the network after it was banned as "undesirable" in 2021. At time of writing, Melkonyants remained in pretrial detention.

Attacks on Human Rights Defenders

Russian authorities continued to harass, intimidate, and prosecute human rights defenders and forcibly shut down human rights groups.

In January, a court ordered the shutdown of the Moscow Helsinki Group, Russia's oldest human rights group.

In March, police raided office spaces affiliated with Memorial, one of Russia's most prominent human rights groups that was forcibly shut down in 2021, and the homes of nine of its staff and board members. Earlier in January, the prosecutor's office opened a criminal case against unspecified Memorial members on "justification of Nazism" charges. In October, a court in Moscow sentenced Oleg Orlov, co-chair of Memorial, to a large fine on "discreditation" charges for a November 2022 social media post on the applicability of the term "fascist" to Russia today. The prosecution appealed the verdict, seeking his imprisonment.

In April, the Moscow City Court ruled to liquidate SOVA, a watchdog on Russian extremism, on the pretext of holding activities outside Moscow.

In August, a court ordered the closure of the human rights NGO Chelovek I Zakon (Man and Law) based in the Mari El Republic, following a Justice Ministry lawsuit, on the grounds of operating outside the region where it was registered, non-compliance with "foreign agents" labeling rules, and alleged discrepancies between its activities and aims listed in incorporating documents.

In December 2022, a court fined the Moscow-based Sakharov Center, a human rights group, 5 million rubles (about US$50,000) for violating "foreign agents" labeling requirements. In August 2023, another court ordered its forcible closure following a Justice Ministry lawsuit alleging several violations, including non-compliance with these requirements. In January 2023, authorities banned the US-registered Andrei Sakharov Foundation as "undesirable."

In July, Russian authorities banned the Human Rights House Foundation, headquartered in Norway, as "undesirable," making cooperation with it a criminal offence for its Russian partners.

In May, a court sentenced Bakhrom Khamroyev to 14 years in prison on terrorism-related charges reportedly for social media posts and for preparing materials related to Hizb ut-Tahrir (HuT), a pan-Islamist movement that seeks to establish a caliphate but publicly repudiates violence to achieve that goal. Khamroyev was affiliated with Human Rights Center Memorial and in recent years defended the rights of migrant workers from Central Asia.

Ill-Treatment in Custody

Russian authorities subjected at least 40 activists and members of persecuted religious minorities to repeated and extended placement in disciplinary cells, according to a Russian human rights watchdog. They subjected such detainees to other forms of ill-treatment, including incommunicado detention during lengthy transfers from pretrial detention facilities to prisons.

In September, opposition figure Alexei Navalny was subjected to the maximum disciplinary penalty of one year. Following his arrest in January 2021, he had already been placed in a disciplinary cell at least 20 times for various terms. Prison authorities also placed historian and rights advocate Yuri Dmitriyev in a disciplinary cell for 15 days, in spite of his reportedly poor health.

Despite risks to those with known health conditions, Crimean Tatars serving sentences in Russia for alleged involvement with HuT have also repeatedly been placed for prolonged periods in disciplinary cells. One has spent some four months in a row in disciplinary cell, and another has cumulatively spent over two years in disciplinary cells since his conviction in 2019.

In January 2023, Andrey Pivovarov, former executive director of Open Russia, was effectively held in incommunicado detention for a month during his transfer from pretrial detention to a penitentiary. Russian authorities ignored his lawyer's and family's inquiries about his whereabouts and well-being, a practice to which the authorities also subjected Vladimir Kara-Murza and numerous others.

Chechnya

Chechen authorities under governor Ramzan Kadyrov continued to eviscerate all forms of dissent, targeting critics and retaliating against their family members, including by forcibly mobilizing men to fight for Russian forces in Ukraine.

In July, armed men in balaclavas violently attacked Elena Milashina, a journalist with *Novaya Gazeta*, and Alexander Nemov, a human rights lawyer, who arrived in Grozny to attend a court hearing in the politically motivated case against Zarema Mussaeva. Mussaeva was found guilty and sentenced to several years in prison. Milashina and Nemov suffered a severe beating, resulting in multiple traumas, including fractures. The assailants also threatened to kill them. At time of writing, an investigation was ongoing.

In February, Moscow authorities arrested Idris Arsamikov, who had previously been tortured in Chechnya for his presumed sexual orientation, on fabricated fraud charges and transferred him to Chechnya. Police in Chechnya refused to disclose his whereabouts or give his lawyers access. Two videos appeared on Arsamikov's VKontakte page, showing him at home denouncing efforts to find him and making other statements that appear to have been forcibly extracted.

In August, a video circulated on social media showing Kadyrov's 15-year-old son beating a suspect detained for destroying the Quran. Kadyrov publicly expressed approval of his son's actions. In October, the boy received the "Hero of the Chechen Republic" governmental award.

Counterterrorism and Counter-Extremism

In mid-2023, some of Alexei Navalny's former allies received lengthy sentences on bogus extremism and related charges following closed trials. They included Lilia Chanysheva, who in June was sentenced to 7.5 years in prison in Ufa, Bashkortostan, on extremism and "destructive NGO" charges; her co-defendant, Rustem Muliukov, who was sentenced to 2.5 years for extremism; and Vadim Ostanin, sentenced to 9 years on the same charge in Barnaul. At time of writing, Kseniya Fadeyeva remained on trial in Tomsk on charges of "aggravated extremism" and participation in a "destructive" organization.

In August, a court sentenced Navalny to 19 years in a maximum-security prison on spurious extremism and other charges. His co-defendant, Daniel Kholodny, former technical director of Navalny's YouTube channel, was sentenced to eight years.

In September, several individuals were arrested on charges of financing an "extremist" organization for donations to the Navalny-affiliated organization "Foundation Against Corruption."

In October, three of Navalny's lawyers were detained on extremist charges for allegedly facilitating contact between Navalny and his aides and supporters while he remains in jail. They face up to six years in prison.

In June, six activists with the opposition youth movement "Vesna" ("Spring" in Russian) were detained on various spurious charges, including extremism. In September, authorities listed 21 Vesna members, including the aforementioned 6, in the registry of "extremists" and "terrorists." In 2022, Russian authorities opened several criminal cases against Vesna activists for organizing peaceful protests against Russia's full-scale invasion of Ukraine. A court banned Vesna as extremist in December 2022 for its legitimate and peaceful civic activism.

In May, authorities arrested Yevgeniya Berkovich, a theater director, and Svetlana Petriychuk, a playwright, on "justification of terrorism" charges for an award-winning play they worked on together about women who became brides of members of Islamic State (also known as ISIS). At time of writing, both remained in pretrial detention.

Russian authorities opened new criminal cases on charges of justification of terrorism against at least two political prisoners already serving prison sentences, based on their alleged comments to fellow prisoners. In August and October, such cases were opened against Azat Miftakhov and Alexei Gorinov. Miftakhov was due to be released after serving a sentence for alleged attempted arson of an empty office of the ruling United Russia party, and Gorinov is serving a seven-year prison sentence for "false information" about Russian forces and for publicly talking about civilian casualties in Ukraine. The new charges may entail up to five years' imprisonment.

In September, a court sentenced a Dagestani journalist, Abdulmumin Gadjiyev, to 17 years in a maximum-security prison on 3 spurious terrorism-related charges; his co-defendants received 17.5 and 18 years. Rights organizations assert the charges were in retaliation for his reporting.

Russian authorities also continued to abuse counter-extremism and counterterrorism legislation to persecute religious minorities. Police raided homes and opened new criminal cases against Jehovah's Witnesses (JWs), banned as "extremist" in Russia since 2017. In 2023, at least 38 JWs were sentenced to up to 7 years in prison and 68 others were sentenced to various penalties not involving imprisonment. Since the 2017 ban, over 410 JWs have spent time behind bars, either awaiting trial or serving a prison sentence.

In 2023, Russian courts continued to issue lengthy prison sentences against people on politically motivated charges of membership in HuT, which was banned as a terrorist organization in Russia in 2003. According to Memorial, as of October 2023, at least 335 people were being prosecuted for alleged HuT affiliation in Russia and occupied Crimea, 115 of whom were sentenced to over 15 years in prison.

Several people were also sentenced, indicted, or detained for their supposed affiliation with Nurdzhular, a group of followers of the late Turkish theologian Said Nursi that Russia banned as extremist in 2008 even though it has no history of incitement or violence.

Russian authorities also continued to expand counter-extremism legislation. Under a June law, possession or distribution of material that falls under the overly broad and vague legal definition of "extremist" can trigger administrative liability, which can then lead to criminal liability for a repeated offence; previously, liability was triggered by possession or dissemination of materials if they were on the authorities' list of "extremist materials."

Climate Change, Environment, and Human Rights

Watchdogs continued to report physical attacks, harassment, and prosecution of environmental activists and groups.

Between April and July, authorities banned five environmental groups, including Greenpeace and the World Wildlife Fund, as "undesirable."

Massive forest fires raged again in different parts of Russia, but the resources allocated by Russian authorities to manage them reportedly remained insufficient. And local authorities allegedly attempted to underreport the extent of forest fires.

In September, the first-ever "climate lawsuit" against the Russian government, demanding a radical reduction of Russia's greenhouse gas emissions, was submitted to the European Court of Human Rights (ECtHR).

Migrants, Statelessness, and Xenophobia

Russian police continued to racially profile non-Slav migrants and ethnic minorities and subject them to unsubstantiated ID checks and detentions, often prolonged, in inhumane conditions. Some have been physically assaulted.

In July, police raided mosques in Moscow region under the pretext of immigration checks, interrupting worship and physically assaulting and verbally insulting worshippers.

In some cases, during raids, police sought out dual Russian nationals among Central Asian migrants and forcibly delivered them to draft offices. In August, authorities in Kaluga region allegedly refused to accept naturalization applications from migrant workers unless they signed military service contracts.

Since autumn 2022, Russian authorities have been actively recruiting Central Asian migrants to sign military contracts, including by luring them with cancellation of deportation orders and simplified naturalization processes or by using coercion and deceit. In several cases, officials issued draft notices to Central Asian nationals who do not have Russian passports and cannot be drafted.

In January, a high-ranking official stated that authorities should prioritize sending dual nationals from Central Asian countries to fight in Ukraine. He later also proposed stripping naturalized Russian nationals of their citizenship if they refuse to fight in Ukraine. In August, the head of the Russian Presidential Human Rights Council proposed synchronizing the naturalization procedure with registration at military draft offices.

At time of writing, parliament was considering a bill—whose official version is available on a Russian governmental website, which in some countries outside Russia can be accessed only with certain types of VPNs—that would allow naturalized citizens to be stripped of their Russian nationality for draft evasion, even if that renders them stateless.

Experts reported a rise in xenophobic racist attacks by neo-Nazis in the country and noted a rise in xenophobic anti-migrant rhetoric in parliament, the media, and wider society.

In late October, there were at least four antisemitic incidents in the North Caucasus, including a mob attack in an airport hunting for Israeli passengers. The police detained 201 people for participating in the airport riots and opened a criminal case. However, they have not acknowledged any of the incidents as antisemitic.

Sexual Orientation and Gender Identity

Russian authorities intensified their crackdown on lesbian, gay, bisexual, and transgender (LGBT) people.

In November, the Russian Supreme Court in a closed hearing deemed the international LGBT movement as an extremist organization and banned it following a lawsuit by the Justice Ministry. The Ministry accused the "LGBT movement" of inciting social and religious discord.

A July law prohibited gender-affirming surgeries and trans health care, dissolved marriages of transgender people, banned changing gender markers in official documents, barred trans people from adopting or taking guardianship of children, and allowed coercive medical interventions on intersex children.

Russia's media and communications regulator, Roskomnadzor, prosecuted streaming services for movies featuring scenes with LGBT people and ordered blockings of websites featuring any LGBT content. In February 2023, Roskomnadzor developed by-laws outlining criteria for defining "gay propaganda."

Authorities used "foreign agent" designations against several LGBT organizations, including Centre T, which focuses on the rights and welfare of trans people. They extrajudicially blocked the websites of LGBT rights groups, including Centre T and Delo LGBT+.

In June 2023, Russia's health minister stated that President Putin instructed the ministry to establish a new psychiatry institute to study the behavior of LGBT people. Human rights defenders are concerned that this could lead to the official introduction of conversion therapy.

Online Censorship, Surveillance, and Privacy

Russian authorities continued to arbitrarily block websites without court orders and further expanded the list of state bodies tasked with doing so. Blocked content included independent media outlets, rights groups, thousands of websites criticizing Russia's full-scale invasion of Ukraine, and content about LGBT and gender-affirming care.

Authorities also continued tightening control over internet infrastructure. A July law requires entities providing internet hosting services to enroll in a state registry. In September, another law entered into force requiring internet exchange points and telecom operators to install deep packet inspection (DPI) technology in their networks allowing the state to directly filter and reroute internet traffic.

In April, Moscow officials acknowledged using video surveillance with facial recognition technology to detain alleged draft evaders. Authorities further expanded the use of facial recognition technology, including at border crossing points and schools.

In December 2022, a personal data leak confirmed that the Moscow city government failed to secure sensitive personal data of millions of children and parents. In February, a new law extended compulsory lifetime DNA data collection for millions of people suspected of any crime or convicted of certain misdemeanors. In

September, a law entered into force allowing Russian security services live access to taxi ride data.

Key International Actors *(see also Ukraine chapter)*

In September, Mariana Katzarova, the first United Nations special rapporteur on human rights in Russia, presented her first report to the UN Human Rights Council, outlining the significant deterioration of human rights in Russia since the full-scale invasion of Ukraine in 2022. In October, the UN Human Rights Council voted to extend her mandate for a year.

Throughout the year, UN institutions issued numerous statements on the human rights situation in Russia. The UN high commissioner for human rights expressed serious concern about Navalny's latest sentence, condemned Kara-Murza's sentence in April, expressed deep concern about "foreign agent" and anti-LGBT legislation, and the forced closure of human rights groups and independent media.

Likewise, UN special procedures, individually or jointly, called for the immediate release of Kara-Murza and Gershkovich, urged Russia to investigate the attack against Milashina and Nemov, urged Russia to drop criminal charges against Orlov, expressed distress over Navalny's gravely deteriorating health and raised concerns about three imprisoned Navalny supporters, and expressed alarm at Wagner's recruitment of inmates and "over the escalating crackdown against civil society."

Two UN human rights treaty bodies issued concluding observations on Russia. In April, the UN Committee on the Elimination of Racial Discrimination expressed deep concern about the unclear definition of "extremist activity" in Russian law and called on Russia to combat racist hate speech, racial hatred, and discrimination. In November 2022, the UN Human Rights Committee expressed deep concern about rights violations in Ukrainian territories occupied by Russia and about a wide range of other rights issues, many of which were previously outlined in this chapter.

In February, the European Union imposed further sanctions against the Kremlin-sponsored Wagner mercenary group for serious human rights abuses in the Central African Republic and Sudan alongside sanctions on Wagner mercenaries under the EU's Mali and Ukraine sanctions regimes. In September, the EU condemned Russia's "elections" in occupied territories of Ukraine as a "violation of international law."

Throughout 2023, the EU issued numerous statements condemning human rights violations in Russia, including the sentencing of Navalny and Kara-Murza. In July, the EU urged Russia to drop criminal "discreditation" charges against Orlov. In June and July, the EU Council announced human rights sanctions against individuals and entities for Kara-Murza sentencing and Navalny's detention and other human rights violations.

The EU issued several statements expressing solidarity with Russia's independent civil society and with those who have been persecuted for criticizing Russia's war in Ukraine. The European Parliament also adopted several resolutions condemning Russia's human rights record.

In February, outlining EU priorities in UN human rights fora, the EU Council condemned violations of international human rights law and international humanitarian law stemming from Russia's full-scale invasion of Ukraine.

In September, the ECtHR handed down a ruling in the case of Maxim Lapunov, the only victim of Chechnya's 2017 anti-gay purge who dared seek justice despite great personal risk. The court found that Lapunov was "detained and subjected to ill-treatment by State agents," which "amounted to torture" and was perpetrated "solely on account of his sexual orientation."

In July, the ECtHR ruled in favor of a Russian national in a case concerning police use of facial recognition technology to prosecute peaceful protesters. The court concluded that using personal data—including from facial recognition technology—to identify and later arrest a protester amounted to an unjustified interference with his private life. It also expressed "strong doubts" as to whether provisions in Russian law provide an appropriate legal basis for processing biometric data.

In October, Russia failed to reclaim a seat on the UN Human Rights Council during a General Assembly election. The General Assembly had suspended Moscow's membership of the council in 2022 due to its full-scale invasion of Ukraine and reported atrocities and rights record at home.

HUMAN
RIGHTS
WATCH
"Join Us or Die"
Rwanda's Extraterritorial Repression

Rwanda

Commentators, journalists, opposition activists, and others speaking out on current affairs and criticizing public policies in Rwanda continued to face abusive prosecutions, enforced disappearances, and have at times died under unexplained circumstances. In January, journalist John Williams Ntwali died in suspicious circumstances. The authorities said he died in a road accident, but they provided no evidence of such an accident and held a hasty trial, essentially behind closed doors, leaving many questions unanswered.

The Rwandan army deployed troops to eastern Democratic Republic of Congo to provide direct military support to the M23 armed group, helping it expand its control over Rutshuru and neighboring Masisi territories. The Rwanda-backed M23 rebels have committed unlawful killings, rapes, and other apparent war crimes since late 2022. Attacks with explosive weapons in populated areas of North Kivu province killed and injured civilians, damaged infrastructure, and exacerbated a catastrophic humanitarian crisis.

Security forces in Rwanda continued to "clear up" the streets of Kigali and detain people deemed "undesirable"—such as street children, street vendors, sex workers, homeless people, and beggars—ahead of high-profile visits and events. People are taken to an unofficial detention facility, Gikondo transit center, under the aegis of the National Rehabilitation Service. Human Rights Watch received information confirming severe ill-treatment and appalling detention conditions at Gikondo transit center, as well as torture in official prisons in Rwanda, throughout the year.

Political Space and Opposition

The Rwanda Patriotic Front (RPF) and its proxies have deployed a range of measures across the globe to silence and target real or suspected opponents. *As Rwanda approaches its 2024 general elections, space for political opposition remains closed, both inside and outside the ruling party.* Senior RPF officials condemned the organization of a traditional clan meeting by a group of influential leaders planning to appoint a chief, denouncing the gathering as an "interference in the unity of Rwandans." According to media reports, after the event on

July 9, senior party officials who attended the ceremony were temporarily detained and questioned after pictures and videos of them dancing at the venue were circulated.

There are over a dozen political opposition members in prison. On December 16, 2022, the High Court's Rwamagana chamber sentenced Théophile Ntirutwa, a member of the unregistered Dalfa-Umurinzi opposition party, to seven years in prison for "spreading false information or harmful propaganda with intent to cause a hostile international opinion against [the] Rwandan Government." This criminal offense is incompatible with Rwanda's regional and international human rights obligations, particularly regarding free speech.

The trial of 10 people related to "Ingabire Day," an event scheduled for October 14, 2021, and organized by the Dalfa-Umurinzi to discuss, among other things, political repression in Rwanda, continued throughout 2023. At time of writing, eight party members were jailed in Kigali's Nyarugenge (Mageragere) prison and one was in hiding. Théoneste Nsengimana, a journalist who was planning to cover the event and is on trial with the group, is also jailed at the same prison. Human Rights Watch received credible information from former prisoners about torture and ill-treatment in Rwanda prisons, including Nyarugenge prison, where some have said they are being held in isolation and beaten.

Christopher Kayumba, the former editor of *The Chronicles* newspaper, who was arrested in 2021 shortly after establishing a new political party, the Rwandese Platform for Democracy (RPD), was released in February. He was acquitted of rape and "sexual misconduct" charges. In November, Kayumba was convicted on appeal and handed a two-year suspended sentence.

In March, the 25-year sentence of Paul Rusesabagina, a high-profile critic and United States resident, was commuted by presidential order. Rusesabagina's enforced disappearance in Dubai, United Arab Emirates, his illegal transfer to Rwanda, and the serious fair trial rights violations—including the interception of privileged communications between Rusesabagina and his lawyers—highlighted the Rwandan government's willingness and ability to target dissidents across its borders.

Freedom of Expression

At time of writing, several journalists and commentators were behind bars in Rwanda. In some cases, they were arrested for speaking out about security force abuses, including unlawful and arbitrary detention, torture, and extrajudicial killings, or for criticizing the ruling RPF and its human rights record.

The trial of blogger and commentator Aimable Karasira continued, on charges of genocide denial and justification and of divisionism. He has spoken about losing family members to both Hutu extremists and the RPF during and after the 1994 genocide. Judges ordered a medical examination into Karasira's mental health, which concluded that he suffers from "depression." Karasira and his defense lawyers accused Rwandan prison authorities of intercepting their communications and denying him access to adequate medical care and his medication, and they requested an independent examination by an international medical team.

In March, an additional 2 years were added to the 15-year sentence of Yvonne Idamange, a Tutsi online commentator and genocide survivor who criticized the Covid-19 lockdown and government-organized genocide commemorations. Her trial was held behind closed doors at the High Court's Special Chamber for International Crimes and Cross-border Crimes, after the prosecution argued she posed a risk to public order.

YouTube journalist Dieudonné Niyonsenga, alias "Cyuma Hassan"—who was sentenced to seven years in 2021, after reporting on the impact of the Covid-19 guidelines on vulnerable populations—remained in jail. Human Rights Watch received information indicating he is being subjected to ill-treatment and held in appalling conditions.

On January 19, Rwanda police reported that journalist John Williams Ntwali died in a road accident in Kimihurura, Kigali, on January 18 at 2:50 a.m. and that the driver of the car involved in the collision had been arrested. In the weeks that followed, Rwandan authorities failed to provide the exact location of the alleged accident, any photo or video evidence, or detailed information on others involved. A hasty trial was held in the absence of independent observers, including journalists, and the driver was convicted of manslaughter and unintentional bodily harm. Ntwali had told several people, including Human Rights Watch researchers, that he was being threatened.

Refugee Rights

Rwanda's support to the M23 armed group in eastern Congo has contributed to the displacement of over 1 million Congolese people. In January, the Rwandan president openly politicized refugee rights by threatening not to host Congolese refugees.

On June 29, the United Kingdom Court of Appeal ruled the UK-Rwanda Asylum Partnership Arrangement—under which the UK plans to expel to Rwanda asylum seekers who arrive irregularly in the UK—unlawful, concluding there is a real risk that asylum seekers sent to Rwanda would be returned to their home countries, where they face risk of persecution or other ill-treatment. The UK government appealed the ruling, and the UK Supreme Court found that the deal was unlawful in November, highlighting Rwanda's poor human rights record and serious defects in its asylum system.

Rwanda continued to target Rwandans around the world, including asylum seekers and refugees, to silence critics and stave off political opposition abroad. The abuse, extensively documented by Human Rights Watch in an October 2023 report, has led to Rwandans practicing self-censorship and living in fear of attacks, including in the UK.

Sexual Orientation and Gender Identity

Rwanda is one of the few countries in East Africa that does not criminalize consensual same-sex relations, and the government's policies are generally seen as progressive. However, in practice, lesbian, gay, bisexual, and transgender (LGBT) people have faced stigma because of their sexual orientation and gender identity.

International Justice

Efforts to hold accountable those responsible for the 1994 genocide in Rwanda continued. In May, a major genocide suspect, Fulgence Kayishema, was arrested in South Africa, after evading justice since 2001. He is alleged to have planned the killings of more than 2,000 men, women, and children on April 15, 1994, at a church in western Rwanda.

In June, a United Nations tribunal in the Hague suspended the trial of Félicien Kabuga for crimes committed during the 1994 Rwandan genocide. He is accused of playing a central role in planning, ordering, and carrying out the genocide. According to media reports, judges said Kabuga, now 90, was "unfit to participate meaningfully in his trial and is very unlikely to regain fitness in the future."

Key International Actors

After the UN Group of Experts on Congo named in June several senior Rwandan army commanders responsible for the Rwanda Defence Force's (RDF) support to the M23 armed group, the European Union in July imposed targeted financial and travel sanctions against nine individuals for "acts that constitute serious human rights violations and abuses" in eastern Congo, including Capt. Jean-Pierre Niragire, known as Gasasira, of the RDF. Earlier that month, the EU said it "firmly condemns Rwanda's support to M23 and Rwanda's military presence in Eastern DRC" and urged Rwanda to withdraw its troops.

In August, the US government imposed financial and property sanctions on six individuals, including senior Rwandan military commander Brig. Gen. Andrew Nyamvumba, for their roles in backing abusive armed groups in the conflict in eastern Congo.

The EU did not publicly speak out against human rights violations committed against activists, journalists, and other critics within the country.

HUMAN
RIGHTS
WATCH
"They Fired on Us Like Rain"
Saudi Arabian Mass Killings of Ethiopian Migrants
at the Yemen-Saudi Border

Saudi Arabia

Killings by Saudi Arabian forces of at least hundreds of Ethiopian migrants and asylum seekers at the Yemen-Saudi border may amount to crimes against humanity. Saudi Arabian authorities conducted arrests of peaceful dissidents, public intellectuals, and human rights activists and sentenced people to decades-long prison terms or death sentences for social media posts. Abusive practices in detention centers, including torture and ill-treatment, prolonged arbitrary detention, and asset confiscation without any clear legal process, remain pervasive. There has been no accountability for Saudi Arabia's role in apparent war crimes in Yemen.

Announced legal reforms are severely undermined by widespread repression under de facto ruler Crown Prince Mohammed bin Salman, known as MBS.

Authorities laundered their reputation, stained by a deplorable human rights record, by funding lavish sports and entertainment institutions, figures, and events. Saudi Arabia's Public Investment Fund (PIF) and the Professional Golfers' Association (PGA) have effectively enabled the Saudi government's efforts to "sportswash" its egregious human rights record through an announced agreement on June 6, which placed the government in an unprecedented position of influence and control of an entire sport, professional golf.

Freedoms of Expression, Association, and Belief

Dozens of Saudi human rights defenders and activists continued to serve long prison sentences for criticizing authorities or advocating for political and rights reforms.

Saudi authorities increasingly target Saudi and non-Saudi social media users for peaceful expression online and punish them with decades-long and even death sentences. On July 10, 2023, the Specialized Criminal Court, Saudi Arabia's counterterrorism tribunal, convicted Muhammad al-Ghamdi, 54, a retired Saudi teacher, of several criminal offenses related solely to his peaceful expression online. The court sentenced him to death, using his tweets, retweets, and YouTube activity as the evidence against him.

Women's rights defenders, including Loujain al-Hathloul, Nassimah al-Sadah, and Samar Badawi, remain banned from travel and under suspended prison sentences, allowing the authorities to return them to prison for any perceived criminal activity. Human rights activist Mohammed al-Rabea, aid worker Abdulrahman al-Sadhan, and human rights lawyer Waleed Abu al-Khair remained in prison on charges that relate to peaceful expression or activism.

Asylum Seekers, Migrants, and Migrant Workers

Saudi border guards killed at least hundreds of Ethiopian migrants and asylum seekers who tried to cross the Yemen-Saudi border between March 2022 and June 2023. Human Rights Watch found that Saudi border guards used explosive weapons to kill migrants and shot at migrants at close range, including many women and children, in a widespread and systematic pattern of attacks. In some instances, Saudi border guards asked migrants what limb to shoot and then shot them at close range. If committed as part of a Saudi government policy to murder migrants, these killings, which appear to continue, would be a crime against humanity.

Saudi Arabia's economy relies heavily on migrant workers. Based on its 2022 census, Saudi Arabia hosts almost 13.4 million migrants, comprising 41.6 percent of the population. Authorities continue to impose one of the most restrictive and abusive *kafala* (visa sponsorship) systems in the region, which remains largely unchanged despite recent reforms. The kafala system gives employers excessive power over migrant workers' mobility and legal status in the country and underpins their vulnerability to a wide range of abuses—from passport confiscation to delayed wages—which can amount to forced labor. Migrant domestic workers also face verbal, physical, and sexual abuse.

Saudi Arabia carries out regular arrests and deportations of undocumented migrant workers, including major arrest campaigns in November 2013 and August 2017. Many workers become undocumented through no fault of their own when their employers report them, sometimes falsely, for "absconding," even when they are fleeing abuse. Migrants are denied the right to contest their detention and deportation.

Yemen Airstrikes and Conflict

The Saudi and UAE-led coalition continue their military campaign against the Houthi armed group in Yemen, which has included unlawful airstrikes that have killed and wounded thousands of civilians.

In January, the United Kingdom's High Court of Justice heard a challenge to the UK government's renewed arms sales to Saudi Arabia.

A 2021 study commissioned by the United Nations Development Programme (UNDP) provided a projected estimate that the protracted conflict in Yemen has killed over 377,000 people directly or indirectly between 2015 and 2021. Key causes of death include inadequate food, health care, and infrastructure. Warring parties have targeted civilian objects, including homes, hospitals, schools, and bridges, internally displacing more than 4 million people in Yemen.

Criminal Justice System

Saudi Arabia has no written laws concerning sexual orientation or gender identity, but judges use principles of uncodified Islamic law to sanction people suspected of having sexual relations outside of marriage, including adultery, and same-sex relations. If individuals are engaging in such relations online, judges and prosecutors utilize vague provisions of the country's anti-cybercrime law that criminalize online activity impinging on "public order, religious values, public morals, and privacy."

An Egyptian doctor is serving a 10-year prison sentence in Saudi Arabia for links with the banned Muslim Brotherhood following what appears to have been an unfair trial. The court imprisoned Sabri Shalabi, 66, despite allegations that Saudi prosecutors based the charges largely on forced confessions and apparently in retaliation for a work-related dispute. A court originally handed down a 20-year prison sentence in August 2022, but it was reduced to 10 years in December 2022 on appeal.

In January, Moroccan authorities extradited Hassan Al Rabea, a Saudi citizen, to Saudi Arabia where he is at serious risk of arbitrary detention, torture, and an unfair trial. Saudi prosecutors' arrest warrant accused him of working with "terrorists" to help him leave Saudi Arabia "irregularly." Saudi authorities have previously targeted other members of Al Rabea's family, including two cousins who were executed in 2019 for alleged protest-related and terrorism offenses and a brother facing a death sentence for alleged terrorism.

Death Penalty

Saudi authorities executed Hussein Abu al-Khair, a Jordanian citizen, on March 12, 2023, after his conviction for a nonviolent drug crime. The judge ignored his allegations that he had confessed only after days of torture and ill-treatment. Under international law, the death penalty should only be imposed for the "most serious crimes" and in exceptional circumstances; international law explicitly excludes drug offenses from such punishment.

In June, two Bahraini Shia men were executed in Saudi Arabia following what Amnesty International described as a "grossly unfair trial" on terrorism-related charges.

Despite statements by Saudi Arabia's Human Rights Commission claiming that no one in Saudi Arabia will be executed for a crime committed as a child, the provision does not apply to *qisas*, retributive justice offenses usually for murder, or *hudud*, serious crimes defined under the country's interpretation of Islamic law that carry specific penalties.

Women's Rights

Saudi Arabia's first codified law on personal status, which was issued on March 8, 2022, International Women's Day, came into effect in June 2022. Although MBS and other Saudi government officials touted the law as "comprehensive" and "progressive," it formally enshrines male guardianship over women and includes provisions that facilitate domestic violence and sexual abuse in marriage.

Saudi women's rights activists long campaigned for a codified Personal Status Law that would end discrimination against women. However, the authorities provided them with no opportunity to offer input, as the bill was not made public before it was adopted. In recent years, Saudi women's rights activists have faced arbitrary arrest and detention, torture, and travel bans.

The Personal Status Law requires women to obtain a male guardian's permission to marry, codifying the country's longstanding practice. Married women are required to obey their husbands in a "reasonable manner." The law further states that neither spouse may abstain from sexual relations or cohabitation without the other spouse's consent, implying a marital right to intercourse.

While a husband can unilaterally divorce his wife, a woman can only petition a court to dissolve their marriage contract on limited grounds and must "establish [the] harm" that makes the continuation of marriage "impossible" within those grounds. The law does not specify what constitutes "harm" or what evidence can be submitted to support a case, leaving judges wide discretion in the law's interpretation and enforcement to maintain the status quo.

Fathers remain the default guardians of their children, limiting a mother's ability to participate fully in decisions related to her child's social and financial well-being. A mother may not act as her child's guardian unless a court appoints her, and she will otherwise have limited authority to make decisions for her child's well-being, even in cases where the parents do not live together and judicial authorities decide that the child should live with the mother.

Saudi Public Investment Fund and Abuses

The crown prince has consolidated economic power in Saudi Arabia, most notably via the country's sovereign wealth fund, the Public Investment Fund (PIF), with approximately US$700 billion in assets under management.

The fund has been directly involved in human rights abuses linked to the crown prince. They include the 2017 "anti-corruption" crackdown that involved arbitrary detentions, abusive treatment, and the extortion of property from former and current government officials, prominent businessmen, and rivals within the royal family as well as the 2018 murder of the Saudi journalist Jamal Khashoggi.

Some sovereign wealth funds are structurally separate and distinct from a government's chief executive. But the crown prince wields significant control over the PIF, one of the largest such funds in the world, and exercises unilateral decision-making with little transparency or accountability over the fund's decisions. While Saudi Arabia's state finances have long been characterized by a lack of transparency and oversight, the restructuring and dramatic expansion of the fund has consolidated—to an unprecedented degree—vast economic power in Saudi Arabia under the crown prince alone.

Technology and Rights

In February 2023, Microsoft announced its intention to invest in a cloud data center in Saudi Arabia to offer enterprise cloud services, despite the government's well-established record of infiltrating technology platforms and ongoing domestic repression.

Saudi Arabian authorities' egregious record on human rights, including their infiltration of X, the social media platform formerly known as Twitter, to spy on dissidents and targeting of human rights activists and political dissidents with sophisticated digital surveillance technology poses problems for companies committing to protect users' privacy rights.

Saudi Arabia's new data protection law and executive regulations grant sweeping powers to government agencies to access personal data and constitute a severe threat to privacy rights. The entities that control data are permitted to disclose data to state agencies based on vague and overbroad "security reasons," which are not defined in the law.

Climate Change Policy and Impacts

By its own admission, Saudi Arabia is "particularly vulnerable" to climate change as an "arid country with a harsh climate and sensitive ecosystem." Water scarcity is common in Saudi Arabia, most land is non-arable, and average rainfall is low. Yet Saudi Arabia remains one of the world's leading producers of fossil fuels.

Key International Actors

The United States provides logistical and intelligence support to Saudi-led coalition forces in Yemen and billions of dollars' worth of weapons. Human Rights Watch previously documented the coalition's use of US-manufactured weapons in at least 21 apparently unlawful attacks under the laws of war.

US President Joe Biden's administration issued a legal position that "recognizes and allows the immunity of Prime Minister Mohammed bin Salman as a sitting head of government of a foreign state"; therefore, he cannot be sued in US courts. No other publicly known accountability measures have been taken for the role of MBS in the brutal murder of Saudi journalist Jamal Khashoggi in 2018.

Negotiations for a trade agreement between the UK and the Gulf Cooperation Council (GCC)—a political and economic coordination body made up of Bahrain, Kuwait, Oman, Qatar, Saudi Arabia, and the United Arab Emirates (UAE)—continued throughout 2023. The UK has released very little information on the timeline and substance of the talks and has not publicly pledged to include detailed rights protections for countries such as Saudi Arabia and the UAE that have dismal rights records, including in regard to migrant workers.

Senegal

During 2023, arbitrary arrests of opposition figures and activists, security force use of excessive force, unjustified restrictions on civic space, and other human rights violations continued in Senegal.

On July 3, President Macky Sall announced he would not run for a third term in the 2024 presidential elections, many having said his candidacy would breach the country's constitution. On July 28, gendarmes arrested prominent opposition leader Ousmane Sonko, head of the political party Patriotes africains du Sénégal pour le travail, l'éthique et la fraternité (Patriots of Senegal for Work, Ethics, and Fraternity, PASTEF), on charges of fomenting insurrection and undermining state security.

Abuse of students remained a serious concern with girls facing high levels of sexual and gender-based violence, including rape, sexual exploitation, harassment, and other abuses, by teachers and school officials. The low retention rate of girls in secondary schools, where most of these cases go unreported and perpetrators are seldom held to account, is linked to these abuses.

Lesbian, gay, bisexual, and transgender (LGBT) people and activists continued to be subjected to smear campaigns and abuse, including arbitrary arrests, threats, and physical assaults. The law punishes any person who commits an "unnatural act" with a person of the same sex with a prison sentence of up to five years.

Exploitation, abuse, and neglect of children living in Senegal's traditional Quranic schools continued. Tens of thousands of these children, known as *talibés*, live in conditions of extreme squalor, deprived of adequate food and medical care.

Excessive Use of Force

During protests in March, May, and June, security forces used excessive force to maintain public order.

On March 16, in Dakar, Senegal's capital, police used tear gas on protesters supporting opposition leader Sonko, ahead of a court case in which he was facing charges of libel. Police forcefully extracted Sonko from his vehicle and drove him to the courthouse. The previous day, March 15, police had also fired teargas at

Guy Marius Sagna, an opposition member of parliament, while he attempted to visit Sonko at his home.

In mid-May, young protestors took to the streets in Dakar's Ngor neighborhood, denouncing an increasingly "repressive state." Security forces responded with excessive use of force, firing bullets and tear gas. The violence resulted in one teenager being killed and 30 people wounded.

Between May 31 and June 3, violent demonstrations broke out in Dakar after Sonko was sentenced to two years in jail on June 1 for allegedly corrupting youth, undermining his chances to run in the 2024 presidential election. On June 2, the army was deployed to strengthen security in Dakar. Demonstrators built barricades, blocked main roads, burned tires, destroyed and looted public and private property, and threw stones at the police, who responded with teargas. Various witnesses reported the presence of armed "thugs" among the security forces, and the opposition has accused the authorities of using armed civilians, alongside security forces, during protests. The media reported similar accounts during these demonstrations and previous ones in Senegal. International media also reported the use of live bullets during the protests in Dakar, leading to the deaths of a 15-year-old boy and a 26-year-old male student.

On June 4, Minister of the Interior Antoine Diome said the violence led to 16 deaths and 500 arrests across Senegal. In a statement on the same day, PASTEF said security forces and "militias" killed 19 people and urged Senegalese people "to defend themselves by all means and to fight back." According to lawyers and the opposition, from May 30 to June 2, in and around Dakar alone, security forces arrested at least 250 people, including children—mostly PASTEF members and supporters, but also civil society activists—and beat some of them.

Crackdown on Media and Dissent

Throughout the year, the authorities cracked down on the media and dissent. Security forces arbitrarily arrested and detained journalists and other dissenting voices. They also restricted access to mobile internet and some social media platforms and banned demonstrations organized by the political opposition.

The National Council for Audiovisual Regulation suspended Walf TV over its coverage of the opposition-led demonstrations in Senegal for seven days on February 10 and again for one month on June 9.

On March 10, security forces arrested Senegal's former prime minister Cheikh Hadjibou Soumare on charges of libel after he asked President Macky Sall in a public letter if he had provided funds to French far-right leader Marine Le Pen. He was released on March 13 and placed under judicial supervision.

On May 16, security forces arrested journalist Ndèye Maty Niang, also known as Maty Sarr Niang, at her home in Dakar and charged her with "calling for insurrection, violence, hatred," and other crimes, following her Facebook posts in which she criticized Senegalese authorities.

On June 1, as protests rocked Dakar and other parts of the country, the interior minister announced restrictions on social media, including Facebook, Twitter, WhatsApp, Instagram, YouTube, Telegram, and Tik Tok, to stop the "dissemination of hate and subversive messages." On June 4, the government extended the restrictions to mobile internet access. Those restrictions prevented journalists, human rights activists, and others from communicating, getting information, or reporting on unfolding events.

During the June protests in Dakar, security forces intimidated journalists and prevented them from covering unfolding events. On May 29, gendarmes stopped a team of three journalists working for Senegalese online media Senegal7, seized their telephones and cameras, and prevented them from filming PASTEF protesters who had gathered in Dakar's Sacré-Cœur neighborhood.

On June 15, the authorities banned an opposition-led demonstration in Dakar. Dakar's prefect said the demonstration, organized by Sonko's supporters, posed threats to public order.

On July 28, gendarmes arrested Sonko on charges of fomenting insurrection, undermining state security, creating serious political unrest, and criminal association, among others.

On July 31, Senegal's interior minister announced the dissolution of PASTEF for rallying its supporters during violent protests in June 2023 and in March 2021. PASTEF condemned its dissolution as "anti-democratic." On the same day, the government also restricted access to mobile data internet services to stop what it called the spread of "hateful and subversive" messages on social media. On

June 6, Sonko, who started a hunger strike in protest against his detention, was admitted to emergency care at a hospital in Dakar.

On July 29, police arrested Pape Alé Niang, the outspoken editor of the news site Dakarmatin, on charges of "insurrection" at his home in Dakar, following comments he made in a live broadcast on his Facebook page about Sonko's arrest on July 28. He was provisionally released after a 10-day hunger strike. This was the third time security forces had arrested Niang since November 2022.

On October 28, Khalifa Sall—leader of the Taxawu party, former mayor of Dakar, and a presidential candidate—denounced the police who prevented his convoy from entering the Fatick region, southeast of Dakar. The police said the 30-vehicle convoy had not been authorized. Khalifa Sall's intent had been to continue his campaign to collect the sponsorships necessary for the approval of his candidacy.

On October 27, security forces arrested PASTEF leader, Amadou Ba, at the end of a television show. At time of writing, Ba's lawyers said no reason for his arrest had been given.

Sexual Orientation and Gender Identity

LGBT people and activists continued to be subjected to smear campaigns and abuse.

Article 319 of Senegal's penal code punishes sexual intercourse termed "acts against nature" between persons of the same sex with up to five years in prison.

On August 15, police arrested 10 young men during a party in a private home in Dakar and detained them for "acts against nature" and possession of digital content that was "contrary to public decency." They were beaten, extorted, and physically abused by the police, then released one month later for lack of evidence. Some were not able to return to their families for fear of stigmatization.

On October 28, in Kaolack, a mob dug up the body of a man suspected of having been gay, dragged it through town, and then burned it in an egregious incident that was caught on camera, and the video was posted on social media. On October 29, Senegal's state prosecutor announced an investigation had been opened. On October 30, four suspects were arrested in connection with the incident.

Abuses against Talibé Children in Quranic Schools

Abuse, exploitation, and neglect of children attending Senegal's still-unregulated, traditional Quranic boarding schools (*daaras*) continued at alarming rates. Tens of thousands of children known as *talibés* are forced by their Quranic teachers in Senegal to beg daily for money, food, rice, or sugar. Many Quranic teachers (also known as *marabouts*) and their assistants continue to set daily begging quotas, enforced with beatings, while subjecting talibés to neglect. Many daaras are housed in decrepit or unfinished buildings without water, sanitation, electricity, or security, exposing the children to health and safety risks. Each year, thousands of talibés, including Senegalese and foreign children, migrate to major cities to attend Senegal's daaras. Thousands of talibés are victims of human trafficking, which under Senegalese law includes the act of exploiting children for money through forced begging as well as the recruitment or transport of children for this purpose.

Despite strong domestic laws banning child abuse, neglect, endangerment, and human trafficking, these are rarely enforced against Quranic teachers. The government has made some efforts to improve daara conditions and remove children from the streets, but sustained commitment by authorities to stop forced begging and abuse of talibés has proven elusive.

Sexual and Gender-Based Violence

Senegalese girls face high levels of sexual and gender-based violence, including sexual exploitation, harassment, and abuse by teachers and school officials as well as rape and sexual abuse by other students.

In March, 27 girls filed rape charges against their Quranic teacher, 34-year-old Serigne Khadim Mbacké, in Touba, central Senegal. On June 5, after several weeks on the run, Mbacké was arrested by security forces.

The government has yet to accept the scale of school-related sexual violence or take concrete actions to tackle school-related sexual violence and protect survivors when and after they report abuses.

Serbia

Independent journalists continued to be subjected to threats and intimidation in 2023. War crimes prosecutions remained slow, inefficient, and marred by delays. Attacks and threats against lesbian, gay, bisexual, and transgender (LGBT) people and organizations continued. Serbia and Kosovo signed a joint declaration on missing persons in May as part of an EU-brokered normalization process, but relations deteriorated after clashes in northern Kosovo later that month linked to a contested election.

Freedom of Media

Independent journalists remain under pressure with an inadequate state response.

In the first half of the year, the Permanent Group for the Safety of Journalists registered 42 cases of threats against journalists and the Independent Journalists' Association recorded three attacks by the end of March.

In March, Stevan Dojcinovic, investigative journalist and editor of the independent news portal *KRIK*, received a death threat on TikTok after a podcast where he mentioned that the price for contract killings had dropped drastically. Authorities were investigating at time of writing.

During a Belgrade protest in March denouncing the European Union's plan for the normalization of relations between Serbia and Kosovo, *FoNet* news agency reporter Marko Dragoslavić was forcibly hooded and punched in the face when leaving the protest. Dragoslavić reported the attack to the police and the case was under investigation at time of writing.

Journalists remained a target of so-called strategic lawsuits against public participation (SLAPP).

In May, the High Court in Belgrade ruled against *KRIK* for publishing an article in 2021 listing those who had sued the outlet for defamation, including a police chief and two employees from the Police Unit for Witness Protection. The court ordered the removal of the article and awarded 374,200 Serbian dinars (about

US$3,643) in damages to the plaintiffs. *KRIK* has appealed the decision. By May, *KRIK* was the target of 12 defamation lawsuits.

In September, the European Court of Human Rights ruled that Serbia violated TV channel *B92*'s freedom of expression when the assistant health minister sued the station over reports alleging she had abused her office in the procurement process for swine flu vaccines. The court held that the *B92* had acted in "good faith and with the diligence expected of responsible journalism."

In March, the retrial of Ratko Romić and Milan Radonjić, two Serbian state security officers accused of participating in the 1999 murder of journalist Slavko Ćuruvija, started. In April, the Belgrade Appeals Court released the suspects from house arrest, following a European Court of Human Rights decision in early April stating that Serbia had violated their rights by holding them in custody for too long.

Pro-government media continued smear campaigns against independent journalists reporting critically on the government.

Accountability for War Crimes

Between January and August, the War Crimes Prosecutor's Office launched three new war crimes investigations involving seven suspects. As of August, 24 cases against 41 defendants were pending before Serbian courts. Ongoing proceedings were marred by significant delays.

In February, following a retrial, the Belgrade High Court found former Bosnian Serb soldier Dalibor Krstović guilty of crimes against civilians, including rape in Kalinovik, Bosnia and Herzegovina (BiH), in August 1992, and sentenced Krstović to nine years' imprisonment.

In April, the trial against Lazar Murlak, a former Bosnian Serb wartime reserve police officer and member of the Sprsko Gorazde Territorial Defence, started at the Belgrade High Court. Murlak is charged with rape of a Bosniak woman in 1992 in Lozje, BiH.

In February, the Belgrade High Court sentenced four Serbian former fighters to a total of 35 years in prison for participating in the 1993 abduction in Strpci, BiH, of 20 non-Serb train passengers, who were subsequently killed.

In July, the Appeals Court in Belgrade ordered a retrial and overturned the November 2022 conviction of Bosnian Serb Danko Vladičić for the killing of an older man and woman in Brod na Drini, BiH, in 1992.

In May, the UN International Residual Mechanism for Criminal Tribunals in The Hague increased the prison sentences of former head of Serbian state security, Jovica Stanišić, and his deputy, Franko Simatović, from 12 to 15 years. They were convicted for their role in forcibly removing non-Serbs from parts of BiH and Croatia in 1992 and 1995 as well as murders, deportation, inhumane acts, and persecution.

Refugees, Asylum Seekers, and Migrants

Between January and September, 1,257 new arrivals registered their intent to seek asylum, but only 150 people lodged asylum applications.

The asylum system remained flawed, with asylum seekers facing difficulties in accessing procedures, low recognition rates, and long delays. Between January and September, Serbia granted refugee status to six people and subsidiary protection to two. Between late February 2022 and late October 2023, Serbia granted temporary protection to 1,387 people, almost exclusively from Ukraine.

By the end of August, 109 unaccompanied migrant children were registered with Serbian authorities. Serbia lacks formal age assessment procedures for unaccompanied children, putting older children at risk of being treated as adults instead of receiving special protection.

In July, the European Court of Human Rights found that Serbia had violated the freedom of movement of a Syrian national to whom Serbia had granted asylum and then denied access to refugee travel documents.

Sexual Orientation and Gender Identity

LGBT people continued to face intolerance, threats, and violence. Between January and September, a domestic LGBT+ support group, Da Se Zna!, recorded 32 incidents of hate-motivated incidents against LGBT people, including seven physical attacks and five threats. In August, President Aleksandar Vučić said that as long as he is president, he will not sign any law recognizing a third gender or same-sex marriage.

In February, unknown assailants attacked three LGBT people in central Belgrade. One victim was stabbed with a knife, and the other two were injured by a broken bottle. The following night, another was injured by security guards at a club.

In May, an unknown person vandalized the Belgrade Pride Info Center by throwing red paint at the Center's window and the Belgrade Pride logo. It was the 18th attack on the center since 2018.

Women's and Girls' Rights

A September report by Council of Europe Human Rights Commissioner Dunja Mijatovic raised serious concerns about the high prevalence of domestic violence and stressed the need for a coordinated institutional response to protect women and girls from violence and provide immediate and long-term support to survivors.

Disability Rights

Children with disabilities continue to be overrepresented in institutional care. Nearly 75 percent of children in institutions in Serbia are children with disabilities. Despite a legal ban, children under the age of 3 continue to be placed in institutional care, including due to socioeconomic reasons, according to UNICEF. In three out of six institutions for children with disabilities across the country, children with disabilities live with unrelated adults, putting them at a potentially greater risk of violence and abuse.

Almost 30 percent of children with disabilities who live in institutions are not enrolled in school; those who are enrolled attend segregated special schools for children with disabilities.

The number of adults with disabilities living in institutions in Serbia increased compared to previous years. The government continues to invest in institutional care for such adults, including by expanding existing institutions, while support in communities remains limited.

Key International Actors

In March, the Organization for Security and Co-operation in Europe (OSCE) Representative on Freedom of the Media Teresa Ribeiro and Head of the OSCE Mission to Serbia Jan Braathu expressed concerns about the targeting of journalists in Serbia and urged authorities to thoroughly investigate all incidents and hold perpetrators accountable for violence and threats.

Council of Europe Human Rights Commissioner Dunja Mijatovic in March called on Serbia to increase safety for journalists and to protect women from violence.

The November EU Commission enlargement report on Serbia said that while authorities had started to implement key judicial reforms, more work and political commitment are needed to implement comprehensive rule of law reforms. The Commission remained concerned about media freedom, noting the continuation of threats, intimidation, hate speech, and violence against journalists and an increase in SLAPPs by members of national and local authorities.

Singapore

Singapore's criminal justice system fell under the international spotlight as the authorities carried out the highest number of executions for drug-related offenses in over a decade, including the first woman put to death in almost 20 years. The government harassed, intimidated, and persecuted civil society activists and independent media practitioners in the lead-up to presidential elections in September, which saw the election of Tharman Shanmugaratnam, a former deputy prime minister and finance minister, to the largely ceremonial post.

Singapore abolished article 377A of the penal code, the colonial-era provision criminalizing same-sex relations between men. The 15th annual Pink Dot pride event on June 24 drew thousands of participants to rally around the theme of "celebrating all families," but marriage equality remains an uphill battle after the government approved a constitutional amendment to bar legal challenges to the current definition of marriage as being between a man and a woman.

Criminal Justice System

Singapore provides for the use of the death penalty for drug-related offenses and other crimes. Despite widespread international condemnation, the Singaporean government continued to defend its renewed use of the death penalty for drug-related offenses following a two-year Covid-related hiatus in executions that ended in March 2022.

As of November 2023, Singapore has executed 16 people for drug-related offenses since executions resumed. On April 26, Tagaraju Suppia was executed for his involvement in the trafficking of one kilogram of cannabis in 2013. The United Nations human rights office, the Office of the High Commissioner for Human Rights (OHCHR), issued an urgent call to not proceed with the execution on grounds that the penalty was not appropriate for a drug trafficking offense and was out of line with "international norms and standards."

During one week between July and August 2023, Singapore conducted three back-to-back executions, including of Saridewi Djamani, the first woman to be executed in the country in almost two decades.

Women's and Girls' Rights

Women and girls in Singapore experience sexual and gender-based violence as well as various forms of workplace discrimination, including a lack of legal protections for pregnant employees. Sexual harassment at work remains prevalent, pushing women to leave their jobs and impacting their financial stability. The Singaporean government has taken a positive step for labor rights by enshrining in law the Tripartite Guidelines on Fair Employment Practices (TGFEP), which seeks to prevent discrimination in the world of work. The government has not ratified the International Labour Organization Violence and Harassment Convention (C190), which requires comprehensive protections to end violence and harassment, including gender-based violence, at work.

Freedom of Expression

Singapore frequently uses overly broad and restrictive laws to silence criticism of the government and restrict the rights to freedom of expression and peaceful assembly.

The Protection from Online Falsehoods and Manipulation Act (POFMA), enacted in 2019, gives the government broad discretionary powers to censor online content. The government used the law repeatedly this year to silence, investigate, and persecute independent media, opposition politicians, and critical civil society actors, forcing them to post subjective government-determined "corrections" and intimidating others to exercise self-censorship.

In May, the government targeted The Online Citizen (TOC) chief editor Terry Xu for publishing an article on TOC's website that made allegations against the police and issued a demand for a correction. The authorities had previously targeted Xu and the TOC numerous times for reporting critical of the government. As a result of the government's legal harassment, the TOC moved its operations out of Singapore.

In June, the authorities used the POFMA against the independent media outlet *Asia Sentinel* for a May 24 article about retaliation against a Singaporean whistleblower. When *Asia Sentinel* refused to publish the POFMA notice, authorities blocked the website in Singapore. In a statement, the media outlet referred to the POFMA as a "draconian provision" deliberately used by the government to silence critics.

In July, the government enacted the Online Criminal Harms Act, which grants additional sweeping powers to restrict and remove online content on overly broad grounds that could undermine freedom of expression.

The Hostile Information Campaigns provisions of the Foreign Interference (Counter-Measures) Act (FICA) provide broad powers to the home minister to require the removal or disabling of online content, publication of mandatory messages drafted by the government, banning of apps from being downloaded in Singapore, and disclosure of information by internet and social media companies. The minister's authority under the law is reinforced by severe criminal penalties and judicial review is limited to only procedural matters. The government can also designate individuals as "politically significant persons" who can be required to follow strict limits on receiving funding and to disclose all links with foreigners. The law's broad language encompasses a wide range of ordinary activities by civil society activists, academics, and journalists who engage with non-Singaporeans.

Freedom of Assembly

The government maintains tight restrictions on the right to peaceful assembly through the Public Order Act (POA), requiring a police permit for any "cause-related" assembly if it is held in a public place or in a private venue if members of the public are invited. The definition of an "assembly" is extremely broad, and those who fail to obtain the required permits face criminal charges. The POA provides the police commissioner with the authority to reject any permit application for an assembly or procession "directed towards a political end" if any foreigner is involved.

Attacks on Human Rights Defenders

The Singaporean government also cracked down on critical views by silencing human rights defenders under the guise of protecting its judicial system.

In a letter to the Singaporean government made public in January 2023, Mary Lawlor, the UN special rapporteur on human rights defenders, expressed deep concern about government suppression and intimidation against human rights defenders Kirsten Han and Rocky Howe for their advocacy opposing the death penalty in Singapore.

In March, the Singaporean High Court suspended the law license of human rights defender and lawyer Ravi Madasamy for five years. Madasamy has played a critical role in defending death row detainees and earned the ire of the government, courts, and legal establishment for his sharp criticisms, which the government has repeatedly claimed undermine the judiciary.

Somalia

An uptick in fighting in several parts of the country resulted in hundreds of civilian casualties and forced almost 650,000 people to flee. While famine conditions were averted, five consecutive below-average annual rains continued to have a devastating impact on the realization of the rights to food and health, with at least 4.3 million people in urgent need of food assistance.

Fighting broke out in the contested town of Las Anod, on the Somaliland-Puntland border, between Somaliland security forces and armed groups linked to the Dhulbahante clan, leaving dozens of civilians dead and forcing over 154,000 people to flee internally or, for many, to Ethiopia.

The armed group Al-Shabab conducted targeted and indiscriminate attacks that killed hundreds of civilians. The offensive against Al-Shabab launched by President Hassan Sheikh Mohamud in 2022 in central Somalia, in which government forces supported clan militia, led to civilian displacement. In March, the president announced a new offensive in southern Somalia.

In June, the African Union Transition Mission in Somalia (ATMIS) withdrew 2,000 of an estimated 20,000 forces from Somalia as part of its expected withdrawal by late 2024. The Somali government requested in September a delay in the withdrawal of an additional 3,000 troops.

The government has not reformed Somalia's outdated penal code. It approved a law granting the abusive national intelligence agency broader powers of detention and surveillance. Authorities throughout Somalia harassed and arbitrarily arrested journalists.

Somalia criminalizes consensual same-sex conduct with up to three years in prison.

Attacks on Civilians

According to the International Committee of the Red Cross (ICRC), an increase in fighting in several parts of the country resulted in greater conflict-related deaths and injuries.

Al-Shabab's targeted and indiscriminate attacks—using improvised explosive devices (IEDs), suicide bombings, shelling, and targeted killings—resulted in a high number of civilian casualties. The armed group conducted attacks in areas that the government had taken control of as part of its operations in central Somalia.

In June, there were clashes between security forces and armed opposition groups in Puntland's capital, Garowe, following a debate in parliament over changes to the voting system, with opposition members accusing the regional president of seeking to extend his term. Media reported that at least 26 people were killed.

Between January and September, 1.5 million people were newly internally displaced, 40 percent of whom were displaced due to conflict, the United Nations reported.

The Somali government did not hand over Al-Shabab cases from military to civilian courts. Authorities throughout the country carried out executions, many following military court proceedings that violated international fair trial standards.

Al-Shabab fighters continued to execute individuals accused of working or spying for the government and foreign forces, often after unfair trials.

In March, the president signed into law a National Security and Intelligence Agency (NISA) bill that granted sweeping powers of arrest, detention, and surveillance with minimal independent oversight to the abusive agency.

Displacement and Access to Humanitarian Assistance

The humanitarian situation remained dire. After Somalia faced five consecutive below-average rains, the Gu rains from March to June were better than forecasted, helping to reduce some of the immense constraints, including food price hikes. However, the rains also resulted in flash floods, forcing tens of thousands to flee in parts of the country.

The UN predicted that between October and December 2023, nearly 4.3 million people are expected to be acutely food insecure; between August 2023 and July 2024, 1.5 million children are expected to be acutely malnourished. Somalia is heavily dependent on food imports.

Al-Shabab continued to besiege government-controlled towns. For 10 days in July, Al-Shabab blocked routes into Baidoa town.

Humanitarian agencies faced serious access challenges due to conflict, targeted attacks on aid workers, generalized violence, restrictions imposed by parties to the conflict, including arbitrary taxation and bureaucratic hurdles, and physical constraints due to extreme weather.

In July, Médecins Sans Frontières (Doctors Without Borders, MSF) announced they were withdrawing from Las Anod due to increased levels of violence, recurrent attacks on medical facilities, and injuries among medical staff.

People across Somalia continue to face high levels of trauma due to prolonged violence and humanitarian crises. However, the availability of mental health services in the country remains limited.

Freedom of Expression

Regional and federal authorities continued to harass, intimidate, and detain journalists.

Abdalle Ahmed Mumin, secretary general of the Somali Journalists Syndicate (SJS), was sentenced by a court in February, four months after his arrest after he raised concerns about a government directive restricting reporting on national security issues. Upon sentencing, the court ordered his release on the basis that he had already served his term. He was rearrested 10 days afterward and only eventually released on March 26.

In August, Mohamed Ibrahim Osman Bulbul, journalist at the privately owned broadcaster Kaab TV and member of SJS, was detained and charged with "bringing the State into contempt" and "circulating false and tendentious news." His detention came a day after he reported on alleged government misuse of funds linked to European Union capacity-building trainings of police. A high court judge stated that he could not be charged under the criminal code and then eventually ordered Mohamed's release in October. According to the Committee to Protect Journalists, the SJS's website was the victim of a cyberattack in August.

Sexual and Gender-Based Violence

The UN continued to report incidents of conflict-related sexual and gender-based violence, including against girls. The UN recorded an increase in gender-based violence from 2022 onward, documenting particularly high rates, notably domestic violence and rape, among displaced women and girls.

At time of writing, the sexual offenses bill of 2018, a progressive sexual violence legislation that stalled following backlash, citing religious objections, has not been presented before parliament. The Somali criminal code classifies sexual violence as an "offense against modesty and sexual honor" rather than a violation of bodily integrity.

Abuses against Children

Grave abuses against children continued to be documented by the UN, including killing and maiming, recruitment and use, and sexual violence. Schools continued to be attacked.

Children continued to be detained on allegations of Al-Shabab affiliation. The independent expert on the human rights situation in Somalia reported that Somali security forces, including members of NISA, increased their arrests and detentions of children in areas recently taken over by the Somali government from Al-Shabab. The independent expert raised concerns about the sentencing to death of six young men by the military court in Puntland, some of whom were children at the time of the commission of the alleged crime.

In July, the federal government adopted age verification guidelines that the UN said are intended to reduce the recruitment of children into armed forces and the detention and trial of children in adult procedures.

A bill to domesticate the Convention on the Rights of the Child was pending before parliament at time of writing.

The UN Children's Fund (UNICEF) estimates that 45 percent of girls are married before age 18. An estimate for boys was not provided.

Somaliland

In February 2023, fighting broke out between Somaliland security forces and armed fighters affiliated with the Dhulbahante clan following months of mounting tensions in the contested border town of Las Anod.

The Human Rights and Protection Group of the UN Assistance Mission in Somalia (UNSOM) documented 552 civilian casualties, including 87 deaths, between late December and June due to the fighting in the town. Amnesty International reported that the fighting had killed at least 100 people and injured over 600, dozens of them civilians, including women, children, and health workers. The ICRC treated 1,700 people with conflict-related injuries.

Amnesty International found that the Somaliland forces had indiscriminately shelled the town, damaging hospitals, schools, and mosques. The UN reported that as of April, the fighting had displaced between 154,000 and 203,000 people, the majority women and children, with most fleeing into Ethiopia's Somali region. Fighting continued at time of writing.

The authorities in Somaliland continued to restrict freedom of expression and media. On May 15, Somaliland police arrested journalist Bushaaro Ali Mohamed near the border with Ethiopia. On August 15, Bushaaro was sentenced to one year in prison, accused of tarnishing the image of state institutions.

Key International Actors

Funding for humanitarian assistance improved in late 2022 but was still underfunded, with the humanitarian response plan only 36 percent funded at time of writing. In April, during a visit to Somalia, the UN secretary-general called on donors to step up their support for the plan.

In September, the EU temporarily halted funding for the UN World Food Progamme, after a UN internal investigation reportedly found evidence of widespread theft and diversion of assistance by landowners, local authorities, and security forces. In March, the EU approved an additional €110 million to support Somalia's armed forces and ATMIS in Somalia.

The United States acknowledged conducting at least 13 airstrikes in support of the Somali national army's operations against Al-Shabab, primarily in central Somalia. In September, the US Africa Command (AFRICOM) stated that it had helped with the medical evacuation of civilians injured in a Somali government operation in El Lahelay. In January, the US gave US$9 million in new military aid to Somali forces, the first direct military support since US forces, including Special Forces, returned to Somalia throughout 2022.

The International Crisis Group reported that Türkiye had also carried out drone strikes in Lower and Middle Shabelle.

Representatives of Somalia's key security partners, the "Quintet," from Qatar, Türkiye, the United Arab Emirates (UAE), the United Kingdom, and the US, met in June and expressed support for Somalia's military offensive and efforts to meet "the technical benchmarks on weapons and ammunition management to enable the UN security council to fully lift the arms control on the Somali federal government."

In February 2023, the UAE and Somalia signed a security agreement strengthening military, security, and counterterrorism ties. The deal apparently allows the UAE to build military bases in Somalia.

South Africa

In 2023, former President Jacob Zuma's corruption trial faced delays, raising questions as to whether Zuma would be held accountable. Members of the VIP Protection Unit of the South African Police Service (SAPS) were suspended for misconduct, facing charges of assault, malicious damage to property, and pointing a firearm at civilians. Environmental challenges remain a concern as air pollution continues to harm the health and well-being of South Africans. Entrenched sexual violence and discrimination prevent the realization of the rights of women and lesbian, gay, bisexual, and transgender (LGBT) people. While guaranteed in legislation, the rights of older people and children have come under threat, and xenophobia against African and Asian foreign nationals continued throughout the year.

Right to a Healthy Environment

Following the March 18, 2022, landmark judgment that the poor air quality resulting from coal and other industrial fossil fuel operations in the Highveld Priority Area in Mpumalanga and some parts of Gauteng violated residents' constitutional right to an environment that is not harmful to their health and well-being, there has been scant progress in the Highveld to meet health-based air quality standards. Instead, it is reported that Eskom, South Africa's largest electricity producer and supplier, is using the current energy crisis in South Africa as an excuse for non-compliance with the country's Minimum Emission Standards. Failure to meet the standards by 2030 would not only cost South Africa 42 billion rands (R) (about US$2.2 billion) and worsen the climate crisis, but also cost lives, with 2,300 deaths projected per year from air pollution.

In June, the Standerton Regional Court imposed an R70 million ($3.7 million) fine—one of the highest on record in South Africa for an environmental offense—on the Lekwa Local Municipality in Mpumalanga for contravening environmental legislation. A condition of the Lekwa prosecution agreement is that the fine will be used to rehabilitate and repair dysfunctional wastewater treatment works in Standerton and other parts of the Lekwa Local Municipality over the next three years.

Rule of Law

The corruption trial of former President Zuma was repeatedly delayed, and there are concerns that such delays are a possible ploy to avoid accountability. At time of writing, the trial was ongoing. On August 11, Zuma was released on special remission, following the expiration of his prison sentence for contempt of court. The remission was for low-risk offenders and aimed at alleviating overcrowding in prisons. It is reported that Zuma spent only 2 months in prison out of a 15-month sentence imposed in February 2021 for his failure to appear before the State Capture Inquiry.

On August 21, the Gauteng High Court in Johannesburg postponed to 2024 the opening of a trial against those accused of the 1982 murders of Eustice "Bimbo" Madikela, Peter "Ntshingo" Matabane, and Fanyana Nhlapo and the attempted murder of Zandisile Musi. The four anti-apartheid activists were members of the Congress of South African Students, collectively known as the "COSAS 4." Christiaan Rorich and Thlomedi Mfalapitsa are the accused in the matter, charged with kidnapping, murder, and crimes against humanity of murder and apartheid for unlawfully and intentionally killing the three students in the context of "a systemic attack or elimination of political opponents of the apartheid regime."

Police Abuses

On July 2, members of the SAPS's VIP Protection Unit viciously attacked three motorists in Johannesburg. In video footage taken by a witness, the officers are seen dragging a victim to the edge of the highway before punching and kicking him on the ground. Identified as members of the deputy president's security detail, the policemen face charges of assault, malicious damage to property, and pointing a firearm. The officers have also been sanctioned under SAPS's disciplinary regulations.

Violence against Women and Girls

Violence against women and girls is widespread, endemic, and an enduring nightmare in South Africa. The World Population Review for 2023 ranks South Africa among the top six countries with the highest femicide rates worldwide. Official crime statistics reveal that between April and June 2023, the police

HUMAN
RIGHTS
WATCH
"This Government is
Failing Me Too"
South Africa Compounds Legacy of Apartheid for Older People

recorded 6,228 counts of murder, averaging 68 murders per day. Of those killed, 1,188 were "women and children," including boys. In the sexual offenses category, an alarming 9,252 cases of rape were reported countrywide during the same period. Many women and girls, especially in the rural areas, find it difficult to access the justice system.

Older People's Rights

Hundreds of thousands of older people do not have access to the community- and home-based care and support services they are entitled to under the Older Persons Act. The government allocates insufficient resources for services, places restrictions on what services nongovernmental organizations (NGOs) can offer, and does not provide enough social workers. The Grant-in-Aid, the social security entitlement for people who require full-time support at home, pays an amount equivalent to less than one day's pay, based on the national minimum wage of R25.42 per hour ($1.36). The Older Persons Grant, the main source of income for 4 million older people on low incomes, increased by 5 percent in 2023 while food prices rose by 14 percent.

Sexual Orientation and Gender Identity

LGBT people, particularly lesbian women and transgender men in townships, are often targets of sexual assault and murder. On March 14, the National Assembly passed the Prevention and Combating of Hate Crimes and Hate Speech Bill to create criminal offenses for hate crimes and hate speech. In August, a revised National Intervention Strategy to combat violence against LGBT people was approved by the cabinet, and the National Task Team that coordinates government and civil society responses has been elevated to the portfolio of the deputy minister of justice.

Children's Rights

Over the last decade, many children have died in pit toilets, and in 2020, the basic education minister, Angie Motshekga, had said that the Basic Education Department planned to eradicate pit latrines by March 2022. However, throughout 2023, pit latrines remained in many rural schools. On March 7, the body of a 4-year-old girl was found in a pit toilet in a school in the Eastern Cape. The police have opened an inquest and an investigation into the circumstances of her death.

Xenophobia

Xenophobic attitudes and violence continued in the post-Covid-19 context in South Africa.

In January, members of the anti-immigrant vigilante group Operation Dudula prevented immigrant patients, in some instances violently, from accessing the Jeppe Clinic in central Johannesburg, saying immigrants should access healthcare services in their countries of origin.

Zandspruit Clinic and Cosmo City Clinic also reportedly faced similar incidents during 2023. Collective Voices against Health Xenophobia—a consortium of progressive civil society organizations, activists, healthcare workers, and researchers working on issues of social justice and challenging xenophobia within the healthcare sector—condemned xenophobic acts and called on the government to uphold South Africa's human rights legislation and international obligations recognizing the right to health for everyone, regardless of immigration status.

Thousands of Zimbabweans who fled political repression and economic deprivation in their country and lived for years in South Africa under Zimbabwean Exemption Permits (ZEPs) faced a renewed risk of expulsion after the Department of Home Affairs (DHA) announced that their permits would be canceled after June 2023. On June 28, the Pretoria High Court ruled the cancellation of ZEPs unlawful and unconstitutional, labeling it an "unjustified limitation of rights" and granted permit holders a 12-month reprieve. On September 18, the DHA initiated steps to appeal the judgment to the Supreme Court of Appeal and lost the appeal. On November 10, the DHA proposed a migration system overhaul. Among the DHA's proposals are that South Africa withdraw from the Refugee Convention and reaccede to it with reservations. This would be a damaging backslide on South Africa's commitments.

In August, a fire in a five-story building in Johannesburg's central business district killed more than 70 people. The building had served as an "informal settlement," primarily for undocumented migrants living with little to no access to electricity, water, or sanitation. In the wake of the tragedy, many South Africans blamed foreign nationals, with some claiming that eviction laws protect criminals by making it difficult to remove people who are occupying buildings without authorization.

Foreign Policy

In August, South Africa hosted the 15th BRICS Summit. Prior to the summit, a court ruled that South Africa was obligated to arrest President Vladimir Putin of Russia should he attend because he is subject to an International Criminal Court arrest warrant for alleged war crimes linked to the war in Ukraine. Putin did not attend.

South African President Cyril Ramaphosa has also been criticized for being silent on human rights violations by members of the BRICS bloc, which includes new members with poor human rights records, such as the United Arab Emirates, Saudi Arabia, and Iran. New and old concerns were raised about how South Africa's association with the bloc could, in the long run, erode the country's rights culture. During the summit, local and international civil society groups protested in Johannesburg against human rights abuses in participating countries.

On July 11, the Extra-Ordinary Summit of Heads of States and Government of the Southern African Development Community (SADC) extended the region's joint military mission in the Cabo Delgado province in northern Mozambique, the SADC Mission in Mozambique (SAMIM), for another 12 months. The mission's mandate is now scheduled to end on July 16, 2024. The South African National Defence Force is the largest contributor to SAMIM; about 600 of SAMIM's 1,000 soldiers come from the South African military.

South Korea

The Republic of Korea (ROK or South Korea) is a democracy that largely respects the civil, political, economic, social, and cultural rights of its citizens. However, several human rights concerns remain, including pervasive and systemic discrimination against women and girls; lesbian, gay, bisexual, and transgender (LGBT) people; racial minorities; migrants; older people; and people with disabilities. South Korea remains one of the few Organization for Economic Co-operation and Development (OECD) countries without an anti-discrimination law.

In 2023, activists raised concerns about the erosion of the rights to freedom of assembly and association as the government cracked down on disability rights demonstrations, labor union protests, and LGBT parades and festivals. President Yoon Suk-yeol pledged to abolish the Ministry of Gender Equality and Family (MoGEF) in a move that activists have called state-sponsored anti-feminism in the face of widespread discrimination and violence against women and girls. The government did not develop a fourth National Action Plan, a comprehensive blueprint on human rights, for 2023-2028.

Over the past year, Yoon strengthened the government's promotion of human rights in North Korea. A South Korean court ruled in February that a same-sex couple should receive the same National Health Insurance Service benefits as a heterosexual couple, recognizing the rights of a same-sex couple for the first time.

Following a string of violent crimes in July and August, the minister of justice called for the maintenance of execution facilities at correctional facilities across the country. While South Korea has not carried out an execution since 1997, 59 people still remain on death row. The government has not abolished the death penalty.

Women's and Girls' Rights

The *Economist* magazine's "Glass Ceiling Index," which assesses women's educational attainment, women in managerial positions, and maternal leave policies, gave South Korea the lowest rank among OECD member countries in 2023.

The government struggled to address digital sex crimes, including the widespread posting of pictures of women and girls without their consent. According to a report released in March by the MoGEF, digital sex crimes targeting children increased between 2019 and 2021. In June, the government's Sexual Violence Safety Survey found that 51 percent of 7,505 women surveyed worry about becoming victims of sexual violence while using public bathrooms or taking taxis alone.

In February, South Korea's Ministry of Justice shot down the MoGEF's plans to revise the legal definition of rape to include nonconsensual sex. South Korean courts have interpreted the penal code very narrowly, often ruling in favor of the perpetrator when there are "mitigating circumstances" such as inebriation.

In October, the National Assembly passed the Protected Birth Bill that promotes anonymous births and adoption or orphanage care as solutions to unregistered births and unwanted pregnancies. Women's rights groups opposed the bill, saying it failed to address the underlying reasons that drive women not to register births, including lack of access to safe abortions, lack of comprehensive sexuality education, inadequate support services for pregnant women and girls, and the stigma of single motherhood.

Freedom of Expression

Though South Korea has a free press and a diverse civil society, the government uses the country's criminal defamation laws to limit scrutiny of its actions. Convictions for criminal defamation are not based on whether what was said was true, but whether it was in the "public interest," and they can result in up to seven years' imprisonment and a fine.

South Korea's draconian National Security Law (NSL) criminalizes the dissemination of materials alleged to be North Korean propaganda and statements thought to praise North Korea and has effectively restricted South Koreans' access to North Korean media. In January, the National Intelligence Service and the police raided the Korean Confederation of Trade Unions, alleging that some of its members had violated the NSL.

Sexual Orientation and Gender Identity

In May, Seoul's city government blocked the organizers of the Seoul Queer Culture Festival from holding its annual pride parade at its usual location in front of City Hall and gave the lot to a vocally homophobic Christian organization. Despite the opposition, over 150,000 people attended the event in July in Seoul's Euljiro neighborhood, according to the organizers.

In June, lawmakers proposed legislation that would extend the right to marry to same-sex couples. Another proposed bill would create civil unions as an alternative to marriage.

Policy on Human Rights in North Korea

Though the government has yet to establish the North Korean Human Rights Foundation as stipulated by the North Korean Human Rights Act of 2016, Yoon reiterated his commitment to its terms. In March, the Ministry of Unification publicly released its annual report on the human rights situation in North Korea for the first time, which Yoon referenced in his address to the US Congress in April. He stressed the collective responsibility to "inform the world of the gravity of North Korea's human rights violations."

In December 2022, South Korea co-sponsored the annual resolution at the United Nations General Assembly condemning North Korean human rights violations and the Human Rights Council resolution on North Korea in April 2023.

In September, South Korea's Constitutional Court overturned a 2020 law amendment that prohibited sending leaflets, information, money and other items from South Korea into North Korea, calling the ban an excessive restriction on free speech. This decision followed complaints from activist groups, including North Korean escapees living in South Korea, that the restrictions were vague and punishments excessive and that the law prevented activists from sending information to North Korea.

Workers' Rights

The South Korean government has not ratified the International Labour Organization (ILO) Violence and Harassment Convention (C190), which would require it to implement measures to end harassment and violence in the workplace. In June, the Federation of Korean Trade Unions and the Korean Confederation of Trade Unions met with the ILO in Geneva to voice concerns that President Yoon had been suppressing labor movements.

Disability Rights

In December 2022 and January 2023, the Seoul Metro and police officers prevented activists with Solidarity Against Disability Discrimination (SADD) from demonstrating on the subway for an increased government budget to protect the rights of people with disabilities. Following the crackdown, the Seoul Metro filed a damages suit against SADD for 601.45 million won (about US$484,000).

Key International Actors

President Yoon has prioritized strategic relations with Japan despite public backlash caused by historical resentment surrounding Japan's occupation of the Korean peninsula. In August, President Yoon met with United States President Joe Biden and Japanese Prime Minister Fumio Kishida at Camp David, the first trilateral meeting of its kind. The three countries agreed to cooperate to counter North Korea's nuclear threats and condemned acts of Chinese aggression in the East Sea but failed to mention the issue of human rights in North Korea. Economically, China is South Korea's top trading partner.

In July, President Yoon pledged to provide military supplies, not just financial and humanitarian aid, to Ukraine, reversing an earlier decision to only provide non-lethal supplies. South Korea also plans to increase its total financial aid to Ukraine to 250 billion won (about $394 million). These policies are expected to further worsen relations with North Korea, one of Russia's allies.

In June, South Korea was elected to the UN Security Council as a non-permanent member for the 2024-2025 term.

South Sudan

South Sudan continued to face a dire human rights and humanitarian crisis. Conflict between government, opposing forces, and their respective allied militias, as well as intercommunal violence, in pockets of the country resulted in the deaths, injuries, and displacement of thousands of civilians.

Authorities failed to ensure accountability for grave violations. Impunity continued to fuel violence, with civilians bearing the brunt of widespread attacks, systematic sexual violence against women and girls, the ongoing presence of children in fighting forces, and state-sponsored extrajudicial killings.

The government failed to meet critical milestones set out by the peace deal, including legislative and institutional reforms ahead of the end of the transitional period and general elections set for December 2024. The country ratified a number of international conventions, including a ban on cluster munitions use, and took steps to limit in law the powers of the National Security Service (NSS), but crackdowns on activists continued throughout the year.

The humanitarian situation worsened, driven by the cumulative and compounding effects of years of conflict, intercommunal violence, food insecurity, the climate crisis, and displacement following the April outbreak of conflict in Sudan. An estimated 9.4 million people in South Sudan, including 4.9 million children and over 300,000 refugees, mostly driven south from the Sudan conflict, needed humanitarian assistance.

During the year, South Sudan lobbied against various forms of international scrutiny, including an arms embargo imposed by the United Nations since 2018, targeted sanctions and travel bans by the UN and other countries, and the investigative and evidence collection mandate of the UN Commission on Human Rights in South Sudan.

Attacks on Civilians and Aid Operations

From January to March 2023, the UN Mission in South Sudan (UNMISS) documented 920 incidents of violence against civilians, during which 405 civilians were killed, 235 injured, 266 abducted, and 14 subjected to conflict-related sexual violence. Between April and June 2023, it also documented 222 incidents of violence affecting 871 civilians (including 128 children), during which 395 were killed, 281 injured, 166 abducted, and 29 subjected to conflict-related sexual violence.

As of August, 22 aid workers were killed as South Sudan remains one of the most dangerous places for aid workers.

According to the UN, in January, violence between Lou Nuer and Murle communities in Jonglei and greater Pibor Administrative Area linked to revenge killings and cattle raiding, led to at least 308 people being killed, 131 injured, 299 abducted, and 4 subjected to sexual violence by organized armed groups and community defense militias.

Authorities have neither investigated nor prosecuted officials accused of instigating and facilitating attacks on civilians and civilian properties in villages in Leer, Koch, and Mayendit counties between February and May 2022. The president launched an investigation, which was finalized by April; but at time of writing, the findings are not public, and no prosecutions of implicated officials are underway.

Child Marriage

The UN Children's Fund (UNICEF) estimates that around 52 percent of girls in South Sudan are married before they turn 18. An estimate for boys was not provided.

Refugees and Returnees

The conflict in Sudan that broke out in mid-April had forced over 300,000 people to flee into South Sudan as of October 27. The majority were South Sudanese refugee returnees. The South Sudanese government allowed access for emergency assistance, but it insisted that no settlements or sites for internally dlsplaced people should be established along the border and that South Sudanese returnees should "return to their places of origin," giving many very limited options. Refugees and returnees experienced poor living conditions in overcrowded humanitarian-run reception or transit centers with limited access to food or water and with poor sanitation, putting them at risk of disease. The situation created further pressure on aid agencies, making the operating environment in South Sudan very challenging.

Civic and Political Space

Civic and political space continued to shrink. Authorities also violated due process and custodial safeguards of accused people. In early January, the NSS arrested six media workers with the state broadcaster, South Sudan Broadcasting Corporation (SSBC), in relation to a leaked video showing President Salva Kiir urinating on himself. Later that month NSS also arrested SSBC staff member Garang John and held him at the NSS Juba headquarters, also known as the "Blue House." All journalists were held in poor conditions and were never charged or allowed access to a lawyer or their families while in detention. They were eventually released at different periods between mid-February and late March.

On February 4, NSS agents and Kenyan police officers abducted Morris Mabior Awikjok, a critic and refugee from Kenya, and renditioned him to South Sudan. At time of writing, he continued to be held in solitary confinement and incommunicado detention at the NSS headquarters in Juba.

In October, the UN Commission on Human Rights in South Sudan reported "entrenched systematic repression" of the media, human rights defenders, and civil society by the state, including through media censorship, intolerable restrictions on civic and political activities, and continued attacks on journalists and human rights defenders.

Legislative Developments

South Sudan passed a series of national laws linked to the implementation of the peace deal and ratified several international instruments. In January, parliament passed the act for a constitution-making process, but progress toward the creation of a new constitution stalled due to a lack of commitment and delays in setting up related mechanisms, among other factors.

The Ministry of Justice prepared legislation for the Commission for Truth, Reconciliation and Healing and for the Compensation and Reparations Authority, but at time of writing, the legislation has yet to be presented before parliament. No steps were taken to establish the Hybrid Court for South Sudan provided for under the peace deal.

In June, South Sudan ratified the African Union (AU) Protocol to the African Charter on Human and Peoples' Rights on the Rights of Women in Africa (the Maputo Protocol) with reservations on several provisions, including those discouraging polygamy and on sexual and reproductive health, particularly the right to decide whether to have children, the number, and spacing and the rights to contraceptives and safe abortion care.

South Sudan also acceded to the international Convention on Cluster Munitions on August 3.

In September, South Sudan enacted a National Elections Act which empowers the president-elect, after the conclusion of parliamentary elections, to nominate additional members to the legislature. In November, the political parties council and national elections and constitutional review commissions were reconstituted.

Authorities revised the National Security Service Act (2014), limiting but not removing the agency's overly broad and vague powers. At time of writing, the bill is undergoing parliamentary review. Human Rights Watch has documented abuses by the NSS and has called for accountability for members of the service and for the agency's powers of arrest, detention and surveillance to be limited.

South Sudan criminalizes consensual same-sex relations with up to 10 years imprisonment.

Key International Actors

Between February 3 and 5, Pope Francis, the leader of the Catholic church, alongside the archbishop of Canterbury, and the moderator of the General Assembly of the Church of Scotland conducted an ecumenical visit to South Sudan. The faith leaders called on South Sudanese actors, including within the church, to shun violence and be more vocal against injustice.

In March, the UN Security Council renewed the mandate of UNMISS for another year. In April, the UN Human Rights Council voted to renew the mandate of the Commission on Human Rights in South Sudan for another year.

In October, the government decided to postpone the visit of the UN Special Rapporteur on the human rights of internally displaced persons on short notice. According to the expert, the government cited critical recent UN reports as the reason for the postponement.

In March, the European Union sanctioned Gatluak Nyang Hoth, the commissioner for Mayendit county, and Gordon Koang Biel of Koch county, under its human rights sanctions regime for “widespread and systematic use of sexual violence as a war tactic.” The two men were also sanctioned by the United Kingdom in December 2022. In July, the EU added James Mark Nando, a major general in the army, to its sanctions list on the same grounds.

In May, the UN Security Council renewed sanctions on South Sudan until May 31, 2024—including targeted sanctions (assets freezes and travel bans) and an arms embargo—and the mandate of the Panel of Experts until July 1, 2024. China and Russia, which have long opposed the South Sudan sanctions regime, and African members of the council, Ghana, Mozambique, and Gabon, all abstained. The council also decided that the supply, sale, or transfer of non-lethal military equipment was exempt from the arms embargo and that actions impeding or distorting pre-election preparatory activities are a new criterion for designating sanctions.

In June, the AU Peace and Security Council called for the lifting of the arms embargo to enable implementation of the peace deal.

Also in June, the United States imposed the first US sanctions issued with a dedicated focus on conflict-related sexual violence on two South Sudanese officials: James Nando, a major general in the army, and Alfred Futiyo, governor of Western Equatoria, affiliated with the Sudan People’s Liberation Movement/Army in opposition.

Under the 2018 peace agreement, the AU Commission has the responsibility to establish the Hybrid Court for South Sudan. However, it failed to do so and seems reluctant to move ahead with the court’s creation or press for greater action by the South Sudanese authorities to establish the court together with the AU Commission.

Spain

The government's pushback policy and failure to offer legal routes to claim asylum at its borders continued to contribute to deaths at sea. Despite multiple calls for accountability, there was no credible investigation into the deaths of more than 20 African men on the Spanish-Moroccan land border in June 2022.

A botched reform of consent laws in 2022 led to controversial reductions in sentences and releases from prison of people convicted of sexual offenses.

The government also took positive steps, passing legislation to improve housing rights, simplify gender recognition procedures for transgender people, strengthen rights for LGBTI people, reduce obstacles to abortion care, and repeal the offense of sedition. A new government was sworn in at the end of November, following snap elections in July.

Although more than one-quarter of the population remained at risk of poverty or social exclusion, poverty rates fell marginally according to midyear data.

Migration and Asylum

The United Nations refugee agency (UNHCR) said that by early November, at least 45,575 people had arrived irregularly by sea to Spain, more than two-thirds to the Canary Islands, while 437 had arrived by land. Caminando Fronteras, a migrant rights group, estimated that 951 people, including 49 children, died trying to cross by boat from Africa to Spain during the first half of the year, primarily on the Atlantic route.

At time of writing, there has been no credible investigation, justice, or reparation for the events of June 24, 2022, when at least 23 African men died while attempting to enter Spain's fenced enclave of Melilla from Morocco. In February, Spain and Morocco announced "intensified" cooperation on migration control. In March, the human rights ombudsperson said 470 pushbacks on June 24, 2022, were unlawful. In May, the commissioner for human rights of the Council of Europe (CoE) called for accountability for the deaths and noted the lack of legal routes to enter Spain's enclaves to request international protection. The commissioner called on Spain to ensure that its cooperation with Morocco did not contribute to further abuses. In August, the UN Committee Against Torture called for an independent investigation into the June 2022 deaths and for measures to prevent the repetition of such events.

A draft law, proposed in February to regularize the migration status of up to 470,000 people following a nationwide petition campaign, was shelved in May.

The dysfunctional digital system for requesting appointments to make asylum and migration-related applications was largely replaced by a clandestine market. In April, the human rights ombudsperson criticized authorities for failing to undertake necessary structural reforms. In June, more than 20 organizations jointly lodged a complaint with the European Commission arguing that the breakdown in the digital appointment system breached European Union law.

Poverty and Inequality

Official data published in June showed 26 percent of the population was "at risk of poverty or social exclusion" in 2022, with 7.7 percent facing "severe material or social deprivation." Although both rates fell from the previous year, about half of single-parent households, largely women-led, remained at risk of poverty and the risk among older people is rising. Detailed analysis showed southern regions were experiencing above average at-risk rates.

By August, falling inflation, coupled with government measures to reduce energy taxes, cap gas prices, and extend a moratorium on utility cutoffs to households considered "socially or economically vulnerable" seemed to alleviate some of the pressure on low-income households.

In January, the human rights ombudsperson called on authorities to fix a breakdown in the system for requesting social security office appointments, noting the specific impact on unemployed people, people awaiting disability assessments, and older people. In March and May, Civio journalists documented a near-complete paralysis of the online system.

In May, the government passed a new housing law to increase public housing provision, introduce clearer private rent increase limits, strengthen tenants' rights, and improve safeguards against "open evictions," in which the occupier is not told the enforcement date. Some housing rights activists welcomed the law's emphasis on a right to housing, while others were critical of the law's failure to include the full set of international human rights law protections against forced evictions or any mention of mortgage-holding owner-occupiers and of its insufficient targets for new public housing.

In June, the government extended to the end of the year a moratorium on evicting people who could demonstrate "social and economic vulnerability" but lifted the bar on increasing rents on privately rented homes, with some exceptions.

In what the human rights ombudsperson called a "humanitarian emergency," at time of writing, authorities had not restored electricity to an estimated 4,500 people, including 1,800 children, in the Cañada Real informal settlement near Madrid, despite a recommendation for immediate measures from the European Committee of Social Rights in October 2022.

Gender-Based Violence, Including Sexual Abuse

By September, 1,205 people convicted of sexual offenses had their sentences reduced and 121 had been released as a result of a loophole in 2022 legislation on rape and sexual consent. In April, the prime minister apologized publicly for these "undesired effects."

As of mid-October, official sources confirmed that 51 women had been killed in gender-based violence during the year.

The human rights ombudsperson's reported in March that it had collected 445 survivor accounts in its ongoing investigation into clerical sexual abuse. In June, bishops at the Spanish Episcopal Conference acknowledged they were aware of the sexual abuse of 927 children in church institutions or activities between 1945 and 2022. Investigations by the newspaper *El País* suggested this was an underestimate and that payment of reparations to victims was slow.

Prosecutors filed sexual assault charges in September against the then-football federation president—who subsequently resigned—for kissing a player without her consent after Spain's team won the Women's World Cup. Women players have long demanded systemic changes to protect and respect their rights, pay them the same as men, and remove abusive coaches and officials from their workplace.

The International Labour Organization Violence and Harassment Convention (C190) came into force in Spain in May.

Right to Health

In February, the UN Committee on the Elimination of Discrimination Against Women said Spanish health authorities violated a woman's rights in 2009 when they performed a cesarean section delivery without her consent. The committee recommended state reparations, systematic improvements to training on informed consent and gender-based violence in reproductive health contexts, and better access to remedies for victims of obstetric violence.

Legal reforms passed in February removed obstacles to abortion care, such as a three-day waiting period and parental consent for girls aged 16 and 17, and limited the right of health professionals to declare "conscientious objection." The CoE commissioner for human rights acknowledged these advances but noted that some regions still had no abortion care in public hospitals. In July, the Constitutional Court ruled that public health authorities in Murcia violated a woman's rights when they failed to ensure her access to public abortion services, directing her instead to private services some 400 kilometers away in Madrid.

Government data attributed more than 3,000 deaths to extreme heat between June and September. In July, the Spanish government established a Health and Climate Change Observatory to study the health impacts of the climate crisis and improve emergency systems.

Sexual Orientation and Gender Identity

In February, parliament passed a new law creating a gender recognition procedure for transgender people based on self-determination without discriminatory medical diagnosis and treatment. The law also expanded access to assisted reproductive techniques, strengthened sexuality education, banned medically unnecessary surgeries for intersex children, and instituted parental recognition for unmarried same-sex couples.

Discrimination and Intolerance

In July, the Interior Minister published data showing that law enforcement had investigated 1,869 hate crimes during 2022, a minor increase over 2021; almost half of the crimes had a racist or xenophobic motive, and one-quarter related to sexual orientation or gender identity.

In July, the government approved an action plan against hate crimes. The Interior Ministry issued guidelines on suspending sporting events in response to racist or xenophobic conduct after instances of racist abuse during football games in the first half of the year. NGOs and civil society groups criticized delays in creating an Independent Authority for Equal Treatment and Non-Discrimination, promised in a 2022 equality law.

Rule of Law

In its yearly *Rule of Law Report*, the European Commission criticized Spain's lack of progress on renewing appointments to the Council of the Judiciary and making needed changes to the appointment process for members and its failure to undertake structural reform to ensure a genuinely independent prosecutor general.

Both the European Commission and the CoE commissioner for human rights noted the lack of progress in reforming a restrictive 2015 public security law that limits the freedoms of assembly and expression, including the work of journalists.

In August, the UN Committee Against Torture recommended that Spain revise its definition of torture to comply with the Convention against Torture and also called for the abolition of incommunicado detention and an end to summary returns and migration pushbacks.

In September, for the first time, a judge ruled that a lawsuit alleging torture and crimes against humanity during the Francoist dictatorship was admissible. Previously, such lawsuits were blocked by a 1977 amnesty law, the reach of which was limited by passage of the 2022 Democratic Memory Law.

After a criminal code reform entered into force in January, an investigating judge dropped sedition charges against five pro-independence Catalan politicians for their actions during the disputed 2017 independence referendum but maintained misappropriation charges against three. In February, the Supreme Court lifted previously imposed bans on holding public office on four pro-independence Catalan politicians and one civil society activist but maintained the bans on four other pro-independence politicians.

In July, the judge investigating the use of Pegasus spyware in 2020-2021 to hack the phones of senior government ministers dropped the investigation, citing a lack of cooperation from authorities in Israel, where the spyware was developed.

Sri Lanka

Regressive government policies and inadequate social protection left many Sri Lankans at risk from the worst effects of the country's economic crisis.

A US$3 billion bailout from the International Monetary Fund (IMF) helped stem the immediate economic crisis in Sri Lanka after it had defaulted on its foreign debt in 2022. However, the government and IMF's response to the economic situation undermined human rights, leaving more than 17 percent of the population moderately or acutely food insecure and in need of humanitarian assistance and 31 percent of children under 5 malnourished, according to the World Food Programme.

President Ranil Wickremesinghe, who came to power in 2022 after his predecessor's departure from office following months-long protests, sought to suppress dissent, ending a moratorium on the use of the draconian Prevention of Terrorism Act (PTA). A proposed new counterterrorism law would give sweeping powers to the police, the military, and the president, and create new speech-related offenses. Other proposed legislation would further constrain freedom of expression online.

In the north and east of Sri Lanka, which was most affected by the 1983-2009 civil war, victims of past human rights violations, their families, and activists campaigning for truth and accountability were subjected to surveillance and intimidation by the police and intelligence agencies.

Economic and Social Rights

Due to the economic crisis, from 2021 to 2022, the country's poverty rate doubled to 25 percent and was projected to rise further.

In March, an IMF loan paved the way for multilateral institutions such as the World Bank and Asian Development Bank to offer new financing. The IMF program focused on raising government revenues and emphasized tackling corruption and improving social protection; however, as structured, it shifted the burden of recovery principally onto people with low incomes, undermining people's economic and social rights.

For instance, as part of the IMF agreement, the government raised electricity tariffs, doubled value-added taxes, and phased out fuel subsidies, contributing to a spike in prices. The reform program included a "social spending floor" requiring that 0.6 percent of GDP be spent on social protection programs, less than developing countries' average of 1.6 percent.

The government's plan of targeted social protection benefits led to the exclusion of many who do not have an adequate standard of living. Amid widespread protests, the government agreed to review almost one million applications for Aswesuma, the new social protection program. Social protection programs such as Aswesuma that target people based on economic status have been criticized for being prone to errors, arbitrary cut offs, corruption, and social mistrust.

In June, in an attempt to reduce its domestic debts, the government announced a policy that would reduce the value of state-run pension funds in which ordinary people hold their savings.

Accountability and Justice

In June, President Ranil Wickremesinghe announced plans to establish a new truth and reconciliation commission, called the National Unity and Reconciliation Commission (NURC), to examine rights violations 14 years since the defeat of the separatist Liberation Tigers of Tamil Eelam (LTTE) in 2009 and over three decades after the suppression of a leftist uprising in the south in 1989.

Victims' groups and civil society organizations said they had not been properly consulted and that the new commission would put them at risk of re-traumatization and further threats from security forces.

The government's ongoing abuses against victims of past violations, their families, and communities undermined the purported goals of the proposed commission. Those campaigning for truth and accountability for crimes committed during the war with the LTTE, particularly the relatives of victims of enforced disappearance, were subjected to surveillance and intimidation by the police and intelligence agencies. Events to commemorate Tamil victims of the war were disrupted.

Successive Sri Lankan governments have appointed similar commissions that collected extensive testimony from victims and witnesses, but none led to accountability or revealed the fate of the disappeared. Instead, the authorities blocked the few criminal investigations into grave abuses that had made some progress in identifying those responsible and initiating prosecutions.

Numerous mass graves, usually discovered accidentally, have not been properly examined to identify the victims or the perpetrators.

The government Office on Missing Persons, set up in 2017 to trace the disappeared, made almost no progress. An April UN Human Rights Committee report criticized the agency's appointment of "individuals implicated in past human rights violations" and its "interference in the prosecution of such cases." Some government officials implicated in alleged crimes remained politically powerful or hold senior official positions.

Government agencies unlawfully occupied property and religious sites of minority Tamil and Muslim communities. In September, a judge from Mullaitivu district resigned and fled the country after receiving death threats following a ruling he handed down against the Department of Archaeology, which had constructed a Buddhist monument on the site of a Hindu temple.

A resolution adopted by the UN Human Rights Council in 2021 to form the Sri Lanka Accountability Project to gather evidence of international crimes for use in future prosecutions is due for renewal in 2024. President Wickremesinghe's office said it hopes the proposed truth commission will convince governments that there is no need for further scrutiny by the council.

The UN High Commissioner for Human Rights Volker Türk said when publishing a September report on Sri Lanka that for any transitional justice process to succeed, "[t]ruth-seeking alone will not suffice. It must also be accompanied by a clear commitment to accountability and the political will to implement far-reaching change."

Freedoms of Expression and Assembly

The authorities clamped down on free speech, including, for example, by holding a comedian in custody for five weeks over comments alleged to be hurtful to religious sentiments.

In September, the government published an Online Safety Bill to prevent the publication of false, threatening, alarming, or distressing statements on the internet, but activists said that it would further restrict speech. If passed into law, the bill would establish an Online Safety Commission, appointed by the president, that could decide whether statements are false or prohibited, order their removal, and participate in police investigations and prosecutions.

A report on Sri Lanka by the UN Human Rights Committee described "severe restrictions on freedom of opinion and expression," including the excessive use of force by police in dispersing peaceful assemblies, the application of counterterrorism legislation against protesters, and the blocking of public access to social media platforms during mass demonstrations against government policies. Restrictions on expression and assembly were particularly severe in the north and east.

The authorities continued to target civil society groups and activists, including human rights defenders. In his report, Türk called for "the immediate end of all forms of surveillance and harassment."

Counterterrorism Laws

The government had pledged to adopt a rights-respecting counterterrorism law following domestic and international criticism of abuses under the existing PTA. In particular, pressure from the European Union, which grants Sri Lanka tariff-free market access in exchange for meeting its human rights obligations under a program called GSP+, led to the government renewing pledges to act on a commitment to repeal the PTA that it first made to the EU in 2017.

However, the proposed replacement legislation, called the Anti-Terrorism Bill, threatens citizens' freedom of assembly and speech and also falls far short of Sri Lanka's international obligations.

The government had first proposed the new law in March but withdrew it for "consultations" following widespread objections that the bill preserved many of the most abused powers of the PTA while also creating abusive new powers. The bill, resubmitted in September, contained minimal changes. Although the Anti-Terrorism Bill has some improvements, it contains vague and overbroad language to include peaceful protest or acts that, while criminal, do not reach any reasonable definition of terrorism. The bill appeared to be designed to give the president, police, and military broad powers to detain people without evidence, make vaguely defined forms of speech a criminal offense, and arbitrarily ban gatherings and organizations without meaningful judicial oversight. In October, following criticism, the bill was withdrawn from parliament, apparently to make further changes.

Women's and Girls' Rights

The impact of the economic crisis was often most severely felt by women, who were in low-paid or insecure employment and faced increasing burdens within the home.

The Muslim Marriage and Divorce Act (MMDA), which governs marriage in the Muslim community, contains numerous provisions that violate the rights of women and girls, including by allowing child marriage without setting any minimum age. The act stipulates that only men can be judges of the Qazi (family) court, makes it easier for men than for women to obtain a divorce, and does not require a woman or girl's consent to be recorded before the registration of her marriage. Furthermore, the penal code permits what would otherwise constitute statutory rape in cases of child marriage that are permitted under the MMDA.

Sri Lanka has among the most restrictive abortion laws in the world, imposing long prison sentences for all abortions with exceptions only for saving a woman's life.

The UN Human Rights Committee expressed continuing concern at the prevalence of violence, including sexual violence, against women, and regretted the low representation of women in politics.

Sexual Orientation and Gender Identity

The penal code prohibits "carnal intercourse against the order of nature" and "any act of gross indecency." These provisions are widely understood to criminalize consensual same-sex activity. Another provision, which prohibits "cheating by personation," is used by police to target transgender people, and the

1841 Vagrants Ordinance contains overbroad and vague provisions that are used to target transgender women and women suspected to be sex workers.

A private member's bill was presented in parliament to decriminalize same-sex relations but had not been brought to a vote by the time of writing.

Key International Actors

The rivalry between China and other powers to assert strategic influence in the region partly forms the context for Sri Lanka's international relations. Key actors include India, the United States, and Japan, which along with Australia are members of the Quadrilateral Security Dialogue, known as the Quad, aimed at countering China. Economic assistance provided to Sri Lanka has partly been viewed by states through the lens of this rivalry.

The EU has continued to push for human rights improvements in Sri Lanka, leveraging its GSP+ program, which grants the country tariff-free access to the EU market conditioned on Sri Lanka's implementation of core human rights conventions.

The Canadian government took a major step by imposing sanctions against two former Sri Lankan presidents, the brothers Mahinda Rajapaksa and Gotabaya Rajapaksa, and two former soldiers, all of whom it said are implicated in "gross and systematic violations of human rights." While the US has sanctioned some Sri Lankan miliary figures, other governments have not done so.

The government's rhetoric on human rights—directed at international audiences—was not matched by actions to end violations. The government did not publish details of its proposed truth commission. However, officials sought the support of foreign governments, including South Africa, Switzerland, and Japan, as well as UN agencies.

The 2021 UN Human Rights Council resolution on Sri Lanka, which will need to be renewed in September 2024, is led by a core group consisting of Canada, Germany, North Macedonia, Malawi, Montenegro, the United Kingdom, and the US.

Sudan

On April 15, 2023, fighting broke out in Sudan's capital, Khartoum, between the Sudan Armed Forces (SAF) and the Rapid Support Forces (RSF), an independent military force, and quickly spread across the country. This followed months of mounting tensions between SAF leader General Abdelfattah al-Burhan and RSF leader Mohamed Hamdan Dagalo ("Hemedti") over the integration of the RSF into the SAF. Burhan and Hemedti had jointly carried out a military coup against the transitional government in October 2021.

Since the fighting started, both forces have repeatedly used heavy explosive weapons in densely populated areas, resulting in numerous civilian casualties and destruction of civilian property and critical infrastructure. As of September, the United Nations reported that at least 9,000 people had been killed since the start of the conflict, most likely a significant underestimation, and 5.4 million forcibly displaced, including 4.1 million internally and over 1 million to neighboring countries.

From late April, West Darfur state was the site of some of the worst attacks on civilians and serious violations of international humanitarian law. Large-scale attacks by RSF forces and allied forces—mostly Arab militia—primarily targeting the ethnic Massalit population took place in multiple towns in the region.

There was also fighting in other parts of the country, including South Kordofan, between the two forces, prompting a dramatic deterioration of the humanitarian situation. As of August, the UN said at least 19 aid workers had been killed. Sudanese community healthcare workers and support networks were also targeted. Twenty million people are estimated to need food assistance in the country. The UN Office for the Coordination of Humanitarian Affairs (OCHA) warned in August that ongoing fighting and widespread bureaucratic impediments hamper the scaling up of humanitarian assistance across the country.

Conflict and Abuses in Khartoum

Since the start of the conflict, both the SAF and RSF have used heavy explosive weapons in densely populated areas across the Khartoum, including Omdurman and Bahri areas, killing thousands of civilians, damaging critical infrastructure, and leaving millions without access to necessities. The fighting destroyed many homes and other civilian objects.

In Khartoum and in towns in Darfur and Kordofan, indiscriminate attacks, including shelling by both parties and SAF airstrikes, killed hundreds. The UN reported that a June 4 airstrike by the SAF in southern Khartoum that hit a refugee center killed at least 10 refugees. In mid-September, Médecins Sans Frontières (Doctors Without Borders, MSF) said at least 49 people were killed and that they had treated over 100 injured after two deadly attacks in a busy market and another in residential area in Khartoum.

On April 15, the Bahri Water Treatment Plant, north of Khartoum, was damaged, leaving residents in the area without water. Water authorities reported that fighters had repeatedly prevented them from accessing the plant due to insecurity, hampering repairs.

Several medical facilities across Khartoum were damaged due to airstrikes or shelling, forcing many of them to close. As fighting intensified in the capital from August onward, humanitarian agencies warned of the risks to the few remaining functioning hospitals. As of October, OCHA said more than 70 percent of health facilities in conflict-affected areas were not functioning.

On July 20, MSF said four of their staff members were stopped by "armed men" who assaulted them with whips and stole their vehicle.

Warring parties also arbitrarily arrested, held incommunicado, and mistreated civilians, including health workers. As of late July, the UN High Commissioner for Human Rights said at least 500 people, including 24 women, were reported missing. He said that many of those detained were reportedly ill-treated and in some cases tortured. In September, the Emergency Lawyers, a group of human rights lawyers, released a report documenting widespread abuses, including extrajudicial killings and torture, committed in detention sites operated by both parties to the conflict.

According to rights monitors, the SAF and RSF have also repeatedly intimidated, attacked, and detained several activists and volunteers facilitating the delivery of aid and other essential services.

In May, SAF military intelligence reportedly detained two volunteers operating an ambulance, accusing them of collaborating with the RSF, and releasing them shortly after. Activists also said the RSF detained three doctors coming to Khartoum to volunteer in a hospital in September.

The conflict saw the systematic looting of aid warehouses and humanitarian goods and property throughout the Khartoum area. The UN secretary-general declared in May that most, if not all, UN agencies and humanitarian partners had faced large-scale looting of their humanitarian supplies. Meanwhile, RSF conducted widespread looting including of private property throughout the capital.

Conflict and Abuses in Darfur

From April 24, RSF and Arab militias carried out attacks against non-Arab communities in El Geneina, the capital of West Darfur. Thousands of people were killed and hundreds of thousands of Sudanese, overwhelmingly from non-Arab communities and specifically the Massalit, were forced to flee to nearby Chad because of the fighting and the abuses. The RSF and allied militias committed widespread killings of civilians in El Geneina, including while they were seeking to flee to safety. And they committed widespread looting and arson and attacked critical civilian infrastructure, including camps for internally displaced people (IDPs), hospitals, and markets. Assailants also targeted local leaders and human rights defenders, searching for them, detaining some, and killing four lawyers who represented victims of the RSF and allied militias' previous attacks in El Geneina.

At least seven other towns in West Darfur state were attacked and burned, some almost completely, between April and July.

On May 28, thousands of RSF and allied militia attacked the town of Misterei, 42 kilometers from El Genaina. They summarily executed at least 28 ethnic Massalit, killed and injured dozens of civilians, and conducted widespread looting before burning much of the town to the ground.

Attacks continued in other parts of West Darfur. In Murnei, the RSF and allied militias killed residents as they fled, looting and burning down the town on June 27. The Darfur Bar Association reported that the attacks in Sirba locality started on July 24 and lasted for several days, with assailants killing at least 200 people, including local leaders, and looting homes before setting them on fire.

Since April, over 300,000 people have fled to Chad, many from West Darfur. As of late July, the UN was recording a significant drop in the number of displaced people still in West Darfur, "reportedly attributed to an increase in the level of internally displaced people (IDPs) who have crossed into Chad."

Fighting between the SAF and RSF also took place in other urban areas of Darfur. In Nyala, the capital of South Darfur, renewed clashes in August left at least 50 civilians dead and forced 50,000 to flee. On September 13, an SAF airstrike in the city killed at least 40 civilians. At time of writing, intense fighting was also reported in El Fashir, capital of North Darfur, with increasing risk to civilian lives.

Conflict-Related Sexual Violence

UN experts raised concerns about the surge of sexual violence during the conflict, including in Khartoum and Darfur.

The Strategic Initiative for Women in Horn of Africa (SIHA), a women's rights group, said in July that they verified more than 70 cases of conflict-related sexual and gender-based violence across the country, largely attributed to the RSF.

In El Genaina, RSF and allied Arab militias raped several dozen women and girls in the city and while people fled fighting between April and June. Survivors who spoke to Human Rights Watch said that their attackers explicitly mentioned their ethnic identity and used ethnic slurs about the Massalit or non-Arabs more generally.

Survivors' access to urgent services, including the clinical management of rape and psychosocial support, were hampered by attacks on medical facilities and organizations providing care for sexual violence survivors as well as by a communications network shutdown in El Geneina and weak health infrastructure in Chad, to where many survivors have fled. Persistent stigma around sexual violence exacerbated barriers to care.

Accountability

Prior to the outbreak of the conflict, the Sudanese civilian political alliance, Forces of Freedom and Change (FFC), signed a framework agreement with military leaders in December 2022, which was not supported by protest groups due to concerns that it downplayed accountability.

Sudan's army leader Abdel Fattah al-Burhan set up a committee to investigate abuses, but only those committed by the RSF.

Former officials under former President Omar al-Bashir, including Ahmed Haroun, who is sought by the International Criminal Court (ICC) on charges of international crimes committed in Darfur, left prison in Khartoum following attacks. The army said that both al-Bashir and former Defense Minister Abdelrahim Mohamed Hussein—both sought by the ICC for international crimes committed in Darfur—were being held at the military hospital prior to the current conflict.

On July 13, the ICC prosecutor announced that his office is probing recent atrocities in Sudan's Darfur region as part of its ongoing Darfur investigation, underscoring the gravity of current abuses.

Refugees and Migrants

As of early August, according to the UN, nearly 1 million people had fled from Sudan to Egypt, Chad, Ethiopia, South Sudan, and other countries since April, with Sudanese nationals comprising two-thirds of those. The others included South Sudanese nationals as well as refugees and asylum seekers, including from Eritrea and Ethiopia.

Those fleeing faced multiple challenges and restrictions on their access to safe and legal routes. As embassies evacuated their diplomatic staff out of the country at the start of the conflict, several reportedly left passports of Sudanese locked in their premises or shredded without offering alternatives, hampering people's ability to flee.

In June, Egyptian authorities required all Sudanese to obtain visas to enter the country, resulting in reduced access to safety for women, children, and older people fleeing.

Prior to the conflict, Sudan hosted more than 1.1 million refugees and asylum seekers during 2021, mostly South Sudanese.

Key International Actors

Despite the gravity of the situation in Sudan, the regional and international response has been underwhelming. To date, the UN Security Council has failed to take any concrete steps to address the conflict or constrain the ability of warring parties to continue inflicting harm on civilians.

On April 15, the UN secretary-general condemned the violence, voicing concerns about the devastating impact of the conflict on the population, and called for immediate cessation of hostilities. The UN Security Council held its session on the situation in Sudan 10 days later.

In response to the outbreak of the conflict, the United States and Saudi Arabia embarked on a process in Jeddah, primarily aiming at facilitating ceasefires and humanitarian access. In May, both the SAF and RSF signed the Jeddah Declaration of Commitment to Protect the Civilians of Sudan, which reiterates the commitment of warring parties to respect international humanitarian law.

On May 11, the UN Human Rights Council held a special session to address the conflict in Sudan, deciding to strengthen the existing mandate of the designated expert of the high commissioner on human rights in Sudan. This move fell short of the demands of Sudanese, regional, and international rights groups that had called on the council to establish a new independent mechanism. Five months later, however, given the further spiraling of the situation and in response to further appeals from Sudanese, regional, and international rights groups, on October 11, the UN Human Rights Council followed up with more robust action, adopting a resolution to establish an independent international fact-finding mission for Sudan. This mission has a mandate to investigate crimes committed by all parties in the context of the conflict, gather and preserve evidence and identify those responsible for abuses, and make recommendations on advancing accountability.

On September 12, the UN High Commissioner for Human Rights and his designated expert on Sudan both reiterated concerns about ongoing widespread violations in the country, including ethnic-based violence, targeted killings, torture, and acts of sexual violence, and emphasized the importance of holding perpetrators accountable.

In June, the US sanctioned three private Sudanese companies and one private Emirati company. About a month later, the United Kingdom applied similar sanctions on business entities affiliated with the SAF and RSF. In September, the US Department of the Treasury sanctioned Abelrahim Hamdan Dagalo, a senior leader in the RSF and brother of the RSF's leader, Mohamed Hamdan Dagalo. Additionally, the US State Department imposed visa restrictions on Abdul Rahman Juma, an RSF commander in West Darfur state. The latest sanctions were the first time that individual sanctions were imposed during the current conflict.

In July, the European Union's high representative for foreign affairs, Josep Borrell, condemned violations of international human rights and humanitarian law and called for those responsible to be held accountable. In February, the EU imposed targeted measures under its human rights sanctions framework against entities identified as linked to the Wagner Group in Sudan and their leaderships. The EU rolled out its new sanctions framework in October, but it has not designated any individuals or entities in connection to the conflict at time of writing.

On June 2, the UN Security Council unanimously voted for a technical rollover of the mandate of the UN political mission in Sudan, UNITAMS, until December 3. Shortly after, Sudan's foreign ministry declared the head of UNITAMS, Volker Perthes, *persona non grata*. Perthes announced his resignation during a briefing to the Security Council on September 13. In his last briefing, Perthes reiterated his calls on the warring parties to end the conflict, denouncing continuous violations of international law, saying, "What started as a conflict between two military formations could be morphing into a full-scale civil war."

At its July meeting, the Intergovernmental Authority on Development (IGAD) quartet (Kenya, Ethiopia, Djibouti, and South Sudan) condemned violations by the warring parties while committing to work with the international community to establish a robust monitoring and accountability mechanism that will be instrumental in bringing perpetrators to justice. The meeting also considered deploying regional peacekeeping forces to protect civilians and guarantee humanitarian access.

Syria

In 2023, Syrians endured severe abuses and hardship due to the ongoing conflict, worsened economic conditions, and general insecurity. The United Nations estimated that, for the first time since the start of the conflict, Syrians in every sub-district of the country experienced some degree of "humanitarian stress." Although conditions remain unsafe, refugee-hosting countries Türkiye and Lebanon unlawfully deported thousands of Syrians back to Syria.

February's devastating earthquakes worsened already dire conditions, especially in hard-hit rebel-held areas of the northwest, where millions were left without access to critical search-and-rescue reinforcements or lifesaving aid for over a week. Despite calls for a nationwide ceasefire, hostilities persisted, resulting in civilian casualties and displacement. Arab states readmitted Syria to the Arab League without demanding accountability or reform.

In positive news for accountability, Canada and the Netherlands filed a joint case at the International Court of Justice against Syria over widespread and systematic torture. Individual accountability efforts continued with war crimes convictions in European courts, and in June, the UN established a new mechanism to address the fate of the over

100,000 missing persons in Syria.

Government-Held Areas (Central, West, and Southern Syria)

Syrian security forces and government-affiliated militias continued to arbitrarily detain, disappear, and mistreat people across the country. Authorities also continued to unlawfully confiscate property and restrict access to areas of origin for returning Syrians.

Despite passing a law in March 2022 criminalizing torture, torture and ill-treatment in government facilities continued and deaths in detention were documented, according to a July 2023 UN Commission of Inquiry (COI) report. In a report issued in August, the commission also documented arbitrary arrests and detention through the application of a draconian cybercrimes law introduced in April 2022.

In late August, initially prompted by worsening economic conditions, anti-government protests spread across the southern Druze-majority province of Sweida and, to a more limited extent, in the former opposition-controlled neighboring province of Daraa. They were the largest protests to take place in government-controlled Syria since 2011, but unlike in 2011, the government had, at the time of writing, refrained from using lethal force against the protesters.

In early September, Syrian President Bashar al-Assad abolished the notorious military field courts, where thousands of people are thought to have been sentenced to death without due process, and referred all pending cases to the military judiciary. Human rights advocates have long called for the dissolution of these courts, but there are concerns that the decision may lead to the erasure of court records and other evidence related to enforced disappearances, hampering efforts of family members to learn the fate of missing loved ones.

Northwest Syria

Opposition-held northwest Syria is home to more than 4.1 million civilians, at least half of whom have been displaced at least once since the start of the conflict. Civilians in these areas are effectively trapped, lacking resources to relocate, unable to seek asylum in Türkiye, and fearing persecution if they attempt to relocate to government-held areas.

In Idlib and western Aleppo, indiscriminate attacks by Syrian-Russian military forces on civilians and critical civilian infrastructure persisted in 2023.

According to the UN COI's August report, Hay'et Tahrir al-Sham (HTS), the dominant anti-government armed group in Idlib, continued to raid and arbitrarily detain activists, journalists, and other civilians voicing critical opinions. Another COI report published in July documented new cases of torture and ill-treatment in detention.

Following credible independent reports that a US military strike killed a civilian on May 3, 2023, in Idlib, Human Rights Watch and 20 other organizations called on the US to ensure a robust investigation, commit to transparency, make amends, and ensure accountability.

Turkish-Occupied Territories of Northern Syria

In the Turkish-occupied territories of northern Syria, various factions of the Syrian National Army (SNA) and the Military Police, a force established by the Syrian Interim Government (SIG) to curb faction abuses, subjected scores of people to multiple abuses with impunity. Abuses included arbitrary arrest and detention, forcible disappearances, torture and ill-treatment, sexual violence, and unfair military trials. In 2023, the US returned Türkiye to its list of countries implicated in the use of child soldiers in response to its support to factions of the Syrian National Army accused of child recruitment.

SNA factions continued to violate civilians' housing, land, and property rights, including by forcefully seizing homes, lands, and businesses. And hundreds of thousands of Syrians who fled their homes during and after Türkiye's successive military operations in the region remain displaced and dispossessed.

Northeast Syria

The Syrian Democratic Forces (SDF), a US-backed Kurdish-led armed group that controls much of northeast Syria, continued to arbitrarily detain civilians, including journalists, according to an August 2023 UN COI report that also documented deaths in detention in al-Hasakeh and Raqqa central prisons.

A 2023 UN report on children and armed conflict concluded that child recruitment had increased in Syria, with cases in the SDF-controlled areas representing more than half of those documented.

As of mid-November, the SDF and Asayish regional security forces continued to arbitrarily detain at least 60,000 suspected members of Islamic State (ISIS) and family members from Syria and nearly 60 other countries. Detention conditions remained life-threatening, degrading, and inhumane. Most detainees are children. At least 39 countries had repatriated or facilitated the returns of about 9,000 of their citizens, including at least 4,000 in 2023 alone. Most repatriations were to neighboring Iraq.

Throughout the year, drone strikes by Turkish forces and hostilities between Turkish-backed local armed groups and the SDF led to civilian deaths and injuries.

A water dispute between Türkiye and the Kurdish-led Autonomous Administration of North and East Syria (AANES), the civilian wing of the SDF, continued to jeopardize the right to water of nearly 1 million people in al-Hasakeh city and its surroundings.

Clashes between the SDF and its Arab-led Deir-al-Zour Military Council began in late August and heavily impacted civilians, with the Office of the High Commissioner for Human Rights (OHCHR) documenting the killings of at least 23 civilians and dozens of arrests by the SDF of people for their alleged involvement in the hostilities.

Economic Crisis and Obstacles to Humanitarian Aid

By mid-2023, over 90 percent of Syrians lived below the poverty line, at least 12 million—more than half the population—could not access or afford enough quality food, and at least 15 million required some form of humanitarian aid to survive. More than 600,000 children were chronically malnourished. More than 12 years of war have decimated Syria's civilian infrastructure and services, severely affecting access to shelter, health care, electricity, education, public transportation, water, and sanitation. According to the UN COI, women and children with chronic conditions and disabilities, including people with untreated injuries dating back to 2019, are particularly harmed by a lack of access to adequate health care in internment camps in northeast Syria. People across the country faced hardship due to severe fuel shortages and rising food prices. According to OCHA, many female-headed households, older people, people with disabilities, and children are disproportionally affected by the compounding drivers of the crisis in Syria.

The Syrian government continued to impose severe restrictions on the delivery of humanitarian aid in the government-held areas of Syria and elsewhere in the country and to divert aid to punish those who express dissent. A lack of sufficient safeguards in procurement practices by UN agencies providing aid in Syria has resulted in a serious risk of financing abusive entities.

In July, the UN Security Council failed to renew the cross-border aid mechanism for Syria when Russia vetoed a resolution on its continuation, closing a nine-year-old avenue for delivering humanitarian assistance to non-government-controlled parts of northwest Syria without the Syrian government's consent. In late

September, after negotiations involving UN agencies, the Syrian government, and HTS, the dominant armed group in Idlib, an agreement was reached. This agreement allowed for the resumption of aid deliveries through the Bab al-Hawa border crossing for six months and extended the use of Bab al-Salam and Al-Ra'ee border crossings for another three months. The Syrian government granted UN agencies permission to use these two border crossings a week after a series of devastating earthquakes struck northern Syria, causing severe disruptions in the UN-led aid delivery system through Bab al Hawa. This disruption left millions in rebel-held areas without access to critical lifesaving aid precisely when they needed it the most.

While the Syrian government's discriminatory diversion of humanitarian aid remains the biggest obstacle to the equitable delivery of assistance to many parts of Syria, complex and wide-ranging sanctions imposed by the US, UK, EU, and others on the Syrian government, officials, and related entities have also at times hampered the principled and impartial delivery of humanitarian aid to communities in need and the rehabilitation of critical infrastructure, such as healthcare and sanitation facilities.

Refugees and Internally Displaced Persons

Displacement remains one of the most dire and protracted consequences of the war. Since the start of the armed conflict in 2011, 12.3 million have been forced to flee the country, according to OCHA, with 6.7 million currently internally displaced across the country. In northeast Syria, hundreds of thousands of internally displaced people live in overstretched and under-resourced camps and temporary shelters, some of which do not receive sustained or sufficient aid.

Against a backdrop of anti-refugee sentiment, Türkiye, which hosts nearly 3.3 million refugees, deported thousands of Syrians to northern Syria in 2023. Turkish border guards indiscriminately shot at Syrian civilians on the border with Syria as well as tortured and used excessive force against asylum seekers and migrants trying to cross into Türkiye.

Between April and May, Lebanese Armed Forces summarily deported thousands of Syrians, including unaccompanied children, back to Syria. Lebanon hosts more than an estimated 1.5 million Syrian refugees who fled since 2011, making it the country with the highest population of refugees per capita in the world.

International Accountability and Justice Efforts

In April, judges in France ordered the trial of three senior Syrian security officials accused of complicity in war crimes and crimes against humanity. In May, France's Court of Cassation concluded that the necessary conditions were met for the French judicial system to take up cases involving Syrian nationals accused of serious crimes committed in Syria. In 2023, other countries, including Germany, the Netherlands, and Sweden, pursued similar cases under their universal jurisdiction laws.

In June, Canada and the Netherlands jointly initiated proceedings against Syria at the International Court of Justice for alleged violations of the Convention against Torture. The court held hearings in October on their request for provisional measures, and on November 16, it issued its order, directing the Syrian government to take all measures within its power to prevent acts of torture and other abuses.

The International, Impartial and Independent Mechanism (IIIM), an investigative body established by the UN General Assembly in December 2016, continued to gather and preserve evidence for future criminal prosecutions.

The Investigation and Identification Team of the Organisation for the Prohibition of Chemical Weapons in The Hague continued to investigate responsibility for the use of chemical weapons in the Syrian conflict. The team has confirmed that Syrian government forces used chemical weapons on multiple occasions.

Women's and Girls' Rights

A June UN COI report highlighted the severe impact of the long-running conflict on women and girls, including challenges for female-headed households, disrupted healthcare access, rising forced marriages, difficulties in securing housing and property rights, and pervasive gender-based violence.

In government-held areas, women face ongoing discrimination in marriage, divorce, child custody, and inheritance under the Personal Status Law. This law denies financial support to women who refuse to live with their husbands without a "valid excuse" or work without their husband's consent, despite 2019 amendments. Although article 548 of the penal code was repealed in 2020, reducing sentences for harming female relatives during alleged "illicit" sexual acts, other provisions still allow reduced sentences for violence against women. Additionally, the penal code unfairly penalizes women for adultery, imposing harsher sentences than men.

Disability Rights

Children and adults with disabilities in Syria face particular challenges to access basic services and have their rights met. According to the Humanitarian Needs Assessment, households with members with disabilities reported spending 50 percent more on health care and medical expenses compared to other households. As of December 2022, children with disabilities are "particularly likely to be deprived of their education," and over 60 percent of school-age children with intellectual or physical disabilities have never attended school or any other form of education.

Sexual Orientation and Gender Identity

Syrian state and non-state actors have subjected men, boys, transgender women, and nonbinary people to sexual violence during the Syrian conflict, resulting in severe physical and mental health consequences. Under article 520 of the penal code, "unnatural sexual intercourse" is punishable by up to three years in prison.

Key International Actors

The UN-led peace process, including the constitutional committee, made no visible progress in 2023. Russia, Türkiye, the United States, and Iran continued to provide military and financial support to warring factions.

Israel has conducted aerial strikes in Syria, including on military targets of the Syrian government's allies Iran and Hezbollah, the Lebanese Shiite political party and armed group. Such strikes targeted both Aleppo and Damascus airports in 2023, at times forcing their temporary closure.

Individuals credibly implicated in atrocity crimes, entities within or affiliated to the Syrian government, and ISIS continue to be under sanctions by the US, European Union, and the United Kingdom.

Tajikistan

Tajikistan's repression of independent and critical voices continued in 2023, with hundreds of nongovernmental organizations forced to close, scores of bloggers detained for their opinions on the government's policies, and religious organizations banned or circumscribed. Several political movements and parties seen as a threat to the government remained banned, including the Islamic Renaissance Party of Tajikistan (IRPT) and Group 24, with some members of both serving lengthy prison terms or subject to forced returns from abroad.

Authorities continued their crackdown on dissenting voices in the Gorno-Badakhshan Autonomous Oblast (GBAO) following violent dispersal of peaceful demonstrations in the region in 2021 and 2022. Tajik officials refused to acknowledge the Pamiri people of Gorno-Badakshan, as a distinct ethnic minority.

Domestic violence against women and girls remains prevalent. Lesbian, gay, bisexual, and transgender (LGBT) people have been targeted and abused by law enforcement.

Civil Society

Following the violent suppression of peaceful protests in GBAO and the continued crackdown on human rights defenders, lawyers, Pamiri activists, and journalists covering the issue, Tajik authorities moved to shut down or nationalize facilities belonging to the Aga Khan Foundation, including NGOs that received funding from the foundation.

In the first half of 2023, Tajik authorities announced the closure of 239 nongovernmental organizations (NGO), following more than 500 closures in 2022, either by court decision or by self-liquidation, following alleged government pressure. At least five of these organizations, including the Pamiri Lawyers' Association and two youth groups, were closed in May in the Gorno-Badakshan region on suspicion of "links with local criminal groups."

In January, a district court in Dushanbe issued a ruling liquidating the Independent Center for Human Rights Protection (ICHPR), an organization working on issues deemed sensitive by the government, including housing rights and legal support to journalists and victims of torture, following a Ministry of Justice inspection of the organization's paperwork. The alleged non-compliance issues included late submission of financial reports and the absence of regional offices stipulated in its governing statute.

In September, Tajik law enforcement detained relatives of members of Group 24, who organized a protest against President Rakhmon during his visit to Germany to meet with Chancellor Olaf Scholz.

Freedom of Expression

In July, Tajikistan's Supreme Court banned the Group 24 website "Novyi Tadjikistan 2" (New Tajikistan 2), deeming it an "extremist" organization, and also banned its authors' pages on Telegram, Facebook, YouTube, and Instagram. Cooperation with the website is punishable by imprisonment of up to eight years.

A week earlier, the Supreme Court banned "Pamir Daily News," an online media outlet focusing on news from GBAO, also deeming it an "extremist" organization. The outlet was among the only media organizations to have covered the crackdown in GBAO in 2022.

In March, independent journalized Khurshed Fozilov was detained by Tajikistan's State Committee for National Security under suspicion of "cooperation with banned organizations." In May, a district court sentenced him to seven years in prison.

In February, Tajik authorities initiated a criminal case against independent journalist and blogger Rustami Joni, who resides in Prague, for allegedly criticizing the authorities' excessive use of force in GBAO.

Deportations and Extraditions

In January, German authorities deported Abdullohi Shamsiddin, a political activist related to the IRPT, despite their awareness that someone with his profile would likely be detained and possibly tortured if returned. In March, Shamsiddin was convicted on charges of "public calls to violent change of the constitutional order of Tajikistan" and sentenced to seven years in prison.

In August, Belarus authorities extradited Nizomiddin Nasriddinov, a member of Group 24, after detaining him in January. Tajik authorities had placed Nasriddinov on an international wanted list in 2017 for his public criticism of Tajikistan's president and government.

In July and September, two Turkish citizens with permanent residency in Tajikistan, Emsal Koc and Kural Voray, were abducted by Tajik police officers and extradited to Turkey against their will. Both had lived and worked in Tajikistan for nearly 30 years as teachers at Turkish schools affiliated with the movement led by the US-based cleric Fethullah Gülen. Koc was to receive his Tajik passport in 2025 and Vural was awaiting the outcome of his application with the United Nations to be resettled in a third country.

Political Prisoners, Torture, and Ill-Treatment

To date, 205 GBAO residents have been sentenced to various terms of imprisonment following closed trials in relation to peaceful protests in the region in 2021 and 2022. Eleven people received life imprisonment sentences, 85 received terms of 10-29 years, and 53 received terms of 1.5-9 years. At least 20 human rights defenders, lawyers, and journalists critical of the government's actions in GBAO in 2022 were imprisoned and serving lengthy sentences at time of writing. Many have complained to their relatives about torture and ill-treatment.

In July, the Vakhdat city court added an extra 10 years to the existing 21-year sentence of Buzurgmehr Yorov, a lawyer who, prior to his imprisonment in 2015, had represented members of the banned IRPT. The trial was conducted behind closed doors without legal representation for Yorov.

Leaders and members of the IRPT previously sentenced to long or life sentences remain behind bars despite continued international calls for their release.

Freedom of Religion

In January, members of the Ismaili community, a Shia branch of Islam prevalent in GBAO, were banned from holding joint prayers in private homes, and Ismaili centers were banned from conducting religious educational activities for children between the ages of 7 and 18, in circumvention of the law on parental responsibility, which allows such instruction with written parental consent.

In August, the Supreme Court rejected the appeal of Jehovah's Witnesses against a previous ban on the organization that categorized it as extremist, despite a 2022 UN Human Rights Committee opinion that such a ban violated international human rights law. The text of the Supreme Court decision has not been made available to the organization.

Violence against Women and Girls

Domestic violence remains largely unaddressed, with authorities failing to implement effectively a 2013 law on the prevention of violence in the family. The Tajik Committee on Women and Family Affairs reported that in the first half of 2023, its resource center received 1,075 complaints alleging domestic violence. Social stigma, economic dependence, impunity for perpetrators, and an insufficient number of shelters hinder survivors' access to help, especially women with disabilities and women in rural areas.

Sexual Orientation and Gender Identity

In May police officers arbitrarily detained at least 8 LGBT activists, confiscated their mobile phones, and verbally and physically abused them. Authorities copied data from their phones and invited other LGBT people in their contact lists to "meetings." One of the detainees, a person living with HIV, was threatened with initiation of a criminal investigation under article 125 of the Criminal Code for "Infecting (others) with HIV," which carries a penalty of up to two years' imprisonment. An NGO that provides legal support to LGBT people was approached by the police and told it should not keep defending the activists.

Conflict at the Kyrgyzstan-Tajikistan Border

Following the border conflict in September 2022 between Tajikistan and Kyrgyzstan forces in which at least 37 civilians were killed, including 5 children, bilateral relations remained tense. Negotiations did continue in 2023 on demarcation and other border-related issues. Both countries committed apparent war crimes in the conflict, leading to the deaths of civilians and widespread destruction of civilian property, as documented in a Human Rights Watch report published in

May. In May, both governments committed to end the use of military drones, which had contributed to civilian deaths, to patrol the border.

Key International Actors

In December 2022, the UN special rapporteur on the situation of human rights defenders, Mary Lawlor, noted in her end-of-mission statement the climate of fear within Tajikistan's civil society and called for the release of all imprisoned human rights defenders.

In April, the UN special rapporteur on freedom of religion or belief, Nazila Ghanea, stated at the end of her visit to Tajikistan that the scope for free exercise of religion in the country fell short of Tajikistan's international human rights commitments and urged Tajikistan to reshape its laws.

In July, several UN experts called on the government to release human rights defenders and journalists convicted on extremism charges connected to the 2022 GBAO events, expressing concern over the apparent use of anti-terrorism legislation to silence critical voices.

In September, President Rakhmon, jointly with the four other Central Asian leaders, met with United States President Joe Biden and separately with German Chancellor Olaf Scholz. After the US meeting the six presidents issued a statement including a commitment to uphold human rights. In June, the Central Asian presidents met with European Council President Charles Michel for the second year in a row. In a joint communique after the meeting, the leaders stressed the importance of cooperation to strengthen the rule of law, democracy, good governance, gender equality, and universal human rights and fundamental freedoms, as outlined in the framework of the European Union Strategy on Central Asia of 2019.

In October, the UN special rapporteur on minority issues, Fernand de Varennes, expressed in his end-of-mission statement particular concern regarding the rights of the Pamiri community in GBAO, including access to education in their mother tongue, freedom of religion, and political representation.

Tajikistan opened negotiations with the EU on an Enhanced Partnership and Cooperation Agreement that emphasizes democratic development and fundamental rights. Tajikistan also applied for the EU's Generalized Scheme of Preferences trade benefits (GSP+) that requires implementation of 27 core international conventions related to labor rights, human rights, environmental and climate protection, and good governance.

Tajikistan has not endorsed the global Safe Schools Declaration.

Tanzania

The government of Tanzania continued its forced evictions of pastoralist Maasai communities from areas in northern Tanzania's Ngorongoro district.

President Suluhu Hassan ended a five-year ban on political rallies and announced steps toward constitutional reform, but the authorities arrested political opposition figures and critics of a controversial government deal for the management of the country's ports. The government failed to implement a 2016 High Court decision to raise the age of marriage for women to 18.

Freedom of Expression and Media

On May 12, Gerson Msigwa, the chief government spokesperson, asked the public to share information with law enforcement officials to aid the investigation to establish the whereabouts of missing journalist Azory Gwanda. Gwanda was picked up from his home in Kibiti in the Pwani region by unidentified people in November 2017 while investigating serious alleged human rights violations. The authorities have not conducted meaningful investigations into his enforced disappearance.

The authorities detained or threatened at least 23 people since June 10, including protesters, after they criticized the Tanzania National Assembly's ratification of an agreement for the management of Tanzania's ports for giving the Emirate of Dubai excessive control of Tanzania's ports. At a press conference on August 11, Inspector General of Police Camilius Wambura described the online criticism of the agreement as "seditious" and said authorities would deal with those critical of the agreement.

In September, police arrested gospel singers Sifa Bujune, Salome Mwampeta, and Hezekiel Millyashi on accusations of promoting an inciteful song. Their arrest was in connection with their song "Mnatuona Nyani" ("You See Us as Monkeys"), which is about police brutality. The three were detained for five days without bail.

Government Opponents

At a meeting with political party leaders in Dar es Salaam on January 3, President Hassan announced the end of a six-year ban on politicians holding political rallies and meetings outside of election periods.

On January 26, opposition leader and former presidential candidate Tundu Lissu returned to Tanzania after a five-year exile. In September 2017, unidentified attackers had shot and wounded Lissu, an outspoken member of parliament and a vocal critic of the president, in Dodoma. Lissu had also been arrested multiple times in 2017, including for "hate speech" and "insulting words that are likely to incite ethnic hatred."

On March 1, opposition politician and Chadema party member Godbless Lema returned from exile in Canada to a cheering crowd. In 2020, Lema fled to Canada with his family after being granted asylum there following the 2020 elections, during which Lema was arrested. On March 5, the president said the government is looking forward to dropping charges against him.

On September 10, police both arrested and released Lissu in Arusha hours before a scheduled political rally on allegations of holding an unlawful assembly and obstructing police.

Right to Education

On June 28, Deputy Minister for Education, Science and Technology Omar Kipanga told the National Assembly that a total of 1,907 teenage mothers had resumed classes by January 2023. Tanzania pledged in February 2022 to adopt guidelines to guarantee that schools ensure adolescent mothers can return to schools by June 2022, in response to strong objections from human rights activists and others. In 2017, the government adopted a discriminatory ban in 2017 prohibiting pregnant students and teenage mothers from continuing their education in public schools.

Land Rights

Human Rights Watch found that since June 2022, the authorities have engaged in abusive and unlawful tactics, including beatings, shootings, sexual violence, and arbitrary arrests to forcibly evict residents in Loliondo division, Ngorongoro district.

South of Loliondo, the government has, since March 2022, implemented a resettlement plan that will forcibly displace herder communities from the Ngorongoro Conservation Area (NCA) to Handeni district, Tanga region, about 600 kilometers away, with little or no consultation with communities affected by the move. As part of the resettlement plan, the government has taken steps to transfer funding for public services, including for health and education, from Ngorongoro district to Handeni, depriving NCA residents of these basic services.

Amnesty International reported that on August 15, security forces arrested 39 community members in the Ngorongoro Conservation Area, following a community meeting in Endulen village, accusing them of attacking journalists attending the meeting. Police later arrested Ngorongoro parliamentarian Emmanuel Lekishon Shangai on allegations that he organized attacks against the journalists.

On January 28, the African Commission on Human and Peoples' Rights concluded its investigation into evictions in Ngorongoro and urged the government to "explore fresh rounds of civil dialogues" with communities in the NCA, the Loliondo division of Ngorongoro, and Msomera village in Handeni.

Sexual Orientation and Gender Identity

In February, the government banned the use of supplementary books with content that "goes against the national morals and traditions"—widely interpreted as content that references homosexuality and lesbian, gay, bisexual, and transgender (LGBT) people—in all schools across the country. On April 17, Minister of Information, Communication and Information Technology Nape Nnauye told the National Assembly that the government had shut down over 3,360 social media accounts and websites that were involved in "promoting homosexuality."

The Sexual Offenses Special Provisions Act of 1998 punishes consensual adult same-sex conduct with up to life imprisonment.

Child Marriage

In June, the High Court ordered the attorney general to comply with the 2016 landmark decision ruling the minimum marriage age for girls of 14 years unconstitutional and directed the government to raise the legal age of marriage to 18 years for both men and women within six months.

Legislative Reform

On March 8, the president announced the creation of a committee for constitutional reforms. In 2012, the government had embarked on a review of the constitution, but the process stalled in 2015 after President John Magufuli took office.

On June 13, the government amended the 2016 Media Services Act, which regulates the media industry and journalism profession, to remove criminal liability for defamation. In the past, the authorities had used the law to restrict the work of journalists and to suspend newspapers for publishing material critical of the government.

On June 8, the National Assembly approved reforms to the structure and operations of the Tanzania Intelligence and Security Services (TISS). The bill, which was not published on the National Assembly's website, reportedly removes oversight of TISS from the attorney general, the ministers of state and foreign affairs, and the chief secretary, transferring oversight to the president and the director general of TISS.

Key International Actors

In March, the government announced a bilateral cooperation agreement on political and diplomatic consultations, security, and energy resources with Namibia, and it agreed to strengthen political and economic relations with South Africa. In the same month, following a visit by United States Vice President Kamala Harris, the US pledged to foster bilateral relations with Tanzania regarding "long-term economic growth for Tanzania, the climate crisis, and ... regional and global challenges."

Thailand

Thailand held a general election on May 14, 2023, under flawed and unfair constitutional and legal frameworks put in place by the National Council for Peace and Order (NCPO) military junta. The reformist Move Forward Party (MFP) won the largest number of seats, but the military-appointed Senate led efforts that effectively blocked it from forming a government.

Srettha Thavisin of the runner-up Pheu Thai Party then formed a ruling coalition that included parties from the previous government of Prime Minister Gen. Prayut Chan-ocha. Even though the new government pledged to promote and protect human rights, impunity for abuses continued unabated. Authorities continued to restrict fundamental rights—particularly freedom of expression and peaceful assembly—and prosecuted human rights and democracy activists, community advocates, environmental defenders, and critics of the monarchy.

General Election, Attacks on Move Forward Party, and New Government

Thailand's general election occurred within the framework of the 2017 constitution written at the behest of the NCPO junta created after the military coup in 2014. A majority of the lower house nominates a candidate for prime minister, but with the 250 unelected members of the Senate and the 500-seat lower house voting, a candidate requires 376 votes, a majority of the combined 750 assembly seats, to become prime minister. The MFP won 151 parliamentary seats but was rejected by most members of the Senate and MPs from the previous government, who claimed the party's proposal to amend penal code article 112, the royal defamation (*lèse-majesté*) law, amounted to an attempt to overthrow the monarchy.

The Constitutional Court decided on July 12 to hear a case against the MFP on whether their policy position to reform article 112 constitutes treason. A court decision was still pending at time of writing, but a ruling against the party could result in its dissolution and criminal prosecution of its leaders. MFP party executives could also be banned from politics for life.

In July, the Constitutional Court suspended MFP leader Pita Limjaroenrat from parliamentary duties pending a ruling on allegations that he violated electoral rules for holding shares in the iTV media company, even though the company has not broadcast for 15 years and was removed from listing on the Stock Exchange of Thailand in 2014.

In September, the Supreme Court banned former Future Forward Party (predecessor party of the MFP) spokesperson and former MP Pannika Wanich from running for political office or holding any political post for the rest of her life because she posted a photo online when she was a college student that the court found disrespectful to the monarchy.

Prime Minister Srettha repeatedly announced commitments to promote and protect human rights, including in his speeches to the Thai parliament on September 11, 2023 and the United Nations General Assembly on September 22, 2023. But the Pheu Thai Party-led government has stated it will not seek to amend Thailand's draconian *lèse-majesté* law to align with international human rights standards and will continue such prosecutions. Srettha also announced that the government-initiated constitutional amendment will leave out demands for monarchy reforms.

Freedoms of Expression and Peaceful Assembly

As of September 2023, at least 1,928 people had been prosecuted since July 2020 for exercising their rights to freedom of expression and peaceful public assembly, according to Thai Lawyers for Human Rights. At least 286 of those charged were children.

Thai authorities continued to use Criminal Code article 112 on *lèse-majesté*, which includes punishments of up to 15 years in prison for each offense. In 2023, authorities prosecuted at least 258 people in relation to various activities undertaken at democracy protests or comments made on social media on *lèse-majesté* charges. Thai authorities used the vague, overbroad Computer-Related Crimes Act and Criminal Code article 116 on sedition to prosecute democracy activists and dissidents.

The government has routinely held outspoken critics of the monarchy in pretrial detention for months. Courts granted bail to some, albeit with restrictive conditions, such as full or partial house arrest, being required to wear tracking devices, or being prohibited from speaking about the monarchy, taking part in political rallies, or traveling overseas. As of September 2023, the government held at least 35 activists in pretrial detention for participating in democracy protests or committing acts that authorities considered to be offensive to the monarchy.

After the Prayut government ordered nationwide enforcement of the "Emergency Decree on Public Administration in Emergency Situation" in March 2020 ostensibly to control the spread of Covid-19, authorities prosecuted at least 1,469 people, primarily for taking part in democracy protests. Police and prosecutors brought charges such as violating social distancing measures, curfew restrictions, and other disease control measures. Most of these legal cases were not revoked after the emergency measures were lifted on October 1, 2022. Violations of the Emergency Decree bring possible penalties of up to two years in prison, or a 40,000 Thai baht (about US$1,080) fine, or both.

Torture, Ill-Treatment, and Enforced Disappearances

Thailand is a state party to the Convention against Torture and Other Cruel, Inhuman or Degrading Treatment or Punishment and has also signed, but still not ratified, the International Convention for the Protection of All Persons from Enforced Disappearance.

On August 24, 2022, the House of Representatives approved and passed the Prevention and Suppression of Torture and Enforced Disappearance Bill. The law became effective on February 22, 2023. However, the government has yet to effectively enforce the law or resolve outstanding cases.

Human Rights Watch documented numerous cases related to counterinsurgency operations in Thailand's southern border provinces in which police and military personnel tortured ethnic Malay Muslims in custody. There are also credible reports of torture being used as a form of punishment for Thai military conscripts. During the five years of NCPO military rule after the 2014 coup, many people taken into incommunicado military custody alleged that soldiers tortured or otherwise ill-treated them during their detention and interrogation.

In highly publicized cases with incontrovertible evidence, justice at times was done. On June 8, 2022, the Central Criminal Court for Corruption and Misconduct

Cases sentenced Pol. Col. Thitisant Utthanaphon to life in prison for torturing to death a suspected drug trafficker in Nakhon Sawan province in August 2021.

But other prosecutions were flawed. On September 28, the Central Criminal Court for Corruption and Misconduct Cases acquitted four forestry officials suspected of abducting and murdering ethnic Karen activist Porlajee "Billy" Rakchongchareon in April 2014. They were only punished with a three-year prison term for dereliction of duties: failing to report Billy's arrest (on a charge of illegal possession of wild honey) and not taking him to the police station. Billy's family and civil society groups pointed to shoddy police work in the investigation as the primary reason the more serious charges failed.

Since 1980, the UN Working Group on Enforced or Involuntary Disappearances has recorded 76 cases of enforced disappearance in Thailand. In recent years, at least nine dissidents who fled persecution in Thailand were forcibly disappeared in neighboring countries. In September 2021, the Working Group raised concerns in its annual report about enforced disappearances in the context of transnational transfers between Thailand and neighboring countries.

Attacks on Human Rights Defenders

The government failed to fulfill its obligation to ensure human rights defenders can carry out their work in a safe and enabling environment.

Cover-up actions, manifested in the form of poor police work and lack of willingness to pursue evidence in the case, effectively blocked efforts to prosecute soldiers who shot dead ethnic Lahu youth activist Chaiyaphum Pasae in broad daylight at a checkpoint in March 2017 in Chiang Mai province.

The police made no progress in investigating violent attacks in 2019 targeting prominent democracy activists Sirawith Seritiwat, Anurak Jeantawanich, and Ekachai Hongkangwan.

Officials regularly intimidated and threatened democracy activists and human rights defenders in Bangkok and other provinces to stop them from organizing or participating in protests, especially during the visits by cabinet ministers or members of the royal family.

Despite the adoption of Thailand's National Action Plan on Business and Human Rights in 2019, Thai authorities failed to protect human rights defenders from reprisals and end the abusive use of strategic lawsuits against public participation (SLAPP). Former National Human Rights Commissioner and Magsaysay Award winner Angkhana Neelapaijit is one of the many activists hit with such retaliatory lawsuits.

Lack of Accountability for State-Sponsored Abuses

On August 22, the Civil Court ordered the police to pay 3 million baht (about US$81,000) in compensation to democracy activist Tanat Thanakitamnuay, who lost his sight in one eye after a police officer shot him with a teargas canister while dispersing an August 13, 2021 rally. But there has been little progress in other cases alleging abuse and excessive use of force by riot police to disperse other democracy rallies in 2020-2023.

Despite overwhelming evidence that soldiers were responsible for most casualties during the 2010 political confrontations with the United Front for Democracy Against Dictatorship, known as the "Red Shirts," which left at least 99 dead and more than 2,000 injured, there has been no action against military personnel or government officials who ordered and carried out the crackdown.

There has been no progress in pursuing criminal investigations of extrajudicial killings related to anti-drug operations, especially the more than 2,800 killings that accompanied then-Prime Minister Thaksin Shinawatra's "war on drugs" in 2003.

Violence and Abuses in the Southern Border Provinces

The armed conflict in Thailand's Pattani, Yala, Narathiwat, and Songkhla provinces, which has resulted in more than 7,000 deaths since January 2004, subsided in the first half of 2023 following an announcement by the Thai military and Barisan Revolusi Nasional (BRN) that both would seek to reduce violence during Ramadan. However, since August, insurgent attacks on military targets and civilians increased despite ongoing dialogue between government representatives and the BRN.

The government has continually failed to prosecute members of its security forces responsible for torture, unlawful killings, and other abuses of ethnic Malay Muslims. In many cases, Thai authorities have provided financial compensation to the victims or their families in exchange for their agreement not to speak out against the security forces or file criminal cases against officials.

Thailand has not endorsed the Safe Schools Declaration. Meanwhile, the BRN has continued to recruit children for insurgent activities.

Refugees, Asylum Seekers, and Migrant Workers

Thailand is not a party to the 1951 Refugee Convention or its 1967 protocol. However, customary international law prohibiting refoulement and Thailand's Anti-Torture law prevent people from being forcibly returned to a place where they likely could face persecution, torture, or other forms of ill-treatment.

Despite the lack of effective protections, Thailand hosts a large number of refugees and migrant workers. The authorities continue to treat asylum seekers as illegal migrants subject to arrest and deportation. As a matter of official policy, authorities refuse to allow Lao Hmong, ethnic Rohingya and Uyghurs, and people from Myanmar and North Korea to be considered for refugee status. In September 2023, the government launched a new National Screening Mechanism to identify asylum seekers and potentially offer them protection, but details about implementation of the new mechanism were not available as time of writing.

Thai authorities have violated the customary international legal prohibition against refoulement by returning refugees and asylum seekers to countries where they are likely to face persecution, particularly to neighboring countries like Cambodia, Laos, Vietnam, Myanmar, and China.

Thai authorities have made no progress in investigating the apparent abduction and, in some cases, killing of exiled dissidents from Cambodia, Vietnam, and Laos in Thailand during the 2014-2023 period. On April 13, 2023, Vietnamese refugee Thai Van Duong was abducted off the street in Pathum Thani province, likely by people working at the behest of Vietnam, and forced back to Vietnam where he is now in jail facing charges in Hanoi. On May 17, 2023, unknown persons shot and killed Free Lao group leader and refugee Bounsuan Kitiyano in Ubon Ratchatani province.

Thailand is holding approximately 50 Uyghurs and several hundred Rohingya in indefinite detention in squalid conditions in immigration detention centers, without adequate food or access to medicine. Some of these individuals have been held for as long as a decade. Two Uyghurs—Mattohti Mattursun and Aziz Abdullah—died in 2023 of health problems in the Suan Phlu immigration detention center in Bangkok.

Despite government-instituted reforms in the fishing industry, many migrant workers still face forced labor, remain in debt bondage to recruiters, cannot change employers, and receive sub-minimum wages that are paid months late. The government has recently made promises to fishing boat owners that would further erode labor protections for workers in the sector.

Thai authorities failed to adequately protect internationally recognized worker rights, such as the right to freedom of association and collective bargaining. Union busting continued in industrial areas, and union leaders faced harassment and dismissal by hostile employers. Non-Thai workers are barred by provisions in the Labor Relations Act 1975 from organizing and establishing labor unions or serving as a government recognized labor union leader.

Gender Inequality

While Thailand enacted the Gender Equality Act in 2015, implementation remains piecemeal, though several court cases have been brought by transgender people.

Sexual Orientation and Gender Identity

Regarding lesbian, gay, bisexual, and transgender rights, on November 21, 2023, the Cabinet approved in principle a draft law on marriage equality and said it would introduce the legislation into Parliament in December. While the draft law was not publicly available at time of writing, it is expected to contain elements of two draft laws—the Life Partnership Bill and the Equal Marriage Bill—that were under consideration by the previous government. If enacted, such a law would make Thailand the first country in Southeast Asia to legally recognize same-sex couples.

Key International Actors

Thailand and the EU started negotiations on a free trade agreement in March, aiming to reach a deal by 2025. The importance of taking up issues of human rights and labor rights in the context of those negotiations is being emphasized by Thai and international civil society groups.

The US, European Union and its member states, and other countries tightened their relationships with Thailand after the Srettha government took office.

On September 22, Prime Minister Srettha announced at the UN General Assembly that Thailand would stand for election to the Human Rights Council (HRC) for the 2025-2027 term despite ongoing and unresolved concerns raised by states and rights groups during Universal Periodic Review (UPR) of Thailand at the HRC in November 2022.

Tunisia

In 2023, Tunisian authorities intensified their repression against the opposition and other critical voices, imprisoning several dozen people on dubious and manifestly political charges.

President Kais Saied continued to wield almost unchallenged power after eliminating nearly all institutional checks and balances on executive power. The new assembly that took office on March 13 had vastly weaker powers under the constitution adopted in 2022 than the parliament that it had replaced. Saied announced local elections for December 24, 2023, to replace the democratically elected municipal councils that he had unilaterally dissolved in March.

With the country facing a severe economic crisis, the president has repeatedly accused his opponents of conspiracy and of fomenting social tensions amid rising food prices. The president has scapegoated Tunisia's small population of Black migrants, asylum seekers, and refugees who have also faced abuses from the security forces.

Political Crackdown

In February, a wave of arrests targeted opponents of various political affiliations, activists, lawyers, judges, and the director of a popular radio station. Most were accused of "conspiracy against state security" and remained in pretrial detention as of September.

The arrests continued throughout the year in the ranks of the opposition and perceived critics of the government, bringing the number of individuals deemed critical of Saied behind bars to at least 40 as of September.

The authorities have also effectively dismantled, without formally banning, the country's largest opposition party, Ennahda. About 20 party members, including its top leaders, Rached Ghannouchi, Ali Laarayedh, and Nourredine Bhiri, were arbitrarily detained.

On May 15, a Tunis court sentenced Ghannouchi to a one-year prison term and a fine on terrorism-related charges in connection with public remarks he made.

Ghannouchi is also being investigated in several other criminal cases, including for accusations of "conspiracy against the state."

On April 18, the police closed Ennahda's headquarters in Tunis and have since prevented access to the party's offices across the country. The same day, the authorities shut the Tunis headquarters of the Tunisia Will Movement party, which hosted activities of the National Salvation Front (NSF), an opposition coalition cofounded by Ennahda.

The authorities imposed at least a dozen travel bans in connection with criminal investigations of opponents and perceived critics, such as President of the Truth and Dignity Commission Sihem Bensedrine and former member of parliament Zied Ghanney, restricting their freedom of movement.

Prosecutions of civilians before military courts have increased since the president's power grab in July 2021. On January 20, six civilians, including four opposition members of the dissolved parliament and a lawyer, were convicted by the military court of appeal and sentenced to up to 14 months in prison on charges that included "insulting public officials" in connection with a protest they held at Tunis airport.

Chaima Issa, one of the leaders of an opposition coalition, is being prosecuted by a military court for comments she made on the radio about the military's role in organizing the elections. Issa was also detained from February to July on a charge of "conspiracy against state security," for which she still faces trial.

Saied's efforts to undermine judicial independence continued. He ignored an administrative court order to reinstate the 57 judges and prosecutors he arbitrarily fired in June 2022. As of September 2023, at least 27 lawyers faced civil or military prosecution in relation to actions they took while defending their clients or for expressing their opinions. Several of them stood accused of "conspiracy against state security."

Freedom of Expression and the Press

Prosecutors have opened criminal investigations against about 20 people, including journalists, political opponents, lawyers, and activists, under Decree 54 on cybercrime, which Saied issued in September 2022. The decree imposes heavy prison sentences for spreading "fake news" and "rumors" online and in the media. And it contains provisions granting authorities far-reaching powers to intercept, monitor, collect, and store data for private communications, without safeguards for human rights protections.

On May 16, journalist Khalifa Guesmi, correspondent of the private Radio Mosaïque FM in Kairouan, was sentenced on appeal to five years in prison on charges of disclosing national security information in connection with his reporting about the dismantling of a presumed terrorist cell. He began serving his sentence on September 3. Also in May, a court released on bail the director of Radio Mosaïque FM, Noureddine Boutar, after three months of detention. Boutar is awaiting trial on charges of "conspiracy against state security" and money laundering.

On July 21, journalist Chadha Hadj Mbarek was arrested in connection with her work with a digital content production company, Instalingo. The company, whose customers include media organizations critical of Saied, has been under investigation since 2021. Haj Mbarek, along with other former Instalingo employees and other defendants, faces dubious "conspiracy" accusations, among others. She was still detained as of September.

Racism and the Rights of Migrants, Refugees, and Asylum Seekers

During comments on February 21 that were made public, President Saied linked undocumented Black African migrants to crime and a "conspiracy" to change Tunisia's demographics. "Hordes of illegal immigrants from sub-Saharan Africa are still arriving, bringing violence, crime, and unacceptable and illegal practices," he said. The UN Committee on the Elimination of Racial Discrimination called Saied's speech racist and considered that such remarks violate the International Convention on the Elimination of All Forms of Racial Discrimination, to which Tunisia is a state party.

Although Black African foreigners have been the subject of discrimination and sporadic racist assaults in Tunisia for years, they suffered a surge in attacks after the president's speech, including violent assaults, robberies, and vandalism by

HUMAN
RIGHTS
WATCH
“All This Terror Because of a Photo”
Digital Targeting and Its Offline Consequences for LGBT People
in the Middle East and North Africa

Tunisian citizens, arbitrary evictions by landlords, and job terminations by employers.

In February, the authorities reportedly arrested at least 850 Black African foreigners indiscriminately, apparently based on racial profiling, including both documented and undocumented people, asylum seekers, and registered students, according to Lawyers Without Borders (ASF).

In 2023, the Tunisian police, military, and national guard, including the coast guard, committed serious abuses against Black African migrants, refugees, and asylum seekers. The abuses documented by Human Rights Watch included beatings, use of excessive force, some cases of torture, arbitrary arrests and detention, collective expulsions, dangerous actions at sea during boat interceptions, forced evictions, and theft of money and belongings.

In July, Tunisian security forces conducted mass and arbitrary arrests of Black African foreigners with both regular and irregular legal status in and around the city of Sfax; in several cases, they used excessive force or engaging in physical or sexual abuse, including against women and children. The security forces summarily and collectively expelled some 2,000 people, according to the UN High Commissioner for Human Rights—of at least 16 African nationalities, including asylum seekers, pregnant women, and children—to remote areas along Tunisia's borders with Libya and Algeria.

Authorities left expelled people stranded at the borders for days to weeks with little access to water, food, or medical care. Many who were expelled to the Algerian border remain unaccounted for. While Tunisian authorities and the Tunisian Red Crescent eventually evacuated over 700 of them from the militarized Libya-Tunisia border zone to International Organization for Migration (IOM) shelters and other government facilities in Tunisia, at least 27 migrants died at the border, according to the Libyan authorities and the UN High Commissioner for Human Rights. Following an agreement between Tunisia and Libya, about 160 people were evacuated to Libya and transferred to detention centers, where they risk facing serious abuse.

Women's Rights

Women's rights regressed under Saied's presidency. His tailor-made constitution, adopted by a national referendum with an official abstention rate of 69.5 percent in July 2022, says women and men are "equal in rights and duties and are equal before the law without any discrimination." Article 5, however, stipulates that "Tunisia is part of the Islamic Umma [community/nation]," making the realization of the purposes of Islam a responsibility of the state. Such provisions could be used to justify attacks on women's rights based on interpretations of religious precepts, as other states in the region have done.

The new electoral law issued unilaterally by Saied in September 2022 stripped provisions from the previous law that aimed to achieve gender parity in Tunisia's elected assemblies. As a result, only 25 women sit in the new assembly of 161 seats.

Tunisian law continues to discriminate against women in inheritance rights, and Saied has expressed his firm opposition to the reform of inheritance laws, which was debated in parliament in 2019.

Despite the 2017 law on violence against women, which set out new support services, prevention, and protection mechanisms for survivors, there are numerous shortcomings in the law's implementation, particularly how the police and judiciary address complaints of domestic violence. The insufficiency of state funding for the law's implementation, as well as the lack of women's shelters, is a critical gap.

Disability Rights

In April 2023, the UN Committee on the Rights of Persons with Disabilities called on Tunisia to review and repeal its laws that deny the right to legal capacity for people with disabilities and to ensure people with disabilities have the right to supported decision-making and individual autonomy. The committee also called on Tunisia to ensure all people with disabilities have the right to accessible quality health services, "in particular sexual and reproductive health services," on the basis of free will and informed consent.

The committee also raised concerns about the scarce participation of women with disabilities in political life and public administration.

Sexual Orientation and Gender Identity

Article 230 of the penal code punishes consensual same-sex conduct between both men and women with up to three years in prison. In December 2022, two individuals, a transgender woman and a gay man, were sentenced by Tunisian courts for homosexuality under article 230 to three years and one year in prison, respectively.

Lesbian, gay, bisexual, and transgender (LGBT) people in Tunisia continue to face discrimination, violent attacks, and online hate speech, including "outing," which has far-reaching offline consequences that threaten affected people's safety.

State actors in Tunisia have also undermined LGBT people's right to privacy and other human rights with digital targeting, namely online harassment, doxxing, and "outing" on public social media platforms. Authorities sometimes rely on illegitimately obtained digital information, such as private photos and chats found on LGBT people's phones during arbitrary phone searches, in prosecutions.

International Cooperation

On July 16, the European Union signed a Memorandum of Understanding (MoU) with Tunisia on a new "strategic partnership" in which the EU pledges to provide a funding package of up to €1 billion (approximately US$1.085 billion) for the country, including €105 million ($114 million) for "combating irregular migration," to be allocated to "border management, ... search and rescue, anti-smuggling and return."

The MoU included neither serious human rights guarantees for migrants and asylum seekers nor provisions to prevent EU aid from reaching entities responsible for human rights violations. The MoU was signed at a time when hundreds of Black African migrants were languishing in the desert along Tunisia's borders after security forces had summarily rounded them up and deposited them there.

On September 13, the EU Ombudsman Emily O'Reilly opened an inquiry about respect for fundamental rights in the MoU between the EU and Tunisia.

On September 22, the European Commission announced the imminent release of €127 million (approximately $US138 million) to support Tunisia's economy, including €42 million (approximately $45.5 million) from the €105 million (approximately $114 million) envelope allocated to border management.

In March, the European Parliament adopted a resolution condemning attacks "against freedom of expression and association, and against trade unions."

Other EU institutions, including the European Council and the European Commission, largely failed to publicly address the grave restrictions on human rights and attacks on migrants' rights throughout the year.

Türkiye

The May 2023 re-election of Recep Tayyip Erdoğan and his Justice and Development Party-led People's Alliance in simultaneous presidential and parliamentary elections consolidated an authoritarian order that routinely and arbitrarily punishes perceived critics and political opponents and exerts strong control over the media and courts. Erdogan won 52.2 percent of the vote in the May 28 second round of the presidential election to secure a third term in office, beating rival Kemal Kılıçdaroğlu of the main opposition Republican People's Party (CHP), who had been backed by an alliance of opposition parties.

Two devastating earthquakes on February 6, affecting Türkiye's southeastern provinces and northwest Syria, left over 50,000 dead in Türkiye, at least 100,000 injured, and hundreds of thousands homeless and displaced. A cost-of-living crisis continued, with extremely high price inflation, which the Turkish Statistical Institute estimated to have risen to 61 percent year-over-year as of October.

Freedom of Expression

The Erdoğan government's control of most media was especially significant in an election year, prompting the international election observation mission led by the Organization for Security and Co-operation in Europe (OSCE) and the Council of Europe to note that during the election campaign, the ruling coalition "enjoyed an unjustified advantage, including through biased media coverage." The observers emphasized that public broadcasters, like TRT, "clearly favoured the ruling parties and their candidates" and that continued restrictions on the freedoms of assembly, association, and expression "hindered the participation of some opposition politicians and parties, civil society and independent media in the election process."

The government-aligned broadcasting regulator, the Radio and Television High Council (RTÜK), regularly issues arbitrary fines to the few television channels critical of the government, notably Halk TV. RTÜK did so for comments made on their platforms during the election period. Among those fined and sanctioned was Tele 1, whose editor-in-chief, Merdan Yanardağ, was arrested on June 27 on the pretext of non-inciteful comments he made concerning Abdullah Öcalan, the jailed leader of the Kurdistan Workers' Party (PKK), during a TV broadcast. Prosecuted for "spreading terrorist propaganda" and "praising crime and criminals," Yanardağ was released from pretrial detention at his first trial hearing on October 4 at which he was convicted and sentenced to 30 months in prison, a sentence he has appealed. The Tele 1 channel was additionally punished for Yanardağ's comments with an unprecedented seven-day broadcasting suspension in August.

Independent media in Türkiye operate mainly via online platforms. The authorities regularly order the removal of critical online content or negative news coverage relating to government ministers, the president, and members of the judiciary. Journalists face prosecution under Türkiye's Anti-Terror Law, as well as under criminal defamation charges, including the widely used charge of "insulting the president," which the European Court of Human Rights (ECtHR) said fails to comply with the right to freedom of expression. At time of writing, at least 43 journalists and media workers were in pretrial detention or serving prison sentences for terrorism offenses because of their journalistic work or association with media. The government significantly expanded online censorship with a series of legislative amendments passed in October 2022.series of legislative amendments passed in October 2022.

Kurdish journalists are disproportionately targeted. In one Diyarbakır trial of 18 Kurdish journalists and media workers accused of "membership of a terrorist organization," 15 spent 13 months in pretrial detention before being released at their first hearing in July. In an Ankara trial of 11 Kurdish journalists, 9 spent 7 months in pretrial detention before being released in May at their first hearing. The two trials continued at time of writing.

Freedoms of Association and Assembly

Tens of thousands of people continue to face unfair trials on terrorism charges on the basis of their alleged links with the movement led by US-based cleric Fethullah Gülen, which the government deems a terrorist organization (Fethullahist Terrorist Organization, FETÖ) responsible for the July 15, 2016 attempted military coup. Many have faced prolonged and arbitrary imprisonment with no effective remedy after mass removal from civil service jobs and the judiciary. The justice minister announced in August that 15,050 remanded and convicted FETÖ prisoners remained in prison.

After the May elections, Türkiye's intelligence agency continued the practice of organizing the abduction and rendition to Türkiye of individuals with alleged associations with the Gülen movement in collusion with authorities in countries with weak rule of law frameworks. In July and September, Tajik authorities bypassed legal extradition processes in abducting Emsal Koç and Koray Vural before they were flown to Türkiye where they were placed in pretrial detention pending trial.

Provincial authorities regularly ban protests and assemblies of constituencies critical of the government, often flouting domestic court rulings that such bans are disproportionate. Police violently detain demonstrators associated with leftist or Kurdish groups. Some are arrested and placed in pretrial detention for resisting the police or failing to disperse.

Attacks on Human Rights Defenders

In September, the Court of Cassation, Türkiye's top appeals court, upheld the baseless conviction and life sentence of human rights defender Osman Kavala as well as the 18-year sentences of Çiğdem Mater, Can Atalay, Mine Özerden, and Tayfun Kahraman on charges of attempting to overthrow the government for their alleged role in the lawful and overwhelmingly peaceful 2013 Istanbul Gezi Park protests. The court quashed the convictions of three others, two of whom (Mücella Yapıcı and Hakan Altınay) were released from prison pending retrial. Kavala has been arbitrarily detained since November 2017 and the others since their conviction in April 2022. President Erdoğan has made repeated public speeches against Kavala throughout the trial and the case demonstrates the Erdoğan administration's high level of political control over Türkiye's courts and flagrant defiance of Council of Europe infringement proceedings against Türkiye over its failure to implement two ECtHR judgments ordering Kavala's release.

At time of writing, in direct contravention of an October Constitutional Court decision ordering his release, human rights lawyer Can Atalay, a defendant in the Gezi trial, remained in prison and unable to take up the parliamentary seat he won on behalf of the Workers Party of Türkiye in the May elections.

The authorities continue to use terrorism and defamation charges to harass rights defenders; sometimes lawyers representing terrorism suspects are also targeted for arrest pending trial and prosecuted on terrorism charges.

Torture and Ill-Treatment in Custody

Allegations of torture and ill-treatment in police and gendarmerie custody and prison since 2016 have rarely been rigorously investigated, and perpetrators even more rarely prosecuted. In the days after the February earthquakes, there were multiple reports of police and gendarmerie beating individuals during the rescue effort, justifying it by accusing them of looting. One man, Ahmet Güreşçi, died in gendarmerie custody in Altınözü, Hatay province, after he and his brother were subjected to torture. An investigation into the gendarmerie is ongoing. Some police ill-treatment has been directed at Syrian refugees and also reflects xenophobic motivation.

Alongside continuing reports of cruel, inhuman, and degrading treatment and over-crowding in removal centers where foreign nationals, including asylum seekers, are subject to administrative detention pending deportation procedures, there were well-documented cases of soldiers and gendarmerie shooting at or severely ill-treating migrants and asylum seekers attempting to cross the border from Syria to Türkiye.

Kurdish Conflict and Crackdown on Opposition

Türkiye has concentrated its military campaign against the PKK with drone strikes in northern Iraq where PKK bases are located and also increasingly in northeast Syria against the Kurdish-led, US-backed Syrian Democratic Forces (SDF), where Türkiye's strikes in October damaged critical infrastructure and disrupted water and electricity for millions of people. Türkiye continues to occupy territories in northern Syria, where its local Syrian proxies have abused civilians' rights with impunity (see Syria chapter). On October 1, in Ankara, a suicide bombing at the entrance to the Interior Ministry was claimed by a unit of the PKK.

The Erdoğan government pursued a highly divisive discourse against the opposition parties during its May election campaign, regularly accusing the CHP of supporting the PKK and circulating a fake video in which a video of CHP's Kemal Kılıçdaroğlu was merged with footage of the leadership of the PKK.

With a closure case against it pending before Türkiye's Constitutional Court, the pro-Kurdish Peoples' Democratic Party (HDP) did not enter the election and instead recommended its supporters vote for another party, the Green Left Party, which ran candidates and won 61 seats. Scores of former HDP members of parliament, mayors, and party officials are in prison on remand or are serving sentences after being convicted of terrorism offenses for their legitimate non-violent political activities, speeches, and social media postings. They include jailed former HDP co-chairs Selahattin Demirtaş and Figen Yüksekdağ, in prison since November 4, 2016, despite ECtHR judgments ordering their immediate release.

Istanbul mayor Ekrem İmamoğlu from the opposition CHP faces two ongoing politically motivated prosecutions that could ban him from politics. At time of writing, his conviction for insulting the Higher Election Board was on appeal and, in a second case that began in June, he is accused of corruption in 2015 during his term as mayor of Istanbul's Beylikdüzü district.

Refugees, Asylum Seekers, and Migrants

Türkiye continues to host the world's largest number of refugees. At time of writing, more than 3.2 million Syrians had temporary protection status, and more than 290,000 people from different non-European countries had a form of conditional refugee status. The Turkish government mostly deems people from Afghanistan, Iraq, and other non-European countries irregular migrants and strictly limits avenues for them to apply for international protection, routinely deporting large groups and publishing statistics that show it. Turkish authorities also conduct mass summary pushbacks at the borders.

During the May election campaign, opposition politicians increasingly weaponized xenophobic anti-foreigner sentiment, particularly directing it at Syrians and Afghans and advocating for the return of Syrians to war-torn Syria. President Erdoğan responded with pledges to resettle 1 million Syrians in Turkish-occupied areas of northern Syria. Since the election, deportation centers have filled rapidly with Syrians, Afghans, and other groups at risk. The practice of men and some boys being unlawfully deported to northern Syria, often after being coerced into signing voluntary return forms, continues in spite of a 2022 ECtHR judgment and a May 2023 Constitutional Court judgment finding forced return under the guise of voluntary repatriation a violation of human rights on several counts.

Women's and Girls' Rights

Two years after Türkiye's 2021 withdrawal from the Council of Europe Convention on Preventing and Combating Violence against Women and Domestic Violence, known as the Istanbul Convention, challenges in providing effective protection to women in Türkiye who report domestic violence are reflected in the high number of murders of women and girls. The We Will Stop Femicide Platform, an association campaigning against murders of women and girls and supporting families of victims, reported 254 femicides in the January to October period.

In September, an Istanbul court dismissed a case brought in 2021 by the prosecutor's office to dissolve the We Will Stop Femicide Platform, rejecting the prosecutor's accusation that the association acted against the structure of the family and "violated law and morality."

Sexual Orientation and Gender Identity

The Erdoğan government made anti-lesbian, gay, bisexual, and transgender (LGBT) hate speech a core part of its election campaign and overall political discourse, appealing to its conservative voter base and fomenting societal polarization while putting LGBT people at great risk. The ninth successive ban on the Istanbul Pride week events in June was accompanied by police arrests of those who attempted to assemble. Authorities regularly and arbitrarily ban other events by LGBT groups.

Local authorities around the country have increasingly been canceling concerts by artists openly supportive of LGBT rights or critical of relevant government restrictions. TV regulator RTÜK has justified imposing fines on digital platforms for airing creative content referring to LGBT people, saying it violates "societal and cultural values," "the Turkish family structure," and "morality."

Climate Change Policy and Impacts

Türkiye is a growing contributor to the climate crisis, which is taking a mounting toll on human rights around the world. While Türkiye ratified the Paris Agreement in 2021, its climate policies and commitments are "critically insufficient" to meet global goals to limit global warming to 1.5 degrees Celsius above pre-industrial levels, according to the Climate Action Tracker, an independent scientific project that tracks government climate action.

Türkiye's failure to set and meet ambitious emission reduction targets is matched by a continuing commitment to running coal-supplied power plants and expanding coal extraction. In July, the destruction of the Akbelen forest in Muğla province to feed local coal power plants was met with strong resistance by the local community and climate activists. Police intervened to disperse protests with tear gas and water cannons, and there were numerous arbitrary detentions.

Key International Actors

The European Union in September announced further financial support to Türkiye for the most vulnerable Syrian refugees provided in return for restrictions on the entry of refugees and migrants to the EU. Although Türkiye is still formally a candidate for EU accession, the process is at a standstill.

In its enlargement report on Türkiye in November, the European Commission stressed that the "deterioration of human and fundamental rights continued," pointing to "serious deficiencies in the functioning of Türkiye's democratic institutions" and Erdoğan's "unjustified advantage" in the presidential election.

In June, the United Nations Committee on the Rights of the Child recommended that the Turkish government "[e]nsure that children under 18 years of age are not detained or prosecuted under anti-terrorism laws," that the minimum age of criminal responsibility be raised from its current level of 12 to "at least 14 years of age," and that the minimum age of marriage be enforced as "18 years without exception."

In September, the ECtHR issued a judgment (*Yalçınkaya v. Türkiye*) with implications for tens of thousands in Türkiye persecuted for their alleged association with the Gülen movement. The court found that being prosecuted and convicted for "membership of a terrorist organization" mainly on the basis of having a mobile phone application called ByLock allegedly used by Gülen followers was an arbitrary application of the law, violating the principle of legality. The judgment also found violations of fair trial and freedom of association rights and ruled that Türkiye needed to implement general measures to prevent thousands of similar cases from coming before the ECtHR.

Turkmenistan

Turkmenistan made no improvements to its dire human rights record in 2023. The country remains closed to international scrutiny. Authorities continue to suppress fundamental rights and freedoms, including freedoms of religion, movement, expression, and association. Recent political reforms have only deepened authoritarian rule. The government does not acknowledge poverty and has failed to take measures to address continued food insecurity.

In December 2022, authorities released several activists imprisoned on politically motivated bogus charges. But many others wrongfully imprisoned remain behind bars, and the fate of dozens of victims of enforced disappearances are still unknown. Torture and ill-treatment persist.

Turkmenistan continues to criminalize adult consensual same-sex conduct, and women and girls face restrictions on their rights.

Parliament and Elections

In January, constitutional reform reverted Turkmenistan's parliament to a unicameral institution and reintroduced the People's Council as the highest body. The council includes representatives of all branches of government, oversees all policy, and is headed by ex-president Gurbanguly Berdymukhamedov.

In March, Turkmenistan held elections for parliament and for local and provincial assemblies. The Organization for Security and Co-operation in Europe (OSCE) did not "carry out systematic or comprehensive observation of the voting." Radio Azatlyk reported voting rights violations at polling stations.

Civil Society

There is virtually no independent civil society in Turkmenistan. Unregistered activities are outlawed, and registration requirements are burdensome. There are no independent human rights organizations, and international monitors cannot freely operate. The government continues to punish all forms of dissent and public criticism.

Activists living abroad and their relatives in Turkmenistan face constant threats of government reprisals. Turkmen rights groups in exile reported that several activists living in exile were deported back to Turkmenistan in 2023 and promptly detained upon their return.

The Turkmen Initiative for Human Rights (TIHR), a Vienna-based group, reported that in August, security officials detained Dovran Imamov, who had been deported from Türkiye, at Ashgabat airport. Imamov, who openly criticized the Turkmen government on social media and participated in anti-government protests in Türkiye, was reportedly being held in pre-trial detention on bogus fraud charges as of September 2023.

In February, Rinat Zainulin, brother of an exiled YouTube and TikTok activist, suffered serious burns after a fire at his house, reported Turkmen.news, a Netherlands-based outlet. The fire occurred on the same day that security officials visited his grandmother and asked for her grandson's address. In September 2022, police arbitrarily held Zainulin for 20 days and forced him to tell his brother by phone that his activities make his "relatives suffer." Zainulin's employer fired him for absenteeism while he was detained.

In December 2022, security services in Turkmenistan questioned the 12-year-old son of Dursoltan Taganova, an activist in Türkiye, at his school and offered him "friendship." Afterward, the deputy principal threatened to hand the boy to police if he remained "stubborn." Radio Azatlyk, the Turkmen-language service of the United States government-funded Radio Liberty, reported that in October 2022, police in Mary province threatened the parents of Merdan Ilyasov, based in Türkiye, with imprisonment in retaliation for his online criticism of the government.

On November 22, Turkish authorities deported Tajigul Begmedova, the head of the THF, from Türkiye, citing a five-year entry ban issued on September 12 on alleged "national security" grounds.

Freedom of Media and Information

There is no media freedom in Turkmenistan. Access to the internet remains severely limited. In April, Turkmen.news reported that three-quarters of global IP addresses in Turkmenistan were blocked and also exposed security services selling access to IP addresses with unfettered internet access.

The authorities block instant messenger apps when they become popular, and in 2023, they blocked ICQ and partially blocked IMO.

Turkmen authorities have ramped up persecution of users and providers of Virtual Private Networks (VPNs) and blocked VPN sites. In November 2022, Radio Azatlyk reported that Turkmenbashi authorities raided the homes and workplaces of suspected VPN users and providers, imposing warnings and arresting some for up to 15 days. In January, security officials in Balkan province raided the homes of VPN installers, detaining and fining 10 individuals. Authorities arrested VPN installers in Ashgabat in October, detaining some for up to 15 days; at least one was fined 15,000 Turkmen manat (about US$4,285). Although Turkmen law does not explicitly outlaw VPNs, it bans "uncertified" encryption programs and punishes "deliberately providing illegal services that provide technical programs" online with a maximum of seven years in prison.

In June, Radio Azatlyk reported that police interrogated and warned local bloggers to post only positive content about Turkmenistan or face arrest.

Economic, Social, and Cultural Rights

Due to a lack of reliable government data, the World Bank does not publish key economic data on Turkmenistan, and statistics regarding poverty and food security are unreliable or nonexistent.

Independent reporting indicates that the availability of subsidized food staples continued to shrink while prices continued to rise, with the government failing to adequately address increasing poverty.

Radio Azatlyk reported shortages of subsidized bread and flour, forcing Turkmen citizens to withstand long queues to purchase rations that were often low quality or expired. The prolonged lack of subsidized staples led to sporadic protests, in some cases turning violent, in Dashoguz province in May and April and in Turkmenbashi in August and June.

Systemic forced labor in Turkmenistan's cotton fields remains widespread. Authorities forcibly mobilize government employees to harvest cotton, threatening to dismiss those who refuse.

Freedom of Movement

Turkmenistan's government continues to interfere with and arbitrarily deny its citizens' right to freedom of movement. Officials regularly bar people from boarding international flights without explanation. They continue to deny passport renewals, through consular services, to Turkmen citizens living abroad.

Turkmen authorities imposed various administrative barriers to renewing and obtaining passports and procuring foreign visas. They temporarily suspended passport services in February 2023 under various pretexts; required travelers to Kazakhstan to submit notarized letters by relatives guaranteeing their return; and required others to sign statements to refrain from activism abroad.

Authorities imposed an arbitrary five-year travel ban on Pygambergeldy Allaberdyev, a lawyer sentenced to six years' imprisonment in 2020 on bogus charges but released in December 2022 under a presidential amnesty.

On November 18, after a lengthy and humiliating security check, Ashgabat airport's border officials prevented Soltan Achilova, an independent journalist and her daughter from traveling to Geneva to attend human rights events, falsely claiming that their passports were damaged.

Political Prisoners, Enforced Disappearances, and Torture

In December 2022, authorities released, under presidential pardon, Khursanai Ismatullayeva and Seryozha Babaniyazov, both sentenced on bogus, politically motivated charges in 2021. But many others remain imprisoned on such charges. At time of writing, they included Nurgeldy Khalykov, Mansur Mingelov, Murat Ovezov, and Murad Dushemov. In March, the government communicated to the United Nations Human Rights Committee that "the pardon of Nurgeldy Khalykov, Murat Dushemov and Mansur Mingelov is being considered."

Political dissident Gulgeldy Annaniyazov, whose 11-year sentence on politically motivated charges ended in 2019, continues to serve a five-year term of forced internal exile.

For more than two decades, dozens of individuals have remained victims of enforced disappearances. Authorities deny them access to families, lawyers, and the outside world. The Prove They Are Alive! campaign, an international coalition that has worked on ending enforced disappearances in Turkmenistan since 2013, has documented at least 162 disappearances in Turkmen prisons, 97 of which are unresolved, including 33 individuals whose prison terms expired at the end of 2022 but whose fates and whereabouts remain unknown.

Freedom of Religion

The Turkmen authorities tightly monitor registered religious groups and forbid unregistered congregations and groups. Individuals who allegedly engage in religious activities beyond state-approved religions are severely punished and sentenced to lengthy prison sentences.

In August, according to the Turkmenistan Helsinki Foundation (THF), Turkmen authorities arrested Ashirbai Bekiev at Ashgabat airport after Russia deported him. Turkmenistan had initially requested his extradition in 2015 on dubious charges of inciting national and religious hatred. In October, a court in Dashoguz sentenced Bekiev to 23 years in prison on spurious "religious extremism" charges.

Azatlyk reported in August that police in Balkan province had raided homes of devout Muslims and confiscated religious literature. In March, police in Balkan province interrogated women and girls who wear hijab.

Also in March, security officials repeatedly summoned and interrogated a man in Mary city for providing Islamic prayer services, according to Forum 18, an independent religious freedom group. Forum 18 further reported that in August, security services detained an imam in Balkan province for teaching Islam to children without state approval.

In October and November 2022, police in Ashgabat detained and threatened bearded young men whom they suspected to be adherents of radical Islam, saying police would bring criminal charges if they did not shave off their beards.

Women's and Girls' Rights

In 2022, a law that banned abortion after five weeks of pregnancy and was reportedly adopted in 2015 was made public. According to Saglyk.org, an online initiative that provides fact-based public health information in Turkmen, abortions are heavily stigmatized and there is no comprehensive sexuality education. In 2021, the UN Population Fund (UNFPA) reported that almost 60 percent of women and girls are denied bodily autonomy, including decision making on health care and contraception. Several sources have reported efforts by authorities to create obstacles to travel abroad by single women under age 40.

Key International Actors

European Union Special Representative for Human Rights Eamon Gilmore and EU Special Representative for Central Asia Ambassador Terhi Hakala visited Turkmenistan in April. They met with officials and reportedly discussed women's rights, the importance of independent civil society, and the government's lack of cooperation with UN human rights mechanisms. During its annual human rights dialogue with Turkmenistan in November 2022, the EU raised a range of issues, including restrictions on the freedoms of assembly, association, and expression; torture and enforced disappearances; and several individual cases. The EU has not yet ratified a bilateral partnership and cooperation agreement with Turkmenistan due to its poor human rights record.

In September, United States President Joe Biden met President Berdymukhamedov during the inaugural summit between the leaders of all five Central Asian governments on the sidelines of the opening session of the UN General Assembly in New York.

During her July visit to Turkmenistan, OSCE Representative on Freedom of the Media Teresa Ribeiro raised concerns about journalists' safety and "restrictions on the free flow of information," including online, and urged Turkmenistan to comply with OSCE media freedom commitments.

The UN Human Rights Committee in April and the UN Committee on the Elimination of Racial Discrimination in August highlighted human rights concerns in Turkmenistan, including restrictions on media and civil society and violations of the freedoms of association, religion, and movement. The Human Rights

Committee also flagged concerns about enforced disappearances, specifically called for release of Khalykov, Dushemov, and Mingelov, and questioned Turkmenistan's request that Türkiye impose visa requirements on Turkmen nationals.

During Turkmenistan's Universal Periodic Review at the UN Human Rights Council in November, a number of delegations urged Turkmenistan to address the issues of enforced disappearances, torture, and arbitrary arrests and detentions; ensure independent civil society and access to information; and criminalize all forms of gender-based violence.

HUMAN
RIGHTS
WATCH
"Our Trust is Broken"
Loss of Land and Livelihoods for Oil Development in Uganda

Uganda

The authorities made progress in addressing certain human rights abuses in 2023 but regressed in other areas. The Constitutional Court nullified repressive provisions of laws previously used by the authorities to restrict freedoms of expression and assembly, but security forces arrested protesters, journalists, and opposition supporters and leaders on trumped-up charges.

Uganda made strides toward addressing workplace sexual harassment but failed to hold perpetrators within the security forces accountable.

The government continued to place restrictions on civil society groups, particularly those working on human rights, while President Yoweri Museveni signed into law the regressive and abusive Anti-Homosexuality Act.

Freedoms of Expression and Assembly

In January, the Constitutional Court nullified section 25 of the Computer Misuse Act, which penalizes "offensive communication." In March, it overturned sections 5 and 10 of the Public Order Management Act, which criminalize unauthorized public meetings and demonstrations.

On May 8, a court dismissed charges of inciting violence against former presidential candidate Kizza Besigye. Police had arrested and charged Besigye in 2022 following demonstrations he led protesting the government's response to inflation.

Despite these court rulings, the authorities continued to threaten to arrest, or arrest, protesters, journalists, and those critical of the government.

On March 28, police in Kampala arrested 11 activists demonstrating against a corruption scandal involving government officials in Karamoja in eastern Uganda. On April 27, police arrested 11 female opposition parliamentarians protesting police brutality in Kampala.

During an event to mark World Press Freedom Day in Kampala on May 3, Minister for Information and Communications Technology and National Guidance Chris Baryomunsi threatened people whom he called "malicious Ugandans" who "spread false information and fake news on social media." A few days later, a joint operation of the police and military arrested five local government officials in the eastern district of Tororo for allegedly staging an unlawful demonstration about the poor status of roads in the area. On June 14, unidentified people assaulted four reporters covering local elections in Bukedea district.

On April 11, the police announced the suspension of officer Yeeko Ogwal for attacking two journalists who were covering a demonstration by medical interns in Kampala. In a statement, the police said Ogwal had been handed over to their Professional Standards Unit for further investigation.

On September 15, police arrested at least four students protesting the East African Crude Oil Pipeline (EACOP) in front of Parliament building in Kampala. They were charged with the offence of "common nuisance," a broadly defined colonial-era offense that carries a punishment of imprisonment for one year. The students were released on bail five days later.

Attacks on Civil Society Groups

On February 6, the Foreign Affairs Ministry informed the Office of the High Commissioner for Human Rights (OHCHR) in Uganda that it would not renew its agreement to host the United Nations entity beyond its three-year term ending in February 2023. The office officially closed on August 5.

On February 12, media reported on a leaked draft report by the National Bureau for Non-Governmental Organizations identifying 22 nongovernmental organizations accused of "promoting homosexuality" and "forced recruitment" of schoolchildren into homosexuality. The report recommended banning groups identified as "promoting LGBTIQ activities" and suggested individual activists should be publicly profiled to prevent them from any further civil society engagement.

Arrest and Harassment of Opposition Leaders and Supporters

On January 24, the authorities charged 12 supporters of the opposition party National Unity Platform (NUP) and remanded them to prison for organizing an "illegal assembly" in Jinja, east of Kampala. A few days later, the General Court Martial sitting in Makindye, Kampala, remanded to prison NUP supporter, Anthony Agaba, also known as Bobi Young, on allegations of "spreading harmful propaganda." Agaba was granted bail in May.

On March 22, police released NUP supporter Hamza Isma Mubiru, also known as Sadam Sadat, who was missing for a month after he was reportedly captured by unidentified armed personnel in the Makindye division of Kampala and charged with terrorism by the police. Eleven other NUP supporters were arrested, charged with terrorism in June, and remanded to prison in Kampala pending their trial.

On September 13, police banned the NUP from holding meetings, alleging that the party's prior meetings had caused "public disorder" and were used to "incite violence and promote sectarianism."

Accountability for Security Force Abuses

On June 30, Uganda's High Court ordered Frank "Kaka" Bagyenda, the former director of the Internal Security Organization (ISO), and 14 ex-security personnel to compensate Musa Nsereko 275 million Ugandan shillings (about US$74,000) for torturing and illegally detaining him for over a year without charge.

On June 13, prosecutors dropped charges against 218 civilians who were arrested when Uganda's military raided the palace of Charles Mumbere, the king of the Rwenzururu kingdom, in Kasese, western Uganda. During the November 2016 raid, the military killed over 100 people, including 15 children, but the government has failed to conduct an independent investigation into the use of force by the police and military.

Sexual Orientation and Gender Identity

On May 26, President Museveni signed a bill into law criminalizing same-sex conduct. It also created the crime of "promotion of homosexuality," introduced the death penalty for several acts considered as "aggravated homosexuality," and increased the prison sentence for attempted same-sex conduct to 10 years. On August 18, prosecutors charged a 20-year old man in Soroti with "aggravated homosexuality" for allegedly having sexual intercourse with a man with a disability.

Over the years, police have carried out mass arrests at lesbian, gay, bisexual, and transgender (LGBT) pride events, LGBT-friendly bars, and at homeless shelters on spurious grounds, and they forced some detainees to undergo anal ex-

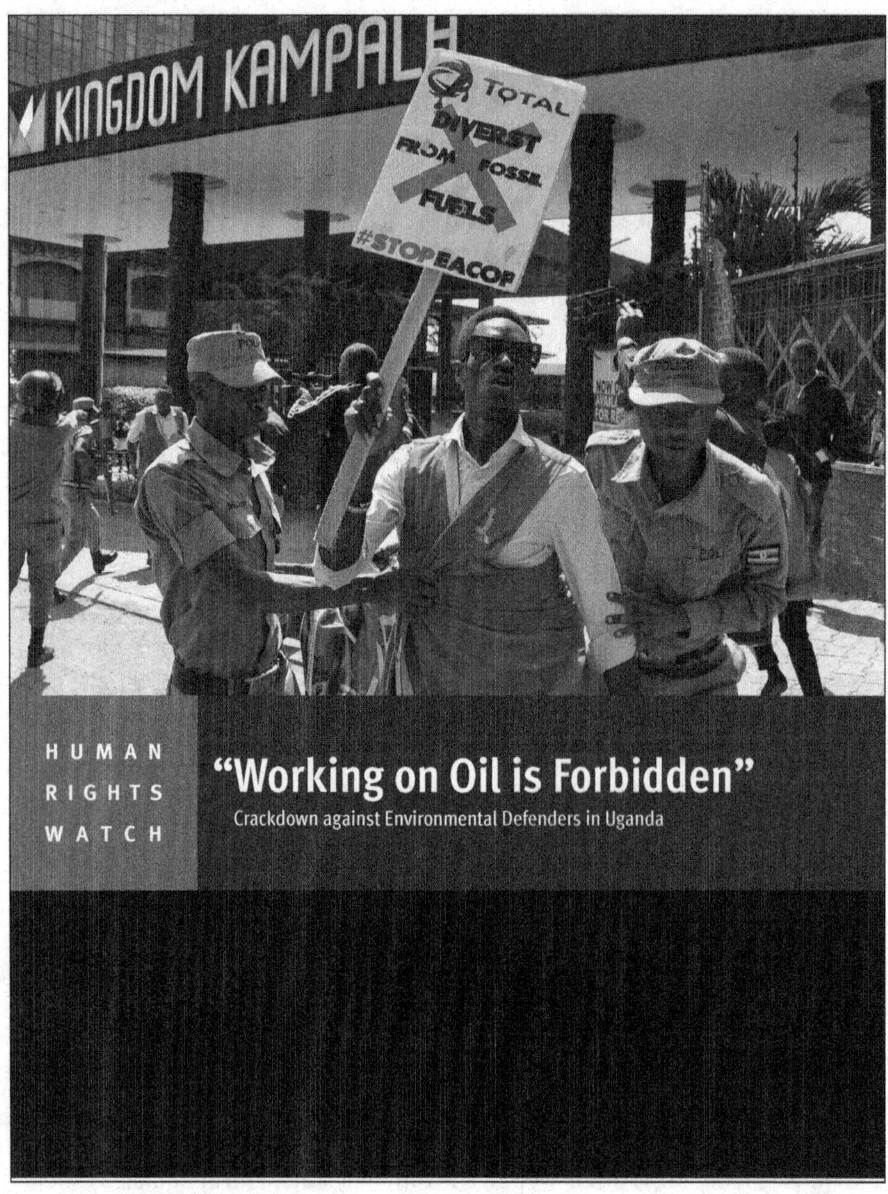
KINGDOM
TOTAL
DIVERST FROM FOSSIL FUELS
#STOPEACOP
HUMAN RIGHTS WATCH
"Working on Oil is Forbidden"
Crackdown against Environmental Defenders in Uganda

aminations, a form of cruel, degrading, and inhuman treatment that can, in some instances, constitute torture.

Women's Rights

On August 7, the government officially deposited for ratification the International Labour Organization (ILO) Violence and Harassment Convention (C190). During negotiations for the convention in 2018 and 2019, Uganda played a key role as part of the African bloc. On May 25, Parliament passed the Employment (Amendment) Bill, which obligates employers to prevent sexual harassment, includes domestic workers in the labor law, and provides protections for casual workers. The bill is now before the president for approval.

Attacks on Students

On June 16, attackers believed to belong to the Allied Democratic Forces (ADF) rebel group attacked Mpondwe Lhubiriha Secondary School in the western district of Kasese, near the border with the Democratic Republic of Congo, killing at least 41 people, including 38 students in their dormitories. At time of writing, five students, believed by the authorities to have been abducted, remain missing. Since 2021, Uganda People's Defence Force troops have been deployed in eastern Congo as part of a joint operation with the Congolese army against the ADF.

Corruption

In April, police arrested and charged Karamoja Affairs Minister Mary Goretti Kitutu and other government officials for allegedly diverting metal roofing sheets meant for a relief program for impoverished communities in the eastern Karamoja sub-region. On April 14, the Anti-Corruption Court granted bail to Kitutu, and on June 29, it committed Kitutu to trial.

Accountability for International Crimes

The 2022 request by the International Criminal Court (ICC) prosecutor to conduct a hearing to confirm charges against Lord's Resistance Army (LRA) leader Joseph

Kony in his absence remains pending. Kony is the only living remaining ICC suspect of LRA crimes.

Uganda's International Crimes Division continued its trial against LRA commander Thomas Kwoyelo, which has dragged on for more than a decade. Kwoyelo has been in prison since he was captured by Ugandan forces in 2009.

Environment and Human Rights

A Human Rights Watch report found that the first stages of a planned oil development, including a pipeline operated and majority-owned by French fossil-fuel giant TotalEnergies, has caused food insecurity and household debt, caused children to leave school, and is likely to have devastating environmental effects.

Key International Actors

On March 24, the governments of Uganda and Rwanda agreed to enhance trade and cooperation during talks in Kigali, Rwanda. In 2022, Uganda and Rwanda reopened their border in Gatuna after relations between the two countries broke down in February 2019.

Following the passage of the Anti-Homosexuality Bill in Parliament, on March 29, UN special rapporteurs and independent experts and Ugandan Parliamentary Working Groups raised "serious concerns about escalating risks to the human rights of LGBT persons in Uganda over the past 15 years."

On April 18, the European Union Parliament condemned the Anti-Homosexuality Bill and urged their External Action Service to "use all necessary diplomatic, legal and financial means to convince the president to not sign the law and establish an EU strategy for the universal decriminalization of homosexuality and transgender identity." In May, EU diplomatic chief Josep Borrell expressed regrets that the bill was signed into law.

On May 29, United States President Joseph Biden released a public statement condemning the Anti-Homosexuality Act, characterizing the legislation as "a tragic violation of universal human rights" and calling for its immediate repeal. On August 8, the World Bank said that it will not consider new loans to Uganda after the enactment of the Anti-Homosexuality Act.

Ukraine

The human rights impacts of Russia's war on Ukraine continued to eclipse all other rights issues in Ukraine. As of September, at least 9,614 civilians had been killed and more than 17,535 injured since Russia's full-scale invasion began in February 2022. Millions more had to flee abroad or were internally displaced.

Throughout the year, Russian forces committed war crimes and other atrocities in Ukraine. They carried out indiscriminate and disproportionate attacks that killed and severely injured civilians and destroyed vital infrastructure and objects of cultural and historical significance. Russian forces' widespread use of torture and their continued attacks on energy-related infrastructure may amount to crimes against humanity, according to a United Nations investigative body. The June destruction of the Kakhovka hydroelectric power station in Khersonska region, reportedly by Russian forces, devastated livelihoods and caused lasting environmental damage. Russian forces repeatedly shelled vital ports and grain facilities in Ukraine, with serious implications for Ukrainians and millions facing hunger worldwide.

In March, International Criminal Court (ICC) judges issued arrest warrants for Russia's President Vladimir Putin and Russia's children's rights commissioner for unlawful deportation and transfer of Ukrainian children from occupied areas of Ukraine to Russia.

Russian forces used both cluster munitions and banned antipersonnel landmines. Ukrainian forces also used cluster munitions, and there is significant evidence they used antipersonnel landmines in 2022, which the authorities pledged to investigate. Ukraine remained one of the world's most mine-contaminated countries, with approximately 174,000 square kilometers contaminated by landmines and explosive remnants of war that may take decades to clear.

Ukraine continued to advance European Union candidacy-related reforms. The government took positive steps toward eliminating certain forms of corruption. Judicial reform advanced, but the outcome of Constitutional Court reform was mixed. Continued institutionalization of children, particularly children with disabilities, remained a concern. The 2022 law on collaboration and its enforce-

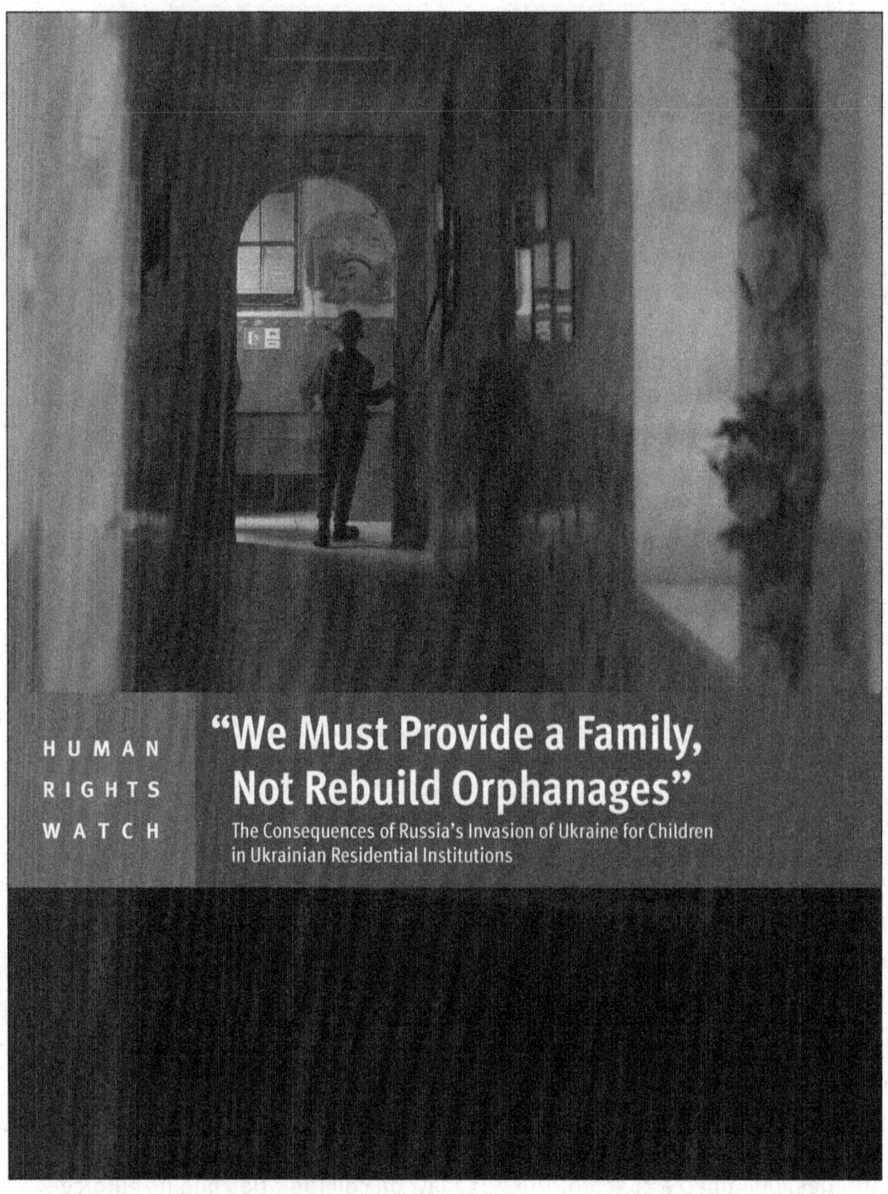
HUMAN
RIGHTS
WATCH
"We Must Provide a Family,
Not Rebuild Orphanages"
The Consequences of Russia's Invasion of Ukraine for Children
in Ukrainian Residential Institutions

ment continued to draw criticism from Ukrainian civil society and international actors alike.

Indiscriminate Attacks

Russian forces continued to carry out attacks using explosive weapons in populated areas, heightening risks for civilians. The attacks impacted civilian infrastructure, including residential buildings, hospitals, and schools. Russia's attacks on energy-related infrastructure caused electricity blackouts and obstructed access to health, education, and other essential services for millions, including people with disabilities.

Throughout the year, Ukrainian forces also carried out some "likely indiscriminate attacks and two incidents that qualify as war crimes," the UN Commission of Inquiry (UN CoI) stated in its March report.

A January Russian attack on a residential building in Dnipro destroyed 236 apartments, killed 45 civilians, including 6 children, and injured at least 80.

A June Russian missile attack on a popular pizza restaurant in Kramatorsk killed 13, including well-known writer Victoria Amelina, and wounded 61. Also in June, a Russian airstrike hit a five-story residential building in Kryvyi Rih, killing 12 people and wounding 36.

Throughout the year, Russian forces repeatedly attacked Odesa with missiles and drones, killing and injuring civilians and damaging and destroying grain terminals, historical buildings, and culturally significant monuments. A July attack in Lviv with a guided missile struck a residential apartment complex, killing 10 civilians and injuring 48. Although Ukrainian military targets were in the vicinity, Human Rights Watch said Russian forces' use of a guided munition with a large, high-explosive warhead on an apartment complex in a residential area should be investigated as a war crime.

Russian forces continued regular artillery bombardments of Kherson city and its environs after retreating to the left bank of Dnipro River following the November 2022 de-occupation of Kherson.

In October, a missile strike on the village of Hroza, in Kharkivska region, killed 59 civilians attending a soldier's funeral. The UN Human Rights Monitoring Mission in Ukraine (HRMMU) investigated the strike, characterizing it as the single deadliest incident for civilians since February 2022, and found no indication of legitimate military targets in the vicinity at the time of the attack. The HRMMU concluded that the strike was likely launched by Russian armed forces, who either failed to do everything feasible to verify that the target was a military objective or deliberately targeted civilians or civilian objects.

The World Health Organization verified more than 1,000 attacks on healthcare workers, vehicles, and facilities since the beginning of the full-scale invasion, the highest number recorded in any humanitarian emergency. In August, five healthcare workers were injured and one killed during Russia's attack on a hospital in Kherson.

Landmines and Cluster Munitions

Since February 2022, Russian forces extensively used at least 13 types of antipersonnel mines in multiple areas, heavily mining its front lines in anticipation of Ukraine's ongoing counteroffensive. This has resulted in an unprecedented situation in which a country that is not party to the Mine Ban Treaty is using the weapon on the territory of a state party to that treaty.

In January, the Ukrainian government committed to "duly study" a Human Rights Watch report about Ukrainian forces' use of rocket-delivered PFM-series antipersonnel mines in attacks on and around Izium in 2022, when it was under Russian control. At a June meeting of the Mine Ban Treaty, to which Ukraine is a state party, Ukraine reaffirmed this commitment.

In addition, both Russian and Ukrainian forces have used at least 13 types of anti-vehicle mines, also called anti-tank mines.

Russian forces continued to extensively use cluster munitions, which have killed and injured hundreds of civilians and contaminated large areas of Ukraine. A July cluster munition attack on a residential district in Lyman, Donetska region, killed nine civilians and injured a dozen more.

Ukrainian forces also continued to use cluster munitions, resulting in an unknown number of civilian casualties. Ukraine has used cluster munitions from its existing stockpiles and received cluster munitions from the United States in July and September. Neither Russia nor Ukraine is a party to the 2008 Convention on Cluster Munitions.

Abuses under Russian Occupation

Throughout the year, Russian and Russian-affiliated forces committed numerous grave abuses against civilians in occupied parts of Zaporizka, Khersonska, Donetska, and Luhanska regions. They carried out enforced disappearances, summary executions of civilians, and unlawful detention and torture, especially targeting civil servants, pro-Ukraine activists and journalists, and other civilians presumed to oppose the occupation.

They also perpetrated sexual violence, forced transfers of Ukrainian adults and children, and looting of cultural artifacts.

Evidence of Russia's apparent war crimes in now de-occupied Khersonska and Kharkivska regions continued to surface, including of torture centers that Russian forces operated in Kherson during their eight-month occupation. In September, the UN CoI reported that Russian soldiers raped and committed sexual violence against women there ranging in age from 19 to 83.

In June, an explosion presumably caused by Russian forces destroyed the Kakhovka dam, flooding dozens of towns and villages on both sides of Dnipro River. Russian authorities restricted access to cities and villages on the Russian-occupied left bank, preventing volunteers from delivering desperately needed humanitarian aid, and did not carry out timely evacuations. At least 50 people reportedly died in the aftermath, 41 of them in Russian-occupied areas. Twenty-four hazardous industrial facilities, sewage treatment facilities, cemeteries, and landfills were flooded, contaminating the surface and groundwater and exposing the local population to communicable diseases.

Russian authorities continued their systematic efforts to coerce residents of occupied areas to accept Russian citizenship. A March law expedited the application process. Those who did not accept Russian passports faced threats and restricted access to employment, medical care, and social benefits.

In September, Russia held local elections in occupied parts of Ukraine, in violation of international law.

Russian authorities in occupied areas continued to try to erase Ukrainian culture and language, including by imposing the Russian curriculum and language of instruction, war propaganda, and military training in schools, in violation of international law. They used detention, torture, and ill-treatment to coerce local educators to cooperate, including to hand over school data. They threatened parents whose children study online in the Ukrainian school system with fines, detention, and deprivation of child custody.

Torture and Ill-Treatment of Prisoners of War

Russian forces committed war crimes against Ukrainian prisoners of war (POWs). A March report by the UN Human Rights Monitoring Mission in Ukraine (UN Monitoring Mission) found that in 32 of 48 detention facilities in Russia and Russian-occupied territories of Ukraine, POWs faced torture and ill-treatment, forced labor, and abhorrent detention conditions. Many were held incommunicado.

Russian authorities committed apparent war crimes by criminally prosecuting Ukrainian POWs, including members of the Ukrainian "Azov" brigade, for participating in hostilities; using torture to extract confessions; and denying fair trials. In March, a court in a Russian-occupied area sentenced POW Maxym Butkevych, a prominent rights defender, to 13 years' imprisonment on bogus charges.

Russian authorities failed to investigate the July 2022 explosion in Olenivka prison—which killed and injured at least 150 Ukrainian POWs—in a Russian-occupied area or allow independent investigators on site.

The UN Monitoring Mission also documented cases of torture and inhuman treatment by Ukraine of Russian POWs and noted in June the "lack of significant developments" in Ukraine's investigations of allegations of extrajudicial executions of Russian POWs. Human Rights Watch is not aware of any ongoing investigations into alleged abuse by Ukrainian fighters of Russian POWs in 2022.

Following her September visit to Ukraine, the UN special rapporteur on torture acknowledged "sincere efforts" made by the Ukrainian authorities to treat Russian POWs held in detention facilities in Ukraine respectfully.

Conflict-Related Civilian Detainees

Russian forces continued to unlawfully detain and forcibly disappear local public officials, civil society activists, volunteers, teachers, and other Ukrainian civilians. Many were forcibly transferred to Russia and Russian-occupied areas, denied access to legal counsel, and held incommunicado without charge, sometimes for months.

Between February 2022 and May 2023, the UN Monitoring Mission documented 77 cases of Russian summary executions of Ukrainian civilians and the widespread practice of torturing and ill-treating of civilian detainees. Of over 900 documented cases of arbitrary detention of civilians during that period, 864 were perpetrated by Russian forces. Of those detained, 260 were civilians held for their perceived political views. More than 91 percent of the 864 detainees described being subjected to torture and ill-treatment, including sexual violence. The UN Monitoring Mission also documented 75 cases of arbitrary detention by Ukrainian security forces, mostly of individuals suspected of conflict-related criminal offences, with 57 percent of those held saying they were subjected to torture and ill-treatment, predominantly in unofficial places of detention.

In May, Ukrainian authorities established a unified registry of missing persons to systematize the collection and sharing of information and to financially support families. By August, the register had the names of 25,000 people disappeared since 2022.

Conflict-Related Sexual Violence

By September, Ukrainian authorities documented 231 cases of conflict-related sexual violence (CRSV) perpetrated by Russian forces in occupied areas of Ukraine and in Russian detention facilities. The true figures are likely much higher, as stigma, shame, and fear of reprisals prevent survivors from seeking help. As of October, 34 Russian servicemen were under investigation by Ukrainian authorities for committing CRSV, 18 cases were on trial, and 2 perpetrators had been sentenced to 12 and 10 years in prison. All proceedings were conducted in absentia. The UN CoI reported in August that Russian authorities had used rape and sexual violence constituting torture against both men and women in detention.

HUMAN
RIGHTS
WATCH
"Tanks On the Playground"
Attacks on Schools and Military Use of Schools in Ukraine

Survivors faced significant challenges in accessing medical, psychosocial, and legal assistance. To address these challenges, in June, parliament considered amendments to criminal legislation concerning the investigation and adjudication of CRSV and a draft law on reparations for victims of war crimes that includes CRSV survivors.

In May, civil society representatives launched a petition to make emergency contraception drugs in Ukraine prescription-free. The Health Ministry was reviewing the petition at time of writing.

Attacks on Education

Throughout the year, Russian forces continued to attack schools and other educational facilities across Ukraine. The Ukrainian government reported that 3,790 educational facilities were damaged or destroyed from February 2022 to September 2023.

Large-scale damage and destruction to schools has had a devastating effect on Ukrainian children's access to education and a profound psychosocial impact on children, parents, and teachers. Ukraine took important measures to prevent schools from coming under attack. Authorities also took steps to ensure that children could continue their education, combining distance and in-person learning, and over 95 percent of students nationwide remained in school.

Children whose regular schools were severely damaged or destroyed relocated to other schools nearby, where in some instances they attended a shortened school day or studied in shifts to accommodate the increased number of students. Many had to switch entirely to remote learning.

Repair and reconstruction of schools were ongoing, with reconstruction efforts varying greatly in different parts of Ukraine, partly due to continuing hostilities.

Children in Institutions

Children in institutions in areas directly affected by the war, forcibly transferred to Russia or Russian-occupied territories, or evacuated to other areas of Ukraine continue to face risks. The war added urgency for Ukraine, with international support, to expand family- and community-based care to ensure that all children in institutions affected by the war, including children with disabilities, are not re-institutionalized.

Impact on Older Civilians

In May, the UN Monitoring Mission documented the disproportionate impact of the war on older civilians. Although older people make up 25 percent of the population, 32 percent of civilians killed from February 2022 to February 2023 were 60 and older (for cases where age was recorded). Some displaced older people had to be accommodated in nursing homes despite living independently before being displaced. Older people in conflict-affected areas had limited access to their pensions and health care.

Crimea

The human rights climate in Russian-occupied Crimea worsened. Russian authorities relentlessly targeted anyone actively opposed to the occupation, particularly politically active members of the Crimean Tatar community as well as lawyers, journalists, and activists. According to the Crimean Tatar Resource Center (CTRC), at least 66 Crimean Tatars were detained and 93 arrested in the first six months of 2023. Of 37 house searches conducted by Russia's security forces, 29 were of Crimean Tatar homes.

Authorities continued to apply, in some cases retroactively, Russia's vague and overly broad counterterrorism and anti-extremism legislation to prosecute Crimean Tatars for alleged ties with organizations such as Hizb ut-Tahrir, which is banned in Russia but not in Ukraine. The prosecution overwhelmingly relied on testimonies from anonymous witnesses and tapped private conversations about religion. Accused were routinely denied due process, including access to lawyers. Since the beginning of the occupation until February 2023, at least 98 Crimean Tatars were being or had been prosecuted for alleged links with Hizb ut-Tahrir, with 73 serving prison sentences ranging between 10 and 20 years.

In January 2023, a military court in Russia convicted the remaining 5 activists from a group of 25 Crimean Solidarity members, who had been under criminal investigation since 2019 on what appeared to be spurious terrorism charges, and sentenced them to 13 years in prison.

Throughout 2023, those serving prison sentences on bogus charges were subjected to ill-treatment. The Crimean Tatar representative body Mejlis' Deputy Chairman Nariman Dzhelial, members of Crimean Solidarity Amet Suleymanov and Server Mustafayev, human rights defender Emir-Usein Kuku, journalist Timur Ibragimov, and activists Rustem Seytmemetov and Zevri Abseitov, among others, were repeatedly denied access to adequate medical care. In February, Dzhemil Gafarov, a Crimean Solidarity activist who was routinely denied necessary medical assistance while serving his sentence, died in a detention facility in Russia.

In January, occupying authorities arbitrarily detained 34 people who gathered near a courthouse in Simferopol to attend a hearing against a group of Crimean Tatars. Of them, 26 were swiftly sentenced to detention for 10 to 16 days and 1 was fined. In August, a court sentenced 22 Crimean Tatars to up to 7 days' detention for gathering outside a courthouse to attend a hearing.

In May, a court in Russia placed Crimean Solidarity activist Leniie Umerova, 25, under arrest on espionage charges. Russian security forces first detained Umerova for alleged violation of migration rules after she traveled to Crimea in December 2022 to visit her gravely ill father. Umerova spent 14 weeks in migration detention. Upon release, she was immediately detained again and charged four times with disobeying police orders.

In her April report, the Council of Europe commissioner on human rights stated that Russia's full-scale invasion of Ukraine "worsen[ed] the already deplorable situation of the Crimean Tatar people in the peninsula."

Russian authorities continued the unlawful practice of forcibly conscripting Crimean residents into Russia's armed forces. By September, authorities had imposed 600 administrative penalties on at least 600 Crimean residents and initiated at least 10 criminal cases on charges of "discrediting Russian armed forces."

In July, authorities unlawfully transferred a Crimean activist, Iryna Danylovych, who had been sentenced in 2022 to seven years on fabricated explosives charges, to a detention facility in southern Russia and repeatedly denied her medical care.

In September, a Russian military court sentenced in absentia the deputy director of Crimean Tatar TV station ATR, Ayder Muzhdabaev, to six years in prison on charges of public incitement to terrorism.

Lack of investigations into enforced disappearances of Crimean Tatars and pro-Ukraine activists when Russia first occupied Crimea in 2014 continued to reinforce the climate of impunity and lawlessness on the peninsula.

Democracy and the Rule of Law

The government advanced EU candidacy-related reforms, taking steps on judicial reform and against corruption.

In March 2023, the Cabinet of Ministers approved a two-year anti-corruption plan, envisaging reforms in numerous government sectors.

In January, the Congress of Judges appointed eight new members to the High Council of Justice (HCJ), reviving its operation since Russia's full-scale invasion. In June, the HCJ appointed 16 members to the High Qualification Commission of Judges, completing the reform of Ukraine's two top judicial entities. Civil society cautiously welcomed these developments except for the inclusion in the commission of two judges whose integrity they questioned.

Reform of Ukraine's Constitutional Court, historically mired in corruption allegations, faced controversy regarding the composition of the special advisory body overseeing candidate vetting. Ukraine's civil society and the Council of Europe's Venice Commission criticized a December 2022 law for failing to ensure meaningful international expert involvement in the advisory body. The European Commission also criticized the law, urging adherence to Venice Commission recommendations, including on increasing the number of experts from six to seven. In July, President Volodymyr Zelensky signed a revised bill enhancing the role of international experts but not increasing their number as recommended.

Law enforcement agencies actively investigated high-level corruption scandals. In June, the head of the Supreme Court was arrested on bribery charges. In January, after a corruption investigation by a Ukrainian media outlet and a criminal investigation that followed, the deputy defense minister was dismissed. In September, Ukraine's defense minister, Oleksii Reznikov, resigned amid months of corruption scandals related to military spending. These scandals involved allegations of the ministry inflating purchasing costs of basic supplies, such as clothes and food, for the army. Six of Reznikov's deputy ministers were dismissed two weeks later. In January 2023, the deputy prosecutor general resigned following a controversy around his vacationing abroad in violation of martial law.

In September, the SBU, Ukraine's security service, arrested controversial oligarch Ihor Kolomoisky on fraud and money-laundering charges.

Ukrainian authorities continued to implement a controversial 2022 law on collaboration with Russian forces and occupation authorities, which international actors and domestic groups criticized as vague, overly broad, and wrongfully putting a wide range of Ukrainian civil servants, doctors, and teachers at risk of administrative and criminal liability. Authorities opened thousands of criminal proceedings under the law, and at time of writing, courts had handed down at least 500 guilty verdicts.

Key International Actors

Ukraine's allies provided extensive military, political, and financial support to the country. Governments and other international actors continued to offer Ukraine evidentiary, technical, and operational assistance to help to bolster its judicial capacity to prosecute war crimes.

Ukraine and other actors pursued multiple pathways for international justice and accountability, including through the principle of universal jurisdiction. For example, in June, a Ukrainian group and an international one filed a criminal complaint with the German Federal Public Prosecutor's Office against four Russian servicemen, including two high-ranking officials, in support of a Ukrainian survivor of CRSV.

Putin did not travel to Johannesburg for the August BRICS summit of the heads of state of Brazil, Russia, India, China, and South Africa. As an ICC member, South Africa would have been obligated to arrest Putin if he had arrived there.

The UN CoI conducted numerous fact-finding missions and publicized its findings, including in a detailed March report that described a wide range of abuses committed by Russian forces in Ukraine, some of which, according to the commission, may have amounted to crimes against humanity. The commission also documented a "small number of violations committed by Ukrainian armed forces, including likely indiscriminate attacks and two incidents that qualify as war crimes."

At least 21 government leaders and officials, including from countries supporting Ukraine's war effort, expressed concern over the US government's decision to transfer cluster munitions to Ukraine. The UN special rapporteur on torture urged the US government to reconsider the transfer, warning of the risk of "serious, indiscriminate harm to civilians both immediately and in the long term." In July, the then-Ukrainian defense minister committed to Ukrainian forces using cluster munitions only "in the fields where there is a concentration of Russian military" and to keeping a strict record of their use.

The UN special rapporteur on torture visited Ukraine in September and characterized Russian forces' use of torture in Ukraine as "orchestrated" and "part of a [s]tate policy to intimidate, instill fear, punish, or extract information and confessions." She commended the Ukrainian authorities' efforts on war crimes documentation and listed obstacles to achieving justice for victims, including the loss of crucial evidence and the need for reform of Ukraine's criminal justice system.

In September, the International Court of Justice (ICJ) began hearings on Russia's preliminary objections in the case that Ukraine lodged concerning Russia's allegations of genocide as grounds for launching the full-scale invasion. This is one of the two cases that Ukraine filed against Russia at the ICJ.

Despite ongoing pressure from civil society and its international allies, Ukraine has not ratified the Rome Statute, which it signed in 2000.

The EU condemned Russia for exacerbating the global food security crisis by withdrawing from the UN-brokered Black Sea Grain initiative, crucial for ensuring the safe export of grain and fertilizers from Ukraine to 45 countries. UN Secretary-General Antonio Guterres also voiced regret regarding Russia's decision and continues to urge Russia to recommit to the initiative.

In May, Guterres' special representative for children and armed conflict met with Russia's children's rights commissioner Maria Lvova-Belova, who was indicted by the ICC over possible war crimes involving illegal deportations and transfers of Ukrainian children to Russia and Russian-occupied Ukraine. Human Rights Watch and other rights groups denounced the meeting.

In June, the European Commission submitted a proposal to the EU Council and European Parliament to establish the "Ukraine Facility," a €50 billion financial instrument for 2024-2027 aimed at providing recovery and reconstruction assistance to and supporting Ukraine in its EU integration. Civil society groups and international partners lobbied for the Ukraine Facility to support a comprehensive reform of the child protection and care system in Ukraine and transition from institutional to family- and community-based care for all children.

In November, the European Commission published its enlargement report on Ukraine, recommending the EU open accession negotiations and noting Ukraine's "powerful reform dynamic despite the ongoing war" and its progress to meet the seven steps attached to its EU candidate status. The commission recommended adopting the enlargement negotiating framework—the next step of the accession process—once Ukraine has implemented remaining key measures related to fighting corruption, de-oligarchization, and the rights of national minorities. In its report, the commission highlighted that Ukraine should work toward ratifying the Rome Statute of the ICC as a matter of priority over the next 12 months. At time of writing, the decision by EU member states on whether to open accession talks with Ukraine was pending and expected in December 2023.

United Arab Emirates

The United Arab Emirates (UAE) invests in a strategy to paint the country as progressive, tolerant, and rights-respecting while carrying out its zero-tolerance policy toward dissent. Many activists and dissidents remain detained, particularly those incarcerated in relation to the "UAE94" case, for exercising their rights to free expression and association. UAE-based migrant workers face widespread abuses, including escalating climate risks, and these abuses contribute to climate injustice in multiple ways.

In 2023, the UAE hosted the United Nations Climate Change Conference (COP28) and sought to use the conference as a means of burnishing its image while continuing to push for the expansion of fossil fuels. There has been no accountability for abuses related to the UAE's leading role in the international coalition conducting military operations in Yemen, and it previously provided support for certain Yemeni forces who have committed grave abuses over the past several years.

Freedoms of Expression, Assembly, and Association

Scores of activists, academics, and lawyers are serving lengthy sentences in UAE prisons following unfair trials on vague and broad charges that violate their rights to free expression and association. In advance of the COP28 climate summit hosted by the UAE, Emirati civil society groups demanded that UAE authorities immediately and unconditionally release all those detailed solely for exercising their human rights, end all abuse and harassment of detained critics, and amend all laws that violate human rights.

As of March 2023, Emirati authorities continued to incarcerate with no legal basis at least 51 Emirati prisoners who completed their sentences between 1 month and nearly 4 years ago. The prisoners are all part of the grossly unfair "UAE94" mass trial of 69 government critics, whose convictions violated their rights to free expression, assembly, and association. UAE authorities used baseless counterterrorism justifications to continue holding them past their completed sentences. Some prisoners completed their sentences as early as July 2019.

In May 2023, Jordanian authorities detained a dual Emirati-Turkish citizen, Khalaf Abdul Rahman al-Romaithi, and extradited him back to the UAE, where he is at serious risk of arbitrary detention, unfair trial, and possibly torture. Al-Romaithi's family and lawyers have not heard from him nor known his whereabouts since May 9.

Ahmed Mansoor, a leading Emirati human rights defender, remained imprisoned in an isolation cell for a sixth year. Human Rights Watch, alongside other human rights organizations, urged the US and other governments to publicly call on UAE authorities to immediately and unconditionally release Mansoor ahead of COP28.

As of March 2023, authorities in the UAE had arbitrarily detained between 2,400 and 2,700 Afghans for over 15 months in the "Emirates Humanitarian City," a humanitarian logistics hub in Abu Dhabi. The Afghans were evacuated to the UAE from Afghanistan.

The UAE deploys some of the world's most advanced surveillance technologies to pervasively monitor public spaces, internet activity, and even individuals' phones and computers, in violation of their right to privacy, freedom of expression, freedom of association, and other rights. The authorities block and censor content online that they perceive to be critical of the UAE's rulers, government, and policies and any topic, whether social or political, that authorities may deem sensitive.

The penal code and Cybercrime Law further curtail space for dissent. Article 174 of the penal code stipulates a minimum prison sentence of five years and a minimum fine of 100,000 dirhams (Dh) (about US$27,225) if the act takes place in "writing, speech, drawing or by statement or using any means of technology or through the media." Two provisions may directly affect the work of journalists based in the UAE. Article 178 provides for sentences of 3 to 15 years in prison for anyone who, without a license from the appropriate authorities, collects "information, data, objects, documents, designs, statistics or anything else for the purpose of handing them over to a foreign country or group or organization or entity, whatever its name or form, or to someone who works in its interest." The Cybercrime Law contains an entirely new section entitled, "Spreading Rumors and False News."

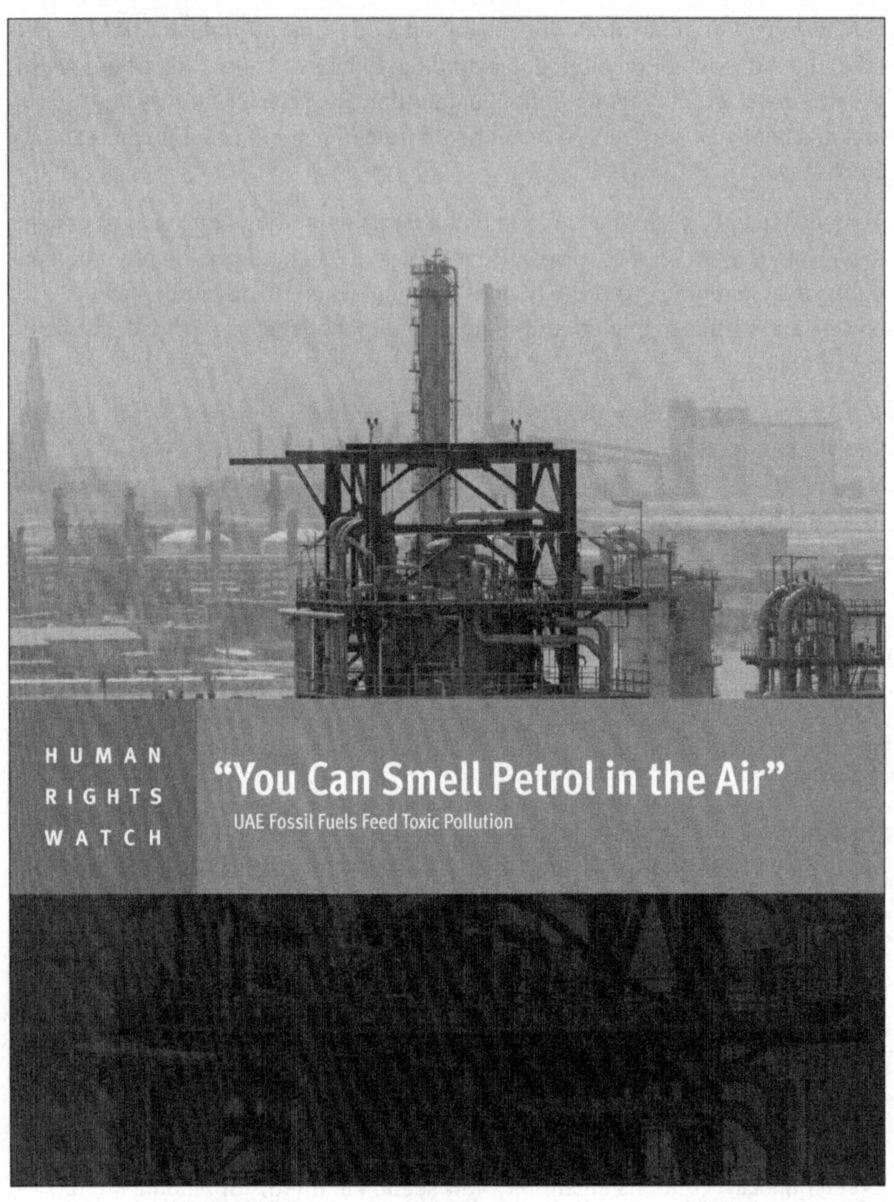
HUMAN
RIGHTS
WATCH
"You Can Smell Petrol in the Air"
UAE Fossil Fuels Feed Toxic Pollution

Migrant Workers

The UAE's *kafala* (sponsorship) system ties migrant workers' visas to their employers, preventing them from changing or leaving employers without permission. Employers can falsely charge workers for "absconding" even when escaping abuse, which puts them at risk of fines, arrest, detention, and deportation, all without any due process guarantees. Many low-paid migrant workers were acutely vulnerable to situations that amount to forced labor, including passport confiscation, wage theft, and illegal recruitment fees. Trade unions are not permitted, which prevents workers from collectively bargaining. The UAE still does not have a non-discriminatory minimum wage.

The labor law allows workers to take on flexible, temporary, part-time, and remote work and also contains explicit language prohibiting sexual harassment and discrimination.

UAE-based migrant workers, who form 88 percent of the UAE population, are exposed to risks of extreme heat without adequate protections. Human Rights Watch documented how extreme heat exposure is a serious health hazard for migrant workers in the UAE. The UAE continues to impose ineffective summer midday bans that prohibit outdoor work between 12:30 p.m. and 3 p.m. between June 15 to September 15, despite evidence of its ineffectiveness in protecting workers. Workers described serious and chronic health conditions that could be linked to extreme heat exposure. Cumulatively, these work conditions often lead to serious health consequences, including heat-related deaths.

Additionally, Human Rights Watch has documented how widespread labor abuses that migrant workers face like wage theft and exorbitant recruitment fees have restricted workers' abilities to support their families back home in climate-vulnerable countries like Pakistan, Bangladesh, and Nepal, including during extreme weather events often linked to climate change.

The authorities issued Federal Decree-Law No. 9 of 2022 concerning Domestic Workers, updating its 2017 law on domestic workers, which guarantees some labor rights. The law now prohibits discrimination and violence against domestic workers by employers and imposes obligations on recruitment agencies to provide information to domestic workers, refrain from charging them with recruitment costs, and refrain from violence against domestic workers. However, it is still weaker than the labor law and falls short of international standards. Moreover, domestic workers continue to report being confined to homes or agency offices, wage theft, and verbal, physical, and sexual violence by employers and recruiters.

Climate Change Policy and Impacts

In November and December, the UAE hosted the UN Climate Change Conference (COP28). The UAE, one of the world's largest oil producers, sought to use the conference as a means of burnishing its image while continuing to push for the expansion of fossil fuels, undermining efforts to confront the climate crisis and protect human rights. Funds from the UAE's vast fossil fuel industry provide the majority of the UAE's government revenue.

The United Arab Emirates' fossil fuel industry contributes to toxic air pollution that creates major health risks for UAE citizens and residents and contributes to the global climate crisis. Migrant workers described breathing air that burned their lungs, feeling out of breath at work, having itchy skin, and other health problems that they believe could be related to toxic air.

On January 12, the UAE appointed Sultan Ahmed Al Jaber as president of COP28. He is the CEO of Abu Dhabi National Oil Company (ADNOC) and founded the state-owned renewable energy company Masdar in 2006. Al Jaber maintained his role at ADNOC while serving as the UAE's special envoy for climate change and leading the conference.

As one of the world's top 10 crude oil producers, the UAE heavily contributes to the climate crisis, which is taking a growing toll on human rights around the globe. The government is planning to expand fossil fuel operations, which, according to the Climate Action Tracker, is inconsistent with the Paris Agreement goal to stay below 1.5 degrees Celsius of warming, necessary to limit the most catastrophic climate outcomes.

Women's Rights

UAE authorities introduced minor amendments to the Federal Personal Status Law in 2019 and 2020: a woman is no longer obliged to "obey" her husband under article 56, and she no longer loses her right to spousal maintenance (*nafaqa*) from her husband if she leaves the marital home or refuses to travel abroad with her husband "without a lawful excuse." However, article 56 still obliges a woman to maintain the home, and article 71 still provides that a woman can lose her right to spousal maintenance from her husband if she abandons the marital home, prevents her husband from entering the marital home, or does not abide by her marital obligations stated in law. A woman is not allowed to move residence with her children without their father's permission.

The Federal Personal Status Law applies to all UAE nationals and foreign nationals except for non-Muslims, who can have their own religious laws apply to them. In November 2021, the Abu Dhabi authorities issued a new law on Civil Marriage and Its Effects in Abu Dhabi providing for a civil marriage with improved protections for women and mostly equal rights between spouses relating to marriage, divorce, and decisions relating to children. However, it only applies to non-Muslim foreign national couples residing in Abu Dhabi; as such, it created a different set of rights, discriminating against women based on their religion, nationality, and where they reside.

Women students attending some state universities face restrictions, including needing parental or male guardian permission for off-campus activities such as joining field trips or leaving campus accommodations.

The 2021 penal code criminalizes consensual nonmarital sex between men and women prosecuted on the basis of a complaint by a husband or male guardian with a minimum sentence of six months' imprisonment. It also criminalizes having a child outside of marriage, punishable with no less than two years in prison for both parents unless the couple marry and register their child separately or together acknowledge the child and obtain a birth certificate and other official documents. The law disproportionately affects women as pregnancy can serve as evidence of the so-called crime and it only allows male relatives to complain about and forgive sex outside marriage.

The Federal Personal Status Law provides that the father is the default guardian of any child with the authority to decide their child's supervision, education, and direction in life. In 2023, the UAE authorities, in a written response to Human Rights Watch, confirmed that it is the obligation of the father, or whoever has legal guardianship over the child according to the child's nationality, to apply for their birth certificate and passport, "as passports are an issue related to the nationality of the country they belong to." Emirati women cannot pass nationality to their children on an equal basis with men.

Sexual Orientation and Gender Identity

The 2021 penal code criminalizes "sodomy" with an adult male. It also continues to criminalize vaguely defined acts, allowing the authorities to arrest people for a wide range of behaviors, including public displays of affection, gender nonconforming expressions, and campaigns promoting the rights of lesbian, gay, bisexual, and transgender (LGBT) people.

Article 411 of the penal code criminalizes and punishes a "flagrant indecent act" and any saying or act that offends public morals with a prison sentence or a fine of Dh1,000 to Dh100,000 (about $270 to $27,000). If it is a repeat offense, the punishment is at least three months' imprisonment and a fine of Dh10,000 to Dh200,000 (about $2,700 to $54,000).

The UAE's federal penal code punishes "any male disguised in female apparel and [who] enters in this disguise a place reserved for women or where entry is forbidden, at that time, for other than women" with one year's imprisonment, a fine of up to Dh10,000 (about $2,700), or both. In practice, transgender women have been arrested under this law even in mixed-gender spaces.

Key International Actors

The UAE invited Syrian President Bashar al-Assad, a leader credibly implicated in rampant atrocities, to COP28. If Assad attends, it would be his first appearance at a global conference since before the outbreak of the Syrian war in 2011.

The United States provided logistical and intelligence support to Saudi and UAE-led coalition forces. A 2022 internal report from the US Government Accountability Office (GAO) found serious gaps in US government oversight of how arms sold to Saudi Arabia and the UAE were being used.

United Kingdom

In 2023, the UK government eroded domestic human rights protections and reneged on important international obligations. The government passed a law further criminalizing protesters and limiting workers' strikes. A new law will ban people who arrive "irregularly" to the UK from claiming asylum or accessing protection, putting them at further risk of harm.

The government again failed to take meaningful steps to tackle institutional racism and address past wrongs, including to fairly compensate Black Britons whose rights were harmed by government policies in what was coined the "Windrush scandal" and to remedy ongoing colonial crimes against the Chagossian people.

The UK's nose-diving domestic human rights record undermined its efforts to promote the rule of law and human rights globally.

Rule of Law and Human Rights

Throughout 2023, the government introduced a number of laws that undermine free speech and democratic rights in the UK.

In April, the government adopted the controversial Public Order Act, further criminalizing people's right to peaceful protest, undermining the freedoms of expression, peaceful assembly, and association. The law came amid an ongoing crackdown on climate change protesters. The year started with at least 13 climate protesters behind bars, serving sentences or awaiting trial. Further jail sentences were imposed in 2023. The Public Order Act was rushed through Parliament ahead of the coronation of King Charles III, and dozens were arrested on the day of the coronation, including six anti-monarchy protesters.

In June, the government introduced an anti-boycott bill to Parliament, which will restrict public bodies, including universities and local councils, from directing investments to avoid contributing to human rights abuses and international crimes, such as divesting from companies complicit in the Chinese government's repression of Uyghurs or in Israeli officials' crime against humanity of apartheid and war crimes linked to Israeli settlements in the occupied West Bank.

In a positive move, also in June, the government dropped plans to repeal the Human Rights Act and replace it with a weaker Bill of Rights. Members of the ruling Conservative party, including a government minister, continued to discuss the possibility of the UK withdrawing from the European Convention on Human Rights.

Asylum and Migration

In July, the UK government adopted the Illegal Migration Act, which bans access to asylum and modern slavery and trafficking protections for anyone who arrives "irregularly" to the UK. People arriving without proper documentation will be automatically detained, including families with children and unaccompanied children—with no right of appeal—pending removal to their home country if it is a "safe country of origin" or to a "safe third country." The act is a flagrant breach of the UK's international obligations, including under the United Nations Refugee Convention.

The UK government continued to defend its controversial asylum deal with Rwanda, despite Rwanda not being a safe third country for asylum seekers. In June, the UK Court of Appeal ruled the deal unlawful, concluding that there is a real risk that asylum seekers sent to Rwanda would be returned to their home countries and subjected to risk of persecution or other inhumane treatment. In July, the government was granted permission to appeal to the Supreme Court. In November, in a significant judgment, the Supreme Court ruled the UK-Rwanda scheme unlawful, as it found that Rwanda is not a safe third country for the UK government to send asylum seekers. The government has vowed to introduce emergency legislation and sign a treaty with Rwanda, but the UK cannot legislate or agree away the facts or its international obligations.

Children and their families seeking asylum face inadequate living conditions in government-provided temporary housing—including rat infestations and mold—affecting their health, well-being, and education. Asylum seekers with disabilities continued to be housed in accommodation without access to adequate support and services.

Rights to Social Security, Food, and Adequate Housing

Despite an ongoing cost of living crisis, the UK government failed to set social security payments at a level that ensures recipients can enjoy their rights and live with dignity. Campaigners called for an independent evaluation to determine adequate social security payments and for the establishment of a legally guaranteed minimum level below which social security payments cannot fall.

Food bank usage increased again. In November 2023, the UK's largest food bank network, Trussell Trust, reported distributing 1.6 million emergency food parcels between April and September, about 16 percent more than in the same period last year. Two-thirds of its parcels were for households with children. The Independent Food Aid Network (IFAN) reported in August that food banks in its network reported an 84 percent increase in need compared to last summer.

Government figures show that homelessness in England reached new heights in 2023. As of the end of March, almost 105,000 households, including more than 131,000 children, were placed in temporary accommodation, rising by 10 percent compared to last year.

Despite an insufficient supply of affordable housing, and more than 1.2 million households on social housing waiting lists in England, state authorities built only 7,644 social housing homes in 2022 compared to 39,562 in 2010. Inadequate levels of housing benefit and social housing construction continued to leave households stuck in temporary accommodation, denying people their right to adequate housing.

Women's and Girls' Rights

In June, a woman was sentenced to 28 months in jail for procuring pills for a medication abortion to terminate a pregnancy beyond the legal timeframe, which is punishable with up to a life sentence. The case sparked calls for an overhaul of outdated abortion laws in England and Wales, which require authorization from two doctors for an abortion, among other barriers. In July, an appeals court halved and suspended the woman's sentence.

In March, media reports revealed that police had referred thousands of women domestic violence victims and child victims of sexual exploitation to immigration

"I Felt So Stuck"
Inadequate Housing and Social Support for Families Seeking Asylum in the United Kingdom
HUMAN RIGHTS WATCH
justfair

authorities between 2020 and 2022. Women's rights groups have long noted that such practices deter victims from accessing essential services and have called for "firewalls" between authorities and the Home Office to facilitate reporting of domestic and other gender-based violence.

Violence against women groups said that authorities continue to fail rape and domestic violence survivors two years after the End-to-End Rape Review revealed worrying decreases in rape prosecutions and convictions. Despite government claims of "significant improvement," few rape victims report to police and prosecutions remain below 2016 levels.

Women continue to experience unequal pay. Data published by the Trade Union Congress in February show that the average woman in paid employment in the UK effectively works for free for nearly two months annually compared to the average man in paid employment.

In March, the International Labour Organization Violence and Harassment Convention (C190) came into effect in the UK, after being ratified by the government in 2022.

Racism and Ethnic Discrimination

Efforts to tackle racism and discrimination suffered setbacks during the year. A survey showed that over one-third of people from minority groups in the UK have experienced racist assaults.

Five years after the "Windrush scandal" became public, the UK government undermined its 30 commitments to right the wrongs experienced by hundreds of thousands of Black Britons from the Windrush generation who were deported, detained, and denied their rights because of repeated policy failings by the UK Home Office. People continue to face serious difficulties accessing the complex and inaccessible Windrush Compensation Scheme—meant to remedy losses and negative impacts on people's lives—with legal aid unavailable to claimants. This has resulted in a low take-up of the scheme and a denial of the right to an effective remedy. A prominent immigration lawyer advocating for people affected by the Windrush scandal faced political and media attacks.

During its UK visit in January 2023, the UN Working Group on People of African Descent raised "serious concerns about impunity and the failure to address racial disparities in the criminal justice system, deaths in police custody, 'joint enterprise' convictions and the dehumanising nature of the stop and (strip) search." The working group also recommended a simplified compensation process for the Windrush generation, who it found had suffered "irreparable harm" with redress being "imperative."

In March, a damning 363-page London Metropolitan police-commissioned report, known as the "Casey report" after author Baroness Casey of Blackstock, found that the London force is institutionally racist and failing Black Londoners, as well as women, children, and LGBT people. Stop and searches and use of excessive force by Met police disproportionately affected Black people.

After several high-profile racially motivated attacks on Black students outside schools, a parliamentary briefing in March called on state-funded schools to comply with anti-discrimination polices and their duty to promote equality. Civil society research from January showed that schools with more Black and ethnic minority students are over-policed in the UK, with students subjected to strip searches by police, often without the presence of an adult.

Sexual Orientation and Gender Identity

In May, after his visit to the UK, the UN independent expert on protection against violence and discrimination based on sexual orientation and gender identity warned that abusive rhetoric by politicians and in the media was creating a climate of hostility against LGBT people in the UK and contributing to a surge in anti-LGBT violence. He also acknowledged the UK's valuable collection of disaggregated data on LGBT people but expressed concern at the government's undermining of protections for the rights of trans women and overrepresentation of LGBT people among the unhoused population.

Environmental and Climate Policies

In 2023, the UK government backtracked on key climate policies. In September 2023, Prime Minister Rishi Sunak announced, on the same day as the UN secretary-general's Climate Ambition Summit, that his government was delaying the

2030 phase-out of new petrol and diesel cars, the 2035 phase-out of gas boilers, and the requirement for landlords to improve the energy efficiency of their homes.

The government also sought to scrap key rules stemming from EU regulations on air pollution that enforce the need to publicly consult on plans to cut emissions.

In June, a London City Hall report showed that areas with large Black and diaspora immigrant communities faced the worst air quality. It follows earlier warning from civil society groups about the need to intensify action to tackle racial disparities of climate change effects in the UK.

Foreign Policy

Since the outbreak of conflict in Sudan in April 2023, the UK has worked closely with international partners to address ongoing abuses and press for credible investigations and accountability. In May, the UK led the convening of a special session at the UN Human Rights Council and later, it successfully led efforts to launch an independent international fact-finding mission for Sudan, responding to calls by Sudanese, regional, and international groups.

In July, the government announced targeted sanctions against six commercial entities linked to the Sudanese Armed Forces (SAF) and the Rapid Support Forces (RSF), but at time of writing, no sanctions had been imposed against military leaders or individuals.

In December 2022, the UK led the first Security Council resolution on the situation in Myanmar and imposed further sanctions targeting the military junta. However, it has not since pushed for a stronger resolution at the Security Council, including one that imposes an arms embargo and sanctions.

In October 2023, the UK, along with Russia, abstained on a Security Council resolution calling for full humanitarian aid access to Gaza and the release of hostages held by Hamas and other Palestinian armed groups. That resolution, which the US vetoed, came after Israel imposed a total blockade on the Gaza Strip, blocking food, water, fuel, and electricity from reaching Gaza's civilian population, following the October 7 Hamas-led attack on Israel.

UK anti-immigrant policies at home have contributed to the government's failure to resettle vulnerable Afghans.

Despite Rwanda's targeting of Rwandans in the UK and support to the M23 who are committing atrocities in eastern Democratic Republic of Congo, the UK appears to be turning a blind eye to ongoing abuses, including by failing to call on Rwanda to end its assistance to the M23.

To date, the government has refused to provide the Chagossian people with full reparations, including their right to return, for its ongoing colonial crimes. The UK is in negotiations with Mauritius over the future of the islands, but there has been no effective consultation with the Chagossians, whom the UK forcibly evicted from the islands over 50 years ago, a crime against humanity.

The UK government is placing ever more priority on concluding trade deals with countries with poor human rights records, such as countries in the Gulf Cooperation Council and India, despite ongoing concerns about the lack of transparency, oversight, and inclusion of concrete human rights protections and commitments.

The UK played a mixed role in multilateral forums. In addition to its leadership on Sudan at the Human Rights Council, the UK ensured ongoing efforts to investigate and advance accountability for abuses in South Sudan, highlighted the violations accompanying Russia's full-scale invasion of Ukraine, and supported a range of other important resolutions, including renewing the mandates on Russia and Belarus, and a joint statement on accountability for the Beirut blast. At the UN General Assembly, the UK led a joint statement condemning the Chinese government's crimes against humanity committed against Uyghurs.

Conversely, the UK continued to undermine the Commission of Inquiry on the Occupied Palestinian Territory and Israel and voted against other resolutions on human rights in Israel and Palestine. The UK also signed a 2030 roadmap for Israel/UK bilateral relations, which commits the UK to shielding Israel from scrutiny at the Human Rights Council and opposes the International Court of Justice's advisory opinion on the legal consequences of Israel's prolonged occupation and repression of Palestinians. They again voted against a resolution on racism, racial discrimination, xenophobia and related intolerance.

United States

Racism, anti-immigrant sentiments, and threats to democracy remained pressing human rights problems in the United States in 2023. The national poverty rate rose dramatically following the choice to cease a pandemic-period child tax credit. Economic inequality also rose, and the racial wealth gap remained high. The incarceration rate also increased, despite the US already having one of the highest rates in the world, with Black people vastly overrepresented in prisons and jails.

In its foreign policy, the US held human rights abusers accountable through targeted sanctions and provided new support to international justice mechanisms such as the investigation of the International Criminal Court (ICC) into the conflict in Ukraine. The US also undermined its stated commitment to human rights by providing military assistance to human rights-abusing states.

The administration of US President Joe Biden banned the government's use of abusive commercial spyware and issued some policies aimed at improving racial equity in efforts to tackle climate change at home and abroad. The US Supreme Court issued decisions reinforcing laws aimed at protecting the right to vote.

However, states enacted an increasing number of laws that restrict access to reproductive care, including abortion, and the rights of lesbian, gay, bisexual, and transgender (LGBT) people. The federal government has not taken sufficient steps necessary to limit global warming, even though the US is among the world's top greenhouse gas emitters. State and federal authorities continued to pursue policies aimed at deterring people from seeking asylum in the US, in flagrant violation of international human rights law, pushing them to take more dangerous routes.

A federal task force documented harassment and threats against election officials, revealing the need to better protect election administrators from intimidation and to address the spread of misinformation and disinformation.

Racial Justice

The racial wealth gap remained stark, with Black families having 24 cents and Hispanic families having 23 cents for every US$1 of white family wealth, and has

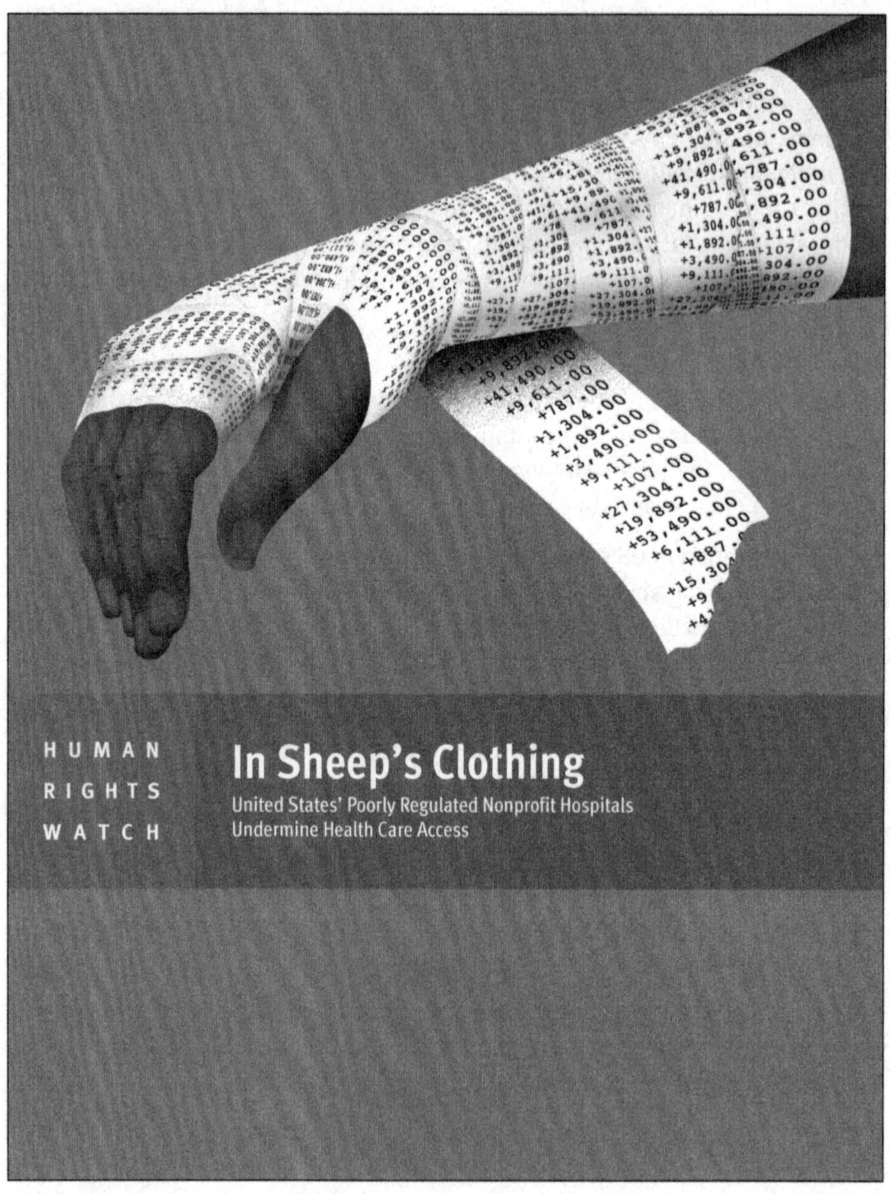
HUMAN
RIGHTS
WATCH
In Sheep's Clothing
United States' Poorly Regulated Nonprofit Hospitals
Undermine Health Care Access

changed very little over the last 50 years. Numerous studies have shown that drastic economic intervention, including reparations in a variety of forms, is needed to address this gap as well as continuing racial disparities in access to adequate health, nutrition, education, employment, and housing, among other things.

In May, US Representative Cori Bush introduced a resolution urging the federal government to provide reparations for enslavement and its legacies and to support existing proposals such as H.R. 40. H.R. 40 is a House of Representatives bill that proposes establishing a federal commission to study and make recommendations on reparations, which has been introduced every congressional session since 1989 but has yet to pass. Congressional leadership did not bring either the new resolution or the House bill to the floor for a vote.

While federal efforts stalled, states made progress on reparations. In May, a California reparations task force, created by 2020 legislation, submitted reparatory proposals to the state governor for consideration. Also in May, Washington state enacted a law to create a downpayment assistance program for people directly affected by past racist housing covenants. In June, the New York state legislature passed a bill to study the economic impacts of enslavement and the government's role in supporting that institution, which the governor had not signed at time of writing.

In July, a lawsuit seeking reparations for the last three known survivors of the 1921 Tulsa Race Massacre was dismissed by an Oklahoma judge. The survivors appealed, and in August, the Oklahoma Supreme Court agreed to hear the case. In October, Hughes Van Ellis, who at 102 was the youngest of the three living survivors, died.

Economic Justice

After two years of historic declines in poverty due to expanded social protection in response to Covid-19, the US Supplemental Poverty Measure, which incorporates the influence of government assistance and geographical cost of living differences, rose dramatically, jumping to 12.4 percent in 2022 from 7.8 percent in 2021. Income inequality in the US is very high compared to other wealthy coun-

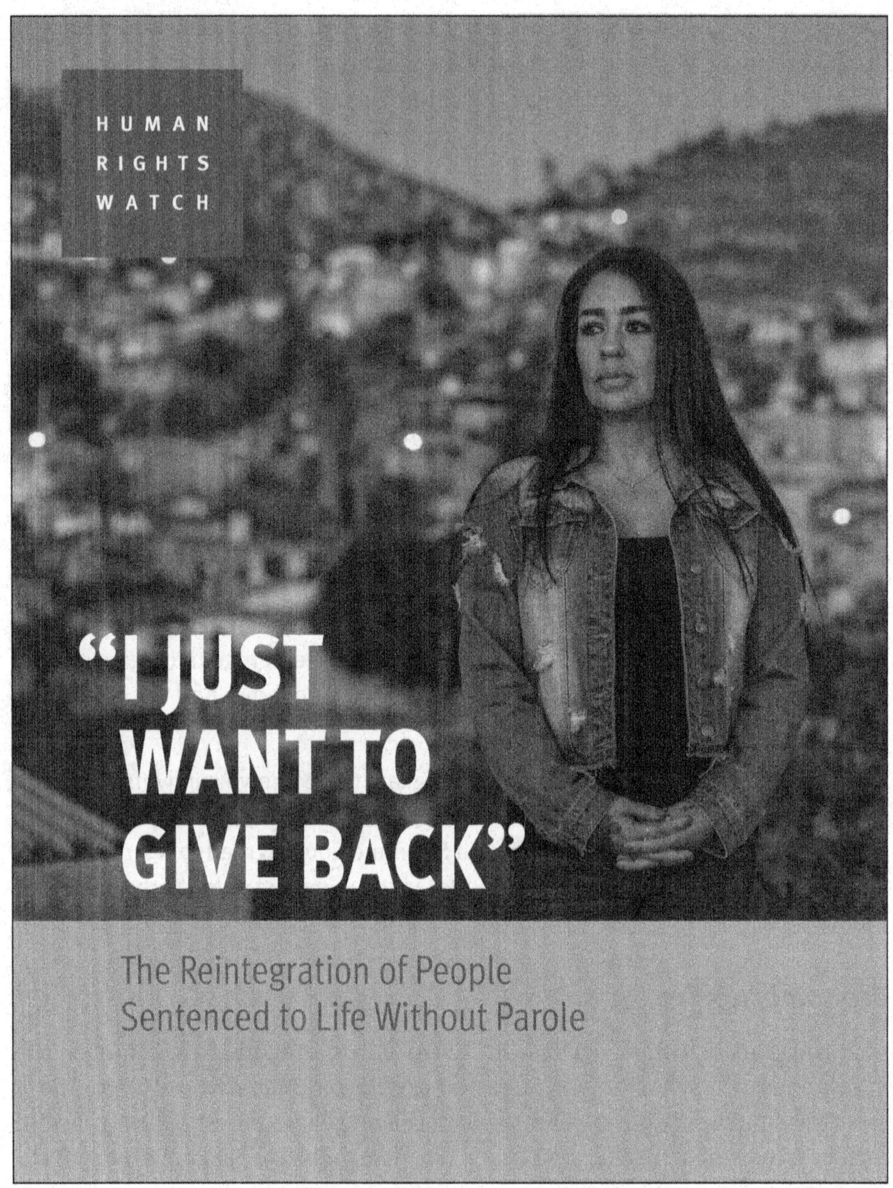
HUMAN
RIGHTS
WATCH
"I JUST
WANT TO
GIVE BACK"
The Reintegration of People
Sentenced to Life Without Parole

tries, with the top 10 percent of earners capturing nearly half of all income and the bottom 50 percent getting just 13 percent.

After taxes and government transfers are considered, the Gini index, a statistical measure of income inequality, for the US has increased by 3.2 percent since 2021. Wealth inequality is similarly stark, with the poorest 50 percent of the US population owning only just 1.5 percent of the country's private wealth.

Criminal Justice

The US has one of the highest incarceration rates in the world, with roughly 2 million people held in state and federal jails, prisons, and immigration detention facilities on any given day, and millions more on parole and probation. Despite some reductions in incarceration rates for Black people, they remain vastly overrepresented in jails and prisons.

In 2021, the most recent year for which such data is available, the rate at which people were incarcerated in jails and prisons nationwide increased for the first time since 2005, although it remained below pre-pandemic levels.

Widespread calls to reduce overreliance on policing and address societal problems instead with investments in housing, health care, and education were largely drowned out by calls for more police funding and the rollback of police reforms. The latter calls were driven by persistent misinformation and misleading narratives about rising crime rates and decreased public safety, often generated and manipulated by law enforcement, despite substantial evidence of the success of reforms and community investments.

Local governments criminalized unhoused communities across the country and expanded forced or coerced treatment to address people living on the streets.

Most US police departments refuse to report data on their use of force, necessitating nongovernmental data collection and analysis. As of September 28, police had killed over 800 people in 2023, similar to numbers in prior years. On a per capita basis, police kill Black people at almost three times the rate they kill white people.

Youth Justice

Children continue to be tried as adults in all 50 states, despite international standards repudiating the practice. Those transferred to the adult system are disproportionately youth of color, with racial and ethnic disparities persisting at almost every point of contact with the justice system, including arrests, pre-disposition detention, and post-adjudication incarceration.

In 2023, three states took steps toward eliminating the sentence of life without parole (LWOP) for children. In total, 33 states and Washington, DC, have now banned it or have no one serving such a sentence. Despite this progress, the US remains the only country in the world to sentence children convicted of crimes to die in prison.

Child Labor

In February, the US Department of Labor reported a sharp increase in child labor violations, and investigations carried out by media outlets showed children, often unaccompanied migrants, working in dangerous and exploitative conditions, sacrificing their health, safety, and education. Some states moved to roll back child labor protections. Longstanding exemptions in US labor laws allow children as young as 12 to work legally in agriculture, the deadliest sector for child workers.

Drug Policy

Overdose deaths continued to rise, reaching another record level. They first surpassed 100,000 in the 12-month period ending April 2021 and increased to 111,355 in the 12-month period ending April 2023. Racial disparities in overdose deaths also continued to widen, with the rate of Black deaths exceeding those of white ones, due in part to racial bias in policies and access to treatment.

Federal and state authorities continue to rely significantly on criminalization to address harmful drug use, even though harm reduction strategies that offer health-centered care and access to voluntary treatment have proven more effective.

In 2022, the Biden administration became the first US administration to invest in harm reduction, but stronger and more robust investments in health-centered approaches are needed. In March, the US Food and Drug Administration approved naloxone, the first over-the-counter drug used to reverse opioid overdose.

Immigrants' Rights and Border Communities

The 2020 Title 42 summary expulsions policy expired in May but was replaced by a new labyrinthine asylum rule. Under Title 42, justified as an emergency measure to combat the Covid-19 pandemic, the Biden administration summarily expelled people 2.3 million times without screening them for asylum.

Under the new asylum rule, many asylum seekers face expedited removals, arbitrary detention, prosecution, and a five-year ban on returning to the US unless they make an appointment at select US land border ports of entry using "CBP One" prior to crossing the border. CBP One is a difficult-to-access phone app that often fails to recognize faces with darker skin tones. This process can take several months and exposes asylum seekers to systematic targeting by cartels and Mexican government officials for kidnapping, extortion, sexual assault, and other harms.

As a candidate, Biden pledged to end private immigration detention, but as of July, 90 percent of the 30,000 non-citizens who are in detention on average each day in the US were held in private facilities.

In June, Texas Governor Greg Abbott ramped up his already ruthless border approach by installing razor wire and buoys with circular saws in or near the Rio Grande. Under Operation Lone Star, high-speed vehicle pursuits and the accidents they cause in communities throughout south Texas are a threat to public safety, with harmful consequences for migrant passengers and Texas residents alike. Human Rights Watch found that at least 74 people have been killed and 189 injured since the policy began in March 2021.

Permission
For
Abortion
DENIED
HUMAN
RIGHTS
WATCH
Access Denied
How Florida Judges Obstruct Young People's Ability to Obtain Abortion Care

Democracy

The battle to defend multiracial democracy in the US continued. In June, the US Supreme Court, in Allen v. Milligan, struck down Alabama's gerrymandered congressional maps, reaffirming that racial discrimination in voting laws, maps, and practices is illegal. Also in June, the US Supreme Court, in Moore v. Harper, upheld the right of people in the US to seek a remedy for voting rights violations in state courts. However, at least 14 states passed laws in 2023 that make it more difficult to vote.

State-level lawmakers continued to undermine democracy by banning books and passing laws that restrict truthful classroom discussions of race, history, sexual orientation, and gender. This censorship has the potential to undermine civic participation by erasing the galvanizing stories of ordinary citizens who organized to promote human rights.

The movement for universal suffrage earned victories. New Mexico and Minnesota passed laws that allow individuals to vote upon release from prison. A federal court overturned Mississippi's lifetime voting ban for individuals convicted of some felony offenses, calling the practice cruel and unusual.

For the first time in US history, a former president faced significant sanctions, including criminal and civil charges, in part for his efforts to overturn the 2020 elections, a serious infringement of the right to vote. New studies by the federal government and civil society groups, revealed vulnerabilities in US democracy, including the need to better protect elections administrators from threats and intimidation, which continued to increase. Since 2020, when the US Department of Justice opened a task force into the matter, 14 investigations into attempts to threaten election workers have been initiated, 9 of which had resulted in findings of wrongdoing at time of writing. The year also revealed the need to better address the spread of misinformation and disinformation through social media platforms.

Climate Change Policy and Impacts

The US remains the world's largest oil and gas producer and historically is the country that has most contributed to the climate crisis. It also remains among the world's top greenhouse gas emitters.

HUMAN
RIGHTS
WATCH
"So Much Blood on the Ground"
Dangerous and Deadly Vehicle Pursuits under Texas' Operation Lone Star

The Biden administration issued an executive order that directs all federal agencies to incorporate the pursuit of environmental justice into their missions and announced the creation of a new policy committee to coordinate efforts to prioritize public health, economic development, and equity in tackling the global plastics pollution crisis. Virtually all plastics are derived from fossil fuels.

However, the US is also on track to be responsible for the world's largest expansion in oil and gas extraction from 2023 to 2050. Fossil fuels are the single largest contributor to global warming and can be linked to human rights harms. These impacts are disproportionately borne by already marginalized communities—including Black, Indigenous, and other people of color and low-income communities—and perpetuate systemic racism.

Women's and Girls' Rights

The June 2022 US Supreme Court decision in Dobbs v. Jackson Women's Health Organization, overturning the constitutionally protected right to abortion, continued to have reverberating negative impacts on women, girls, and other people in the US who can become pregnant.

As of September 15, 22 states had banned abortion or restricted access to abortion at earlier stages and 14 states had enacted laws that criminalize healthcare providers who perform abortions. Some states also made it a crime for anyone, including healthcare providers, to assist pregnant people in obtaining an abortion. As a result, approximately 22 million women and girls of reproductive age, as well as other people who can become pregnant, now live in US states where abortion access is heavily restricted or inaccessible.

In August 2023, a federal appeals court, attempting to reconcile two conflicting lower court opinions issued within minutes of each other—one revoking the approval of mifepristone, a safe and effective drug used for medical abortions, and the other keeping it available—ruled that access to the drug should be limited in certain contexts: when mailed and prescribed via telemedicine. The US Department of Justice and the manufacturer appealed the decision.

Racial disparities in access to health care continue to leave millions of women of color at risk. Cervical cancer is a highly preventable and treatable disease, yet over 4,200 women die from it each year in the US, disproportionately Black women in the South.

Disability Rights

People with disabilities are three times less likely to be employed, and those who are employed often earn less than their peers for doing the same work. Public spaces, including transit systems and voting locations, often remain inaccessible.

Wellness checks for mental health crises by police are still prone to have fatal and harmful consequences for people with mental health conditions. Authorities have been slow to adopt alternative approaches featuring nonpolice emergency response teams.

Older People's Rights

In January, the Centers for Medicare and Medicaid Services (CMS), fulfilling a 2022 Biden commitment, announced it would audit the appropriateness of nursing homes' schizophrenia diagnoses to reduce the misuse of antipsychotic drugs to control behavior, known as "chemical restraints." In August, CMS proposed minimum nursing home staffing levels of only 3 hours of direct care per resident per day, lower than the minimum 4.1 hours per day recommended by a CSM-funded study and the Institute of Medicine.

Sexual Orientation and Gender Identity

At the state level, lawmakers introduced hundreds of bills aiming to restrict the rights of LGBT people—more than in any prior year—and dozens of them were enacted into law.

The majority of these efforts have targeted transgender people, particularly transgender children in schools. As of September 2023, 22 states ban at least some best-practice medical care for transgender children, and 5 of these states criminalize such care as a felony offense; 23 states prohibit transgender children from participating in sports consistent with their gender identity; 11 states ban various discussions of sexual orientation and gender identity in schools; and 9 states prohibit transgender people from using bathrooms consistent with their gender identity in K-12 schools, with some of these bans encompassing other public facilities as well.

Positive developments have failed to keep pace. Michigan is the only state where lawmakers adopted a comprehensive LGBT-inclusive nondiscrimination law in 2023, making it the 22nd state to do so. The US has failed to enact comprehensive federal legislation that would expressly protect LGBT people from discrimination in areas such as education, housing, public accommodations, and federally funded programs.

Technology and Human Rights

The US continues to lack a human rights-centered federal data protection law, leaving personal data open to abuse by both government and private actors, particularly commercial tech sector actors with advanced data collection, profiling, and targeting abilities.

Numerous federal agencies are considering how to regulate powerful new technologies, including artificial intelligence (AI). Regulations should contain rights protections and enforcement mechanisms and be informed by civil society inputs on human rights harms.

Workers recruited by digital labor platforms to provide ride-hailing and delivery services continue to experience low, unpredictable wages and unsafe working conditions.

The Biden administration in March issued an executive order banning government agencies from using commercial spyware that has been misused to target political dissent or perpetuate discrimination and marginalization. Commercial spyware continues to be a pervasive threat to human rights and human rights workers globally, including Human Rights Watch staff.

Guantanamo

At time of writing, 30 foreign Muslim men remained detained at the US military detention center at Guantanamo Bay, Cuba, including 5 charged with involvement in the attacks on September 11, 2001. Talks stalled on a deal for the five

9/11 accused to plead guilty in exchange for life sentences, after President Biden rejected the men's requests for care to help them recover from Central Intelligence Agency (CIA) torture and to not serve their sentences in solitary confinement. A judge found one 9/11 defendant not mentally competent to stand trial.

Two detainees from Malaysia agreed to plead guilty before Guantanamo's fundamentally flawed military commissions in connection with the deadly 2002 bombings in Bali and a 2003 bombing of a Marriott Hotel in Jakarta, Indonesia. They were expected to be transferred to Malaysia after sentencing in January 2024.

Two other men awaited trial and a third awaited sentencing at Guantanamo. Nineteen have never been charged. Only one man still held at Guantanamo has been convicted by a military commission.

Foreign Policy

President Biden strongly criticized the Hamas-led attack on southern Israel on October 7 that resulted in the killing of hundreds of Israeli and other civilians. He committed increased support for Israel's defense beyond already approved annual military aid. Such security assistance and arms transfers violated US domestic laws and policies that condition US military aid on ensuring partners are not in violation of international law. US officials publicly and privately urged Israel to minimize civilian harm in its military response and allow humanitarian assistance into Gaza.

The US continued to provide significant military and economic support to Ukraine in 2023 in opposition to Russia's full-scale invasion in February 2022. In July, President Biden authorized the sharing evidence of international crimes being committed in Ukraine with the ICC. Also in July, Biden approved the transfer of US cluster munitions to Ukraine. These weapons are banned by an international treaty due to the dangers they pose to civilians, but neither the US nor Ukraine are parties to that treaty.

After conflict broke out in Sudan in April, the US Treasury imposed sanctions on a leader of the Rapid Support Forces (RSF) armed group and visa restrictions on an RSF commander in West Darfur state. Three private Sudanese companies and a private Emirati company were sanctioned under a May executive order. The

State Department set up a "Sudan Observatory" with civil society to document atrocities in the conflict.

At the United Nations Human Rights Council in October, the US supported a successful resolution to establish an international fact-finding mission for Sudan. At the UN Security Council that same month, the US co-sponsored with Ecuador a resolution, which was then adopted, to authorize a Kenya-led multinational security force to Haiti; it also vetoed a resolution that both condemned Hamas and called for all sides involved in the hostilities in Israel and Palestine to comply with international humanitarian law. In November, the US abstained from voting on a UN Security Council resolution calling for extended humanitarian pauses in Gaza and the release of Israelis held hostage. The US abstention allowed the resolution to be adopted.

In March, Secretary of State Antony Blinken formally determined that all parties to the conflict in northern Ethiopia had committed war crimes. He noted that the Ethiopian government forces and its allies, including Eritrea, were responsible for crimes against humanity. In late June, the administration notified Congress that the government was no longer engaging in a "pattern of gross violations of human rights," allowing it to qualify for US and international financial assistance, despite the ongoing commission of abuses.

In June, India's Prime Minister Narendra Modi received a state dinner at the White House and delivered a speech to a joint session of Congress, despite increasing human rights abuses by his party and its supporters.

A new Conventional Arms Transfer Policy announced in February allows the State Department to deny a sale if a country would "more likely than not" harm civilians with US weapons. In September, the State Department created a Civilian Harm Incident Response Group (CHIRG) to analyze allegations of US military aid being used to harm civilians in recipient countries.

The Egyptian government receives $1.3 billion in US military aid annually. Although Congress has conditioned a portion of these funds on actions that include strengthening human rights, in September, the Biden administration used a national security waiver to allow $235 million to go to President Abdel Fattah al-Sisi's government. Another $85 million was withheld because of Egypt's poor record on political prisoners. In September, members of Congress changed course and placed a hold on the previously approved $235 million following the indictment of Senator Robert Menendez for allegations of corruption that benefited the Egyptian government.

Iran released five Americans imprisoned on unproven charges in exchange for five Iranians imprisoned in the US. In parallel, the US Treasury issued a waiver allowing Iran access to $6 billion in frozen Iranian oil revenue via banks in Doha for humanitarian use. However, in October, the US reportedly blocked access to these funds following the Hamas attacks in Israel.

In Latin America and the Caribbean, the Biden administration prioritized efforts to restrict the flow of migrants and refugees traveling north. While the Biden administration took steps to defend the right to vote in Brazil and Guatemala and to limit deforestation in the Amazon, its responses to other pressing human rights situations, including in Mexico and Cuba, often prioritized domestic implications and politics, undermining its credibility on human rights.

Uzbekistan

Uzbekistan's human rights record deteriorated in 2023, with a notable increase in the harassment and prosecutions of bloggers and journalists, a persistent lack of justice for human rights abuses committed during the Karakalpakstan events in 2022, and changes to Uzbekistan's constitution that allowed President Shavkat Mirziyoyev to stand for re-election in snap presidential elections in July. Promised legislative reforms were further stalled.

The Justice Ministry continued to deny registration to independent human rights groups. Consensual same-sex relations between men remains criminalized, and impunity for torture and ill-treatment persists. In April 2023, Uzbekistan adopted legislative amendments criminalizing domestic violence and increasing protections for women and girls. Domestic violence remains a pervasive and serious problem.

Presidential Elections

Uzbekistan held a national referendum in March that ushered in a new constitution allowing President Mirziyoyev to run for two additional seven-year terms. After snap presidential elections on July 9, the Organization for Security and Co-operation in Europe (OSCE) Office for Democratic Institutions and Human Rights (ODIHR) election monitoring mission noted that the vote "lacked genuine competition" and involved "significant procedural irregularities." Authorities denied registration to the independent Truth, Progress, and Unity Party, preventing its leader, Khidirnazar Allakulov, from participating.

Accountability and Justice

On August 4, an Uzbekistan court sentenced two police officers to seven years in prison for torture and another to three years in prison for perjury and leaving a person in danger resulting in his death in connection with the Karakalpakstan events. No other law enforcement officers have been held accountable for the 21 deaths and many serious injuries that occurred during the events, nor has the parliamentary commission tasked with investigating human rights abuses reported its findings.

In two separate trials related to the Karakalpakstan events, a Bukhara court in January and March convicted 61 defendants, including lawyers and journalists, on "rioting" and other charges, and sentenced them to up to 16 years in prison. Of the 61 defendants, 15 were given non-custodial sentences. On appeal, 35 defendants had their sentences reduced. One defendant who had received a six-year prison sentence in January, Polat Shamshetov, unexpectedly died in custody four days after his conviction.

In early May, an Uzbekistan court convicted in absentia Aman Sagidullaev and Neitbai Orazbaev, ethnic Karakalpaks living in exile, on multiple charges, including attempting to overthrow the constitutional order. It sentenced them to 18 and 12 years in prison, respectively.

Torture and Ill-Treatment

Torture and ill-treatment persist as a serious problem. On March 21, 12 police officers were sentenced to 3 to 4 years in prison for torture after beating a 32-year-old man to death in pretrial detention in Shakhrihan district, Andijan.

The Karakalpak blogger and lawyer Dauletmurat Tazhimuratov, who was sentenced to 16 years in prison, testified that law enforcement officers beat him in custody, including with a stun gun, and stood on his head, causing him to lose consciousness. Authorities failed to effectively investigate his claims of torture. Tazhimuratov's lawyer, Sergey Mayorov, reported in mid-April and again in mid-September that Tazhimuratov continued to face abuse and restrictions in prison.

Authorities continued to ignore a May 2021 opinion issued by the United Nations Working Group on Arbitrary Detention calling for the immediate release of Kadyr Yusupov, a former diplomat imprisoned in January 2020 for five-and-a-half years on charges of treason.

Freedom of Speech

There was a serious decline in respect for freedom of speech and the media. In March, approximately 40 journalists and bloggers signed an open appeal to President Mirziyoyev raising concerns about censorship, pressure, and intimidation. Citing pressure, multiple bloggers and independent journalists announced in 2023 that they would cease their work. Defamation and insult, including insulting the president, remain criminal offenses. In October, a Samarkand regional court sent a 19-year-old to prison for 2.5 years for insulting the president online.

In May, Elmurod Odil, a blogger from Kashkadarya region, was sentenced to 15 days' administrative arrest for hooliganism and disobeying authorities after he tried to film a meeting between silk farmers and local authorities. He claimed police beat him in custody.

Ferghana region police arrested the outspoken and critical blogger Olimjon Khaidarov in late July on charges of extortion. Slander and insult charges were added later. On December 1, an Uzbekistan court sentenced Khaidarov to eight years in prison and ordered his social media accounts blocked.

In early August, a Tashkent court sentenced Abduqodir Muminov, an investigative blogger, to seven years and three months in prison on multiple criminal charges, including large-scale extortion. At his appeal hearing, Muminov said he had been tortured in detention.

The blogger Otabek Sattoriy continued to serve a six-and-a-half-year prison sentence for alleged extortion. In February, the UN Working Group on Arbitrary Detention issued a decision in favor of Sattoriy, calling for his release and that he be provided reparations.

Civil Society

Uzbek authorities obstruct independent human rights activism. The Justice Ministry continues to deny registration to independent groups, including Human Rights House, an independent human rights organization in Tashkent, often on trivial grounds. Authorities made no effort in 2023 to pass a stalled draft code for nongovernmental organizations (NGOs), but they adopted new regulations on the receipt of foreign funding for NGOs.

Several people were barred from entering Uzbekistan, including journalist Shahida Tuleganova on April 5; Isokzhon Zakirov, an activist who had fled Uzbekistan under former President Islam Karimov, in March; and Galym Ageleouv, a rights monitor from Kazakhstan, in May.

The women's rights activist Irina Matvienko temporarily fled Uzbekistan in May after receiving an anonymous death threat. The UN Special Rapporteur on the Situation of Human Rights Defenders Mary Lawlor noted her alarm and called on Uzbek authorities to "promptly [and] effectively investigate the incident."

Uzbek authorities continue to deny legal rehabilitation to more than 50 people, including human rights defenders, who, between 2016 and 2019, were released from prison after having served politically motivated sentences.

Freedom of Religion

Uzbek authorities restrict religious freedom by preventing registration of religious communities, subjecting former religious prisoners to arbitrary controls, and prosecuting Muslims on broad and vaguely worded extremism-related charges. The last includes charges under Criminal Code article 244-1, part 3, for storing or sharing materials containing "religious extremist" content on social media networks. Jehovah's Witnesses has made multiple attempts to register in Tashkent and Samarkand since 2021, all unsuccessfully. On Easter Sunday, April 9, police raided a Baptist church in Kashkadarya, detaining and beating several worshippers, according to the international religious freedom watchdog Forum18.

A Tashkent court sentenced the blogger Hojiakbar Nosirov to 15 days' administrative arrest for "distributing material inciting religious hatred" after he claimed in a video that Muslims should not eat certain yogurt because it could contain carmine, a red coloring agent, and is therefore haram.

Sexual Orientation and Gender Identity

Consensual same-sex sexual conduct between men is criminalized with up to three years in prison. Police target gay and bisexual men and transgender women with arbitrary detention, prosecution, and imprisonment. Lesbian, gay, bisexual, and transgender (LGBT) people face discrimination and harassment from state and non-state actors.

Uzbek police and courts have relied on the conclusions of forced anal examinations in prosecutions of gay men for consensual same-sex relations. Such exams are a form of violence and torture, according to the World Health Organization.

Women's and Girls' Rights

Violence against women and girls, including sexual violence, remains pervasive in Uzbekistan. In April, Uzbekistan adopted a new law amending Uzbekistan's Criminal and Administrative codes that offers better protections for women and girls from abuse as well as strengthened measures to address child abuse. Domestic violence was made a standalone offense. The law increases sanctions for sexual violence, including against children, and introduces administrative sanctions for sexual harassment and stalking. Women's rights activists helped to draft the bill, but some of their recommendations were rejected.

In June, the OSCE senior gender adviser concluded a three-day visit to Uzbekistan. She stressed in meetings with Uzbek officials the need to "strengthen accountability" and "punish perpetrators" of gender-based violence.

Forced Labor

Independent cotton harvest monitors found no evidence of systematic, government-imposed forced labor for the second consecutive year. Isolated incidents of forced labor and extortion in the cotton fields persisted. Restrictions on independent trade unions and rights groups continued to threaten Uzbekistan's progress. Agricultural workers and farmers faced constraints on their right to organize and bargain collectively.

Key International Actors

In mid-April, the EU special representatives for human rights and Central Asia, Eamon Gilmore and Terhi Hakala, respectively, met senior Uzbek officials, including President Mirziyoyev, in Tashkent. They discussed media freedom, the Karakalpakstan events, and progress on ending torture and domestic violence.

After visiting Uzbekistan in March, UN High Commissioner for Human Rights Volker Türk urged an "after action" review of the Karakalpakstan events, calling for "accountability for the loss of lives." Türk also called for the decriminalization of same-sex relations and better protections for media workers.

In June, the EU Sub-Committee on Justice and Home Affairs, Human Rights and related issues expressed concerns about increased government control over NGOs receiving foreign funding and raised several cases of harassment or detention of journalists, bloggers, and activists.

On September 19, United States President Joe Biden met with President Mirziyoyev on the sidelines of the UN General Assembly during the first US-Central Asia presidential summit, but he did not prominently raise rights concerns.

On October 2, the European Parliament adopted a resolution on Uzbekistan expressing concern about constitutional provisions allowing the president to extend his time in office and Uzbekistan's poor human rights record. The resolution called for a "genuinely independent, impartial and effective investigation into the events" of July 2022 in Karakalpakstan.

On November 8, Uzbekistan appeared before the UN Human Rights Council for its fourth Universal Periodic Review. States recommended that the Uzbekistan government address impunity for torture, ensure NGOs and journalists can work without harassment, and address violations of LGBT rights in law and practice, among other actions.

Venezuela

Venezuelans continued to suffer repression and a humanitarian crisis. More than 270 political prisoners are behind bars. About 19 million people are in need, unable to access adequate health care and nutrition. More than 7.7 million Venezuelans have fled the country, generating one of the largest migration crises in the world.

On June 27, International Criminal Court (ICC) judges authorized the resumption of an investigation into alleged crimes against humanity in Venezuela. In September, the United Nations Fact-Finding Mission (FFM) found serious human rights violations that continued the same patterns of conduct that the FFM had previously qualified as crimes against humanity.

Several government actions, including the designation of a new National Electoral Council (CNE) and the disqualification of presidential candidates, increased concerns about the possibility of free and fair elections.

Negotiations between Nicolás Maduro's government and the opposition resumed in October 2023, reaching an agreement related to political rights and electoral guarantees.

Authorities harass, persecute, and jail union workers, journalists, and human rights defenders, restricting civic space. Persistent concerns include the lack of protection for Indigenous people; lesbian, gay, bisexual, and transgender (LGBT) people; and the rights of women and girls.

Abuses and Repression of Dissent

While the same patterns of abuse continue, there has been a shift from the widescale repression of protesters in the streets to a seemingly more selective repression that includes surveillance, harassment, and criminalization. However, as the FFM found, Maduro's government continues to have the capacity to resort to the "hardline" tools of repression, such a torture and killings, "to stifle dissent."

More than 15,800 people have been subjected to politically motivated arrests since 2014, and about 270 remained in detention, the legal aid organization Foro

Penal reported in October. Five political prisoners, including journalist Ronald Carreño, were released on October 18 after the government and opposition resumed negotiations.

The UN Office of the High Commissioner for Human Rights (OHCHR) and the FFM continued to document cases, albeit a decline in number, of killings, short-term enforced disappearances, arbitrary detentions, torture and ill-treatment, and sexual and gender-based violence against opponents of the Maduro government.

The Special Action Forces (FAES), a police unit that engaged in serious human rights violations, was dissolved in 2022 and replaced by the Directorate of Strategic and Tactical Actions (DAET) after continued international pressure. DAET has similar functions and modus operandi as FAES, with former FAES officials who have been involved in gross human rights violations holding key roles, according to the FFM.

Right to Vote

Venezuela made little, if any, progress in implementing recommendations made by European Union election monitors in 2021 in anticipation of the 2024 presidential elections and 2025 legislative and regional elections.

In late June, the Comptroller General's Office added to its list of electoral disqualifications a 15-year ban for opposition candidate María Corina Machado.

The Supreme Court continued to impose ad hoc leaders on opposition parties. In August, it ordered new leaders for the Venezuelan Communist Party.

The government-controlled National Assembly elected all new members of the CNE in August, after pro-government members resigned. New members include Elvis Amoroso, who, as comptroller general, disqualified opposition candidates, and Carlos Quintero, whom the United States sanctioned in 2017 for his role, as a CNE member, in weakening elections.

On October 17, the government and opposition agreed to honor political parties' right to choose their presidential candidates and to hold the presidential elections in the second half of 2024, along with other electoral guarantees.

Also in October, opposition parties held their first primary elections since 2012, electing Maria Corina Machado as the opposition presidential candidate. Days later, the Attorney General's Office launched an investigation into the primary organizing committee for alleged fraud and the pro-government Supreme Court suspended "all effects" of the primary election.

Impunity for Abuses

The judiciary stopped functioning as an independent branch of government in 2004. There has been no meaningful justice for crimes committed with the knowledge or acquiescence of high-level authorities.

In June, ICC judges found that Venezuelan courts are not investigating possible crimes against humanity to the extent of an intended investigation at the ICC, therefore greenlighting the resumption of the investigation. At time of writing, Venezuela was appealing the decision.

In July, OHCHR reported "prolonged delays" in the investigation of deaths during 2014, 2017, and 2019 protests. Only 8 of the 101 deaths the office documented during security operations have been brought to trial.

In September, the FFM had reasonable grounds to believe that far from dismantling structures involved in abuses, Venezuelan authorities have "promoted" individuals responsible for them.

Humanitarian Emergency

HumVenezuela, an independent platform of civil society organizations monitoring the humanitarian emergency, estimated that from March 2020 to March 2022, 66 percent of Venezuela's population needs humanitarian assistance and 65 percent have "irreversibly lost or exhausted their means of livelihood."

Venezuela has the highest prevalence of undernourishment in South America, according to the 2022 UN *Regional Overview of Food Security and Nutrition*.

In August 2023, over 72 percent of people were unable to access public health services when needed, compared to 65.5 percent in July 2021. Medicine shortages stood at 26.3 percent by August 2023, the humanitarian organization Convite estimated. Despite a reduction in shortages, medicines are unaffordable to many.

Lack of electricity and running water undermine hospital services. Deteriorated infrastructure and lack of basic services in rural areas have pushed people to move to urban centers.

Due to illness and the lack of basic services, food, and school supplies, over 26 percent of children between 0 and 17 years old are out of school.

At time of writing, the UN had greenlighted the creation of the fund for humanitarian aid using the government's frozen assets abroad, to which the government and the opposition agreed in 2022.

Refugee Crisis

More than 7.7 million Venezuelans have left Venezuela since 2014, of whom about 6.5 million relocated within Latin America and the Caribbean. The number crossing the Darién Gap, a dangerous jungle on the Colombia-Panama border, skyrocketed, owing in part to visa restrictions that effectively closed safer routes. Over 440,000 Venezuelans crossed the Darién Gap between January 2022 and October 2023.

Many Venezuelans were fleeing harsh economic conditions. Some were escaping persecution, including by security forces and gangs.

Unemployment or inadequate income, inability to regularize their immigration or refugee status, and discrimination and xenophobia drive many to keep heading north.

In October, the US announced the resumption of direct deportations of Venezuelans.

Freedom of Association

In 2023, restrictions on civic space increased, resulting in the erosion of the right to freedom of association and undue constraints on labor and civil society organizations.

Several trade unionists have been subject to intimidation, arbitrary prosecution, and detention. On August 1, six Venezuelan union leaders who had led protests for labor rights and fair salaries were sentenced to 16 years in prison on charges of conspiracy and criminal association. UN special rapporteurs denounced a "chronic misuse of counter-terrorism measures against those advocating for the rights of workers."

On August 4, the Supreme Court named an interim president of the Venezuelan Red Cross, tasked with overseeing its restructuring. Courts have established ad hoc boards for unions, federal associations, and political parties.

Attacks on Human Rights Defenders

On January 24, the National Assembly advanced a bill giving the executive branch broad powers to control, register, sanction, and dissolve nongovernmental organizations (NGOs). NGOs, OHCHR, the FFM and UN special rapporteurs expressed concern. At time of writing, the bill remained pending.

At time of writing, Javier Tarazona, from the NGO Fundaredes, arrested in July 2021 after exposing links between Venezuelan security forces and armed groups, remained in prison.

Freedom of Expression

The authorities have stigmatized, harassed, and repressed the media, closing dissenting outlets. Fear of reprisals leads to self-censorship. In September, the civil society organization Espacio Público reported 261 violations of freedom of expression in 2023; censorship and intimidation were the most common.

In January, *El Nacional* director Miguel Otero reported the detention of journalist José Gregorio Meza and said four other journalists from the outlet were summoned to testify about "certain works published by the media."

Armed Groups

Armed groups—including the National Liberation Army (ELN), the Patriotic Forces of National Liberation (FPLN), and groups that emerged from the Revolutionary

Armed Forces of Colombia (FARC)—operate mostly in border states, brutally enforcing curfews and regulations governing everyday activities.

Fundaredes reported in 2023 that armed groups and criminal gangs are expanding extortion in the border area with Colombia, threatening civilians' lives and properties.

Mining and Indigenous Peoples' Rights

Mining is one of the leading drivers of deforestation in the Venezuelan Amazon. Environmental and human rights organizations have accused security forces of collaborating with illegal miners, including by providing mercury for gold mining, and indiscriminately targeting civilians with disproportionate use of force.

In September, soldiers clashed with suspected illegal miners in the Yapacana national park, resulting in two fatalities and six people injured.

Journalists and SOS Orinoco, an NGO, reported that Indigenous people living close to gold mines are experiencing severe poisoning from mercury. Some have been forcibly displaced.

Sexual Orientation and Gender Identity

Venezuela has no comprehensive legislation protecting people from discrimination based on sexual orientation and gender identity.

In March, the Supreme Court decriminalized consensual same-sex conduct by military personnel.

On July 23, police raided a club frequented by LGBT people and arrested 33 on noise level and public indecency charges. Of those arrested, 30 were granted "conditional parole" after 72 hours, and 3 were released 10 days later. Activists accused authorities of "criminalizing" people for their sexual orientation.

Disability Rights

Venezuelan law prohibits discrimination against people with disabilities and requires accessible public parks and buildings. But there is still prejudice and minimal access to public transportation, including because of drivers unwilling to transport people with disabilities. Access to public health services for people with disabilities is difficult and private services are unaffordable.

Women's and Girls' Rights

Abortion is criminalized except when the life of the pregnant person is at risk.

Sexual and reproductive health services for women and girls are suffering a loss of capacity, HumVenezuela reported. Contraceptives and menstrual hygiene products are unaffordable.

According to UNFPA, Venezuela has a high maternal mortality rate, with 125.4 maternal deaths per 100,000 live births, as well as a high adolescent pregnancy rate of 97.7 per 1,000 girls and women aged 15-19.

Venezuela lacks the regulations and gender-sensitive protocols needed to implement the Organic Law on Women's Right to a Life Free from Violence, the UN Committee on the Elimination of Discrimination against Women reported in May.

The Observatory of Femicides of the Center for Justice and Peace (Cepaz), an NGO, documented 160 femicides and 93 attempted femicides between January and July. No official data on femicides has been released since 2016.

Key International Actors

After visiting Venezuela in January, the UN High Commissioner for Human Rights flagged human rights challenges in the "civil, political, economic, and social spheres." The UN Office for the Coordination of Humanitarian Affairs (OCHA), which oversees the UN's humanitarian work in Venezuela, estimates that 7 million Venezuelans in the country are in need of assistance.

In addition to noting cases of torture and delays in investigations, OHCHR flagged the following for the UN Human Rights Council: unlawful and arbitrary detentions; restrictions on civic space; obstacles to free participation in political affairs; and economic and social challenges that have contributed to the humanitarian emergency.

During June, days before the ICC's decision on the resumption of the investigation into alleged crimes against humanity, the ICC prosecutor visited Venezuela and signed a memorandum of understanding with Maduro, agreeing to establish an in-country office.

In September, the FFM issued its fourth report concluding that, while the state has adopted less overt coercive tactics, it still possesses the capacity to resort to harsh measures to suppress dissent; therefore, international scrutiny should persist.

Brazil invited Maduro to a South American leaders' meeting in May. President Luiz Inácio Lula da Silva implied that democracy is thriving in Venezuela, calling the undermining of democratic institutions there a "constructed narrative." His remarks prompted negative reactions by local and international NGOs.

In Bogotá in April, Colombian President Gustavo Petro convened an international summit aimed at reigniting negotiations between the Venezuelan government and opposition.

Also in Bogotá in April and again during the EU-CELAC Summit in July, the EU high representative for foreign affairs (HRVP), Josep Borrell, recalled the need to implement the EU Electoral Observer Mission's recommendations. Jointly with the presidents of Colombia, Brazil, Argentina, and France, the HRVP encouraged the resumption of negotiations and expressed support for lifting sanctions on Venezuela if transparent and inclusive elections take place in 2024. In July as well, the European Parliament strongly condemned political disqualifications of candidates.

In July, a prosecutor in Argentina launched an investigation into potential crimes against humanity in Venezuela, following a criminal complaint filed by the Clooney Foundation for Justice under the principle of universal jurisdiction.

On August 8, during the first day of an Amazon Summit, Venezuela, along with seven other Amazon countries, signed the Belém Declaration, establishing a collective agenda to protect the Amazon environment.

In October, shortly after the government and opposition reached an agreement, the US relieved some sanctions by granting six-month licenses related to Venezuela's gas and oil sector. Failure to abide by the terms of the October agreement will lead the US to "reverse" them.

In November, the Council of the EU decided to extend its restrictive measures, including individual travel bans and asset freezes, for six months, until May 14, 2024, instead of one year.

In December, the Maduro government held a referendum on the creation of a Venezuelan province in the Essequibo, a territory controlled by neighboring Guyana that has been in dispute for over a century including in ongoing proceedings before the International Court of Justice. The Maduro government said that 10 million people participated in the referendum and over 90 percent voted in favor. Governments in Latin America, Europe, and the US urged Maduro to de-escalate the situation, fearing an international armed conflict. At time of writing, Guyana and Venezuela had agreed to initiate talks.

Vietnam

Vietnam systematically suppresses citizens' basic rights to freedom of expression, association, peaceful assembly, movement, and religion. Independent labor unions, human rights organizations, and political parties are prohibited. The Communist Party of Vietnam (CPV) has ruled the country for almost five decades and severely punishes anyone who challenges its monopoly on power.

The government prohibits independent press and media. Authorities systematically block access to sensitive political websites and social media pages, and they regularly pressure social media and telecommunications companies to remove or restrict content critical of the government or the ruling party.

In early 2023, during a high-stakes anti-corruption investigation related to the handling of the Covid-19 pandemic, Nguyen Phu Trong, the general secretary of the CPV, forced the resignation of President and former Prime Minister Nguyen Xuan Phuc and two deputy prime ministers. However, this rare political shakeup did not help improve the country's abysmal rights record.

Freedom of Expression

Critics of the government face police intimidation, harassment, restricted movement, arbitrary arrest and detention, and imprisonment after unfair trials. Police regularly hold political detainees for months without access to legal counsel and subject them to abusive interrogations. Party-controlled courts sentence community leaders, online free speech advocates, and civil society activists to long prison sentences on bogus national security charges.

Vietnam currently holds more than 160 people in prison for peacefully exercising their basic civil and political rights. During the first 10 months of 2023, the courts convicted at least 28 rights campaigners and sentenced them to long prison sentences. They included Truong Van Dung, Nguyen Lan Thang, Tran Van Bang, Bui Tuan Lam, and Dang Dang Phuoc.

At time of writing, police were holding at least 19 other people in pretrial detention on politically motivated charges, including human rights defender Nguyen Thuy Hanh and former political prisoners Nguyen Hoang Nam and Le Minh The.

In 2023, Vietnam did not cease its repression of nongovernmental organization (NGO) activists. In May 2023, police arrested leading environmentalist Hoang Thi Minh Hong on bogus tax evasion charges. Hoang Thi Minh Hong was an Obama Foundation Scholar in 2018, and former United States President Barack Obama praised her environmental leadership. Environmental campaigner Dang Dinh Bach, who was sentenced to prison in January 2022 on politically motivated tax evasion charges, remained behind bars. In August, common prisoners were sent into the cell of Dang Dinh Bach and prominent political prisoner Tran Huynh Duy Thuc to intimidate and threaten to use violence against them, family members told the press. Dang Dinh Bach was reportedly hit on the head from behind for trying to tell his family on a phone call how he was being treated in prison. In September, a court convicted and sentenced Hoang Thi Minh Hong to three years in prison.

Freedom of Media and Access to Information

The government prohibits independent or privately owned media outlets and imposes strict control over radio stations, television stations, and print publications. Authorities block access to websites, frequently shut down blogs, and require internet service providers to remove content or social media accounts deemed politically unacceptable.

The Vietnamese authorities constantly request social media companies, including Meta (Facebook and Instagram), Google, and TikTok, to remove content that criticizes the government or CPV leaders. According to the Ministry of Information and Communications (MIC), during the first three months of 2023, Meta "blocked and removed more than 1,096 posts with bad content (a 93% compliance rate [with government requests])"; "Google removed 1,670 violating videos on YouTube (a 93% compliance rate [with government requests])"; and "TikTok removed 323 violating links and removed 47 accounts and channels that often posted bad contents (a 91% compliance rate [with government requests])."

Similarly, according to the government, in July, "Facebook blocked and removed more than 224 posts that spread wrong information and propagandize to oppose the Party and the States, brand name, individuals and organization (a 90% compliance rate with [government] requests)"; "Google removed 1,052 violating videos on YouTube, a 91% compliance rate with [government] requests"; and

"TikTok removed 19 violating links that published wrong information and pessimistic contents, a 90% compliance rate with [government] requests."

Human Rights Watch reached out to TikTok, Google, and Meta for comment on the Vietnamese government's claims about the volume of content taken down from their platforms. TikTok and Google did not respond directly to the Vietnamese government's numbers and referred Human Rights Watch to their content removal policies and transparency report. Meta did not respond to Human Rights Watch's inquiry.

In June, the *Washington Post* reported that Meta cooperated with the Vietnamese government to stifle free speech. Two former employees of Meta told the newspaper that that Meta "has adopted an internal list of Vietnamese Communist Party officials who should not be criticized on Facebook" and that this list "is kept private even within the company and has not been publicly reported on before." They also alleged the list is included in guidelines used in controlling online content and "was shaped in large part by Vietnamese authorities." Meta failed to address these specific allegations in response to the *Washington Post*'s questions.

Freedom of Religion and Belief

The government restricts religious practice through legislation, registration requirements, and surveillance. Religious groups must get approval from, and register with, the government and operate under government-controlled management boards. While authorities allow government-affiliated churches and pagodas to hold worship services, they ban religious activities that they deem contrary to the "national interest," "public order," or "national unity." In practice, these restrictions include many ordinary religious functions.

The police monitor, harass, and sometimes violently crack down on religious groups operating outside government-controlled institutions. Unrecognized religious groups—including independent Cao Dai, Hoa Hao, Christian, and Buddhist groups—face constant surveillance, harassment, and intimidation. Followers of independent religious groups are subject to public criticism, forced renunciation of faith, pretrial detention, interrogation, torture, and imprisonment. As of September 2021, Vietnam acknowledged that it had not officially recognized about 140 religious groups with approximately 1 million followers.

Children's Rights

Violence against children, including sexual abuse, is a serious problem in Vietnam, including at home and in schools. Numerous media reports have described cases of guardians, teachers, or government caregivers engaging in sexual abuse and physically beating children.

According to Children Bureau Chief Dang Hoa Nam, "in the first four months of 2023, telephone calls to national number 111 [for reporting child abuse] with content related to school violence had increased 11%" compared to the first four months of 2022.

Vietnam has sought to combat violence against children by organizing campaigns in various provinces, including a month of actions for children in June, providing trainings to local authorities and school staff, carrying out awareness-raising campaigns, and organizing training sessions for children.

Women's and Girls' Rights

Violence against women and girls, including sexual abuse, is pervasive in Vietnam. According to UN Women, "The National Study on Violence against Women in Viet Nam in 2019 shows that nearly 2 in every 3 women (nearly 63 per cent) have experienced one or more forms of physical, sexual, emotional and economic violence as well as controlling behavior by a husband/partner in their life. More than 90 per cent of women who experienced sexual and/or physical violence by their husband/partner did not seek any help from formal services or authorities."

According to state media, in cases of domestic violence in Vietnam, 74 percent of victims are women and 11 percent of victims are children.

In July, the 2022 revised Law on Prevention and Combatting Domestic Violence came into effect. The revised law provides additional protections for victims of domestic violence. It increases the number of acts that constitute domestic violence from 9 to 16, provides victims of domestic violence with additional rights, and increases punishment for abusers.

Sexual Orientation and Gender Identity

In recent years, the Vietnamese government has taken modest steps to recognize the rights of lesbian, gay, bisexual, and transgender (LGBT) people, including by removing prohibitions on same-sex relationships and legal gender change. In 2022, the health ministry formally declared that being gay or transgender is not a disease.

In June, the National Assembly passed a resolution stating that it will give its opinion on the Gender Change Law project at its eighth session in October 2024.

Key International Actors

US-Vietnam relations strengthened significantly over the year. On September 10, President Joe Biden visited Hanoi. During this visit, the US elevated its relations with Vietnam to a "Comprehensive Strategic Partnership" but said little about Vietnam's worsening rights record. A US-Vietnam human rights dialogue in November did not result in any notable pledges or changes to policy. The US is Vietnam's largest export market and counts among its citizens the largest overseas Vietnamese community in the world, which accounts for a significant portion of family remittances sent to Vietnam.

Vietnam seeks to balance its relationship with the US and China, but Vietnam's relationship with China remains complicated. One week before Biden arrived, CPV General Secretary Nguyen Phu Trong welcomed the Chinese Communist Party's International Department head Liu Jianchao and pledged continued close friendship between the two parties. In June, Vietnam's Prime Minister Pham Minh Chinh visited Beijing.

However, territorial tension between the two countries continues, with Vietnam regularly and strongly opposing China's unilateral actions in disputed areas of the South China Sea. In July, Vietnam banned the movie "Barbie" because one scene displayed a map that Hanoi viewed as the nine-dash line map used by China to claim sovereignty over the disputed areas, which has been rejected by Vietnam.

August 2023 marks the three-year anniversary of the bilateral free trade agreement between the European Union and Vietnam (EVFTA). In April, a delegation from the European Parliament's Subcommittee on Human Rights visited Vietnam and expressed serious concerns about the human rights situation in the country, urging Vietnam to respect its human rights obligations, including pursuant to its commitments under the EVFTA.

The EU discussed human rights concerns with Vietnam during a series of bilateral meetings, including the human rights dialogue, and mentioned Vietnam in statements at the UN Human Rights Council. Despite Vietnam's utter disregard for the EU's public and private diplomacy, the bloc has yet to consider taking more persuasive measures, such as targeted sanctions or the suspension of the EVFTA.

In August and September, the EU and other local delegations urged Vietnam to halt imminent executions.

In 2023, Australia and Vietnam celebrated the 50th anniversary of their diplomatic relationship. Vietnamese leaders welcomed Australia's Governor-General David Hurley in April, Prime Minister Anthony Albanese in June, and Minister of Foreign Affairs Penny Wong in August. In July, Australian citizen and pro-democracy activist Chau Van Kham was released after more than four years of arbitrary detention. But Chau Van Kham's co-defendants, Vietnamese activists Nguyen Van Vien and Tran Van Quyen, remain behind bars. Vietnam and Australia held discussions about potentially upgrading their relationship to a "Comprehensive Strategic Partnership" in the near future.

Japan remains Vietnam's most important bilateral aid donor and its fourth largest trading partner. In 2023, Vietnam and Japan celebrated the 50th anniversary of their diplomatic relations. In May, Prime Minister Pham Minh Chinh visited Japan and met Prime Minister Fumio Kishida. Japan pledged another 61 billion Yen (about US$407 million) in development aid for Vietnam. In November, during Vietnam President Vo Van Thuong's visit to Japan, the two countries upgraded their relationship to a "Comprehensive Strategic Partnership." As in previous years, Japan refrained from publicly commenting on Vietnam's poor human rights record.

DAIHATSU
10
HUMAN
RIGHTS
WATCH
"Death is More Merciful
Than This Life"
Houthi and Yemeni Government Violations of the Right to Water in Taizz

Yemen

The last United Nations-brokered truce in Yemen ended in October of 2022. While there have not been significant airstrikes or major military offensives since the truce began in April 2022, the warring parties—including Houthi forces, the Yemeni government, and the Saudi- and United Arab Emirates (UAE)-led coalition—have continued to commit serious international human rights and humanitarian law violations in Yemen.

Violations include unlawful attacks that have killed civilians; restrictions on freedom of movement and humanitarian access to and from Taizz, Yemen's third-largest city; arbitrary detentions; and forced internal displacement. Saudi border guards have carried out mass killings of Ethiopian migrants at the Yemeni border, which may amount to crimes against humanity.

Throughout the nine-year conflict in Yemen, parties to the conflict have perpetrated widespread violations of international humanitarian law and international human rights law, causing extensive civilian harm. The conflict has included unlawful attacks, including likely war crimes, targeting homes, hospitals, schools, and markets, a number of which were carried out deliberately and indiscriminately. However, the parties to the conflict, powerful state allies like the United States, the United Kingdom, and France, and UN institutions have failed to hold rights violators accountable. Under customary international law, warring parties are obligated to provide "full reparation for the loss or injury caused" for their violations of international humanitarian law.

Yemen is one of the world's largest humanitarian crises, with more than 21 million Yemenis in need of assistance and suffering from inadequate food, health care, and infrastructure. Despite this, all parties to the conflict have taken actions that have harmed civilians. The Saudi- and UAE-led coalition has attacked food, water, and health infrastructure. The Houthis have imposed an abusive siege on Taizz, and have blocked water from entering the public water network. The Yemeni government and the Houthis impose unnecessary restrictions and regulations on humanitarian organizations and aid projects, creating lengthy delays. And in Aden, the Yemeni government and the Southern Transitional Council have failed to fulfill Aden residents' right to electricity and water.

Harms against Children in Armed Conflict

Yemen's protracted armed conflict and humanitarian crisis severely impact children. Eleven million children in Yemen need humanitarian assistance, more than 3.1 million are internally displaced, and more than 11,200 have been killed or maimed, according to UNICEF. Parties to the conflict have attacked hospitals and schools, causing disruptions to health services and children's education. Yemen's laws explicitly permit corporal punishment of children in the home.

Warring parties' attacks on water and food infrastructure and their weaponization of water have had especially harmful impacts on children. Many children have had to drop out of school to make time to travel and queue to bring water to their families.

The Houthis and the Saudi- and UAE-led coalition have committed serious violations against children throughout the war. Indiscriminate attacks have destroyed schools and hospitals and killed or injured thousands of children. Warring parties, including the Houthis and government forces, have recruited and deployed over 4,000 children in combat, according to the UN.

Landmines

Landmines and explosive remnants of war continue to be a major cause of civilian casualties. In the first quarter of 2023 alone unexploded ordinance caused 121 civilian casualties, according to the UN Mission to support the Hudaydah Agreement. On March 23, Save the Children stated that child casualties from landmines and unexploded ordinance (UXO) increased eight-fold from 2018 to 2022, and increased noticeably during the truce, highlighting the deadly legacy of the conflict. According to Save the Children, a child in Yemen was killed or injured by landmines or other UXOs every two days, on average, during 2022.

Houthi forces continue to use anti-personnel landmines in violation of the 1997 Convention on the Prohibition of the Use, Stockpiling, Production and Transfer of Anti-Personnel Mines and on their Destruction, to which Yemen is a party. Houthi forces' use of mines in areas containing objects critical for survival, including farmland, water sources, and water infrastructure, has exacerbated the humanitarian crisis and contributed to the starvation of civilians, according to Mwatana for Human Rights, an independent Yemeni organization, and Global Rights Compliance. Houthi forces have not shared any maps with mine removal authorities, violating their obligations under the Mine Convention.

Mine removal authorities have not followed the International Mine Action Standards in their removal of landmines, explosive remnants of war, and improvised explosive devices.

Arbitrary Detention, Torture, and Enforced Disappearance

All parties to the conflict, including Houthi forces, the Yemeni government, the UAE, Saudi Arabia, and various UAE and Saudi-backed Yemeni armed groups have arbitrarily arrested, forcibly disappeared, tortured, and ill-treated detainees across Yemen. Hundreds of Yemenis have been detained at official and unofficial detention centers across the country.

On May 25, Houthi forces stormed a private residence in Sanaa where Yemeni Bahais were meeting, and detained and subsequently disappeared 17 people. The group was targeted solely on the basis of their religious beliefs. Eleven of the individuals remain disappeared. Houthis have systematically arrested and disappeared Bahais and forced Bahais into exile.

UAE-backed forces, in particular the Southern Transitional Council (STC), continued to arbitrarily arrest and forcibly disappear individuals and maintain at least two informal detention facilities.

While Yemen's internationally recognized government and the Houthis released a combined 887 detainees as part of an exchange in April, many more individuals, including human rights defenders and activists, continued to be arbitrarily detained and disappeared by multiple parties to the conflict.

Blocking and Impeding Humanitarian Access

The Houthis and the Yemeni government impose unnecessary restrictions and regulations on humanitarian organizations and aid projects, creating lengthy delays. Human Rights Watch has documented many cases of aid interference and obstruction by Houthi forces, including but not limited to lengthy delays for approval of aid projects, blocking aid assessments to identify people's needs, attempts to control aid monitoring and recipient lists to divert aid to those loyal to the authorities, and violence against aid staff and their property. The Yemeni government has impeded much needed aid through the imposition of complex bureaucratic requirements on aid agencies that have impacted millions of civilians' ability to access it.

Civilians in the city of Taizz have been severely harmed by Houthi aid obstruction. Residents have faced a dire humanitarian crisis since 2015 when the Houthis closed off all major roads into and out of the city. The International Committee of the Red Cross stated in March 2022 that "the severity of food and water needs is dangerously acute in Taizz." The road closures have severely restricted the flow of essential goods, including medicine and food, as well as humanitarian access into the city. In 2022, the Houthis rejected a proposal by the UN special envoy's office to reopen the roads. Since that time, there has been little to no progress in reopening the roads and allowing greater humanitarian aid to enter the city.

Rights to Food and Water

Yemen has long been one of the most water scarce countries in the world and has a long history of food scarcity. The war has exacerbated Yemen's existing food and water crisis. At the end of 2022, UN agencies reported that 17.8 million people in Yemen—more than half of the population—did not have access to safe drinking water, sanitation, and hygiene services, and 17 million were food insecure, with 6.1 million facing "emergency" levels of food insecurity.

According to Mwatana for Human Rights and Global Rights Compliance, the warring parties have repeatedly carried out attacks on food and water infrastructure across Yemen, including targeting farms, irrigation works, and fishing boats, in violation of the international humanitarian law prohibition on attacking, destroying, removing, or rendering useless objects indispensable to the survival of the civilian population.

Droughts and floods, exacerbated by climate change, have also worsened the water crisis in Yemen. Extreme weather events have destroyed irrigation facilities, leading to the loss of agricultural livelihoods, and placed additional pressure on other water and land resources.

According to the International Rescue Committee, skyrocketing food prices in recent years have left more than half of the population in need of food assistance, while the sharp depreciation of the Yemeni rial has made imported food, cooking oil, and other necessities more expensive, and has dramatically reduced households' purchasing power.

Women's and Girls' Rights

Yemeni women continue to face restrictions on their freedom of movement in areas under Houthi control, where authorities require them to be accompanied by a *mahram* (male relative) in order to travel. The mahram requirement bars women from traveling without a male guardian or evidence of their written approval. Increased Houthi restrictions related to the mahram requirement have prevented Yemeni women from working, especially those who must travel, according to Amnesty International. These restrictions also apply to Yemeni women working for humanitarian organizations, which has made it more difficult for them to conduct fieldwork and has impacted access to aid for Yemeni women and girls.

UN human rights experts have detailed the Houthis' "systematic violations of women's and girls' rights," including their rights to freedom of movement, freedom of expression, health, and work, as well as widespread discrimination.

In practice, women and girls in the south also face movement restrictions. Some women have reported being stopped at checkpoints when traveling without a mahram from one governorate to another in government-controlled Yemen. According to a coalition of Yemeni NGOs, hotels, particularly in cities like Aden and Taiz, prevent Yemeni women from staying unless they have a mahram. Amnesty International also reported that prison authorities across Yemen as a customary practice do not allow women to leave prison upon completion of their sentences unless they have a male guardian to accompany them on release. If their families refuse to receive them, they release them only to women's shelters.

Sexual Orientation and Gender Identity

Yemen's penal code prohibits same-sex relations. Article 264 punishes anal sex with 100 lashes and one year in prison if participants are not married. If married, the same article prescribes death by stoning. Article 268 punishes sex between women with up to three years in prison.

Abuses against Migrants

Saudi border guards killed at least hundreds of Ethiopian migrants and asylum seekers who tried to cross the Yemen-Saudi border between March 2022 and June 2023. If committed as part of a Saudi government policy to murder migrants, these killings, which appear to have continued, would be a crime against humanity. Human Rights Watch found that Saudi border guards have used explosive weapons to kill many migrants and shot other migrants at close range, including many women and children, in a widespread and systematic pattern of attacks. In some instances, Saudi border guards asked migrants what limb to shoot, and then shot them at close range.

Houthi forces' role in coordinating security and facilitating access to the border for smugglers and migrants in Saada governorate, coupled with its practice of detaining and extorting migrants, amount to torture, arbitrary detention, and trafficking in persons.

Since the armed conflict began in Yemen in 2014, both the government and the Houthi armed group have detained migrants in poor conditions and exposed them to abuse.

In June the International Organization for Migration (IOM) estimated that if first-quarter 2023 trends continued more than 160,000 migrants would arrive in Yemen during the year.

Accountability

There has been virtually no accountability for violations committed by parties to the conflict. Since the UN Human Rights Council narrowly voted to end the mandate of the Group of Eminent Experts on Yemen in October 2021, there has been no independent international mechanism to monitor the human rights situation in Yemen and lay the foundation for accountability for abuses.

On July 26, over 40 civil society organizations and victim and survivor associations from Yemen launched the Yemen Declaration for Justice and Reconciliation (the Declaration), in which they set forth their common vision for achieving justice and reconciliation in post-conflict Yemen. The declaration underlined that grievances caused by the war have not been sufficiently addressed by parties to the conflict or by the international community.

Mwatana for Human Rights and Yale Law School's Lowenstein International Human Rights Clinic found that the warring parties have failed to effectively provide reparations.

Thus far, negotiations between the Houthis and Saudi Arabia have not included discussions of accountability.

Key International Actors

On April 7, 2022, President Abdo Rabbu Mansour Hadi transferred his presidential authority to an eight-member presidential leadership council, with Yemeni politician Rashad al-Alimi serving as president of the council. The council is backed by Saudi Arabia and the UAE, while Houthi forces continued to receive support from Iran.

Arms sales to Saudi Arabia, the UAE, and other coalition members continued from Western countries including the US, the UK, France, Germany, Italy, Canada, and others.

An internal report from the US Government Accountability Office (GAO) found serious gaps in US government oversight of how arms sold to Saudi Arabia and the UAE are being used. In September, the *Washington Post* found that the US Army's Security Assistance Command had been training Saudi border guards for the past eight years in a program that concluded in July.

In February, international donors pledged US$1.2 billion to the humanitarian response, $3.1 billion less than the $4.3 billion needed for humanitarian programming.

Zambia

When Hakainde Hichilema was elected president of Zambia in 2021, there were hopes that he would improve the human rights situation in the country. However, there has been growing intolerance for political opposition and dissent, cases of arbitrary detention and censorship, and threats to the rights of freedom of expression and freedom of assembly.

In February 2023, the police arrested opposition leader Chishimba Kambwili after a group of youths protesting the high cost of living assembled outside his residence in Lusaka, the capital. At various points during the year, authorities used the Public Order Act to disrupt opposition activities, including refusing in some cases to grant authorization for opposition meetings and rallies.

According to the United Nations Children's Fund (UNICEF), some 29 percent of girls (and 2 percent of boys) are married by 18 in Zambia.

Zambia criminalizes consensual same-sex conduct with up to life imprisonment.

In August, President Hichilema became the chair of the Southern African Development Community (SADC) Organ on Politics, Defence and Security Cooperation.

Freedom of Assembly

Writing in the *Washington Post* on March 28, President Hichilema said "my government has returned our democracy to health, shoring up the civil liberties the people demanded: the right of assembly, an end to defamation laws that challenged free speech, and removing the death penalty."

However, a month earlier, opposition leader Chishimba Kambwili was arrested and charged with unlawful assembly after a group of youths protesting the high cost of living assembled outside his residence in Lusaka. He was released after spending a night in detention.

On June 28, the Law Association of Zambia (LAZ) condemned "increased incidents of police brutality against members of the opposition." The statement followed the arrests of opposition presidential hopeful Emmanuel Mwamba, opposition member and blogger Rizwan Patel, and former State House Special Assistant for Politics Christopher Zumani Zimba.

In response, the Minister of Home Affairs and Internal Security stated that the government "remains committed to upholding the principles of democracy, human rights, and the rule of law," and that the "government will continue to foster an environment that encourages open discourse, respects freedom of expression, and ensure that law enforcement agencies operate within the confines of the law."

In January, police stopped a meeting of the former ruling Patriotic Front (PF) party, arguing the PF had not obtained permission to gather. In April, the PF applied to the High Court for judicial review of alleged abuse of power by the Zambia Police Service in cancelling the January meeting. Zambia police also denied clearance to the PF to hold a public rally on August 26, citing security concerns. The Inspector General of Police said that the PF could only hold a public rally at the end of September. The police also denied the Socialist Party permission to hold a rally in Kitwe on October 7, citing "security concerns" and "insufficient manpower."

In August, LAZ criticized the government for denying the opposition the right to freely operate, and for using the Public Order Act to violate citizens' constitutional rights of association, assembly, and expression. Section 5(4) of the act requires that anyone intending to assemble or convene a public meeting, procession, or demonstration, give the police seven days' notice. Although the provision does not require formal prior approval from the authorities, the police have interpreted it to mean permission is required before any public assembly can proceed.

In October, Zambian police thwarted planned protests against the rising cost of living that had been organized by a group calling itself "protest movement."

Also in October, police forced their way into the home of opposition Patriots for Economic Progress leader Sean Tembo and arrested him for "hate speech." Tembo had urged the police to wait for the arrival of his lawyers. Tembo previously had been arrested on the same charge in September and detained for six days in violation of his right to be brought before a court of law within 48 hours.

In October, 13 leading civil society and human rights groups issued a joint statement expressing concern over the "failure by public authorities to protect the rights to freedom of expression and freedom of assembly." They urged the government to "quickly enact the Access to Information Bill and the Public Gatherings Bill in order to safeguard the right to freedom of expression and assembly in the country."

In April, the UN Human Rights Committee expressed concern about allegations of "restrictions on peaceful assemblies, such as cancelling assemblies at the last minute, arbitrary arrests, bodily injuries, deaths and property damage, especially during peaceful anti-government protests and political gatherings organized by the opposition." The Human Rights Committee is the body of 18 independent experts that monitors implementation of the International Covenant on Civil and Political Rights by state parties.

Freedom of Association

In January, the ruling United Party for National Development (UPND) party stated that the Public Order Act would be amended to allow every Zambian citizen including those in the opposition to gather freely, without hinderance. Among the restrictive laws that President Hichilema promised to repeal is NGO Act No. 16 of 2009. The law unduly restricts the activities of nongovernmental organizations (NGO) and civil society groups that operate in the country and subjects them to excessive and unwarranted controls, including by placing them under the authority of a government-dominated NGO Registration Board that has the authority to interfere in their activities. However, nearly two years into his term, his administration has not fulfilled this promise.

In June, the *Daily Mail*, a state-owned newspaper, dismissed a photojournalist who had taken pictures of people queuing up for mealie meal when some parts of the country were experiencing shortages of the basic food commodity. The journalist was accused of sabotaging the government.

In October, the Independent Broadcasting Authority wrote to Hot FM Radio Station telling the radio station to "strengthen its international controls." This was after the station had hosted Dr. Sishuwa Sishuwa, a leading Zambian academic and critic of the government. The broadcasting authority stated that the academic's assertions had "the potential to cause disunity in the country."

The UN Human Rights Committee, in its concluding observations on the fourth periodic report of Zambia, expressed concern about reports that "opposition political parties have been denied access to public media and that some private radio stations have been forced to stop broadcasting programs featuring opposition political leaders."

By-Election Violence

In April, political violence was reported in a by-election campaign in Serenje district in Zambia's Central Province. Supporters of the ruling UPND allegedly attacked the president of the Socialist Party, Fred M'membe, and his supporters who had gathered at a campaign rally. M'membe reportedly used his gun to disperse the crowd. On April 9, M'membe was arrested for unlawful discharge of a firearm and assault. He was charged together with two other suspected Socialist Party members for allegedly assaulting nine UPND members.

Religious leaders under the Christian Churches Monitoring Group called on the Electoral Commission of Zambia (ECZ) to take action against the UPND and the Socialist Party for violating the provisions of the Electoral Code of Conduct by engaging in violence during the by-election campaign.

On August 22, M'membe was summoned to Ibex Hill police station in Lusaka and charged with the additional offense of "acts intended to cause grievous bodily harm" relating to the April by-election violence. M'membe told the media that his arrests were "a clear attempt to silence prominent critics of the UPND government."

Restrictions on the Former President

In September, police stopped a church service that was to be attended by former Zambian President Edgar Lungu and his wife Esther, citing security concerns. Earlier, in the same month, President Hichilema had denounced alleged coup plotters who he claimed were planning to undermine the country's democratic rule and stability by trying to illegally seize power. The president had written on Facebook that: "to colleagues that think we are timid by being kind and that they can break the laws and entertain thoughts of illegal takeover of government including undemocratic coup d'état, our only word is that; We are coming for you and we will not allow you to make Zambians start running around as is the case in some places."

On September 7, the authorities denied Lungu's request to travel to South Africa for medical purposes.

On September 16, Lungu was reportedly removed from a plane and stopped from travelling to South Korea to attend a World Peace Conference. The Ministry of Information and Broadcasting stated that government took the action because he did not get travel clearance from cabinet.

Also in September, media reported that police told Lungu to stop jogging in public with supporters, with officers describing his weekly runs as "political activism." The authorities told Lungu that his exercise sessions accompanied by members of his Patriotic Front party amounted to "unlawful assembly," and advised him to seek police approval for future jogging events.

Cleanup of Lead Contamination in Kabwe

Kabwe, the capital of Zambia's Central Province, is one of the world's worst pollution hotspots because of contamination from a former lead and zinc mine. In March, the Ministry of Green Economy and Environment outlined its vision of Kabwe as a "Green City" with "buried lead surfaces" at a roundtable conference organized by a civil society alliance, the Alliance for Lead-Free Kabwe, of which Human Rights Watch is a member. However, the ministry has not taken any public steps to implement this vision, nor has it acted on the president's directive to establish a technical committee for the planning of the mine cleanup. In July, youth activists released a video in which they describe life in a dangerously polluted town and advocate for comprehensive cleanup of the former mine site.

Lead is a toxic metal with no safe level of exposure; children are especially at risk. It causes stunted growth, learning difficulties, memory loss, developmental delays, and many other irreversible health effects. It can also cause coma and death.

Key International Actors

In March, United States Vice President Kamala Harris visited Zambia, discussing debt restructuring with President Hichilema and announcing a range of private sector commitments worth more than US$7 billion aimed at supporting climate resilience, adaptation, and mitigation.

In July, the UN Human Rights Council adopted Zambia's Universal Periodic Review (UPR) outcome. During the UPR, Zambia received and supported recommendations to, among other things, amend the Public Order Act to ensure the full enjoyment of freedom of expression, assembly and association, and take measures to end child marriage.

In September, Hichilema became the chair of the SADC Organ on Politics, Defence and Security Cooperation. As chairperson, he nominated former Zambian Vice President Nevers Mumba as the head of the regional bloc's Electoral Observer Mission (SEOM) to Zimbabwe. The mission's preliminary report found that the August 23 elections in Zimbabwe "fell short of the requirements of the Constitution of Zimbabwe, the Electoral Act, and the SADC Principles and Guidelines Governing Democratic Elections (2021)." Hichilema did not attend President Emmerson Mnangagwa's inauguration in Harare following the disputed election.

In September, the president visited China to engage in discussions on restructuring the country's external debt. Around two-thirds of the US$6.3 billion debt that Zambia is in the process of restructuring with its official creditors is owed to the Export-Import Bank of China. At the meeting, Hichilema and Chinese President Xi Jinping signed several bilateral agreements, including on economic cooperation and investment, and reportedly discussed Chinese investment in Zambia's energy, mining, and infrastructure sectors.

CCC
HUMAN
RIGHTS
WATCH
"Crush Them Like Lice"
Repression of Civil and Political Rights Ahead of Zimbabwe's
August 2023 Election

Zimbabwe

Many observers considered Zimbabwe's August 23 elections, which Emmerson Mnangagwa won, as falling short of constitutional requirements, the Electoral Act, and international election standards such as the Southern African Development Community (SADC) Principles and Guidelines Governing Democratic Elections. There were also concerns about the impartiality of the Zimbabwe Electoral Commission prior to and during the elections. The climate of threats, intimidation, repression, and violence against political opponents severely undermined the electoral environment.

The government's failure to investigate and prosecute abuses primarily committed by ruling ZANU-PF party supporters and state security forces entrenched the culture of impunity, especially ahead of the August 23 elections.

Repression of Civil Society Organizations

On January 22, Zimbabwean authorities announced they had revoked the registration of 291 nongovernmental and civil society organizations for "noncompliance with the provisions of Private Voluntary Organisations Act."

This was in concert with the government's efforts to enact repressive laws in 2023, most notably an amendment to the Private Voluntary Organisations (PVO) Act. In February, President Mnangagwa claimed that the PVO Amendment Bill was necessary to protect and defend the country's sovereignty from destabilizing foreign interests.

Once signed, provisions of the act would allow the government to cancel the registration of organizations deemed to have "political affiliation." Such organizations would have little to no recourse to judicial review, with criminal penalties ranging from heavy fines to imprisonment for some violations.

United Nations experts called on President Mnangagwa not to sign the bill into law, stating that "the restrictions contained therein will have a chilling effect on civil society organizations, particularly dissenting voices." In September, it was reported that Mnangagwa had sent the bill back with reservations to Parliament for reconsideration, but it was unclear why he returned the bill.

On July 14, the president signed into law the Criminal Law Codification and Reform Amendment Bill 2022, commonly referred to as the "Patriotic Bill." The law, seen as a grave threat to the freedoms of association and expression, empowers the National Prosecuting Authority to prosecute anyone it considers to be undermining the country or using false statements to paint a negative picture of the country to foreign governments. A leading nongovernmental organization, Zimbabwe Lawyers for Human Rights, argued that the provisions of the law were "vague, lack certainty, are imprecise, and are thus prone to abuse by law enforcement [and] could be interpreted broadly and subjectively to criminalize the legitimate conduct of those asserting their freedom of expression."

On election night, government security forces raided the offices of the Election Resource Centre (ERC) and the Zimbabwe Election Support Network (ZESN), arresting nearly 40 staff and volunteers and confiscating laptops, phones, and other equipment. The two civil society organizations had trained and deployed accredited observers to every constituency, district, and province in the country. The raid and arrest prevented an independent, nonpartisan verification of the official results as announced by the Zimbabwe Electoral Commission. A spokesman for the police told local media that the raid was because the two organizations were conducting an illegal parallel vote tabulation exercise.

Arrest, Detention, and Prosecution of Government Critics

Authorities in Zimbabwe continued weaponizing the law against critics of the government, denying those arrested the presumption of innocence, the right to bail, and access to a fair trial.

On May 17, six University of Zimbabwe students were arrested for staging a peaceful protest in Harare, Zimbabwe's capital. The protesters were demanding an end to the persecution of opposition politicians, including the release of opposition politician Job Sikhala. The students were charged with "criminal nuisance and disorderly conduct." They were released on bail after two months in detention.

Sikhala, a former member of parliament (MP) and opposition Citizens Coalition for Change (CCC) party interim vice chairperson, has been incarcerated since June 14, 2022, at Chikurubi Maximum Security Prison, on the outskirts of Harare.

He is charged with inciting violence, and several appeals for bail have been denied. A lawyer familiar with his detention conditions said that Sikhala has been subjected to leg irons; his lawyers and relatives have at times been denied access, prompting a court application in one instance; and his party colleagues have been prevented from visiting him. While in detention, Sikhala's health has deteriorated.

Prominent Zimbabweans, foreign diplomats, and other individuals signed a petition calling on President Mnangagwa to end Sikhala's unlawful detention "without bail and without trial, and also more broadly to ensure that the judiciary is not used as a political weapon in which differential treatment is given to those apprehended by the state depending on real or perceived political affiliations and intentions."

On April 28, Jacob Ngarivhume, leader of the small opposition party Transform Zimbabwe, was sentenced to four years in prison for inciting public violence over a 2020 protest call he posted on X, formerly known as Twitter. Ngarivhume had posted a video calling for anti-government protests over the state of the economy and rampant corruption.

Opposition MP Joanah Mamombe and activists Netsai Marova and Cecillia Chimbiri were abducted, tortured, and sexually assaulted on May 13, 2020. The three had participated in an anti-government protest in Harare. However, they were charged with faking their abduction and communicating falsehoods. In July 2023, the High Court found that the evidence against the three was "grossly unreasonable, irrational characterized by bias and malice" and ordered that they should be set free. The National Prosecuting Authority indicated they would appeal the decision to the Supreme Court.

In early August, ahead of the general election, a CCC supporter was killed during clashes with suspected ZANU-PF supporters in the township of Glen Norah, Harare. Police said they had arrested 11 people in connection with the CCC supporter's death and the court charged them with "public violence," a lesser offense than homicide.

Sexual Orientation and Gender Identity

Lesbian, gay, bisexual, and transgender (LGBT) people have faced police harassment and sexual and physical assaults. In September, a man committed suicide in fear of police arrest for sodomy. The Criminal Law Act makes acts of "sodomy" punishable with of a maximum of 10 years' imprisonment. Zimbabwe's laws prohibit same-sex marriage.

Lack of Accountability for Abuses

In 2023, there was a pattern of arrests, charges, and criminal proceedings that amount to attacks on the rights to freedom of expression and peaceful assembly, without any accountability.

On January 14, police arrested, detained, and beat with batons Costa Machingauta (the opposition CCC MP for Budiriro, Harare) and 25 others. They were charged with participating in an illegal gathering and disturbing public peace in what police said was an illegal meeting at the MP's house in Harare.

On March 4, police shut down the show of a popular musician, Wallace Chirumiko. Popularly known as "Winky D," the reggae-dancehall artist had released an album that contained lyrics against social and political injustice, corruption, and the economic meltdown in Zimbabwe.

The authorities' continued shutting down of meetings and gatherings of the opposition, artists, critics, and human rights defenders violated the right to freedom of assembly.

Women's and Girls' Rights

Zimbabwe has a very high rate of child marriage, with 34 percent of girls married before age 18.

A troubling feature of the election was the low number of female candidates, and the number of women in Parliament has been declining. The African Commission on Human and Peoples' Rights expressed concerns about violence against women voters and candidates ahead of the last election.

Land Rights

Reports continued to emerge of communities affected by the government's designation of their land for mining and commercial projects without adequate consultation. In July, a court ordered Labenmon Investments, a Chinese mining company, not to prospect or conduct exploration or any form of mining activity in four villages in Mashonaland East province without following due process and the law.

Zimbabwe Lawyers for Human Rights represented communities in Mutoko, Mashonaland East province, against another Chinese mining company, Zim Win Mining Private Limited, which had started lithium mineral exploration activities in their area, resulting in displacement and damage to land and livelihoods. The lawyers asked the Chinese company to "cease and desist from coercing or unduly influencing the villagers to sign any consent forms," which were vague and lacked specifics as to the "consequences of such mining operations on their livelihoods, farming activities, environmental impact and the exact nature of compensation for the negative effects of the mining."

Key International Actors

Multiple election observation missions, including those from the European Union and the United States, expressed deep concerns about the country's electoral process and stated that the process did not meet regional and international standards for credibility. In September, the EU announced its intention to suspend support for the Zimbabwe Electoral Commission in light of concerns about its independence. The preliminary report of the SADC Electoral Observation found that "some aspects of the 2023 Harmonised Elections fell short of the requirements of the Constitution of Zimbabwe, the Electoral Act, and the SADC Principles and Guidelines Governing Democratic Elections (2021)."

In May, the UN special rapporteur on the situation of human rights defenders urged Zimbabwe to end the judicial harassment of education and labor rights defenders.

A September 20 statement by the US Embassy in Zimbabwe expressed concern at reports of continued politically motivated post-election violence and intimidation, reiterating that "every person ... has the right to live free of fear and to be treated fairly under the law."

When President Mnangagwa was sworn in on September 4, only Presidents Cyril Ramaphosa of South Africa, Filipe Nyusi of Mozambique, and Felix Tshisekedi of the Democratic Republic of Congo, out of the 16 SADC heads of state, attended the ceremony. Other SADC members sent representatives to the inauguration, with the exception of Zambia.